"AN ACCOUNT OF THINGS ACCOMPLISHED"

"AN ACCOUNT OF THINGS ACCOMPLISHED"
An Exposition of the Gospel according to Luke

Donald T. Williams

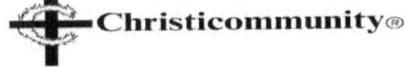

Copyright Page

An Account Of Things Accomplished: An Exposition of the Gospel according to Luke

Copyright 2024, Donald T. Williams. All rights reserved.

ISBN: 979-8-9877278-2-9

DEDICATION

This book is dedicated to the memory of Dr. Paul R. Van Gorder, pastor of Colonial Hills Baptist Church, East Point, GA., in the 1960s, and then later an associate teacher with the Radio Bible Class. His careful weekly treatments of the biblical text first showed me what expository preaching could be and led me as a high–school student to pray, "Father, it would be really neat if some day you would let me do for others what this man is doing for me." That was my first inkling that I might be called to the ministry. I hope he would not be appalled to think of this book as a fruit of that moment!

Table of Contents

INTRODUCTION

AN ACCOUNT OF THE ACCOUNT

The series of sermons that lies before you has been preached three times: at the First Evangelical Free Church of Marietta, GA., in the 1980s, at Trinity Fellowship of Toccoa, GA., in the 1990s, and at University Church in Athens, GA., in the 2020s. With each successive iteration, it was updated, revised, refined, and (hopefully) improved. Each time there were people who felt that there was something about its approach and the insights that approach produced, something about its faithfulness to the text and its focus on the need of the church for a renewed vision of the glory of the Gospel and of the Savior, that deserved a wider audience. Why should you want to be part of that audience?

First, because Luke is in some respects the most comprehensive of the Gospels. Each of the four canonical accounts of the life of our Lord is essential, and each has its own unique contribution to make to a full stereoscopic vision of the glory of God in the face of Jesus Christ. I can put it no better than in the following poem (too recent to be included in my collected verse, *Stars through the Clouds*[1])

FOUR IN HAND

> Matthew, Mark, Luke, and John
> Wrote what they had heard and seen
> When the Master walked upon
> The waters blue, the meadows green.

> Matthew, Mark, Luke, and John
> Wrote what they had seen and heard
> When priest and peasant stumbled on
> The sound of the eternal Word.

> Matthew wrote to scattered Jews;
> Mark to Roman legionnaires;
> Luke became the Gentiles' muse;
> John to all sang Heaven's airs.

> Matthew wrote what he recalled;
> Mark recorded Peter's story;
> Luke by research was enthralled;
> John leaned on the breast of Glory.

---

[1] Donald T. Williams, *Stars through the Clouds: The Collected Poetry of Donald T. Williams*, 2nd ed. (Lynchburg, VA: Lantern Hollow Press, 2019).

Matthew wrote of Christ the King;
Mark, the sacrificial Lamb;
Luke the Son of Man would sing;
John, the Word, the great I AM.

With deep, quadrangulated sight
They wrote for all and all as one.
Thus we receive the Gospel light
From Matthew, Mark, Luke, and John.

Luke was not, like the other three Evangelists, an eyewitness. He gives us, not a personal memoir, but a researched study that encompasses input from many eyewitnesses, undoubtedly interviewed as he met them on his travels with the Apostle Paul. We go to Matthew for Jewish background, Mark for narrative punch, John for pondered profundity. Luke gives us a unified synthesis of all three features, put together with a scholar's eye and written in prose that, even in translation, sings the song of redemption with heart–piercing poignancy. What the church needs, in our day as in every day, is a fresh vision of who Jesus is. If I could turn to only one Gospel to get it, Luke might just be the one.

Second, you should want to be part of that audience because sound expository preaching is always the need of the moment, and it is not at all easy to find. I am not immune to repeating the often–told preacher joke that I first heard from Walter Kaiser: "I preached a topical sermon once. The topic was the need for expository preaching." Why is expository preaching so important? Because that vision of who Jesus is and what it means to follow Him has to come from the Word, and sound exposition lets the Word set the sermon's agenda and speak for itself. It offers accurate teaching each week and a balanced diet of that teaching extended through time. Again, I can probably put it best with a poem:

HOMILETICS 101

Nothing less can speak to our condition,
Not prooftexts, pretexts; we must have the Word:
There is no power but in exposition.
The Text is captain of the expedition,
The Apostle's accents are what must be heard,
For nothing less can speak to our condition.
The finger on the verse, the fair rendition,
Then, not to brandish, but to thrust, the Sword:
There is no power but in exposition.
When heralds mind the message and the mission,
Not feelings only—mind and heart are stirred,
And nothing less can speak to our condition.

Can mere opinion lead to true contrition
When bone and marrow splitting's not incurred?
There is no power but in exposition.
Such splitting, like the atom: in that fission
The power is unleashed, the Faith conferred.
For nothing less can speak to our condition;
There is no power but in exposition.[2]

Having degrees in both theology and literature and having spent my career teaching both subjects puts me, I hope, in a unique position to be able to listen to the Text. When I see where the author is going (theology) and how he is getting there (literature) and find that this vision focuses my understanding of his message on precisely what meets the spiritual needs I share with my contemporaries, I know I have something that can benefit the church. If I discern with some richness and accuracy the original meaning of the Text and can apply it in a sermon that I need to hear myself, I have some hope that others may benefit by hearing it too.

What does the church need to hear right now? I have addressed that question directly and in greater detail elsewhere.[3] The Evangelical movement has lost its way, letting the Gospel it received from the New Testament via the Reformation slip through its fingers. To put the larger answer in a nutshell, we need to get back to the Gospel. That means getting back to Jesus. That means getting back to an accurate vision of who He is. And there can be no better way of doing that than engaging afresh with this Gospel that so insistently asks the eminently pertinent question: "What manner of man is this?"

One should imagine these chapters as sermons being preached. I am a scholar as well as a pastor, so I have included the apparatus of scholarship for those who are interested.[4] These are sermons, not lectures, for all that, though based on a measure of scholarship. The Scripture quotes unless otherwise noted are from the NASB, though when I quote from memory, it might be the old King James. There are also elements of style here that are appropriate for the oral medium of the sermon but which I would not employ (at least, not to the same extent) in prose meant just for reading. A more lavish use of alliteration, repetition, parallelism, antithesis, even colloquialism, than one expects to find in plain professional prose reflects the orality of the homiletic origin of these meditations—appropriately, I hope.

---

[2] Williams, *Stars through the Clouds*, op. cit., 385.

[3] Donald T. Williams, *Ninety-Five Theses for a New Reformation: A Road Map for Post-Evangelical Christianity* (Toccoa, GA: *Semper Reformanda* Publications, 2021).

[4] Like footnotes, for example.

So imagine me stepping up to the pulpit in the sanctuary of your church. I put down my notes, solemnly open my Bible, and nervously clear my throat. And then I say ...

AN ACCOUNT OF THINGS ACCOMPLISHED

Luke 1:1, *Inasmuch as many have undertaken to compile an account of the things accomplished among us, 2 just as those who from the beginning were eyewitnesses and servants of the Word have handed them down to us, 3 it seemed fitting for me as well, having investigated everything carefully from the beginning, to write it out for you in consecutive order, most excellent Theophilus, 4 so that you might know the exact truth about the things you have been taught.*

Introduction

The Gospel according to Luke has been called "the most beautiful book ever written." I hope in the coming months as we work through its text together that we will begin to see why this is so. But it is not only beautiful, it is also powerful—for the Gospel is as Paul tells us *"the power of God for salvation to them that believe"* (Rom. 1:16). And it is not only powerful but also practical, for the Gospel is not only the key to eternal life but also to a meaningful existence in this life here and now. So let us take our bearings as we make our beginning by examining Luke's own formal introduction to his work. What kind of book did he set out to write? What did he want to accomplish in our lives by writing it? What can we learn from the study of it? Such are the questions that must occupy us as we begin. So we will look at Luke's predecessors, his program, his purpose, his public, his perspective, and his passion as they are revealed in these opening verses—his prologue.

I. Luke's Predecessors (vv. 1–2)

Luke did not of course write in a vacuum. He mentions that *"many have undertaken to compile an account of the things accomplished among us, just as those who from the beginning were eyewitnesses and servants of the Word have handed them down to us"* (1:1–2). Who are these "many" who have been telling the story of Jesus before him? The "eyewitnesses and servants of the Word" are the Apostles, who are identified by Luke in Acts as eyewitnesses to the resurrection (1:21–22) and servants of the Word (6:2, 4). Their function was to hand down the Gospel in authoritative form. But the "many" of verse 1 cannot be the Apostles, for there were not "many" of them, and possibly only Mark had produced a written Gospel before Luke wrote. So how did this transmission work?

In the earliest days of the Church of course there was no written New Testament, and not every congregation even had its own Apostle. There would, however, have been many Christians who collected and circulated notes on the Apostles' preaching and teaching, some perhaps in written, most in oral form. At first the Church was dependent on oral tradition as the Gospel was passed from mouth to mouth. This meant it was dependent on memory, which is inexact. It was not as inexact for them as it would be for us, though, because the early Christians lived in a more orally oriented culture than we do, less dependent on written texts, and had thus developed trustworthy techniques for preserving and transmitting information accurately in oral form. The teacher would repeat a sound bite from Jesus' teaching or His life until his disciples could repeat it accurately from memory. Only when he was satisfied that they could do so reliably would they then be permitted to teach the same content to others. We probably see this practice reflected in Paul's instructions to Timothy. *"The things which you have heard from me in the presence of many witnesses, these entrust to faithful men, who will be able to teach others also"* (2 Tim. 2:2). The "many witnesses" here would be people who could verify that the tradition was being handed on accurately. So even in those early days without a written New Testament, there was a message that had reliable integrity; we're not talking about the "telephone game" here.[5]

Nevertheless, as the Apostles and other eyewitnesses were gradually martyred, there was felt an increasing need for someone to write the Gospel, the story of what God had done in Christ for our salvation, down in a more permanent, more reliable, and more authoritative form. Mark was probably the first to do so, based on notes from the Apostle Peter. Luke, writing under the aegis of the Apostle Paul's authority, took a slightly different approach. Rather than giving an account based mainly on one witness like Mark (depending on Peter) had done and Matthew and John would do, Luke, who had not been an eyewitness himself, carefully interviewed all the living witnesses he could find so that he could write everything out in order. *"It seemed fitting for me as well, having investigated everything carefully from the beginning, to write it out for you in consecutive order"* (verse 3). And that leads us to our second point.

II. Luke's Program **(v. 3)**

Luke's predecessors were those who told the story before; his program was to investigate everything carefully. His Gospel is unique in that it is not a personal memoir but a carefully researched history, using the accepted standards of Greek secular historians of the day. Luke was the friend, personal physician, and traveling companion of the Apostle Paul, writing under his apostolic authority. He would have known John Mark (2 Tim. 4:11). Probably when accompanying Paul on visits to Jerusalem he interviewed the surviving witnesses, including Mary (his is the only Gospel to include her personal memories in his well–known version of the Christmas story). He says he investigated everything "from the beginning." And so his is the only Gospel to give us details about the birth of the forerunner, John the Baptist. Then he wrote it all out "in consecutive order." His account is not just a compilation of various sayings and stories but a well–thought–out narrative whose theme could be said to be "On to Jerusalem!"

---

[5] For a detailed treatment of this process, see Richard Bauckham, *Jesus and the Eyewitnesses: The Gospels as Eyewitness Testimony* (Grand Rapids, MI: Eerdmans, 2006), 252–7.

Just as Tolkien's *The Hobbit* and *The Lord of the Rings* give us the fictional journeys of the hobbits Bilbo and Frodo "there and back again,"[6] so Luke presents Jesus as on a historical quest which would reach its climax in the atonement wrought in Jerusalem. After the birth narratives, the book is organized around ministry in Galilee (3:1–9:50), ministry on the way to Jerusalem (9:51–19:28) and ministry in Jerusalem (19:29–the end). The pivotal verse is 9:51. "*He resolutely set his face to go to Jerusalem.*" Satan (4:13, 10:17–20, 13:16–17, 22:3, etc.), the Jewish leaders, His own family, and even His own disciples (11:52–54, 13:14, 13:31–33, 15:1–2, 19:39, 20:19–20, etc.) try to keep Him from getting there, but nothing can stop Him from fulfilling His destiny. On His arrival in Jerusalem, He throws down the gauntlet in the triumphal entry, and everything builds from there to the inevitable climax in the Crucifixion and Resurrection. The story of Jesus is the story of the conquest of Satan's kingdom by the kingdom of God.

Luke then has given us the most comprehensive of all the Gospels. This is borne out by the statistics. Just think of the number of scenes described by Luke alone: the Annunciation, the visit to Elizabeth, the manger, the shepherds, Simeon and Anna, the encounter with the rabbis in the Temple at the age of twelve, Christ weeping over Jerusalem, the walk to Emmaus, the Good Samaritan, the Prodigal Son. By one calculation, there are a total of 172 sections (or pericopes, to use the fancy word that biblical scholars use—these are the "sound bites" we mentioned earlier) in the Synoptic Gospels (Matthew, Mark, and Luke). Mark has only 84 of the total; Matthew has 114; and Luke has 127. He gives us the most complete and rounded picture of the whole story.[7]

If you could only have one Gospel, which one would you pick? Mark for his simplicity and narrative punch? Matthew for his emphasis on Jesus' public teaching? John for his theological profundity? Of course, we want and need them all, but the question is worth asking for the light it sheds on what each one contributes to the whole picture. A good choice would be Luke for the most comprehensive and systematic account of the whole of Jesus' life and ministry. Luke's program was to investigate everything thoroughly from the beginning and set it out in order.

III. Luke's Purpose (v. 4)

If Luke's program is to investigate everything carefully, what is his purpose? Why does he do this? What is the purpose behind it? Luke writes to Theophilus so that he might "*might know the exact truth about the things you have been taught*" (verse 4). So Luke's stated purpose is just that: for his readers "to know the exact truth" about what they have been taught. The word translated "know" is not the regular γινωσκω (*ginwskw*) but the intensified form επιγινωσκω (*epiginwskw*), to know

---

[6] J. R. R. Tolkien, *The Hobbit* (1937; NY: Ballantine, 1973), title page.
[7] Alfred Plummer, *The Gospel According to Luke*, 5th ed. (The International Critical Commentary (Edinburgh: T&T Clark, 1923), xxxv.

thoroughly or to know well—to have not just theoretical knowledge but personal acquaintance with something. And the word translated "exact truth" is ασφαλεια (*asphaleia*), which means not just having the bare content but rather having a sure and certain grasp of the truth. So Luke's purpose is not just to give his readers information, but rather a confident assurance that they have accurate and sure knowledge of the things accomplished and fulfilled in Christ. (It is more than information—not less.)

Do you know what Jesus did? Do you understand what it accomplished? Do you not just "know" these things but have a well-grounded confidence that you know and understand the real truth about them—what Jesus really did, what He really said, what it means in itself, and what it means for us? That should be very important to us, who think that our eternal destiny and the meaning and purpose of our lives here and now depend absolutely on what Christ has done for us. We should therefore want very much to read Luke very carefully indeed. And so, as God gives us the grace to do so, we will. His purpose is to give us the exact truth about the things we have been taught. (Note, by the way, that this purpose as expressed is more in keeping with Lydia McGrew's contention that Luke is giving us solid history rather than the looser narratives we expect from Greco–Roman biographies.[8])

IV. Luke's Public (v. 3b)

Okay, we've looked at Luke's predecessors, his program, and his purpose. Let's also think a bit about Luke's public. "Theophilus," the name of Luke's stated audience, is a word that means "friend of God." Was this an actual individual or a symbolic reference to the fact that Luke was writing to people who love God? Most scholars think it was an actual individual. There are two main reasons for this conclusion. First, Theophilus was actually a very common proper name in the First Century. But second and more importantly, in the language of his prologue Luke is obviously going out of his way to situate himself among the Greek historians of his day, and the dedication to an individual of a book actually meant for the general public was an accepted practice among ancient Greek historians like Herodotus or Thucydides.[9]

If Theophilus was an individual, what was he like? Almost certainly he was not a Jew. He has a Greek name, for one thing. And Luke, more than any other Evangelist, goes out of his way to avoid or provide translations or substitutes for Hebrew names and titles that would have been unfamiliar to a Gentile audience. Where the other Gospels have rabbi he will have διδασκαλος (*didaskalos*, "teacher"). What the other Gospels call "scribes" he calls "lawyers," etc. There is less emphasis on Old Testament quotations and the fulfillment of Old Testament prophecy than in Matthew, which was

---

[8] Lydia McGrew, *The Mirror and the Mask: Liberating the Gospels from Literary Devices* (Tampa, FL: DeWard, 2019).

[9] Luke is clearly situating his narrative as belonging with the best of ancient *history*; it does not follow that he is adopting all the *techniques* associated with ancient Greco-Roman *biography*. See McGrew, op. cit., for the many reasons for rejecting the latter conclusion.

written for a Jewish Christian audience. And the prologue which we have read today is unlike anything else in the New Testament. All of a sudden you are reading an almost classical Greek. I can often go a page or two or more in my Greek New Testament without having to look up any Greek words in the dictionary. Suddenly in these four verses I am looking up every other word. It sounds like the prolog to Herodotus or Thucydides. For Luke is setting his history alongside theirs as part of the universal history of the world, not just the story of some local Palestinian cult. Luke's audience is the educated, cosmopolitan Greek of his day. So that is the frame of mind into which we should try to put ourselves as we read. For that makes us more aware of Luke's particular perspective on his material.

V. Luke's Perspective

Am I going to keep perpetuating these pedantic points patently presented by a palpable procession of potent and possibly pestiferous Ps? Precisely. The next one is Luke's perspective. Luke's perspective on the Gospel is the one you would expect from a disciple of the Apostle Paul: It is a missionary perspective. All four of the Gospels have this emphasis, to be sure, and Matthew has the classic passage, the Great Commission of chapter 28. But Luke has a continuing emphasis throughout his narrative that the defeat of Satan by the Savior is for *all men*. For Mark, Jesus is the First and Last Action Hero; for Matthew, he is the Jewish Messiah; for John, he is the Son of God; for Luke, he is the Savior of the *World*. Examples of this universal, world–encompassing missionary perspective include the fact that Luke takes Jesus' genealogy back not just to Abraham, the father of Israel, but to Adam, the father of all mankind. Luke mentions non–Jews more than anyone else: the Samaritans, for example (9:52–56, 10:30–37), and Gentiles in general (2:32, 3:6, 7:9, 13:29, 24:47). And we must remember that the Gospel of Luke is really only part one of a two–part work. That whole work, Luke–Acts, is truly a geographically oriented narrative, "there and back again." In Luke's Gospel we move from Galilee to Samaria to Jerusalem; then in Acts the movement is reversed, from Jerusalem to Samaria, and from there out all the way to the uttermost parts of the earth (Acts 1:8). There and back again; in and then out again. It's a wonderfully apt narrative structure when you see it. That is where Luke's narrative is going: out to the whole world. That is where he wants his readers to go. Oh. That would be us.

VI. Luke's Passion

Finally, in seeing Luke's program, his purpose, his public, and his perspective, we see Luke's passion: It is evident on every page: It is like that of his mentor the Apostle Paul, who said, *"Woe is me if I preach not the Gospel"* (1 Cor. 9:16): It is to tell the story of Jesus; to tell the story of Jesus as the Savior of the World. And for Luke, to tell that story is to praise and magnify and glorify its central character. The God who did all of this needs to be worshiped! Luke would have agreed with John Piper that evangelism needs to exist because worship does not—not everywhere, not yet. (Piper actually said "mission needs to exist," but it amounts to the same thing.[10]) Evangelism and mission will continue to exist as long as and wherever worship does not. Luke and Piper are definitely on the same page here.

How does Luke communicate this emphasis? His Gospel begins and ends with worship in the Temple; it alone preserves hymns of praise like the *Magnificat*; and more than any other Gospel it emphasizes that those who receive the blessings of salvation from Christ "glorify God." It starts with the shepherds, who went back to their fields *"glorifying and praising God for all that they had seen* (2:20). Then the people who saw the healing of the paralytic lowered through the roof (5:25), the members of the funeral procession who witnessed the raising of the widow's son of Nain (7:16), the woman who was bent double and who was made erect again in the synagogue (13:13), the one leper out of ten who came back to give thanks (17:15), the blind man who was sitting by the road outside of Jericho and received his sight (18:43), these and many others: All of them are specifically recorded as having responded by giving glory to God. *"And they were all filled with astonishment and began glorifying God; and they were filled with fear, saying, 'We have seen remarkable things today"* (5:26).

They gave glory to God when they saw. So should we as we read. Why? Because it needs doing for its own sake, and because only thus will the Great Commission be fulfilled. Evangelism must exist whenever and wherever we realize that worship does not. And only being filled as Luke was with a passion for the glory of God can motivate and sustain us in that task. We should have a deep love for lost men and women and an urgent passion for their souls, but if that is all we have, we will get discouraged and depressed when so many of them fail to respond. Worse, we are liable to give them the impression that the Gospel is about them. No. It is about Jesus! Everything He said and everything He did shows us a vision of the glory of God in the face of Jesus Christ. And it all climaxes in the Cross and the Resurrection, which show it most of all. Yes, we get eternal life in the bargain, but why is that such a good thing? Because it lets us go on looking into the face of Jesus forever! That is why Luke writes the story and why we need to read it and why we need to tell it. To see Jesus as Luke presents Him is to worship Him, to give Him glory, and it is to see that evangelism needs to exist because worship does not. Not everywhere. Not yet.

Conclusion

Did Luke, the Missionary Evangelist, have a passion for souls? Oh, yes. Most definitely. But he had that passion because first he had a passion for Jesus and therefore for the very story of Jesus itself, because it is wondrous and glorious and true and deserves to be told to the salvation of men and the glory of God. May God give us a like

---

[10] John Piper, "The Supremacy of Godin Missions through Worship," *Mission Frontiers*, July-August 1996, https://www.missionfrontiers.org/issue/article/the-supremacy-of-god-in-missions-through-worship.

passion as we delve into the story told so beautifully and accurately by the Gospel according to Luke.

GOOD NEWS FOR ZACHARIAS

Luke 1:5 In the days of Herod, king of Judea, there was a priest named Zacharias, of the division of Abijah; and he had a wife from the daughters of Aaron, and her name was Elizabeth. 6 They were both righteous in the sight of God, walking blamelessly in all the commandments and requirements of the Lord. 7 But they had no child, because Elizabeth was barren, and they were both advanced in years. 8 Now it happened that while he was performing his priestly service before God in the appointed order of his division, 9 according to the custom of the priestly office, he was chosen by lot to enter the temple of the Lord and burn incense. 10 And the whole multitude of the people were in prayer outside at the hour of the incense offering. 11 And an angel of the Lord appeared to him, standing to the right of the altar of incense. 12 Zacharias was troubled when he saw the angel, and fear gripped him. 13 But the angel said to him, "Do not be afraid, Zacharias, for your petition has been heard, and your wife Elizabeth will bear you a son, and you will give him the name John. 14 "You will have joy and gladness, and many will rejoice at his birth. 15 "For he will be great in the sight of the Lord; and he will drink no wine or liquor, and he will be filled with the Holy Spirit while yet in his mother's womb. 16 "And he will turn many of the sons of Israel back to the Lord their God. 17 "It is he who will go as a forerunner before Him in the spirit and power of Elijah, to turn the hearts of the fathers back to the children, and the disobedient to the attitude of the righteous, so as to make ready a people prepared for the Lord." 18 Zacharias said to the angel, "How will I know this for certain? For I am an old man and my wife is advanced in years." 19 The angel answered and said to him, "I am Gabriel, who stands in the presence of God, and I have been sent to speak to you and to bring you this good news. 20 "And behold, you shall be silent and unable to speak until the day when these things take place, because you did not believe my words, which will be fulfilled in their proper time." 21 The people were waiting for Zacharias, and were wondering at his delay in the temple. 22 But when he came out, he was unable to speak to them; and they realized that he had seen a vision in the temple; and he kept making signs to them, and remained mute. 23 When the days of his priestly service were ended, he went back home. 24 After these days Elizabeth his wife became pregnant, and she kept herself in seclusion for five months, saying, 25 "This is the way the Lord has dealt with me in the days when He looked with favor upon me, to take away my disgrace among men."

Introduction

Christmas will be here before you know it. Do you have your shopping done? Started? As we look forward to the celebration of Advent, I would like to begin a "pre–Advent" series, as it were, by surveying the Christmas narratives in Luke's gospel. And I would like to start at the beginning, with parts of the story that don't usually get much attention. They instruct us by rooting the coming of our Lord in both the Old Testament revelation and contemporary Jewish worship.

The whole Old Testament was indeed one long preparation for the coming of Messiah. In Gen. 3:15 we have the first promise of a coming Savior, who would crush the head of the Edenic Serpent, reversing for His people the effects of Adam's rebellion. Then Abraham was called to form a nation who would know God, and whose history, culture, and religion would enable the whole world to make sense of the Messiah when he came.

The most interesting part of that story as it relates to this passage may be the way the nation of Israel began: with the first of a series of supernatural births (Isaac, Samson, etc.) which would culminate in the familiar ones in Luke. Isaac should not have been born, naturally, and neither should Samson or Samuel. They establish a pattern of a supernatural birth preceding a critical moment in the history of God's people and a new revelation of His saving power. Now in the New Testament the same phenomenon reappears in John the Baptist and is turned up a notch to a new level in Jesus. The supernaturally enabled births of John and Jesus did not happen out of the blue but were recognizable as the last steps in a pattern God had used of old to create His people and raise up deliverers for them.

The whole history of Israel—Passover, Exodus, Sinai—revealed the person of God and the nature of His covenant. Then the Davidic kingdom was a foreshadowing of the rule of Messiah, who would arise from David's line to bring the Kingdom of God to men. And the Prophets promised a coming one—Davidic King (2 Sam. 7:16), Son of Man (Dan, 7:13–14), Suffering Servant (Isaiah 53), Wonderful Counselor, Mighty God, Everlasting Father, Prince of Peace (Isaiah 9:6)—who would deliver God's people in an ultimate and climactic sense.

Now after centuries of waiting we have finally entered the last stage of this process. For 400 years now the Prophets have been silent. Rome rules the world with an iron fist, and the Jews ask, "When will the promised King come to deliver us?"—little understanding their need for deliverance from a much greater Enemy than Rome. So an obscure priest named Zacharias comes to Jerusalem to take his turn in the Temple service. There are too many descendants of Levi by now for them all to serve regularly, so most of them wait a lifetime for their one opportunity to offer up incense upon the altar. This moment then was the climax of Zacharias's whole life; it would have been felt as such even if no angel had appeared. As he enters the holy place, a crowd of the devout and those who would appear devout gather in the courtyard to pray. A bell rings to signal that Zacharias has placed the incense upon the flames, symbolic of the prayers of the people rising up to God. A dead silence falls—but it lasts longer than they were expecting. The people wait for the priest to reappear and pronounce God's blessing upon them. But nothing happens. They begin to grow nervous. What's going on?

Well, inside, Zacharias has been confronted by a being who looks like a man, but who exudes a more than human aura of power, who simply and suddenly was there without having come, and who says to him, *"Fear not!"* You will have a son, and name him John. And he will be the Forerunner of Messiah foretold of old. And Zacharias remembers the very last prophecy of the Old Testament, Malachi 4:5–6, and realizes that his son will be its fulfillment. *"Behold, I am about to send you Elijah the prophet before the coming of the great and terrible Day of the Lord. And he will restore the hearts of the fathers to their children and the hearts of the children to their fathers, lest I come and destroy the land with a curse."* And thus he realizes that he himself would very likely live to see at least the childhood of the Messiah of Israel.

Most people whom I've heard preach on this passage emphasize Zachariah's lack of faith, as if whether or not you believe the next angel who appears to you without having to be struck dumb for a while were a real–life issue for you. Well, he ought to have believed, and so should we. But I want to focus on something much more important, and which I think was Luke's primary point as we move on toward the actual birth narratives of the Christmas story: What does this passage tell us about the coming Forerunner, and what does *that* tell us about the promised Messiah he was coming to introduce and about the kind of faith we should have in Him?

To answer that question, try asking this one. If you are a parent, try to remember when you first heard the news you were going to have a baby. If you are not a parent yet, try to imagine it. Oh, the questions that go through your mind! Will it be a boy or a girl? Will it be healthy? Will it look like me? What kind of person will it grow up to be? Then you hear the heartbeat, feel the kicking, and the questions all come back again. Now imagine Zacharias actually getting answers to those questions which point to the greatness not only of John but also of the One for whom he was coming to prepare the way. What did he learn about his coming son? He learned four things, each one of which can still prepare us for faith in the coming Messiah: John would be . . .

I. Great In The Sight Of God

Zacharias was told, first, that John would be great in the sight of God (verse 15a). In men's eyes, he was only a flash in the pan. A prophet who began with great promise and a huge following, he came to a bad end, came to nothing. He wrote no books, appeared on no talk shows, appeared on no lists of the pastors with the 10 largest Sunday Schools in America. (Oh, wait . . . neither did Jesus!) Yet in God's eyes John was great. In fact, Jesus said that he was the greatest man ever born of woman. What did Jesus mean by that? Well, think of Jesus' own criterion of greatness: *"He who would be great among you, let him be the servant of all"* (Mark 10:43, cf. Luke 22:26). John was a perfect exemplar of this radical definition of greatness, because it fell to him to utter the most noble words ever to come from the mouth of man: *"He must increase, but I must decrease"* (John 3:30). Jesus must increase, but I must decrease! To say that of Jesus and truly to mean it is to be great in the eyes of God. Is that the way we feel about Jesus? Or is our concern, even in His service, that *we* increase, that people say how spiritual, or what great men and women of faith, or great Bible teachers or visionary leaders *we* are?

May it never be! Rather, let us decrease into greatness. Did you hear me?" Let us *decrease into greatness*, just as John did!

II. Dedicated To God

Secondly, John would be wholly dedicated to God: He would drink no wine or strong drink (15b). The point of this is not that John was a teetotaler, nor that we should be; rather, John's abstaining from alcohol was a cultural symbol of the thing we should be emulating: the fact that he lived a totally dedicated life. Almost certainly it means that he took a Nazirite vow (not to be confused with Nazarene) as a sign of his radical dedication to the Lord. That vow is described in Numbers 6. *"When a man or woman takes a special vow, the vow of a Nazirite to dedicate himself to the Lord, he shall abstain from strong drink . . . neither shall he drink any grape juice or eat fresh or dried grapes . . . and all the days of his vow no razor shall pass over his head. He shall be holy"* (Num. 6:1–8). In other words, he gave up something that his culture considered a blessing from God as a sign of his radical dedication to Him.

This shows us a second reason for John's greatness: He was utterly single–minded in the pursuit of his goal, that Jesus would increase, and he would decrease. Nothing was allowed to compete with this; nothing would be in his life which did not contribute to this end, nothing which would hinder his single–minded devotion to his purpose for existing. And here again he serves as an example for us. There may be things that are innocent in themselves that I have to give up in order more effectively to serve the Lord, either permanently or for a time. The Bible does not mandate teetotalism, but I have had to give up alcohol in order to teach at Toccoa Falls College. I don't think hot showers are sinful, but I have to give them up while I am ministering in African villages. If I made either of these things into an issue, if I refused to serve unless I could have them, I would not be as devoted to the Lord as John was—more importantly, not as devoted to Him as He deserves me to be. What might be in that category for you? I have no idea—but it is a question John the Baptist's example puts to us. Is there anything you would find it hard to give up in order to serve the Lord, or even in order to serve Him better? Well, don't give it up ostentatiously to prove your spirituality! But do identify such things and pray that God will enable Jesus to increase in your life while they decrease.

III. Filled With The Holy Spirit

Third, John was filled with the Holy Spirit from his mother's womb (verse 15c). I must confess I do not fully comprehend this. It is not the norm for how the Spirit comes to indwell us. But clearly John was marked out by God as a special instrument of His purposes from the beginning. He had an unusual sensitivity to spiritual things, which allowed him to recognize his Lord and leap for joy even as a fetus in Elizabeth's womb when Mary came into the room on a visit in her own first trimester of pregnancy. Surely John's being filled with the Spirit even in his mother's womb had something to do with that.

What does this tell us about our relationship to the Holy Spirit? For one thing, it suggests that the sign of being filled with the Spirit is not speaking in tongues (which John is never recorded as having done) or any other manifestation that calls people's attention to itself. It is how we relate to Jesus. It is whether we say with full meaning and fervency, "He must increase, and I must decrease." That is the clearest sign of John's being full of the Spirit, and really the only one we need. For the Spirit has one purpose: to glorify Jesus. *"When He, the Spirit of truth comes, He will guide you into all the truth; for He will not speak on His own initiative, but whatever He hears, He will speak; and He will disclose to the world what is to come. He shall glorify me; for He shall take of mine and shall disclose it to you"* (John 16:13–14). "He must increase, and I must decrease." That is the authentic voice of the Holy Spirit speaking! Does it speak in us? Does it do so clearly and unequivocally? Well, if we cannot be like John from the womb, we can still recognize this as another sign of his greatness and recognize with it the importance of being filled with the Spirit, i.e., completely under His control, submitted to His influence, yielded to His purposes in our lives, from this point on. For then Jesus will increase, and we will decrease. And that is where our true greatness lies.

IV. A Witness

John would be great; he would be dedicated; he would be filled with the Holy Spirit. Fourth, John would be a witness (v. 16–17). The last of the Old Testament Prophets was also the first of the New-Testament Witnesses. He would turn back many, make the people ready for the Messiah, prepare His way. Many in Israel wanted to do this. The Essenes separated themselves from society to purify themselves in the desert, believing that if they could just somehow make themselves worthy enough, Messiah would come. Had not the Rabbis said that "When all Israel repents, then will Messiah come?" Had they not said, "If even one Jew should repent perfectly in his heart, then would Messiah come?"[11] But these people, zealous and sincere, did not pursue righteousness with understanding, i.e., by faith, but as if it were by law.

Repentance is not the Cause of Messiah's coming but its Effect. When God was ready to send Him, he also sent the Forerunner to preach repentance. And Israel as a whole rejected this message. Was Gabriel's prophecy false? No. Look at John 1:35–37. *"And again the next day John was standing with two of his disciples, and he looked upon Jesus as He walked, and said, "Behold the lamb of God!" And the two disciples heard him speak, and they followed Jesus"* (John 1:35–37). The core of Jesus' band of twelve disciples were former disciples of John. One may well believe that the same was true of many of the seventy and the 500 who were faithful to the Lord. There was no "John–the–Baptist" movement left in the world once the Ephesian disciples had been baptized in the name of Jesus. But this is not what makes John a failure; it is what makes him a great success, the greatest of all the Old-Testament prophets. And it is what makes the least in the

---

[11] Qtd. in Plummer, *The Gospel according to St. Luke*, op. cit., 89.

Kingdom of Heaven greater than him. For now, we too are to be witnesses to the fact that God still grants repentance and forgiveness in Jesus' name, to prepare our own generation for His coming—whether His coming to their hearts in faith now or to the world when He comes again.

Conclusion

We have seen something of the greatness of this last of the Old Testament Prophets and first of the New Testament Witnesses. But Jesus also said, "He who is least in the Kingdom of Heaven is greater than he." Least in the Kingdom of Heaven: if greatness comes by decreasing that Jesus might increase, then that is an honor to aspire to indeed.

THE ANNUNCIATION TO MARY

Luke 1:26 Now in the sixth month the angel Gabriel was sent from God to a city in Galilee called Nazareth, 27 to a virgin engaged to a man whose name was Joseph, of the descendants of David; and the virgin's name was Mary. 28 And coming in, he said to her, "Greetings, favored one! The Lord is with you." 29 But she was very perplexed at this statement, and kept pondering what kind of salutation this was. 30 The angel said to her, "Do not be afraid, Mary; for you have found favor with God. 31 "And behold, you will conceive in your womb and bear a son, and you shall name Him Jesus. 32 "He will be great and will be called the Son of the Most High; and the Lord God will give Him the throne of His father David; 33 and He will reign over the house of Jacob forever, and His kingdom will have no end." 34 Mary said to the angel, "How can this be, since I am a virgin?" 35 The angel answered and said to her, "The Holy Spirit will come upon you, and the power of the Most High will overshadow you; and for that reason the holy Child shall be called the Son of God. 36 "And behold, even your relative Elizabeth has also conceived a son in her old age; and she who was called barren is now in her sixth month. 37 "For nothing will be impossible with God." 38 And Mary said, "Behold, the bondslave of the Lord; may it be done to me according to your word." And the angel departed from her.

Introduction

Six months have passed since Zacharias was struck dumb while ministering in the Temple. So far, no one but he and Elizabeth knew that anything out of the ordinary was afoot. But then Gabriel was sent to an encounter which would come to be portrayed more than any other in Western art: the Annunciation to Mary of Jesus' conception, incarnation, and birth. His message was one for which Israel had waited throughout her history. Yet it came not to Annas or Caiaphas the high priests or to Herod the king or to some zealous Pharisee or learned Scribe or high–placed Sadducee, but to a simple peasant girl who was destined to become the most celebrated woman in history. But the story is not about Mary, not primarily: Like all of Scripture, it is about Jesus. So let us try to hear Gabriel's words as they would have sounded to Mary, the better to understand how the New Testament would develop them. For thus they reveal Christ to us. They reveal His humanity, His identity, His majesty, His personality, His destiny, His perpetuity, and His divinity.

I. His Humanity (v. 31, "*conceive . . . a son*")

First to be revealed is His humanity. Mary would conceive in her womb and bring forth . . . a son (v. 31). And He was the son of Mary, a very human son, with DNA that she provided. The term "virgin birth" is really a misnomer. The miracle was in Jesus' virginal *conception*; the birth itself, once the egg began growing and dividing, was perfectly normal and natural. Jesus was completely human: He grew in the womb and was born just like all of us. He kicked his mother in the ribs, made her short of breath in the last trimester, and gave her morning sickness, quite possibly, and awful back pains, no doubt. Once He was born, He was just as dependent, on things like the warmth of Mary's arms, the nourishment of her mother's milk, and the work of Joseph's hands to keep Mary fed so she could produce that milk, as any of us have ever been. He was just as weak and helpless as we were as newborns. He could not walk or even crawl; He could not talk. He did not look up at the Shepherds from the manger or the Wise Men in the house and deliver lectures in advanced theology; He did not explain to His mother at her breast the science behind lactation. He dirtied the first–century equivalent of diapers. He was as weak and helpless as we were in our own infancy which we cannot remember and as our children were in theirs, which we can remember—sin only excepted. We marvel at His deity, and rightly so. But the real marvel is deity revealed in humanity, through weakness. So, if we can accept that, it is no wonder that He still makes his strength perfect in our weakness.

The takeaway here then is twofold. First, we are reminded of the profound depths of God's love for us as shown by God the Son's identification with us in our humanity. Think about what that means. How would you like to go from your present level of competence, from the fact that you can actually do a reasonable facsimile of "adulting," back to the helplessness of being a newborn, or before that, a fetus, and have your growing up to do all over again? Jesus gave up the enjoyment of omnipotence to go there. And it was real. He loves us that much. And second, when we are reminded by both Scripture and experience that God's strength is perfected in our weakness—as my foot was reminding me quite recently when healing from surgery—we mustn't complain about that *modus operandi*. Do you struggle with it? I certainly do. But God hasn't asked us to participate in any aspect of that plan that He wasn't willing to go through Himself. And we are not going through any aspect of it with which He cannot fully sympathize, not just in an abstract way through His omniscience, but practically through real life experience. I preach the sermon I need to hear. If it helps you too, there is no extra charge!

II. His Identity (v. 31, "Jesus")

First then we see His humanity. The second thing to be revealed is His identity. They were to call His name Jesus (verse 31). Jesus is a Hellenization of the Hebrew name Yeshua, which was the same name as Joshua, the successor of Moses, the war hero who had led the Israeli army in the conquest of the Promised Land. It meant, literally, "Yahweh saves." So it meant Savior, Redeemer, Hero. It was a name that already had a history before this baby got it. You give a name like that to express your aspirations for the character and life you hope your child will have—as when _____'s grandparents named her father Jefferson Lee Davis. That would have meant something to his generation in the South! Like Joshua, Jesus meant Savior: but from what He would save his people, and how, was not yet guessed. It would drive a metaphorical sword through Mary's heart when she realized it. For this child would be the last step on the journey that led the human race from the Tree of Knowledge to the Tree of Life by way of the Tree of Calvary. He would save his people from their sins.

Dear friends, let us not forget who Jesus is, for that is the key to what faith in Him is all about. Yes, He gives meaning and purpose to our lives; yes, He gives us peace in the midst of our emotional struggles; yes, He sometimes gives us practical help in the answer to our prayers; yes, He gives us a sound epistemological place to stand amidst the miasma of Post–Modern relativism (I throw that one in for philosophy nerds like myself). All these benefits are real, and they are all important, but they are not the central focus. None of them is the critical element that gives access to all the rest. Mary was to call His name Jesus, for He would save His people from their sins.

III. His Majesty (v. 32, "great")

We see then His humanity and His identity. The third thing to be revealed is His majesty: He would be great, says verse 32. The Greek root μεγα (*mega*) shows up in English as a prefix, in words like megabucks, megatons, megawatts, megastar: a huge pile of money, *beau coups* of pounds, a humongous charge of electricity, a celebrity that impresses the masses. Now, Jesus was certainly great in the sense of being powerfully impactful and magnificently glorious. You see it in His great miracles of healing and even bringing back the dead; you see the glory peek out at moments like the Transfiguration. But He was not content to manifest that kind of greatness. In fact, Jesus would radically redefine greatness forever. How did He put it Himself? *"He who would be great among you, let him be the servant of all. As ye see me doing,"* he said with towel and basin (Mark 10:43, cf. Luke 22:26). As He was facing the Cross, he prayed, *"Father, the hour is come. Glorify thy Son that the Son may glorify Thee"* (John 17:1). We see His glory most profoundly not in His miracles but in His death. If greatness lies in servanthood (think about John the Baptist from last week), the Suffering Servant of Isaiah must surely be the greatest of all.

Do you have to keep reminding yourself what true greatness really is? Do you get yourself into trouble when you forget to do so? Every time I get up in this pulpit, I have to suppress the hope that you will think I am a great preacher and a brilliant expositor. I hope that isn't my main motivation, but I would be lying if I said it wasn't present. But where was John the Baptist's greatness as we saw it last week? *"He must increase, and I must decrease."* I wonder if a great deal of the impotence of contemporary Christianity doesn't come from our forgetting this lesson. So remember this about Mary's Son: He earned and merited and deserved and manifested all the glory and majesty in the normal sense that you can imagine and more, but showed His greatness most profoundly in weakness and suffering. We follow in His train.

IV. His Personality (v. 32, "Son of the Most High")

His humanity, then, and His identity and His majesty, are revealed by Gabriel's words. Fourth is something about His personality: He would be the Son of the Most High (verse 32). Now, the meaning of this phrase to Mary's mind at the time was probably not sonship in the full Trinitarian sense, though that is a possible and very logical extension of what she would have heard that was later shown to be fully justified. "Son of X" was a Jewish idiom with which she would have been very familiar. James and John were the "sons of thunder," that is, thunderous people. Judas was "the son of perdition," a quintessentially lost person. A "son of stripes" in the Old Testament was one who deserves a beating, i.e., one who is guilty. So "son of" something means "like," or "characterized by," that thing. If you look up X in the dictionary, you see the Son of X's picture next to the definition. Jesus then would be godly, like God in character, so much so in fact that the author of the Epistle to the Hebrews would call him the *"exact representation" of God's nature"* (1:3). If you want to know what God is like, look at Jesus. The full depths of this truth will be revealed later. But He is the one who is supremely both Son of God and Son of Man.

And He came to save us from our sins so that we could become sons (and daughters) of the Most High. The end of being saved from our sins is that we should be like Him. We should start becoming like Him now and we will be fully so when we see Him face to face. Wow! Think about that as we continue to look at our Savior in this sermon and beyond. It becomes more challenging and more daunting with every word that comes out of His mouth and every deed that He does. But the God who revealed such a Savior to Mary—His grace is sufficient even for this.

V. His Destiny (v. 32, "throne of David")

We see then His humanity, His identity, His majesty, and His personality. The next thing to be revealed was Jesus' destiny: He would be given the Davidic throne (verse 32). Jesus was a King before he was anything else. Messiah means "annointed one," again, like David. *"Now the Lord said to Samuel, 'How long will you grieve over Saul since I have rejected him from being king over Israel? Fill your horn with oil and go; I will send you to Jesse the Bethlehemite, for I have selected a king for myself among his sons.'"* And Jesse brought all his sons except David, who was tending the sheep. But Samuel insisted that he be called in too. *"And the Lord said, 'Arise, anoint him, for this is he'"* (1 Sam. 15:1, 12). That is what the word Messiah would have meant to Mary. We think of Christ as Savior, as the friend of sinners, and rightly so. But the first form the Gospel took was "Repent, for the *King*dom of Heaven is at hand." Had you asked the Apostles to summarize it they would have said, **"κυριος χριστος"** (*kurios Christos*), "Jesus Christ is Lord."

But wait a minute. Didn't I just get done arguing that saving His people from their sins was essential to Jesus' identity and central to His Gospel, based on His name? Yes. But His Lordship is not an optional truth tacked on to his Saviorhood; if anything it is the other way around. We distort the Gospel when we see the two concepts as rivals or even as alternatives. Jesus is able to be Yeshua, Yahweh saves, *because* He is Lord. It is because He is Lord that He has the authority to save. There is no such thing as a Jesus who is Savior without being Lord. He is either Lord of all or He is not Lord at all. Bow before him as Lord, in other words, and you will discover that He has pardoned you your treason, your former loyalty to His Rival the Usurper, and restored you to citizenship and service in God's Kingdom. But bowing, accepting Him as the true King, is the only way truly to discover this. The notion of accepting Jesus as Savior now and dealing with His Lordship later is a modern innovation created by well–meaning evangelists eager for decisions. But it is foreign to the biblical Gospel, as the way the very terms are packed in Gabriel's announcement shows us.

VI. His Perpetuity (v. 33, "forever . . . no end")

Gabriel has revealed Jesus' humanity, His identity, His majesty, His personality, and His destiny. The next thing that is to be uncovered is Jesus' perpetuity, for His Kingdom will have no end (v. 33). All human kingdoms, all human kings, have one thing in common: they end. Where is the splendor of Nebuchadnezzar, the glory that was Greece, the grandeur that was Rome, the promise and ideal that was Camelot? They are all now nothing more than dust blown in the wind, ink–smudges preserved on parchment. "Think'st thou that Alexander [that is, Alexander of Macedon, Alexander the Great] looked so i' the earth?" Hamlet asks Horatio, holding up the skull of Yorick. "And smelled so? Pah!"[12] "I met a traveler from an ancient land," wrote Shelley,

> Who said Two vast and trunkless legs of stone
> Stand in the desert. . . . Near them, on the sand,
> Half sunk, a shattered visage lies, whose frown
> And wrinkled lip and sneer of cold command
> Tell that its sculptor well those passions read
> Which still survive, (stamped on these lifeless things).
> The hand that mocked them and the heart that fed.
> And on the pedestal these words appear:
> "My name is Ozymandias, king of kings;
> Look on my works, ye mighty, and despair!"
> Nothing beside remains. 'Round the decay
> Of that colossal wreck, boundless and bare,
> The lone and level sands stretch far away.[13]

But this King will be different, and so His kingdom will be different. People gladly give their lives for kingdoms that are destined to pass away in a few hundred years, and which will probably become horribly corrupted before that. How much more should we spend them for this King and this kingdom? For that is a sacrifice that will not be wasted! And therein lies the grounds of Hope.

VII. His Divinity (v. 34–35)

---

[12] William Shakespeare, "Hamlet," act V, scene i, lines 218-20; *Shakespeare: The Complete Works*, ed. G. B. Harrison (NY: Harcourt, Brace, and World, 1968), 927.
[13] Percy Bysshe Shelley, "Ozymandias," 1818, *English Romantic Poetry and Prose*, ed. Russell Noyes (NY: Oxford Univ. Pr., 1956), 981.

All right, then. We have seen something of Jesus' humanity (He was Mary's son), His identity (He was Jesus, "Yahweh saves"), His majesty (He gloried in the Cross), His personality (He was also the Son of the Most High), His destiny (He would ascend David's throne), and His perpetuity (He would occupy it forever). Finally and climactically, and as a kind of summation of all the rest, we see Christ's divinity. How could all this be, asks Mary, since I know not a man? The Holy Spirit would come upon her, the Power of the Most High would overshadow her, the Glory of God would fill her. And *therefore* the holy offspring that would be born from her would be the Son of God. Mary the ancient Jewess would have recognized in Gabriel's answer the echoes of Exodus 40:34, when at the dedication of the Tabernacle the Cloud had *overshadowed* the Tent of Meeting. The very same word, επισκιαζω (*episkiazo*) is used in the Septuagint, the Greek translation of the Old Testament, and here in Luke's Gospel. The implication of Gabriel's words was that for the next nine months, Mary's womb would be the Holy of Holies. The Glory that had departed from the Temple would now reside *there*—in Mary's womb. Now we must indeed hear the phrase "Son of God" in the strong sense that Christ would be God himself in human form. In the last book of the Narnia series there is a stable that was bigger on the inside than on the outside, and the children are told that once in their world a stable held something that was bigger than the whole world as well.[14] As the medieval Christmas play puts it, "*Stabulo ponitur qui continet mundum*": "That which contains the world is placed in a stable."[15] And before that? Mary's womb would be the Holy of Holies. The deity of Christ could not be expressed more profoundly than that.

And what is the takeaway from all of this? That Christ is to be worshiped as God, served and obeyed as King, and trusted as Savior. That He is God means that there is no end to how true those claims are, and thus no limits to the whole–souledness of that worship, no limits to the devotion of that service and obedience, or the confidence of that trust. All this we get just from Gabriel's Annunciation to Mary of His coming. And Luke is going to spend twenty–four chapters, and the Apostles the entire New Testament trying to unpack it. So stay tuned! This story is only beginning.

Conclusion

The key to understanding Gabriel's words are to hear them as Mary would have heard them. But the next step is to consider how *we* hear them. Now, what would you say to news like that? What *do* we say to news like that? It is very easy sitting at a safe distance. But what if it were your womb? What if it were your fiance? What if it were your parents who would have to be told, in a world in which the stigma of unwed motherhood had not yet been blunted at all? Would they believe your story about an angel? What if this news was going to change your life forever so that it would never be

---

[14] C. S. Lewis, *The Last Battle*, 1956 (NY: HarperTrophy, 1984), 177.
[15] "The Service for Representing Herod," *Medieval Drama*, ed. David Bevington (Atlanta, GA: Houghton Mifflin, 1975), 64.

the same again? (Oh, wait. Guess what? It has! It does! It will!). I must therefore ask you very soberly whether you are now willing to say about the current situation in your life what Mary said in v. 38: *"Behold the bondservant of the Lord. Be it so unto me according to your word."* If you can, then come to the Lord's Table. For the Lord announced here will meet you there, according to his Word.

THE VIRGIN BIRTH OF CHRIST

Luke 1:26 Now in the sixth month the angel Gabriel was sent from God to a city in Galilee called Nazareth, 27 to a virgin engaged to a man whose name was Joseph, of the descendants of David; and the virgin's name was Mary. 28 And coming in, he said to her, "Greetings, favored one! The Lord is with you." 29 But she was very perplexed at this statement, and kept pondering what kind of salutation this was. 30 The angel said to her, "Do not be afraid, Mary; for you have found favor with God. 31 "And behold, you will conceive in your womb and bear a son, and you shall name Him Jesus. 32 "He will be great and will be called the Son of the Most High; and the Lord God will give Him the throne of His father David; 33 and He will reign over the house of Jacob forever, and His kingdom will have no end." 34 Mary said to the angel, "How can this be, since I am a virgin?" 35 The angel answered and said to her, "The Holy Spirit will come upon you, and the power of the Most High will overshadow you; and for that reason the holy Child shall be called the Son of God. 36 "And behold, even your relative Elizabeth has also conceived a son in her old age; and she who was called barren is now in her sixth month. 37 "For nothing will be impossible with God." 38 And Mary said, "Behold, the bondslave of the Lord; may it be done to me according to your word." And the angel departed from her.

Introduction

The virginal conception of our Lord and Savior Jesus Christ—popularly known as the "virgin birth"—has been a cherished doctrine of the Church since the beginning, and it was elevated to the status of a shibboleth during the "fundamentalist" controversies of the early Twentieth Century in America. When men claiming still to be teachers of the Church first began casting doubt on the historicity of the miracle stories in the New Testament, the virgin birth of Christ became something of a litmus test for orthodoxy among conservatives. If someone were inclined to the view that the supernatural elements in the Gospel story were mere mythological elements added by superstitious early believers, the virginal conception of Jesus would be one of the first places that view would show itself. And so, in the 1920s, this doctrine necessarily became a subject more of apologetics than of theology. Having been impressed by the rich theological insight of early fundamentalist stalwart J. Gresham Machen's classic book *Christianity and Liberalism*,[16] I remember how much I looked forward to reading his book on *The Virgin Birth of Christ*,[17] and how disappointed I was when I did. It was a useful book, certainly, a detailed refutation of every liberal interpretation of Jesus' conception, and of every half–baked historical argument against the reliability of Luke's account of it then abroad. But it had relatively little to say about the meaning of the virgin birth for understanding Christ or the Christian faith.

---

[16] J. Gresham Machen, *Christianity and Liberalism* (1923; Grand Rapids, MI: Eerdmans, 1981).
[17] J. Gresham Machen, *The Virgin Birth of Christ* (NY: Harper, 1930).

We have continued to inherit from that period an emphasis on the fact of the virgin birth to the relative neglect of its meaning. The first emphasis was necessary, is still needed, and is not wrong. But this ought we to have done without neglecting the other, as Jesus himself might say (Mat. 23:23). I would like to try to redress that imbalance just a wee bit this morning, as we spend a second week on the Annunciation. I will give a fuller exposition to a couple of important ideas that we introduced in the last message.

Thesis: Gabriel's presentation to Mary of our Lord's virginal conception enhances our understanding of both Christ's nature and His mission, of what He was and of why He came.

I. His Deity

It is obvious that the story of Jesus' virginal conception is related to claims about His deity. Though Mary was His mother, His father was, by implication, not Joseph but God himself. But if we look at this claim too quickly, without considering the real import of Gabriel's language, we might easily come away with a very inadequate notion of Jesus' relationship to the Divine—i.e., that he was some sort of divine–human hybrid, half God, half human. But the Church has always maintained that he was much more than that, and something much harder to imagine: One Person with two complete Natures, united but neither mixed nor confused: fully God and fully Man.

There are many reasons for this difficult doctrine, too many for us to discuss today. But one of them is certainly a careful understanding of Gabriel's language in this passage. An accurate understanding of that language has to be rooted in salvation history. What would a devout Jewish girl of the last years of the first century BC, illiterate, but with a mind thoroughly nourished on the Old Testament story and even its very language by a rich oral culture—what would she have made of those words? That is the question we asked and answered last time, and which we will dwell on again this week. What would Mary have thought when she asked how she could possibly have a son without having "known" a man, and she heard, *"The Holy Spirit will come upon you and the power of the Most High shall overshadow you; and for that reason the holy offspring shall be called the Son of God. And behold, even your relative Elizabeth has also conceived a son in her old age, and she who was called barren is now in the sixth month. For nothing will be impossible with God."*

Two things about this statement would have resonated powerfully in her mind. One is that she was being connected with a familiar Old-Testament pattern of miraculous conceptions and births as a way of marking out key moments in the history of redemption, key points in God's progressive revelation of Himself to His people. A whole series of very important people were born to mothers who should not have been able to have them: Isaac, Joseph, Samson, Samuel. If we think of his preservation rather than his conception itself as making his coming into the world miraculous, we could add Moses to the list. In most of these cases a barren woman miraculously conceives a son who will play a key role in the development or deliverance of Israel. In one case, Abraham and Sarah having Isaac, the husband was also sterile, so there was a double miracle—but in each case a husband was involved. And now Mary's relative Elizabeth and her son John the Baptist have been added to the list. The Forerunner will be the next to the last member of this series. And that leads us to Mary. As we saw in week one of these pre–Advent messages, her son would be the climax of the series, the exclamation point to the sentence the others constitute. And therefore, in her the miracle is taken to a new level; it goes one step further. Jesus will be part of this series, its climax, but, as the climax, also different from all His predecessors. In His case, there will be no human father involved at all. It is not just that barrenness or sterility is being healed, but that the whole normal and natural process of conception is being bypassed or transcended. *"And for that reason the holy offspring shall be called the Son of God."* God, not Joseph, will be his father. What exactly does this mean?

The second Old–Testament motif that would have rung like a bell in Mary's mind carries the answer to that question. For Gabriel uses a very curious word when he says that *"The Holy Spirit will come upon you and the power of the Most High shall overshadow you."* The word *overshadow* takes us back to the dedication of the Tabernacle in Exodus 40:34. *"Then the cloud covered the tent of meeting, and the glory of the Lord filled the tabernacle."* The cloud is the pillar of cloud by day and pillar of fire by night that was the visible sign of God's presence with Israel in the wilderness. And if that is not clear enough, the Hebrew parallelism links its covering of the tabernacle with the tent being filled by the shekinah, the glory of God. As we saw last week, the Septuagint translation of the Hebrew uses the same Greek word for the word translated "cover" in the NASB that Luke ascribes to Gabriel in Luke 1:35 and is translated "overshadow." The connection cannot be anything but deliberate.

In other words, the cloud is the sign of God's presence. When it overshadows the tabernacle at its dedication and fills it with the Glory, it means that God has accepted the tent as the place where He will meet his people and be worshiped by them, as the place where He will "dwell" in their midst. Do you see what it meant when Gabriel applied the same sacred language to Mary? Mary did. It means that God is about to visit his people in a very personal way. It means that for the next nine months, Mary's womb is going to be the Holy of Holies. God himself will be there. And when you put all this together, it means that the boy's other name was entirely appropriate, and literally so: Immanuel, "God with us" (Mat. 1:23). This child, born with a completely human nature derived from His mother, would also be, personally, God Himself. Fully God and fully Man: The fully orthodox language of the Creeds is already here in embryonic form as it were. *"And for that reason the holy offspring shall be called the Son of God."*

II. His Sinlessness

A second truth about Christ that is implied here is His sinlessness (or holiness, to use the word that actually appears in the text). It is clear that our Lord's virginal conception is related to his sinlessness. But again, the precise nature of that relationship is often misunderstood. I have run into people who seem to think that for Christ to be sinless he had to be conceived without sex—for anything that can feel that good must be inherently sinful, even between two faithful married people! Others' thinking seems to suppose that sin is somehow transmitted genetically, and that breaking that transmission by leaving Joseph out of the process was supposed to help. Both views profoundly miss the point, being ignorant of biblical teaching on how sin is transmitted from one generation to another. Sin is not inherited genetically from Adam; it is imputed to us by virtue of his headship over the human race.

Romans 5:19 tells us that sin came to the human race from one man, Adam, the same way righteousness does through one man, Christ. *"For as through the one man's disobedience the many were made sinners, even so through the obedience of the One the many will be make righteous."* And Romans 4:3–5 has already explained how Christ's righteousness comes to us. *"'Abraham believed God and it was <u>counted</u> to him as righteousness.' . . . To the one who does not work but believes in Him who justifies the ungodly, his faith is <u>reckoned</u> as righteousness."* The key words are *counted* and *reckoned*. They are the basis of what is called the Doctrine of Imputation. God does not force us to become righteous first and only then accept us as His children. If He did so, it would create a catch–22 that would prevent us from ever being saved. He counts us as righteous on the basis of Christ's perfect obedience and sacrifice on our behalf, and therefore reckons us as such and accepts us as such, with the result that we are able to start becoming actually righteous with His help. The theological way of saying this is that Christ's righteousness is *imputed* to our account. Actual (or a better word would be "experiential," for imputed righteousness is actual)—experiential righteousness flows from imputed righteousness, not the other way around. It is backwards from the way human beings normally think, for we assume that we must somehow make ourselves righteous (even if it be with God's help) before we can be counted as righteous. It is backwards from the way human beings normally think, but it is clearly the way God thinks—and the way He works.

What allows Christ's righteousness to count for us is our relationship to Him: He is our Lord, our Head, our Representative—which is what Paul means in Romans 5 when he calls him the Second Adam. For Adam was all those things to the human race. He was our head; he was not just the first man, he was Representative Man. As head of the race, he had the authority to make decisions, not just for himself, but for the whole human race. And so when he chose sin, he was choosing it for all of us. And his choice counted. Think of the way our representative democracy works. We can't all go to Washington to vote on every issue, so we elect a representative, a congressman or woman, to go there as our representative and vote on our behalf. Because he was duly elected, his vote counts as ours. If we do not like how he voted, we can try to replace him with someone who will represent us better. But as long as he is in office, his vote counts as that of our district. In just that way, Adam had the legal authority to speak and act for us. (Theologians call this his "federal headship," by the way, which is related to why we call our national government the "federal" government.) So when Adam chose sin, he acted for us; and when Christ chose righteousness and when He paid the penalty for our earlier choice, He was also acting for His people, for believers. That is why His sacrifice counts as the payment for our sins and why His righteousness can therefore be imputed to us. And this is the key not only to salvation but to the Christian life as well. Just as God imputes Christ's righteousness to all believers, leading to actual deeds of righteousness, so God imputed Adam's sin to all of his descendants, leading to actual acts of sin on their part. That is really how it works.

A lot of people object that it is unfair for us to be counted guilty of Adam's sin when we did not personally choose it. But three things can be said in response to that objection. First, this is the way the universe works. The language of Romans 5 is pretty plain about that. Second, we underestimate the meaning of the reality that we were "in Adam" when he made that choice to sin. Can you really tell me in all honesty that, if you had been there, you would have chosen differently? You know this? I didn't think so. In a mysterious but real sense you were there, and you did not choose differently. And third, the imputation of Christ's righteousness as our new Head and Representative is way beyond fair—it is grace. We have nothing to complain about!

Sin then is not transmitted biologically at all. If it were, Jesus could have caught it from Mary just as well as from Joseph. Instead, Adam's sin was not imputed to Jesus because Jesus was not "in Adam." He was the new Adam, a new head, a fresh start for the human race. And that is why Joseph was excluded from the process that led to the creation of Jesus' human body and human nature: not because Jesus could not have been sinless if He had a biological father, but as *a sign that the link with Adam had been broken.* Jesus was not born of a virgin so He could be sinless; he was born of a virgin to show He was sinless. The issue was not so much biological as dynastic, in other words. Jesus was not descended from Adam through the male line because a change of dynasty was taking place. Jesus was the Seed of the Woman, and therefore human, but He was not the Seed of Adam. He was the new Adam, a fresh start, an alternative head for humanity. Adam's guilt was not imputed to Christ because Adam was not Christ's head. And Jesus' virginal conception is therefore a sign miracle, a sign that a fresh start was being made. It was to emphasize Jesus' relationship with Adam and with us as being different from that of any other child who was ever born.

Now, this might sound like some pretty abstruse theology, but it has profound practical implications. It means that we can have complete confidence in Jesus as the one Mediator between God and Man (1 Tim. 2:5). He is the new Adam. He is our King. He is fitted by His nature and His relationship to us, as shown in the form of His birth, to fill this role. It means we can have complete confidence in faith alone as the means by which we receive God's salvation. Salvation in its very conception and design, even down to the conception, nature, and birth of our Savior and Mediator, is such that it cannot be performance–based. The only cure for imputed guilt is imputed righteousness. Righteousness in action flows from righteousness imputed, just as sin in action flowed from Adam's guilt imputed. It cannot be the other way around.

And, finally, Jesus' virginal conception understood thus gives us the ultimate motivation to live in such a way as to please our King. How does it do that? Because it helps us understand how much we truly owe to Him, how radical our dependence on Him really is. You are free—free from the intolerable burden of having to manufacture your own righteousness. It is His—all His—and the totality of that "all" is conveyed most clearly by that technical but beautiful and life–imparting theological word, *imputation*. It is ironic: The less performance–based our concept of salvation is, the more we are freed to perform in the service of our Lord. If we understand this, it means that we serve out of gratitude, not out of guilt. Then our service becomes a benefit, not a burden. It is adoration, not obligation, a delight, not a duty, a desire, not a debt. It is a privilege that carries no pressure because we do it as sons, not slaves, as children, not churls. Good works become a blessing, not a bondage, once we fully grasp that our performance not only has nothing to do with our acceptance by God but theoretically cannot be its basis. And this is the key to a victorious Christian life that knows fully the joy of salvation.

Conclusion

When we think of our Lord, the Lord of Glory, lying in that feeding trough, and remember that His mother had not known a man, let us be reminded of His wonderful nature and glorious mission—Immanuel, God with us, and also fully Man, the second Adam, fit to be our Representative and Head. He came to give us the opportunity to transfer our allegiance from Adam so that we could be represented before God not by Adam's disobedience but by Christ's obedience. And that is a fresh start indeed, which fully justifies the words of the carol: "Joy to the World."[18] Amen.

---

[18] Isaac Watts, "Joy to the World," *Trinity Hymnal*, (Atlanta, GA: Great Commission Publications, 1990), 105.

A VISIT TO ELIZABETH

Luke 1:39 Now at this time Mary arose and went in a hurry to the hill country, to a city of Judah, 40 and entered the house of Zacharias and greeted Elizabeth. 41 When Elizabeth heard Mary's greeting, the baby leaped in her womb; and Elizabeth was filled with the Holy Spirit. 42 And she cried out with a loud voice and said, "Blessed are you among women, and blessed is the fruit of your womb! 43 "And how has it happened to me, that the mother of my Lord would come to me? 44 "For behold, when the sound of your greeting reached my ears, the baby leaped in my womb for joy. 45 "And blessed is she who believed that there would be a fulfillment of what had been spoken to her by the Lord."

The Magnificat

46 And Mary said: "My soul exalts the Lord, 47 And my spirit has rejoiced in God my Savior. 48 "For He has had regard for the humble state of His bondslave; For behold, from this time on all generations will count me blessed. 49 "For the Mighty One has done great things for me; And holy is His name. 50 "And His mercy is upon generation after generation toward those who fear Him. 51 "He has done mighty deeds with His arm; He has scattered those who were proud in the thoughts of their heart. 52 "He has brought down rulers from their thrones, And has exalted those who were humble. 53 "He has filled the hungry with good things; And sent away the rich empty–handed. 54 "He has given help to Israel His servant, In remembrance of His mercy, 55 As He spoke to our fathers, To Abraham and his descendants forever." 56 And Mary stayed with her about three months, and then returned to her home.

Introduction

Just before our passage this morning, Mary had received the most astounding news ever delivered to mortal man or woman: she would be the mother of the Messiah, and, as such, the mother of the incarnate Son of God. If an angel told you something like that, what would you do? You couldn't sit still; you would have to talk to someone or burst. But who are you going to tell? We have romanticized Mary's situation to the point that we have forgotten what a hard life she had chosen when she said, *"Behold the maidservant of the Lord. Be it so according to your will."* Who is she going to tell? Joseph? Her parents? Can you imagine that conversation? "Uh, Guess what, Mom? Dad? I'm pregnant. I'm going to be an unwed mother—but, not to worry, an angel said it's Okay." Yeah, right. You and I believe her because we've got the whole history of Christ, including His resurrection and His Spirit's transformation of our lives, behind us. Joseph and Mary's parents did not. Okay, let's just put those conversations off a bit. Right now, there is only one person who can be counted on to understand. And so Mary hurries off to visit Aunt Elizabeth. Whether it was to put off telling her parents or because she *had* told them and they felt a need to get her out of town, Elizabeth is the one person in the world she can really talk to right now. It was a mercy in more ways than one that she got to go.

Now, lots of stuff happened in the three months of that visit that are not recorded. The account we have is in the story because here, at the very outset of His earthly life, even before He was born, it gives **three responses to the coming of Christ.** There is one by each of the three main characters in this little vignette, one each by John, Elizabeth, and Mary. They are here because, taken together, they form a definitive pattern, a practical set of trustworthy signs of Christ's presence with His followers. Indeed, I will argue, our Lord cannot be present to a receptive and faithful heart without producing these three responses. Is the Lord effectually present in a life? In a congregation? These three signs will tell you, because they are the natural, appropriate, and inevitable responses of a believing heart to *who He is*. And who He is, is what Luke is at pains to reveal throughout his Gospel. What are they?

I. Joy

The first is that the infant **John the Baptist leaped for joy.** This is important. John does it in verse 41, and Elizabeth remarks on it in verse 44. "*When Elizabeth heard Mary's greeting, the baby leaped in her womb; and Elizabeth was filled with the Holy Spirit. . . . . 'For behold, when the sound of your greeting reached my ears, the baby leaped in my womb for joy.'*"

Well, what is Joy? Joy is different from Happiness, which is more dependent on circumstances; Jesus was a man of sorrows and acquainted with grief, but those experiences are not incompatible with Joy. Joy is the ability to praise God and rejoice in His love in spite of our circumstances, It is the ability to praise God and rejoice in His love even in the full acknowledgement of the grievousness they sometimes have. So prominent is this response to Christ in both the Gospel narratives and in the Epistles which explain them that its absence in so many contemporary believers and their churches is a troubling and perplexing wonder indeed. To see that, let's get just a brief survey of those biblical passages.

In Mat. 2:10, the Wise Men saw the star and rejoiced with exceeding great Joy. In Luke 2:10 the angels announced Christ's birth as news of great Joy to all peoples. The Lord Himself said He had come to bring life, and that more abundantly (John 10:10), for the word "Joy" does not have to be present for the concept to be implied. In Mat. 25:21 He promises to say to his faithful servants, "*Enter into the Joy of your master.*" In John 15:11 He came that his Joy might be in his disciples and their Joy be made full. In Gal. 5:22, the fruit of the Spirit Christ sends as His Representative includes love, Joy, peace, etc. Paul commands the Philippians to "*Rejoice in the Lord always, and again I say, 'Rejoice'*" (Phil. 4:4). John writes to us in his first epistle so that our Joy may be made complete (1 John 1:4). Peter speaks in 1 Peter 1:8 of "*Joy unspeakable and full of glory.*" When the lame man in Acts 3:16 was healed by Christ through his servants Peter and John, he started "*walking and leaping and praising God.*"

Now, none of us here are lame in body this morning (though I was a little for a while not long ago), but we are all lame and worse in spirit, yea, *"dead in trespasses and sins."* Does having our crippled, twisted souls straightened and strengthened into new life not make us leap for joy within? Yes, yes, of course it does—unless we have forgotten what we were like before. No one in the Gospels met Christ without a strong response. No one. It was either bitter anger and hatred, or joy and love inexpressible. If He causes neither in you, then you have not met Him! You have only met a phantom you have created in our own mind to protect you from the shocking and astounding Reality of the Son of God.

Now, what am I doing here? Am I pressuring you to manufacture in yourself a false counterfeit of genuine Christian joy so you can feel better about your spirituality? Go wash your mouth out with soap! If that is what you get out of this, it would be better if I had never spoken. What then am I saying? Don't try to feel joy (or any other emotion). You will only push the real thing away that way. Rather, choose to focus your attention on those things that we should be joyful about: the beauty of Christ's person, the elegance of the plan of salvation, the forgiveness of your sins (yes, yours, even yours!), the profundity of God's love shown by the Sacrifice that gave you that forgiveness. *"For God commendeth His love in this, in that while we were yet sinners, Christ died for us"* (Rom. 5:8). Do you remember my series on Second and Third John last year? There we learned that Joy is the emotional residue left behind in the psyche by indwelling truth and outworking love, which are the effects and the signs of Christ's work in your life. Joy is the byproduct of His presence in your life in those ways. Focus on those realities and not on your response to them, and by God's grace, in time, the response will flow.

II. Being Filled With The Holy Spirit

The first response to the presence of our Lord was that John that Baptist leaped for joy. The second response is that **Elizabeth was filled with the Holy Spirit** (v. 41). This too is the result of responding to Christ with faith. It is related to Joy, which is part of the Fruit of the Spirit, and it is simply a way of talking about the presence of Jesus in your life. How so? The Holy Spirit is Jesus' own personal agent and representative. We make the doctrine of the fullness of the Spirit too difficult. It really is a meaningful way of talking about the presence of *Jesus* in your life. For it is He who sends the Holy Spirit. *"John answered and said unto them, 'As for me, I baptize you with water; but One is coming who is mightier than I. . . . He will baptize you with the Holy Spirit'"* (Luke 3:16). *"But I tell you the truth,"* Jesus said, *"it is to your advantage that I go away. For if I do not go away, the Helper will not come to you; but if I go, I will send Him to you"* (John 16:7). As Christ further explains in what may be the most crucial passage for understanding the Holy Spirit and His work, *"But when He, the Spirit of truth, comes, He will guide you into all the truth. . . . He shall glorify me, for He shall take of mine and shall disclose it to you"* (Jn. 16:13–14). And what does Peter say in his Pentecost sermon? *"Therefore, having been exalted to the right hand of*

God, and having received from the Father the promise of the Holy Spirit, He [Jesus] has poured forth this which you both see and hear" (Acts 2:33). And, furthermore, Jesus sends the Spirit to each heart which He Himself enters. "*If anyone does not have the Spirit of Christ, he does not belong to Him*" (Rom. 8:9).

The Spirit's ministry is to take what belongs to Jesus and reveal it to us, to glorify Jesus, as we saw in John 16:13–14; in other words, it is to make Jesus real to us. The Holy Spirit is the personal Agent and Representative of Christ, sent by Christ to His people to represent Him in their lives between the Ascension and the Second Coming. In the mystery of the Trinity, the Holy Spirit is a stand–in for Jesus who is as good as the real thing—better, actually, in that He can be present with all Christ's people at once. He is, in other words, the *way* Jesus is present with all His people even though He is currently located at the right hand of the Father in Heaven, not physically here on earth. Therefore, the fullness of the Spirit is not some strange mystical experience *in addition* to knowing Christ. It simply *is* knowing Christ. It has no necessary connection to speaking in tongues or any other particular Gift (for the Spirit distributes the Gifts severally as *He* will) but everything to do with Christ being formed in us. For what we see in these verses is that the Holy Spirit is simply Christ's personal Representative and Agent who mediates Christ's presence to His disciples after Christ's ascension until He returns. The closer to Jesus you are, the more full of the Spirit you will be. To know the fullness of the Spirit, therefore, draw near to Christ.[19]

III. Praise

The third Response is that **Mary praised God** (vv. 46–55). Mary was probably illiterate, since at that time only boys would have been sent to synagogue school, but she had absorbed the content and the spirit of the Old Testament through a rich oral culture. And so in response to the Spirit in her own heart she spontaneously uttered the Magnificat, one of the most beautiful hymns of praise to Christ ever composed, in which the very style and rhetorical structure of the Psalms is reproduced. Luke's almost classical Greek becomes suddenly very Hebraic as he quotes it, worthy to take its place in the Psalter alongside the greatest Messianic hymns written by David, the Sweet Singer of Israel. It continues the theme of Joy (verse 47), for praise is Joy overflowing in expression. As Dr. Dan Orme once said (one of my very favorite of his quotes), "Joy is Peace dancing; Peace is Joy at rest."[20]

Mary's hymn praises God for his Grace, in Old-Testament terms, to be sure (since the radical form Redemption would take had not yet dawned on her, or anyone else), but Grace unmistakably. Look at verses 48–50: "*For He has had regard for the humble state of His bondslave; for behold, from this time on all generations will count me blessed. For*

---

[19] For more on the work of the Spirit in relation to Christ, see Donald T. Williams, *The Person and Work of the Holy Sirit* (Nashville, TN: Broadman, 1994; rpt. Eugene, Or: Wipf & Stock, 2002).
[20] The late Dr. Alan Dan Orme was the founding pastor of University Church, Athens, GA, the church where this series was last preached.

the Mighty One has done great things for me; and holy is His name. And His mercy is upon generation after generation toward those who fear Him." Grace of course is unmerited favor. We see it in Mary being blessed despite her humble state, in God doing great things for her, not as reward for her superlative piety, as some Roman Catholic rhetoric would lead us to expect, but out of His *mercy*. Mary sees herself not as some kind of super saint worthy to receive this blessing, but as a recipient of Grace—unmerited favor. In this, she is an example to us. This is an infallible sign of Christ's presence among a people, that they praise God, and praise Him specifically for his Grace, His *unmerited* favor—because Christ is its supreme expression.

Mary also praises God for His mighty power (verses 51f), because this power is used to bring His Grace to bear on the lives of men. "*He has done mighty deeds with His arm; He has scattered those who were proud in the thoughts of their heart.*" The result is that "*He has brought down rulers from their thrones, and has exalted those who were humble.*" And she praises Him for His covenant faithfulness, because he has done all of this in accordance with the way "*He spoke to our fathers, To Abraham and his descendants forever*" (verse 55). Again and again, as we follow Jesus through His earthly ministry, we will find that He causes people to give glory to God. This has not changed to this day among those who truly know Him.

Conclusion: The Proper Use Of The Paradigm

Now, I want us to put this little vignette to its right use. I want it to be an encouragement to us to respond to Jesus authentically as Elizabeth, John and Mary did. But it may be a discouragement if we are not careful. What we are seeing here is a classic, definitive, perfect, paradigmatic instance of the natural emotional response of redeemed sinners to their faith to Christ. It is crystal clear, and it is pure. But in our own lives, I'm willing to bet the response has never been clear or pure; it has often been anything but clear or pure. It is muddy and mixed and scandalously undependable, to the point that we might, in comparing ourselves to this portrait, become discouraged and wonder if we have met Christ at all. But I think that if those of us who are truly Believers could look at our lives objectively, we would see Joy in the Lord, we would see the fullness and fruit of the Spirit, and we would see that we have praised Him truly if imperfectly on many occasions. The fruit of love, joy, and peace may be green and knotty, it might not be as thick on the boughs as it should, but it is there on the branches in ways that would not be so had Christ not impacted our lives. We should perhaps be encouraged that in vile, wretched, hopeless and inexcusable Sinners like ourselves we can see these signs at all.

Let me give you an example of what I mean. My freshman year in college I was a music major, first–chair clarinet in both the concert band and the orchestra at Taylor University as well as taking private lessons. I was practicing more than I ever had in my life, and I was getting powerfully discouraged. "I've never practiced harder," I complained to my teacher, "But I'm only getting worse." "No you're not," he responded. "You are actually improving a lot. But what is happening is that your understanding of where you should be is climbing faster than your ability to get there. The gap between the two is growing, and that is why it feels like you are going backwards. But you are actually making great progress." He was right. I've seen the same thing happening to people in their spiritual walk. Is that an accurate description of where you are? I don't know, of course. But if you really are serious about following the Lord and are nonetheless discouraged, it very well might be. If you are really serious about following the Lord and not just being a spiritual slacker, I'm inclined to think it probably is. Be encouraged!

Yes, be encouraged. But encouragement is no grounds for complacency. Do what Paul said to do: Always be pressing forward to the high calling in Christ Jesus (Phil. 3:13–14). Why? Because our labor is not in vain in the Lord. When we see Him face to face, these responses of Joy, Fullness, and Praise, in purity and power, will define us completely. And to the extent that we come to know Him and learn to live by faith in Him, we will find them growing in us even now. That is one way to measure whether we are growing. To the extent that we are, our testimony will have credibility, for these things are the definitive evidence of His Presence in our lives—just as when Mary brought Him in embryonic form into the house of Elizabeth, and there was Joy, the Fullness of the Spirit, and the spontaneous Praise of God. May it increasingly be so in our lives.

THE PROPHECY OF ZACHARIAS

Luke 1:57 Now the time had come for Elizabeth to give birth, and she gave birth to a son. 58 Her neighbors and her relatives heard that the Lord had displayed His great mercy toward her; and they were rejoicing with her. 59 And it happened that on the eighth day they came to circumcise the child, and they were going to call him Zacharias, after his father. 60 But his mother answered and said, "No indeed; but he shall be called John." 61 And they said to her, "There is no one among your relatives who is called by that name." 62 And they made signs to his father, as to what he wanted him called. 63 And he asked for a tablet and wrote as follows, "His name is John." And they were all astonished. 64 And at once his mouth was opened and his tongue loosed, and he began to speak in praise of God. 65 Fear came on all those living around them; and all these matters were being talked about in all the hill country of Judea. 66 All who heard them kept them in mind, saying, "What then will this child turn out to be?" For the hand of the Lord was certainly with him.

Zacharias's Prophecy

67 And his father Zacharias was filled with the Holy Spirit, and prophesied, saying: 68 "Blessed be the Lord God of Israel, For He has visited us and accomplished redemption for His people, 69 And has raised up a horn of salvation for us In the house of David His servant – 70 As He spoke by the mouth of His holy prophets from of old – 71 Salvation from our enemies, And from the hand of all who hate us; 72 To show mercy toward our fathers, And to remember His holy covenant, 73 The oath which He swore to Abraham our father, 74 To grant us that we, being rescued from the hand of our enemies, Might serve Him without fear, 75 In holiness and righteousness before Him all our days. 76 "And you, child, will be called the prophet of the Most High; For you will go on before the LORD to prepare His ways; 77 To give to His people the knowledge of salvation By the forgiveness of their sins, 78 Because of the tender mercy of our God, With which the Sunrise from on high will visit us, 79 to shine upon those who sit in darkness and the shadow of death, To guide our feet into the way of peace." 80 And the child continued to grow and to become strong in spirit, and he lived in the deserts until the day of his public appearance to Israel.

Introduction

John the Apostle tells us that in the beginning was the Word, and the Word was with God, and the Word was God (John 1:1). When that eternal Word came into the world, His coming generated other words, which were true just as He is the Truth. Some of them were spoken by Zacharias, the father of John the Baptist, at the very moment he recovered his speech after the nine month's wait due to his hesitancy to believe the angel's announcement of John's birth. They shed some interesting light on the coming Messiah and on His mission. They are cast in very Old–Testament language of course, and that very fact helps us reconceptualize Salvation in more biblically accurate terms

51

perhaps than some of the ones we have become familiar with. What do they tell us about the coming One? They tell us something about what Christ came to save us from, what He came to save us by, and what He came to save us for.

I. What Christ Came To Save Us From

The first thing they help us to see is what Christ came to save us from: An Enemy, a powerful enemy who hates us. *"Blessed be the Lord God of Israel, For He has visited us and accomplished redemption for His people. And has raised up a horn of salvation for us In the house of David His servant, As He spoke by the mouth of His holy prophets from of old: Salvation from our enemies, And from the hand of all who hate us"* (vv. 68–71). No doubt the others in the room thought Zacharias was referring to Rome. But this verse is an allusion to Psalm 106:10. *"So He saved them from the hand of the one who hated them and redeemed them from the hand of the enemy."* This connection hints that even Zacharias may have seen deeper than Rome. For that psalm is a rehearsal of Israel's history from the standpoint of her captivity in Babylon. Why is she in Babylon? Because again and again she has sinned. *"We have sinned like our fathers. We have committed iniquity, we have behaved wickedly. Our fathers in Egypt did not understand thy wonders. They did not remember thine abundant kindnesses, but rebelled by the sea, at the Red Sea"* (Ps.106:6–7). God has allowed Israel to be oppressed as a result. *"Therefore the anger of the Lord was kindled against His people and He abhorred His inheritance. Then He gave them into the hand of the nations"* (v. 40–41). But God has always sent deliverance in the past, and will again in the future, in spite of Israel's unworthiness. *"Nevertheless He looked upon their distress when He heard their cry, and He remembered His covenant for their sake"* (v. 44–5).

The whole thrust of Psalm 106 then is that it is Israel's sin and unbelief that is her real enemy. Israel's sin and unbelief, in other words are the real reason why she has been conquered and taken into captivity—her sin and unbelief, not Pharaoh or Nebuchadnezzar. It is her sin and unbelief that gives her oppressors their power over her. Indeed, Zacharias will go on in Luke 1:77 to define the deliverance (or salvation) that Messiah will bring as forgiveness of sin. He will *"give to His people the knowledge of salvation by the forgiveness of their sins."* This is a rather strange thing to say if it is all about overthrowing the Babylonian, or now the current Roman, oppressor. Zacharias's son would fulfill this prophetic vision by identifying Israel's deliverer as *"The Lamb of God who taketh away the sins of the world"* (John 1:29). So it is sin which is the real enemy, and behind sin lies Satan, the Enemy of our Souls.

We know that Satan is God's enemy, but it would be helpful to remind ourselves that he is ours too. As God is love, Satan is the embodiment of hatred. God might love you and have a wonderful plan for your life, but Satan hates you and wants you to be miserable. To move from those clichés to a better and more biblical manner of speech, let us say that God wants to share His life with you, to give you joy unspeakable, and indeed His own glory; Satan wants you to share his misery, for, as Mephistopheles reminds us in Marlowe's Faustus, "Misery loves company."[21] Satan is a powerful adversary, perfectly capable of disguising himself as an angel of light when he is really a roaring lion seeking whom he may devour. And because Satan is behind it, sin too is your enemy, and sin too is aggressive: Gen. 4:7 describes it as crouching at the door, desiring Cain like a beast of prey. It is not just a neutral choice sitting there quietly in the path just in case you might happen to come by and pick it up; it is after you. Yes, sin is aggressive; it lusts for us, but we must master it.

By describing salvation as being from an Enemy who hates us, Zacharias reminds us of the importance of these biblical metaphors. We picture good and evil as simply neutral choices just lying there waiting for us to make up our minds. But sin is not passive; because Satan is behind it, it is an active principle, dynamic, aggressive and predatory. And we are not neutral either; we are twisted in the direction of sin already, due to the corruption of our natures caused by the Fall. Why do we have such trouble shaking loose of our besetting sins? One reason is our substitution in our own minds of tamer pictures for the biblical ones describing the Enemy. This allows us to trust in our own wisdom and strength rather than fleeing to Jesus alone as the all–sufficient Deliverer. He came to save you from your mortal enemy. He came to give you salvation from your enemy, from the hand of the one who hates you. He came to give you the knowledge of salvation by the forgiveness of your sins. Flee to Him! Cling to Him! That is your only refuge in the time of temptation. He is your only hope. You will cling to Him in so far as you understand what He came to save us from.

II. What Christ Came To Save Us By

Zacharias also helps us to restore our vision of what Christ came to save us *by*: the Forgiveness of Sins. He came *"To give to His people the knowledge of salvation by the forgiveness of their sins"* (verse 77). The knowledge of salvation is in the forgiveness of sin, he says. As we have already seen, this is a rather strange thing to say if we, like all of Zacharias's uninspired neighbors and even Jesus' own disciples right up to the Ascension, view the Roman Empire (or any other set of temporal circumstances) as our primary enemy. God wants to deliver us from our Enemy, Satan, who hates us. So what prevents Him from doing so? What keeps Him from just up and raiding Satan's kingdom and taking us out of it? Two things: our Sin and His Justice.

And we are sinners. We know it because Scripture convicts us. *"All have sinned and fallen short of the glory of God"* (Rom. 3:23). *"There is none that is righteous, no not one"* (Rom. 3:10). We know it because the Holy Spirit convicts us, as Jesus sent Him to do. And we know it because, if we were honest, our own hearts would convict us. Which of us at this very moment is obeying the Great Commandment, to love the Lord our God with *all* our heart, *all* our soul, and *all* our mind? (Mat. 22:37). We won't even talk about

---

[21] Christopher Marlowe, "The Tragical History of Doctor Faustus," *The Norton Anthology of English Literature*, ed. Stephen Greenblatt et al. (NY: Norton, 2013), 517.

our neighbor as ourself. Really: *as you love yourself*. That is what it says. And if we cannot obey even those two Commandments in their apparent simplicity, how are we, apart from grace, going to follow the more elaborated list of Ten that fleshes them out in detail?

We are sinners. And God is a God of justice. These two truths in combination are terrible news, but news we have to hear and accept before we are ready to understand the Good News that is the Gospel. God is just. He is not a cosmic Tyrant and Bully. He is not, in other words, the enforcer of arbitrary rules imposed by sheer power only because He could. His own moral character is the source of the moral Law of the universe. It is therefore as absolute as He is in His uncreated and transcendent holiness. He can no more ignore the Law or sit passively by while it is broken or wink His eye at those who violate it than He can cease to be. That is why the God of all the universe must do right, and that is why *"The soul that sinneth, it shall die"* (Ezek. 18:4), because *"The wages of sin is death"* (Rom. 6:23). Therefore, God can no more pretend that sin didn't happen than He can lie—for that would be a lie. He can no more waive its penalty out of mere soft–hearted kindness than He can do any other evil—for a great evil and affront to justice that would be. Therefore, if there is to be forgiveness, there must be atonement. If there is to be forgiveness, a price must be paid. If there is to be forgiveness, the moral books of the universe must somehow be brought back into balance. And that is why, *"Without the shedding of blood, there is no remission of sin"* (Heb. 9:22).

That is why the death of Christ was necessary, and that is why His incarnation was necessary. Christmas is necessary so that Good Friday and Easter can come. Christ must take on our nature so he can serve as our Substitute. He must die to take our penalty and wipe out our guilt so that God can receive us back as his own and shield us from our deadly enemies forever more, in spite of our previous willful entanglement with them. To do this He must relate to us as the Second Adam, our Representative before God, as we saw in our study of the Virgin Birth above. And He must ever live as the Head of our restored humanity and Mediator between us and the Father so that His perfect obedience can not only count for us but also come to live in us. Thus Zacharias anticipates the Pauline doctrine of Justification by Faith alone as the only way to salvation, Christ's merit imputed to us as the only ground of justification and the only door to sanctification. And that is what Christ came to save us *by*.

III. What Christ Came To Save Us For

A third reality Zacharias can help us reconceptualize is what Christ came to save us for: Himself. He came to die so that God could "grant" us to serve Him without fear. He will *"grant us that we, being rescued from the hand of our enemies, Might serve Him without fear, in holiness and righteousness before Him all our days"* (verse 74–5). The result is that *"the Sunrise from on high will visit us, to shine upon those who sit in darkness and the shadow of death, to guide our feet into the way of peace"* (verse 78–79). To serve the God of Heaven without fear, and more, to bask in the light of His presence and glory, in peace: That is what we were made for.

This, as Paul emphasizes in his correspondence with Timothy, is perhaps the greatest of His gifts. *"I thank Christ Jesus our Lord, who has strengthened me because He considered me faithful, putting me into service, even though I was a blasphemer and a persecutor and a violent aggressor. And I was shown mercy because I acted ignorantly in unbelief. But the grace of our Lord was more than abundant, with the faith and love which are found in Christ Jesus"* (1 Tim. 1:12–14). Service is not to Paul an obligation but a privilege, not something Paul has to do because he was saved, but rather itself the thing for which he is thankful. He and Zacharias are therefore definitely on the same page here.

We tend to view salvation negatively, as release from eternal punishment. And this view is true, though incomplete. But Zacharias and Paul help us to see it also as positive, as saved not just from but for. What greater gift could there be than the ability to serve God without fear? Service is not something we ought to do if we are especially zealous Christians; it is something we get to do as the fulfillment of our redemption. And because our trust is not in the inadequacy of our own righteousness but wholly in the supreme gift of Christ's, we can do it without fear. I don't have to worry that my service will be unacceptable, because it too is covered by the Blood. My righteousness is not my own, but it is from the One of whom the Father said, *"This is my beloved Son, in whom I am well pleased."* I need only to be faithful, and I will hear those blessed words, "Well done, thou good and faithful servant." God has rescued us from our Enemy so that we can serve Him without fear. It doesn't get any better than that!

Zacharias also pictures this great salvation in terms of light dawning (v. 78b–79a) and peace (v. 79b). It comes to us *"Because of the tender mercy of our God, with which the Sunrise from on high will visit us, to shine upon those who sit in darkness and the shadow of death, to guide our feet into the way of peace."* Once again, Zacharias helps us see the positive (for) as well as the negative (from) aspects of salvation. The English word for peace is more negative: peace in our mind is simply the absence of conflict. But the Hebrew *Shalom*, the word that would have been in Zacharias's mind (and in his mouth before Luke translated it), is positive: not just the absence of conflict but the presence of harmony, not just the absence of strife but the presence of harmony, of God's rich blessing enjoyed in security and contentment. That is a light dawning, indeed; that is what it means to serve God without fear. It really doesn't get any better than that. For that is what Christ came to save us for.

Conclusion

The preposition is a neglected part of speech that is often the key to unlocking the deep truths of the Word. Christ came to save us *from, by,* and *for: From* our Enemy who hates us, not Rome but Satan and sin; *by* the forgiveness of our sins, purchased by the infinitely precious blood of Christ on the Cross; *for* fellowship with God, *for* the glad service of God without fear in dawning light and ever–deepening *shalom; for* inclusion in the love that the Father has for His beloved Son, in whom He is well pleased; *for* that moment when we finally hear the Lord's voice saying, *"Well done, thou good and faithful servant"* (Mat. 25:21).

From; By; For. Let us allow these words to sink deep into our minds and transform our thinking. The more we come to picture salvation as Scripture does, the more we will realize what a great salvation the Lord came to that stable to bring us. The more we come to picture salvation as Scripture does, the more we will realize what a great and marvelous and all–sufficient Savior we have. Then we will flee to Him indeed, and then we will serve Him with joy. Then we will celebrate His birth with real understanding. Joy to the world! Amen.

"FEAR NOT!"

Luke 2:1 Now in those days a decree went out from Caesar Augustus, that a census be taken of all the inhabited earth. 2 This was the first census taken while Quirinius was governor of Syria. 3 And everyone was on his way to register for the census, each to his own city. 4 Joseph also went up from Galilee, from the city of Nazareth, to Judea, to the city of David which is called Bethlehem, because he was of the house and family of David, 5 in order to register along with Mary, who was engaged to him, and was with child. 6 While they were there, the days were completed for her to give birth. 7 And she gave birth to her firstborn son; and she wrapped Him in cloths, and laid Him in a manger, because there was no room for them in the inn. 8 In the same region there were some shepherds staying out in the fields and keeping watch over their flock by night. 9 And an angel of the Lord suddenly stood before them, and the glory of the Lord shone around them; and they were terribly frightened. 10 But the angel said to them, "Do not be afraid; for behold, I bring you good news of great joy which will be for all the people; 11 for today in the city of David there has been born for you a Savior, who is Christ the Lord. 12 "This will be a sign for you: you will find a baby wrapped in cloths and lying in a manger." 13 And suddenly there appeared with the angel a multitude of the heavenly host praising God and saying, 14 "Glory to God in the highest, And on earth peace among men with whom He is pleased." 15 When the angels had gone away from them into heaven, the shepherds began saying to one another, "Let us go straight to Bethlehem then, and see this thing that has happened which the Lord has made known to us." 16 So they came in a hurry and found their way to Mary and Joseph, and the baby as He lay in the manger. 17 When they had seen this, they made known the statement which had been told them about this Child. 18 And all who heard it wondered at the things which were told them by the shepherds. 19 But Mary treasured all these things, pondering them in her heart. 20 The shepherds went back, glorifying and praising God for all that they had heard and seen, just as had been told them.

What we have today is not so much a traditional sermon as a Christmas meditation on the meaning of the birth of Christ in Luke's familiar narration—an attempt to lift it out of our traditional holiday associations and see it afresh. It is not that all of those associations are wrong—but they are way too familiar and comfortable. If you had been there, you would have found these events anything but that.

C. S. Lewis said, "There comes a moment when people who have been dabbling in religion ('Man's search for God') suddenly draw back. Supposing we really found him? We never meant it to come to that! Worse still, supposing he had found us?"[22] The Christian faith in general and Christmas in particular are the proclamation that He has found us. And when He did, it was, for a moment, as threatening to the Shepherds as Lewis' quotation suggests. Before they could rightly hear the good news of joy to all

---

[22] C. S. Lewis, *Miracles: A Preliminary Study* (NY: MacMillan, 1947), 96–7.

peoples in verses 10–11, they had to get scared out of their wits in verse 9. Why did the angel begin with "Fear not?" Because he was frightening. Angels are not cute and cuddly and encounters with them are not "precious moments" but profound shocks to the system. Why? Because they shine with the reflected glory of the greatness of the majesty of God.

An angel is a more intense concentration of the glory of the Creator which David says is declared by creation, specifically the heavens (Ps. 19:1). Probably, none of you has ever seen even this lesser declaration as our ancestors did, for the night sky is damped, even in the remotest areas of N. America, by the "light pollution" created by the electric lights of our cities. Even in the remotest places you can go East of the Mississippi, like camping on top of Albert's Mountain off the Appalachian Trail in North Carolina, a place you can only reach by a couple days of stiff hiking or by being lowered from a helicopter, the lights of Greenville, S.C. streaming up from over the horizon in the East blank out half the glory the heavens were able to declare to David. Once, I saw the stars much as he must have, in a village in the Andes with no artificial illumination stronger than a kerosene lamp even over the horizon. And I thought I was going to die! They were not twinkling prettily but pulsating dynamically as if they were going to bore holes right through you. It was very exciting but also a little frightening. But the angel who appeared to these Shepherds—men who were used to the night sky in all its pristine splendor—was more than a little frightening. They were "sore afraid." What must it have been like? Let's imagine one of those shepherds telling his story:

SOLILOQUY: THE SHEPHERD

I was never before a man of many words.
What I had to say could be expressed
In curses mumbled at the wayward herds
Or loudly shouted at the boys from town.
The buyers of mutton might just be addressed
Not much more civilly, as up and down
We haggled over whether I would die
Of hunger or live yet another year.
The sky at night was simply the night sky,
A thing to be ignored. I knew to fear
Then only hunger and the hungry wolf.

I've learned a lot since those days of both fear
And hunger, and had more of both than ever.
There was no moon that night, and yet the stars
Shone with a light the like of which I'd never
Seen before. Not since I was a child
Had I taken notice of the way their light

On a clear, frosty night, out in the wild,
Can fill you up with hunger—no, with fright—
Well, something else that's both, and yet is neither.
They'd seemed then like a thousand eyes, whose sight
Could see clean through a man and leave no secrets.
Their piercing gaze had never bored as deep
As it did on that night. They seemed so near!
I told myself it was just lack of sleep,
That they could not be *really* getting closer.
But as I tried to explain that to the sheep,
The endless blackness which is seen to lie
Between the stars to keep them separate
Was in a moment squeezed out of the sky,
And I was knocked flat on m y face by light
That thundered like the sea—or by a choir
Of voices that shone brighter than the sun,
And burnt me to the bone with searing fire.

I'd always joked that when Messiah came
I'd ask him what he meant to do about
The price of sheep. If that was not his game,
I'd know he was a Christ of no concern
To me. But I was in no way prepared
For angels, with their messages that burn
Behind them after they are gone, and drive
You down the dark, deserted roads at night
To see a baby lying in the hay.
Still less was I prepared for such a sight
As that was. Yes, he had to do with sheep
Alright (the Lamb of God the prophets called him!),
And with their price. The one he paid was steep:
It was himself, and I purchased the sheep.

Of course, I didn't find that out 'til later.
That night I only knew I was afraid,
And hungry for I knew not what. But listen!
I've seen forty summers bloom and fade
Since then, and I would rather know that fear
Than all the ease that Caesar now enjoys
In his bright palace. Soon—perhaps this year—
I go to join my fathers, hungry still
With an eternal hunger. But the bread

I found that night in Bethlehem will fill
Me then as earthly meat has not. I am
Invited to the Supper of the Lamb![23]

Can we get back to the place where we can see the world like the shepherds did? Maybe part of the way. Poetry can help. We also try to compensate for our visually impaired concept of the sky by our greater theoretical knowledge of it. The sun, our own neighborhood star, is 300,000 times the mass of the earth. The energy which it lavishes on the insatiable sponge of space comes from the conversion of 974 million tons of hydrogen into 970 million tons of helium every second. Four million tons of matter a second is thus transformed into energy. An infinitesimal bit of that reaches the earth and fuels all the life in its biosphere. The sun is 93 million miles away from us. That energy, traveling at the speed of 186,000 miles per second, takes 8 minutes to reach us. The next nearest star system, Alpha Centauri, is 4.3 light years away. If it went supernova right now, we would not even know it until June of 2028. Our galaxy, the Milky Way, contains 100 billion such stars. The known universe contains an estimated 100 billion galaxies. Not even to mention quasars, pulsars, black holes . . .

Alright, then: The idea of God means that the Power that made and maintains and controls all these vast unimaginable forces is a Person—who can see into your heart right now. If you find that a comforting thought—if you are not threatened by it to the point of extinction and reduced to dust and ashes—then you are dead or deaf or just plain stupid. If the Being who is as absolute in power and intelligence as He would have to be to be the Creator and Maintainer of this universe is just as absolute in burning moral purity, as the Bible clearly teaches, then what must He think of us? Our standard defense against such thoughts is to say, "I'm not so bad." Do we really suppose such an argument has any force with a Being such as we are describing? That you are, after all, only a *petty* sinner? Hmmm.

In an earlier version of this message preached in another church, someone accused me of "scare tactics." Just preach the love of God, she urged. But my point is precisely to magnify the love of God by beginning with the reality of God. We want to get to verses 10–11: *But the angel said to them, "Do not be afraid; for behold, I bring you good news of great joy which will be for all the people; for today in the city of David there has been born for you a Savior, who is Christ the Lord."* But the only doorway that leads to an adequate appreciation of vv. 10–11 leads through v. 9. *"And an angel of the Lord suddenly stood before them, and the glory of the Lord shone around them; and they were terribly frightened."* We have such a superficial grasp of God's love because we have tried to get to the Good News by making an end run around the "fear not." It is just as it is in that

---

[23] Donald T. Williams, *Stars through the Clouds: The Collected Poetry of Donald T. Williams*, 2n ed. (Lynchburg, VA: Lantern Hollow Press, 2019), 141–2.

most misunderstood sermon of all time, Jonathan Edwards' "Sinners in the Hands of an Angry God."[24] All the infamous imagery of God dangling the sinner over the flames of Hell like a spider over a campfire is there to say, "Look: God hates sin this much. And he *still* sent His Son to save us!" So His love must be a powerful and profound force indeed if it can overcome His hatred of sin.

In other words, it is only when we have seen God as *God* and ourselves as He must see us that we are in a position to get the impact of what the birth of Christ means: We have a Savior! Now we can understand why the Gospel is called Good News: Nothing less could transform the glory and reality of God from the threatening idea it ought to be to the comfort it is. Hence my poetic summary of the whole history of religion:

WITNESSES

We sensed that there was something. In the sky
It somehow seemed to be, or in the wind —
A Voice, a subtle message in the dew,
Something in our hearts that would not lie
Quiet when we knew that we had sinned.
(How did we know that it was sin? We knew.)

Something. Power hidden in the earth
To push the blades and buds up in the spring.
At first we gave each face of it a name;
So sky and field and river each gave birth
To its own god, and men began to bring
The blood they shed to cover up their shame.

And they did right, though they did not know why
Until the Voice called out to Abraham
To leave his father for an unknown land.
A cave for burial he had to buy,
A mountain–thicket where he found a ram,
Sore feet, the burning sun, and blowing sand,

More mysteries than answers he could learn,
A son to whom he could bequeath the trial,
An oath, but not one acre he could claim
Were all that wanderer got in return —
Plus one thing more that made it all worthwhile:

---

[24] Jonathan Edwards, "Sinners in the Handa of an Angry God," 1741, *The Works of Jonathan Edwards* (Edinburgh: Banner of Truth, 1974), 2:7–12.

He saw through all that flickers to the Flame.

And so his seed would bear the message, "Hear
Oh Israel, the Lord your God is One!"
And camp at Sinai when the Flame came down.
Though all too easily the holy fear
Engendered by the way they had begun
Was lost, at least they got their piece of ground.

And there they stayed, and there they read the Law,
And studied, and debated every word,
And kept alive at least some memory
Of who they were and what their fathers saw.
But what the Flame had shown, the smoke had blurred,
And most of them would finally fail to see

The Thing they'd waited for through all those years,
The Something we had groped for in our fears.
The hopes, the blood, the altars—who'd have guessed
That this would be the answer to our quest?
The smoke of Sinai slowly cleared away
To show a Baby lying in the hay.[25]

So let the glory of the Lord shine round about you and be sore afraid. And then listen to the angel's words, the message of Christmas: *"Fear not, for behold I bring you good tidings of great joy, which shall be to all peoples. For unto you is born this day in the city of David a Savior, who is Christ, the Lord."*

Amen.

---

[25] Donald T. Williams, *Stars through the Clouds*, op. cit., 116–117.

WHAT SIMEON SAW

Luke 2:21 And when eight days were completed before His circumcision, His name was then called Jesus, the name given Him by the angel before He was conceived in the womb. 22 And when the days for their purification according to the Law of Moses were completed, they brought Him up to Jerusalem to present Him to the Lord 23 (as it is written in the Law of the Lord, "Every first–born male that opens the womb shall be called holy to the LORD.") 24 and to offer a sacrifice according to what was said in the Law of the Lord, "a pair of turtledoves or two young pigeons." 25 And behold there was a man in Jerusalem whose name was Simeon; and this man was righteous and devout, looking for the consolation of Israel; and the Holy Spirit was upon him. 26 And it had been revealed to him by the Holy Spirit that he would not see death before he had seen the Lord's Christ. 27 And he came in the Spirit into the temple; and when the parents brought in the child Jesus to carry out for Him the custom of the Law, 28 then he took Him into his arms, and said, 29 "Now, Lord, Thou dost let thy bond–servant depart in peace, according to thy word; 30 for my eyes have seen thy salvation 31 which Thou hast prepared in the presence of all peoples, 32 'a light of revelation to the gentiles,' and the glory of thy people Israel." 33 And His father and mother were amazed at the things which were being said about Him. 34 And Simeon blessed them and said to Mary His mother, "Behold this child is appointed for the fall and rise of many in Israel, and for a sign to be opposed— 35 and a sword will pierce even your own soul—to the end that thoughts from many hearts will be revealed." 36 And there was a prophetess, Anna the daughter of Phanuel, of the tribe of Asher. She was advanced in years, having lived with a husband seven years after her marriage 37 and then as a widow to the age of eighty–four. And she never left the temple, serving night and day with fastings and prayers. 38 And at that very moment she came up and began giving thanks to God, and continued to speak of Him to all those who were looking for the redemption of Jerusalem.

Introduction

We look again today at a question we have examined from many angles in our pre–Advent, Advent, and now post–Advent series over the last few weeks: What is the true meaning of Christmas? It is easy to miss. One thinks of the child's picture of the manger scene. The Sunday School teacher asks, "Who is that short fat guy in the corner?" "Oh, that's Round John Virgin." Or the version of the carol, "The Catalog's roaring, the poor baby wakes." And then there is this masterpiece from the old Pogo comic strip:

> Deck us all with Boston Charley,
> Walla Walla wash and a Kalamazoo.
> Dora's freezing on the trolley.
> Swaller dollar cauliflower, alley–garoo!

Well, now that the pretty wrapping paper is trash, half the toys are broken, and most of the stomachs are rumbling with indigestion, we may wonder if we have done much better. Simeon understood it as well as anyone ever has, and he teaches us to see Jesus in five different but complementary ways: as the consolation of Israel, as the Lord's Christ or Messiah, as salvation embodied, as a light of revelation to the Gentiles, and as the glory of God's people Israel.

I. The Consolation Of Israel (v. 25).

"And behold there was a man in Jerusalem whose name was Simeon; and this man was righteous and devout, looking for the consolation of Israel." Consolation is the Greek word παρακλησις *(paraklesis)*, related to παρακλητος *(parakletos)*, paraclete or "comforter," one of the titles of the Holy Spirit. Well, why did Judah need to be consoled? Because she has had one of the saddest stories of any nation: hundreds of years in captive slavery, forty more of wilderness wandering, finally getting her Promised Land only to lose it and spend seventy years in exile, returning from that only to fall under Roman subjection, seeing her capital sacked and her temple destroyed twice. And it doesn't end with biblical times: She was scattered for millennia, with her people persecuted in ghettoes and made scapegoats for all the world's problems. They finally became the targets of the Holocaust, and its survivors are still unable to feel secure in the borders of their ancestral Land. She has been a nation of sorrows and acquainted with grief — an eloquent picture of the human condition, with all its pathos concentrated in one nation and its history.

One can understand then why the rabbis interpret Isaiah's great Suffering Servant passage as a reference to corporate Israel and her experiences rather than to an individual Messiah. It is not. The discussion actually begins in chapter 52:13, not chapter 53. And there we read an interesting comparison: *"Just as many were astonished at you, my people, so His appearance was marred more than any man."* It is true that the words "my people" are not in the original. But whom is Isaiah addressing? Israel! Who else? So the addition of the phrase in our translation is justified. The Servant is being compared to Israel ("you"), which means He cannot *be* Israel. It is therefore indeed a clear prophecy of the suffering of Christ in our atonement. But we can still understand why the rabbis are tempted to take it the other way. Nevertheless, Simeon saw more clearly than they do. He believed God's promise of One coming who would wipe away all those tears and make all the sorrows and burdens of their existence — and ours — worthwhile. And he saw Him in Mary's arms.

II. The Lord's Christ (v. 26)

"And it had been revealed to him by the Holy Spirit that he would not see death before he had seen the Lord's Christ." Second, Simeon saw Jesus as the Lord's Christ, that is, the Lord's Messiah or, literally, the Lord's Annointed One. This is a phrase familiar from the Old Testament in its more literal translation, for David refused his opportunities to kill Saul on the grounds that he would not lift up his hand against the Lord's

Annointed—the very same phrase. It refers here, then, as it did there, to the fact that this Baby would grow up to be King of Israel, specifically a Davidic king. All that David promised but delivered imperfectly and only for a while, this Baby would deliver perfectly and forever: justice, righteousness, well–being, peace, *shalom*. Now that is a Promise to cling to and a fulfillment to get excited about indeed!

But was Simeon right about this? The primary reason modern Jews reject Jesus' claim to be the Messiah is that the Messiah was supposed to bring Peace on Earth, and, well, just look around you! No peace, no Messiah; the real one obviously hasn't come yet. And if we looked only at the prophecy that He would be the Prince of Peace, taken out of the context of the rest of the biblical revelation about Christ, we would have to admit the force of their argument. Fortunately, there is enough context to help us see that the world is not yet at peace because it is still in rebellion against this King, who has not yet stepped in finally to subdue it because He is still giving it time for repentance. But He has not failed of His promise: He *has* brought peace personally and individually to the hearts of His subjects already, a peace that passeth understanding. The others are still being given the opportunity to repent, to submit willingly to His rule before it is imposed by force. So the peace has come and is coming: personally and internally now for believers, universally and objectively later when the King comes again. Yes, Simeon was right: this baby was the Lords' Christ, the Anointed One, the Messiah—the Prince of Peace.

III. Thy Salvation (vv. 29–30)

The Consolation of Israel; the Lord's Messiah; now comes "Thy Salvation." *"Now, Lord, Thou dost let thy bond servant depart in peace, according to thy word; for my eyes have seen thy salvation."* What Simeon says here is really interesting, for it is not what I suspect we would have said if we were making this up. We might have seen in Jesus the one *bringing* salvation; but Simeon saw not that but the salvation itself—lying in Mary's arms. And while it is true that Christ brings salvation, it is more profoundly true that He constitutes it. Richard Sibbes put it most succinctly: "Christ himself is nothing else but salvation clothed in our flesh. So old Simeon conceived of him, when he held him in his arms."[26] And Jesus Himself put it most profoundly: *"This is life eternal, that they might know thee, the only true God, and Jesus Christ whom thou hast sent"* (John 17:3). The great thing about being saved and having eternal life is not living forever—it is knowing God in Christ and living forever so we can keep on doing that!

So that is why we worship Christ. He is our all in all. He is our portion. He is our God! But even in our worship of Christ, we often treat him merely as a means to an end: forgiveness, a clear conscience, release from the flames of Hell, eternal life. And while He does bring those things, and while they are wonderful things indeed to have, they

---

[26] Richard Sibbes, "The Soul's Conflict with Itself and Victory over Itself by Faith," 1635. *Works of Richard Sibbes*, 6 vols. Ed. Alexander B. Grossart (Edinburgh: Banner of Truth Trust, 1973), 1:1259.

are but the side effects of the real salvation, which is just *Him*. Like eternal life itself as we just explained, they are valuable most of all as the means of something else, while He is not a means at all, but the something else for the sake of which every other gift of salvation is worth having. The other gifts are valuable because they remove the barriers that sin has put between us and the One who is altogether lovely. We appreciate forgiveness because it restores our friendship with God, and especially with God revealed to us as the Friend of Sinners in His Son. Simeon seems to have understood this. "My eyes," he said, looking at the tiny baby lying in front of him, "have seen thy salvation." Having seen Jesus, Simeon had seen it all. What do *we* see when we look through the eyes of this text?

IV. A Light Of Revelation To The Gentiles (v. 31)

The Consolation of Israel; the Lord's Messiah; Thy Salvation; that's not all. Next is a Light of Revelation to the Gentiles. "*Now, Lord, Thou dost let thy bond servant depart in peace, according to thy word; for my eyes have seen thy salvation which Thou has t prepared in the presence of all peoples, 'a light of revelation to the gentiles.'*" Salvation, as Paul tells us, is of the Jews (Rom. 9:4–5). But Simeon, inspired by the Holy Spirit, understood something that most of the Jews of his generation had missed: The coming of Christ means that the Abrahamic covenant Promise of blessing to all people will now finally be fulfilled. This was the mystery of Eph. 3:4–6, which no one else would see as clearly until Paul arose to explain it. It was, in Paul's words, "*the mystery of Christ which in other generations was not made known unto the sons of men as it has now been revealed to His holy apostles in the Spirit: to be specific, that the gentiles are fellow heirs and fellow members of the Body and fellow partakers of the Promise through the Gospel*" (Eph. 3:4–6).

Now, of course, Gentile salvation had been revealed, in the Promise that through Abraham all the families of the earth would be blessed; but it was not revealed in the sense of being fully understood until Christ had risen — fully understood not until after Peter's vision, the conversion of Cornelius, and the Jerusalem Council — except by Simeon. What does this mean for us? Two things. First, we are reminded that the Great Commission is our commission. It was part of God's plan from the beginning, and the coming of Christ makes its fulfillment possible. A Christian who is not doing something toward evangelizing his neighborhood and the world — a church that is not doing something toward those ends — is still living in the Old Testament half understood, as if Christ had not come to make is full meaning inescapably clear. Second, through Simeon's insight, we realize what our inclusion means: As Paul put it, we are fellow heirs, members of the Body, and partakers of the Promise with Israel. What Promise? The ones made to Abraham and all the Old-Testament saints. Those are the Promises now fulfilled in Christ for Jew and Gentile alike. Therefore, we may now all read both the Old Testament and the New. They are ours! We may read them with full assurance that they belong to us. We can read every word of them, every prophecy, every promise, every declaration of God's love for us and of His plans for our blessing and eternal fulfillment, and say with blessed confidence, "Because of Jesus, this is mine!"

V. The Glory Of Thy People Israel (v. 32b).

The Consolation of Israel; the Lord's Messiah; Thy Salvation; a Light of Revelation to the Gentiles: What could be better than that? Good question. Simeon called the infant Jesus *a light of revelation to the gentiles, and the glory of thy people Israel.* This last phrase, "glory of thy people," is parallel with a light of revelation to the Gentiles, the peoples or nations who are not Israel. So "the glory of thy people" therefore refers to Israel as a nation, to national Israel. What does it mean for Christ to be their glory? It means that what makes them special, what gives their existence and their history its significance, is their connection to Jesus. That is their glory, their legitimate claim to fame. To them were given the promises; through them came the fulfillment. They were made the people of God so that all could become the people of God. To them was given the Law; through them came the One who made keeping it possible by keeping it perfectly Himself. They were given animal sacrifices so that we might all understand and believe in the Lamb of God who taketh away the sins of the world (John 1:29). They were given a temple of stone so that our hearts of stone might become temples of living flesh. They were given an earthly land so we might be given an eternal kingdom. They were entrusted with the message so that through them might come the Messiah. What makes them special, what gives their existence and their history its significance, is their connection to Jesus. He is the glory of God's people, Israel.

Though this applies primarily in context to Israel, it contains a principle which applies to us as well: What makes *us* special? What gives our lives significance? It is our connection to Christ as well. What are you living for? There is only one thing that will sustain you though all the sorrows and tragedies and even the petty hassles and frustrations of even this life, much less make life so good it is worth living for all eternity. For who would bear the whips and scorns of time, the proud man's contumely, the oppressor's wrong, the pangs of despised love, the laws delay, the insolence of office and the spurns that patient merit of the unworthy takes? Hamlet's description of this life, or one side of it, rings terribly true.[27] What makes all that worthwhile? What lets us face it with gladness and courage and even joy? Money? Fleeting pleasure? Earthly fame? You know how empty those answers are! There is only one purpose that can make life worthwhile in the long run: to see the glory of God in the face of Jesus Christ, to see more of it, and, seeing it, to share it with others. To know Christ; to make Him known! What makes us special? What gives our lives significance? It is our connection to Christ! He is the glory of thy people Israel. He is the glory of our lives. And they will lose their significance, they will cease to be special, they will cease to matter the moment

---

[27] William Shakespeare, "The Tragedy of Hamlet, Prince of Denmark." act III, scene i, lines 56f, *Shakespeare: The Complete Works*, op, cit., 906.

we forget it. He is the glory of University Church. And it will lose its significance, it will cease to be special, it will cease to matter the moment we forget it.

Conclusion

What can we say of these things? The meaning of Christmas is that God has given to us the Consolation that makes all our sufferings worthwhile. The meaning of Christmas is that God has given to us a King worth following. The meaning of Christmas is that God has given to us a Savior who not only brings but is our salvation. The meaning of Christmas is that God has given to us an invitation that applies to all nations. The meaning of Christmas is that God has given to us a guarantee of the meaningfulness, yea, the glory of our lives if we belong to Christ. What can we say to that?

> Were the whole realm of Nature mine,
> That were a present far too small.
> Love so amazing, so divine,
> Deserves my soul, my life my all.[28]

Yes, it does

---

[28] Isaac Watts, "When I Survey the Wondrous Cross," *Trinity Hymnal*, rev. ed. (Atlanta, GA: Great Commission Publications, 1990), 252.

JESUS IN THE TEMPLE

Luke 2:39 When they had performed everything according to the Lae of the Lord, they returned to Galilee, to their own city of Nazareth. 40 The Child continued to grow and become strong, increasing in wisdom, and the grace of God was upon him. 41 And his parents used to go to Jerusalem every year a the Feast of Passover. 42 And when he became twelve, they went up there according to the custom of the feast. 43 And as they were returning, after spending the full number of days, the boy Jesus stayed behind in Jerusalem. And his parents were unaware of it, 44 but supposed him to be in the caravan, and went a day's journey; and they began looking for him among their relatives and acquaintances. 45 And when they did not find him, they returned to Jerusalem, looking for him. 46 And it came about that after three days they found him in the temple, sitting in the midst of the teachers, both listening to them and asking them questions. 47 And all who heard him were amazed at his understanding and his answers. 48 And when they saw him, they were astonished; and his mother said to him, "Son, why have you treated us this way? Behold, your father and I have been anxiously looking for you." 49 And he said to them, "Why is it that you were looking for me? Did you not know that I had to be in my Father's house?" 50 And they did not understand the statement which he had made to them. 51 And he went down with them and came to Nazareth; and he continued in subjection to them; and his mother treasured all these things in her heart. 52 And Jesus kept increasing in wisdom and stature and in favor with God and men.

Introduction

There is perhaps no passage in all the Bible more tantalizing to the curiosity than this one. From His circumcision at eight days old to the beginning of His public ministry in his thirties, we glimpse in specific terms only one day of Jesus' life: this one. Surely Mary could have told Luke more about Jesus' childhood. If she was like any mother I ever met, she *must* have told Luke more about Jesus' childhood! So why did he choose to include only this episode? Probably because this episode from Jesus' childhood has something to teach us about who Jesus was and what His mission was, while the rest of His childhood and adolescence was perfectly normal and uneventful. If we did know more about it, it probably wouldn't tell us anything we really need to understand.

It is insightful to compare the sober historicity of Luke, who is the only Gospel writer who tells us anything about Jesus' childhood at all, with the apocryphal gospels, which have no compunctions about gratifying our curiosity. They give us dramatic vignettes indeed: The time when Jesus and his playmates were molding animals out of clay, and Jesus threw his bird up into the air and it flew away; the time the neighborhood bully tried to pick a fight with Jesus, but when he went to punch Him his hand just withered up and fell off! The trouble with these accounts is that they are obviously pious fiction, and not very good even as that.[29] That boy in the apocryphal gospels was an obnoxious show–off who did not exactly turn the other cheek. He did not grow up to be the Jesus we know from the Gospels, who was not a wandering magician but a frail human being whose miracles—wrought only after the Holy Spirit came on Him at His baptism—gave glory to God because He did only what He saw the Father doing.

The reality was much more prosaic. Jesus would have gone to synagogue school from the age of six to twelve to learn to read the Torah. After his bar mitzvah at thirteen, He was probably apprenticed to Joseph in the carpenter's shop. After Joseph's death He probably supported his family for several years as a carpenter—perhaps beginning His public ministry only when his brothers were old enough to take over the family business. We do not know the details, but two Scripture passages give us the general idea. Isaiah 53:2 says that *"He grew up before him like a tender shoot, and like a root out of dry ground. He had no stately form or majesty that we should look upon him, nor appearance that we should be attracted to him."* He looked like a normal kid, in other words. If you had watched His childhood unfold, He might have struck you as a bit unusual, precocious and well–behaved perhaps (though even that would not always be obvious, as we shall see), but you would have seen nothing to tell you He was the Son of God. And Hebrews 4:15 says that *"We do not have a high priest who cannot sympathize with our weaknesses, but one who has been tempted in all points like as we are, yet without sin."* To outward eyes he would have just looked normal. He went through everything that other kids go through. He cried when he was a baby. How else is even a sinless baby supposed to let its mother know it is hungry or needs its diaper changed? If they would have had little league baseball back then, He would have struck out as often as anyone else. (Missing a baseball is not a sin.) When He was a teenager, he was probably awkward around girls and got zits. All this we may guess, but one thing we know from our passage today: He got into trouble with his parents, who, like the parents of every other teenager who has ever lived, did not understand him.

How Jesus came to recognize that He was different and to understand what that difference meant is a mystery that no story even of Scripture can help us to penetrate. It is not something that we can ever fully comprehend. Can you explain how *you* came to know that you are you? But sometimes you could get a glimpse of the mystery in Jesus' case if you knew where and how to look. And so Luke gives us here one example from Jesus' childhood that can help us to see certain things about Jesus. In this story we can see His priority, His prowess, His problem, His practice, His progress, and His promise. (You will note that once again I have alliterated my points with six Ps, and I hope you also note that they are all different P words from the ones I used last time I did that, in sermon I. Precisely.)

---

[29] See F. F. Bruce, *Jesus and Christian Origins outside the New Testament* (Grand Rapids, MI: Eerdmans, 1974), 87.

I. His Priority

First, His priority: What was Jesus' priority? His first priority was the things of God (verse 49). It was to be about his Father's business, as the King James puts it. Yes, this is the same person who would later say that His very meat and drink was to do the will of the Father, who would choose death, if need be, rather than let the Father's will go undone, as He showed us in Gethsemane. It was something He felt as a matter of necessity: He *had* (Greek δει, *dei*) to be about His Father's business. So central was this to His personality that He seems to have been genuinely surprised that his parents would not have known this. How could they not know where He was? It was obvious to Him; there was no question!

And what was His Father's business? It had Scripture as its center and its starting point. Since Jesus grew in wisdom, it is clear that the continual experience of His divine omniscience was one of the things He laid aside when he took on our nature. He had voluntarily adopted the limitation of having his infinite mind operate through a finite human brain. And so we find Him immersed in a deep theological and exegetical discussion with the greatest Bible scholars in the land. And He wasn't just lecturing them. He was asking questions as well as answering them. Do we grasp what this means? Jesus as a human being had to study the Bible to understand His own mission! I've always wondered if it wasn't Isaiah 53 that they were discussing.

Now, do not miss the application of this point. If even Jesus needed not only to read the Bible but also to think about it, study it, and *discuss* it, how much more do we need to be doing the same thing? What incredible arrogance it is if we are trying to lead the Christian life without doing so! If you are following Jesus' example, it means you will not only be a regular and serious Bible reader, it means that you will be landing on the doorstep of the best Bible scholars you can find and asking them questions. Part of your elders' job is to be one of those people for you. Make sure they are men who understand their role so, and then if one of them is a professional, full–time pastor, make sure you give him the study time he needs to be able to fulfill it.

II. His Prowess (v. 47, cf. v. 52)

His Father's business was Jesus' priority. Finding it in Scripture was also His prowess. The people who heard the boy Jesus discussing the Bible with the rabbis were impressed by His understanding and His answers. I think the word "understanding" is a key word here. What impressed them was not just his Bible knowledge, but his *understanding*. Maybe He could have been captain of the quizzing team at His local synagogue, but what made Him stand out was the intelligence of His questions. What He said made you think; it made you see things in a new way. What impressed people was his insight into the Bible and his practical application of it. Years later it would be no different. *"Never man spoke like this man"* (John 7:46). He taught with authority, not as the scribes (Mat. 7:29).

This is Jesus making His first public impression. What made Him stand out? What made Him different? What made people notice Him? It was not grandiose miracles or moving rhetoric, though He would show Himself capable of both before He was done. It was—and it continued to be—his *insight* into the Scriptures! If we want to be more like Jesus, maybe we should start by asking God to give us more of that.

III. His Problem (vv. 48–50)

Okay, Jesus' priority was to find and do the will of the Father, and His prowess was the ability to do that in Scripture. What was Jesus' problem at this point? It was the same problem every other adolescent boy in the history of the world has faced: His parents did not understand Him! Only, in his case, they *really* didn't understand Him. Jesus was sinless, but this passage makes us realize that to be sinless is not always to look sinless in the eyes of others; to be sinless is not always to stay out of trouble. If you cannot hear the exasperation in Mary's voice in verse 48, *"Son, why have you treated us this way? Behold, your father and I have been anxiously looking for you,"* if you do not realize that Jesus was in a big heaping mess of trouble, then all I can say is that you have never had a mother.

Jesus, being sinless, had not been deliberately disobedient or blamefully negligent. He really seems to have thought that His parents would know what He was doing, and to have been genuinely surprised when they did not. Verse 49 is not insolence, which would be incompatible with the clear biblical teaching that Jesus was sinless, but sincere surprise. *"Why is it that you were looking for me? Did you not know that I had to be in my Father's house?"* Maybe he had said something to them before they left for Nazareth, and they just didn't catch it. We do not know. But we do know that this was a continuing problem even after Jesus grew up. When Mary heard during Jesus' public ministry something that gave her the idea he wasn't eating right, she did what any other mother would do: She sent his brothers to straighten him out! (Mark 3:21). They were to make sure he was eating properly, three square meals a day with lots of vegetables, and probably try to get him to wear the First–Century equivalent of a sweater.

Now, I want you to appreciate and sympathize with the difficulty of this thing on both sides. How would you like to try to raise the Son of God? He is sinless, but He is a kid. He is sinless, but that doesn't mean He doesn't have to be potty trained. He is sinless, but that doesn't mean He comes out of the womb already knowing things like what good manners consist of. He is sinless, but that doesn't mean He will never get himself into trouble! So how do you go about raising him? What are the precedents? Mary's job could not have been an easy one.

And we must recognize the difficulty for Jesus, too. He is in trouble, but it is not His fault. It is never His fault, but He is in trouble anyway. Do you think this was the only time that happened? Now, it is hard enough to respect your parents when they know more than you do. It is hard enough to obey them and submit to them when you really know deep down that they are right. What if they are wrong and you know *that*? I want you to appreciate this point so you will be in a position to be adequately impressed by the next one:

IV. His Practice (v. 51)

How did Jesus handle this difficult situation, the problem created by His priority and His prowess? He obeyed His parents. That was His practice. He obeyed His parents! He was in subjection to them. His meat was to do the will of his Father, and part of that was *"Honor your father and mother"* (Exodus 20:12). If you don't think it is very hard to show respect and submission to people in legitimate authority when you know they are wrong, when you know they are completely off base and clueless and don't have a leg to stand on but they simply can't or won't admit it (but it's not such an important issue that you would be sinning to go along with them, and they are still legitimately in authority, so you just have to suck it up and do what they say anyway), then you have either lived a very sheltered life or just never bothered to submit to authority in such a situation. I tell you, I am more convinced that Jesus really was the sinless Son of God when I read verse 51 than maybe at any other point in the Bible. *And He went down with them and came to Nazareth; and He continued in subjection to them.* A twelve–year old did that! Would I have done it? Definitely not. Would you? Can you do it now? Have I done quit preaching and went to meddling? I have swallowed my pride and done it as an adult a few times for people in authority over me with what I hope was a pretty good grace, but never without a great struggle—a struggle I hope they were blissfully unaware of. When I was twelve? It wasn't going to happen. I might have ultimately had to obey, but they were definitely going to know what a struggle it was. The character Calvin from the cartoon strip "Calvin and Hobbes" was sadly a pretty accurate portrait of my boyhood.

Jesus was tested in every point like as we are. *Every* point! The difference is that He was without sin. I think this was one of the biggest tests. Why did He have to go through it? First, He did it because it was necessary as a part of a full human life, without which the statement in Hebrews 4:15 about His being tempted in every way like us could not have been made. But more importantly, He did it because it was a necessary part of His preparation for the Cross. Listen to the words of Hebrews again: *"Although He was a son, He learned obedience from the things that he suffered. And having been made perfect, he became to all those who obey him the source of eternal salvation"* (Heb. 5:8–9). My friends, that submission was part of the price of our redemption.

V. His Progress (v. 52)

That was Jesus' practice in response to His problem; and in it He made progress. Jesus, who at twelve showed a maturity beyond what I have managed as an adult, *increased* in wisdom and stature and favor with God and man (verse 52). This verse used to confuse me. "How can a person who is perfect make progress?" I used to ask. But the answer is really not all that difficult. He progressed from being a perfect boy to being a perfect man. Don't miss the practical point of this: Jesus showed he was perfect by continuing to *grow*. And he grew in a number of areas. First was wisdom. Wisdom is the crown of intellectual virtue. Intelligence is just processing speed. Knowledge is the possession of information. Understanding is seeing how those bits of information relate to each other. But wisdom is knowing how to use your intelligence, knowledge, and understanding in creative and constructive ways that bring glory to God and benefit to man. If Jesus grew in wisdom, surely we should want to do the same. And how do you grow in wisdom? There is only one way, the way that Jesus did it: You *submit* to God and his Word in the midst of the difficult and challenging experiences of life.

Saying that, we might seem to have said enough. But Luke goes on to make sure we do not miss the fact that Jesus' growth touched every area of his life. He grew in stature, that is, he grew physically. Think for a moment about the implications of the fact that he probably worked as a carpenter before the invention of power tools. He grew in favor with God, which is to say he grew spiritually. And he grew in favor with men, which is to say he grew socially. If we want to be Christlike, then we should ask God to help us grow in wisdom and in all these other areas of our lives as well. If Jesus as a perfect human being needed to grow, how much more do we?

VI. His Promise

Why does Luke include this story in his telling of the Gospel? Ultimately it is because to understand Jesus' Priority and his Prowess, his Problem and his Practice in dealing with it, and his Progress in those things, is to understand the Promise this young lad held out to us as our future Redeemer. And what was that promise? *"We do not have a high priest who cannot sympathize with our weaknesses, but one who has been tempted in all points like as we are, yet without sin"* (Heb. 4:15). To understand this incident from Jesus' boyhood is to see the promise of a sympathetic Savior.

The one thing we know about Christ's boyhood is that He had the same problems we did, and he had them worse. Can we possibly believe He was never tempted to sass Mary or Joseph, to talk back to them? He was tempted in all points like as we are. Of course He was! And with more excuse than we have. Yet He learned obedience through the things that He suffered. He did this so He would be qualified to be a perfect Sacrifice, but also so that He would be able to be an effective Mediator. There is nothing we face in life about which we have to worry that maybe Jesus will not understand it. We cannot even say, "Well, of course he is omniscient, but that is only a very abstract kind of understanding." No. He has been there. He had not just omniscient knowledge but actual human *experience* of our temptations. He has added to his perfect omniscient knowledge the *life experience* of these things *in the flesh*. *"We do not have a high priest who cannot sympathize with our weaknesses, but one who has been tempted in all points like as we are, yet without sin."*

Because of experiences like the one Luke has recorded for us here, and because of how He handled them, Jesus is able to offer us three things we desperately need. The first is **Forgiveness,** for which he paid His blood, blood which was worthy to be that of a perfect sacrifice because His obedience had been not only perfect but real, experienced and tested in the nitty–gritty of life. The first thing Jesus gives us is forgiveness, and the second is **Understanding.** He really does know what it is like to be tempted. He knoweth our strength that we are dust (Psalm 103:14), because he wore that dust for more than thirty years. The first thing Jesus gives us is forgiveness, the second is understanding, and the third is **Strength.** Not only was He tempted in every point like as we are, but He was yet without sin. He has already successfully resisted every temptation you are ever going to face, and He makes that same power available to us when we trust Him completely. When you are tempted and you ask Him for help, you are asking the help of One who has already been there and done that. You are asking the help of One who had already conquered—and therefore One through Whom we can be more than conquerors through Him who loved us so (Rom. 8:37).

Conclusion

We learn from this passage in a new way what it means to say that *"We do not have a high priest who cannot sympathize with our weaknesses, but one who has been tempted in all points like as we are, yet without sin"* (Heb. 4:15). And what is the conclusion Scripture draws from that lesson? It is in the very next verse. *"Let us therefore draw near with boldness to the throne of grace, that we may find mercy and may find grace to help in time of need."* May this fascinating episode in the life of our Lord encourage us to do so indeed. We can begin by drawing near to Him in Communion.

THE PREACHING OF JOHN THE BAPTIST, PART I: REPENTANCE

Luke 3:1 Now in the fifteenth year of the reign of Tiberius Caesar, when Pontius Pilate was governor of Judea and Herod was tetrarch of Galilee and his brother Philip was tetrarch of the region of Ituraea and Trachonitus, and Lysaneus was tetrarch of Abilene, 2 in the high priesthood of Annas and Caiaphas, the Word of God came to John, the son of Zacharias, in the wilderness. 3 And he came into all the district around the Jordan preaching a baptism of repentance for the forgiveness of sins, 4 as it is written in the book of the words of the prophet, "The voice of one crying in the wilderness, 'Make ready the paths of the Lord; make his way straight.' 5 Every ravine shall be filled up and every mountain and hill shall be brought low, and the crooked shall be made straight and the rough places smooth, 6 and all flesh shall see the salvation of God." 7 He therefore began saying to the multitudes who were going out to be baptized by him, "You brood of vipers, who warned you to flee from the wrath to come? 8 Therefore, bring forth fruits in keeping with repentance. And do not begin to say to yourselves, 'We have Abraham for our father,' for I say to you that God is able from these stones to raise up children to Abraham. 9 And also the axe is already laid at the root of the tree. Every tree therefore that does not bear good fruit is cut down and cast into the fire." 10 And the multitudes were questioning him, saying, "Then what shall we do?" 11 And he would answer and say to them, "Let the man who has two tunics share with him who has none, and let him who has food do likewise." 12 And some tax gatherers also came to be baptized, and they said to him, "Teacher, what shall we do?" 13 And he said to them, "Gather no more than what you have been ordered to." 14 And some soldiers were questioning him, saying, "And what about us, what shall we do?" And he said to them, "Do not take money from anyone by force or accuse anyone falsely, and be content with your wages."

Introduction

Perhaps no prophet in the history of Israel stirred up more excitement and anticipation than John the Baptist. To understand why, we must know something about the history of Israel. For if John was the person they thought he might be, then his coming meant that the whole history of the Jewish nation was coming to its climax.

That history begins with the call of Abraham about 2,000 BC. The Abrahamic Covenant is recorded in Gen. 12:1–3. Abraham was to leave his home and go to a land that God would show him, and God would make him a great nation through whom every family in the earth would be blessed. From then on, his descendants would be God's chosen people, a people with a special identity and a special mission, to bring that blessing into the world. God proceeded to reveal progressively to them who He was and what that blessing entailed. He delivered them from bondage in Egypt and gave them the Law through Moses about 1500 BC. This was a critical moment in that progressive revelation, as God's moral character as well as his power and his grace were coming into sharper focus. Then about 1,000 BC we come to the reign of David and the

Davidic Covenant of 2 Sam. 7:16. David's house would endure forever, and from it would come a future king who came to be known as the Messiah, the Anointed One. But Israel was rebellious and fell into idolatry. The nation was divided, the Northern Kingdom passed out of existence, and the Southern Kingdom of Judah was exiled to captivity in Babylon around 600 BC. A remnant was allowed to return to the Land in 536. Cured of their idolatry by the experience of exile, they waited for the Davidic king and the Davidic kingdom to be restored to them according to God's promise. But they forgot that the promised Blessing was not just for them, but rather for the whole world. So they focused on an earthly kingdom while they became a vassal state in subjection to various human empires, culminating in Alexander the Great's conquest of the world in about BC 325.

Alexander conquered the world and wept that there were no more worlds to conquer. But he died at the age of 32 and his empire was divided among his squabbling generals. Judea fell to the lot of Ptolemy of Egypt, who allowed her a limited amount of self–rule. Still, their subjugation grated on the Jews, and they longed for the promised deliverer. But things would get much worse before they got better. In 170 BC Judea was conquered by Syria and Antiochus Epiphanes desecrated the Temple in Jerusalem. Soon the fragments of Alexander's one–world empire were reunited under Roman rule. The Maccabees revolted but were crushed, and the Jews once again found themselves an occupied territory, though the Romans allowed them limited autonomy under a puppet king (Herod the Great at the time of Jesus' birth). By the time of Jesus' ministry, the real power was vested in the Roman governor; even the two corrupt high priests were essentially under his thumb. Judea groaned under this servitude, and the longing for the promised deliverer, a king like David who would free her from foreign rule and restore the glory of the Solomonic empire, had reached a fever pitch.

They ought to have read their own Scriptures better, but perhaps it is understandable given their trials how the Jews had come to concentrate on what seemed like the military and political aspects of the Old–Testament prophecies to the neglect of other elements: Christ's fulfillment of the whole Law and the sacrificial system, for example. But they kept a spiritual emphasis in their messianic expectations to this extent: They believed that God would send the Messiah in response to their *Repentance*. The rabbis they were listening to at this time had said things like this: "If all Israel would repent for only one day, the Son of David would come forth." "If Israel would observe only one Sabbath according to the ordinance, forthwith would the Son of David come." And perhaps most tellingly, given the depths of their desire, they said, "All the stages are past, and all depends solely on repentance and good works."[30] It was with these words of their own rabbis resonating in their ears that they heard the ringing challenge of John the Baptist: *"Repent, for the Kingdom of Heaven is at hand!"*

---

[30] Quoted in Alfred Plummer, *The Gospel according to St. Luke* (Edinburgh: T&T Clark, 1922), 89.

When John called Judea to repentance, then, the Jews knew that he was calling them to prepare for the coming of their long-anticipated deliverer, and they thought that this repentance would in fact be the thing that would usher Him in to their midst. They therefore heard those words with an excitement which would be hard for us to imagine today. That is why every class of society was so persistent with their questions about what they should do. They believed that, if they did it well enough, they could bring the Messiah on to the scene. Little did they know—though John tried his best to tell them—that God was preparing to do a greater thing in Israel than they could even begin to imagine: to liberate not just them but, in accordance with his original promise to Abraham, the whole world; and to liberate it from bondage, not just to Caesar, but to Satan, Sin, and Death. With this background in mind, we are ready to get the real impact of what John had to say to them.

Thesis: John came to prepare Israel for the Messiah by turning on their heads some of their most basic assumptions about the Messiah and His Kingdom. And those assumptions center on the idea of *Repentance*. What are the radical points John was trying to make about it?

I. Repentance Is Not A Meritorious Act

First, repentance is not a meritorious act. Notice a subtle difference between what John actually said and what the Jews, controlled by their preconceived notions, were able to hear. Contemporary Jewish theology emphasized that people should repent so that the Kingdom could come. John said something very different: Repent, for the Kingdom is coming! In other words, the Kingdom *is* coming; *therefore*, repent! Do you see the difference? It is central to the whole New Testament concept of salvation. For the Jews, repentance was itself a meritorious act which was capable of meriting a response from God, a response which, because He was just, would in fact obligate him to send the Messiah. For John, the Messiah was coming, not in response to the people's repentance, but as the expression of the Divine Initiative of God's Grace. God does not respond to our repentance by sending the Messiah; we respond to his sending the Messiah by repenting. For the Jews (and all human beings following the mind of the "natural man" since), if we make ourselves righteous enough, God will bless us. For John (and Jesus and the Apostles), this misses the point completely. The Biblical way is, if we accept God's gracious blessing by faith alone, it will make us righteous.

Any righteousness that we have, then, is always the effect of God's grace, never its cause. This is not a trivial distinction. It is sitting right on the watershed between salvation by grace and salvation by works, between God's way of grace and the way that seemeth right unto a man but the end thereof is death (Prvb. 16:25). Biblical repentance is not our turning over a new leaf to change ourselves and make ourselves more worthy. It is relinquishing all claim to self and to our own righteousness and giving ourselves over completely to Christ so that *He* can change us and make us worthy. John's language is subtly but beautifully out of step with contemporary Jewish assumptions and consistent with the doctrine of salvation as the New Testament would proceed to develop it in the Apostolic exposition of the Messiah God would actually send.

II. True Repentance Results In A Changed Life

First, repentance is not a meritorious act. Second, true repentance results in a changed life. This is the point of verse 8: *"Bring forth fruit in keeping with repentance."* Every time the Bible overturns the human propensity to believe in works righteousness, it simultaneously guards against the natural man's reaction to that overturning: to assume that the doctrines of Grace alone and Faith alone are really just a license to sin. That is the caricature of Biblical doctrine known to theologians as *Antinomianism*. It is amazing to me how efficiently we are able to ignore the beautifully balanced way in which the Bible presents this truth. We either make salvation dependent on our works, our own efforts to create our own worthiness, or we imply that people can live any way they want and still get to heaven as long as they mouthed the right words once at a church altar. The Bible will not let us go down either path. It will have none of either error, and the language of even its simplest and as yet undeveloped fore-gleams of the Gospel such as we have here are perfectly clear on the matter.

Let's make sure *we* get the distinction clear, then. Repentance is not us changing ourselves to make ourselves more worthy of God's grace. It is allowing God to change us by His grace. Either way, we change. Or I should say, only the second way do we really change in a way that is spiritually significant. God does not accept us because we have changed to an adequate extent, nor is our acceptance based on that change. He changes us because He has already accepted us in Christ, and the change is based on that acceptance. John's preaching is thus entirely consistent with Paul's later and fuller development of the same ideas in Romans 3.

III. Repentance Is A Personal And Individual Issue

First, repentance is not a meritorious act. Second, true repentance results in a changed life. Third, repentance is a personal and individual issue. John was known as The *Baptist*. He came preaching not only repentance, but a *baptism* of repentance for the remission of sin. What would this have meant to contemporary Jews? They were already familiar with the rite of baptism. Proselytes—Gentiles who wished to become Jews in order to worship the true God—were required to undergo a ceremonial washing with water before they were received into full fellowship. All Jewish males had to be circumcised, but proselytes had to be circumcised *and baptized*. The implication is that because they were not born Jews, they needed extra purification.

Well, then, that makes this one of the more radical elements of John's preaching. He was the first to ask born Jews to be baptized. Why? He was in effect asking his converts to accept the fact that, because of their sins, they had no more claim on God than a Gentile did! Had they understood, they would have been saying to God that they were approaching him on the basis of His grace alone. John's baptism then is precisely parallel with his telling the Jews, "Don't even think of saying, 'Abraham is our father.' God is able to raise up children to Abraham out of these stones" (Luke 3:8) Your ancestry does not give you a spiritual leg up, in other words. Is Abraham your father? Were your parents Christians? Were you raised in the church? Were you baptized as an infant? Fine. *You* are still a sinner. *You* still have to repent and personally accept salvation by grace alone through faith alone. John's baptism in the context of first–century Judaism and of his own preaching is the most eloquent object lesson imaginable of the truth that God has no grandchildren. The point of it is that, no matter who you are, repentance is for you.

IV. Repentance Is A Decision Not To Be Put Off

First, repentance is not a meritorious act. Second, true repentance results in a changed life. Third, repentance is a personal and individual issue. Fourth, repentance is a decision not to be put off. This is the point of verse 9. *And also the axe is already laid at the root of the tree. Every tree therefore that does not bear good fruit is cut down and cast into the fire."* The axe is already aimed at the tree roots. Trees without good fruit are headed for the brush pile and the fire. It is a graphic depiction of what are ultimately the fires of Hell. What does it mean? It means that you need to repent even if you are descended from Abraham. And you need to do it now, because the arrival of the Messiah is the arrival of a crisis moment when we are all going to have to decide what our ultimate allegiance is. We are all sinners in need of grace; we are all brands that need to be snatched from the burning. John makes the urgency of repentance graphically plain.

V. The Fruits Of Repentance Must Be In Accordance With The Word Of God

First, repentance is not a meritorious act. Second, true repentance results in a changed life. Third, repentance is a personal and individual issue. Fourth, repentance is a decision not to be put off. Finally, the fruits of repentance must be in accordance with the Word of God. John's answers to the questions about what specific fruits of repentance he had in mind for various groups are most intriguing in verses 10–14. *And the multitudes were questioning him, saying, "Then what shall we do?" And he would answer and say to them, "Let the man who has two tunics share with him who has none, and let him who has food do likewise." And some tax gatherers also came to be baptized, and they said to him, "Teacher, what shall we do?" And he said to them, "Gather no more than what you have been ordered to." And some soldiers were questioning him, saying, "And what about us, what shall we do?" And he said to them, "Do not take money from anyone by force or accuse anyone falsely, and be content with your wages."*

These answers are one more example of how radically John was turning the whole Jewish conception of the Messiah and his Kingdom on its head. For they all undercut the assumption that God was going to send a military Messiah. If a military Messiah were coming, if Christ was really about overthrowing the Roman Empire and restoring Jewish hegemony, then John's advice makes no sense at all. If we are preparing for a rebellion against Rome, why tell the people who work for the Romans—the tax collectors and the soldiers—to stay in their jobs and just do them honestly? If Christ were going to be the kind of military Messiah the Jews were expecting, the logical thing for collaborators to do as an act of repentance would be to resign, to change sides in preparation for the struggle that was coming.

John's answers must have seemed very confusing to the people asking the questions. But they were so convinced that their understanding of the Old Testament was right that they probably translated them into "bide your time." But let us not miss the point. Repentance is not something that happens in a vacuum. The question "What shall we do?" is a good question to ask. But it must drive us to Scripture, and the answer must be consistent with the whole tenor and direction of the Scripture as well as with its individual statements. "Good works," works that are the fruits of true repentance, are not just anything we might think is nice. They must be done in response to God's Word, in accordance with God's Word, by God's grace, and for God's glory. Otherwise, our good intentions are quite capable of doing more harm than good, of hindering the work of the kingdom rather than furthering it.

Conclusion

The whole Christian life, said Martin Luther, must be a life of repentance.[31] John the Baptist helps us to understand why this is so and what it means. First, repentance is not a meritorious act. Second, true repentance results in a changed life. Third, repentance is a personal and individual issue. Fourth, repentance is a decision not to be put off. Finally, the fruits of repentance must be in accordance with the Word of God.

Repentance is not changing our ways so that God will accept us; it is changing our ways in response to the fact that God has accepted us in Christ. Therefore, it can be a joyous thing, a way in which we express our love for the Savior who gave His all for us. May God help us to experience that joy in greater measure. For since Christ has come, because He still stands at the door and knocks, John's exciting words are still true: The Kingdom of Heaven is at hand! What does that mean for us? Where do *we* need to repent? What ways do we—do you—need to change in response to that fact? Let us each ask the Holy Spirit to give us the answers to that question as we close.

---

[31] The first of his famous ninety-rive theses was "Our Lord and Master Jesus Christ, in saying, 'repent ye,' etc., intended that the whole life of believers should be penitence." Qtd. in John Warwick Montgomery, *In Defense of Martin Luther* (Milwaukee, WI: Northwestern Publishing House, 1970), 20.

THE PREACHING OF JOHN THE BAPTIST, PART II: THE COMING ONE

Luke 3:15 Now while the people were all in a state of expectation and all were wondering in their hearts about John, as to whether he might be the Christ, **16** *John answered and said to them all, "As for me, I baptize you with water; but One is coming who is mightier than I, and I am not fit to untie the thong of his sandals. He will baptize you with the Holy Spirit and with fire.* **17** *And his winnowing fork is in his hand to thoroughly clear his threshing floor, and to gather the wheat into the barn; but the chaff he will burn with unquenchable fire."* **18** *So with many other exhortations also he preached the Gospel to the people.* **19** *But when Herod the tetrarch was reproved by him on account of Herodias, his brother's wife, on account of all the wicked things which Herod had done,* **20** *he added this to them all, that he locked John up in prison.* **21** *Now it came about when all the people were baptized, that Jesus also was baptized, and while he was praying Heaven was opened,* **22** *and the Holy Spirit descended upon him in bodily form like a dove, and a voice came out of Heaven, "Thou art my beloved Son; in thee I am well pleased."*

Introduction

Last week we saw how John came striding out of the desert to prepare the way for Christ by preaching a baptism of repentance for the remission of sins. We saw the radical nature of that message and that baptism, how they stood the expectations of the Jews on their heads and called them to forsake their religion of merit for the Gospel of Grace that God was bringing. It called them to forsake their hope in a military Messiah, accepting instead the Savior from sin that God was sending. Today as we conclude our study of John's ministry, the focus shifts from that preparatory repentance to the One whose coming it responded to and to His mission. And, meeting Him here at the very beginning of His public ministry, we see Him, not as a military Messiah, but as the Lamb of God who taketh away the sins of the world (John 1:29). It tells us three things about Him and the nature of His mission.

I. He Came To Bear Our Sins

Jesus declared his intentions at the very inception of his public ministry by beginning it with a profound symbolic act: He came to be baptized by John (verse 21). What exactly did this mean? A number of theologians—beginning with John himself—have had a hard time understanding this. John, we read in the other Gospels, tried to dissuade Jesus. "I have need to be baptized by you, and you come to *me*?" But Jesus insisted that it was necessary "to fulfill all righteousness." And so John agreed.

What was the problem? Well, John's baptism, as we saw last time, was a baptism of repentance for the remission of sins in preparation for the Messiah's coming. So what need did the Messiah Himself have of it? Specifically, what need did Jesus have of it? He was sinless. He had done nothing for which he needed to repent. Surely John felt the incongruity of his giving such a baptism to Jesus. When Jesus over–rode his objections, we do not know whether he understood it or not. He may have yielded out of sheer faith and obedience.

Whatever solution to the dilemma might have been in John's mind, we know that later theologians have offered their explanations. One is that this passage simply proves that the very earliest Christians did not think of Christ as sinless. But that solution is clearly incorrect, for two reasons. In the first place, it simply shifts the difficulty from why Jesus asked for the baptism to why John objected to it. That gets us nowhere. In the second place, it is in conflict with some of the very earliest testimony to Jesus' messianic status. When Peter said, "Depart from me, for I am a sinful man," his statement would be meaningless apart from its implied contrast between Peter and Jesus: the contrast between one who was a sinner and One who was not, one who was a sinner and One whose holiness called that sin out by contrast. No, there is no evidence that the early Church ever thought of Christ as anything but sinless.

Others have suggested that Jesus perhaps requested baptism to show his support for and approval of John's ministry, giving the baptism his own unique, private meaning as it were. There are at least two problems with this view as well. First, there is simply no evidence in the text that this baptism ever meant anything to anybody except repentance for the remission of sins. And second, it makes no sense of Jesus' own explanation. How would showing support for John "fulfill all righteousness"?

There is only one explanation that really does make sense in the context not only of the passages which record the baptism but also of the total New Testament witness to the meaning of Christ's whole career. The Baptist himself hints at it in his words recorded in the Apostle John's account: *"Behold the Lamb of God, who taketh away the sins of the world"* (Jn. 1:29). Why did Jesus request a baptism of repentance which He did not need? It was an expression of his identification with those who did need it. It was a profound expression of his solidarity with a sinful race. It was thus a declaration at the outset of his ministry of what his central role would be. By accepting our *baptism*, he formally identified himself with us in our *need*, that is, in our *sins*, and took on the role of Substitute as One who could stand in our place *as sinners*. His identification with us was so strong that He gave up his heavenly glory and took on our very nature (sin excepted) in the Incarnation. Now He literally stands in our place, the place we should have occupied, the place of repentant sinners. It was our sins, not His, that He was confessing in that baptism. But from now on in a sense they *would* be His, and that is why He would bear their punishment on Calvary. This was the offer He was making, and God the Father accepted it with pleasure, approval, and pride: *"Thou art my beloved Son; in thee I am well pleased"* (verse 22).

Now, we must not miss the fact that, not only does Jesus' baptism by John help us understand His work and His mission and our atonement, but it also has important implications for how we understand Christian baptism. Christian baptism is different from John's—those who had received only John's baptism but not been baptized in the name of the Father, the Son, and the Spirit, were not yet fully Christians (Acts 19:1–7). But certainly Christian baptism was built on John's. It was in fact the fulfillment of John's baptism; it is more but not less. And the important connection between the two at this point is this whole concept of *identification*. As Christ identified Himself with us and our sins in this passage, so we identify ourselves with Him in His death and resurrection. We see this in Rom. 6:4–5. *"Therefore we have been buried with Him through baptism into death, in order that as Christ was raised from the dead through the glory of the Father, so we too might walk in newness of life. For if we have become united with Him in the likeness of His death, certainly we shall be also in the likeness of His resurrection."*

Just as Jesus identified himself with us in our sin, so by the same symbolic act we identify ourselves with Him in His death, burial, and resurrection. Bu undergoing John's baptism, Jesus was saying, "I identify myself with these people. I accept their sins as if they were my own. I authorize the Father to impute or reckon them to my account so that my death will atone for them and my righteousness can then be counted or reckoned as theirs." And so when we are baptized, we are saying, "I identify myself with the Lord Jesus Christ. I accept His death as my death, the basis on which God forgives my sins. And therefore His resurrection is the hope of my resurrection. I accept Him as my Lord and Savior and publicly identify myself with Him. In doing so, I publicly identify myself with His people, with His Gospel, with His Kingdom and with His cause. These realities are now mine, just as my sins became His." The parallel is powerful. In believer's baptism, this is what we are saying to the whole world. "As Christ identified himself with me so long ago, so I now identify myself with Him. I am His and He is mine, and I want the whole world to know it!" For those Evangelicals who practice infant baptism, this is what they are claiming by faith for their children, believing that it will become their possession and their identity when they ratify this covenant being made for them by personally accepting Christ with their own faith when they are old enough to do so with understanding.

By the way, if that is you, this morning, have you made that personal commitment? Did your parents have you baptized when you were a baby? Okay. But have you since then publicly confessed Jesus as *your* Lord and believed in your heart that God raised Him from the dead? You don't have to be a certain age—you just have to understand what you are doing and want to do it. Talk to your parents if you aren't sure, and then meet with an elder to be sure you understand, and then make that public confession of your own faith in Christ when we are given that opportunity at the end of the service. When is the right time to start that process? It is *now* if the Lord is speaking to your heart. Or have you never been baptized, but you believe in Christ and are trusting Him as your Savior and Lord? Then you need to follow Him in believer's Baptism to make that particular public statement of *your* personal identification with Him. The elders will be happy to meet with you and confirm your understanding of the

Gospel and schedule that opportunity for you. Whatever your church's practice of baptism, then, whether Believer's Baptism by Immersion or Infant Baptism, let it proclaim this message of identification with Christ and His people clearly and with understanding. And if we have been baptized into such an identification, then let us live in the light of it.

II. He Came To Grant Us The Blessings Of The Kingdom

Alright, then, Jesus came to be our sin–bearer, and He did that so that, having dealt with our sins, He could also grant us the blessings (and the curses, if we do *not* repent) of the Kingdom. John baptized people with water, but the One who was coming, the One mightier than John, would baptize them with the Holy Spirit and with fire (verse 16). In other words, when Christ came, He would grant people the reality of which John's baptism was only the symbol. The Holy Spirit is the One who brings us even now in this life wonderful foretastes of the blessings of the Kingdom Christ came to bring. John baptized (symbolically) with water; Jesus would baptize (really) with the Holy Spirit.

What does it mean to be baptized in the Holy Spirit? That has become a needlessly controversial question. To answer it, we need simply to remind ourselves what the Holy Spirit came to do. Well, what are the ministries assigned to the Holy Spirit in the New Testament? To be given the Holy Spirit is to be joined to Christ intimately as the body is joined to its head, for the Spirit is the vital power which flows form the Head to unite and animate the members of the Body. To be given the Holy Spirit is to be regenerated, brought from spiritual death to life. It is to begin the process of sanctification, being brought into conformity with the very character of Christ. It is to be sealed for salvation, protected by the power of God. It is to enter into a communion with God the Father through the Son that is as potentially as intimate as anything that can be imagined, for the Holy Spirit comes to indwell us, to live inside of us as the very personal agent and representative of Christ Himself. It is to be granted boldness of access to the throne of God in prayer. It is to be granted an inheritance with all the saints, to be made a partaker of eternal life. It is to be given spiritual gifts that make us able to serve and edify the Body in our own unique way. All these things Christ will give to those who are his when he "baptizes" them with the Holy Spirit. In other words, he gives them to us when we become Christians, when we receive him as Lord and Savior by faith. The water that was used by John as a symbol of this *coming* reality continues in Christian baptism as a powerful symbol of what has now become a *present* reality. That is what it means to say that Christ will baptize us with the Holy Spirit.

But what does it mean to say that Christ will baptize people with fire? I think this statement has been often and tragically misunderstood. People tend to associate it with the tongues of fire at Pentecost, with revival "fire," and thus to see it as parallel with the prophecy that the coming Messiah would baptize his people with the Holy Spirit. The associations with Pentecost have given rise to the assumption that being baptized with the Holy Spirit must be something "extra" that happens subsequent to conversion. But look at the context! In the immediate context there is another reference to fire. The Coming One has his winnowing fork in his hand, and He will gather the wheat into the barn—but the chaff He will burn with unquenchable fire (verse 17)! Clearly and without question, this is the fire of eternal judgment. It is impossible that the fire into which Christ will baptize people in the very same passage could suddenly mean something different without any explanation. Neither John who said it, Luke who wrote it, nor the Holy Spirit who inspired it were such incompetent communicators as that.

What John is saying then is that when the Messiah comes, it will be a time of decision for everyone. Everyone is going to be undergo a baptism. It can either be a baptism with the Holy Spirit that confers all the blessings and benefits of the messianic kingdom, or it will be a baptism of unquenchable fire which brings the curse of the Kingdom on those who reject its authority. And what is the difference between the wheat, carried to the barn by the Spirit, and the chaff which burns forever? It is faith and repentance. It is how we respond to this One that God is sending. And that is why John's message is, "Repent! For the Kingdom of Heaven is at hand." Have you done so? Now that Christ has come, the decision is inescapable. And he came to identify himself with us in our sins! Surely we can come to him with confidence that he will never cast us out. But come we must, or our destiny will be with the chaff.

III. There Is A Connection Between Christ's Sin–Bearing And The Baptism With The Spirit

Okay, Christ came to bear our sins and to give us the blessings (or curses) of the Kingdom through the baptism of the Holy Spirit. Finally, there is a connection between Christ's sin–bearing and the baptism with the Spirit.4 What is that connection? John had promised that the One who was coming would baptize with the Holy Spirit. And in verse 22, the Spirit comes visibly to rest on Christ as the Father's response to His acceptance of His mission as sin–bearer. It is not that the Spirit was absent from Christ before, but now He comes on Him specifically to empower Him for His public ministry. The Spirit was given to Jesus to enable Him to serve. And when He was exalted, He was given that same Spirit to bestow on His own people (Jn. 16:7, Acts 2:33). The implication is that the Spirit not only brings to us the blessings of the Kingdom, but He also empowers us for sacrificial service in the Kingdom as well. For He is the same Spirit who came upon Christ here, to enable His sacrificial service of love.

This is why the Spirit is connected so closely with baptism: not that baptism confers the Spirit magically, but because baptism symbolizes the identification with Christ that is central to the relationship we have with Him. It is that identification that causes Him to baptize us with the Spirit—or results from His baptizing us with the Spirit (both statements are true). This reinforces the teaching that baptism with the Spirit is not something "extra" added to salvation later, but is a way of talking about conversion itself. It is tied to the very identification with Christ as your personal Lord and Savior that is the essence of your relationship with Him, and the initiation of which baptism symbolizes. This therefore means that all believers should see themselves as called to sacrificial Kingdom service and should therefore explore the ways in which they have been empowered for that service—in the language of the Epistles, they should seek to discover their spiritual gift or gifts. It is as much a part of our identity as those who have been baptized with the Holy Spirit as it was a part of Christ's, on whom the Spirit came.

Conclusion

All right then: In baptism we symbolize our identification with Christ in His death, burial and resurrection, our identification with Him and thus with His people, with His Gospel, with His Kingdom and with His cause. That identification is so close that it involves Christ sending the Holy Spirit as His personal Representative and Agent to indwell us and to give us foretastes of the Kingdom's blessings and power for its service. This all goes back to Christ's own baptism at the outset of His ministry, and the profound identity with us in our sins that it expressed. And that is why for us, while baptism is not a requirement for salvation, it is a required expression of salvation.

Baptism is the central symbol in this passage that pulls all these truths together. Baptism is like the old silver certificates we used to use as money in this country. The silver certificate certified that there was one dollar worth of silver on reserve in a federal bank to back up the money, and you could take that certificate to the bank and trade it in for the silver. The paper bill was actually worth nothing in itself; it was valuable because of what it represented. So the water of baptism is like the paper, and the Holy Spirit is the silver in the vault. The water does not save you. It only symbolizes the fact that Christ has saved you by bearing your sins and sent the Spirit to those who believe. Apart from the reality, the identification with Christ which baptism symbolizes—apart from faith, in other words—it is only counterfeit money.

Communion, the Lord's Supper, works in exactly the same way. The bread and wine are the paper; the Lord Jesus Christ is the silver in the vault; and faith is the connection between them. To eat and drink without faith is to spend counterfeit money; to eat and drink with faith is to commune with Christ. And so I invite you in that spirit to come to the Table and share with us in this feast in honor of the Christ who came to identify with us, to bear our sins, and to baptize us with the Holy Spirit.

XII—Luke 4:1–13

THE TEMPTATION OF JESUS

Luke 4:1 And Jesus, full of the Holy Spirit, returned from the Jordan and was led about by the Spirit in the wilderness 2 for forty days, being tempted by the devil. And he ate nothing during those days, and when they had ended he became hungry. 3 And the devil said to him, "If you are the Son of God, tell these stones to become bread." 4 And Jesus answered him, "It is written, 'Man shall not live by bread alone.'" 5 And he led him up and showed him all the kingdoms of the world in a moment of time. 6 And the devil said to him, "I will give you all this domain and all this glory, for it is handed over to me and I give it to whomever I wish. 7 Therefore, if you worship before me it will all be yours." 8 And Jesus answered and said to him, "It is written, 'You shall worship the Lord you God and serve Him only.'" 9 And he led him to Jerusalem and had him stand on the pinnacle of the Temple and said to him, If you are the Son of God, throw yourself down from here; 10 for it is written, 'He will give his angels charge over you to guard you;' 11 and 'On their hands they will bear you up lest you strike your foot against a stone.'" 12 And Jesus answered and said unto him, "It is said, 'You shall not put the Lord your God to the test.'" 13 And when the devil had finished very temptation, he departed from him until an opportune time.

Introduction

Last time we saw Jesus at His baptism, the inauguration of His public ministry, declare Himself to be a sin–bearer by identifying with sinful mankind in our baptism, a baptism of repentance for the remission of sins. That identification was complete. Not only did He humble Himself to be take on our nature and be born in a stable, to bear our sins, and to die our death for us, but He also submitted Himself to being "tempted in all points like as we are, yet without sin" (Heb. 4:15). As we saw back at the Temple ("Jesus in the Temple," chapter IX), this was not Jesus' first trial or temptation, and it will not be His last. But it was one of the most significant, and therefore I want to draw your attention to seven lessons it has for us. (Yes, seven points in one sermon is a personal record. But do not fear! I have no intention of trying to break it any time soon.)

I. The Rationale Of The Temptation

Why is this event happening now in the life of Christ, coming hard on the heels of His baptism? Each of the major characters involved had a reason for being there. For Jesus it was simply obedience, submission to the will of the Father. For verse one says He was led there by the Spirit. Jesus had already set Himself on the path that led to Calvary, and if this was another step on that road, so be it. His identification with sinners logically entails the experience of temptation, and it might as well come now as any other time. In fact, God's people have frequently experienced a vulnerability to Satan's assaults that comes right after a great spiritual victory. Christ Himself was no exception.

Had He not just heard His Father say, *"Thou art my beloved Son, in Whom I am well pleased"*?

For God the Father, it was a necessary time of testing for His Son. The period of 4forty days in the desert reminds us of the forty years of Israel's trial in the wilderness. So the point of it is to test and to prove the depths of the identity with sinners as their sin–bearer that was expressed and approved at Christ's baptism. It was good for this commitment to be confirmed at the outset of Jesus' public ministry in a deeper way than could be achieved merely by a symbolic declaration of intent. Also, Jesus had been sent to undo, to reverse for those with the faith to accept it, the rebellion of the first Adam. Part of that reversal must be enacted here: As Adam yielded to Satan's advances, so Jesus must resist them. In no other way could His identification with us be complete; in no other way could He be one to whom we could come with confidence knowing that He understands all our trials.

For Satan, there was the same motive as for any temptation: malice against God and man. But in this case, there was an added reason. It was an attempt to divert Christ from His purpose and thus to protect Satan's own kingdom from the threat which this coming Messiah represented. This will become more evident as we proceed to look at the particular form this temptation took.

II. The Reality Of The Temptation

To complete his identification with us, Jesus would have to experience a temptation as real as ours are. But at this point a number of people have had a theoretical difficulty with this passage. If Jesus was God and sinless, indeed incapable of sin, how could the temptation be real? How could a perfectly holy Person even *be* tempted? How could an omniscient mind be tricked? How could an omnipotent will be overcome? How could it be a real temptation unless there was a real possibility of Jesus falling? Many people have found these to be difficult questions indeed.

The first thing that needs to be noted in response to this problem is that the Bible says Jesus was tempted. So, whether we can explain how it could be so or not, we are required to believe that the temptation was real. But there is more that can be said. While as God Jesus was incapable of sinning, as man He was quite capable, just as Adam was. How Jesus' two natures, the divine and the human, worked together in his one Person is a mystery we can never plumb completely. But we can understand that because Jesus' human nature was real, therefore His temptation was real. The bait that was offered Him was attractive to Him: to eat when He was hungry, even at the price of abusing His divine power, to (apparently) achieve His mission of liberating the kingdoms of the world from Satan without going through the agony of the Cross. Just spend a few minutes with Him in Gethsemane if you don't think that was an attractive proposition. In that the bait was attractive to his human nature, the temptation was real. But because He steadfastly rejected it, He did not fall.

Another point that is often missed is that there was a sense in which temptation was actually *harder* for Jesus to bear than it is for us, not easier. How could that be? I mean it was at least emotionally harder to endure, if not harder to resist. Imagine a heart absolutely pure and completely unjaded, a conscience never tainted and never seared at all. You cannot? Neither can I. But that is who Jesus was; that was the emotional life that would be challenged and threatened by this experience. Imagine then how His sinless and holy soul must have recoiled at the very suggestion of disobedience. We see the strength of his reaction when the temptation comes through Peter. *"Lord, far be it from you . . . ." "Get thee behind me, Satan!"* (Mat. 16:23). Have you ever reacted to a temptation that strongly? It cannot have been a pleasant experience to undergo.

We cannot fully understand it, then, but we can conclude that this temptation was very real and was a great trial for the Lord. And that leads us to:

III. The Rigors Of The Temptation

There are at least two indications in the text that Jesus' temptation was not only real to Him but also quite rigorous, yea, strenuous, for Him. In the first place, it took place over a period of forty days. What we are given in the description of it would not have taken forty minutes. We can safely assume it is a summary. In the second place, we notice that Matthew's account has the temptations in a different order. Compared with Luke, he has the last two reversed. What this suggests is not that one of the Gospels is wrong, but that Jesus did not get a simple set of three suggestions in order, one, two, three, and then it was over. What we are given is just a representative sample of the arguments Satan used and the rebuttals Jesus made. All these suggestions and probably more were being constantly intertwined for forty days with such intensity that Jesus did not even stop to eat. He was so preoccupied that he did not even notice His hunger and weakness until the very end. And then, when He is at his weakest, Satan comes in with his final assault.

There is an ironic and instructive contrast here which takes us back to the theme of Jesus as the Second Adam who is reversing or undoing what Adam had done on behalf of the human race so long ago. Adam fell in Paradise under the most ideal conditions; Jesus stood in the wilderness under the most adverse conditions. This tells us at least two things when we come into temptation. First, there is no excuse for us. But second, and more importantly, what a strong Deliverer we have! Nothing we have ever faced compares to what Christ has already overcome. Let us run to Him and seek His aid, for He understands what we are going through and *in Him* we are more than conquerors. The victory He won alone here He can win for us now if we flee to Him and rest under His protection.

IV. The Rhetoric Of The Tempter

The three appeals Satan tried in our summary of this temptation were both typical of Satan's normal tactics used on all of us and strategically adapted to his particular intended victim. They were designed to drive a wedge between Jesus and the Father and divert Him from His mission.

"If you're really the Son of God, tell these stones to become bread." Temptation always includes the insinuation of doubt. Are you really the Son of God? Did God really say you would die if you eat the fruit? Faith is the key. You are not going to disobey God as long as you really trust him. You cannot deliberately disobey him while you are consciously trusting him. The two acts are inherently incompatible. So Satan is always trying to cast doubt on some aspect of God's Word or His character or both. This is something that people who think that the doctrine of salvation by faith alone apart from works will lead to moral laxity do not understand. Faith is not just mental assent to a set of formulae; it is an active trust in our heavenly Father. Real faith tends to drive out sin by its very nature. And that is why temptation is always allied with doubt. In Jesus' case, the doubt was very specific: Am I really the Son of God? Do I really believe the Voice that came at my baptism? That is why it would have been wrong for Jesus to turn the stones to bread. Surely it was not wrong for Him to eat, and I do not know that it was even inherently problematic for Him to have supernaturally provided bread for Himself. But to do it now, after what Satan had just said, would be an act of unbelief. To need to prove one's Sonship by means of a miracle is by that very act to admit that one is doubting the Father's word. And this was something that Jesus resolutely refused to do.

"See all these kingdoms? Bow down and worship me and they are yours." As with the bread, Satan usually appeals to a legitimate desire. Every good gift comes from above (James 1:17), and every good thing was made by the Father as a gift for us. As C. S. Lewis points out, pleasure is a good thing in itself. Satan is reduced to having to tempt us to take good things in the wrong way, at the wrong time, in the wrong amounts, or for the wrong reasons.[32] Jesus had been sent to get those kingdoms. Of course He wanted them. That wasn't the problem. The problem was that the way proposed for Him to get them was the way of compromise, compromise of His loyalty to the Father as the one true God. And this Jesus resolutely refused.

"If you are the Son of God, cast yourself down from the Temple." Satan knows that the half–truth is the most effective lie, and so he often quotes Scripture, especially to pious people. "It says right in the Bible that the angels will protect you, so jump!" The full passage is Psalm 91:11–12. *"For He will give His angels charge over you to guard you in all your ways. They will bear you up in your hands lest you strike your foot against a stone."* But notice that Satan leaves out a key phrase: The angels were charged to guard God's servant "in all his ways." They were there to guide his feet in the right paths—and jumping off of the Temple was certainly not one of those paths. We must not be misled by Scripture quoted out of context or quoted to make a point that is contrary to the

---

[32] C. S. Lewis, *Mere Christianity* (NY: MacMillan, 1943), 49.

message of the whole Bible. Presumption does not become faith just because somebody can tie it to a prooftext! And that was a game that Jesus resolutely refused to play.

V. The Response Of The Tempted

Jesus' response to Satan's rhetoric can be summed up in one word: "No." That is an important lesson in itself. But there are also lessons for us in how that "no" was said.

In the first place, it is noteworthy that Jesus never stooped to arguing with the Devil. He might well have done so. He could have pointed out that the passages had been taken out of context or misapplied, or that a fundamental misunderstanding of the Messiah's nature and mission was implied by Satan's suggestions. But Jesus does not do so. Why? Well, what would be the point? It's not as if Satan cares about the truth. He's not going to say, "Oh, I'm sorry, I see that you are right. My mistake. Carry on." He is totally unscrupulous. Even if you won the argument, he would never admit it, but would just go on twisting things to his own advantage. Jesus understood that it is best not to let that game ever get started.

Now, I do not mean to exclude rational argument from the field of ethics. We need to know the Scriptures well enough to spot their misuse, and we must apply our reason in doing so. And there are times when we must think through issues to discern what God's will is, what the right application of his Word is. But the time to do that is before we are being tempted! For there is also a time to recognize that we are not dealing with a teachable adversary, but with one who is not really interested in discussing the issue but rather in persuading us to do something we know we shouldn't be doing. An important key to dealing with temptation is to learn to discern the difference. Rational argument is necessary in dealing with the search for truth. It is worse than useless in dealing with temptation. This means that we must think through the issues rationally and biblically *in advance* so that we know when we are being tempted and can make the appropriate response for that situation.

And what is the appropriate response? That is the second thing to notice about Jesus' example here. He just said "no." Well, no, it was more than that. He spoke with the authority of command in the words of Scripture. The only answer to Scripture misapplied or taken out of context is Scripture rightly applied in its original meaning. Jesus' answers all boil down to this: "Whatever you say, I know on the basis of Scripture already thought through and accepted that God has said not to do this. That is the bottom line. God said not to. And that is all that matters to me."

For us, this is supremely important. Even the Archangel would not give a railing accusation against Satan but said, *"The Lord rebuke thee"* (Jude 1:9). How much more do we need the power and authority of the Word in dealing with that adversary? Even Christ himself availed himself of it. In the Word of God we too have the authority to say, "No!" and make the answer stick.

VI. The Recurrence Of The Temptation

Surely one of the most sobering verses in this whole passage is verse 13: *"And when the devil had finished very temptation, he departed from him until an opportune time."* Jesus had defeated Satan soundly, but that did not mean that the temptation was over. Even Jesus had only a respite until the attacks of Satan resumed. And these same suggestions resumed in more subtle and painful ways, coming sometimes through people that Jesus loved, including Mary and Peter. We can expect no less. There is no final victory in this life, and pride goeth before a fall. So we need to be ready for a recurrence. There will always be one until we see Christ face to face.

VII. The Ramifications Of The Temptation

We have seen many ramifications of this story of the Temptation in the Wilderness, but let me re–emphasize three of them in closing. First, the Christian life from beginning to end is a life of spiritual warfare, not of permanent rest and recreation. If this story had been fiction, verse three would have read, "And then, having defeated Satan soundly, Jesus lived happily ever after." It doesn't exactly say that. *"And when the devil had finished very temptation, he departed from him until an opportune time."* In real life that other ending is coming for believers, but it is not yet. It is coming when we see Him face to face. And not before.

Second, Satan is not defeated by argument but by the authority of God in his Word. As we have seen, that does not mean there is no place for argument, for rational debate and analysis. But it means it needs to happen in advance. The moment of temptation is too late for us to try to think through the issues. It is the very worst time to be doing that, for then reason is most likely to degenerate into rationalization. And so we must prepare for the inevitable temptations beforehand by learning the Scriptures well in context so that we can recognize Satan's lies for what they are and counteract them with the Word. We need to be fortifying ourselves with truth before the next attack of Satan begins.

Finally, and most importantly, we must remember that we have a Savior who can be trusted to be both sympathetic and sufficient. He understands what we are going through, for He has been there. And He is able to deliver, for He has already won the victory Himself. He is an example of how to defeat the Enemy, but He is more than that. He is a very present help in time of trouble. And so let us run to the throne of grace when that time comes, with alacrity and joy. For the One who is in us is greater than the one who is in the world (1 John 4:4).

Conclusion

How can we sum up Jesus' impressive triumph and the practical lessons that flow to us from it? Let me try to do it with a sonnet:

> "And if the Voice at Jordan really said
> That you were his beloved Son, when on

94

Your shoulder came the Spirit—you need bread?
Just ask! He'd make a loaf for you from stone.
Now, you were sent to take—I'll not say, 'steal'—
The kingdoms over which I rightly reign.
I'm not unreasonable. Let's make a deal:
No need for either of us to suffer pain.
Salvation's (as you know) by faith. Let's make
It easy for the people to believe.
It says right in the Bible you'll not break
A bone, so jump! The angels will receive . . ."
Thrice, "No," the only answer Satan heard:
Three times, the simple power of the Word.[33]

---

[33] Donald T. Williams, *Stars through the Clouds*, op. cit., 143.

PROPHET WITHOUT HONOR

Luke 4:14 And Jesus returned to Galilee in the power of the Spirit, and news about him spread through all the surrounding district. 15 and he began teaching in their synagogues and was praised by all. 16 And he came to Nazareth, where he had been brought up; and as was his custom, he entered the synagogue on the Sabbath and stood up to read. 17 And the book of the prophet Isaiah was handed to him. And he opened the book and found the place where it is written, 18 "The Spirit of the Lord is upon me, because he anointed me to preach the Gospel to the poor. He has sent me to proclaim release to the captives and recovery of sight to the blind, to set free those who are downtrodden, 19 to proclaim the acceptable year of the Lord." 20 And he closed the book and gave it back to the attendant and sat down; and the eyes of all in the synagogue were fixed upon him. 21 And he began to say to them, "Today this scripture has been fulfilled in your hearing." 22 And all were speaking well of him and wondering at the gracious words that were falling from his lips, and they were saying, "Is this not Joseph's son?" 23 And he said to them, "No doubt you will quote this proverb to me, 'Physician, heal yourself! Whatever we heard was done at Capernaum, do here in your home town as well.'" 24 And he said, "Truly I say to you, a prophet is not without honor save in his home country. 25 But I say to you in truth, there were many widows in Israel in the days of Elijah, when the sky was shut up for three years and six months and a great famine had come over all the land; 26 and yet Elijah was sent to none of them, but only to Zarephath in the land of Sidon, to a woman who was a widow. 27 And there were many lepers in Israel in the time of Elisha the prophet; and none of them was cleansed, but only Naaman the Syrian." 28 And all in the synagogue were filled with rage as they heard these things, 29 and they rose up and cast him out of the city, and led him to the brow of the hill on which their city had been built in order to throw him down the cliff. 30 But, passing through their midst, he went his way.

Introduction

Two messages ago we saw Jesus at his Baptism accept the role of Sin Bearer, in response to which he was officially anointed as Messiah by the Holy Spirit. We saw last time how that commitment was tested by Satan at the Temptation in the Wilderness. Now Luke will show us that commitment being tested in another way, by the response to Jesus' preaching, in which He proclaims himself to be the Messiah in a way that doesn't exactly fit His audiences' expectations and preconceived notions.

We must realize that Luke is not giving us a strict chronology here. Lots of encounters, including the wedding at Cana, which happened during this Galilean ministry, and much of the content of Jesus' preaching, have been omitted (Cf. Mat. 13:53, etc.) so that Luke can focus our attention on this theme of testing, which confirms Jesus' commitment to being the kind of Messiah God actually intended to send. Luke cuts to this scene at Nazareth because it was an extreme case of what was typical of Jesus' whole ministry: acceptance and popularity at first, which turns into rejection when people realize that Jesus is not quite what they were expecting, not quite what they were hoping for—and they are not willing to adjust their expectations to the reality of what God had actually given them. (I assume none of us ever have this problem? Ahem.) As John says, *"He came unto his own, and his own received him not"* (John 1:11). It must have hurt, and it must have cut especially deeply here, in Jesus' own hometown. But neither devil nor man can deflect Him from what He has come to do. Today, then, we look at the role of rejection in Jesus' life and ministry. (I don't suppose any of you have ever had to deal with that? Oh, you have? It hurt like . . . the place of eternal punishment? Join the club! We are in very good company.) So how did Jesus handle rejection? What does it tell us about Him? What does it tell us about His mission and His kingdom? And what does it tell us about ourselves and our relationship to Him?

I. The Phenomenon Of Rejection

First let's look at The Phenomenon of Rejection. What was the nature of the rejection Jesus faced, and how did it come about? Why did it happen? Well, it is not hard to imagine the high anticipation with which the Nazarenes must have anticipated Jesus' visit to their town—and how it quickly turned into a disappointment just as fierce. We have to remember that at this time Nazareth was a really small town, with all the small-town dynamics we have come to know and love. (Modern Nazareth has been turned into a sizeable city by the religious tourist trade. But if you go there, you will see in the middle of it what they call "Nazareth Village," which is a reconstruction of the town Jesus grew up in. It is tiny.)

Okay, then the Nazarenes would have known Jesus growing up—and known Him really well, probably better than you know the kids on your street. They had probably liked Him. They knew He was precocious, both intellectually and spiritually; they knew He had promise—you could not have avoided knowing that about the boy who was on his way to impressing the rabbis in the Temple at the age of twelve—but miracles? They had never seen anything like that. He had seemed quite ordinary in that way. But now they were hearing astonishing things about Him from places like Capernaum. So I think they were excited and probably prepared to be impressed. Local boy makes good! They were no doubt sticking their chests out rather absurdly as they filed into the synagogue that Sabbath. And at first, things seemed to go really well. Their initial reaction to Jesus' sermon was quite positive. *And all were speaking well of him and wondering at the gracious words that were falling from his lips, and they were saying, "Is this not Joseph's son?"* (verse 22). So what went wrong between verse 22 and verse 23? Why does Jesus suddenly seem to start going out of his way to insult them?

The custom in the synagogue at this time was that the speaker would read the passage and then give a short explanation and exhortation based on it, which was followed by a question-and-answer period between him and the congregation. Jesus' sermon is summarized in verse 21. *"Today this scripture has been fulfilled in your hearing."* It is a forthright claim to be the very Messiah Isaiah was predicting. And the Nazarenes were at first quite ready to accept it. Hey, this will make people shut up with that stupid proverb, "Can anything good come out of Nazareth?"! This will really put us on the map. We'll probably all get cabinet posts, or at least lucrative contracts, in the new regime. The Messiah is our boy!

I can't help thinking of Shakespeare's Falstaff when he hears his friend Prince Hal has become king Henry V. He assumes he can still take the same liberties he was allowed to take when Hal was prince; he assumes that with his boy on the throne he will be able to get away with anything. "We are made men. Take any man's horse! The laws of England are at my disposal"[34] Falstaff was in for a bitter disappointment: "I know you not, old man!"[35] What else could the new king have done? I wonder if Shakespeare wasn't echoing Jesus' *"Depart from me; I never knew you!"* delivered to the Goats when they are separated from the Sheep — after assuming that they were of course going to be accepted on the basis of all the things they had done in Jesus' name. The Nazarenes are an acute instance of this very type of presumption.

Verse 23 and following then belong to the question–and–answer session, where undoubtedly these false assumptions on the part of Jesus' audience had begun to come out. Let's hear it again. 23 *And he said to them, "No doubt you will quote this proverb to me, 'Physician, heal yourself! Whatever we heard was done at Capernaum, do here in your hometown as well.'* 24 *And he said, "Truly I say to you, a prophet is not without honor save in his home country.* 25 *But I say to you in truth, there were many widows in Israel in the days of Elijah, when the sky was shut up for three years and six months and a great famine had come over all the land;* 26 *and yet Elijah was sent to none of them, but only to Zarephath in the land of Sidon, to a woman who was a widow.* 27 *And there were many lepers in Israel in the time of Elisha the prophet; and none of them was cleansed, but only Naaman the Syrian."*

Whoa! It had become obvious that the home–town folks thought they deserved special treatment, favoritism, partiality, because of their position in Jesus' life. And they were wondering when they were going to get it. They were wondering why they were not getting it now. What about all the miracles that had happened in Capernaum? When were *they* going to all get healed? Probably there were some early advocates of the "health–and–wealth" theology present who expected to "name it and claim it" then and there. When Jesus started trying to explain that it didn't work that way, it was not something they were prepared to hear. Look, there were lots of widows and lepers in Israel in the old days, but who got healed? Not the people you would have expected; actually, it was people you would least have expected. Naaman the Syrian? Give me a break! Not so fast. Being from my hometown does not give you an inside track.

---

[34] "The Second Part of King Henry the Fourth," Act V, Scene v, lines 142-3; *Complete Works*, op. cit., 694.
[35] Ibid., Scene v, line 51, p. 695,

Nothing is harder to take than disappointed expectations. The surest way to get people really angry is to have them perceive that you have promised them something and then refuse to deliver it. Well, Jesus had not in fact promised any special treatment to the Nazarenes, but that fact was quickly lost in their reaction. Who ever let mere facts stand in the way of a good hissy fit? They felt they had it coming, and here was Jesus letting them down. Who did He think he was? Isn't this Joseph's boy? Why, we knew Him when he was a young whippersnapper underfoot in the carpenter's shop! Let Him remember who He's talking to! And so their disappointed expectations turned into such anger that they were ready to throw Him off a cliff.

II. The Function Of Rejection

The Phenomenon of Rejection then leads us to consider the Function of Rejection in Jesus' life—and ours. Rejection by the world—sometimes even by our loved ones— is something that happens to all God's people at some point, beginning with their Master Himself. What matters is how we respond to it, for that will tell us where our true loyalties lie. So how did Jesus respond to this reaction on the part of His old friends and neighbors? There is real sadness in the proverb He quotes: "*A prophet is not without honor save in his own country.*" Maybe the people of Nazareth weren't the only ones with disappointed hopes that day. Surely Jesus had a right to have expected something better from His old friends and neighbors! So the first thing we learn is that it is Okay to be hurt by rejection, and to admit that it hurts. Even Jesus did not pretend that it did not matter. If He was affected, He gives us permission to be as well. And when we are, He gives us the assurance, just as He did at the Temptation, of a Master and a Friend who will truly be able to understand.

But, just as He had done at the Temptation, Jesus, in spite of his pain, resolutely refused compromise. Indeed, here He chose a very painful rejection over compromise. In fact, he even refused to gloss over the conflict; He went out of this way to force the issue. Are you going to accept me as a sin–bearing Messiah or not? Are you going to put your faith in me so that I can perform miracles here, or make the miracles a condition of your acceptance so that I cannot because of your unbelief? His brief Old–Testament history lesson has a sharp theological point to it. Who can expect the Messiah's favor, who has a right to special treatment, who deserves an exclusive place in the kingdom? How about his family? No. How about his hometown? No. How about the Jewish nation? No. As John the Baptist had said, God is able to raise up children to Abraham out of these very stones (Luke 3:8)! There is only one group that can have such an expectation: those who do not have it; those who do not think of it as a right or as something they deserve. The poor in spirit, Jesus would call them in the Sermon on the Mount (Mat. 5:3). *They* will inherit the kingdom! Or, to put it in another way, consonant with the preaching of John the Baptist that is still ringing in our ears at this point in Luke's narrative, we could say it is *repentant sinners.*

I'm afraid we are still all too prone to the same error committed by Jesus' townspeople here. Have you not heard it in too many believers' voices? Do you not hear the claim to be special there? We are Bible–believing Christians! We are separated believers! We are fully immersed Baptists! We are cultured and educated Presbyterians! We preach the full Gospel! We've been entirely sanctified! We belong to the one true Church! Have you ever been guilty of this? I have. Some of these are good things; some are things we should be. But they confer no special status in the kingdom. They do not entitle us to any special spiritual privileges. There is only one way to be part of that kingdom, and that is to come together at the foot of the Cross as people who have no claim whatsoever to be there except the Lord's gracious pardon proclaimed to repentant sinners. Sinners saved by grace! Beggars telling other beggars where to find bread! If you want to be anything in the kingdom, you had better start by being that. The moment you think you have become something more, you show yourself to be something less.

There is no principle that is closer to the heart of this kingdom than this. It is for sinners who have no claim to be there but their need and God's grace. If Christ was not willing to compromise this principle for His aunts and uncles and neighbors and boyhood friends, what makes us think He will be willing to compromise it for us? Sinners saved by grace! Beggars telling other beggars where to find bread! That is who we are. If we come with other expectations, will we not be in danger of rejecting the real King and the real kingdom? Come as a repentant sinner and you may get incredible miracles and healing and provision for this earthly life—along with temptation and trials and persecution—thrown in. Come for the miracles, thinking your "faith" gives you a right to them, and you may end up as disillusioned as the citizens of Nazareth.

This rejection also raises the issue of the Lordship of Christ. The people of Nazareth would all have said that they accepted the Messiah's authority. But the moment His agenda didn't match theirs, they were ready to throw Him off a cliff. God was not sending them a Savior who was here to advance their agendas. God was not sending us a Savior who was here to advance *our* agendas. Often the best thing He can do for us is to replace them. He offers us the fulfillment of being part of *His* agenda, which is to do the will of the Father, to live for the glory of the Father. Are we really so foolish as to think that health and wealth here and now, or being the Big Fish in the Small Pond which is the church (the only pond small enough where we could get away with it)—are we really so foolish as to think that is better? That it can even compare? The world is full of people who think so. God forbid that any of us should be among them!

Many people react positively to Jesus as long as they don't face the issue of His Lordship. Maybe that is why they expend so much energy in putting a full acceptance of it off as long as possible. But when the real Jesus, the Messiah God actually sent, comes into your life, He brings the issue of His Lordship with him, and sooner or later you are going to have to face it. It is as Lord that He has the authority to issue the pardon that we have been speaking of. If we want Him as anything less, we are still playing the same stupid, self–serving, sad, and futile game as the Nazarenes in this passage.

Conclusion

And so what of us? On what basis do we presume to come to Christ? Let us never forget the only basis that gives us access to Him. Sinners saved by grace! Beggars telling other beggars where to find bread! Let us remember whence we come and to Whom we are coming. Why? By giving up our own agendas we are included in a glory far greater than anything we can imagine. In other words, blessed are the poor in spirit, for theirs is the kingdom of heaven.

POWER AND AUTHORITY

Luke 4:31 And he came down to Capernaum, a city of Galilee. And he was teaching them on the Sabbath. 32 And they were amazed at his teaching, for his message was with authority. 33 And there was a man in the synagogue possessed by the spirit of an unclean demon, and he cried out with a loud voice. 34 "What do we have to do with you, Jesus of Nazareth? Have you come to destroy us? I know who you are—the Holy One of God!" 35 And Jesus rebuked him, saying, "Be quiet and come out of him!" And when the demon had thrown him down in their midst, he came out of him without doing him any harm. 36 And amazement came upon them all, and the began discussing with one another, saying, "What is this message? For with authority and power he commands the unclean spirits, and they come out!" 37 And the report about him was getting out into every locality in the surrounding district.

Introduction

In the three episodes leading up to this passage, Luke has been studying Jesus' dedication to His mission as the Sin–Bearer for His people. It was declared at His Baptism, when He identified Himself with sinners by insisting on a baptism of repentance for the remission of sins which He did not personally need. It was demonstrated, tested, and proved at His Temptation in the Wilderness, And it was tested again at His rejection by His hometown synagogue in Nazareth. Luke now continues by presenting us with a series of events which portray Christ's ministry as a continued confrontation with Satan through which the identity and the worthiness of the Savior are revealed. Today we examine the first of them, an event which demonstrates His *power* and His *authority*.

I think many of us who have been believers for some time miss some of the impact of these accounts because we already assume the deity of Christ as a starting point. Given that He is the Son of God, we rather expect Him to do amazing things. But perhaps that assumption comes a wee bit too easily; perhaps we take it a little bit too much for granted. Therefore, I would ask you today to exercise your imagination and pretend that you are one of these people in the synagogue at Capernaum. Pretend that you are completely ignorant of who Jesus is. You hope He may be the Messiah, but you think of the Messiah as a charismatic military leader who will overthrow the Roman Empire and replace it with a Jewish one centered in Jerusalem. Contemporary Judaism has not taught you to identify the Messiah with the Suffering Servant of Isaiah or with the glorious Danielic Son of Man. You do not necessarily expect Him to be the Son of God. So you have come out of curiosity, probably expecting nothing more than a sermon with some rather rousing political overtones. How do you react to what you are about to see and hear? What does it tell you about this man?

What it tells you is that you have no intellectual categories big enough to hold what you have just seen. He speaks with authority, not as the scribes: That is, He really seems to know what He is talking about, as if He were speaking from first–hand knowledge. But who could have first–hand knowledge of *these* things? Hmmm. And then He speaks with a different kind of authority, casting out a demon with a simple Word. What kind of message is this? What manner of man is this? These are questions that require a thoughtful answer.

I. Two Types Of Authority

What does it mean to say that Christ spoke with authority, that He had authority? It can mean at least two different things, and we see both of them in this passage. For there are at least two different kinds of authority. We might call them the authority of possession verse the authority of position, or the authority of counsel verse the authority of command. Let me illustrate the difference in a man I knew who had both in my own life.

Dr. Dale Heath, my Greek professor at Taylor University, was an expert in Greek, an authority on biblical languages. He did not cause the genitive singular of λογος (*λογος*) to be λογου (*logou*) or the first–person plural, present active indicative of λυω (*luo*) to be λυομεν (*luomen*). He did not dictate that it be so; but when he reported this fact to you, you had better listen and would be well advised to believe it. He delivered such facts with an authority that was based on much training and on dependable first–hand knowledge that had been demonstrated consistently over time. He had actually worked with sho' 'nuff ancient Greek manuscripts. He did not need to speak about Koine Greek tentatively or apologetically or with a lot of hems and haws or ifs, ands, and buts; he knew whereof he spoke. He spoke with authority because he *was* an authority. That is the sense of the word in its first use in this passage, when the people were "amazed" at Jesus' teaching in verse 31.

But Dr. Heath was not only my Greek professor. He was also my supervisor, because I had a work–study job as his teaching assistant. In this role, he had authority over me in a different sense. He could say, "Don, scramble a sample of ten of these vocabulary words into a matching quiz for the first year class," or "Don, go to the library and look this word up in Liddell and Scott and bring me back a list of the citations they have for it," or "Don, grade the objective portion of this test by such–and–such criteria," and I had to do it, in precisely the manner and within the time frame prescribed. In the first case, Dr. Heath's *possession* of knowledge gave him the authority of *counsel*; in the second, his *position* as supervisor gave him the authority of *command*. And that is the second use of the word, in verse 36: With authority and power Jesus commands the unclean spirits, and they come out. Well, Jesus had both kinds of authority in a way that was unprecedented in all this congregation's experience.

II. Christ And The Authority Of Counsel

We do not have the words Jesus spoke here that caused the people of Capernaum to attribute to Him the authority of counsel, but we have plenty of other samples of his teaching we can look to. And what we find is that Jesus was the greatest authority on theology who has ever lived. To avoid anticipating passages we will look at in detail in their proper place in this series, I will take my examples from the other Gospels. Again, pretend you are hearing these words for the first time—not just *your* first time but the first time they were ever said. What will you realize? You will realize that every time this man opens his mouth, something gets settled for all time: Something gets said so simply yet profoundly that there can be no going behind it or around it for those who truly love and seek the truth. Other thinkers like the Apostle Paul may bring out further implications of it, but it will have been Jesus who laid it down and gave them the impetus for that further development. Once He has spoken, we must go on from there; there can be no going back.

Do you doubt this? Just listen to Him. Here he is on theology proper, the doctrine of God. *"God is spirit, and those who worship him must worship him in spirit and in truth"* (Jn. 4:24). *"Pray then in this way: 'Our Father, who art in heaven . . ."* (Mat. 6:9ff). *"If you knew me, you would know the Father also"* (Jn. 8:19). He is also the greatest authority on ethics who has ever lived. We are still trying to plumb the depths of the Sermon on the Mount. And what of anthropology, the doctrine of man? *"And this is the judgment, that the light has come into the world, and men loved darkness rather than light because their deeds were evil. For everyone who does evil hates the light, and does not come to the light, lest his deeds should be exposed"* (Jn. 3:19–20). Nailed us! And as for soteriology, the doctrine of salvation: *"For God so loved the world that he gave his only begotten Son, that whosoever believeth in him should not perish, but have everlasting life"* (Jn. 3:16). *"From that time Jesus began to show his disciples that he must go to Jerusalem and suffer many things from the elders and chief priests and scribes, and be killed, and be raised up on the third day"* (Mat. 16:21). *"For even the Son of Man did not come to be served, but to serve, and to give his life a ransom for many"* (Mk. 10:45). *"I am the door. If anyone enters through me, he shall be saved, and shall go in and out and find pasture. . . . I am the good shepherd. The good shepherd lays down his life for the sheep"* (John 10:9, 11).

I say it again: Jesus was the greatest authority on theology who has ever lived. Every time this man opens His mouth, something gets settled for all time; something gets said so simply yet profoundly that there can be no going behind it and no going around it. Other thinkers like Paul will bring out further implications of it, but it will have been Jesus who laid it down and gave them the impetus for that further development. Once He has spoken, we must go on from there; there can be no going back. He was the greatest authority on theology who ever lived because he spoke from an intimate, first-hand acquaintance with those truths that no one else has ever had or will ever have. What does that tell us about who He was?

III. Christ And The Authority Of Command

But what really got the people's attention here was the other kind of authority that Jesus showed, the authority of command. The encounter with the demon might have seemed like a chance meeting, but it was not by chance. Demonic activity had risen to a fever pitch in the First Century in response to the threat that Satan's kingdom felt from this man. Either this fellow's demon had been dormant recently—otherwise he would never have been allowed into the synagogue—or he just wandered in off the street. In either case, it was the demon, as much as the congregation, who was in for a shock.

The New American Standard, like all our other modern translations, is much too timid with its translation here. *"What have we to do with you?"* they write. Way too dignified. And they have left out a word. What this man let out with was an ear–piercing "AAUUUGGGGHHHHH!" The demon was apparently not expecting to see Jesus there. He let out a scream of absolute terror. *"Have you come to destroy us? Get away from me! I know who you are: the Holy One of God!"* People are probably scurrying back out of the way as fast as they can, leaving this man and Jesus facing each other in the middle. They are terrified of demons. Demons, on the other hand, are afraid of no one. But this demon is terrified—of Jesus! And he has told us why: because Jesus is the Messiah. Now what is Jesus going to do?

What the people expected Jesus to do was to begin an elaborate exorcism ritual full of gobbledy–gook, rigmarole, and mumbo jumbo. That's what the Jewish exorcists they were familiar with would have done. There would be intricate charms designed to protect the exorcist and intricate prayers and incantations designed to force the demon to do his bidding. It was all very impressive—when it worked. But Jesus was impressive in a different way. One simple sentence, one command, and it was all over. They had never seen or heard of a demon tucking tail and running like that! Once again, our translation is entirely too tame, intimidated I suppose by people's expectations that the Bible's language be elevated and dignified. This was not a dignified moment; it was intense spiritual warfare. ""*Be quiet and come out of him!*" Not hardly. A much more accurate and idiomatic translation would be something like *"Shut up! You're outta here!"* In good King James English, the word for "be quiet" might be rendered, *"Be thou muzzled"*—or, even more accurately, *"Stuff a rag in it!"* Jesus turned on this demon with a fierceness that matched its fear, that showed its fear to be well justified. Wham! And it was over. Just like that.

IV. The Power Of Christ

Christ's way of exercising His authority over this demon points out not only His authority but also His power. Authority did not seem an adequate word the second time, and so the people added "power" to it as they were trying to figure out what in the world they were dealing with here. We might define power as the ability to make one's commands stick. "I can call spirits from the vasty deep!" boasts Owen Glendower. "Why, so can I, and so can any man," replies Henry Hotspur. "But will they come when you do summon them?" A very good question; and one that is like unto it is, will they go when you dismiss them? In Shakespeare's "Henry IV part I,"[36] Glendower wisely forebears to put his claim to the test. Jesus had no such hesitation.

Authority and power need to go together if either is to be effective. Once when I was a senior in high school our band director had to be away and left me in charge of the rehearsal. He had given me the authority; I was authorized to lead the session. But I was frustrated because the other students weren't taking the rehearsal very seriously. They were horsing around, making mistakes on purpose—acting like high–school students. Go figure. Then the choir director poked her head in the door to check on us, and suddenly the group got very serious and started applying themselves most earnestly to my direction. Why? Because *she* had clout!

Authority is the right to say certain things; power is the ability to back those words up. Jesus in this passage demonstrated the fact that He had both in a measure the people had never seen before. They had no categories big enough to hold what they were seeing. Who has the authority and the power to command demons and get this kind of response? Not an exorcist! They have to have elaborate charms to protect themselves. Who has the authority and the power to command demons and get this kind of response? There are only two possibilities: God or Satan. But how can this man be either?

The logic of the answer awaits further encounters to come out. It can't be Satan, or his kingdom would be divided. So the only answer is that we are looking at God in human flesh. It would take time for such an answer to be worked out, and Jesus Himself would have to help with statements like *"Before Abraham was, I AM"* (John 8:58) and *"I and the Father are one"* (John 10:30). At this point, Luke is simply beginning to give us a series of encounters that insistently ask the question. *"What is this message?"* these people ask. And the question will keep ringing: "What manner of man *is* this?" It is a question we would do well to keep posing today. Maybe, like Luke, we should work harder at posing it before leaping too quickly to the answer. (You will understand that I am not asking you to *doubt* that Answer, but rather to more fully appreciate it.)

Conclusion

We, who have already read the rest of the Book, can see the answers already in the question. This passage teaches us at least two things. First, Jesus is the highest authority there is on the things that matter. He wrote the Book! Well, more accurately, He had His personal agent and representative, the Holy Spirit, inspire its writers. The Old Testament is the preparation for His coming. The New Testament is the record (the Gospels) and explanation (the Epistles) of that coming by the Apostles, His appointed spokesmen. It was a good saying attributed to Martin Luther: "The whole Bible is about

---

[36] Act III, Scene 1, lines 52–4; *Complete Works*, op. cit., 635.

Christ only everywhere."[37] Jesus is the highest authority there is on the things that matter. Only a fool would not consult Him. Suppose you had to write a term paper in American History on the First Gulf War, and George Bush the Elder offered to help you with it. You'd be an idiot to turn him down. Suppose you wanted to know the meaning of life and how to live it to the full as it was meant to be lived? What is the ultimate answer to life, the universe, and everything? Well you can try to figure out what to do with "42," or you can come to Jesus of Nazareth.

Second, Jesus has the right to rule. He not only has the right to rule, He is destined to rule, and He has the power to rule. When "advice" comes from an authority as high as this, to hear is to *obey*. Only a fool would fail to listen; only a bigger fool would hear and then refuse to obey. Well, the world is replete with fools. But the day is coming when every knee will bow before Christ, some in joy, others in the kind of terror shown by the demon in this story. You can bow in joy or in terror, but everyone is going to bow. Today He is giving us the opportunity to serve Him by choice and be in that first group who bow in joy. Will you take it? For those who own Him as their Lord and highest Authority now, His words become true now, and do not even have to wait for that Day: "*I have come that they might have life—and have it more abundantly*" (John 10:10).

---

[37] Luther may well have said it. It is the kind of thing he would have said. But honesty compels me to admit that I have not been able to track the reference down.

THE GREAT PHYSICIAN

Luke 4:38 *And he arose and left the synagogue and entered Simon's home. Now Simon's mother in law was suffering from a high fever, and they made request of him on her behalf.* **39** *And standing over her, he rebuked the fever, and it left her. And she immediately arose and waited on them.* **40** *And while the sun was setting, all who had any sick with various diseases brought them to him; and, laying his hands on every one of them, he was healing them.* **41** *And demons also were coming out of many, crying out and saying, "You are the Son of God!" And rebuking them he would not allow them to speak because they knew him to be the Christ.* **42** *And when day came, he departed and went to a lonely place. And the multitudes were searching for him, and came to him, and tried to keep him from going away from them.* **43** *But he said to them, "I must preach the kingdom of God to the other cities also, for I was sent for this purpose."* **44** *And he kept on preaching in the synagogues of Judea.*

Introduction

Throughout all four of the Gospels people frequently ask about Jesus, "What manner of man is this?" We have certainly been asking that question in our study of Luke's Gospel, even when we have not articulated it as such. What manner of man is this that you cannot study His life or come to know Him without asking, "What manner of man is this?" What manner of man is this who submits to a baptism of repentance without confessing any sins? What manner of man is this on whom the Holy Spirit descends like a dove? What manner of man is this to whom a Voice from Heaven says, "You are my beloved Son in whom I am well pleased"? What manner of man is this who puts so much energy and concentration into resisting temptation that He forgets to eat for forty days? What manner of man is this who refuses to compromise even when it alienates His own hometown? What manner of man is this who teaches with authority, not as the scribes? What manner of man is this who casts out demons with a simple word of command? And today we ask it again: What manner of man is this who heals with a touch? As we try to answer that question we must consider His ministry of healing, His motive for healing, His methods of healing, and also the message of healing and the meaning of healing in Jesus' life.

I. The Ministry Of Healing

The ministry of healing certainly had an important place in Jesus' mission. Part of the prophecy from Isaiah he had used to announce his purpose at the synagogue of Nazareth in Luke 4:18 was giving sight to the blind. That literal physical healing of actual physical blindness, and not just a spiritualized "enlightenment," was an important aspect of the fulfillment of that promise, is showed by multiple examples from Jesus' life, though of course it also has reference to giving spiritual insight to people blinded by sin. Nevertheless, starting with Peter's mother–in–law, physical healing was the aspect of Jesus' ministry that attracted the most attention and gave Him the opportunity to deliver His spiritual message to a larger audience. The point of it is that in the coming of this Messiah *all* the effects of the Fall are to be reversed, including physical illness.

But though physical healing had an important place in Jesus' ministry, it did not have the central place. When Jesus tears Himself away from the crowd in verse 43, He does not offer as justification that He had to *heal* in other cities too. He was sent to preach the Gospel, the good news, of the kingdom, that is the rule, of God, in every city. Preaching the Gospel of the kingdom was primary; healing was secondary. It was important, as a means to the end of preaching the Kingdom and as a living illustration of it and for its own sake; but it was still secondary. And even more basic and important than either was making atonement for our sins—for that was to *bring* the kingdom He had been preaching.

Healing was present in Jesus' earthly ministry then as a sign that the true Healer was here and as a foretaste of the complete reversal of the effects of sin that the atonement would make possible, but which will be fully manifest only when Christ returns. That is one reason why Jesus had reminded the Nazarenes that of all the lepers in Israel in the days of Elisha, only Naaman the Syrian was healed. Healing is one of the side–effects of the atonement, but it is not the central thing. There are two mistakes, therefore, that we can make concerning miraculous physical healing today. One is to believe that Christ no longer heals in response to the prayers of His people. The other is to make healing so central to the atonement that it can be "claimed" automatically by faith in the same way as the forgiveness of sin. Each of these errors, in its own way, is simply cruel. One takes away hope, and the other gives a false and unrealistic hope that often only adds guilt to the suffering people are already experiencing.

II. The Motive For Healing

What then was Jesus' motive for healing? There are a number of reasons for the emphasis that healing had in the Lord's earthly ministry. One was to vindicate His claim to be the sight–restoring Servant Isaiah had prophesied. One was to show the connection between the atonement and the curse, one of the effects of which (disease) is being undone. These are important purposes served by the healing stories in the Gospels.

But when the Gospels speak of Jesus' personal motives for healing, of the emotional wellsprings of His willingness to labor so tirelessly at it, two feelings stand out. One is simple compassion for the suffering of the victims. "*And Jesus was going about all the cities and villages, teaching in their synagogues and proclaiming the gospel of the kingdom, and healing every kind of disease and every kind of sickness. And seeing the multitudes, he felt compassion for them*" (Mat. 9:35–36). In Luke we see this compassion in a couple of ways. First we see it in the individual attention he gave to the people he healed, laying hands on each one individually. *And while the sun was setting, all who had any sick with various diseases brought them to him; and, laying his hands on every one of them, he was healing them* (Luke 4:40). Then we see it is His staying up all night to meet their needs. *And when day came, he departed and went to a lonely place* (verse 42).

So Jesus' compassion stands out, not only by being mentioned but also by being demonstrated practically in His actions. But there is another motive that also came into play. Of everything that Jesus did, we know that his meat and drink was to do the will of His Father and glorify Him (John 4:34). In Luke, the thing that moves Jesus to begin His ministry is that *"the Spirit of the Lord was upon Him"* (4:18). The Holy Spirit during Jesus' earthly life functioned as the Liaison between Him and the Father when the Father was not speaking from Heaven, saying *"This is my beloved Son."* The Spirit provided both direction and power that came from the Father. So this is Luke's way of saying what Jesus said in John's Gospel: His meat and drink was to do the will of the Father. His motive then was twofold: compassion for the people and zeal for the Father's will and for His glory.

For us too, then, compassion for people and zeal for God's glory must be the twin motives that drive whatever ministry the Father gives us. It cannot be just one or the other; it has to be both together. If either is lacking, true healing of body or soul will not occur, for neither can be true, whole, or sustainable without the other. Zeal for God's glory that does not involve real compassion for hurting people will not promote God's glory at all but is very liable to be mistaken for self–righteousness—because it is very likely to *be* self–righteous. If you really care about God's glory you must care about what He cares about. And compassion that is not rooted in and sustained by devotion to the glory of God will also fall short. It may be misguided in its application, and even if it is not, it will fail to address the deeper needs that underlie our merely physical suffering. Like Jesus, we have to keep the two together.

III. The Methods Of Healing

Jesus used at least three methods in his healing ministry, and each of them has something to teach us. Often he healed simply with a word, as with Peter's mother in law in verse 39. Here, as with the exorcism we saw last time, there is an instructive contrast with contemporary Jewish exorcists and miracle workers, the "faith healers" of their day. Here is a formula that was actually used by one of those guys, as reported in the Talmud: To cure a fever, you must tie an iron knife by a braid of the victim's hair to a thornbush. Repeat over the bush on successive days Exodus 3:2, 3:3, 3:4, and finally 3:5. Then cut down the bush while reciting a secret formula. (What is the formula, you ask? It is not revealed. It is secret.) Do this, the rite promises, and the fever will die with the thornbush.[38] Hmmm. Chances are that by the time that rigmarole was finished the fever would have subsided naturally anyway. The power and authority of Christ stand out by contrast in such bright relief that no commentary is really needed. Remember the

---

[38] Alfred Edersheim, *The Life and Times of Jesus the Messiah* (1886; Grand Rapids: Eerdmans, 1971), 1:486.

casting out of the demon in the Synagogue of Capernaum? Boom! You're outta here! The same kind of unprecedented authority and power is used with disease.

Another method Jesus employed was healing at a distance, as with the centurion's servant who will be healed when we get to chapter seven. This is another sign of the astounding power and authority Jesus had. He does not even have to be present to pull off a healing. When the centurion's messengers get back to the house, they find the boy in good health. In some accounts it is noted that the healing occurred at precisely the time when Jesus, who had not been there, had pronounced it.

But by far the most common method, indeed Jesus' preferred method, is healing by a touch (verse 40). He goes out of his way to do this. He does it even with lepers, the last people you would want to touch; He does it even when it is less efficient, as in this passage. That is why He ends up spending all night at it. Why? Because there was something at stake here more important than healing people's bodies. Touching them was a way of personalizing the act, of establishing a relationship with the one being healed—or at least giving him the opportunity to enter into one. Why not just snap His fingers and heal everyone in Judea in one fell swoop? He could have, surely, if He can heal with a word and at a distance. Why leave *this* town with people who are yet unhealed? (That's why they were looking for him the next morning.) Because there was something more important than physical cures at stake. And that leads us to the next point.

IV. The Message Of Healing

What was the message of Jesus' healing ministry? We have already hinted at it, but let us bring it into focus at this point. That message had at least three parts. Every healing Jesus performed was an Expression of Mercy, it was Evidence of Messiahship, and it was an Offer of Meeting. It was **an Expression of Mercy**. Each healing was an acted parable, saying, "God cares." It was **Evidence of Messiahship**. Every healing was an acted sermon, declaring, as Jesus had declared at Nazareth, "This day is fulfilled in your ears, not just Isaiah but *all* the prophecies and promises of the Old Testament." And it was **an Offer of Meeting**. That was the reason for the laying on of hands. It is all because then as now the primary issue was not physical health and comfort but a relationship with Christ.

Don't misunderstand me. If you or someone you love is hurting from or hindered by a physical illness or disability, that is a very significant thing to you. I've been there a number of times, so believe me, I know! I do not mean to minimize physical suffering, but the point still needs to be made: There is something even more important here than that. And what could that be? Every healing in Jesus' ministry was an opportunity for someone to accept Jesus as God's Messiah. Look for this issue to come increasingly to the fore in future healing narratives. And let us make sure it stays at the forefront in our own lives, when we seek healing for ourselves or for others we care about. Ask for physical healing by all means; work for it if you can. But don't lose sight of the even more significant healing that Christ offers too. Physical healing is an expression of mercy, and for that we are grateful; it is evidence of Jesus' messiahship, and from that we receive encouragement and joy; but it is also an offer of meeting, a chance for the beginning or the deepening of our relationship with Christ, and for that we bow in worship and adoration. Amen.

V. The Meaning Of Healing

We have looked at the ministry of healing, which had an important but not the primary place in Jesus' earthly labors; the motive for healing, which was compassion for people and zeal for the Father and His glory; the methods of healing, which focused on physical touch in order to make the healing personal; and the message of healing, which was an expression of mercy, evidence of Messiahship, and an offer of meeting. Alright, then, what is the meaning of Jesus' healing miracles for us today? We can answer that question with a series of questions.

1. Does God still heal miraculously today? Yes. He is still the same God, and the Christ He sent is still present in our lives through His personal Representative and Agent, the Holy Spirit. All healing comes from God, always, whether it happens naturally through the body's own repair mechanisms, whether it happens naturally through the aid of medicine, or whether it happens miraculously. But there is no automatic guarantee of healing in this life just because we have enough faith. Paul had to bear his thorn in the flesh with the realization that God's grace was sufficient. And sometimes God heals us by releasing us from a diseased and failing body to come and be with Him in spirit until He gives us the ultimate healing of the Resurrection of the Dead when Christ returns. Unless Christ returns first, this will eventually be the answer to all our prayers for healing. Even Lazarus was resurrected only to face the prospect of getting sick and dying all over again. There may be many healings, even miraculous ones, along the way to encourage us and to give us foretastes of what is coming, but we will not be *finally* healed until we see Christ face to face.

2. If Jesus is so compassionate, why doesn't God always heal us when we ask Him in faith? We could restate that question in another way: Why didn't He heal everyone in Judea in the First Century? It's really the same question, isn't it? Surely part of the answer is that if He had done so He would have left the first–century Judeans satisfied—and still in their sins. Even those He did heal did not all follow Him. Of the Ten Lepers, only one returned to give thanks. God knows that we are not mature enough to handle automatic guaranteed healing. We would stay babes in faith if we had faith at all; people would be "believing" for all the wrong reasons. God sends us healing to encourage us, but if it always came, we would cease to share in the groaning of creation. We would then minister with less compassion for a lost and needy world with which we could no longer identify, and we would cease longing for our full redemption when Christ returns as it deserves to be longed for. And none of those things would be good. Each would be worse than any sickness we are called to endure.

3. Finally, what does healing mean when it does come? It is an acted parable saying that Jesus cares. It is an acted sermon saying that Jesus is the Messiah and that the words of Isaiah are fulfilled in your ears. It is a demonstration that God cares about the whole man, not just the spirit but the body too, not just Sunday but the rest of the week too, not just "religion" but all of life. It is a down payment on a future when there will be no more tears. It is an opportunity to grow closer to the Lord. And, finally, it is an opportunity to worship Him, to ask in awe, "What manner of man is this?" And to ask it with a wee bit of a greater inkling of the answer.

Conclusion

God's interest in the whole man, body as well as spirit, is shown by the healing ministry of Jesus. It is also shown by the physical elements of bread and wine by which we celebrate the Lord's Supper, that feast which points forward to the Marriage Supper of the Lamb, when sickness will be no more. Let us think of the Lord's Supper in those terms today as we recommit ourselves to him by partaking of it.

FISHERS OF MEN

Luke 5:1 Now it came about that while the multitude were pressing around him and listening to the word of God, he was standing by the Lake of Gennesaret. 2 And he saw two boats lying at the edge of the lake, but the fishermen had gotten out of them and were washing their nets. 3 And he got into one of the boats, which was Simon's, and asked him to put out a little way from the land. And he sat down and began teaching the multitudes from the boat. 4 And when he had finished speaking, eh said to Simon, "Put out into the deep water and let down your nets for a catch." 5 And Simon answered and said, "Master, we worked hard all night and caught nothing, but at your bidding I will let down the nets." 6 And when they had done this, they enclosed a great quantity of fish, and their nets began to break. 7 And they signaled to their partners in the other boat, for them to come and help them. And they came and filled both of the boats so that they began to sink. 8 But when Simon Peter saw that, he fell down at Jesus' feet, saying, "Depart from me, for I am a sinful man, oh Lord!" 9 For amazement had seized him and all his companions because of the catch of fish which they had taken. 10 And so also James and John, sons of Zebede, were partners with him. And Jesus said to Simon, "Do not fear; from now on you will be catching men." 11 And when they had brought their boats to land, they left everything and followed him.

Introduction

As we have studied Luke's Gospel we have been confronted in a profound way with the question, "What manner of man is this?" What manner of man is this who submits to a baptism of repentance without confessing any sin; on whom the Holy Spirit descends in the form of a Dove; who will not compromise despite intense pressure from Satan and Synagogue; who casts out demons and heals diseases with a word or a touch; whose teaching is with authority, not as the scribes? Today Luke continues his examination of that question, but begins to address another one as well: Whatever manner of man this may be, what does it mean to be a follower of such a One as this? For us, that is a very pertinent question indeed. To answer it, we need to understand some important features of the story we have just read. And the first one is the story of the connection being established here.

I. The Story Of The Connection

What is the story of the connection between Jesus and Peter? It is obvious that this is not their first encounter. In fact, they must have met even before the healing of Peter's mother–in–law that we looked at last week. Their first meeting is recorded in John 1:35–42. It apparently took place right after Jesus returned from the Temptation in the Wilderness, before leaving on his first preaching tour. He reconnected with his cousin John the Baptist, who at that meeting pronounced him *"The Lamb of God who taketh away the sins of the world"* (John 1:29). One of John's disciples, Andrew, heard him say this, followed Jesus, and became His disciple. The first thing he did after that was to introduce Jesus to his brother, Simon. Probably not too long after that, Jesus met the Bar–Jonah boys again, along with their friends and business partners the Zebedees, James and John, in Mat. 4:12–23. (Mat. 4:17 and 4:23 probably refer to the same preaching tour that we read about last week in Luke 4:43.) Once again, they are called to be Jesus' disciples, and they accept. Then Jesus is off preaching again. On a stop in Capernaum, their hometown and Jesus' base of operations at this stage, he heals Peter's mother–in–law and is pursued by the multitudes as we saw last week. Probably on a subsequent return trip, after verse 43 of chapter four, the incident happens that is told about in our passage today.

So what did this "acceptance" by these four men mean? It meant that they acknowledged Jesus as the Messiah and were supporting Him in his "bid" for that office as they understood it. Simon and Andrew may have offered him their house as a home base. But they had not yet entered into what today we would call "full–time Christian service." It is obvious that when the Luke 5 passage begins, they are still living at home and working their secular jobs as fishermen; they have just been out fishing all night and are cleaning their nets. After what happens today, that will no longer be the case. Something will impel them to leave everything and follow Jesus in a way that they have not done so far. What was it, and why did it have that effect? That is the subject of our study today.

Okay, Jesus is back in town, and the people are thronging about Him on the shore much as they did the last time He was here when He had healed so many of them, and Simon's boat makes a good platform from which to teach them. What was He teaching them? What were Simon Peter and his friends listening to as they worked on their nets over to the side? The general content of Jesus' preaching at this point was that the Kingdom of Heaven is at hand, that to enter it you need a greater righteousness than that practiced by the Pharisees, and that therefore you should repent, accepting the rule of God that is coming through Christ himself. To Peter and his friends, it probably sounded vaguely messianic, and they no doubt listened approvingly. What it really meant was about to hit them in a way they did not expect. When Jesus was done, going out into the deep water was a good way to bring the session to a close and get away from the crowd—the same persistent people we saw back in Luke 4:42. No doubt Peter was happy to oblige and figured that casting the nets again was a good excuse. Well, he was in for quite a surprise.

II. The Surprise Of The Catch

After the story of the connection comes the surprise of the catch. As far as any serious fishing was concerned, Peter knew that no such thing was going to happen. It was now mid–morning, the worst time to fish. The best time was sunrise and right before, and Peter knew that there had been no fish out there at that time. There was no way you would catch any now. There weren't any fish in the area. All Peter's long years

116

of professional experience told him it was hopeless. Yet he obeyed—maybe just to humor Jesus or provide an excuse for His breaking up the meeting. And then—what's this? The net is about to break and swamp the boat! Even with the help of the other boat, they were barely able to get this stupendous haul of fish safely back to shore. I would love to have been able to see the expression on Jesus' face as He watched these men of little faith struggling with their sudden good fortune. I wonder if He shook his head over them; I wonder if He sighed; I wonder if He had to stifle a laugh. It may have been a combination of all three, mingled with the one thing that was never absent from that face: a profundity of outflowing love.

Commentators have bestowed much ink on trying to figure out what the nature was of this miracle. We know there should not have been any fish there to catch. Did Jesus create a school of fish *ex nihilo,* out of nothing? Did He summon them from wherever they were in the depths of the lake? Or did He just happen to know through His omniscient insight that they had showed up? In one sense it doesn't matter, but in another I think the context suggests a particular answer. To have merely known about the fish connects with nothing that has been happening; to have created them would be superfluous. Luke has been giving us a series of examples that illustrate Jesus' *authority,* his Lordship. Demons obey Him; fevers obey Him; Peter obeys Him; *now the fish obey Him.* I think He summoned them, and they answered His call. The message of the miracle is that the One who is sovereign over Creation is here before us. And Peter is about to show us that he fully got the point.

III. The Psychology Of The Characters

So the story of the connection and the surprise of the catch raise the question of the psychology of the characters. Peter had seen other miracles—the miracles of healing—already, and had no doubt been (he thought) duly impressed by them. But this one hit home in a new way. Fishing was his business, his profession. He knew that there was no way those fish ought to be in that net, no way they *could* be in that net. But there they were. What manner of man is this who summons a school of fish without even saying a word, and they obey him? Only one Person in the universe has that kind of authority, and Peter's response shows that he knew who it was. How much of the full meaning of it he had worked out in his head as yet is doubtful, but his reaction is the reaction of a pious Jew who has just seen God. *"Depart from me, for I am a sinful man, oh Lord!"* (verse 8). It echoes Isaiah 6:1–8. *"Woe is me, for I am undone! For I am a man of unclean lips, and my eyes have seen the Lord of Hosts."*

Both passages, Isaiah talking about himself and Luke talking about Peter, are encounters with the living God in which a man is being called into His service. In both, the man is struck with an overwhelming sense of his own unworthiness to be in that service. In both, God does not disagree with the accuracy of the man's cry of unworthiness but accepts him anyway out of grace and sends him forth as His messenger. Oh, yes. The very same thing is happening on both occasions because it is the very same Person with whom the sinful man is dealing. And while Peter might not yet have fully understood it, he sensed it right down to the very marrow of his bones.

The appropriateness of this miracle to Peter's situation is truly remarkable. Not only was it elegantly designed to get his attention, much as the healings might especially impress a physician, or a raising from the dead an undertaker, or the feeding of the five thousand a farmer, but it was also simultaneously designed to answer the questions Peter must have been silently asking himself. He was probably sitting there wanting to go with Jesus and wondering how he could. What would happen to his business? How would he support his extended family? And who was he to think he was worthy to be one of the Messiah's closest associates anyway? In one brilliant stroke Jesus blows all of those questions out of the water. Yes, I know you aren't worthy. I want you anyway. And I can provide for you better than you can provide for yourself. It is no wonder that it is at this point that Peter, Andrew, James, and John leave everything to follow Jesus "full time."

Now, for all I know, Christ has called you to serve him right where you are, in whatever business or profession you are pursuing. After all, Jesus had 500 true disciples back then, but only twelve of them were expected to quit their jobs and follow him around full time. The ratio is probably not much different today. But if he *were* calling you to leave everything and go to Bible school or seminary to prepare for the ministry or the mission field—or to do something difficult and challenging right where you are—how can you read this account and not say yes? How can you believe this account and even hesitate? For it is the same God who called Isaiah, and whose Son called Peter, who calls to us to follow him today.

IV. The Substance Of The Calling

Well, the story of the connection, the surprise of the catch, and the psychology of the characters are all here to help us focus on the substance of this calling that Peter received. Peter and his friends were called to be fishers of men. This was not just a cute metaphor Jesus made up for being an evangelist. It was a phrase that had strong messianic overtones from Jeremiah 16:16. "'Behold, I am going to send for many fishermen,' declares the Lord, 'and they will fish for them* [i.e., for the exiled and scattered people of God].'" Jeremiah was initially talking about God bringing all the scattered Jewish exiles back to the Land in a more radical and complete way than Cyrus would. It was understood as something the Messiah would do in the Last Days. So that is how Peter and his friends would have heard it: Jesus was calling them to be the fulfillment of that prophecy! It was a foreshadowing of the Great Commission, when all Christ's followers are given the identity and the mission of being disciple–makers. I've tried to show what it must have felt like in the following sonnet:

FISHERS OF MEN

Two boats of fish, crammed to the gunwales, full:

A week of work accomplished in one day!
Yet it exerted hardly any pull.
We left them in the sun and walked away.
We *had* to follow Him. How could we stay?
He'd called the fish into our nets, and then
He called to us. You ask, what did He say?
Just, "Come! From now on, you will fish for men."
To doubt He was the Christ would be a sin.
There was no way we should have caught those fish!
But there they were, with gill and scale and fin,
As many and as big as we could wish.
But, this man–fishing: What's that all about?
I've got a feeling we will soon find out.[39]

So Peter's calling was a foreshadowing of the Great Commission, when all Christ's followers are given the identity and the mission of being disciple–makers. And so when we come to Christ we too become fishers of men. We are all called to fish, and therefore to learn to fish better. To neglect Bible reading and prayer and public worship is to fail to mend our nets and keep them in good repair. To sin is to tear holes in them. Many fail to catch significant numbers of fish for those reasons, but others who have avoided those failings also become ineffective fishermen simply by their failure to obey the command of this passage: Let down the net!

Oh, we have many reasons why we do not. But to all those reasons the Lord's answer is simply to repeat the command, "Let down the net." "But we aren't very skilled fishermen." Well, if Peter had not been taking care of his nets he would have been in no position to answer the call. But was it Peter's skill that caught these fish? No. Let down the net! "But I've labored all night and caught nothing." Let down the net! "But the fish are too slippery, they won't listen." Let down the net! "But I am not worthy. Who am I to tell people what to believe?" Let down the net! There is no promise of success. The Lord did not say, "Let down the net and you will have a big catch." But there is hope in the command when we remember who gave it. It is our responsibility to let down the net; it is His part to fill it with fish, to call the fish in. But we must let down the net. When was the last time you shared the Gospel—not just talked vaguely about your "spirituality" but shared the Good News of salvation in Christ? Let down the net!

V. The Sequel To The Commission

After the story of the connection, the surprise of the catch, and the psychology of the characters leads to the substance of the calling, we finally get the sequel to the commission. When Peter and company finally got the fish to the shore, their next move was in one sense amazing, and in another sense seems inevitable. They left everything

---

[39] Donald T. Williams, *Stars through the Clouds*, op. cit., 147.

and followed Jesus. Imagine the scene. You've got two boats loaded to the "gills" with the catch left sitting in the sun. Now, I know what the businessmen in the congregation are thinking. Here's a whole lot of merchandise with a very short shelf life, and they just leave it? That "stinks." Well, it sounds "fishy" to me too. But before I "spawn" any more fish puns, let me move on to the point. They left that "school" of fish to sit at the feet of Jesus.

Seriously, imagine the commitment these guys are making at this moment. They have just made the biggest catch of their career. They've got work to do! If you don't think those boats full of fish weren't worth some serious money, you haven't eaten at Red Lobster lately! And they walked away from it, just like that, and never gave it a second thought. (I doubt the fish actually spoiled. Lots of neighbors and hopefully many of the poor probably got a free dinner out of the deal, which is an interesting footnote to the story.) But the disciples? They just walked away from it all, just left those two boatloads of fish baking in the hot Judean sun! Why? To follow Jesus. Do you really think they made a mistake? I let them tell their own story in the following villanelle:

THE PROFESSIONALS
(Commentary, Luke 5:5)

"We've toiled all night and caught no fish as yet;
　　　Our eyes are drooping and our muscles ache.
　　　But at your bidding, we'll let down the net."
(Though, just 'twixt you and me, I doubt we'll get
　　　A single tug at this end of the lake.
　　　We've toiled all night and caught no fish as yet.)
"A better preacher we have never met,
　　　But teaching *us* to *fish*? That takes the cake!
　　　Still, at your bidding we'll let down the net."
(I don't know why we're doing this. I'll bet
　　　He's never fought this hard to stay awake.
　　　We've toiled all night and caught no fish as yet.)
And yet, somehow I don't think we'll regret
　　　Obeying *him*, though seaweed's all we'll take.
　　　So, "At your bidding we'll let down the net."
Then, without warning, every line was set
　　　So taut we were afraid the line would break:
　　　We'd toiled all night and caught no fish as yet,
But, at his bidding, we let down the net.[40]

How does this relate to us? We are not all called to full–time "vocational" Christian service, but we are all called to full–time Christian living and

---

[40] Ibid., 145.

total Christian commitment. Are we living that way? What's holding us back? And if the Lord should, say, call you to the mission field, would you go? What's holding you back? Nothing more than a boatload of smelly old fish.

Conclusion

What if the Lord should call us to the mission field or some other full–time ministry? What should hold us back? *Nothing* should hold us back except the realization that He has called us to stay and help send others while living a life of full Commitment to Him here. What manner of man is He? Such a man that the privilege of being his disciple is worth leaving anything—worth leaving everything—for. May we be prepared to do so when he calls us. For, like the story we have studied today, the Lord's Supper, which shows forth Christ's death until He come, is an encouragement to that commitment in that it is a reminder of how much He gave for us. For at His bidding, they let down the net. *"And when they had brought their boats to land, they left everything and followed him."* Amen.

XVII — Luke 5:12–26

YOUR SINS ARE FORGIVEN

Luke 5:12 And it came about that while he was in one of the cities, behold, there was a man full of leprosy. And when he saw Jesus he fell on his face and implored him, saying, "Lord, if you are willing you can make me clean." 13 And he stretched out his hand and touched him, saying, "I am willing; be cleansed." And immediately the leprosy left him. 14 And he ordered him to tell no one, "But go and show yourself to the priest and make an offering for your cleansing, just as Moses commanded., for a testimony to them." 15 But the news about him was spreading even farther, and great multitudes were gathering to hear him and to be healed of their sicknesses. 16 But he himself would often slip away to the wilderness to pray.

17 And it came about one day while he was teaching that there were some Pharisees and teachers of the Law sitting there, who had come from every village of Galilee and Judea and from Jerusalem, and the power of the Lord was present for him to perform healing. 18 And behold, some men went carrying on a bed a man who was paralyzed, and they were trying to bring him in and set him down in front of him. 19 And not finding any way to bring him in because of the crowd, they went up on the roof and let him down through the tiles with his stretcher, right in the center, in front of Jesus. 20 And seeing their faith, he said, "Friend, your sins are forgiven you." 21 And the Scribes and the Pharisees began to reason, saying, "Who is this man who speaks blasphemies? Who can forgive sins but God alone?" 22 But Jesus, aware of their reasonings, said to them, "Why are you reasoning in your hearts? 23 Which is easier, to say, 'Your sins have been forgiven you,' or to say, 'Rise and walk'? 24 But in order that you may know that the Son of Man has authority on earth to forgive sins"—he said to the paralytic—"I say to you, rise, take up your stretcher, and go home." 25 And at once he rose up before them and took up what he had been lying on and went home, glorifying God. 26 And they were all seized with astonishment and began glorifying God; and they were filed with fear, saying, "We have seen remarkable things today."

Introduction

Last time we saw the Lord call Peter and his friends to follow him and become fishers of men. Luke follows this story with several examples of Jesus showing Peter and his friends just what He meant by that. Today we would like to examine the first two, the healings of a leper and of a paralytic. Next time we will look at a third: the call of Levi (or Matthew), a despised tax collector, to join the inner band of disciples and be also a fisher of men. In other words, to be a fisher of men, to be a disciple of Jesus, you have to be ready and willing to minister both *to* and *with* people you might not otherwise want to touch.

I. The Cleansing Of The Leper (vv. 12–16)

The cleansing of the leper reveals three facts about the Lord that are relevant to His followers.

1. HIS POWER. We've already seen Jesus' power over temptation, over demons, over disease, and over nature (the fish). What does this encounter add to that? Well, first we see **His power over leprosy.** To us, this might just seem to be another example of Jesus' power over sickness. But to the first–century Jews who observed this healing, it was a special case. Leprosy was incurable and very serious, leading to the mutilation of the body as the extremities were literally worn away due to the loss of feeling in the nerves. It made a person ceremonially unclean. None of the contemporary "faith healers" would even attempt a cure of leprosy; it was considered incurable except by God himself. So Jesus' cure of this man was unprecedented in the experience of those who witnessed it. It was one more indication to His disciples that the Person they were following was more than just a man sent by God; He was in some sense God himself. Peter, in other words, was being given one more opportunity to respond as he had done at the unaccountable draft of fish.

But we also see something else here: **Jesus' power or authority over the Law.** It was against the Law to touch a leper, but Jesus does it anyway in order to heal him. Yet then, having ignored the Law Himself, Jesus turns around and upholds it as far as the leper himself is concerned, commanding him to show himself to the priest and make the requisite sacrifice. What is going on here? Why the seeming inconsistency? We cannot appeal to the distinction between the "moral" law and the "ceremonial" law, because both of these rules belong to the ceremonial law, and, besides, it was still in force until the veil of the Temple was split anyway. Yet, if Jesus was simply footloose about the law, why bother insisting on the priestly examination and the sacrifice? The answer is that the King is here, one who has the authority to make exceptions. Jesus did not need the protection which the prohibition of touching lepers was designed to give, and His desire to personalize the healing through touch was more important than adherence to the letter. In effect, Jesus bypasses the letter of the Law to uphold the spirit of it. It is good for this man to be touched; it is also good for him to keep the Law as concerning himself, for otherwise he will not be able to re–enter society. For us that would likely be a rationalization. But the Law of God is not something passed by a legislature. It is the revelation of the will of the King, and therefore the King (and only the King) has the authority to suspend it for His own purposes. One who is able to heal leprosy, one who is even greater than the Law — what manner of man is this?

2. HIS PERSONALITY (verse 13). So the first thing revealed is Jesus' power, over leprosy and over the Law; the second is His personality. Jesus did not need to touch this leper in order to heal him. He has already shown Himself capable of healing with a word, even from a distance. So why do it? Because, as we saw some weeks ago, touching is a way of establishing a relationship, of expressing identification, and of showing compassion. Ultimately that was the reason for this gesture; to heal in such a way that it was an expression not just of power but of compassion for this suffering individual. Doing it that way was important enough to Jesus that He was willing to suspend His own Law to do it, important enough that He didn't care what anyone else thought about it. If we are going to be fishers of men for a leader like this, we had better learn to do the same kinds of things for the same reasons—not suspending the Law on our own authority but being willing to get our hands dirty and go out of our way to make contact with what society considers the untouchable.

3. HIS PRIORITIES (verse 16). The third thing revealed by this miracle is Jesus' priorities. Jesus was obviously not in pursuit of popularity as such. Otherwise He would have encouraged word-of-mouth advertising instead of actually forbidding it in many cases, as here. But the leper could not help himself, and so he told about what had happened to him anyway, the word got out, and the crowds increased. So what was Jesus' reaction? "Oh boy, the crowds are increasing, our constituency is growing, so let's build a bigger sanctuary and add all their names to our direct–mail fundraising file." Not exactly. He would often slip away to pray, to be alone with the Father. Now, a lot of Jesus' fishers need to pay attention at this point. Many of us act as if popularity were an end in itself, as if it were what we were actually in the ministry for. A more attentive follower of Christ was the great Reformer Martin Luther, who when asked why he had stayed an extra hour in his prayer chamber reportedly explained that it was because he had so much to accomplish that day. Ministry is not about us, it is not about numbers and influence, it is not even ultimately about the lost. It is ultimately about God. If we forget that, nothing else we do really matters. Jesus' example here can help us remember it.

APPLICATION: What is the message of all this to Peter and his friends who are now observing as Christ models man–fishing for them? They should be learning that in order to be a fisher of men you have to get your hands dirty. Christian ministry is not something that can happen in an ivory tower. To be effective in it you have to get involved with people; you have to be willing to touch the untouchable. The point is made physically here with the leper; it will be made in a different way next time with the calling of Levi, who as a Tax Collector was considered a moral leper by his society, a Collaborator with the hated Romans. There is no real ministry without risk, without exposure. It is costly. Dr. Francis Schaeffer of L'Abri fellowship put it like this:

"Don't start a big program. Don't suddenly think you can add to your church budget and begin. Start personally and start in your homes. I dare you. I dare you in the name of Jesus Christ. Do what I am going to suggest. Begin by opening your home for community. . . . L'Abri is costly. If you think what God has done here is easy, you don't understand. It is a costly business to have a sense of community. L'Abri cannot be explained merely by the clear doctrine that is preached; it cannot be explained by the fact that God here has been giving intellectual answers to intellectual questions. I think those two things are important, but L'Abri cannot be explained if you remove the third. And that is that there has been some community here. And it has been costly. In about the first three years of L'Abri all our wedding presents were wiped out. Our sheets were

125

torn. Holes were burned in our rugs. . . . Blacks came to our table. Orientals came to our table. It couldn't happen in any other way. Drugs came to our place. People vomited in our rooms, in the rooms of Chalet Les Melezes which was our home, and now in the rest of the chalets of L'Abri. How many times has this happened to you? You see, you don't need a big program. You don't have to convince your session or your board. All you have to do is open your home and begin."[41]

Perhaps not everybody is called to take the kind of risks the Schaeffers took. But there is no man–fishing that follows Jesus without some kind of risk. I have seen churches with dress codes, churches which would have gone into apoplexy if the "wrong" kind of person came there to be saved. This is less than Christian discipleship; it has missed the lessons in being fishers of men that Jesus wanted Peter and his friends to understand.

Okay, then, someone is going to say, if we do not hide from the world, if we are going to be willing to go out into it and get our hands dirty, how will we maintain our own purity and avoid compromise with the world? I would have to ask, purity from what? What a lot of Christians call "purity" is a very artificial construct that has very little to do with the way Jesus actually loved and ministered. It is mainly an excuse to avoid the way Jesus actually loved and ministered, to avoid real, risky following of our Lord. On the other hand, yes, there is a moral purity, rooted in a purity of devotion to the One who leads us into these non–antiseptic situations, with which we do need to be concerned. And the answer to preserving that is not in preserving it so much as in *nourishing* it. That is what Jesus shows us in verse 16. *"But he himself would often slip away to the wilderness to pray."* Our connection with God has to be strong to maintain us in all the challenges of life. So like Jesus, we must make the pursuit of that connection a priority. If I do not love the Lord and pursue fellowship with Him, what do I have to offer anyone else? To be a fisher of men we have to be a disciple; to be a disciple is to attend to and follow Jesus' example. This we must never forget.

II. The Healing Of The Paralytic (vv. 17–26)

This episode is remembered from Sunday School for the quaint details of the friends lowering the paralytic through the roof, and rightly so. Who wouldn't want to have friends like that? But the main point as with all these stories is what it tells us about Jesus. And the point that sticks out here is Jesus' astounding act of forgiving the man's sins before He healed him. This is another of those "What manner of man is this?" moments, as the Pharisees were quick to perceive. Who does Jesus think he is? No one can forgive sins—except God alone.

We must begin by stressing the rightness of the Pharisees' case—as far as it went. Let's say that ____ runs his big truck over _____'s compact car and smashes it into

---

[41] Francis A. Shaeffer, *The Church at the End of the Twentieth Century* (Downers Grove, Il: InterVarsity Press, 1970), 108.

oblivion, receiving only negligible damage himself in the process, and I say, "That's Okay, ____, don't worry about it; I forgive you." Now, that surpasses even my usual arrogance, as _____ would be quick to notice. I forgive him? It wasn't my car that was destroyed. It won't be my insurance payments going up—and maybe _____ only has liability anyway. Who am I to let _____ off the hook for destroying someone else's car? It is none of my business. I cannot extend the forgiveness because the offense was not committed against me. There is only one Person in the universe who is in a position to have the right to assume that *every* offense is an offense against Him personally, and that is God. So who does Jesus think He is to be assuming God's prerogatives?

That was a very good question. The Pharisees' premise was in fact correct, and Jesus does not challenge it. In fact, his whole answer accepts it as true and foundational. But he turns around and answers their question, as was his custom, with a question of his own: Which is harder, to say, "*Your sins are forgiven*" or to say, "*Rise, take up your bed, and walk*"?

Now, that is an interesting question. Jesus obviously expects the answer to be that it is harder to say, "Rise." But how is it harder? Forgiving a third party is actually harder to *do*. Only God can do that, while lots of powers in the universe may be able to heal. Even Satan has a limited power to do miracles, as proved by the Egyptian wizards' rods which turned into serpents. But while forgiving a third party is harder to *do*, it is easier to *say*, because forgiveness is invisible. How do you prove whether it has really happened or not? "Rise" is harder to say because everyone will immediately see whether or not you can back it up. Jesus' healing of the paralytic does not strictly prove that He has the right to forgive, for it is theoretically possible that the power to heal came from Satan.

What it does do is force the audience to take Jesus seriously. They cannot just dismiss him as a crank. They are now in fact faced with the famous "trilemma" which C. S. Lewis explained so well in *Mere Christianity*.[42] There are only three possibilities: Jesus is Lord, he is a Liar, or he is a Lunatic, to have said what He has said. To finish the argument—this part is left implied—we would have to say that the Lunatic option is ruled out by the healing. Jesus is either Lord, or he is a Liar, claiming to speak for God when he is really using the power of Satan. And that option is ruled out by His goodness. Jesus' logical gambit has removed the option of dismissing Him and forced the audience into a choice: He is either God or He is demonic. No wonder the people said, "We have seen remarkable things." The word inadequately translated "remarkable" is παραδοξος (*paradoxos*), from which we get the English word *paradox*. It means something unexpected, something so astonishing it just doesn't make sense— because the Pharisees were not prepared to accept the correct conclusion, that Jesus was

---

42 C. S. Lewis, *Mere Christianity*, op. cit., 54-6.

in fact God in human flesh . . . and therefore that He had the authority to forgive sins. And that was the heart of His ministry.

Application: Christ here goes out of his way to make the forgiveness of sin the central issue. So if we are to follow Him as fishers of men, we must not forget what is central either. If we are to fish for men, *the Gospel is our net*, and *forgiveness is the bait*. It is man's deepest need, whether he recognizes it or not. Yet today many of us, even who believe this, hesitate to deal with it forthrightly for fear of offending our audience. For there are people today who deny that there is any such thing as sin. And until you see sin as your central problem, the Gospel is hardly good news to you. But we must believe the Gospel strongly enough to believe that, whatever they say, deep down people do still wrestle with guilt and long to be free from it.

So let's not get embarrassed or tongue–tied about the fact that the Gospel has to do with sin and guilt and is the only solution to this problem. Let us continue to present Jesus as the only solution to man's biggest problem, sin, believing that despite our denials it still is our biggest problem and that therefore this message will indeed hit home. To be a fisher of men who follows Jesus is to follow Him in raising the issue of forgiveness precisely in those situations where people have forgotten it in their focus on other things. And I must begin by honestly remembering that forgiveness is *my* greatest need, that Jesus has met it completely, and by rejoicing in that fact.

Conclusion

What manner of man is Jesus Christ? He is one who identifies with sinners, who says no to Satan, who bosses demons around, who fills fishnets, who touches lepers, who forgives sins, and who accepts sinners. He is one who raises the issue of sin and forgiveness when no one else does, even if it is controversial. And He calls us to follow Him and pay attention to these things so that we too can be fishers of men. So we must begin by putting ourselves in the place of Peter and his friends, the newly called fishers of men, as they watch Jesus model their job for them. And we must ourselves accept the fact that we are forgiven sinners because Jesus died on the Cross for our sins, and we must become so appreciative of this fact that we can't help sharing it. For until you begin to feel that way, you do not yet understand what the Christian faith is all about.

NOT RIGHTEOUS BUT SINNERS

Luke 5:27 And after that, he went out and noticed a tax–gatherer named Levi sitting in the tax office, and he said to him, "Follow Me." 28 And he left everything behind and rose and began to follow him. 29 And Levi gave a big reception for him in his house. And there was a great crowd of tax–gatherers and other people who were reclining at the table with them. 30 And the Pharisees and their scribes began grumbling at his disciples, saying, "Why do you eat with the tax–gatherers and sinners?" 31 And Jesus answered and said unto them, "It is not those who are well who need a physician, but those who are sick. 32 I have not come to call the righteous but sinners to repentance."

Introduction

We have been looking at three incidents in the life of our Lord that illustrate what it means to be a fisher of men. They immediately follow the acceptance by Peter and his friends of the call to be fishers of men, and they amount to Jesus teaching this role to His new disciples by example. Last time we saw how the cleansing of the leper makes the point that man–fishers need to be separated from the world but not isolated from it. As the Lord touched the leper, so we must not be afraid to get our hands dirty in ministry if we are to be fishers of men. Then follow two incidents that make the point that the primary issue involved in man–fishing, the primary thing Jesus came to give us and therefore the primary thing the Gospel offers, is the forgiveness of sins. The first was the healing of the paralytic, where, as we saw last time, Jesus goes out of his way to raise the issue of forgiveness. The second is the calling of Levi (or Matthew, a name by which he is also known and under which he wrote the first Gospel), which we will examine today. To understand this exchange, we must think about the Attitude of the Rabbis, which is the background to the story; the Attack of the Pharisees, which sets up Jesus' response; and the Answer of the Christ, which is the point we need to take away.

I. The Attitude Of The Rabbis

There were basically two theological parties in mainstream Judaism at this time: the Sadducees and the Pharisees. The Sadducees were what today we would call theological liberals. They were secular–minded people who downplayed the supernatural elements of Yahwism and went so far as to deny the doctrine of the resurrection of the dead outright. (That's why the Sadducees were "sad, you see.") You don't hear much from them in the New Testament, though Caiaphas and Annanias were Sadducees, and their scholars did challenge Jesus once on the resurrection with their story about the seven brothers who all married the same woman, and whose would she be in the resurrection? Jesus' answer was that in the Kingdom we will neither marry nor be given in marriage but be like the angels—that basically that they were missing the point of both marriage and of the resurrection. (We'll deal with that when and if we ever get there.) You don't hear much about the Sadducees because they were usually too secular–minded to be all that interested in one more nut claiming to be the Messiah; hence most of Jesus' debates were with the Pharisees, as in this passage.

The Pharisaic party were what today we might call the conservatives, or maybe even the puritans. They saw themselves as the guardians of the true Jewish traditions. They generally have a bad name amongst Christian believers today because they spend so much time in the Gospels being refuted and even made fools of—and deservedly so, given their judgmental and legalistic attitudes. But we must also remember that they were at least enough on the same page with Jesus to *be* arguing with him; they at least perceived that they and Jesus had something to discuss. They were at least participating in the same conversation. The Pharisees were dead wrong at many points, but at least they and Jesus inhabited the same universe of discourse. Most of the early Jewish converts—like the Apostle Paul, for example—were from the Pharisaic party. If they were wrong, at least they were wrong about the right things, you might say—as we will see here in their attitudes toward three very specific things relevant to this encounter.

1. Their Attitude to Repentance. The very crux of the difference between Jesus' understanding of theology and that of the Pharisees lies here. For the Pharisees, repentance is itself a meritorious act whereby a sinner turns himself back to the Law. They at least understood that people are sinners who need to be forgiven. But in their mind, we must merit forgiveness through good deeds, fasting, alms, and the study of the Law. What must a sinner do to be pardoned? Or, to put the question as one of them did to Jesus on another occasion, "What must I do to be saved?" Here is a typical Pharisaic answer to that question: "If [a man] had been accustomed daily to read one column in the Bible, let him read two; if he had been accustomed daily to learn one chapter of the Mishnah, let him learn two."[43] Well, why not three? Why not four? Where does it end? This has an interesting corollary: for all practical purposes, only Pharisees—professional students and teachers of the Law as they were—could be saved! There was little hope for the despised "people of the earth," the *"am ha–aretz."* God was ready to receive them if they would repent, but they had to make not only the first move but travel all the way back themselves through their own efforts. Theoretically they could make it, but the Pharisees weren't holding their breath. You can imagine they were not thrilled with Jesus' idea that all the prodigal son had to do was confess his sin to receive far more acceptance than he was capable of imagining. They weren't thrilled with Jesus' declaration that the Publican—a tax collector!—was justified just for beating his breast and crying, "God, be merciful to me, a sinner." They wanted nothing to do with Jesus' idea that salvation was by grace, by free grace, and grace alone.

---

[43] Edersheim, *Life & Times of Jesus the Messiah,* op. cit., 1:513.

2. Their Attitude to Tax–Collectors. The Pharisees looked down their noses at sinners in general, as we have seen. Think of the "righteous" man in the Parable of the Publican: *"I thank you, Lord, that I am not like other men . . . ."* But the tax–collectors (i.e., the Publican in the parable) were the lowest of the low. This attitude actually had a basis in fact and was really understandable. For tax–collectors like Levi were hated Collaborators with the Roman oppressor. They were the first–century equivalent of Scalawags—even worse than Carpetbaggers. Not only were they collaborating with the Roman overlords, but they were notorious cheats who were getting rich off of the misery of their fellow Jews. The whole system was corrupt. The tax–collector owed the Romans a certain quota, and anything he collected over that he got to keep as his compensation. Is that a recipe for corruption or what? And the tax laws were so complicated that the poor citizen had no way of knowing how badly he was being cheated. (Oh, wait. . . . No, let's not make any analogies to our current tax code. That would take us too far afield from our topic. I hereby officially resist that temptation.) It was easy for the collector to be arbitrary, and you just felt helpless and full of impotent rage while the tax collector got rich off of you. At least our system is better than that. It is no wonder these people were resented and vilified as the scummiest scum of the earth. Everybody felt that way about them, but, the Pharisees added a theological twist to the general hatred: Of all the despicable and hopeless sinners, the tax–collector was the most despicable and the most hopeless. It was considered simply impossible that one should repent—according to the Pharisaic definition of meritorious repentance. These then are people who by definition cannot ever be saved. In the Pharisees' eyes, being a tax collector is the unpardonable sin. They were fit to be tied when Jesus sent the Publican, the tax collector, in the parable home justified rather than one of them.

Let's pause just a second here to realize what an astounding thing the call of Levi was. It was astounding that Jesus *would* do it, and just as astounding that He *could* do it. Here is a man who has seared whatever conscience he might have had so that he could live with himself while he got rich not only by cheating his fellow countrymen, not only at their economic expense, but by betraying them to the hated Romans. Not exactly what we would call disciple material! Yet one call from Jesus, two words from Jesus, and he leaves everything, risking the wrath of his former employers, and joins the disciples right then and there. He walks out of the tax office and leaves all those ill–gotten gains sitting on the table, like the other disciples did their miraculous draught of fishes just a few days earlier. And his next official act is to throw a big party and invite all his wretched tax–collector friends to meet Jesus—who astonishes everybody, probably including his own disciples, by accepting the invitation. It may be the most radical conversion, the most precipitous transformation of character, the most profound sudden reorientation of a heart, on record—until the same thing happened to that feared persecutor of the church, the murderous Saul of Tarsus, after the resurrection. What manner of man is this that He can work such a revolution in a person's heart just by saying, "Follow me!" Has He said it to you?

Who would have thought old Levi would be able

To leave that money lying on the table?

He wasn't, until Jesus changed his mind;

He was not, after that, to stay behind![44]

3. Their Attitude to Righteousness. Okay, the Pharisees thought of repentance as a meritorious act whereby one could make oneself worthy of forgiveness. They thought of tax collectors as irreformable reprobates for whom there was no hope. In both ideas, their thinking could not have been more different from Jesus'. What was their view of righteousness? In their own way, the Pharisees hungered and thirsted after righteousness, but it was not the righteousness of God, but rather an artificial righteousness of their own self–serving definition. The very name *Pharisee* means "righteous," in the sense of "separatist." Righteousness was an outward observance of Law and Tradition so complicated that only Pharisees, who had dedicated their lives to the study of the Law in all its technicalities, could attain it. The common people were utterly incapable of understanding that righteousness, much less practicing it. So the Pharisees gloried in their superior attainments in this outward and legalistic "righteousness" and looked down their noses on those who could not compete with them in practicing such artificial skills. Ceremonial purity was a big part of this whole game. Thus we see the Pharisees in the Gospels obsessed with elaborate rules of ritual washing, etc. The most important rule of all was to avoid all contact with sinners. Especially you would be defiled if you *ate* with them. For table fellowship implies acceptance. And this must be avoided at all costs. And just look at Jesus and His disciples! Eating not only with sinners but with the very worst kind of sinner imaginable. Shameful! Embarrassing! Inexcusable! Inconceivable! And this ignorant and unclean multitude who do not know the Law think He might be the Messiah? Heresy! Abomination! [Pause for ceremonial rending of garments.] The very idea!

II. The Attack Of The Pharisees

Understanding the attitudes of the Pharisees then helps us to put their attack on Christ into perspective. Here was a man who implicitly claimed to be the Holy One of Israel, and he is blithely violating every standard of holiness that the Pharisees held dear. How can he possibly be eating, not only with sinners, but with a big bunch of the worst of the whole lot, and claim to be a person who loves God and upholds righteousness? The Pharisees were so completely scandalized they could hardly contain themselves.

But their response is interesting. They address it, not to Jesus himself, but to the disciples. Their question, "Why do you eat with the tax–gatherers and sinners?", is designed to appeal to very deep–seated assumptions about what is right and wrong that they can assume the disciples share with them. Their purpose is twofold: with respect

---

[44] Donald T. Williams, *Stars through the Clouds*, op. cit., 149.

to the disciples themselves, it is to try to drive a wedge between them and Jesus. "Do *you* want to be seen with tax collectors? This is how your Master plans to overthrow the Roman oppressor? By buddying up to their stooges and making friends with those who have already betrayed us to them? Seriously?"

With respect to the overhearing crowd, the Pharisees' purpose is to discredit Jesus and destroy any credibility he might have as a candidate for Messiah. "How can you follow this guy as Messiah? He eats with *tax collectors*! Collaborators! He's not even on the right side in this war. How is he going to help us win it?" And they knew their audience well. Their strategy was one that could be expected to be very effective. What they had not reckoned with was the radical genius and the profound theology of their Opponent, who overheard their innuendoes and answered for Himself in ways that exposed the shallowness of their hearts and the inadequacy of their assumptions in ways that were most embarrassing. It would not be the last time.

III. The Answer Of The Christ

This is one of those embarrassing moments when you have just made a case that sounds brilliant and irrefutable and impresses your audience most wonderfully—until someone has the audacity to utter one simple sentence that exposes its fatal flaw for all to see and makes it all come crashing down to the ground in utter ruin. Why are you *eating* [pause for dramatic shock—ooh, gross!] with tax collectors and sinners? What is the matter with you? Answer: *"It is not those who are well who need a physician, but those who are sick. I have not come to call the righteous but sinners to repentance"* (verse 32). And your mouth just drops open, and you stand there staring stupidly. What can you say in answer to that? The Pharisees were left standing stupefied, but the people who overheard had the opportunity to realize that they were being presented with a concept of what repentance is and how it relates to forgiveness that was radically and profoundly different from anything they had ever heard—and one that made repentance and forgiveness possible for sinners like them.

The Pharisees said if we repent, by which they meant make ourselves worthy, God will send the Messiah. "If all Israel would but repent, then would Messiah come. If all Israel would keep but one Sabbath perfectly, then would Messiah come."[45] Then Jesus shows up while they are still waiting for that to happen with His own agenda. The Jews said, we must make ourselves worthy, and in response to that, God will send His Messiah to give us the (earthly) kingdom. Jesus said, you simply accept me and I will grant you forgiveness and count it as worthiness of the (heavenly) kingdom. The Jews said, the Messiah comes to save the worthy and judge the unworthy. Jesus said, those who think they are worthy delude themselves, forfeit salvation, and come into judgment—because self–righteousness is the worst form of unrighteousness. I came to save the unworthy, whose primary need is forgiveness, and who know it. And this

---

[45] Qtd. in Plummer, *The Gospel according to St. Luke*, op. cit., 89.

forgiveness is a free gift granted (as Paul would explain later) by grace alone through faith alone.

The paralytic on his mat could not perform any of the Rabbinic acts of righteousness to merit forgiveness. Jesus just up and gave it to him out of the blue when he wasn't even asking for it. He did not say to Levi, "Reform yourself first, clean up your act, and then you can follow me." He just said, "Come!" And Levi just up and left everything and came, and he was accepted immediately. Now, Levi did become a different man. He started by leaving his sinful employment to follow Christ. But he did this because Christ had already accepted him, not in order to be accepted. And that is the bottom line, the watershed between God's way of salvation by Grace and man's way of righteousness by works.

Conclusion

The offer of forgiveness reveals Jesus Christ as the One with the right to bestow it—as God. The acceptance of that forgiveness reveals Levi as a saved man. The refusal to admit their need of it reveals the Pharisees as condemned men. And Jesus' acceptance of that redeemed and forgiven sinner Levi's hospitality reveals his readiness to accept the worst of us without reservation if we will only turn to Him. All this reveals the forgiveness of sins as the heart of Christ's mission and explains why His path took him inexorably to the Cross. What does your response to it reveal about you?

Note one more thing: Jesus expressed his acceptance of Levi/Matthew's repentance by table fellowship. It was a profoundly symbolic and meaningful gesture in that culture, and it can be for ours as well, as you might realize if you ever mistakenly tried to sit down at the "cool" table in your high–school cafeteria. Jesus sat down with Levi and broke bread with him and didn't care whom it scandalized. Do you realize He is still doing that? This same Jesus who accepted Levi's invitation to break bread together now offers His own invitation to you. We call it the Lord's Supper. If you can respond to Jesus in repentance and faith and follow Him, it is for you. Come and dine.

WINESKINS

Luke 5:33 *And they said to him "The disciples of John often fast and offer prayers; the disciples of the Pharisees also do the same; but yours eat and drink."* **34** *And Jesus said to them, "You cannot make the attendants of the bridegroom fast while the bridegroom is with them, can you?* **35** *But the days will come when the bridegroom is taken away from them; then they will fast in those days."* **36** *And he was also telling them a parable: "No one tears a piece from a new garment and puts it on an old garment. Otherwise, he will both tear the new, and the piece from the new will not match the old.* **37** *And no one puts new wine in old wineskins. Otherwise, the new wine will burst the skins and it will be spilled out, and the skins will be ruined.* **38** *But new wine must be put into fresh wineskins.* **39** *And no one, after drinking old wine, wishes for new; for he says, 'The old is good enough."*

Introduction

In our last couple of looks at Luke's Gospel, we saw that the religious leaders of Jesus' day did not approve of His claim to be able to forgive sins. They understood that it entailed a claim to be the One against whom all sins are committed, a claim to be God; and they were not prepared to go there. Neither did they approve of His associates, for He ate with tax collectors and sinners. They were definitely not prepared to go there! Today we discover that they did not approve of Jesus' style of piety either. It seems that He and His disciples did not fast enough to suit them. Translation: They were way too happy and were having way too much fun. To understand what the Pharisees disapproved of—and what God does approve of—we need to examine carefully three things: the Fasting of the Pharisees, the Feasting of the Friends, and the Forms of the Future.

I. The Fasting Of The Pharisees (v. 33)

To understand what fasting meant to the Pharisees, we need to understand their place in the development of the Jewish religion. Originally in the Old Testament, fasting was only required on the Day of Atonement. It was understood to be included in the "humbling" or "afflicting" of oneself that is mentioned in Lev.16:29. *"And this shall be a permanent statute for you: In the seventh month, on the tenth day of the month, you shall humble your souls, and not do any work, whether the native or the alien who sojourns among you."* Though it was required only on that one day, it could be undertaken voluntarily at any time as an expression of mourning or of repentance. Mourning: *"And they mourned and wept and fasted until evening for Saul and his son Jonathan and for the people of the Lord and the House of Israel, because they had been taken by the sword"* (2 Sam. 1:12). Repentance: *"And it came about that when Ahab heard these words that he tore his clothes and put on sackcloth and fasted"* (1 Kings 21:27). These practices continued until the time of the Babylonian Captivity.

During the Babylonian Captivity is when the seeds of what would become Pharisaism were planted. During this period, of course, there was no Temple, and hence no sacrifices. The Synagogue grew up to take the place of the Temple and continued after the Temple was restored. After the destruction of Herod's Temple, the Synagogue survived as the locus of Jewish worship to this day. Meanwhile, during the exile, because of its already established associations as an expression of repentance, fasting gradually became accepted as a substitute for the no longer available blood sacrifices as something that could remove sin and gain God's favor. Like repentance, it came to be falsely understood as an act meritorious in itself.[46] By the First Century, the Pharisees, as a sign of their righteousness, were fasting regularly twice a week, on Mondays and Thursdays, and doing it very ostentatiously. Hence we have Jesus' instructions for His disciples to be different: *"And whenever you fast, do not put on a gloomy face as the hypocrites do, for they neglect their appearance in order to be seen fasting by men. Truly I say to you, they have their reward"* (Mat. 6:16). The spin the Pharisees put on their practice was that anyone who did not do this obviously did not love God or care about true religion. Where there is no fasting, they assumed, there must be no devotion.

In terms of our immediate scene here in Luke 5, it is apparent that John's disciples had continued the Pharisaic practice, though doubtless he had taught them not to view their fasting as meritorious: They were looking for the Lamb of God who would take away the sins of the world. We can hope that for them fasting was what it had originally been intended to be, part of being "poor in spirit." Nevertheless, their custom allowed Jesus' opponents to portray them unfairly as being on their side. I have a sneaking suspicion that Levi had the audacity to throw his notorious reception for Jesus and the other tax collectors and sinners on a Monday or a Thursday. If Jesus and his disciples were thus partying with sinners while everyone else with a reputation for piety was fasting, it would certainly explain why this question comes up right after the one we looked at last time about Jesus eating with sinners. Oh, my! The scandal! The scandal! On the count of three, let us all ceremonially (and sanctimoniously) rend our garments! (Some Pharisees actually wore a pre–torn place in their robes loosely stitched together so they could perform that ritual easily whenever the occasion presented itself).

So here come the Pharisees: *"The disciples of John often fast and offer prayers; the disciples of the Pharisees also do the same; but yours eat and drink!"* (5:33). What Jesus' opponents were really saying then in their question was, "How can you people *possibly* claim to be good Jews, devoted to the Law, and serious about righteousness?" The meaning of their complaint was, "You are not religious!" For them, the Law and the Traditions they had placed as a hedge around the Law were indistinguishable. Therefore, this passage is the first appearance of a common theme in their attacks which would continue into the period of the early church: "You are really undermining Moses;

---

[46] Cf. Edersheim, *Life and Times*, op. cit., 1:512.

you are against the Law!" (Wait. Moses never said we had to fast like y'all do. Never mind.) You still hear the same charge in Acts 6:11 and 21:21. On his visit, the Jerusalem church warns Paul that some people *"have been told about you that you are teaching all the Jews who are among the Gentiles to forsake Moses, telling them not to circumcise their children nor to walk according to the customs."* (Fasting would be included in the "customs.")

Jesus had a broad and well–rounded response to this attack, which had three elements. One was to insist on the distinction between the Law of God and the Traditions of Men. *"Then some Pharisees and scribes came to Jesus from Jerusalem, saying, 'Why do your disciples transgress the tradition of the elders?' . . . And He answered and said to them, 'Why do you yourselves transgress the commandment of God for the sake of your tradition?'"* He concludes, *"You hypocrites! Rightly did Isaiah prophesy of you, saying, 'This people honors me with their lips, but their heart is far from me. In vain do they worship me, teaching as doctrines the precepts of men'"* (Mat. 15:1–9). A second was to distinguish between destroying the Law and fulfilling it. *"Do not think that I have come to abolish the Law or the Prophets; I did not come to abolish, but to fulfill"* (Mat. 5:17). Jesus was fulfilling the *real* Law, which meant getting back to its spirit as well as its letter and its real meaning as opposed to traditional Pharisaic interpretations of it.

The third element, the one which is developed in this passage, is to argue that the change in God's economy that comes with the arrival of the Messiah (the "bridegroom" in Jesus' analogy here), the change that comes with the transition from Promise to Fulfillment, brings with it and demands a change in the outward forms of religious expression. Jesus makes this point with His characteristic use of bold metaphor and concrete imagery: *"No one tears a piece from a new garment and puts it on an old garment. Otherwise, he will both tear the new, and the piece from the new will not match the old. And no one puts new wine in old wineskins. Otherwise, the new wine will burst the skins and it will be spilled out, and the skins will be ruined. But new wine must be put into fresh wineskins"* (verses 36–38). The wine represents genuine spiritual life and the wineskins the outward forms (rituals and spiritual disciplines and practices) through which it is expressed. In other words, the old wineskins won't hold this new wine, the new cloth won't fit in the old garment, and it's no time to be fasting when the Bridegroom is here! And that leads us to the next point. The Fasting of the Pharisees is contrasted with the Feasting of the Friends.

II. The Feasting Of The Friends (vv. 34–35)

Jesus' reply had a point. The Old Testament and the Jewish piety that developed from it had a purpose: to prepare for the coming of the Messiah. Now that He is here, all of that is passing away. The fasting is over; the feast has begun! Verse 35 is often misunderstood as mandating fasting for Christians today. *"But the days will come when the bridegroom is taken away from them; then they will fast in those days."* But it does not have an imperative verb; it merely predicts that until the Marriage Supper—that is, between the Cross (the "taking away") and the Marriage Supper of the Lamb—

Christians are going to have occasions for fasting that parallel the original Old Testament spirit of fasting for sorrow or repentance. And they will no doubt take advantage of them. But still they live in anticipation of the Feast, for the Bridegroom is present in their lives through his personal agent and representative, the Holy Spirit.

For us today, then, fasting is a good spiritual discipline if practiced in the right spirit, because we do not yet see the Bridegroom face to face; but it is not something commanded or required. We must not miss the fact that the burden of this whole passage is that the central emotion of Christian experience is *Joy*. In the long run, the Feast is a more accurate expression of our faith than the Fast, though there is a time and place for fasting while we wait for the Bridegroom to come for us. When we do fast, we should wash our faces and anoint our heads and be so cheerful that no one notices. We are doing it before God, not before men as a form of pious "virtue–signaling." That would undermine any spiritual value the practice might otherwise have had! We must not forget that, while our Lord was (falsely) accused of being a glutton and a drunk, no one ever thought to accuse him of being too ascetic. That charge would have been too laughable to make.

So then, the outward forms of religion that we adopt should be ones in which Joy is the dominant note, as if we worshipped the One who came to give life and give it more abundantly (John 10:10), as if we worshipped the One whose Apostle Paul commanded us to rejoice in the Lord always and again I say rejoice (Phil. 4:4), as if we worshipped the One whose beloved Disciple John wanted our Joy to be made full (1 John 1:4). We are sinners who have been forgiven, orphans who have been adopted, lost men and women who have been given meaning, purpose, and identity. Rejoice! Celebrate! Party down! Find a Pharisee to scandalize! That is to be a true disciple of Jesus. What does this really look like? That question takes us from the Fasting of the Pharisees and the Feasting of the Friends to the Forms of the Future.

III. The Forms Of The Future (vv. 36–39)

The change in God's economy that comes with the arrival of the Messiah, the change that comes with the transition from Promise to Fulfillment, brings with it and demands that we accept a change in the outward forms of religious expression. The old wineskins won't hold this new wine; the new cloth won't fit in the old garment. Why not? Because the radical nature of Christian Joy will burst those old wineskins right down the middle. And this is Good News. Everything now must reflect the Good News, the Gospel, which is so good that it is full of joy unspeakable and full of glory (1 Pet. 1:8). Really? Yes! No more animal sacrifices, because Christ has now paid for our sins once and for all completely. Good News! No more mandatory circumcision, because the preparatory role of Israel has been completed and salvation is now being thrown open to the Gentiles. The nations can now be saved without becoming Israelites. Good News! No more ceremonial law with its ritual cleanliness and dietary restrictions for the same reason. You can now eat cheeseburgers! Good news! The radical nature of

Christian Joy cannot be tacked on to business as usual like a new patch on old cloth. It must itself become the new cloth out of which our lives are made. It must become the center of life, and everything else — *everything* — has to be fit into that. Everything has to shout, "Good News!"

What are these new wineskins? They are not spelled out in this passage. And the New Testament in general does not spell them out in terms of a new set of specific "pious" religious practices but rather in terms of qualities of life. Think of the fruit of the Spirit: love, joy, peace, etc. (Gal. 5:22). Everything is to reflect that, and we are free to use our creativity to make it so where we don't have specific instructions. We do have some instructions. We are told not to forsake the assembling of ourselves together (Heb. 10:25). When we meet for public worship, of course there will be Word and Sacrament, praise and exhortation, confession of sin and rejoicing in forgiveness, prayers of petition and the singing of hymns. We follow the example of the First–Century church in all of that, but no specific mix or order or style of those things is specified — except that in the end, it all needs to reflect and communicate the Good News and the joy of the Lord. People who lead worship and participate in worship as if they are bored with it are denying the Gospel. They are trying to serve lukewarm water in old wineskins. And we have it on good authority that God will spew it out of His mouth.

When we have our private devotions, the same principles apply. There will of course be Bible study and prayer. We will wrestle with our problems and grieve for others who are hurting and groan under our own suffering and let the Lord deal with everything that is going on in our lives. But because the Lord is near when we do these things, the joy of the Lord should never be far from the surface in all of it. The best description I've ever seen of it is Pippin's insight into Gandalf's character during the siege of Minas Tirith:

> Gandalf . . . came and stood beside Pippin, putting his arm around the hobbit's shoulders and gazing out of the window. Pippin glanced in some wonder at the face now close beside his own, for the sound of that laugh had been gay and merry. Yet in the wizard's face he saw at first only lines of care and sorrow; though as he looked more intently he perceived that under all there was a great joy: a fountain of mirth enough to set a kingdom laughing, were it to gush forth.[47]

This is ultimately a portrait of Christ: a man of sorrows and acquainted with grief who scandalized the Pharisees by going to Levi's party; a man who wept at Lazarus's grave but who nevertheless came to give us life, and that more abundantly (John 10:10). He showed neither a despairing depression nor a glib and facile happiness but a profound sorrow encased in an even deeper joy. You cannot really have one without the other. Christians who are joyless or those marked by a superficial smugness are both giving the world a terrible portrait of Jesus. I hope Luke's Gospel is helping us

---

[47] J. R. R. Tolkien, *The Return of the King* (Boston, MA: Houghton Mifflin, 1956), 33.

get back to the real picture. He came to give us *that* life. That is why it should increasingly become a portrait of us while we wait for Him, a portrait that should be reflected in our worship practices. The world's real suffering and sorrow produces great empathy and sympathy in us, but cannot crush our joy, a joy we are able to offer in its stead. Why? Because we live in anticipation of the biggest Party ever thrown. Let the celebration begin!

Conclusion

We will not stop the celebration as long as we have the Bridegroom. And, having died for sin once, He dies no more. He will never be taken from us again. And He is coming! He is coming to be with us, no longer indirectly through the mediation of the Holy Spirit, but directly, immediately. We shall see Him face to face! Then we will have the main course of this banquet. But the feast of which that main course is a part has already begun. Already we are nibbling on the appetizers; already the guests have begun to gather as the Gospel draws them to Christ. That is what worship is. And so our worship today is a part of that grand celebration. Let us proceed in that spirit as we share the appetizer known as "The Lord's Supper" together. Amen.

LORD OF THE SABBATH

Luke 6:1 Now it came about that on a certain Sabbath he was passing through some grainfields, and his disciples were picking and eating the heads of grain, rubbing them in their hands. 2 But some of the Pharisees said, "Why do you do what is not lawful on the Sabbath?" 3 And Jesus answering them said, "Have you not even read what David did when he was hungry, he and whose who were with him? 4 How he entered the house of God and ate the consecrated bread, which it is not lawful for any to eat except the priests alone, and gave it to his companions." 5 And he was saying to them, "The Son of Man is Lord of the Sabbath." 6 And it came about that on another Sabbath, he entered the synagogue and was teaching, and there was a man there whose right hand was withered. 7 And the Scribes and the Pharisees were watching him closely to see if he healed on the Sabbath, in order that they might find reason to accuse him. 8 But he knew what they were thinking, and he said to the man with the withered hand, "Rise and come forward!" And he rose and came forward. 9 And Jesus said to them, "I ask you, is it lawful on the Sabbath day to do good or to do harm, to save a life or to destroy it?" 10 and after looking around at them all, he said to him, "Stretch out your hand!" And he did so, and the hand was restored. 11 But they themselves were filled with rage, and discussed together what they might do to Jesus.

Introduction

We've been seeing lately that the Pharisees did not approve of our Lord's style of personal piety, his outward religious expressions. Last week their complaint was about fasting. This week it is the observance of the Sabbath. Naturally we look to a passage like this for teaching on the Sabbath. But it really sheds a powerful light on at least three issues: the Sabbath itself, the Savior who is Lord of the Sabbath, and the Scriptures which reveal them both.

I. The Sabbath: How Should We Keep It?

For the origins of Sabbath observance, we must of course look back to the Old Testament. It is part of the Ten Commandments in Exodus 20:8–11. Six days we are to labor and do all our work, and then the seventh is a "Sabbath" to the Lord our God. In it neither we, our family, our domestic staff, nor our animals are to do any work. Why? Because God himself worked for six days and rested on the seventh, and therefore He blessed that day and hallowed it, that is, sanctified it and set it apart as special. As people who follow Him, who live a lifestyle based on His character, we are to follow suit. Then Exodus 31:13–17 defines the Sabbath as a *sign* of the covenant between God and Israel and reemphasizes that it is to be observed by "complete rest"—not bed rest, but rest from one's normal weekly work. To ignore this would be to give a sign that one was outside the covenant, and so the penalty was death. Exodus 34:21 stipulates that the Sabbath is to be observed even during plowing time and harvest time. Especially busy periods of the year when there is pressure at work and "life is just a little bit hectic right now" are not to be used as an excuse or a rationalization for skipping the Sabbath observance.

Now, here is a fact you may not be expecting: In all these earliest references the stress is on *rest* and *refreshment*; worship *as such* is not even mentioned. Well, if everybody has the same day off from work, it would be natural for regular worship to be scheduled on that day, and it would not be inappropriate as a remembrance of the God who created and who rested and gave us the Ssabbath. And that seems to be exactly what happened. But worship was not the *primary* point of the Old–Testament Sabbath. Few modern Christian Sabbatarians seem to have noticed that.

Okay, then, the primary purpose of the Sabbath is rest, refreshment, and re–creation. But worship is implied as a secondary purpose in Leviticus 19:30, which parallels keeping the Sabbath with revering the sanctuary. This is confirmed by Leviticus 23:37–38, where the Sabbath is included in a list of days set aside as "holy convocations, to present offerings by fire." So worship on the Sabbath is not just convenient; it is also appropriate, and, indeed, commanded. In all these passages, the emphasis is on setting one day out of seven apart for rest and worship. Little or nothing is said as to the details of how this is to be done.

Of course, the Pharisees could not leave it at that! They felt obligated to work out in exhaustive detail just how one is to keep the Sabbath in their zeal to "put a hedge around the Law." (That was their infamous strategy for making sure they did not transgress the Law. If it says not to take God's name in vain, for example, we won't pronounce it at all—so we can't very well take it in vain, now, can we?) How did they apply this "hedge" principle to the Sabbath? Well, how far could you walk on the Sabbath before it became "work"? The "Sabbath Day's Journey" was calculated at 2,000 cubits, or about 1,000 yards—a little over half a mile. Of course, you could extend that limit by a curious legal fiction. If you needed to travel farther than that from home on a Sabbath, you could place an object of your property within 2,000 cubits of your destination in advance. This would extend the boundaries of your "house," so that the official count of cubits would not begin until you passed that point.[48] You can see how the inherent legalism of the Pharisaic mentality was given free reign. These are actual rules that were applied by Pharisaic Jews in Jesus' day. I am not making this up!

Well, what are some additional ways a hedge was built around the Sabbath? How much could you carry in your hand without it constituting a "burden" and thus work? An amount equal to the weight of a dried fig. ("If it weighs the same as a du . . . ." Oh, never mind.) If a person in one place had his hand stretched forth into another place and filled with fruit, and the Sabbath "overtook" him, he should drop the fruit

---

[48] H. Porter, "Sabbath Day's Journey," *The International Standard Bible Encyclopedia*, ed. James Orr (Grand Rapids MI: Eerdmans, 1946), 2634.

rather than risk "carrying a burden." Women should not wear ornaments on the Sabbath because they might be tempted to remove them in order to show them off, and thus momentarily "carry a burden." It was wise not to look in a mirror on the Sabbath, because you might be tempted to pull out a gray hair, and that would be work. If you arrive at your place of rest just as the Sabbath begins, you should unpack only what may be handled on the Sabbath. To prevent your beast from working, you may untie the ropes and let the rest fall to the ground by itself. To make sure you avoided work, you must not climb a tree, ride, swim, clap your hands, or dance on the Sabbath. If you have been in modern Israel on a Sabbath, you may have encountered the "Sabbath protocol" for elevators. They are automatically programmed to stop at every floor so you won't have to "work" by mashing the button for yours! You realize at that moment that I am really *not* making all this up. I haven't found it yet, but there must be a prohibition of smiling in the traditions somewhere! And here is a provision quite relevant to the Pharisees' controversies with the Lord: You could wear a bandage or plaster on the Sabbath if and only if the object of it was to prevent further injury, but not if its purpose was to promote healing, for that would be work. The only exception to this would be if there was immediate danger to the person's life.[49] I don't guess the man's withered hand in the synagogue quite made the cut.

This legalistic, uncharitable, and wrongheaded approach hardly even needs a critique. Merely to describe it is to see its absurdity as an attempt to practice the Law in the spirit in which it was originally given. To confuse such traditions of men with the Law of God and to impose this confusion on the consciences of others is not only evil in itself, but it does tremendous damage, creates huge stumbling blocks to faith, and brings the name of God into disrepute. And it discourages people from looking to the Bible for practical wisdom for life.

Contemporary Christians are generally too lazy to generate or observe that many rules, but a few of them have managed to catch the Pharisaic spirit quite nicely. One thinks of strict Sabbatarians, who insist that only worship or other religious activity may be pursued on the Sabbath. You may remember Eric Liddell in "Chariots of Fire" scolding the little boy for playing soccer on Sunday and then refusing to run in an Olympic race scheduled for Sunday. We must truly admire his genuine evangelistic zeal, his belief that he could glorify God by running track, and his willingness to make costly sacrifices rather than violate his conscience. But at the same time, we must question the wisdom of his application of Scripture. The original purpose of the Sabbath was rest from our *work*. Surely, for the little schoolboy, that would have meant not doing sums or parsing verbs. It is inconceivable that he thought of soccer as "work." Ironically, Liddell was preventing him from fulfilling the true intent of the original

---

[49] The rabbinic rules are summarized in two treatises of The Mishnah, "Shabbath" and "Erubin." *The Mishnah*, ed. Herbert Danby (Oxford: Oxford Univ. Pr., 1933; rpt. Peabody, MA: Hendrickson, 2019), 100–136.

ordinance! Equally Pharisaic are those like the Seventh-Day Adventists who insist that because God said to worship on the seventh day, we must therefore worship on Saturday rather than Sunday. As if they even knew what the seventh day from Creation is by accurate count; as if Paul had not explicitly forbidden us in Colossians 2:16 from judging one another over such things! The human capacity for ingenuity in using the letter of the Law to circumvent or even overturn its spirit is truly amazing.

Unfortunately, most contemporary Evangelicals have avoided these errors only by flying from them to another place just as unbiblical: They treat the Sabbath as nothing special at all. Therefore, all of us need to pay attention once again to the example of Jesus. He had no patience with the Pharisaic hedge around the Law; He would walk right through it without blinking an eye. There was no place in Jesus' approach for legalism and judgmentalism on the details. For the Pharisees, the disciples were working by both harvesting the grain (picking it) and processing it (rubbing it between their hands). Jesus' response was, if it is not irreverent to put it this way, "Good grief! Get a life!" This was not just laxity, nor was it mere orneriness, a rebellious desire to get the goat of the religious establishment. It was the consistent living out of a positive principle: to cut away the traditions of men and get back to the simplicity of the Old Testament.

In verse 9, then, Jesus is really asking the Pharisees to remember that the purpose of the Sabbath was positive, not negative. Is it for doing good or not? You tell me. His message here is very consistent with His words in Mark 2:27—"*The Sabbath was made for man, and not man for the Sabbath.*" It was made for man's rest and refreshment; therefore, sports and recreation are not only Okay, but they help to fulfill that purpose. It was made for worship; therefore, it should be characterized by celebration and the joy we spoke of last time. So sports and other forms of recreation are perfectly Okay as long as they do not conflict with or interfere with the stated hours of worship in the church. And above all, the Sabbath was not made for judging others who do not keep it in exactly the same way that we do. We should set the Sabbath aside as "holy," i.e., as "special." We should take advantage of it to make sure we do not neglect the assembling together of the Saints. To neglect this is disobedience. But we should not turn it from a blessing into a burden as we do so. This is a warning I charge you to heed seriously! For the human capacity—and therefore our capacity—for ingenuity in using the letter of the Law to circumvent or even overturn its spirit *is* truly amazing. May the grace of God and the spirit of Christ enable us to do better! So let it be written; so let it be done.

II. The Savior: Who Is He?

The second question this passage raises is the most important but requires the least explanation. Not "the Sabbath: how should we keep it," but "the Savior: Who is He?" The answer does not need a lot of explanation, but it is supremely important, and we must make sure we do not miss it. Jesus of course claims to be "Lord of the Sabbath."

What does this mean? To his Jewish audience, the Sabbath was the memorial of Creation and of God's rest when Creation was finished. To be Lord of the Sabbath surely means on a practical level that Jesus has the authority to reject the Pharisees' teaching on how to keep it and substitute His own example. But it means much more than that. Lord of the Sabbath? Who would have that kind of authority? Hmmm. To be Lord of the Sabbath is to be Lord of the completed Creation. It is one more way that Jesus claims to be no one less than God himself. No wonder the Pharisees were looking for opportunities to catch Him up, accuse Him, and discredit Him! Well, if they were wrong about the Sabbath, maybe they were wrong about Jesus too. Do we accept Him as Lord of the Sabbath? Then we must follow Him, not just in His approach to this issue, but in everything. And that leads us to our final question, which may have the most practical import of all: "The Scriptures: how do we interpret them?"

III. The Scriptures: How Do We Interpret Them?

Jesus here is not only teaching us how to keep the Sabbath; in doing so, He is also teaching us how to read the Bible. And the lesson He is giving us here can surely be summarized in this principle: **Do not attempt to apply the letter of any passage of Scripture until you have first grasped the spirit of it!** The Pharisees are the perfect negative example in their approach to the Sabbath. And Jesus is the prefect positive example not only in his general approach to the Sabbath question but also in his treatment of the biblical texts dealing with the shewbread. How does this work?

Jesus refers his opponents to 1 Samuel 21:1–6, a passage which requires a prior knowledge of Leviticus 24:5–9. When the shewbread was removed from before the altar, it was then given to the priest, who is the only person with a right to eat it. When the priest gave this bread to David in 1 Samuel 21, it had already been set aside for him. He was therefore giving up his own bread for the sake of helping David. (Since it was consecrated bread, he had scruples about the ceremonial purity of David's men—hence the question about whether they had been "kept from women." That is an incidental fact about the priest, not the point of the passage.) It would have been wrong for David to *take* the shewbread for himself, but did Leviticus forbid the priest from *giving* it to him, from choosing freely to yield his own right to eat the bread for David's sake? Evidently not. Jesus' point is that David's eating is parallel to that of the disciples. That is, both had the potential to offend people with a scrupulous conscience, but neither actually breaks the letter of the Law (that is important). Both acts are right, and the rightness is seen when the spirit of the Law is understood.

From Jesus' example as a Bible reader here we can derive **four basic and important rules** for dealing with any ethical question. **First,** we must **ascertain what biblical commands or principles apply** to the issue. For the Sabbath, we followed this rule by discussing the references to it in the Creation narrative and its treatment in the Law of Moses. For the showbread, it was the passages in Leviticus and Second Samuel. **Second,** we must ask ourselves, and let the Scriptures answer by context, **for what**

145

purpose were those commands originally given, or those principles originally laid down? Jesus discerned clearly what our treatment of the Old–Testament passages has already implied: The Sabbath was made for man, not man for the Sabbath. That was His way of stating the positive nature of the institution. God intended it to be a blessing, not a curse or even a burden. His treatment of the showbread seems very consistent: The showbread was made for the priest, not the priest for the showbread. Therefore, he could be charitable with it and give it to David if he chose. **Third,** we must safeguard ourselves by remembering that **while our proper applications of the text to situations that exist today may go beyond the letter, they must never contradict the letter** (unless it has been superseded by later revelation, as in the New Testament's repealing of the Ceremonial Law). So Jesus did not just ignore the Sabbath or the provisions about the showbread (He was in the synagogue on the Sabbath!), but rather applied them in ways more in keeping with their original purpose. And fourth and most importantly, we must remember that **the final and ultimate purpose of all Scripture is to glorify God by revealing and pointing us to Jesus Christ.** Therefore, Jesus with his Gospel of Grace is the highest vantage point, the ultimate frame of reference, from which to view all of Scripture, the ultimate criterion by which every interpretation must be judged. Jesus applied this principle when He proclaimed that the Son of Man was Lord of the Sabbath. And so should we.

Remember then the basic rule and the four principles of sound interpretation derived from it, modeled on the very practice of the Lord, and use them whenever you are reading the Scriptures and trying to understand their application to the problems of modern life. Do not attempt to apply the letter of any passage of Scripture until you have first grasped the spirit of it! And in order to do so, first, ascertain what biblical commands or principles apply to the issue. Second, ask yourself, and let the Scriptures answer by context, for what purpose were those commands originally given, or those principles originally laid down? Third, safeguard yourself by remembering that while our proper applications of the text to situations that exist today may go beyond the letter, they must never contradict the letter of the Law. Look to Jesus in this passage and elsewhere as your role model as you do so. And finally, remember that the final and ultimate purpose of all Scripture is to glorify God by revealing and pointing us to Jesus Christ. Thus you will understand and use the Scriptures as our Lord intended and in accordance with His example.

Conclusion

The very fact that we are here on a Sunday instead of a Saturday is eloquent testimony to the greatness of our Lord Jesus Christ, the Lord of the Sabbath, the Lord of Creation, the Lord of Redemption. On a Sunday He entered Jerusalem on the colt of a donkey and proclaimed Himself Lord. On a Sunday He rose from the dead and proved Himself to be Lord. And that is why the early Church felt compelled to move the day of rest and worship (still one out of seven) to the first day of the week. In so doing they honored the spirit of the Law (to point to Jesus as the Christ) without violating the letter (to set aside every seventh day). And in so doing they gave us a reminder, every time we meet, of the greatness of our Lord Jesus Christ, the Lord of the Sabbath. Let us praise Him!

BLESSINGS AND WOES

Luke 6:12 And it was at this time that he went off to the mountain to pray, and he spent the whole night in prayer to God. 13 And when day came, he called his disciples to him and chose twelve of them, whom he also named as Apostles: 14 Simon, whom he also called Peter, and Andrew his brother, and James and John, and Philip and Bartholomew 15 and Matthew and Thomas, James the son of Alphaeus and Simon who was called the Zealot, 16 Judas the son of James, and Judas Iscariot, who became a traitor. 17 And he descended with them and stood on a level place, and there was a great multitude of his disciples and a great throng of people from all Judea and Jerusalem and the coastal region of Tyre and Sidon 18 who had come to hear him and to be healed of their diseases; and those who were troubled with unclean spirits were being cured. 19 And all the multitude were trying to touch him, for power was coming from him and healing them all. 20 And turning his gaze on his disciples, he began to say, "Blessed are you who are poor, for yours is the kingdom of God. 21 Blessed are you who hunger now, for you shall be satisfied. Blessed are you who weep now, for you shall laugh. 22 Blessed are you when men hate you and ostracize you and cast insults at you and spurn you name as evil for the sake of the Son of Man. 23 Be glad in that day and leap for joy, for behold, you reward is great in heaven; for in the same way their fathers used to treat the prophets. 24 But woe to you who are rich, for you are receiving your comfort in full. 25 Woe to you who are well fed now, for you shall be hungry. Woe to you who laugh now, for you shall mourn and weep. 26 Woe to you when all men speak well of you, for in the same way their fathers used to treat the false prophets."

Introduction

We've been how Luke's purpose in his Gospel is to tell the story of Jesus in such a way as to reveal him as the Messiah of Israel and the Savior of the World. So far Luke has done this mainly by showing us a selection of Jesus' deeds and his words in explanation of those deeds, which had a tendency to raise questions. Who do you think you are, forgiving other people's sins? Why don't you fast? Why do you heal on the Sabbath? What manner of man *are* you? etc. Now Luke will give us an extended sample of Jesus' actual teaching, in a discourse that is sometimes called "The Sermon on the Plain" to distinguish from the similar and more familiar "Sermon on the Mount" in Matthew. We will examine the opening section of it today.

I. Its Relation To The "Sermon On The Mount" (Mat. 5–7)

A question about this passage that has to be addressed is that of its relationship to the very similar "Sermon on the Mount" of Matthew 5–7. The two sermons have a great many points in common: the Beatitudes, the House built on the Rock, etc. More than that, the two sermons even have the same basic three–point outline: The Blessings of the Kingdom (the Beatitudes), The Behavior of the Kingdom (the stuff in the middle), and an Exhortation to Obedience rather than Foolishness based on the first two points as a conclusion (the parable of the house built on the rock or the sand). But there are also some important differences. The sermon in Luke is much shorter overall, though it has some points that the Matthean version leaves out (i.e., the woes). In Matthew, Jesus blesses the poor *in spirit* in the third person; in Luke, He blesses the poor plain and simple in the second person. In Matthew, Jesus goes *up* a mountain to preach the sermon; in Luke, He comes *down* a mountain to a level place (hence "The Sermon on the Plain"). With differences like these, how can both accounts of the sermon be completely true?

There are two logical possibilities to explain these two documents. One is that they are two different accounts of the same sermon. If that is so, then either one of the Gospel writers was confused about the location, or the discrepancy between going up and coming down is solved by taking different spots on the same mountain as a vantage point. If they are the same sermon, that is in fact almost certainly what happened. You can visit the "mount" of the Sermon today. There is a chapel on top of it, The Church of the Beatitudes. But the topography of the mountain is what matters. It starts uphill from the shores of the Sea of Galilee, goes up for a while, levels off, and then goes up some more to the top. The level place (or "plain") halfway up is the only place where a crowd could have gathered for the sermon. So all you have to do to solve the difficulty is just go look at the spot. Mountain? Level place? Which is it? Both. Both, plain and simple. Both writers are speaking accurately, just emphasizing different aspects of the same geological feature. But if it's one sermon, the differences in wording still have to be accounted for. Two different translations into Greek of the same Aramaic original, two different summaries of the same longer material: Those explanations take us a long way to reconciling the two accounts. Some scholars still try to maintain that neither could be simply a different summary of the same material, but rather that each Gospel writer is putting his own "spin" on Jesus' original words. And that is where the second possibility comes in.

I think the second possible explanation is also important to keep in mind: that Jesus often used the same material with a slightly different application on more than one occasion. He was, after all, an itinerant preacher who was speaking in a different town every day or so. It is inconceivable that He did not re–use his material often in that kind of ministry, and He was under no more obligation to say exactly the same thing to every audience than I am when I use the same outline with different groups at different times. A lot of liberal students of the Gospels create a lot of problems in the text simply by making assumptions about Jesus' ministry that are contrary, not only to the doctrine of inspiration, but to plain common sense. He must have said everything once and once only, or if He ever repeated anything He must have done it verbatim? On what other assumption can you conclude that one of the Gospels must have got it wrong? Give me a break! The alleged "discrepancies" between the two accounts then are mainly the product of unrealistic assumptions about what Jesus' ministry must have been like. I preached a version of this sermon twenty–five years ago—same outline, different congregation. If I preached it again in Toccoa rather than Athens next week, I guarantee that two people reporting on the two sermons would have some differences even if they were both perfectly accurate, and liberal scholars of the future would try to prove that one of them had gotten something wrong. That is a scholarly game too pointless, too stupid, and, quite frankly, too boring to be played.

Two important conclusions follow from this line of reasoning. The first is that there is no reason not to see both sermons as accurate summaries of Jesus' teaching. There is no need, much less any good reason, to obsess over discrepancies in either the place or the content. The second is that Luke's version should be studied as a text in its own right and not thought of simply as a condensation or abridgement of Matthew's material. That is the approach that we are going to take in this series. So let us read and study these words carefully. To begin, let me make some general observations on the text of the sermon.

II. Some General Observations On The Text

The first thing to notice is that this sermon is addressed to Jesus' disciples (verse 20a, *"turning his gaze"* on the disciples), though others were there to overhear it. This is an important observation, because with it the apparent difference with Matthew becomes much more interesting ("you poor" versus "the poor in spirit"). Luke's version brings out the disciples, not people in general, as the primary audience. So it is not recommending poverty as such. Rather, here as in Matthew, it is the specific kind of poverty characteristic of Jesus' disciples—*you* poor—the poor *in spirit*—which is being blessed.

We should also notice in passing the skill expended on the composition of this discourse as a whole. The woes carefully parallel the blessings: the poor correspond to the rich, the hungry to the full, those who weep to those who laugh, those who are hated and despised to those who are loved and approved. Each series of blessings or curses, moreover, is climactic. The emphasis is therefore placed on the last member of each series: how we are received by men. If we are received like the prophets, i.e. rejected and mistreated, for Jesus' sake, we are blessed. If not, if we have the approval of those who persecuted the prophets and will eventually kill Jesus, then we are cursed. So the ultimate point of the whole is not being rich or poor, hungry or full, happy or sad, as such, but it is how we relate to Jesus in a world that is opposed to Him and which can be expected to treat us as it did Him.   Riches and happiness bought at the expense of aligning ourselves with the world against Jesus is a woeful thing because it will lead to our being cursed in eternity, with all that illusory current blessing reversed. Poverty or hunger or sadness that is the result of being on the side of Jesus and the prophets is blessed, not because they are good things in themselves, but because they will be rewarded in eternity with the reversal of all our present distress. We will miss this, which is actually the main point of the passage, if we focus on each beatitude or curse separately, rather than seeing the two series as wholes, as the rhetoric of the sermon intends.

III. The Teaching Of The Passage

What is Jesus trying to teach us here then? Surely it is that **believers can expect this life to be a struggle**, involving the possibility of poverty, hunger, sorrow, and rejection. The pictures of the Christian throughout the New Testament bear this lesson out. We are athletes, farmers, soldiers. The appeal of the New Testament Gospel is not, "Come to Jesus and He will solve all your present problems," but rather, "Come join the right side in the cosmic spiritual War! Then you will experience all the deprivations and challenges of the life of a soldier, but you will have the joy of being on the right (and winning) side." We are encouraged to count the cost before doing so. It may involve poverty, hunger, sorrow, rejection, and death. But those who undergo such things for Jesus' sake are blessed anyway because great is their reward in heaven.

The Christian life is depicted as a struggle, but the second point is that **the joy of following Christ outweighs the struggle**, so that, even if we are poor, we may consider ourselves to be blessed to be Jesus' disciples. Surely our future reward is one reason why this is true. (The fact that we dismiss it contemptuously as "pie in the sky" shows how secular we have really become.) But the statement about being blessed is in the present tense! Not just "will be blessed," but rather "already are blessed." Being poor with Jesus is a happier condition than being rich without Him, *right now*. Being hungry with Jesus is a happier condition than being full without Him, *right now*. Weeping with Jesus is a happier condition than laughing without Him, *right now*. Being rejected by men with Jesus is a happier condition than being accepted without Him, *right now*. Why? Because with Jesus we already enjoy the forgiveness of sins, a clean conscience, a sense of purpose in life—and best of all, a personal relationship with Jesus Himself—right now. A bigger house and a fancier car, filet mignon rather than a Big Mac, fortuitous personal circumstances, and such popularity that you are elected homecoming queen: All of this amounts to precisely nothing in the scale of value next to the kingdom of God, next to knowing Jesus as your Savior, Lord, and Friend. For what shall it profit a man if he should gain the whole world and lose his own soul?

Okay, the Christian life can be expected to be a struggle, but the joy of knowing Jesus outweighs the struggle. It follows from all this, in the third place, that **the world is deluded about the source of true happiness**. Wealth, pleasure, popularity—all of these are good things, but all of them are empty without Christ. If they are the best you've got, then woe to you! Nobody has ever captured the richness of this irony better than Edward Arlington Robinson.

> Whenever Richard Cory went downtown
> We people on the pavement looked at him.
> He was a gentleman from sole to crown,
> Clean–favored and imperially slim.

And he was always modestly arrayed,
And he was always human when he talked.
But still he fluttered pulses when he said
"Good morning," and he glittered when he walked.

And he was rich, yes richer than a king,
And admirably schooled in every grace.
In short, we thought that he was everything
To make us wish that we were in his place.

And so we worked and waited for the light
And went without the meat and cursed the bread,
And Richard Cory one calm summer night
Went home and put a bullet through his head.[50]

Woe to you who are rich! Woe to you who are full! Woe to you who laugh! Woe to you who are well thought of by the men whose fathers killed the prophets! Not because wealth or a good diet or happiness or popularity are to be shunned in themselves—but woe to you who have chosen these things rather than Christ! You are of all men most to be pitied. True happiness comes from having a purpose great enough to make life fulfilling, and the only purpose great enough to do that is Christ and His Kingdom.

Okay then, Jesus' followers can expect this life to be a struggle. But the joy of following Christ outweighs that struggle even here and now because the world is deluded about the ultimate source of happiness. And finally, Jesus is teaching us here that **there is coming a Day when it will be made plain who has made the right choice**. At present the lies of the world succeed because man looketh on the outward appearance (1 Sam. 16:7). But one day all that will be stripped away and what we know deep down in our hearts even now will be undeniable. Then the true poverty of those who have chosen to live for riches will be revealed. Then the true starvation of those who have chosen to live for their bellies will be revealed. Then the true sorrow of those who have sought happiness in the world will be revealed. Then the true rejection of those who have lived for popularity will be revealed. Woe to those who have chosen these things! But on that Day, praise God, the true Wealth of those who gave up everything for Jesus will be revealed. Then the true Fullness of those who were hungry for His sake, the true Joy of those who mourned for His sake, the true Acceptance of those who suffered ostracism for His name, will also be revealed. Blessed are those who have chosen the kingdom of God and His righteousness—blessed are those who have

---

[50] Edward Arlington Robinson, "Richard Cory," *Modern British and American Poetry*, ed. Louis Untermeyer (NY: Harcourt, Brace, & World, 1955), 20–21.

chosen the King! Let us therefore choose rightly now, for in that Day we will be stuck for all eternity with the choice that we have made.

Conclusion

Why is there so little of the joy of the Lord in Christians today? It is because to a certain extent we have believed the lies that the Lord was combating here. We are seeking blessedness, happiness, in a place where it cannot be found. We are seeking it in things. We do not lack the joy of the Lord because we have wealth or food or enjoy good times or have good reputations. But we definitely lack it because we look for it *in* those things, and we most definitely lack it if we have bought those things at the price of compromising our allegiance to Christ and His kingdom and its principles. We are exposed constantly to this lie. Use this deodorant or toothpaste, drive this car, and you will be happy! We know better, but it has snuck in under some of our radars anyway. So let me tell you something from the Lord in this passage: It is a lie! To counteract it, let me simply repeat what the Lord has said to us today:

"Blessed are you who are poor, for yours is the kingdom of God. Blessed are you who hunger now, for you shall be satisfied. Blessed are you who weep now, for you shall laugh. Blessed are you when men hate you and ostracize you and cast insults at you and spurn you name as evil for the sake of the Son of Man. Be glad in that day and leap for joy, for behold, your reward is great in heaven; for in the same way their fathers used to treat the prophets. But woe to you who are rich, for you are receiving your comfort in full. Woe to you who are well fed now, for you shall be hungry. Woe to you who laugh now, for you shall mourn and weep. Woe to you when all men speak well of you, for in the same way their fathers used to treat the false prophets."

Blessings or woes? Which will it be? The choice is yours. Amen.

LOVING YOUR ENEMIES

Luke 6:27 *"But I say to you who hear, love your enemies, do good to those who hate you, 28 bless those who curse you, pray for those who mistreat you. 29 Whoever hits you on the cheek, offer him the other also; whoever takes away your coat, do not withhold your shirt from him either. 30 Give to everyone who ask you, and whoever takes away what is yours, do not demand it back. 31 And just as you want people to treat you, treat them in the same way. 32 And if you love those who love you, what credit is that to you? For even sinners love those who love them. 33 And if you do good to those who do good to you, what credit is that to you? For even sinners do the same. 34 And if you lend to those from whom you expect to receive, what credit is that to you? Even sinners lend to sinners in order to receive back the same amount. 35 But love your enemies and do good, and lend expecting nothing in return; and your reward will be great and you will be sons of the Most High. For He himself is kind to ungrateful and evil men. 36 Be merciful, just as your Father is merciful. 37 And do not judge, and you will not be judged; do not condemn, and you will not be condemned; pardon and you will be pardoned. 38 Give, and it will be given to you; good measure, pressed down, shaken together, running over, they will pour it into your lap. For by your standard of measure it will be measured to you in return."*

Introduction

We've been listening to Jesus' teaching in the "Sermon on the Plain" (corresponding to Matthew's "Sermon on the Mount"). We saw last time that it has a three–part outline: the Blessings of the Kingdom (the Beatitudes), the Behavior of the Kingdom (the part we examine today), and an exhortation to obedience in the parable of the house built foolishly on the sand or wisely on the rock. We saw last time that the parallels between the blessings and the woes, in two climactic series, are focused on how we relate to Jesus. It is better to be poor, hungry, mourning, and unpopular with Jesus than to be rich, full, laughing, and popular without Him. The Christian life can be expected to be a struggle. The joy of following Jesus outweighs that struggle. The world is deluded about the source of true happiness or blessedness, seeking it in wealth, food, laughter, and popularity. And a time is coming when it will be revealed who has made the right choice. Blessed are you if you chose Jesus, even if it means poverty etc. Woe to you if you chose wealth and popularity over Jesus! Such were the lessons of the first point in Jesus' sermon. You really want to bow to Jesus as the true King and be a citizen of His Kingdom! And to the extent that you really know Him, you *will* want to.

We come today then to the heart of Jesus' teaching on the behavior to be expected of those who are citizens of the Kingdom of Heaven, and it contains some of the most radical and most misunderstood words ever uttered. Since they came from the lips of our Lord and constitute the center of this formal teaching addressed to His disciples, we had better be sure we get them right. The version of Jesus' sermon on this topic as reported by Luke can help us greatly in coming to that understanding.

I. Blunders In Interpretation

There are two equal and opposite errors in the interpretation of this passage that have unfortunately dominated the history of the church's understanding of it. The first is the naive view that takes every word literally, leading to pietism and pacifism. It is a difficult view to combat because people who hold to it often take Jesus' words very seriously indeed, sometimes at great personal sacrifice, and, moreover, such a literal approach sounds radical and deeply spiritual. But it cannot be right, for the simple reason that it would create a conflict with other passages of Scripture. If a literal pacifism, a radical non–resistance, were in fact the New Testament ethic, then John the Baptist would have erred greatly when he told the soldiers who asked him what they should do to perform deeds worthy of repentance that they should be content with their wages and take nothing by force. He would have had to tell them to resign their commissions. Well, some might say, but he was the last of the *Old* Testament prophets, and the New Testament ethic of Christ was not yet in effect. Oh, really? Then why does the Apostle Paul tell his disciple Timothy to be a good *soldier* of Jesus Christ? If pacifism were indeed the New Testament ethic, then he might just as well have told Timothy to be a good prostitute for Jesus! One of the most basic rules of Evangelical hermeneutics (the science and art of interpretation) is that we are required to find a reading of such passages that does justice to all of them while allowing us to keep all of them in the Bible. I will attempt such a reading before we are done today. And you must search the Scriptures diligently to see if it be so.

The other common error is a reaction to the first. It ironically agrees with the first error in taking the passage literalistically, but then denies that it is relevant for believers today. This ethic is actually impossible to implement in the real world, they argue. So it must be a millennial ethic designed for a different dispensation, the way we will live after Christ returns, perhaps, but not something we are required to practice today. This approach has even more problems than the first one. These words were addressed by Jesus—who knew perfectly well that He was not going to bring in the kingdom immediately in the way His disciples expected—to His disciples, as we saw last week. There is not the slightest hint in the text that He did not mean them to take it seriously. There is therefore not the slightest hint that He did not mean for *us* to take it seriously. Besides, what good would this be as a millennial ethic? In the Millennium, there will be no need to turn one's other cheek.

We've got to do better than this. And therefore, we must give our attention to our next point: the background to a proper understanding.

II. Background To A Proper Understanding

Two features of the context are the key to understanding this passage. First is the immediate literary context, and second the broader cultural context.

156

In the **immediate context** of The Sermon on the Plain, Luke has already brought out very clearly the identity of the enemies we are talking about. *"Blessed are you when men hate you and ostracize you and cast insults at you and spurn your name as evil for the sake of the Son of Man"* (verse 22). These are not enemies in general, much less someone who is trying to mug you or your family. They are people who have rejected and mistreated you *for the sake of Christ.* Surely the lesson here is that everyone who mistreats you, everyone who persecutes you for your Christian faith, is a potential convert. Their very persecution of you for Christ's sake makes the Gospel the bone of contention. The Gospel is precisely already the issue; it is already in the foreground of the discussion. Therefore, such people are to be treated accordingly. They should get a very different kind of push–back from us than what they are expecting! This does not mean you are supposed to let your family be robbed or put at risk, nor that you should cheerfully contribute to the maintenance of the habit of the drug addict who mugs you in the night. Of course, such people are potential converts too, and they should therefore be treated with all the kindness we can muster. But what form is that kindness to take? For that we need the next point.

In the broader **cultural context**, we have to remember that Jesus was an ancient near–eastern peasant speaking mainly to other ancient near–eastern peasants. We therefore need to know something about their habitual style of speaking, their typical use of language. We discover that they were prone to the use of strong language, bold metaphors, dramatic hyperbole (exaggeration for effect). A passage that illustrates this point very well is Matthew 5:27–29. In the context of his discussion of adultery, Jesus says, *"If your right eye makes you stumble, tear it out and throw it away."* For some reason, almost no one, not even the stoutest Anabaptist, takes this injunction literally. If they did, you would see a whole lot of one–eyed Christians running around! Almost everyone either misses the connection of this verse with the topic of adultery (Jesus had just said that *looking* on a woman to lust after her was committing adultery in your heart) altogether or understands that Jesus was speaking hyperbolically. He did not mean for us literally to mutilate ourselves in order to avoid sin. Rather, he was just making the point in the strongest and most dramatic way he could that the issue of adultery in the heart is very serious and not to be taken lightly, that sexual purity is extremely important.

Alright, why then would we not take the language of turning the other cheek in exactly the same way? Jesus is telling us not to be belligerent or vengeful; He is telling us to bend over backwards, as it were, (to use a more modern and less radically hyperbolic metaphor) to avoid conflict. He is not saying that there is no circumstance in which one can rightly defend oneself, still less that we can never use force (otherwise what would we do with the cleansing of the Temple, which involved some rather violent action with a scourge on His part?). Neither is He saying that we should become complete idiots in our financial dealings when He commands a radical generosity. What then is he saying? Perhaps we are now ready to understand it.

III. Behavior Of Kingdom Citizens: Redemptive Love

I think the key to the whole passage is verse 36: As citizens of the Kingdom, we are to be merciful *as our Father is merciful*. We are not private persons, free to pursue our own good and to attack and avenge our own enemies. We are ambassadors of Christ the King, whose first responsibility and therefore whose first priority is to show His love and communicate His Gospel. Therefore, personal vengeance, vindictiveness, even bitterness are absolutely forbidden. This is seen in the logic of the whole passage.

First, verses 27–28 lay down the **principle** (love your enemies). *"Love your enemies, do good to those who hate you, bless those who curse you, pray for those who mistreat you."* Then verses 29–30 are dramatic and hyperbolic **illustrations** of that principle. *"Whoever hits you one the cheek, offer him the other also; whoever takes away your coat, do not withhold your shirt from him either. Give to everyone who ask you, and whoever takes away what is yours, do not demand it back."* Verse 31 is a **summary** of the principle, widely known as the Golden Rule. *"And just as you want people to treat you, treat them in the same way."* Verses 32–34 give the **rationale** for this behavior. *"And if you love those who love you, what credit is that to you? For even sinners love those who love them. And if you do good to those who do good to you, what credit is that to you? For even sinners do the same. And if you lend to those from whom you expect to receive, what credit is that to you? Even sinners lend to sinners in order to receive back the same amount.* Then in verses 35–6 we have a **recap** of why this all matters that ties it back into our purpose as Ambassadors of the Kingdom representing Christ and His Father. *But love your enemies and do good, and lend expecting nothing in return; and your reward will be great and you will be sons of the Most High. For He Himself is kind to ungrateful and evil men. Be merciful, just as your Father is merciful."*

We do all of this as Ambassadors of Christ who represent Him and His Father before men. Therefore, we are not to apply those examples naively, but neither are we to ignore them. While personal vindictiveness is forbidden, positive goodness to others, including our enemies, is commanded. This means a generosity that goes beyond normal worldly expectations—we are not to lend or give only when we expect to get something out of it. How else would we represent Christ and His heavenly Father? But we must understand the "everybody" who asks as hyperbole too, for it is often not loving at all to give people everything they ask for.

This application without naivety is confirmed by the rest of Scripture, which puts helpful **limits** or boundaries around how literally we are supposed to understand and apply these words. How do we know how far to go? The rest of Scripture tells us. The hyperbolic giving and lending of verse 30, *"Give to everyone who ask you, and whoever takes away what is yours, do not demand it back"* is limited by 1 Tim. 5:8. *"If anyone does not provide for his own, and especially his own household, he has denied the faith and is worse than an unbeliever."* It is likewise limited by 2 Thessalonians 3:10. *"If anyone will not work,* *neither let him eat.*" We are to aid genuine need, but not encourage or subsidize laziness. The hyperbolic non-resistance to evil of verse 29, "*Whoever hits you on the cheek, offer him the other also,*" is limited by Romans 13:4, which tells us that the State does not bear the sword in vain as a minister of God for promoting good and restraining evil. It is not therefore inherently wrong for it to use coercive force, even, when necessary, deadly force. If the State is the servant of God when doing so, then it is not wrong for a Christian to serve as a policeman or a soldier. He has higher loyalties which might limit that service in ways that would not happen for other citizens, but we want his influence to be there in that service.

In personal conduct, then, we are to bend over backwards to avoid vindictiveness, but we can see a number of actions that in the right circumstances are not incompatible with the modeling of redemptive love even to those trying to injure us for Christ's sake. They include **rebuke**, as Paul turned on Ananias rather sharply when he had commanded Paul to be struck and said, "*God will strike you, you whitewashed wall! Do you sit to try me according to the Law and in violation of the Law command me to be struck?*" (Acts 23:3). It includes **escape**, as when the disciples snuck Paul out of Damascus by lowering him over the city wall in a basket to escape a plot against his life (Acts 9:25). It includes **appeal to legal redress**, as when Paul refused to leave quietly after the Philippian magistrates had beaten him contrary to his rights as a Roman citizen (Acts 16:37). It even includes the **use of police and military power** to protect ourselves and our loved ones, as when Paul was rescued by the centurion from the Jewish mob in Jerusalem and escorted in protective custody to Caesarea by a troop of Roman legionnaires to protect him from another plot against his life (Acts 23:23–31). We can— and must—use all these things and still do them in a way that expresses redemptive love, and still be people who are different from the world.

Now, I have had to point out these limits in order to give the full balance of Scripture. But with them I must also give a warning: If you use them to evade your responsibility to be any different from the world, you wrest Scripture to your own condemnation. We may act to protect and defend the innocent, or even within limits to defend ourselves, but never in a vengeful or vindictive manner. If you can't use restraint against the violent in that manner, then you had better let him keep on hitting you indeed! We had better make sure that in understanding the point of this passage without naive literalism we do not lose its point altogether, for it certainly has one.

IV. The Basis Of Redemptive Love

Why must we go beyond the kind of self-serving love the world shows? We have already seen this point, but it is so important that we need to emphasize it again. It is because we are representatives of Christ, who represents our Heavenly Father. "*But love your enemies and do good, and lend expecting nothing in return; and your reward will be great and you will be sons of the Most High. For He himself is kind to ungrateful and evil men. Be merciful, just as your Father is merciful*" (Luke 6:35–36). We must understand the necessity of showing our family resemblance, to be "sons of the Most High." Note well: To seek personal vengeance is to deny Christ before men. To hold a grudge is to deny Christ before men! To indulge in bitterness is to deny Christ before men! And this we must not do. Rather, we must positively show the love of Christ. And this cannot be done through a mechanical and outward imitation, no matter how much effort we put into it. It can only be done as Christ lives within us, because we really are sons and daughters of the Father through faith in Him.

Conclusion

No passage of Scripture has been more copped out on by the Church than this one. Pacifism looks spiritual but is naive and irresponsible and is thus practically (though not intentionally) a cop–out. But even worse is the average Evangelical who uses the excesses of the pacifist tradition to justify ignoring the passage altogether! What is difficult, impossible apart from the Holy Spirit, but necessary if the Church is to preach the Gospel convincingly, is responsible redemptive love which shows us to be ambassadors of Christ. For He set us the example in the Cross, which we celebrate in Communion this morning. Let us contemplate His love in that light, and ask Him to make it live in us, as we partake.

"DOING WHAT I SAY"

Luke 6:39 And he also spoke a parable to them: "A blind man cannot guide a blind man, can he? Will they not both fall into a pit? 40 A pupil is not above his teacher; but everyone, after he has been fully trained, will be like his teacher. 41 And why do you look at the speck that is in you brother's eye but do not notice the log that is in your own eye? 42 Of how can you say to your brother, 'Brother, let me take out the speck that is in your eye,' when you yourself do not see the log that is in your own eye? You hypocrite, first take the log out of your own eye, and then you will see clearly to take out the speck that is in your brother's eye. 43 For there is no good tree that produces bad fruit, nor, on the other hand, a bad tree that produces good fruit. 44 For each tree is known by its own fruit. For men do not gather figs from thorns, nor do they pick grapes from a briar bush. 45 The good man out of the good treasure of his heart brings forth what is good, and the evil man out of the evil treasure brings forth what is evil; for his mouth speaks from that which fills his heart. 46 And why do you call me, 'Lord, Lord,' and do not do what I say? 47 Every one who comes to me and hears my words and acts on them, I will show you what he is like: 48 He is like a man building a house, who dug deep and laid a foundation upon the rock. And when a flood rose, the torrent burst against that house and could not shake it, because it had been well built. 49 But the one who has heard and has not acted accordingly is like a man who built a house upon the ground without any foundation; and the torrent burst against it and immediately it collapsed, and the ruin of that house was great.

Introduction

We come today to the conclusion of our Lord's sermon on the Christian life as summarized by Luke: "The Sermon on the Plain." Two weeks ago we saw the Blessings of the Kingdom: that the joy of being a Christian outweighs poverty, pain, and persecution. Last time we saw the Behavior of the Kingdom: not passivism or pacifism, not non–resistance, but a redemptive love that goes far beyond the expectations of the world. Today in conclusion Jesus addresses the Bottom Line of the Kingdom: commitment to Him as its King. The words of Jesus (and His Apostles)—the ones in this sermon and the others throughout the New Testament too—are central to the Christian life. In this conclusion to His sermon, Jesus gives us three ways in which we are to relate to those words and be affected by them: Seeing what He says, Being what He says, and Doing what He says.

I. Seeing What He Says (vv. 39, 41)

The first thing is to see what Jesus says. By seeing, of course, we mean understanding. Hearing (or reading) His words, understanding them, and accepting them must logically precede doing anything about them. So Jesus begins His conclusion with the first step to understanding: admitting our lack of it. He begins by asking us to see ourselves as blind people in need of a guide. *And he also spoke a parable to them: "A blind man cannot guide a blind man, can he? Will they not both fall into a pit. . . . And why do you look at the speck that is in your brother's eye but do not notice the log that is in your own eye? Or how can you say to your brother, 'Brother, let me take out the speck that is in your eye,' when you yourself do not see the log that is in your own eye? You hypocrite, first take the log out of your own eye, and then you will see clearly to take out the speck that is in your brother's eye."*

Most people see in these verses a warning against hypocrisy—trying to deal with your neighbor's speck around your own log—and rightly so. But there is a more general point that comes out also when we see these words as the conclusion to Jesus' sermon about the blessing, the behavior, and the bottom line of the Kingdom of God. The absolutely essential place where we must begin if we are to follow Jesus' teaching here is with the need to admit our blindness apart from Christ. We will not hear His words as we ought, we will not internalize them as we ought, and we will not follow them as we ought as long as we think we can get by with our own wisdom or the wisdom of the other blind guides who offer themselves to us. Admitting our blindness is the first step to seeing what he says.

Why is this so hard? Because our blindness of course is not absolute. Even a pagan or an atheist can see that $2 + 2 = 4$. He says, "$2 + 2 = 4$. I have no idea why; it just seems to work." The Christian whose eyes have been opened says, "$2 + 2 = 4$, it is reliably 4, and this is a beautiful example of the profound rationality of the glorious mind of God." They both get the same sum, but for only one of them is it an act of worship. But they do both see that the answer is four. A little light gets in past the logs in our eyes, even the eyes of the natural man. And that is what makes admitting our blindness to spiritual things so difficult. We can see, and we can see that we can see, some things. How do we know that there is more to be seen? Well, we can start by being open to the possibility.

A person was once asked how he liked his new glasses. "I like them just fine," he replied, "except that everything looks sharper than it really is." Even with his vision corrected, he was still allowing his previous, default setting to define reality! I can relate to this difficulty well, because I did not get my first pair of glasses until I was in the seventh grade—and I should have gotten them several years earlier. But my distance vision had deteriorated gradually, so I had no idea how bad it really was until I put the glasses on. I remember being fascinated by all the extra wrinkles my elderly spinster teacher, Miss Mims, had suddenly acquired. I kept putting the glasses on and taking them off and putting them back on, marveling at the difference they made in what I could see, marveling at all the detail I had been missing without ever knowing it. It wasn't exactly like having a log removed from my eye, but it was like having a very thick film removed. So I have an inkling of what Jesus was talking about. I had no idea how blind I was because I could still see well enough to get by (though not as well as I thought I was); and if you have never considered this whole issue of spiritual

162

blindness, you may have no idea how blind you are either—even while putting yourself forward as a guide or an eye surgeon!

Our spiritual vision is distorted by sin, and until we come to Christ, the master Ophthalmologist, we have no way of knowing how much. It is our sin, and our sinful commitments, that are the logs that keep us from seeing the truth. This is easy to illustrate, though the easiest logs to see may not be (probably will not be) the ones in our own eyes. Think about the abortion issue, for example. All the light of genetics, embryology, and logic is on one side of that debate, giving consistent and clear testimony to the fact that the human fetus is from conception an individual human being by every scientific criterion that can be brought to bear. And yet this light can make no headway, blocked by the logs of our society's sinful commitments to sex without responsibility and personal convenience as its highest values. In another area, Hebrews 10:25 tells us very explicitly not to forsake the assembling of ourselves together. But there are people in whom the light of that verse is impotent against the logs of personal pride and the refusal to be reconciled with their brethren, or of their refusal to submit to any authority or live with any accountability. I am not talking about overt and intentional rebellion. The people I have in mind can read right past that verse without seeing anything contradictory to their lifestyles, just as many secular people really can't seem to see that abortion is murder.

Now, these particular spiritual blind spots are obvious—if they do not happen to be yours. The difficulty is that we all have our own logs and our own resulting blind spots. And, sadly, the very nature of blind spots is that you do not—indeed, you cannot—see them. If you knew they were there, they would not be blind spots anymore! So this is a problem you cannot solve for yourself. You must turn to somebody else—perhaps another brother or sister in Christ to help you identify your blind spots, and then to Christ Himself to remove them. We all desperately need two things: a guide and a "log–odectomy." And Christ alone is the only fully adequate answer to both needs. He gives us the first through a systematic study of his Word, looking not for a "blessing" so much as for truth and its application to all the questions and problems of life, possibly applied to one of our own blind spots with the aid of a brother or sister who does not happen to share it—hopefully not one with his own logs that need to be removed. (We need to take that warning seriously too.) Christ gives us the log–odectomy in response to sincere prayer asking Him through his Word to identify and remove the specific blind spots that still remain in us. For either to happen we must begin by admitting our need—whether we can "see" it or not!

II. Being What He Says (vv. 40, 43–45)

Seeing what Christ says is necessary but not sufficient. Christian truth is not merely "academic," but it is all meant for use in the "real world." Intellect must lead to action, or we cannot really claim even to have "seen." But even action is not enough: Transformation is the goal. That is why Jesus in verse 40 gives us the principle that the purpose of discipleship (that is the kind of "pupil" he has in mind) is becoming like the teacher or master. *"A pupil is not above his teacher; but everyone, after he has been fully trained, will be like his teacher."* Verse 40 lays down the principle, that we should be like Jesus, and verses 43–45 illustrates it with the pictures of trees and fruit and good or evil treasuries in the heart. *"For there is no good tree that produces bad fruit, nor, on the other hand, a bad tree that produces good fruit. For each tree is known by its own fruit. For men do not gather figs from thorns, nor do they pick grapes from a briar bush. The good man out of the good treasure of his heart brings forth what is good, and the evil man out of the evil treasure brings forth what is evil; for his mouth speaks from that which fills his heart."*

An apple tree produces apples; an orange tree produces oranges; a Jesus tree produces little Jesuses, with Jesus–like character from which flows Jesus–like actions. We are to become good trees producing good fruit because our very nature is becoming more Christlike, good men and women bringing good things out of the treasuries of our hearts because that is what is really in there. Citing chapters and verses is not enough; even acting on them in an outward and mechanical manner is not enough. Being like Jesus is the goal, and nothing less will do.

How do we become more like Jesus? By *being* His disciple. By recognizing our need of Him as guide and eye surgeon and submitting to Him as such. By spending time with Him in His Word and practicing what He preaches, not in outward straining to fit a mold but in faith and in dependence on His Holy Spirit to truly transform us from within. It is by the lifelong process of being His disciple. There are no shortcuts.

This then is how we should measure our spiritual progress. Are you more like Jesus than you were a year ago? How would you tell? Well, do you love the unlovable, redemptively and even sacrificially, more than you did a year ago? Do you think like Jesus more than you did a year ago? Do your priorities reflect His more than they did a year ago? Is your meat and drink to do the will of the Father? Are you more like Jesus than you were a year ago? If not, what have you been doing? You have just wasted an entire year of your life! What have you achieved in a year like that? Nothing but blind, aimless wandering, getting nowhere while leading other blind people into the ditch, and trying to operate on their eyes in the dark! Let us not be satisfied to be professing believers; let us be His disciples indeed and so become more like him.

III. Doing What He Says (vv. 46–49)

First we learn to see what Jesus says; then we proceed to being what Jesus says; and finally we come to doing what Jesus says. The emphasis on being what Jesus says does not take anything away from doing what He says. Rather, it is what makes it possible, for the only doing that counts spiritually is the doing that flows from this being. If we are truly seeing what He says and becoming what He says, then we will not be going through the motions but will truly be doing what He says. This is where the rubber meets the road. Then we will not just be theoretically committed to forgiving our debtors, but actually accepting them back into fellowship and closing the books on their offenses. Then we will not just be theoretically committed to the truth of Scripture but actually studying and living by the whole teaching of the whole Bible. Then we will not just be theoretically committed to evangelism but actually giving sacrificially to missions and witnessing for Christ effectively ourselves because now we are truly representing Him in more than just our words. The question we must ask ourselves this morning is, "How much of our commitment to these things is merely theoretical?" If the answer is "too much," you will not change it by taking my words as a guilt trip. Please don't do that! You will change it by truly seeing what Jesus says, being what He says, and then doing what He says.

The consequences of seeing, being, and doing—or not—are laid out graphically in verses 46–49, the familiar parable of the two houses. *"And why do you call me, 'Lord, Lord,' and do not do what I say? Every one who comes to me and hears my words and acts on them, I will show you what he is like: He is like a man building a house, who dug deep and laid a foundation upon the rock. And when a flood rose, the torrent burst against that house and could not shake it, because it had been well built. But the one who has heard and has not acted accordingly is like a man who built a house upon the ground without any foundation; and the torrent burst against it and immediately it collapsed, and the ruin of that house was great."*

The wise man built his house upon the rock, the foolish on the sand. What we are building of course is our lives. If they are not built on the solid foundation of what Jesus says, and built on that foundation by seeing, being, and doing, then we will see everything we have spent our lives on come to nothing. Other foundation can no man lay, says Paul, "building" on this metaphor, than that which is laid, which is Christ (1 Cor. 3:11).

When I was still in school and in need of summer jobs, I worked for a two–bit outfit called Hayes Construction Company. We were building an addition on to a lady's house. After we had poured the foundation and laid the sub–flooring and were starting up with the frames for the walls, she came out into the addition, saw what it looked like, got a look of consternation on her face, and went back into the house for a tape measure. It seems Mr. Hayes had poured the foundation three feet short of where the plans dictated! They proceeded to have a very interesting discussion which decorum, good manners, and respect for the house of God forbids me to repeat verbatim here. Guess what? Because we had not built on the right foundation, all that work could have been for nothing. She would have been within her rights to make us tear the whole thing up and start over. (Instead, she agreed to let him finish the project for a greatly reduced price. But that part is not parallel to the parable!) As we were finishing it the rest of the summer, the nice lady would bring lemonade out to us workers (whom she knew not to be at fault). She never gave any lemonade to Mr. Hayes.

You get the point. The foundation is important! Indeed, it is the most important part of any building. And the foundation of life is the Word of Christ, and the only building on that foundation that matters is seeing, being, and doing what those words say.

Conclusion

What the Lord is saying here is, "Take me seriously!" Do not just go through the motions of religion. It is a waste of time. It *matters* whether you see what He is saying, whether you are letting Him guide you and take the logs out of your eyes. It matters whether you as a result are becoming like Him so that you can truly do what He says, not in mechanical conformity but because it flows from the treasure of your heart. Much is at stake: whether your life will be fulfilled or futile, whether it will be worthwhile or wasted, whether it will be erected on the Rock or sunk in the sand. The storm is coming. How will your house withstand the flood?

A MAN UNDER AUTHORITY

Luke 7:1 *When He had finished all his discourse in the hearing of the people, He went to Capernaum. 2 And a centurion's slave, who was highly regarded by him, was sick and about to die. 3 When he heard about Jesus, he sent some Jewish elders, asking Him to come and save the life of his slave. 4 When they came to Jesus, they earnestly implored Hm, saying, "He is worthy for you to grant this to him, 5 for he loves our nation, and it was he who built us our synagogue." 6 Now Jesus started on His way with them, and when He was not far from the house, the centurion sent friends, saying to Him, "Lord, do not trouble Yourself further, for I am not worthy for You to come under my roof; 7 for this reason, I did not even consider myself worthy to come to You, but just say the word, and my servant will be healed,. 8 For I also am a man placed under authority, with soldiers under me; and I say to this one, 'Go!' and he goes, and to another, 'Come!' and he comes, and to my slave, 'Do this!' and he does it. 9 Now when Jesus heard this, He marveled at Him, and turned and said to the crowd that was following Him, "I say to you, not even in Israel have I found such great faith." 10 When those who had been sent returned to the house, they found the slave in good health.*

Introduction

If we are saved by grace through faith (Eph. 2:8); if faith is the victory that overcomes the world (1 John 5:4); if the just shall live by faith (Rom. 1:17); if whatever is not of faith is sin (Rom. 14:23); if we are crucified with Christ, and it is no longer we who live but Christ who lives in us, and the life we live in the flesh we live by faith in the Son of God who loved us and gave Himself for us (Gal. 2:20); then it is of the utmost importance that we know and be clear about what faith is. Fortunately, the nature of true faith is one of Luke's major themes, and we come to the first of several passages that treat it today. *"Now when Jesus heard this, He marveled at Him, and turned and said to the crowd that was following Him, 'I say to you, not even in Israel have I found such great faith.'"* The centurion is presented to us as a role model who demonstrates three components of the faith that brings us into a relationship with Christ and unleashes the power of the Gospel: the Admission of Unworthiness, the Acceptance of Authority, and the Ascription of Excellence.

1. The Admission Of Unworthiness (vv. 6–7)

The first component of true faith the centurion shows us is the admission of unworthiness. It stands out in ironic contrast to the Jews' insisting that he was worthy for Jesus to grant his request, He sees it differently. *"Lord, do not trouble Yourself further, for I am not worthy for You to come under my roof; for this reason, I did not even consider myself worthy to come to You."* He does not just admit his unworthiness; he makes rather a point of it.

The first thing to notice in understanding the significance of this admission is the **Prevalence of Unworthiness**. Its recognition is a common feature in people who have had a real encounter with God. You see it in Jacob's prayer when he was returning from his sojourn with Laban: *"I am unworthy of all the lovingkindness and of all the faithfulness which you have shown to your servant; for with my staff only I crossed this Jordan, and now I am become two companies"* (Gen. 32:10). You see it in Job, who had earned a reputation for being a righteous man. But when he saw himself in contrast to the holiness of God, his righteousness seemed but filthy rags" *"I have heard of You by the hearing of the ear, but mow my eye sees You; therefore, I abhor myself and repent in dust and ashes"* (Job 42:5–6). You see it in Isaiah, whose response to seeing God high and lifted up was *"Woe is me, for I am undone! I am a man of unclean lips . . . for my eyes have seen the Lord of Hosts"* (Is. 6:5). And less than a chapter ago we saw it in Peter, whose response to the miraculous draft of fishes was *"Depart from me, for I am a sinful man"* (Luke 5:8). The greater the vision of God, the clearer the understanding of it on the part of the man, the deeper will be the sense of unworthiness to be granted such a great gift.

The prevalence of unworthiness makes us want to grasp the **Point of Unworthiness** for our understanding of true biblical faith. Faith is not simply a theoretical belief in a set of theological propositions. It is that, of course, but it is more than that. It is a trust and commitment that takes hold of God's promises and brings us into a relationship with Christ. And this is a vital, living relationship with One who is a figure of majesty and glory beyond our ability to comprehend. It is a relationship with the High King of Heaven, before whom our place is on our faces in the dust. And it is a relationship with One who has nevertheless paid the ultimate price for our redemption. And therefore, the admission of unworthiness is a necessary ingredient of true saving faith. To feel worthy of such love is simply to confess that we know nothing of it at all.

Grasping the prevalence of unworthiness and the point of unworthiness highlights the **Paradox of Unworthiness**. It is hinted at indeed by the irony of this passage, where the centurion's forthright confession of his unworthiness is set up by the Jews' praise of his very worthiness. For so it often plays out. The most worthy are the very ones who feel their unworthiness most acutely. It fits the pattern perfectly that the Apostle Paul, the most powerful evangelist and the most profound theologian of the apostolic church, a man who was faithful through beatings and shipwrecks, saw himself as the chief of sinners (1 Tim. 1:12–15). When practiced rightly, this seeming self–abnegation is the path to the greatest assurance of God's acceptance and the greatest joy. Why? Because the focus is not on our lowliness but on Christ's exaltation. We lose ourselves in His greatness and His glory. I say it again: To feel worthy of such deep love from such a high Being is simply to confess that we know nothing of it at all.

II. The Acceptance Of Authority (v. 8)

The first component of true biblical faith shown by the centurion is the admission of unworthiness. The second is the acceptance of authority. He not only affirms Jesus' authority; he does it in terms that show that he understands what he is doing. *"Just say the word, and my servant will be healed, For I also am a man placed under authority, with soldiers under me; and I say to this one, 'Go!' and he goes, and to another, 'Come!' and he comes, and to my slave, 'Do this!' and he does it."*

The true acceptance of authority goes against the grain of fallen human nature. The poet A. E. Housman expressed our default setting perfectly:

> The laws of God, the laws of man,
> He may keep that will and can;
> Not I: Let God and man decree
> Laws for themselves and not for me.
> And if my ways are not as theirs,
> Let them mind their own affairs.
> Their deeds I judge and much condemn,
> Yet when did I make laws for them?
> Please yourselves, say I, and they
> Need only look the other way.[51]

That default setting is one of the key traits the Holy Spirit has to overcome if we are to put our faith in the Lord Jesus Christ. For if faith is the empty hand that grasps hold of a saving relationship with Jesus, the Jesus who is Lord of Lords and King of Kings, then it must perforce entail the acceptance and embracing of His right to rule. It is only as the King that He has the authority to grant us a pardon for our rebellion and receive us anew as the citizens of His Kingdom. So we are embracing not only His right to rule in general, but also specifically His right to rule over *us*.

We saw that there was a paradox of unworthiness: The more worthy a person actually is, the less worthy he feels, the more fully he appreciates his real unworthiness of the favor he has been granted. In like manner there is a paradox of accepting Christ's authority: It is only in slavery to Him that we find perfect freedom. There and only there are we free to be what we were created to be: the servants, companions, and sons and daughters of God. So just as the person who thinks he is worthy of God's grace shows by that thought that he knows nothing of it, so the person to whom Jesus is anything less than Lord shows that he knows nothing of Him nor of true faith in Him. The second mark of true faith shown by the centurion is the acceptance of authority.

III. The Ascription Of Excellence

---

[51] A. E. Housman, "The Laws of God, the Laws of Man," *Modern British and American Poetry*, op. cit., 465.

The third component of true biblical faith shown by the centurion is the ascription of excellence. A life lived by faith in Jesus is a life of praise, a life of worship, a life of adoration, a life lived to the glory of God. What else could it be? This point is not stated directly in the passage, but surely it is implied by what we do see in this centurion. How do we see it?

We see it implied first in his admission of unworthiness rightly understood. The admission of your own unworthiness is only meaningful and saving when it implies by contrast the worthiness of Christ. The admission of your own unworthiness is only meaningful and saving when it flows from an awareness of the worthiness of Christ There is nothing particularly spiritual about reveling in your own worthlessness for its own sake. There is nothing particularly spiritual about self–loathing as such. There is nothing particularly spiritual about demeaning oneself for any other reason or in any other context. The whole point of admitting our own unworthiness is to point ourselves and others to the supreme worthiness of Christ.

We see the ascription of excellence also implied in the centurion's explanation of his understanding of Jesus' authority with reference to his own. "I have authority over soldiers and servants," he says. What does that mean? "I tell them to do something, and they have to do it." This statement is only relevant to his request for the healing of his servant if we get the unstated conclusion to it, unstated but strongly implied: "I have authority over a hundred soldiers; you have authority over the universe. I can tell a few people what to do; you; you can command Nature, the elements. You can even [if we anachronistically but accurately add our modern understanding of medicine] tell germs and viruses what to do, and they will have to do it." Or, if we translate it into another form of modern parlance, "You da man!"

What do we conclude from these implications? If true biblical faith is not just a theoretical belief in certain theological truths; if it is more, the empty hand of trust that takes hold of God's promises as they are expressed *in Jesus;* then praise is a necessary ingredient of all true biblical faith. We are talking about Jesus here! So wonderful is the One we know by faith that religion that does not rush to rejoice is false faith. So wonderful is the One we know by faith that deeds which do not declare His glory are but Pharisaic self–righteousness and futile striving after wind. So wonderful is the One we know by faith that any theology which is not doxology is the worship of a lesser God. The final mark of true biblical faith is the ascription of excellence.

Conclusion

We see then that faith is not a bare theoretical belief even in the right set of theological opinions but the trust which commits. It is the empty hand of trust that takes hold of God's promises and unites us to Christ. Therefore, faith which embraces, not just a theory, but the Lord of Glory, cannot help but discover itself in the admission of unworthiness, the acceptance of authority, and the ascription of excellence. May God grant us that kind of faith today! Amen.

THE WIDOW'S SON OF NAIN

Luke 7:11 And it came about soon afterwards, that He went to a city called Nain. And his disciples were going with him, accompanied by a large multitude. 12 Now as He approached the gate of the city, behold, a dead man was being carried out, the only son of his mother, and she was a widow; and a sizeable crowd from the city was with her. 13 And when the Lord saw her, He felt compassion for her, and said to her, "Do not weep." 14 And He came up and touched the coffin; and the bearers came to a halt. And He said, "Young man, I say to you, arise!" 15 And the dead man sat up and began to speak. And Jesus gave him back to his mother. 16 And fear gripped them all, and they began glorifying God, saying, "A great prophet has arisen among us!" and "God has visited His people!" 17 And this report concerning Him went out all over Judea and in all the surrounding district. (NASB)

Introduction

John the beloved disciple tells us that, if everything about Jesus were to be told, the whole world could not have contained the books (John 21:25). Therefore, those incidents that are included have been selected for a reason. Every miracle story — like this one, for example — is not just another impressive narrative but was chosen by the Gospel writer to tell us something we need to know about Jesus. This one obviously tells us that He could raise the dead. But it tells us a lot more than that. I see at least four important concepts here that are relevant to all disciples who follow Jesus Christ today.

1. The Compassion Of Christ (v. 13)

And when the Lord saw her, He felt compassion for her, and said to her, "Do not weep."

You know, like the Lord, I passed a funeral on the road myself the other day: a hearse followed by a long line of cars all burning their headlights in broad daylight. I followed our quaint Southern custom of pulling off the road and stopping until they were past to honor the deceased and show respect to his loved ones. I did not begrudge showing that much respect; but because I did not know the people involved, I hardly gave it a second thought, and I continued on my way as soon as they were past. Jesus, on the other hand, took a different approach: He flipped on His own lights, as it were, turned His car around, and joined the procession to the gravesite.

Since His funeral party was not ensconced in two-ton steel projectiles, Jesus was able to make His way immediately to the side of the grieving mother, a widow who had lost not only her husband but now her only son—which may well have meant her only prop for existence. And Jesus felt compassion for her and said something very interesting: "Do not weep."

We've all said something like that in awkward situations: "Don't cry." But what in the world do we mean by it? Sometimes we really mean, "Don't cry—you're making me uncomfortable." Sometimes we ironically mean, "I wish you didn't need to cry—but go ahead; there's nothing else we can do." And if we are really kind and empathetic we may join the weeper in her tears. Christ set us an example in this when he wept at the tomb of Lazarus. He was going to do something much more radical than that, but first He joined the suffering people in their tears. He did not skip that step! But there is also a third scenario that some of us have enacted, perhaps when rushing to the side of one of our children when they were little. Then, "Don't cry" may mean, "Your cry for help has been answered. So you can stop crying now: *I am here!*" This poor widow could not have known she was in a position to hope for anything more than the second meaning: "I sympathize." But this third one was what Jesus was really saying, as she would soon discover to her everlasting astonishment and joy.

What is the point? There is sorrow, tragedy, and pain in every life in this room sufficient to make us all cry if we were to think about it too long and hard. "Man is but dust," said John Donne, who has been "coagulated and kneaded into earth by tears."[52] But the Lord Jesus Christ, representing God the Father, still says to us—He says it this very moment as we read this passage—"Do not weep!" And what does He mean? He means, "I join you in your tears here and now. I too was a man of sorrows and acquainted with grief. I was tempted in all ways like as you are. I know! In understand!" But He says more than that: "The day is coming when all your tears will be wiped away." In its fullness at the Second Coming, we will hear—by foretaste and down payment even now, we may hear—Jesus saying, "Your cry for help has been answered. So you can stop crying now: *I am here!*" Jesus, representing the Father, says it to us. And we, representing Jesus, should be saying it for Him with meaning to others: "Do not weep! Don't cry!" For Christ is here; and we are here on His behalf.

The first lesson this passage highlights for us is then the compassion of Christ, and by implication the compassion that should be ours. But the second one is . . .

II. The Power Of Christ (vv. 14–15)

And He came up and touched the coffin; and the bearers came to a halt. And He said, "Young man, I say to you, arise!" And the dead man sat up and began to speak. And Jesus gave him back to his mother.

As a Minister of the Gospel, I have often had to preside at funerals. There one has the great privilege of offering comfort, sympathy, support, and hope based on the glorious Gospel of salvation in Jesus Christ. But there is also in such moments a feeling of impotence. I can offer hope for the future if the deceased was a believer, but I cannot reverse what has happened in the immediate past. I can offer comfort for the present, but I cannot fill the gap that has been left in people's lives. But the point of this passage is that Jesus could. The amazing point of this passage is that Jesus did. The astounding

---

[52] John Donne, *Devotions Upon Emergent Occasions*, "Meditation VIII" (1624), in Alexander M. Witherspoon and Frank J. Warnke, eds., *Seventeenth Century Prose and Poetry*, 2nd. ed. (NY: Harcourt Brace Jovanovich, 1982), 64.

point of this passage is that Jesus can. The glorious point of this passage is that Jesus will. For *the dead man sat up and began to speak.*

The power manifested by any victory is revealed by the greatness of the Foe who has been defeated; so also the glory that accrues to the Victor is coordinated with the majesty of the Foe overcome. I recall in 1980 when the University of Georgia defeated Notre Dame in the Sugar Bowl to win the national championship, that Coach Vince Dooley was carried off the field by his team in celebration. The following year, I was present in Sanford Stadium when the "Dawgs" defeated the Richmond Spiders—that year's homecoming patsy—by a rather astronomical score for those days of Dooley's conservative, three–yards–and–a–cloud–of–dust offense. The margin of victory was much greater, but somehow nobody seemed to think it was much of a big deal. Coach Dooley had to walk off the field on his own two legs. The power manifested by any victory is revealed by the greatness of the Foe who has been defeated.

Well, what is the Enemy being overcome here? Jesus overcomes the futility, the finality, the irrevocable void, of Death. In Greek mythology, Hades, the god of the Underworld, the god of the Dead, is the most hated of all the immortals, because he is the only god who never answers prayer. Never.

The exception that proves the rule is the story of Orpheus and Eurydice. Orpheus was the greatest of mortal musicians. When his beloved wife, Eurydice, died, he simply could not accept the finality of that loss. So he took his harp and journeyed to the Underworld. There he played so beautifully, sang so poignantly of mortal sorrow, that tears of molten iron ran down the implacable face of Hades, and for the only time ever recorded, he relented. Eurydice would be permitted to follow Orpheus back into the world of the living, the world of the sun. But he must not look behind him until they had both safely emerged from the darkness of Hades' realm back into the sunlight. So imagine what he is feeling as he begins the long walk through the tunnel. He sees the small point of light at the end, he sees it turn into a disc, and he begins to hear faint footsteps, growing ever more solid, as Eurydice begins to resume physical form as light begins to seep back into the cave. How he wants to look and see her again, to verify that it is her footsteps that he hears! But he dare not. And now they have almost emerged. One more step and the quest will be achieved—life snatched back from the grave! But at that moment she stumbles against a stone and cries out, and by instinct, without thinking, he turns to catch her and keep her from falling. But he has broken the ban, he has violated the requirement, he has transgressed the taboo. It is one step too soon—one lousy step! And so he turns only to see her for one intolerably heartbreaking moment reaching for him as she evaporates, loses the substantial physical form she had so briefly recovered, and fades back into the mist, forever lost in the darkness.

Hades is the only god who never answers prayer. And that is the hardest thing about Death to accept: that impenetrable stone wall suddenly erected across your path, that steel door slammed in your face. No matter how important and essential the deceased was to your life, you aren't getting him back. That is what makes Death the great and final Enemy: "The last enemy to be defeated is death" (1 Cor. 15:26). And *that* is what Jesus overcame! No wonder the people were filled with terror and awe when the dead man sat up and began to speak.

The second lesson we learn from this passage is the power of Christ. And the third is . . .

III. The Paradigm Of Christ's Acts

The third thing we must see in this passage as a whole is a paradigm, a basic pattern or grid for understanding all the acts of Jesus as we read about them in the New Testament. What does this victory tell us about Jesus? And how does it do this telling? This deed and others like it do two things: they Announce His Character, and they Anticipate His Coming.

First, the miracle stories in the Gospels **Announce Christ's Character**. They tell us who He is. C. S. Lewis analyzed this aspect of the miracle stories brilliantly in his great apologetic work, *Miracles*.[53] What does it tell you when water is turned into wine — suddenly and immediately, without the normal apparatus of a grapevine and a wine vat? It tells you that the Reality which pagans ignorantly worshipped as Bacchus, the god of wine — the Reality of which Bacchus was only a faint and corrupted reflection in the minds of men — that Reality has come, is here! What does it tell you when Jesus multiplies the loaves and fishes? It tells you that the Reality which pagans ignorantly worshipped as Ceres, the god of harvest — the Reality of which Ceres was only a faint and corrupted reflection in the minds of men — that Reality has come, is here! What does it tell you when Jesus stills the winds and the waves? It tells you that the Reality which pagans ignorantly worshipped as Poseidon, the god of the sea — the Reality of which Poseidon was only a faint and corrupted reflection in the minds of men — that Reality has come, is here! And what does it tell you when Christ raises the dead? It tells you that One who is stronger than Hades, greater than all the false gods, One stronger even than Fate, has come, and now stands before you. If you are an ancient Jew you know that it must be Jehovah. If you are an ancient Greek you realize that your whole concept of what deity is has just been shattered and now has to be rebuilt from scratch. And what if you are a modern secular American? Oh, my.

The first thing the miracles stories do is to announce Christ's character: He is the Son of the living God. But a second thing the miracle stories in the Gospels do is to **Anticipate Christ's (second) Coming**. For Scripture itself teaches us to read such passages in terms of the principle of the Pledge or Down Payment. Paul tells us that when we accepted Christ we were *"sealed in Him with the Holy Spirit of promise, who is given as a pledge of our inheritance"* (Eph. 1:13–14). Another way of seeing the same principle is in terms of a Foretaste. Hebrews describes us as having *"tasted the good word*

---

[53] C. S. Lewis, *Miracles: A Preliminary Study* (N.Y.: MacMillan, 1947), 116–21, 140ff.

of God and the powers of the age to come" (Heb. 6:5). So what Christ does in the Gospel miracles is to give us a glimpse, a sneak preview, as it were, of what He is going to do on a cosmic scale when He returns. I remember how excited some of us were when the first previews of Peter Jackson's *Lord of the Rings* movies started showing up in the theaters or on television. Well, some of us don't think the movie quite lived up to our expectations. But *these* previews are not going to disappoint! When we look back to the miracle stories of the Gospels, or when we look to the no less supernatural and astounding miracle of our own regeneration right now, we should connect these things together as an eloquent whole that both whets our appetite for the future and builds our faith in the meantime. May God allow them to work, to make it so, in our lives.

The third thing this passage gives us is a paradigm for understanding Christ's acts: the paradigm of the Pledge, the Down Payment. And the fourth thing it shows us is . . .

IV. The Promise Of Christ (v. 16)

And fear gripped them all, and they began glorifying God, saying, "A great prophet has arisen among us!" and "God has visited His people!"

God has visited His people! And because that visit of old was not an isolated event but a paradigm, we know He will visit us again to complete the work that was begun then. Therefore, the Compassion of Christ, the Power of Christ, and the Paradigm by which we should read His actions lead us to our last point: the Promise of Christ, the Hope that He gives us for the future. When I read this passage and others like it, I know that the Day is coming when Jesus will finally say to all of us, "Do not weep." The comfort He gave to this widow then, the comfort He gives to His disciples even now, all point to that Day which is coming. So when I read this passage, I know that a Day is coming when all the injustices, the futility, and the petty hassles of life will be no more. When I read this passage, I know that a Day is coming when the whips and scorns of time, the proud man's contumely, the oppressor's wrong, the pangs of despised love, the law's delay and the thousand natural shocks that flesh is heir to[54] will be no more. When I read this passage, I know that a Day is coming when my grandfather and grandmother whom I buried, my father and mother, and my mentor Dr. Orme, whom I saw buried, will stand before me in glorified flesh. When I read this passage I know that a Day is coming when my experience in the summer of 1994 will be reversed.

For about thirty minutes that summer, time was frozen for me in the churchyard of the Headington Quarry parish church as I knelt at the grave of C. S. Lewis. Never has the weight of our mortality bowed me down more severely than at that moment. For I had been hanging on every published word of this man for over twenty–five years. He had saved me from apostasy when I was a doubting and questioning high school student; he had taught me how to think like a Christian. I literally owed this man my

---

[54] "Hamlet," act III, scene i, lines 56f, *Shakespeare: The Complete Works*, op, cit., 906.

life and had come to feel I knew him and loved him as a friend. And here he was only six feet away. But the barrier of Death was a more solid wall between us than the stone slab of his tomb or the steel walls of his casket: Had I broken through those barriers the distance would still have been infinite and unbridgeable. I had been closer to him with my nose in one of his books on the other side of the Atlantic. I was looking for a closer connection, but I was absolutely stymied. *That* is what Death has done to us! And so the truth of the words carved on the stone was carved also into my soul: "Men must endure their going hence."

THE GRAVE OF C. S. LEWIS

> There was a marble slab, the evidence
>> Of burial, with writing on the stone
>> Which said, "Men must endure their going hence."
> The mind that had restored my mind to sense
>> Was here reduced to elemental bone;
>> There was a marble slab, the evidence.
> That well of wisdom and of eloquence
>> Was now cut back to just one phrase alone
>> Which said, "Men must endure their going hence."
> No monument of rich magnificence
>> Stood fitting one who had so brightly shone;
>> There was a marble slab. The evidence
> That plain things have their power to convince
>> Was in that simple block with letters strewn
>> Which said, "Men must endure their going hence."
> The weight of Time was focused there, intense
>> With wrecked Creation's universal groan:
>> There was a marble slab, the evidence,
> Which said, "Men must endure their going hence."[55]

But that was not the last word to be uttered. For in the silence of that moment I could also hear the voice of Izaak Walton applying to Lewis the words he had originally written for seventeenth–century poet and pastor John Donne:

"He was earnest and unwearied in the search of knowledge; with which his vigorous soul is now satisfied and employed in a continual praise of that God that first breathed it into his active body, that body that was once a temple of the Holy Ghost and is now become a small quantity of Christian dust."

---

[55] Donald T. Williams, "The Grave of C. S. Lewis: Headington Parish Church, Oxfordshire. Villanelle no. 15," *Christianity and Literature* 44:2 (Winter 1995), 180; rpt. in *Stars Through the Clouds: The Collected Poetry of Donald T. Williams.* Op. cit., 350.

"But I shall see it reanimated!"[56]

The fourth lesson we learn from this passage is the promise of Christ.

Conclusion

Christians are people of joy because even in the midst of their greatest sorrows they are people of hope. Why? Because of the way the compassion of Christ, the power of Christ, the paradigm by which we understand Christ, and hence the promise of Christ are revealed by stories such as this one. Because already it lets us hear Jesus say, provisionally "Do not weep! Help has arrived! I am here!" Because on that Day Jesus will say, finally and forever, "Do not weep! Help has arrived! I am here!" I know that Day will come because when I read Luke's Gospel I know that *this* day *came*. That is the hope the Bible gives us. Let us share it with the world, by saying, with our mouths and with our deeds as Jesus' representatives, "Do not weep." And let us praise the Father for it.

---

[56] Izaak Walton, *The Life of Dr. John Donne* (1675), in Alexander M. Witherspoon and Frank J. Warnke, eds., *Seventeenth Century Prose and Poetry*, 2nd. ed. (NY: Harcourt Brace Jovanovich, 1982), 271.

JUST THE FACTS

Luke 7:18 And the disciples of John reported to him about all these things. 19 And summoning two of his disciples, John sent them to the Lord, saying, "Are you the Expected One, or do we look for someone else?" 20 And when the men had come to him, they said, "John the Baptist has sent us to you, saying, 'are you the Expected One, or do we look for someone else?'" 21 At that very time he cured many people of diseases and afflictions and evil spirits; and he granted sight to many who were blind. 22 And he said to them, "Go and report to John what you have seen and heard: 'The blind receive their sight,' the lame walk, the lepers are cleansed, and the deaf hear, the dead are raised up, the 'poor have the Gospel preached to them.' 23 And blessed is he who keeps from stumbling over me."

Introduction

What can possibly have been wrong with John the Baptist in this passage? He was the last of the Old Testament prophets. He was the Forerunner of the Messiah. He was the first to announce Jesus as the Lamb of God who taketh away the sins of the world (John 1:29). So what in the world is he doing now in verse 20 wondering whether he had made a big mistake in saying all that? There is an answer that makes sense once you understand John's Jewish background, once you understand where he was coming from. This is a passage about the power of preconceived notions. It is a topic so important that Luke is hitting it for the second time, as you will realize if you can recall our discussion of blind spots a few weeks ago, when Jesus warned about the blind leading the blind and trying to do eye surgery when they needed log–odectomies themselves. (See the sermon "Doing What I Say," Luke 6:39–49, above.) Well, if Luke thought it that important, I'm going to hit it again too. What does this passage have to add?

I. The Problem Of Preconceived Notions

In order to understand what was happening here, we must remind ourselves of some of the particular preconceived notions to which first–century Jews were subject. For they were so strong that they were able, in the case of John apparently, to obscure the truth and raise doubts about it even in sincere and godly people who were the recipients and channels of special revelation! First–century Jews, as we know, were looking for a military Messiah who would overthrow Roman occupation and restore to Israel the glory of the Davidic kingdom and the Solomonic empire. How did they ever come to hold such a view? Well, the Old Testament is full of prophecies about the coming of Christ. But the interpretation of those prophecies was never clear until Christ had in fact come and fulfilled them.

You see, the Old Testament talks about the Messiah, which means "anointed one." This is the Son of David who would reign on his throne forever. It also mentions a Prophet like Moses, the Suffering Servant of Isaiah, and the Son of Man of Daniel. Now that Christ has come, we know that all these figures are one and the same person, our Lord. But there is not one single verse in all the Old Testament that identifies them in that way. From just reading the Old Testament you cannot tell whether they are supposed to be one person or four. (This is an important point to realize about the very nature of biblical prophecy, by the way: It is not intended to let us predict the future, but rather to enable us to *recognize* God's fulfillment *when it happens.* We ought to remember that when we are generating confident dogmas about the interpretation of those prophecies that deal with our Lord's Second Coming!)

Jews at the time of Jesus all held to a view of those messianic prophecies that did not identify the four figures but took them as separate persons. The basic assumption was a scenario something like this: The Messiah would be the new king to overthrow Rome and re–establish the kingdom, the Prophet like Moses was going to be his press secretary, and the Suffering Servant would be a warrior whose self–sacrifice in the war with Rome would allow the Messiah to achieve victory. This did not of course turn out to be the correct interpretation. But until Christ came, there was no way to disprove it based on the Old Testament alone. It was not the "clear teaching of Scripture." It was an assumption! But people did not realize that it was an assumption and therefore did not treat it like an assumption. Denying this view, insisting on the identity of the four figures, especially of the Messiah with the Suffering Servant, was the "heresy" that caused the Jewish religious establishment to reject Jesus' messianic claims and ultimately have Him executed. This shows us how important it is to know the difference between what Scripture says and our own assumptions read into the text. It can be a matter of spiritual life or death!

Well, the Roman occupation was the Jewish preoccupation, and John the Baptist was no exception. God had revealed to him that Jesus was the Messiah, and also this little bit about taking away sins (the Lamb of God who taketh away the sins of the world, John 1:29), which John had obediently proclaimed even though he apparently did not completely see how it fit in with the "obvious" truth that the days of Rome's rule were numbered. But now doubts had begun to creep in—could he have gotten it all wrong somehow? Because Jesus did not seem to be acting very messianic. All these miracles and healings and all this parabolic teaching was all well and good, but when was the revolution going to start? As Dorothy L. Sayers has him say it in her wonderful series of plays on the life of Christ, *The Man Born to be King*, "When will the long spears go up to Jerusalem?"[57] Or, to use the words that are recorded, *"Are you the Expected One, or do we look for someone else?"* Preconceived notions can be a huge problem indeed.

Well, we modern people don't have any preconceived notions that hinder our reception and understanding of God's Word, do we? Yeah, right. If you have ever tried

---

[57] Dorothy L. Sayers, *The Man Born to be King* (Grand Rapids, MI: Eerdmans, 1943), 107.

to do any witnessing, you know that no matter how clearly you explain the Gospel of salvation by grace through faith alone, modern people already "know" that a God of love would not require the blood of Christ as the grounds of our forgiveness and that any salvation we do receive has to be on the basis of our works—and theirs are surely good enough. It is all but impossible to keep our words from going through that grid and being translated into those terms, no matter what we say—unless the Holy Spirit is powerfully at work in the person's life.

Okay, at least we Christians have gotten rid of all of our preconceived notions, haven't we? I hope that particular preconceived notion isn't one of yours! Could you have any preconceived notions? What are they? Well, if you knew what they were, they wouldn't be preconceived notions, now, would they? That's the problem; that's what makes them so powerful and hard to defeat. It is much like the blind spots we were talking about a few weeks ago, the logs sticking out of our eyes as the blind being led by (or, worse, leading) the blind.

I don't know what your preconceived notions are, but here are some that I have encountered operating powerfully in Christians who ought to know better. Many of us still have the same set as the non–Christians we already discussed, only in a more subtle and less blatant form. We believe in salvation by grace through faith, but we get discouraged and doubt God's work in our lives because we are really still living as if it had to be achieved by our works. Here is another one: Many people have the unspoken assumption that godliness is all about our emotions rather than our thoughts or actions. They spend an incredible amount of energy trying to engineer and maintain a very artificial emotional state which they confuse with sanctification, even though all kinds of ungodliness can still hide in their lives quite compatibly with it.

On a different front, many of us assume that the particular brand of theology we were taught is obviously biblical, and everything else is in error. You wonder how Pentecostals can so blatantly read their experience into the Text? Well, I have known some of God's Frozen People who read their lack of experience into the Text. And there are some Calvinists who very efficiently read the Westminster Confession into the Text! It is not as easy to keep the Text in charge of our thinking as we think it is. And how about this one: "If God loves me, then I won't have any problems in my life, so if I do, they must stem from my lack of faith. For if I had perfect faith, I would also have health and wealth and would be able to 'blab it and grab it.'" Where do people get this stuff? It is not in the Bible—but once you have adopted it as a preconceived notion, you can find it there anyway in ways that are simply astonishing—to those who do not share that *particular* preconceived notion. You begin to see what a huge problem this is—as big potentially to us as it was to John. Unchecked, our own preconceived notions can take us to the point where we too are capable of asking, *"Are you the Expected One, or do we look for someone else?"*

II. The Power Of Preconceived Notions

To realize the problem and the power of preconceived notions is a sobering thing indeed. Why are they so powerful? Their power over us comes from at least three sources. The first is one we have already mentioned: they are by their very nature hidden. They are like a pair of built–in glasses that make us see everything with spiritual astigmatism. But because they are built in, it never occurs to us to take them off and see what the world, or the Bible, would look like without them. The second is our own nature. This has two aspects. The first is that the Natural Mind, the mind of the Old Man, does not receive the things of the Spirit of God, neither can it know them, being spiritually discerned (1 Cor. 2:14). And while the process of renewing our minds begins when we accept Christ as Lord and Savior, it is not yet completed in any of us. Therefore, there is a part of our minds that is susceptible to worldly preconceptions. The second aspect of our own natures that makes preconceived notions so powerful is our pride. We would rather rationalize them than admit we are wrong. The third overall reason for their power is not only their hiddenness and our natures but the fact that Satan is at work to enhance their influence in our lives, to keep us unaware of them and to encourage us to continue following them blindly.

The power of preconceived notions is seen in a number of biblical examples, especially the one we are examining today. John the Baptist had many advantages as a student of the Word of God. He was filled with the Holy Spirit from his mother's womb. He was raised by Zacharias, the most godly priest of that generation. He was a cousin of the Lord Jesus Christ. To him the Father had revealed Jesus as the Lamb of God. And he had been an eyewitness of Christ's character. Nevertheless, with all these advantages, he was capable of asking, *"Are you the Expected One, or do we look for someone else?"*

How much more must we be concerned about the power of preconceived notions, who operate without many of those advantages? The disciples were also people with many advantages. They were personally chosen by Christ. They followed Him, lived with Him, for three years. They were eyewitnesses not only of His character but also of His miracles. They heard His teaching from His own lips and had the opportunity to ask all the questions they wanted. They were eyewitnesses of the Resurrection. And yet, just as He was ready to go back to Heaven, they were asking, *"Is it now that you will restore the Kingdom to Israel?"* (Acts 1:6). The same preconceived notion that had led John astray was still potent in their own minds after all of that. How much more must we be concerned with the power of preconceived notions to hinder our walk with the Lord?

The effects of preconceived notions that are not identified and dealt with can be profound. Because of them a sincere servant of God who was filled with the Holy Spirit and who was a diligent student of Scripture could be so out of synch with God's program that he teetered on the brink of apostasy. He was so out of synch with what God was doing that he wrestled with an almost debilitating doubt. And he was on the verge of allowing that doubt to dishonor Christ and affect the faith of others. We are vulnerable to all these effects as well. Therefore, we had better pay close attention to the next point:

III. The Prescription For Preconceived Notions

How can we combat an enemy so hidden, so powerful, so insidious? Jesus' answer to John's question contains some answers: First, go back to the facts; and always, go back to your relationship with Jesus.

1. Go Back to the Facts (verse 22). *"Go tell John what you see and hear."* The Old Testament prophets had performed miracles, healings, even resurrections. But these were usually done for isolated individuals. Never before had there been such a wholesale application of supernatural power as was seen in Jesus' ministry. And as the Old–Testament allusions in his answer show, they were all quite specifically signs of the Messiah's ministry. They were quite sufficient to prove that Jesus' claims were valid. However confused John might be by his approach, it did not change the facts.

Doubts are often based on theories, expectations, what–ifs. These are all things that are lower in the scale of warrants for belief than facts are. "It is always a capital mistake, Watson," Sherlock Holmes says more than once, "to theorize in advance of the facts."[58] So, while preconceived notions can cause us to see things in Scripture that are not there and to ignore things that are there, if we remind ourselves that we might be influenced by them and therefore pay close attention to the facts of the Text, asking God to show us where we might be wrong, we have the opportunity to realize that there might be a disconnect between what we think we ought to be seeing in Scripture and what we are in fact seeing — or maybe between what we think we ought to be seeing, what we are in fact seeing, and what is really there. The distress from noticing this disconnect is called "cognitive dissonance." It is an opportunity to become aware of our preconceived notions and to allow the Text of Scripture to correct them. It is an opportunity we need to be constantly on the lookout for. We must understand the insidious nature of preconceived notions and therefore be vigilant in looking for this opportunity. We must always be going back to the facts.

2. Go Back to your Relationship with Jesus (verse 23). *"Blessed,"* said the Lord, *"is he who keeps from stumbling over me."* Whenever we catch ourselves stumbling over Jesus, whenever something hinders our relationship with him, it should be a sign to us that a preconceived notion may be operating in us. Therefore, it is a sign that some serious self–examination, some serious questioning of our own assumptions, is in order. When you go back to the facts, you are ultimately going to be left with this question: Do you trust Him? Or do you trust yourself? It ultimately boils down to one of those two options. His ways are not your ways. He is infinitely wise; you are sinful and

---

[58] See for example Sir Arthur Conan Doyle, "A Study in Scarlet," *The Annotated Sherlock Holmes*, 2 cols., ed. Willia, S. Baring-Gould (NY: Clarkson N. Potter, 1997), 1:167; cf. "The Adventure of the Second Stain," 1:311, etc.

foolish. Therefore, it is a perfectly rational expectation that you are sometimes going to wonder what He is up to! When you do, don't stumble over Him. He deserves your trust. He earned it by going to the Cross for you. That is the chief, the most important, of the Facts we are to keep going back to.

Conclusion

If John the Baptist had a problem with preconceived notions, you can bet that we do too. No matter how biblical your thinking, no matter how biblical your theology, it is not perfect. It stands in need of correction. We must never forget that! Sooner or later, like John, you are going to have a problem with what Jesus is doing in your life. When you do, recognize the possibility of preconceived notions at work in your life. Go back to the facts. Go back to your relationship with Christ. And do not stumble over Him!

JESUS AND JOHN THE BAPTIST

Luke 7:24 And when the messengers of John had left, He began to speak to the multitudes about John. "What did you go out into the wilderness to look at? A reed shaken by the wind? 25 But what did you go out to see? A man dressed in soft clothing? Behold, those who are splendidly clothed and live in luxury are found in royal palaces! 26 But what did you go out to see? A prophet? Yes, I say to you, and one who is more than a prophet. 27 This is the one about whom it is written, 'Behold, I send my messenger before your face, who will prepare your way before you.' 28 I say to you, among those born of women there is no one greater than John; yet he who is least in the kingdom of God is greater than he." 29 And when all the people and the tax gatherers heard this, they acknowledge God's justice, having been baptized with the baptism of John. 30 But the Pharisees and the lawyers rejected God's purpose for themselves, not having been baptized by John. 31 "To what then shall I compare this generation, and what are they like? 32 They are like children who sit in the market place and call to one another. And they say, 'We played the flute for you and you did not dance; we sang a dirge, and you did not weep.' 33 For John the Baptist has come eating no bread and drinking no wine, and you said, 'He has a demon!' 34 The Son of Man has come eating and drinking, and you say, 'Behold, a gluttonous man and a drunkard, a friend of tax gatherers and sinners!' 35 Yet wisdom is vindicated by all her children."

Introduction

Last time we left John the Baptist languishing in prison, hearing exciting things about Jesus' ministry, maybe feeling a bit left out, and not hearing some of the things he thought he should have been hearing. We left him thinking, "Okay, all this healing and all these parables are great, but where is the Kingdom? Let's get organized, let's get moving! Rome is still in control! When are we going to overthrow the Roman Empire and bring in the *Kingdom*?" And therefore, he had sent his disciples to ask the Lord, *"Are you the One who is coming, or do we look for another?"*

We saw the way John's question flowed from his preconceived notions—ones that he shared with almost every first–century Jew, including Jesus' own disciples, who did not get rid of theirs until the Day of Pentecost. Even at the Ascension they were asking, "Are we going to do it now? Are we going to restore the Kingdom to Israel now?" (Acts 1:6). In all of that, we saw the problem and the power of preconceived notions. And in Jesus' answer to John's question, we saw a prescription for what to do about our preconceived notions: to go back to the facts (*"Tell John what you see and hear"*) and to go back to your relationship with Christ (*"Blessed is the one who does not stumble over me"*).

Now in the passage that is before us today, John's disciples have been dispatched to bring Jesus' answer back to him. We meanwhile are not given much time to wonder how he is going to respond to it. For as John's disciples leave, Jesus immediately turns to the crowd, to the people who have been overhearing this little exchange. And he has something to say to them—and therefore to us. Let's see if we can hear it. It tells us something about Jesus' Concern, about John's Character, and about a Generation at the Crossroads.

I. Jesus' Concern

In the midst of what must have been a rather tense (and disappointing) encounter, Jesus shows a touching concern for His cousin's reputation. John had been out of line, and Jesus' answer to His disciples necessarily contained what could only be heard as a rebuke: *"Blessed is the one who does not stumble over me,"* which of course implied that John was in danger of stumbling. It also sounds very much like Jesus telling John to remember his place. Well, the people had unavoidably overheard this conversation, even though it should ideally have been conducted privately. But so what? John had asked for it, hadn't he? Besides, he was being phased out anyway. His ministry was basically over, so what difference did it make? Well, it made a lot of difference to our Lord. The crowd had overheard a message intended for John's ears only, and one that did not exactly put him in a complimentary light. So Jesus moves quickly to put this situation right, to make sure that they do not misunderstand or leave with a lower estimation of John's character or his importance. The bottom line? *"I say to you, among those born of women there is no one greater than John; yet he who is least in the kingdom of God is greater than he."*

There is surely a lesson for us in our Lord's example here. John had just gone from being the most exciting and popular religious figure of his day to being a prisoner, on the sidelines and eclipsed by the rising popularity of Christ himself. John's star was on the wane, his life was at risk, and it was dangerous now to be known as his friend. When he had said in one of his better and more theologically profound moments that *"He must increase, and I must decrease,"* I doubt that this was what he had in mind! But despite the potential political ramifications, the Lord serves notice that there is one friend who is not going to desert John, even at this moment when he least deserves that loyalty—for John's own loyalty to Christ had been wavering. Does the Lord's response here not bring your heart up into your throat? For he is *our* Lord too! As Paul put it to Timothy, even *"If we are faithless, He remains faithful, for He cannot deny Himself"* (2 Tim. 2:13). Oh, let us trust in Him and let us follow Him! For he said, *"You are my friends if you do whatever I command you"* (John 15:14). The favor of the crowd is fickle; but the friendship of Christ is forever!

There is here perhaps a faint echo of Jesus' own word in the Sermon on the Mount: *"Blessed are you when men say all manner of evil against you falsely for my sake."* Why blessed? Because that's how their fathers treated the prophets. But also because whatever men may say about us must now be weighed against the Lord's word, *"Well done, thou good and faithful servant!"* (Mat. 25:21). And, put into that balance, the words of men fall to the ground as less than empty air. Look what Jesus says about John even when John had not been exactly faithful! But, John's doubts aside—they had earned him a rebuke that should have been private—look what Jesus said about John publicly. How would you respond to an earthly boss who went out of his way to affirm you publicly when people thought they had a reason to doubt where you stood? Would this win your gratitude? Inspire your loyalty? Motivate you to service that would make his good words about you true? You know it would. And this is our Lord! The favor of the crowd is fickle; but the friendship of Christ is forever.

Satan understands how much our reputations matter to us. He twists that good and honorable motive into one of his chief ploys. If you do this—or do not do that—you are a sissy, a wimp, uncool. When Satan says such things to you, remember Jesus' turning to the crowd to speak about John at this moment. For then you may know that Christ says to you also, "I understand. I care. Do not faint, because I know differently. And the day is coming when you will be vindicated by me before the whole universe." At the Day of Judgment when all the nations are gathered—including the ones who called you names—when Jesus is revealed as the King of kings and Lord of lords and every knee is bowed, He will put his arm around your shoulder and say in front of them all, "This is my good and faithful servant _____. I am pleased with him! John the Baptist was great, the greatest prophet who ever lived. But in the gracious accounting of the Kingdom, this servant of mine is greater than that!" Ah, my friends, do not live for the fickle praises of men. Live for that day! For the favor of the crowd is fickle; but the friendship of Christ is forever.

II. John's Character

As we try to understand fully what Jesus said about John here, I want you to appreciate our Master's consummate skill with words, His absolute mastery of rhetoric, in this speech. You must picture this as an interactive exchange. It was probably a lot like the "call–and–response" style of African–American preaching we are familiar with. Jesus begins where the people are and uses rhetorical questions to get them with him, and then suddenly takes them to a surprising and paradoxical place they had not expected to go. *"What did y'all go out into the wilderness to see?"* he asks them. *"A reed shaken by the wind?"* Well, that is just about the silliest description of John the Baptist you can imagine. That scruffy–looking, leather–wearing, locust–eating, desert–living, sin–denouncing, repentance–calling prophet, who challenged Herod's illegal marriage and was so politically incorrect that he got himself arrested and thrown into prison? Yeah, right! You have to imagine the crowd laughing and responding, "No way!" Just as Jesus wanted them too.

"Well, what did you go to see? A man dressed in soft clothing?" More laughter; more raucous denials. The very idea! *"People who dress like that are in the king's palace!"* And now the heads are nodding in the affirmative. Jesus has these people in the palm of His hand. *"Okay, what did you go out to see? A Prophet?"* "That's right! Yes, sir! Amen! Preach

it, brother!" And so now comes the perfect time to hit them with the punch line. Oh, yes, he was a prophet, all right, but not just any prophet. He was the voice crying in the wilderness, *"Prepare ye the way of the Lord!"* He was the greatest prophet who ever lived. And you know what? The very least member of the Kingdom of God is greater than that!

I guess if you want people to swallow a paradox like that, you had better build them up to it! You and I are greater than John? Everyone in the Kingdom is greater than he was? Does that mean he is not in the Kingdom? No, that is the wrong question to ask; it misses the point entirely. John himself, *as a member of the Kingdom*, is a greater thing than John considered *as the greatest prophet* who ever lived.

Two kinds of greatness are in view here, in other words, and John had both. In the first sense, he was great because he had a very important job to do and he did it supremely well, achieving fame even in the eyes of men thereby. This is greatness of accomplishment, and by that standard there is no prophet, indeed no person, who has ever risen higher. But the greatness conveyed by Grace is infinitely higher than that. By the gracious accounting of the Kingdom, the very least person who knows Christ as his Savior has a higher status than that of prophet, even the greatest prophet. We are children of God! Friends of Christ! Joint–heirs with Christ! In the person of Christ, our Head, we sit at the right hand of the Throne on high! By His Grace, and by His Grace alone, we (and John) will be enabled to hear Him say without untruth, *"This is my good and faithful servant, in whom I am well pleased"* (Mat. 25:21). He will share his glory with us. *"I say to you, among those born of women there is no one greater than John; yet he who is least in the kingdom of God is greater than he."*

III. A Generation At The Crossroads (vv. 29–35)

We've seen the concern of Jesus and the character of John; now we see a generation at the crossroads.; By this time, everyone has forgotten all about the fact that John was rebuked, just as Jesus intended. And now those whose hearts were enlightened by the Spirit can contemplate the potential meaning of God's grace for their own lives. This of course presents you with a choice; it places you at a spiritual crossroads—as Jesus also intended. You have two and only two options: you can "justify" God, or you can attempt to "justify" yourself. "Acknowledge God's justice" in the NASB is literally "Justify God." "Justify" is the same word we use in soteriology, the doctrine of salvation. Its noun form is "justification." It means "to declare righteous." So we can declare that God is righteous and accept His purpose for us, the blessing of the "greatness" of the Kingdom that comes only by grace, unmerited favor. Or we can try to justify ourselves like the Pharisees did. If we insist on that, we refuse God's purpose for us, but we do not escape His righteousness, which now has no choice but to condemn us.

Make sure you follow the logic of this exchange. The only reason for justifying oneself and rejecting God's gracious purpose for us could be a most appalling perverseness of heart—unfortunately one typical of fallen human beings. That is the point of the children calling out in verse 32: Their friends illustrate the attitude required in those who justify themselves. The children's friends are very hard to please! We played the flutes and you wouldn't dance; we sang a dirge and you wouldn't mourn. What do you want? John was ascetic, and you said he had a demon; Jesus ate and drank, and you accused Him of gluttony and drunkenness. What do you want? If you *will* not be pleased, then you must remain unblessed. In this case, to remain unblessed is to remain in the curse of your sins. What other alternative is there?

I'm afraid we meet an awful lot of this attitude still, and it shows up very often in relation to the Church. If the people aren't too friendly and hence "pushy," they're too stand–offish; the preaching is either too shallow or too deep; the service is too formal or too informal; the congregation is too big or too small; etc, etc., etc. Do we realize what a spiritually dangerous condition this attitude is? We see it in the world of course, but we also see it in people who are saved, or who think they are. We must understand how closely allied this attitude is to the one that causes us to reject God's purpose for ourselves. For even if we are saved yet so as by fire (1 Cor. 3:15), this attitude cannot help but deprive us of the full experience of the blessings of the Kingdom. In its fullness, it will deprive us of them altogether.

The bottom line in verse 35 is that *"wisdom is vindicated by all her children."* What does that mean? The "children" of wisdom would be the deeds, the responses, the lives that she gives birth to. The modern equivalent to this proverb would be something like, "The proof is in the pudding." Which is the right choice? Justifying God or justifying yourself? Well, just look at the joy of those who justify God and have received the blessings of God's grace that elevate them to a position of favor with the Father that John as a prophet could never have reached. And compare it with the self–involvement and the performance–driven bondage of those who try to justify themselves. It's not really that hard of a choice. The proof is in the pudding. Wisdom is vindicated by all her children.

Conclusion

Jesus then has used the rhetoric of His preaching to bring us to a spiritual crossroads. One path justifies God, the other ourselves. The Lord has given us every reason to follow Him down the Calvary Road. He has shown us how He treats His friends. The favor of the crowd is fickle; but the friendship of Christ is forever. He has shown us the greatness that awaits the small and the humble in His Kingdom, with its accounting of grace. *"I say to you, among those born of women there is no one greater than John; yet he who is least in the kingdom of God is greater than he."* He has analyzed profoundly the self–involved and self–refuting and self–defeating attitude that leads us to reject His gracious offer. *"And they say, 'We played the flute for you and you did not dance; we sang a dirge, and you did not weep.'"*

And now we must choose. Wisdom is vindicated by all her children! Choose wisely.

FORGIVEN MUCH—LOVED MUCH

Luke 7:36 Now one of the Pharisees was requesting him to dine with him. And he entered the Pharisee's house and reclined at the table. 37 And behold, there was a woman in the city who was a sinner; and when she learned that he was reclining at the table in the Pharisee's house, she brought an alabaster vial of perfume, 38 and, standing behind him at his feet, weeping, she began to wet his feet with her tears and kept wiping them with the hair of her head and kissing his feet and anointing them with the perfume. 39 Now, when the Pharisee who had invited him saw this, he said to himself, "If this man were a prophet, he would know who and what sort of person this is who is touching him, that she is a sinner." 40 And Jesus answered and said to him, "Simon, I have something to say to you." And he replied, "Say it, Teacher." 41 "A certain moneylender had two debtors: one owed five hundred denarii, and the other fifty. 42 When they were unable to repay, he graciously forgave them both. Which of them therefore will love him more?" 43 Simon answered and said, "I suppose the one whom he forgave more." And he said to him, "You have judged correctly." 44 And turning toward the woman, he said to Simon, "Do you see this woman? I entered your house; you gave me no water for my feet, but she has wet my feet with tears and wiped them with her hair. 45 You gave me no kiss, but since the time I came in she has not ceased to kiss my feet. 46 You did not anoint my head with oil, but she has anointed my feet with perfume. 47 For this reason I say to you, her sins, which are many, have been forgiven, for she loved much; but he who is forgiven little, loves little." 48 And he said to her, "You sins have been forgiven." 49 And those who had been reclining at the table with him began to say to themselves, "Who is this man who even forgives sins?" 50 And he said to the woman, "Your faith has saved you. Go in peace."

Introduction

Certainly, one of the chief things that believers in Christ have to be thankful for is the forgiveness of their sins. This anonymous woman is possibly the outstanding example in all of history of such gratitude. The best way to understand her example is to look at the way this incident functions in the context and the flow of Luke's narrative. So let us think about the Setting of the Scene, the Scene itself, and the Significance of the Scene for understanding Jesus and our own relationship to him.

I. The Setting

Frist, the setting: Why is this story placed right here in Luke's unfolding of the narrative of Jesus's ministry? You say, "Well, it happened next. Duh!" A simple, common–sense response. This is where it happened: between the encounter with John the Baptist's disciples and the preaching tour of chapter eight. And I do not doubt that, as far as it goes, this answer is true. But we must remember John's observation that if everything Jesus did and said had been written down, the whole world could not have contained the books (John 21:25). Lots of things may have happened or got said after our last passage and before the next one. So why put any of them in this spot? And if we are going to include something, why *this* story? I don't think Luke made any of these decisions by accident. When anything shows up, it is usually a testimony to two things: first, the Gospel writer's estimation of its importance, and, second, the fact that it advances or develops a theme he is working with, either throughout his narrative as a whole or in this particular section of it. Our passage today does this both in the larger context of Luke's Gospel and in the immediate context as well.

First, the idea of forgiveness is important to all the Gospel writers, because Jesus was the Lamb of God who taketh away the sins of the world (John 1:29), and He came to give his life a ransom for many (Mat. 20:28). So each Gospel devotes about half of its space to Passion Week and the Resurrection—as much as to the other thirty–odd years of Jesus's life all put together! But they also include particular episodes throughout the whole period of Jesus's ministry in which forgiveness itself, or people's attitudes toward forgiveness, get highlighted. Sometimes, as with the Paralytic Let Down through the Roof, Jesus goes out of his way to inject the topic into a scene where everyone else was thinking of something else. Before he heals this paralytic, out of the blue, as it were, he up and forgives his sins. Sometimes there is a Parable, such as the Prodigal Son, which brings out the Father's forgiveness of the Prodigal and the Elder Brother's problems with it. Sometimes, as with the Woman Taken in Adultery, Jesus turns the tables, bringing forgiveness where condemnation was expected. Here, as the Woman breaks the Alabaster Jar, Jesus takes the opportunity to make sure we (and Simon the Pharisee) do not miss what this whole scene is about: being forgiven, appreciating that forgiveness, and being able to forgive.

In the immediate context, this incident follows the discourse about John the Baptist in Luke 7:24–35. One theme of that conversation was the contrast between those who justify God (i.e., declare him righteous), and those who justify themselves (verse 29–30). To justify God is to condemn yourself, and ironically to be justified by God. To justify yourself is to reject God, and therefore to be condemned by God. What follows in our passage today then is an extended example of these very two kinds of people: the Woman, who justifies God, and the Pharisee, who justifies himself—or tries to. You really can't.

II. The Scene

So much for the setting. What about the scene? As we analyze the scene being played out before us, we can divide it into two parts: the Cast of Characters and the Complications.

Cast of Characters. The cast includes one of the few Pharisees whose name is actually remembered: **Simon.** He thought himself a religious and pious man. As was typical of his sect, he was zealous for the Law to the point of a legalism that bled over into self–righteousness, as legalism tends to do. His party was at loggerheads with Jesus over a number of issues, the proper manner of keeping the Sabbath and the proper attitude toward sinners being among the chief. Why he had invited Jesus to dinner is not clear. Was it out of curiosity and an open mind? Or was it a trap all along, the kind of opportunity for Jesus to put His foot in His mouth that the Pharisees were always trying to arrange and then being disappointed by? At any rate, Simon was a poor host, omitting many of the basic courtesies toward guests that were standard in that day. If he was trying to trap Jesus, he must have thought the sinful woman wandering in was just the break he was looking for—which may explain why she gained entrance so easily. Normally she could hardly have expected to get in to such a house at all.

Then there is **the Woman.** Though Luke does not use the word *prostitute*, the phrase "woman who was a sinner" was a common Greek euphemism for a prostitute. She was apparently well known as such in that town. She was probably a very recent convert—certainly no one had yet had any opportunity to notice a change in her lifestyle. Jesus may well not have even known she had become a follower of His until she showed up. This was a woman who had long ago gotten over any sense of shame she had ever had. But now God was transforming that vice into a virtue: she was not the least bit embarrassed or ashamed to show her love for Christ.

And that leads us to **our Lord** Himself. He appears as we have already come to know Him: compassionate toward repentant sinners, sharp and aware of what is going on and of what people are thinking, able to think quickly on His feet and turn any wrinkle in events to spiritual advantage. If we didn't know Him, we might think, "Here's a controversial outsider being given an opportunity by the Establishment to gain some respectability; surely He will take full advantage of it." But we do know Him, and therefore we know He will do no such thing. He will tell the truth and He will do the truth as He sees it, and if the Establishment is offended by that, so be it.

The Complications that cause the drama in this scene come from the very act of bringing this particular set of characters together. Put these three characters in a room, and something is going to happen! Well, as long as we're thinking of this tableau as a scene, let's think a little about the blocking. The custom at this time was to "recline" at the table. You would lean on benches on one elbow, with the other hand free to reach for the food as you faced the table with your feet stuck out behind. [At this point Dr. Williams demonstrates the posture on a bench conveniently placed next to the pulpit.] That's how the Woman was able to come up behind Jesus and anoint His feet: they were not stuck under the table as they would be today but stuck out behind Him. Well, here she is, bawling, kissing His feet as she anoints them with both tears and perfume, and wiping them with her hair, loose and let down—a fact that would have had even stronger connotations then than it does today. She was making a scene indeed! There was nothing dignified about it. She had, to put it mildly, not yet learned how to act in public, much less in church. I suspect this would be embarrassing enough to you if *anyone* was carrying on like that over you in the middle of a meal—but a Streetwalker? Oh, my!

I think we have to have at least a little bit of sympathy for poor Simon the Pharisee. Let's be honest: Would you be completely comfortable with this happening in your home? You've invited the preacher over for Sunday dinner and a well–known Lady of the Evening barges into your house off the street and starts carrying on in such a fashion—over me, for example. And you're not even a Pharisee! Simon must have been near apoplexy. I'm afraid he might have even had a conniption. No, this is worse than that. I think we are all the way up to a hissy fit. And you would have had one too, and so would I. Let's not pretend any different.

But Simon does have one problem that I hope you and I would not have added to this embarrassing scene: He makes a fatal assumption about the meaning of it all. *"If this man were a prophet, he would surely know who and what sort of person this is who is touching him, that she is a sinner."* It is supremely ironic: Simon thinks Jesus can't see the obvious about this woman, and that it proves he is not even a prophet, much less the Messiah. But Jesus' response shows that he sees beyond the obvious to the secret thoughts of her heart—and Simon's. His prophetic credentials then are actually affirmed by the very thing that seems to threaten them. Meanwhile, the woman continues with her embarrassing attentions—the verbs in verse 38 are present participles, which indicate ongoing action—and Jesus is not the least bit embarrassed. He lets her continue while He asks Simon one of his patented innocent–sounding questions that turn everything upside down. And that leads us inexorably to the point of it all.

III. The Significance Of The Scene

So here's the significance of the scene. Jesus leads off with one of His classic parables. Two men owe money, and both are forgiven their debts. Which one, he asks then, will appreciate it more? Simon has the sinking feeling that he has just painted himself into a corner. We can hear it in the grudging concession in the word "suppose." *"I suppose the one who was forgiven more."* And now the trap is ready to spring, but its jaws will not close on the one Simon was hoping for.

The parable is, first of all, a wonderful picture of salvation by grace through faith apart from works. Neither of the men in the story paid any of their debt. Their freedom from it was all owing to the graciousness of the lender. But the emphasis is not on the forgiveness so much as on their response to it. Who will love more? The one forgiven more. He is not forgiven because he loves; he loves because he was forgiven. His love is the sign of his forgiveness, a response that flows naturally from it. The Woman then is not forgiven much because her love for Jesus is so great. Rather, she has such great, expressive love because she has been forgiven an awful lot, and she knows it. Simon does not forfeit forgiveness because he does not love Jesus. Rather, he feels no love because he does not think he needs very much forgiveness—if any.

The point is in the contrast. The Woman justifies God, agreeing with His standard of holiness that condemns her, and therefore receives an astonishing forgiveness, and therefore shows that she is aware of this in her outpouring of extravagant love. Simon justifies himself, thinks he needs no forgiveness, and so sees no reason even to give Jesus the customary water to wash His feet or oil to anoint His head. Note that it is not the actual number or seriousness of sins forgiven that determines how much a person loves Jesus, but rather the person's own estimation of how many and how serious they were. I don't think Jesus is actually agreeing that Simon is less sinful than the Woman. The Lord normally had a much more severe attitude toward self–righteousness than He did toward what a Pharisee would consider grosser, less respectable sins. He is just taking Simon's own estimation of the situation as true for the sake of argument. The point is that, whatever their relative level of sinfulness, the Woman enters into the joys of the Kingdom on a profound level because she justifies God and condemns herself in her own mind. Because he justifies himself in his own mind, Simon refuses God's purpose for him and the joys of the Kingdom pass him by.

I wonder if we do not have many Simon the Pharisees in the church today? Thay are way too ready to condemn others whose sinfulness is less respectable than theirs than anyone conscious of his own need for forgiveness has any right to be, incapable of understanding the need to be demonstrative about one's love of Jesus. It is as if they thought that maybe Christ had to die on the Cross for other people's sins, but for theirs all he would have needed to do was maybe to get a splinter from the Cross in his finger. The sobering thing about this encounter with Simon and the Woman is that these Simon the Pharisees emerge as people who show no evidence of having been forgiven at all.

Γνωθι σεαυτον, *"Gnothi seauton,"* the ancient Greeks advised us, "Know thyself." Well, if you do not know yourself as a sinner, you do not know yourself at all. We therefore need to pursue a certain amount of regular meditation on our own sinfulness, about how much we are forgiven. We often are given an opportunity to do so in our worship services here. We do this, we remind ourselves of the depressing fact of our own sinfulness, not in order to put ourselves down, but so that we may better and more adequately exalt the Savior who has forgiven us so much so freely, to exalt Him in the unimaginable riches of His Grace. When John Newton, the converted slave trader who helped William Wilberforce abolish the slave trade in England and wrote "Amazing Grace" in the meantime reached old age, he was suffering from dementia and a good bit of memory loss. The once–great preacher and Bible scholar was almost silenced. But even then he continued his own testimony to the amazing grace of his Master, Jesus, with all the mind he had left. "Two things I remember," he is reputed to have said. "I am a great sinner; and I have a great Savior."

Guilt will get you nowhere in the pursuit of godliness. Gratitude for grace will. Extravagant love for Jesus who has shown us such extravagant grace: This is the motivational engine that drives truly vibrant Christianity! Is that engine running in your life?

Conclusion

What are we supposed to take away from this story? I am not suggesting that we become undignified for the sake of indignity, as many of our Charismatic brethren seem to do. But better to lose our dignity than our joy—or our souls. How is it that this Woman was not embarrassed to show that she loved Jesus, to act in such a way in front of other people? That phrase, "in front of other people," is the key, isn't it? How many mistakes, how many failures, how many missed opportunities flow from worrying about what other people are going to think of us? I don't think this Woman was aware of the other people at all. I think that in the light of how much she had been forgiven, all she saw was Jesus.

But here is an even more astounding thing. If this Woman was not embarrassed to give such effusive a demonstration of love, Jesus was not embarrassed to receive it. Think about that!   And listen to me: Jesus is not embarrassed to be your Savior. Jesus is not embarrassed to be your Savior! (Neither is the Father to be your God—Heb. 11:16). He ought to be, but He isn't. And that is one of the best definitions of Grace you will ever hear. We serve Jesus, not Simon the Pharisee! When we tap into this dynamic, we are no longer thinking about such excuses as whether we have any talent or training that the Lord can use. We are no longer asking, "Who am I to speak to others about the love of Jesus?" When you know you have been forgiven of this much (and we all have, even if our sins are more respectable), you *have* to show your love for Him somehow.

This is the motivational engine that drives truly vibrant Christianity! There is no substitute for it. Is that engine running in your life? If you have been forgiven, let it run.

GOSPEL FARMING

Luke 8:1 And it came about soon afterwards that He began going about from one city and village to another, proclaiming and preaching the kingdom of God; and the twelve were with him, 2 and also some women who had been healed of evil spirits and sicknesses: Mary, who was called Magdalene, from whom seven demons had gone out, 3 and Joanna the wife of Chuza, Herod's steward, and Susanna, and many others who were contributing to their support out of their private means.

4 And when a great multitude were coming together and those from the various cities were journeying to him, he spoke by way of a parable: 5 "The sower went out to sow his seed; and as he sowed, some fell beside the road; and it was trampled under foot, and the birds of the air ate it up. 6 And other seed fell on rocky soil, and as soon as it grew up it withered away because it had no moisture. 7 And other seed fell among the thorns; and the thorns grew up with it and choked it out. 8 And other seed fell into the good soil, and grew up and produced a crop a hundred times as great." As he said these things he would call out, "He who has ears to hear, let him hear!"

9 And his disciples began questioning him as to what this parable might be. 10 And he said, "To you it has been granted to know the mysteries of the kingdom of God, but to the rest it is in parables, in order that 'seeing they may not see, and hearing they may not understand.' 11 Now the parable is this: the seed is the Word of God. 12 And those beside the road are those who have heard; then the devil comes and takes away the word from their heart so that they may not believe and be saved. 13 And those on the rocky soil are those who, when they hear, receive the word with joy, But these have no firm root; they believe for a while, and in time of temptation fall away. 14 And the seed which fell among the thorns, these are the ones who have heard, and as they go on their way they are choked with worries and riches and pleasures of this life, and bring no fruit to maturity. 15 And the seed in the good soil, these are the ones who have heard the word in an honest and good heart, and hold it fast, and bear fruit with perseverance."

Introduction

We come today to one of the most familiar, yet fascinating and "fertile" (ahem) passages in the Gospel of Luke: the Parable of the Sower, or, just as pertinently, of the Soils. So let's think a little about what this passage can teach us. We'll look at the Prologue to the Parable, the Purpose of the Parables, and the Point of this Parable.

I. The Prologue To The Parable (vv. 1–3)

The first three verses actually have no connection to our topic today except proximity in the chapter, but they are worth a passing comment. For they show us Jesus' ministry in its practical and day–to–day details. We see in verse 1 that there was a systematic effort to spread the Gospel throughout the cities and towns of Judea. *"And it came about soon afterwards that He began going about from one city and village to another, proclaiming and preaching the kingdom of God; and the twelve were with him.*" And we discover in verses 2 and 3 how Jesus and his disciples were supported—by donors who had independent means. With him also were "*some women who had been healed of evil spirits and sicknesses: Mary, who was called Magdalene, from whom seven demons had gone out, and Joanna the wife of Chuza, Herod's steward, and Susanna, and many others who were contributing to their support out of their private means.*" We seldom think of this, but without this support network, how would thirteen men have been able to wander around the countryside and maintain themselves for three years without jobs? Those who play this crucial role for missionaries today should be encouraged by Luke's recognition here of their forebears. It is a crucial and important ministry they perform.

In addition, these verses add to the mounting evidence for Luke's reliability as a careful historian. It is very unlike early fictional accounts of Jesus' ministry like the apocryphal gospels, in which the work would be supported more piously, by ongoing miracles. Luke has Jesus' ministry rooted in practical reality. And the names he gives are interesting too. Joanna was the wife of an important government official, a cabinet secretary as it were, and has been independently verified from secular records, while of Susannah we know nothing but the name. And then others remain anonymous. A writer of pious fiction would have given names to the woman at Simon's house, the centurion and his son, the widow of Nain and her son. Luke gives the names when he knows them and omits them when he does not—according to what was in his sources, not according to whom he thinks we would be more interested in (surely the widow or the woman with the phial) or what would seem more appropriate to narrative art. But let us let these passing thoughts pass and then pass on to things of more than passing interest—like the purpose of the parables.

II. The Purpose Of The Parables (v. 10)

Verse 10 has given a lot of people problems. "*To you it has been granted to know the mysteries of the kingdom of God, but to the rest it is in parables, in order that 'seeing they may not see, and hearing they may not understand.'*" Many cannot believe that Jesus would *want* to conceal the truth from the multitudes. This seems to the pious to be incompatible with the purely loving and altruistic and benevolent image we have of Him. But we must not forget the doctrine of Judicial Hardening, which is given in passages like Isaiah 6:9–11 (from which the Lord quotes here) or Isaiah 29:9–14. "*They become drunk, but not with wine; they stagger, but not with strong drink. For the Lord has poured over you a spirit of sleep. He has shut your eyes, the prophets, and covered your heads, the seers. And the entire vision will be to you like the words of a sealed book. . . . Because this people draws near to me with their words and honors me with their lips, but their hearts are far from me . . . therefore the wisdom of their wise men shall perish and the discerning of their discerning men shall be concealed.*"

When people refuse to listen to the Word of God, the ultimate punishment of this greatest of sins is to be deprived of the ability to hear it. It is as if God, after exhausting His infinite patience with us, says, "Okay, you want to harden your heart? You want to blind yourself? Fine. I'll help you!" There is no more awful fate, no heavier punishment, no more horrible judgment that can befall us. And Jesus came to reveal the whole character of the Father—His justice as well as his love, His wrath as well as his grace. How we respond to Him determines which side of His character He will show to us. The crowd in their superficiality and fickleness—they were a lot like the first three types of soil in the parable, weren't they? Hmmm, maybe not a coincidence—had certainly made themselves liable to this judgment. To complain of Jesus' attitude here is to commit blasphemy; it is to make ourselves out to be more pious than God!

My difficulty with verse 10 is at an entirely different point. I have a hard time seeing how the parables are supposed to accomplish their alleged purpose of concealing the mysteries of the kingdom from the crowd! They are, on the contrary, among the most effective teaching techniques ever used in the entire history of education. What do you think? Does the parable of the Good Samaritan conceal from you who God thinks your neighbor is? Do the parables of the Prodigal Son and the Lost Sheep conceal from you God's concern for the wayward? Does the parable of the House Built on the Rock conceal from you the critical importance of a Bible-based life? No, of course not. You don't even need a lot of interpretation to see the point of them, which seems as plain as the proverbial nose upon the face. So what gives here?

Part of the answer is to remember how familiar these parables have become for us who have known the Lord for any length of time. Indeed, even for those who have not, they have become part of the store of legend and fable in Western culture. But what if we were hearing them for the very first time? Would the meaning of the parable of the soils be self-evident? Probably not. The principle behind Jesus' cryptic statement is this: the Parable plus the Key to its interpretation (which Jesus gave the disciples when they asked Him to explain it later) reveals spiritual truth clearly and powerfully. The Parable without that Key may remain just a nice story. We could make it an equation: Parable plus Key equals Understanding; Parable minus Key equals head scratching, especially for those not in tune with the mind of Christ. The parable then reveals the truth powerfully to those who make the effort to understand it, i.e., to the disciples, who bothered to ask for the explanation. The rest felt vaguely taught but probably were unable to tell you exactly what. Rather than pursuing the answer, they just shrugged their shoulders and walked away. Seeing they did not see, and hearing they did not understand.

In other words, the parable reveals the truth to the teachable while it leaves the rest in darkness, but without excuse. For they could have hung around for the question-and-answer session too if they had wanted to. The point is that you can be one of those to whom it is granted to know the mysteries of the kingdom just by wanting to be. Let's make sure we are in that group!

III. The Point Of The Parable

The key to this parable then is to see that the seed is the Word of God and the soils are the people who hear it. The point of the parable therefore is the importance of hearing teachably. When the Word of God comes to you, how will you respond to it?

There are two critical elements in the parable: the seed and the soils. Seed needs soil to grow, but the seed is the only part that contains a principle of life within itself. The soil in itself is inert. The soil adds only receptivity to that principle, a hospitable environment in which it may grow—or the opposite. So the choice of the seed metaphor is a wonderful way of capturing the mystery of the relation between God's initiative and our response. The life being in the seed pictures *Sola Gratia*, the fact that salvation is by God's grace alone. And the role of the receptivity or lack of it in the soil pictures *Sola Fide*, faith alone as the way we respond to God's grace. But the main emphasis of this picture is on the different types of soil, the different ways we can respond to God's Word as the carrier of his Grace. There are four.

1. The Roadside Rejecter *"And those beside the road are those who have heard; then the devil comes and takes away the word from their heart so that they may not believe and be saved"* (verse 12). The worst case is the seed that fell by the road. Satan takes away the Word and it never even has a chance to geminate. These people are definitely not saved. These are people who just don't listen. Either they violently reject the message or just turn a politely deaf ear to it. Their brains just have no sticking places for these notions. There may be some of you here today. Your parents brought you, or you just came to church out of cultural habit. You are listening, but you do not hear. These words, you tell yourself, are for someone else. They don't apply to you. Oh, really? If that's what you think when you hear the Gospel, then maybe you should be listening, if only because the Text is talking about you right now! Are your ears burning? Please give yourself a chance to understand that this voice telling you to be cool and not take the message to heart is Satan taking the Word away to your everlasting hurt. Don't let him do that! If you must rebel against something, rebel against that voice. You might find a kind of freedom you would otherwise be incapable of imagining.

2. The Stony Stumbler *"And those on the rocky soil are those who, when they hear, receive the word with joy, But these have no firm root; they believe for a while, and in time of temptation fall away"* (verse 13). The rocky soil represents people who seem to hear the Gospel, but in fact they are having only an emotional response to it that never reaches the will, the mind, or the heart. They might even seem to believe for a time. But "for a time" is the key phrase. In Greek it is for the καιρος *(kairos)*, a word for time that could be translated "for the moment." Their response is so shallow that it has no permanence. They have not faith but a fad. The Word in them is only able to produce illusory results that do not stand the test of time. These people are not saved either, for the plant of faith dies and withers away as if it had never been. Not faith, but a fad. Is there anyone like that here today? The Christian faith is not a game. It is a matter of life or death. What you call your belief can be seen as true faith only by testing and trial. Jesus has no place for fair-weather friends. Do not pretend that you have put your faith in Him unless you are prepared to deny yourself, take up your cross daily, and follow Him! Anything else is just a game whose only outcome can be your own spiritual death. Hear the Word and let it sink in deep so that it changes your life! Examine yourself whether you be in the faith. Do not allow yourself to run the risk of being a Stony Stumbler.

3. The Briar-Bush Babe in Christ *"And the seed which fell among the thorns, these are the ones who have heard, and as they go on their way they are choked with worries and riches and pleasures of this life, and bring no fruit to maturity"* (verse 14). The people among the thorns are a sad bunch, though not so tragic as the first two soil types. Some of these people may be saved, for they are not said to die or wither away, but simply never to mature, i.e., bear fruit. They may be saved *"yet so as by fire"* (1 Cor. 3:15), but they have wasted their lives by being too focused on the cares, riches, and pleasures of the world. They think possessions, position, prestige, power, and pleasure are things that will enhance their lives, but they sadly discover that these things are nothing but kudzu. These things are necessary, they may be part of our calling, and some may be good gifts to be enjoyed. But when we make them our main purpose, they begin to act like kudzu: to choke us, stunt us, smother us, and all but deprive us of real life. They will not bring you true happiness in this life, and they will send you to the back of the line in the next. Do any of us recognize ourselves in this portrait? Then let us ask ourselves why gardeners have hoes. Let the Lord use His to chop away the clutter so you can begin to focus on the things that really matter: His Word, His people, His message, His mission, and ultimately Himself.

4. The Black Dirt Believer *"And the seed in the good soil, these are the ones who have heard the word in an honest and good heart, and hold it fast, and bear fruit with perseverance"* (verse 15). These folk don't need much explanation, but maybe their fruit does. What is the fruit they bear? Surely the fruit of the Spirit: love, joy, peace. Certainly the fruit of the Christian: good works that bring glory to God and a good testimony along with them that brings people into his kingdom. Definitely a sense of fulfillment in this life, and in the next, the chance to hear the most beautiful words that will ever be spoken: *"Well done, thou good and faithful servant"* (Mat. 25:21). Who wouldn't want to be a Black-Dirt Believer? Well, the way to become one is to hear the Word with a good and honest hear and hold it fast with perseverance.

Conclusion

Let us all be like that good soil. Let the Word of God take deep root in you and encourage the plant of faith it produces to grow by holding that Word fast and meditating on it day and night. Read it and meditate on it daily; hear it weekly at least. Fertilize if with fellowship. Prune it with prayer and good preaching. Water it with worship. Weed it with witnessing. Hoe it with the habit of never just filing it away but always looking for ways of putting into practice. Harvest it with the help of the Holy Spirit, until it brings forth fruit a hundred–fold to the glory of God and your own eternal joy. For unto you it is granted to know the mysteries of the kingdom of God. Amen.

MORE ON GOSPEL FARMING

Luke 8:16 *"Now no one after lighting a lamp covers it over with a container or puts it under a bed, but he puts it on a lampstand in order that those who come in may see the light.* *17* *For nothing is hidden that shall not become evident, nor anything secret that shall not be known and come to light.* *18* *Therefore, take care how you listen. For whoever has, to him shall more be given, and whoever does not have, even what he thinks he has shall be taken away from him."* *19* *And his mother and his brothers came to him, but they were unable to get to him because of the crowd.* *20* *And it was reported to him, "You mother and your brothers are standing outside wishing to see you."* *21* *But he answered and said to them, "My mother and my brothers are these who hear the Word of God and do it.*

Introduction

Last time, in our study of the Parable of the Soils, we saw the importance of how we hear and heed the Word of God. Both our eternal destiny and the fruitfulness of our spiritual lives here and now depend on the receptivity or fertility of the soil of our hearts into which the Seed of the Word falls. So we looked at the Roadside Rejecter, from whom Satan steals the Seed away. We saw the Stony Stumbler, who seems to believe for a time but falls away. We examined the Briar Bush Babe in Christ, kept unfruitful by his entanglement with the weeds of the world. And we rejoiced in and aspired to be the Black Dirt Believer, who brings forth fruit thirty or sixty or even a hundred–fold. The most important thing to understand at the outset about the passage before us today is that it is a continuation of this theme of the importance of how we receive the Word, first in precept and then by example. We can divide it into two parts, each with its own way of advancing that theme: The Unhidden Beacon and the Unbidden Busybodies.

I. The Unhidden Beacon (vv. 16–18)

First, the Unhidden Beacon. *"Now no one after lighting a lamp covers it over with a container or puts it under a bed, but he puts it on a lampstand in order that those who come in may see the light. . . . Therefore, take care how you listen. For whoever has, to him shall more be given, and whoever does not have, even what he thinks he has shall be taken away from him."*

Jesus is still talking about the importance of how we hear the Word of God, but this fact is often obscured for the inexperienced or inattentive reader by the fact that He shifts His metaphor from Seed to Light. It might seem like a new subject, but it's actually a new way of talking about the old one. Seed as the Word produces fruit when it is planted, and Light as the Word produces vision when it is lit in our lives. Like Seed, Light is an active agent. It is the nature of a seed to grow, and it is the nature of light to shine. Therefore, if the Seed has been planted, watered, fertilized, and hoed, there should be growth and fruit. If the Light has been kindled and held up where you can see it, there should be illumination of the surrounding darkness. When these things don't happen, there is obviously a problem. Just as you don't plant a seed without expecting to get some fruit from it, so you do not light a lamp without expecting to see better what it shines on. You don't light a lamp and then hide it away; you put it on a lampstand so it can shine throughout the room.

The obvious implication of this word picture is that a "closet Christian" is an unnatural thing, almost a contradiction in terms. Where you seem to have that phenomenon, when you seem to have a person who professes to know Christ but does not increasingly manifest the fruit of the Spirit, or when you have a person who professes to know Christ but who still walks in darkness, when you have a person who professes to know Christ but nobody can tell, there is something seriously wrong. Either like the Stony Stumbler this person is not really a Christian at all, or like the Briar Bush Babe he or she is allowing the weeds of the world — riches, fame, power, pleasure, etc. — to choke the Seed's growth or put a shade over the Light.

Now, often an observer cannot tell which is which — is this person a carnal Christian or not a real Christian at all? Most sobering, the person who is playing such games with God can't tell which he is either. Do you assume that you can be a half–way Christian, live like the world, and still be saved "yet so as by fire" (1 Cor. 3:15)? Scripture does not assume any such thing! It teaches that there are such people, but it gives you no assurance that if you are playing such games you are going to be one. Many in the last day will say, "Lord, Lord, did we not believe in you, did we not do this, that, or the other thing for you?" only to hear, "Depart from me. I never knew you" (Luke 13:27). Either way, such a life makes about as much sense as lighting a candle or turning on a flashlight and then sticking it under the bed or in a closet.

But our main purpose here is not to dwell on the negative — the Lamp under the Bushel — but rather to focus on the positive picture we are given of the Christian life: the Lamp that is set on a Lampstand, illuminating the darkness all around itself for all the world to see. The purpose of lighting a lamp is to allow people to see, not so much the light itself, as to see everything else in that light. Remember what C. S. Lewis said? "I believe in Christianity as I believe that the sun has risen, not only because I see it, but because by it I can see everything else."[59] So what is this Light of which we are speaking? As background to this passage, we must remember that God is light and in Him is no darkness at all (1 Jn. 1:5). We must remember that Jesus, the eternal Son of God, is the Light of the World (Jn. 1:4–5, 9). We must remember that when Christ is in us, His Word enlightens the believer, who also becomes a little light in the darkness, letting his light so shine before men that they may see his good works and glorify his father who is in heaven (Mat. 5:14–16).

---

[59] C. S. Lewis, "Is Theology Poetry," *The Weight of Glory and other Addresses,* ed. Walter Hooper (San Francisco, CA: HarperSanFrancisco, 1980), 140.

So what do we see in this light? We see the glory of God in the face of Jesus Christ (2 Cor. 4:6). We then see the whole world either as related to and serving, or else as obscuring, that glory, to be evaluated, and thus approved or disapproved, praised or condemned, embraced or repudiated, in precisely those terms. And we see this light in order to share it. In other words, if we make Bible knowledge an end in itself, that would be like turning on a flashlight and just shining it straight into our own eyes. We would only blind ourselves and not help anyone else. Accurate knowledge of the Bible is important, not so we can become walking concordances to impress our friends or be the Big Fish in the Small Pond of the church, but so that we can see and rejoice in the glory of God in the face of Jesus Christ and so that our little light can help others to see it and rejoice in it too.

The story is told of a man who met a friend who was scouring the sidewalk under a streetlamp. "I've lost one of my contact lenses," he explained. So the man got down on his hands and knees and helped his friend go over every square inch of the area, to no avail. Finally in desperation he asked, "Where were you standing when you lost it?" "On the other side of the street," came the reply. "Then why are we looking over here?" he asked in astonished exasperation. "Oh," the friend explained, "this is where the light is." If what I am telling you today stays in this room, either because this is the only place where I talk about it or live it, or because you are satisfied to have it so, we are about as dumb as that man. It is important that we talk about it here. This is where we hand out the seed. This is where we hand out the flashlights and the batteries. But we are supposed to be handing out the seed to sowers and the flashlights to scouts and guides. Put the light where the lost contacts are!

Do you only act—and talk—like a Christian in front of other believers? Only on Sunday? Only when it is not inconvenient or embarrassing? We need to take the light to where the lost are! You might as well be looking on the wrong side of the street—or turning your flashlight on and then sticking it in the closet.

Okay, how do we make sure that we are shining as we should? Look again at verse 18: "*Therefore, take care how you listen. For whoever has, to him shall more be given, and whoever does not have, even what he thinks he has shall be taken away from him.*" What will be added or taken away? The light by which you yourself see; the light by which you could be helping others to see. The way to shine as we should is to make sure that we hear the Word of God aright, like last week's Black Dirt Believers. Take care how you listen!

How should we listen? Let me suggest six ways. First, we should listen **attentively**. A little boy was once heard saying to his father after one of my sermons, "Wow! Dad, you were right. The time really does pass faster if you pay attention!" That is a true story. Well, to listen rightly we must first be listening. If you do not already have the habits of regular Bible study and prayer and of listening to good expository preaching by a faithful minister of the Word, well, you really can't listen better when you are not listening at all! Second, we should listen **prayerfully**. The Holy Spirit who inspired the Word is our ultimate teacher (Jn. 16:3). He must illumine our minds and hearts if our study of the Word is to be spiritually profitable. Without His aid you can translate the original Greek brilliantly and analyze it profoundly and profit not at all. Third, we must listen **reverently**. The Seed is the Word of God; it is God himself who is speaking to us. We should listen as if we actually thought that was so. Fourth, we must listen **obediently**. Jesus promised that if anyone is willing to do the Father's will he would know of the doctrine whether it be of God (Jn. 7:17). Fifth, when it comes to the Word preached and expounded, even by faithful men, we must listen **critically**. We must be like the noble–minded Bereans who searched the Scriptures daily to see if these things were so (Acts 17:11). Finally, we must listen **consistently**. Paul told Timothy to preach the Word in season and out of season (2 Tim. 4:2). If that is how preachers are supposed to preach, then that is also how we all are supposed to listen.

Attentively, prayerfully, reverently, obediently, critically, consistently: What will happen if we listen like that? The first consequence of how you hear the Word of God today is how you will hear it tomorrow. *"For whoever has, to him shall more be given, and whoever does not have, even what he thinks he has shall be taken away from him."* If you hear receptively today, you will hear with greater receptivity tomorrow. If you harden your heart today, you will hear with a harder heart tomorrow. And the end result of that is that you will become either a lamp set on a lampstand giving light to all who come into the house, or your own light will be extinguished at worst or wasted—put under a bushel—at best. Let's be bright beacons! For then we will fulfill our purpose: to see and rejoice in the glory of God in the face of Jesus as it is reflected by the whole of creation, and to help others to see and rejoice in it as well. What could be better than that?

II. The Unbidden Busybodies (vv. 19–21)

So much for the Unhidden Beacon, which is really the heart of this passage. Next we come to a moment that illustrates it: the arrival of the Unbidden Busybodies. *And his mother and his brothers came to him, but they were unable to get to him because of the crowd. And it was reported to him, "You mother and your brothers are standing outside wishing to see you." But he answered and said to them, "My mother and my brothers are these who hear the Word of God and do it."*

This troubling story about the Lord's apparently dismissive treatment of his mother is here in Luke's text, I think, for thematic rather than chronological reasons. It appears at this moment in Luke's Gospel because it illustrates the point Jesus was making about the importance of hearing the Word aright. In Mark 3 and Matthew 12, on the other hand, it is placed *before* the parable of the Sower, not right after it. The best explanation for this discrepancy is not that the two accounts are contradictory but rather that they are simply being organized according to a different plan, with Luke grouping stories about Jesus thematically at this point in his Gospel. To understand Jesus' behavior here we have to get the background from Mark 3:20–21: "*And he came home, and the multitude gathered again to such an extent that they could not even eat a meal. And when his own people heard of this, they went out to take custody of him, for they were saying, "He has lost his senses."* That was the trip his family was on when they showed up here! It goes a long way toward explaining Jesus' brusque treatment of them. At this point in Jesus' career, they were not listening to Him aright! Certainly they were not listening reverently, certainly not obediently. So it is little wonder that He turns and says, "*My mother and my brothers are these who hear the Word of God and do it.*"

What is Luke's point in putting this exchange here? Surely it is to highlight, bring out, and make inescapable the lesson that **how you hear the Word of God will determine the kind of relationship you have with Jesus.** It makes all the difference between whether you will be part of His family or whether you are a stranger who doesn't really get Him even if you grew up with Him in your house. It also emphasizes that the kind of hearing that is good is the kind that leads to doing. *My mother and my brothers are these who hear the Word of God **and do it.**"* Note the emphasis on those last three words, "*and do it.*" I wonder if James, the Lord's half–brother who was one of the family members hearing this, was remembering this moment when, after his own conversion, he exhorted his readers twenty years later to *"Prove yourselves doers of the Word, and not merely hearers who delude themselves"* (James 1:22). Remembering this sad moment in his own career, he would have known very personally the importance of the difference!

Where does this leave us? It leaves in a truly astounding place: The humblest believer who listens well to the Word of God and puts into practice what he hears with a humble and loving spirit is closer to Jesus than his earthly mother or his brothers—closer to Jesus than the Virgin Mary! Did you hear that? Can you believe it? These are the words of Jesus. This is a promise of intimacy that takes your breath away! And it applies to you. Happily, we know that Mary and James were later added to that intimate circle themselves. But even they had to come into it the same way that we do: by hearing and doing the Word of God. *"Ye are my friends,"* Jesus said elsewhere, *"if ye do whatsoever I command you"* (John 15:14).

Conclusion

In conclusion: Oh, wow! What more could Jesus have done to motivate us to hear the Word of God often, carefully, prayerfully, reverently, obediently, and consistently, than by giving us this seemingly rude response to his mother and his brothers? To read Scripture, to hear it accurately expounded, to receive it and let it put down deep roots in the soil of our hearts, to let it shine out from our lives like a lamp on a stand, to *practice* it before men, is to be invited into the most intimate fellowship with Jesus Christ—to be His mother or His brother—to be His friend! It is to be right now and today what His real earthly mother and brothers should have been, and eventually became. But to spurn God's Word or to ignore it or to treat it lightly is to spurn that fellowship and to be excluded from it. Therefore, *"be careful how you listen,"* for *"my mother and my brothers are these who hear the Word of God and do it."*

Amen!

THE STILLING OF THE STORM

Luke 8:22 *Now it came about on one of those days that he and his disciples got into a boat and he said to them, "Let's go over to the other side of the lake." And they launched out.* **23** *But as they were sailing along, he fell asleep. And a fierce gale of wind descended upon the lake, and they began to be swamped and to be in danger.* **24** *And they came to him and woke him, saying, "Master, Master, we are perishing!" And being aroused, he rebuked the and the surging waves, and they stopped, and it became calm.* **25** *And he said to them, "Where is your faith?" And they were fearful and amazed, saying to one another, "Who then is this who commands even the winds and the water, and they obey him?"*

Introduction

In the last few times we've had together we have been studying Jesus' teaching on the importance of hearing the Word of God aright, hearing it with a teachable spirit. Today we begin to look at a series of incidents which show the Word of God not simply as a word of wisdom, doctrine, or redemption, but also as a word of authority, power, and command. And the first of these incidents is the familiar story of The Stilling of the Storm. It highlights two truths: the Commanding Character of the Captain, and the Fickle Faith of the Followers.

I. The Commanding Character Of The Captain

First, the commanding character of the Captain. In this story we have represented graphically in concrete action a doctrine that our minds can never completely and fully grasp in the abstract: the two natures in one person of our Lord Jesus Christ (called by theologians the "hypostatic union"). He was the God–Man, not half God and half Man, but fully God and fully Man, two natures united in one person without mixture or confusion, not the pouring of Godhood into a finite man, but the taking up of Manhood into Divinity. This truth is beyond anything our intellects can adequately comprehend. How can one person be infinite and finite at the same time? Omnipotent and weak? Eternal and born in a manger? Immortal yet crucified, dead, and buried? Holy and a friend of sinners? It is more than we can get our heads around, more than our limited powers of analysis can comprehend, but we can see the truth of it being acted out in front of us frequently in the Lord's earthly life. There are some things that can be profitably said in explanation of these conundrums, but today we simply want to follow our text in portraying their truth in all its paradoxical profundity. This incident is one that shows both sides of it most clearly.

1. His Humanity. The first side is His humanity. Scripture tells us that the Lord was tempted in all points like as we are, yet without sin. The Gospel narratives emphasize the physical trials of Jesus' life in the narrative leading up to this passage. He has just gone through a strenuous time of ministry in which, as we saw last week, he didn't even have time to take out for a meal. *"And He came home, and the multitude gathered again, to such an extent that they could not even eat a meal. And when His own people heard of this, they went out to take custody of Him, for they were saying, 'He has lost His senses'"* (Mk. 3:20–21). This boat trip was apparently undertaken at the end of such a day (Mk. 4:1, cf. 4:35). And though Jesus had places like Mary, Martha, and Lazarus's house in Bethany where he could sometimes rest, during most of the three years of his ministry he was apparently camping out, roughing it—he had *"no place to lay his head"* (Mt. 8:18–20), a comment which Matthew puts right before this very boat trip.

What then is the point of all this? Jesus was not sleeping through the storm, as some pious interpreters would have it, because of the incredible depth of calm and peace in his soul. He was bone tired. His great, unbearable weariness, indeed his weakness, is stressed as the reason he was asleep—so exhausted that he slept right through a storm that was threatening to wreck the boat! The disciples lived with Jesus. They experienced his humanity close-up and first-hand. They knew he was fully man; they never doubted it. They couldn't. That is why the Gnostic heresies that emphasized Jesus' divinity to the exclusion of his humanity, that treated his humanity as an illusion, were made up by pious fools who had never known the real Jesus. You never get a hint of anything like that from the eyewitnesses. They knew and could never deny or doubt that Jesus was fully Man.

2. His Divinity. Right next to Jesus' humanity we see His deity. In fact, it was the very inescapability of Jesus' humanity that made the equally inescapable evidence of His divinity all the more astonishing. The disciples had already seen the miraculous draught of fishes. They had already seen demons cower and crawl in abject fear. They had already seen the lame walking, the blind seeing, and the dead raised and living. Nevertheless, these things happened at special crisis moments, while they saw their master's humanity day in and day out, hour by hour, as He ate, drank, slept, and relieved Himself in the bushes just like everybody else. So they still found the miracles astonishing; they never quite got used to them. And this one hit home especially hard for a couple of reasons.

First, as with the miraculous draft of fishes, these men knew the sea. Many of them had lived and worked on it their whole lives. They knew its power; they knew that, like the men in "A Perfect Storm," they were in "deep" trouble (if you'll pardon the expression) and might well not have survived. And they knew what many un–nautical modern readers miss: There is no way that furious waves driven by a vicious wind are going to suddenly become a complete calm, a surface clear as glass, once they have been stirred up. Even if the wind had stopped on Jesus' orders, the waves ought to have continued to surge for a long time anyway, perhaps for hours. What Jesus did here was absolutely inexplicable and completely unprecedented. What kind of man could do this? It's no wonder they were asking that question!

Second, as serious religious Jews looking for the consolation of Israel, these men knew the Old Testament. They would not have had the technical expertise in it that the Scribes and Pharisees had, but they had absorbed its content and its very language and turns of phrase through synagogue school and a rich oral culture. And so they knew that in the Old Testament the sea is often used as a symbol of nature's wildest, most uncontrollable realm. They knew that there was only one Person who could say to it, "*Thus far shall you come, but no further; here shall your proud waves stop!*" (Job 38:11). They knew who it was that "*dost still the roaring of the seas, the roaring of their waves*" (Ps. 65:7). They knew who had made a path right through the Red Sea for their fathers and commanded the same waters which had been held back to drown the Egyptians (Ps. 106:6–12). They knew that there was only one Power in the universe sufficient to command the winds and the waves—and it was not a man! Only Moses had ever done anything remotely approaching this—but he had told the people right as he was doing it, "*Stand by and see the salvation of* **Yahweh**, *which* **He** *will accomplish*" (Ex. 14:13, emphasis added). And Jesus by contrast had just up and rebuked the winds and the waves in His very own voice and by His very own authority. What kind of person can do such a thing? **What manner of man is this**?

3. Fully God and Fully Man. That indeed is the question as we try to put these two truths, the inescapable humanity *and* deity of Christ, together: What manner of Man is this that even the winds and the waves obey him? What manner of Man is this who does what only God can do, more *directly* even than Moses had done? How could the fully incarnate, that is, embodied, that is, fleshed–out Man whose exhausted flesh we just woke up from an irresistible sleep suddenly make us think that God himself is here in the boat? Again, it was the very inescapability of Jesus' humanity that made the equally inescapable evidence of His divinity all the more astonishing. It just did not compute. **What manner of Man is this** that even the winds and the waves obey him?

What we see here is that the doctrine of two natures in one person, the full Humanity and full Divinity of the person of Christ, is not some later embellishment, a rationalization made up by over–intellectual Greeks, but was implicit in the Gospel story from the beginning. The Gnostic heresies that emphasized Jesus' divinity to the exclusion of his humanity, that treated his humanity as an illusion, were made up by pious fools who had never known the real Jesus. And modern heresies that claim Jesus' divinity was added to the story of a simple carpenter by naive mythologizers were made up by *im*pious fools who never knew the real Jesus. A person claiming credibly to be God simply would not show weakness. A godly person claiming merely to be a prophet would avoid Old Testament allusions that could be nothing less than blasphemous— yet, far from avoiding them, Jesus goes out of his way to bring them up. And a prophet merely acting for God would do things in God's name, but Jesus says, "*I command you . . .*"

The upshot? You cannot say He was simply an appearance of God, like an Old–Testament theophany; you cannot say He was just a great prophet, but really just a man after all. All such answers are too simple. The only doctrine that works, the only doctrine that gets in all the facts, is the one the Church came up with and codified in the Nicene and Athanasian Creeds and the Definitions of the Council of Chalcedon. The disciples were not there yet. They were still in the head–scratching stage. What manner of Man is this that even the winds and the waves obey him? But this was head–scratching that would lead inevitably to the full doctrine of the two natures, fully God and fully Man—because the only explanation of Jesus that fits in all the facts is that this is just the way it was.

II. The Fickle Faith Of The Followers

The disciples were not there yet. In fact, they were farther from being there than they knew, further than they should have been. Jesus' question to them is one we should ask ourselves as well: *"Where is your faith?"* I find it a curious question. Had the disciples not recognized that they had a problem? Had they not come to the right place with that problem, to Jesus? Do they not seem to recognize that if anyone is going to keep them from perishing it has to be Him? This would pass for pretty sound faith among an awful lot of believers today! Yet Jesus' question implies that their faith was somehow defective. How so? The text gives us a couple of hints.

The disciples' faith was good as far as it went. They knew they had a problem, and they brought it to Jesus—and so should we. But they seem to have brought it to him with a certain lack of confidence in what He might be able to do about it. There was a level of desperation in their voices that was not rational or justified for people who have Jesus in their boat. Interestingly, Luke says that they were "in danger" (verse 23). But the disciples say, "We are perishing!" (verse 24). They are not the same thing. I take it that Luke was writing from a critical distance with objectivity, and the disciples were speaking in the present with understandable but undue desperation. They ought to have come to Jesus with more confidence in what He could do.

The second defect in their faith is evident in the wonderful question they ask at the end: *"What manner of Man is this that even the winds and the waves obey him?"* I say their question is wonderful because it was at least intelligently and pertinently phrased, and it therefore helps drive us to the answer, and would eventually help to drive them there as well. But at the moment, it reveals that, despite everything they had seen and heard, they still did not have an adequate understanding of who Jesus was. Such an understanding is a necessary component of a truly robust, spiritual, and healthy faith in Christ.

What then do we learn from Jesus' question? We learn a useful and important definition of faith: **Faith is an understanding of who Jesus is that produces confidence in His solution of our problems.** Let me repeat that. Faith is an understanding of who Jesus is that produces confidence in His solution to our problems.

Do you understand? Biblical faith is not an emotion, it is not a leap in the dark, it is not just constitutional optimism, it is not a religious "experience" that may be not much different from a drug trip, it is not a psychological trick we play on ourselves, it is not wishful thinking, it is not presumption or a form of intellectual blindness or naivety or any of a number of other things that sadly pass for faith in modern Christianity. Faith is an informed and correct answer to the question, *"What manner of Man is this that even the winds and the waves obey him?"* It answers, *"Thou art the Christ, the Son of the living God!"* And on the basis of that answer, on the basis of its truth, it means a confidence in, trust in, and commitment to His solution to the problems of life. Faith accepts Jesus' diagnosis of those problems: They are not ultimately due to lack of education, lack of money, bad luck, or the unfairness of others (though any of these things may be contributing factors). They are ultimately due to sin. And faith embraces His solution: His death on the Cross for us, and our death to self for Him. And finally, faith means confidence in the ability of obedience to His Word to correct the consequences of sin, in so far as they can be healed in this life. Why do we say, "Lord, Lord," if we do not do what He says? Faith is an understanding of who Jesus is that produces confidence in His solution of our problems.

Conclusion

Do you wrestle with guilt? Do you need direction for life? Guidance in setting your priorities, determining what is really important? Do you have trouble coping with everyday hassles? Are you torn by bitterness, anxiety, fear? The answers to all those problems are here, in this Book! Why do we not read them? And if we read, why do we not apply them? Because we do not really think they will work. Why not? We lack confidence in Christ's solutions because we have not really come to grips with who He is. We need first to ask the disciples' question afresh: What manner of man is this? And we must not be content with repeating the right formulae in answer to it. We must really believe them! Our problem, as theirs was, is simple: unbelief. It is often unbelief walking around disguised as faith because it is able to say the right words. But faith is an understanding of who Jesus is that produces confidence in His solution to our problems. We profess to believe that Jesus is Lord. May God help us to live by faith, that is, to live as if we really thought it was true.

THE GERASENE DEMONIAC

Luke 8:26 And they sailed to the country of the Gerasenes, which is opposite Galilee.
27 And when he had come out onto the land, he was met by a certain man from the city who was
possessed with demons, who had not put on any clothing for a long time, and was not living in
a house, but in the tombs. 28 And seeing Jesus, he cried out and fell before him and said in a loud
voice, "What have I to do with you, Jesus, Son of the most high God? I beg you, do not torment
me!" 29 For he had been commanding the unclean spirit to come out of the man. For it had
seized him many times. And he was bound with chains and shackles and kept under guard, but
he would burst his fetters and be driven by the demon into the desert. 30 And Jesus asked him,
"What is your name?" And he said, "Legion," for many demons had entered him. 31 And they
were entreating him not to command them to be cast into the abyss. 32 Now there was a herd of
many swine feeding there on the mountain. And the demons entreated him to permit them to
enter the swine. And he gave them permission. 33 And the demons came out from the man and
entered the swine, and the herd rushed down the steep bank into the lake and were drowned.
34 And when the herdsmen saw what had happened, they ran away and reported it in the city
and out in the country. 35 And the people went out to see what had happened. And they came
to Jesus and found the man from whom the demons had gone out sitting down at the feet of Jesus
clothed and in his right mind; and they became frightened. 36 And those who had seen it
reported to them how the man who was demon possessed had been made well. 37 And all the
people of the country of the Gerasenes and the surrounding district asked him to depart from
them, for they were gripped with fear; and he got into a boat and returned. 38 But the man from
whom the demons had gone out was begging him that he might accompany him; but he sent him
away, saying, 39 "Return to your house and describe what great things God has done for you."
And he went away, proclaiming throughout the whole city what great things Jesus had done for
him.

Introduction

Last time we left the Disciples marveling at the stilling of the storm and asking,
"What manner of man is this that even the winds and the waves obey him?" Had they
had the ears to hear, they might have heard the waves lapping against the shore saying,
"You ain't seen nothing yet!" For no sooner do they reach the shore than they encounter
another demoniac. It is a familiar story but a rich one, and almost every element in it
has something to teach us, including the fact that it is one more example of the power
and authority of the Word of God at work in Jesus. Let us take them one at a time.

I. The Setting

The first element that helps us understand the significance of this event is the
setting. This passage presents us with one of the most puzzling textual problems in the
Greek New Testament. For Matthew has the incident taking place at Gadara, Mark at

Gerasa, and in Luke, some manuscripts say Gerasa and some Gergesa. But the problem is not just with the name of the city but whether the event could have taken place in any of them. For clearly it has to happen right on the shore of the lake. Jesus meets the demoniac immediately upon landing, and the pigs have to be able to run off the cliff into the water. Yet Gadara is seven miles inland, and Gerasa is even worse, about forty miles away. There was no city of Gergesa; it did not exist. Is the text hopelessly confused, if not fictitious? At the turn of the last century, liberal scholars thought so with such confidence that they heaped ridicule on the Gospel authors. But by now, History should have taught us that, when it comes to Scripture, that is always a bad idea. The only one who ends up deserving ridicule is the critic.

The solution is not difficult at all once you have all the facts. More thorough knowledge of Palestinian geography has revealed that there was a village named Kersa in the right place. *Kersa* could easily go from Aramaic into Greek as *Gerasa*. Gergesa is probably descended from a misspelling by a later scribe. As for Gadara, it turns out that the Gadarenes owned property at Kersa—Gadara is where the owners of the pigs lived. In the Jewish mind, that really makes Kersa part of Gadara. So all the discrepancies are reconciled if we are just patient enough to discover all the relevant data.[60] As Sherlock Holmes says more than once, "It is always a capital mistake, Watson, to theorize in advance of the facts."[61]

What is the significance of this little excursion into archaeology and philology? It should reinforce our confidence in the truth and reliability of Scripture. The confident ridicule of the text of the 1890's just isn't possible without dishonesty today. (That does not mean it doesn't happen!) Ninety per cent plus of the alleged "errors" and "discrepancies" and "contradictions" you read about in a certain type of commentary have perfectly reasonable solutions that are known—many have been known for years. For the other ten per cent, we are still waiting. But we ought to be waiting with confidence. It would be dishonest of us to pretend that there are no problems. But it would be foolish to conclude that any of them are irresolvable. Surely the clear verdict of the history of interpretation is that it is always wise to give the benefit of the doubt to the Text rather than the critic! And this is an important realization when you are contemplating the theme of Luke's larger context as we have been seeing it the last few weeks: how we hear and respond to the Word of God.

II. The Demoniac

Next is the demoniac himself. This demoniac is similar to the one we met at Capernaum. The demon has the exact same reaction to Jesus: recognizing Him as the Son of God and worrying about what Jesus might do to him. But this man's case was

---

[60] The data is discussed in most of the commentaries on this passage. See also Gleason Archer, *Encyclopedia of Bible Difficulties* (Grand Rapids, MI: Zondervan, 1982), 324–6.

[61] See for example Sir Arthur Conan Doyle, "A Study in Scarlet," *The Annotated Sherlock Holmes*, op. cit., : 1:167; cf. "The Adventure of the Second Stain," 1:311, etc.

much more serious, if demon possession is capable of such a distinction. He was possessed by a multitude of demons rather than just one, perhaps (though we know very little about how such things work), producing the more severe effects described in verses 27 and 29. He had notoriously defied all attempts of his neighbors to control him.

The thing that strikes me about this man's condition is how parallel it is to the seemingly less extreme case of every non–believer. Satan does not take complete outward control of a man's body through a complete inward domination of his spirit *in this life* very often. But if sinners are really the slaves of Satan, as Scripture clearly teaches, then they are already on a path that leads to the place where this demoniac already was before his deliverance. Maybe that is what Hell will be like.

Think about what it means to be demon possessed. This man was in the first place deprived of his reason. He did not know who he was or where he was or what he was doing. Probably his breaking of the chains was not through supernatural strength from the demons but is parallel to the impressive feats of strength sometimes performed by people on drugs such as Angel Dust, which deprives them of the knowledge or awareness of the pain and damage they are causing themselves when they push their muscles beyond their safe limits. Well, non–Christians may often appear, compared to this, to be in their right minds. But they are in principle committed to ignoring or denying their own reason in order to persist in their stubborn denial of God's truth (the Word of God again!), which is simply the truth of what is. They have no choice but to hold to contradictions or try to rationalize irrational views.

The parallels continue. The demoniac was deprived of his own will; the non–believer, who thinks he is in control of his life, is really the slave of Satan. The demoniac was deprived of fellowship, driven out from the community; the non–believer is separate from the people of God and the covenants of promise, the only basis for a lasting and healthy community that can survive the ravages of time. The demoniac was deprived of his dignity, having been unclothed for a long time; the non–believer often seeks only to satisfy his animal desires, or, if he aspires to something more than that, he has no basis for such aspirations, having rejected the One who is the source of all Goodness, Truth, and Beauty. The demoniac was deprived of his own personality, for when asked, he did not give his own name, but the demons spoke for him; the non–believer is on a path that leads to the same place, for he has rejected the Person who is the source of all personhood. The demoniac was preemptively deprived even of life, living symbolically among the tombs; the non–believer is dead in his trespasses and sins (Eph. 2:1), spiritually dead though his body still functions.

Are these parallels merely clever and arbitrary? I don't think so, and the conclusion is devastating. The natural man, the sinful and fallen human being apart from Christ, differs from a demoniac in principle not at all, but only in degree! There is no more hope for them apart from Christ than for one already fully possessed. But in Christ there is hope even for these. Look again at verse 35: "*And they came to Jesus and found the man from whom the demons had gone out sitting down at the feet of Jesus clothed and in his right mind; and they became frightened.*" Apart from Christ, you already suffer from the beginning phases of all the deprivations of real and full humanity that marked the demoniac and are on a path that will take you to the place where your experience of those deprivations will be total. In other words, you are on the road that leads to Hell. That is what Satan has in mind for you. He won't often make it clear by possessing someone dramatically as he does here—the road to Hell for most of us is gentle and smooth and paved with good intentions. But this is the place to which that road leads. And in Christ there is restoration of all that Satan and sin have taken away. All! "*And they came to Jesus and found the man from whom the demons had gone out sitting down at the feet of Jesus clothed and in his right mind; and they became frightened.*"

You cannot deliver yourself from this bondage and this fate. Your only hope is in Christ. Come to Him today! For if you do not, eventually the illusion that seems to divide you from the man in this story will fade away and leave you naked in the cemetery of the universe. God sometimes allows demonic possession, in other words, so we can see that it is simply "sin writ large."

III. The Demons

The next set of characters is the demons themselves. Even they give unwilling testimony to the sovereignty and the saviorhood of Christ, the only One adequate and able to deliver us from such Satanic oppression—and to the authority and power of His Word. They are in terror of the Lord as the one with both the ability and the authority to punish them. Their ultimate fear is of the Abyss, the "*bottomless pit*" of Revelation 20:3. They knew that Christ is the One who will eventually lock them there, and when they saw Him they apparently thought that time might already have come. He knew it was not yet, and so He permitted them to go into the pigs. What manner of man is this, that even the winds and the waves obey him? You think that's a hard question? What about this one? What manner of man is this that demons are terrified of Him? What manner of man is this, who holds the keys to the Abyss? What manner of man is this, indeed?

IV. The Pigs

Next we come to the infamous Gadarene swine. I have a lot of sympathy for the pigs, to tell you the truth. Here they are innocently wallerin' and gruntin' and rootin', and out of nowhere comes a swarm of demons like a thousand angry wasps. Can you imagine the oinking and squealing as that humongous herd of horrendously hurtin' hogs hurtled headlong down the highway to their death by drowning? Why did the Lord allow that? Some people actually see an ethical problem in this story. Why would, how could, a supposedly morally perfect Messiah allow this destruction of the private property of others, not to mention this destruction of animal life?

In answer to this question, some have responded with a question of their own: what were Jews doing with pigs in the first place? Swine–herd is not exactly a kosher profession! Bu while it takes us a way, I don't think that answer really gets at the heart of the question. There was a significant Gentile population in Galilee—"Galilee of the Gentiles"—after all. The swine may well have belonged to them. But even if they did not, there is a more profound point that needs to be raised. The only adequate response is to deny the false premise that lies behind the objection. Who says the pigs did not belong to Jesus? He was the Creator, the Lord of Glory! Everything belongs to Him and is only held in trust by what we call its human owners. Of course the pigs were His, to be disposed of as He saw fit.

Why then did he choose to allow this thing to happen? The ultimate answer may lie beyond us. Like earthquakes, shipwrecks, etc., the loss of the pigs may be seen simply as a result of the Fall, part of the insoluble mystery of evil. But there is one suggestion about Jesus' decision here that seems to me to have merit. It is possible that such an impressive visual effect was necessary in this case to demonstrate to the demoniac's neighbors that his cure was real and that they could safely take him back. After all, he had apparently had moments before when he was quieter and able to be subdued. How else would they have gotten the chains on him for him to break in the first place? And he had always broken them and returned to the tombs, with who knows how much violence and destruction of limb and property in the process. So anybody with any sense would have slapped him right back in a straitjacket this time as well, unless there were a dramatic demonstration to prove that the demons were really gone. Without this final touch—without going the whole hog, as it were—it is possible that Jesus knew the man would not really be restored to his place in the community.

V. The People

Finally we come to the people. Their response is remarkable: "*Depart from us! Get away from here!*" That's gratitude for you. This is not like Peter's similar words, "Depart from me for I am a sinful man." There is no confession of sin. Peter was expressing his sense of unworthiness; these people just wanted to get rid of Jesus because they were afraid He was going to upset the local agricultural economy. They represent the essence of worldliness. They had been offered redemption from bondage to Satan, all that was given to the demoniac, the privilege of sitting at the feet of Jesus, of having the Lord of Glory in their midst. And all this was outweighed for them by the death of a few pigs. Well, before we look down our noses at them, we'd better ask ourselves if *we* really want Jesus around. He never comes without upsetting things, from money lenders in the Temple to our safe, secure lives. Are we up to the adventure of a life with him? That is not a trivial question! I hope we are.

Conclusion

In verse 39, Luke subtly answers the question posed at the end of the Stilling of the Storm, as well as the ones raised by implication by the Healing of the Gerasene Demoniac: "*What manner of man is this that even the winds and the waves obey him?*" For Jesus tells the man to go and tell what great things *God* has done for him, and he goes and tells what great things *Jesus* has done for him. What an example this anonymous demoniac is to us! He helps us see in radical and unvarnished terms what every un–believer is: in bondage to Satan. He helps us realize what salvation is: release from that bondage, which means the restoration of reason, will, personality, relationships, and life. He helps us realize what our response to all of that should be: to sit at Jesus' feet and to hear His Word aright and to proclaim what great things He has done for us. Let us who know Him all rededicate ourselves to that task; and if you have never accepted Him as your own personal Savior and Lord, may you be helped even now to find Him whom to know is life eternal.

JAIRUS' DAUGHTER AND THE WOMAN WITH AN ISSUE OF BLOOD

Luke 8:40 And as Jesus returned, the multitude welcomed him, for they had all been waiting for him. 41 And behold, there came a man named Jairus, and he was an official of the synagogue. And he fell at Jesus' feet and began to entreat him to come to his house. 42 For he had an only daughter, about twelve years old, and she was dying. But as he went, the multitudes were pressing against him. 43 And a woman who had a hemorrhage for twelve years and could not be healed by anyone 44 came up behind him, and touched the fringe of his cloak. And immediately her hemorrhage stopped. 45 And Jesus said, "Who is the one who touched me?" And while they were all denying it, Peter said, "Master, the multitudes are crowding and pressing upon you." 46 But Jesus said, "Someone did touch me, for I was aware that power had gone out from me." 47 When the woman saw that she had not escaped notice, she came trembling and fell down before him, and declared in the presence of all the people the reason why she had touched him, and how she had been immediately healed. 48 And he said to her, "Daughter, your faith has made you well. Go in peace." 49 While he was still speaking, someone came from the house of the synagogue official, saying, "Your daughter has died. Do not trouble the Teacher any more." 50 But when Jesus heard this, he answered him, "Do not be afraid any longer. Only believe, and she shall be made well." 51 And when he had come to the house, he did not allow anyone to enter with him except Peter and John and James, and the girl's father and mother. 52 Now they were all weeping and lamenting for her. But he said, "Stop weeping, for she has not died, but is asleep." 53 And they began laughing at him, knowing she had died. 54 He, however, took her by the hand and called, saying, "Child, arise!" 55 And her spirit returned and she rose immediately, and he gave orders for something to be given her to eat. 56 and her parents were amazed; but he instructed them to tell no one what had happened.

Introduction

We come today to two stories so intertwined that they demand to be studied together: the raising of Jairus' daughter and the healing of the woman who had the issue of blood. The way they are intertwined raises some interesting questions. Why did Jesus go out of His way to elicit a public confession of healing from the woman, but then turn around and forbid Mr. and Mrs. Jairus in effect to make one by commanding them not to tell anyone what had happened to their daughter? Why this difference in treatment of two sets if people on the very same page? In the answers lies an understanding not only of the incidents in themselves, but also of the way in which Jesus treated people as individuals. I wonder if that might have anything to do with how He relates to us? Let's take a look at both of them, starting with the woman.

I. The Woman With The Issue

First let's look at the woman with the hemorrhage. And the first thing to notice about her is what she wanted.

1. The Wish of the Woman (verses 43–44, cf. Mark 5:25–29). What did this woman want? Obviously, to be healed of an incurable disease. Mark's version of the story mentions the fact that she had spent all of her money on many physicians who had done her no good—a fact that Dr. Luke, possibly sensitive to the reputation of the medical profession, did not feel it necessary to include! But there was more to it than that. Why did she just want to touch the hem of Jesus' robe? Now that is a more interesting question than you might think.

All pious Jews were required to have a tassel on the corner of their robe by the Law in Numbers 15:37–41.

> *The Lord also spoke to Moses, saying, "Speak to the sons of Israel and tell them that they shall make for themselves tassels on the corners of their garments throughout their generations, and that they shall put on the tassel of each corner a cord of blue. And it shall be a tassel for you to look at and remember all the commandments of the Lord so as to do them and not follow after your own heart . . . in order that you may remember to do all my commandments and be holy to the Lord your God.*

This tassel was worn by all Jews out of obedience; it would have been worn by Jesus. But the Pharisees had big, gaudy, ostentatious tassels as a symbol of their holiness.[62] Sadly, this spoke of a piety they falsely claimed to possess rather than the sanctity they should have been seeking. But the point is that the tassel had become a symbol of Jewish spirituality. The woman's motives now begin to become clear. She had faith in Jesus as the Messiah, but it was obviously a faith mixed with a good measure of superstition. She thought if she could just touch His tassel, His spiritual power might be transferred or "rub off," and that this would heal her.

There is also another necessary piece of background information we need in order to understand this woman fully. According to Lev. 15:25, her bleeding made her ceremonially unclean. *"Now if a woman has a discharge of blood many days, not at the period of her menstrual impurity . . . she shall continue as though in her menstrual impurity; she is unclean."* Nobody was supposed to touch her. So another reason she tried to touch Jesus' garment rather than simply asking for healing was probably that she was embarrassed and wanted to receive healing and sneak away without attracting any attention. It was not so much humility that led her to this strategy as superstition mixed with inadequate desire. She wanted to be healed, and she had faith enough to believe that Jesus' spiritual power might be able to do it, but she did not (yet) have the faith or understanding to believe that she could have much more: a relationship with Christ!

2. The Question of the Christ (verses 45–46). Understanding what the woman was up to helps us to understand Jesus' question: "Who touched me?" It was undoubtedly not simply a request for information. Jesus' awareness of the activation of His healing power (which was almost certainly not triggered in the superstitious way

---

[62] Edersheim, *Life and Times*, op, cit., 624.

the woman had intended) and Mark's comment in 5:32 that Jesus looked around at her both imply that He was well aware of what was going on. The question was not to satisfy His own curiosity, but to create an opportunity for the woman. He wanted to complete a process that her superstitious faith had been sufficient to begin but could not have brought to its conclusion without growing beyond itself. Jesus was glad to heal her physical ailment, which was not something to belittle in its seriousness (especially when we consider its implications for her ceremonial purity and hence her social standing in the community). But Jesus wanted to give her much more than that. He wanted her to look Him in the eye and hear Him say, "Go in peace." Physical health is not to be despised, but Jesus came to give us something much greater than that: His peace, His *shalom*: the full experience of the blessing of peace, harmonious relationship, *friendship* with God.

3. The Lessons of the Lord (verses 47–48). There are then at least three things the Lord teaches us by his treatment of this woman. First is that **salvation is by faith, not by magic.** He goes out of his way to prevent her intended escape as if to say, "Hey! It's not my tassel; it's me!" It is not physical contact with my magical power but your faith, your trust in me as Messiah, that has saved you. The churches have developed—in some cases been given by the Lord—a number of things to help people be incorporated into fellowship with one another and with Christ. Baptism and Communion were established by Christ himself. We have added things like confirmation, church membership, going forward at an altar call, etc. Some of these things are necessary; all can be helps. But if we think that they have power to save in themselves, if we divorce them from the personal faith in Christ as Lord and Savior that they are designed to foster, they become mere tassels and our faith mere superstition.

Second, **salvation is** not so much the alleviation of particular troubles—even of the flames of Hell—as it is **a personal relationship with God** as Father through the Lord Jesus Christ. It is interesting that in verse 47, the woman claims only to have been healed. In verse 48, Jesus uses the larger word: Her faith has *saved* her. Healing, relief from felt needs, is not the main thing. The main thing is allegiance to Christ as Lord, becoming part of his Kingdom.

Third, we learn that **true faith involves confession** (verse 47). It is when the woman declares before all the people what Christ has done for her that she receives His blessing. As Paul put it, *"if we confess with our mouths that Jesus is Lord and believe in our hearts that God has raised him from the dead, we shall be saved"* (Rom. 10:9–10). There are still many Christians who just want to touch the tassel, but not necessarily to come face to face with the Lord. They may be saved if faith is present, however shallow or confused. But Jesus says to them, "Who touched me? Where are you? Come forth and be counted!" And He will not let us rest until we do.

II. Jairus' Daughter

223

Meanwhile, we are still on our way to Jairus's house. Let's remind ourselves of what happened when they got there.

When he had come to the house, he did not allow anyone to enter with him except Peter and John and James, and the girl's father and mother. Now they were all weeping and lamenting for her. But he said, "Stop weeping, for she has not died, but is asleep." And they began laughing at him, knowing she had died. He, however, took her by the hand and called, saying, "Child, arise!" And her spirit returned and she rose immediately, and he gave orders for something to be given her to eat. and her parents were amazed; but he instructed them to tell no one what had happened. (verses 51–56)

The huge question that jumps out at us from this story is why, after having just gone out of His way to elicit a public confession from the woman, did Jesus work so hard to suppress the one that so naturally would have been forthcoming from Mr. and Mrs. Jairus after the raising of their daughter from the dead? The answer lies in the difference in the audience and what they could have been expected to do with that confession. When Jesus told the mourners that the girl was only asleep, they laughed at Him. Really, they ridiculed Him. Why had He said she was asleep? Not that she wasn't really dead. But what was a permanent and irreversible condition to men was nothing more serious than sleep to Him. And He knew that He was going to wake her up from that sleep. But the mourners outside, unlike Jairus himself, neither had faith in Jesus nor were they really even open to it. Therefore, Jesus' handling of the situation in this case becomes an act of judgment on their unbelief.

Imagine the situation. The mourners have just ridiculed Jesus for saying the girl was asleep. So he goes in with only Peter, James, and John, and the parents and raises her from the dead. But the Jairuses are not supposed to tell anybody what happened. Yet the girl is alive and has a healthy appetite. So what are they going to tell the crowd? "Hey, what's up with your daughter? I thought she was dead. What in the world happened?" and what is Jairus going to say in response to that? "You wouldn't believe me if I told you."

What would the crowd think after that? They could only think that the girl had been asleep after all. What else could they conclude? And they would feel extremely foolish and ashamed for what they had said to Jesus. It's not that Jesus is trying to deceive them. But they have shown themselves not ready for the truth, not open to the truth, not eligible for the truth. Can't you just picture Jack Nicholson popping up to shout at them, "You can't handle the truth!" They got the only truth they were willing to receive, the only truth they were prepared to accept.

Do you understand what has just happened here? These people have just blown the opportunity to participate in one of the greatest of the triumphs of the Kingdom of Heaven, a resurrection from the dead! Yet because of their unbelief, they are only given what they are able to receive. They are left with what they were really asking for all along: a strong taste of dust in their mouths.

The consternation this crowd must have felt levels a pertinent and hard question at us. What truths are we really prepared to receive about Jesus? Do we live a safe but boring Christian life that leaves us comfortably mired in mediocrity if not actual sin and self–destructive habits? Have we become satisfied with fruitlessness and futility? Or maybe we are desperate for a spiritual reality that is always just beyond our reach? Why are we stuck in this rut? Could it be because we are Okay with Jesus as a Savior from a very distant and theoretical Hell but not prepared to deal with Him as Lord of the here and now? Are we prepared to reckon with the gentle Jesus meek and mild but not the radical claimant to the throne who goes around insulting respectable religious leaders when He's not flipping over tables in the Temple?

It is a dangerous thing to mock at the Word of God! It may lead to the loss of the opportunity to hear and believe it later. It just may be that Christ will only give us what we are able and willing to receive. He saw in the Woman the potential to accept a salvation beyond anything she was even able to imagine, and He went out of His way to draw that kind of faith out of her, to strengthen her to look without fear into His intimidating but finally compassionate and loving face. His forbidding of Jairus to tell anyone what happened in the house in effect leaves the mocking mourners trapped in their mockery and in the stubborn unbelief that fed it. What does He see as He watches the truth of His Word impact you and me this morning?

That simple hemorrhaging woman calls to me. There was only a mustard seed of real faith in her superstition, but it was enough. There was only a mustard seed of real faith in her superstition, but she was willing for Jesus to call it forth and let it blossom into the real thing. Those sophisticated mocking mourners, on the other hand, nag at me. Jesus left them in the position of the dwarfs in C. S. Lewis's conclusion to the Narnia books, *The Last Battle*. Sitting under the bright sky in Aslan's country, they believe they are in a dark and filthy stable. How, they ask, can they see what ain't there? And when Lucy tries to share some violets with them, they reject it as stable litter and thistles. No matter what the children or even Aslan himself try to do for them, they refuse to be "taken in." "You see," said Aslan, "they will not let us help them. They have chosen cunning instead of belief. Their prison is only in their own minds, yet they are in that prison, and so afraid of being taken in that they cannot be taken out."[63] They are a graphic picture of what happened to the crowd at the aborted funeral. Brothers and sisters, let us make sure that we do not end up like them!

Conclusion

This passage by bringing together these two contrasting stories brings together two themes that Luke has been working with if your mind can reach back far enough in

---

[63] C. S. Lewis, *The Last Battle* (1956; NY: Harper Collins, 1984), 185–6.

this series (or if your fingers can turn back in the book—to sermons XXIX and XXXI). One is the question of how we respond to the Word of God, if you can remember back to the Parable of the Sower and the Seed. Second is the meaning of faith. Faith is an understanding of who Jesus is that produces confidence in His solution to our problems, as we saw in the Stilling of the Storm. Today we reinforce the importance of how we hear the Word while adding a new wrinkle to our understanding of faith. **Part of the meaning of faith is being willing to receive what God has to give you.** Jesus questioned the Woman with the Issue of Blood to draw out that faith. He found it present in Mr. and Mrs. Jairus, but utterly lacking in the mourners at Jairus's house. What will He find in us?

THE MISSION OF THE TWELVE

Luke 9:1 And he called the twelve together and gave them power and authority over all the demons and to heal diseases. 2 And he sent them out to proclaim the kingdom of God and to perform healing. 3 And he said to them, "Take nothing for your journey, neither a staff, nor a bag, nor bread, nor money, and do not even have two tunics apiece. 4 And whatever house you enter, stay there, and take your leave from there. 5 And as for those who do not receive you, as you go out from that city, shake off the dust from your feet as a testimony against them." 6 And departing, they began going about among the villages preaching the gospel and healing everywhere, 7 Now Herod the Tetrarch heard of all that was happening, and he was greatly perplexed, because it was said by some that John had risen from the dead 8 and by some that Elijah had appeared, and by others that one of the prophets of old had arisen again. 9 And Herod said, "I myself had john beheaded, but who is this man about whom I hear such things?" And he kept trying to see him. 10 And when the apostles returned, they gave an account to him of all that they had done. And taking them with him, he withdrew by himself to a city called Bethsaida.

Introduction

Everyone is interested in beginnings, and rightly so. For to understand the origin of a thing is to understand much about its nature, purpose, and destiny. It is therefore curious that theologians have never been able to agree on when the Church began. One reason for this difficulty is that the Church is so rich and multifaceted an organism. If we define it as the Bride of Christ (and surely this definition is biblical and correct), then it had its beginnings before the foundations of the earth when the Father covenanted with the Son to give Him a people for His name. If we define the Church as the redeemed people of God (and surely this definition is biblical and correct), then you could say it began with the slaying of the animals outside of Eden to provide a covering for Adam and Eve. If we define it as spiritual Israel (and surely this definition is biblical and correct), then it began with the Call of Abraham. If we define the Church as the followers of Jesus Christ (and surely this definition is biblical and correct), then it begins with the calling of the disciples. If we mean the Church as we now know it, called out from the Gentiles and empowered by the Spirit as a witness to the Resurrection in the last days (and surely this definition is biblical and correct), then it began of course at Pentecost. But if we define the Church as a group called together by Jesus Christ to be sent out by Him, then perhaps the Church has its beginning in the passage we have read today.

There is therefore much we can learn from this passage about our identity and our mission as the Church of Jesus Christ. For that mission has not changed from of old. Here we see something about our **calling**, about our **conduct** in pursuit of that calling, and about the **consequences** of our following that calling. First, the calling itself.

I. Our Calling (vv. 1–2)

Our mission and our calling as revealed by this passage is twofold: to preach and to heal. *"And he sent them out to proclaim the kingdom of God and to perform healing"* (verse 2).

1. Preaching. Like Jesus' first disciples, we are commissioned to proclaim the Gospel of the Kingdom. The phrase "Gospel of the Kingdom" in Greek is an idiom that means the good news of the rule or reign of God in the affairs of this world. The good news is not first that Jesus has saved us from our sins. That is pretty good news, of course, but it does not come first. The Good News is first that Jesus is Lord, with all that this sovereignty implies. It is because He is Lord that His death takes away the guilt and the penalty of sin and that His resurrection confers eternal life on all who bow and follow him. It is as Lord that He has the authority to grant us a full pardon for our rebellion against His kingdom. Therefore, God commands all men everywhere to repent and believe. Some of us are called to preach this message formally from the pulpit; all of us are called to deliver it informally as ambassadors of Christ. It is the Good News that has been entrusted to us to deliver to all the world.

2. Healing. How does healing relate to this Good news? Healing should not be confused with the Gospel. The Gospel is the Good News that Jesus is Lord and as such offers pardon for our sins based on His atoning sacrifice. But healing is included in the disciples' mission because it is a *fruit* of Jesus' Lordship. The atonement is the death of the Lord Christ erasing the guilt and remitting the penalty of sin for all who believe. Healing is simply the practical extension of the Lordship of Christ over the effects of sin, ameliorating those temporal effects wherever we can. All pain and suffering are the results of sin, sometimes direct, often indirect. Not every painful thing that happens to you is a direct judgment on a particular sin, as both Job and the man blind from birth in John's Gospel teach us; but pain in general is in the world in general because of sin. Every sickness, every tragedy, everything that is not right is ultimately traceable back to Adam's sin and the Curse it unleashed on the world.

But now Christ as Lord has come to reassert His dominion over His creation, usurped by Satan. The Gospel takes away the *guilt* of sin immediately when we believe. Healing—physical, psychological, social—you see it is more than just *medical* healing—deals with the *effects* of sin that remain behind during this life even after the guilt has been nailed to the Cross. This reassertion of Christ's dominion will be complete when Christ returns, for then every disease will be healed and every tear will be wiped away. But even now we give testimony to its coming reality by ministering Christ's love to whomever we can touch. That is why the Church has always been active in setting up hospitals and orphanages and soup kitchens and schools. In those organized ministries of mercy, or in the individual giving merely a cup of cold water in Jesus' name, we like the first disciples show that the Good News we preach is more than just words.

Now, we no longer live in the time of the Apostles, who had gifts of miraculous healing. Though God still heals, sometimes miraculously, we do not have the apostolic authority to wield that power at will. But we are to do what God enables us to do. You may not have the opportunity to exorcise demons, but you can oppose Satan and all his works and everything he stands for at every level, from personal habits to politics. You may not have the gift of miraculous healing, but you can visit the sick, the elderly, or the prisoner, with encouragement. You can care for an invalid relative. You can open your home to an unwed mother. You can support those organized ministries that try to help people in need. You can give to University Church's deacon's fund. You can put your arm around a suffering friend instead of passing by in embarrassment. You can offer a cup of cold water in Jesus' name. You can do *something* to bring healing to a fallen and sin–ravaged world.

Now, this is our calling just as much as preaching the Gospel is, as our Lord in this passage makes plain. *"And he sent them out to proclaim the kingdom of God and to perform healing"* (verse 2). Healing in this broad sense is in fact intimately related to preaching the Gospel, never to be separated from it. We must neither identify healing with the Gospel nor must we allow them to be separated. Remember the Woman with the Issue of Blood? To confuse healing with the Gospel would be to let her slink away after touching Jesus' tassel with her flow of blood stopped but no relationship with Jesus, no salvation established. To separate them would be to say, "Go in peace," but leave her blood flowing. When we confuse healing with the Gospel, as the Social Gospel movement did in the early Twentieth Century and as many Social Justice Warriors do today, we fall into liberalism and our greatest need, the forgiveness of sin, inevitably gets lost in the shuffle. (Remember that healing is alleviating suffering of whatever kind.) Historically that has always been the result. Conservatives have been vigilant against that confusion, rightly so; but we need to be just as vigilant against the opposite error. For once we have allowed the separation of healing from the Gospel, we have lost our credibility as disciples of the One who said, *"Repent, for the kingdom of heaven is at hand"* and who sent his disciples out to preach—and to heal.

We have a Word to speak and a Work to do, in other words, and they must always be kept together, for the Work is the Word lived and the Word is the Work explained. All this is simply to preach the gospel of redemption from sin through the blood of Jesus Christ and to live as if we actually thought He really was Lord. We must work for what He worked for, preach what He preached, and oppose what He opposed. And this is the calling of the individual Christian and of the corporate Church still and will be until Christ comes. *"And he sent them out to proclaim the kingdom of God and to perform healing."*

II. Our Conduct In Pursuit Of That Calling (vv. 3–6)

The Lord's instructions for His disciples in this mission also teach us something about our conduct in pursuit of our mission of preaching and healing. *And he said to* them, "Take nothing for your journey, neither a staff, nor a bag, nor bread, nor money, and do not even have two tunics apiece. And whatever house you enter, stay there, and take your leave from there. And as for those who do not receive you, as you go out from that city, shake off the dust from your feet as a testimony against them" (verse 3–5). What does this teach us? It teaches us something about our conduct with reference to people in general, with reference to our fellow believers, and with reference to those who oppose us. What it teaches is not obvious to us who are not familiar with first–century Jewish customs, but it becomes obvious when we learn a little bit about them.

1. With Reference to People in General (verse 3). "*Take nothing for your journey, neither a staff, nor a bag, nor bread, nor money, and do not even have two tunics apiece.*" Why did Jesus forbid his disciples to take anything for their journey, including even a bag? What was the point of this? It has nothing to do with traveling without a suitcase. The word translated "bag" is the Greek πηρα (*pera*), which refers to a very particular kind of bag. The *pera* was a beggar's bag, where the beggar would put the money he had collected. There were traveling preachers in the ancient world, religious hucksters who went around begging as they preached. I suppose it was the equivalent of our collecting an offering during the service in American Christianity, and the *pera* was the equivalent of the offering plate. (Aren't you glad we don't do that at UC? Aren't you also glad we do have an offering box for those who do want to give? I am!) Well, these preachers were notorious for asking for money — like certain televangelists we have today. I think Jesus wanted the disciples to bend over backwards not to look like those people.

To translate this into contemporary terms, evangelists should not be asking non–Christians for money — even if they have to do without necessary things! We may share our needs with God's people and accept their support. But the last thing an unbeliever needs to be hearing from us is an appeal for money that will reinforce his belief that money is what we are really after! How dare we make appeals for money on religious television, especially when the programming is evangelistic in nature? For such programs are broadcast to the general public. Those televangelists who do so (not all of them do) might as well be wearing a *pera*, a begging bag, around their necks! They are disobedient to the Lord's command, and they bring the Gospel into disrepute and cause the enemies of God to blaspheme.

2. With Reference to our Fellow Believers (verse. 4). "*And whatever house you enter, stay there, and take your leave from there.*" What is the point of staying in one house? The principle here is that we should prefer permanent relationships to free circulation, commitment and accountability to being spiritual free–lance artists. Could these houses which welcomed Jesus' representatives, obviously houses belonging to people who believed in Him as the Messiah, have been the forerunners of the later house churches in each of these towns? I bet they were. God's will is that his servants who are proclaiming the Gospel of the Kingdom today be loyal and accountable to a specific local church in their ministry. Church hoppers never accomplish anything for the kingdom.

3. With Reference to Opposition (verse 5). "*And as for those who do not receive you, as you go out from that city, shake off the dust from your feet as a testimony against them.*" At this point in the New Testament history, the Church as the people of God had not yet become formally distinct from Israel as a nation. So the rejection and opposition dealt with here is really opposition that comes from within the Church. Therefore, the principle that is enunciated here is that when opposition to the very Gospel itself comes from within the professing Church, separation becomes necessary. How is this seen here? It is in that dust the disciples were to shake off their feet. Shaking the dust off your feet was not an original gesture with Jesus, but this application of it was. Pharisees who traveled outside of Israel would always shake the dust of the Gentile nations off of their feet when they crossed the border coming home. Now, to shake *Jewish* dust off is a radical gesture indeed! It is saying, "You are really pagan; you must be treated as those who are outside of true Israel. For you have rejected God's Messiah."

Whether it comes from classic Protestant liberalism, cultic Pharisaism, or the new Post–Modernism, those who deny the very Gospel itself—those who deny that Jesus is the true Son of God come in human flesh, those who deny that He rose bodily and objectively from the dead, those who deny that salvation is by grace alone through faith alone in His atoning death alone, apart from human works—Those who deny these central truths are not to be tolerated in the Church or treated as if they were really members of the Church. The Gospel is so central to the Church's identity that allegiance to its truth comes even before maintaining the outward unity of the organization. If we do not preach the Gospel in purity and maintain our message with integrity and practice it through the works of mercy we looked at earlier, we will be but an anemic shell of the Church we were supposed to be.

III. The Consequences Of Pursuing Our Calling (vv. 6–9)

What were the consequences of the disciples' following the Lord's instructions here? They were very interesting. *And departing, they began going about among the villages preaching the gospel and healing everywhere, Now Herod the Tetrarch heard of all that was happening, and he was greatly perplexed, because it was said by some that John had risen from the dead and by some that Elijah had appeared, and by others that one of the prophets of old had arisen again. And Herod said, "I myself had john beheaded, but who is this man about whom I hear such things?" And he kept trying to see him* verse 6–9).

I find it very interesting that it was not the ministry of Christ as such, but the ministry of the Twelve, that caused Herod to sit up and take notice. It was the mission of the twelve that attracted his attention. In other words, the disciples were reaching more people than Christ had Himself. More people were hearing about Jesus, thinking about Jesus, and wanting to see Jesus. In Herod's case, unfortunately, this did not lead to conversion. But until we get people at least that far, until people are hearing about

231

Jesus in such a way that they are thinking about Him and wanting to know more about Him, there is no opportunity for conversion. And there were many others who did come to faith in Christ as a result of this mission.

Why is this not happening to the same extent today? Why does transfer growth far outweigh conversion growth in most of our churches, when they are growing at all and not declining or plateaued? One reason is that we have forgotten the definition of the Church implied by this passage: a group brought together by Jesus Christ *for the purpose of being sent out* by Him. And we have forgotten the purpose and the plan of that sending: to preach the Gospel and to heal, that is, to show some substantial reality of the difference the Gospel makes, maintaining our integrity before the Church and the watching world as we do so.

Now here is a question we need to ask ourselves as individuals and as a congregation. I think if we have a hard time answering it, we have a problem. What are we doing to get people outside these walls hearing about Jesus, thinking about Jesus, and wanting to see Jesus? What are we doing to show them some substantial reality of the difference the Gospel makes to that end? I do not presume to tell you what your answer should be, but I believe I am obligated by Jesus' action in this passage, by His bringing His disciples together to send them out to preach and to heal, to ask the question and tell you that you do need to have an answer.

Conclusion

Bottom line: We have a Word to speak and a Work to do, and they must always be kept together; for the Work is the Word lived and the Word is the Work explained. If you are a child of God through faith in Jesus Christ today, I invite you to use the Lord's Supper as a covenant with God, recommitting yourself to Christ and to this understanding of who you are and what your calling is in Him. Amen.

THE FEEDING OF THE 5,000

Luke 9:10 And when the apostles returned, they gave an account to him of all that they had done. And taking them with him, he withdrew by himself to a city called Bethsaida. 11 But the multitudes were aware of this and followed him. And welcoming them, he began speaking to them about the kingdom of God and curing those who had need of healing. 12 And the day began to decline, and the twelve came and said to him, "Send the multitude away so that they may go into the surrounding villages and countryside and find lodging and get something to eat; for here we are in a desolate place." 13 But he said to them, "You give them something to eat!" And they said, "We have no more than five loaves and two fish, unless perhaps we go and buy food for all these people." 14 (For there were about five thousand men.) And he said to his disciples, "Have them recline to eat in groups of about fifty each." 15 And they did so, and had them all recline. 16 And he took the five loaves and the two fish, and looking up to heaven, he blessed them and broke them and kept giving them to the disciples to set before the multitude. 17 And they all ate and were satisfied; and the broken pieces which they had left over were picked up, twelve baskets full.

Introduction

The very familiar story we have read today is the only miracle (except the Resurrection) to be recorded in all four Gospels. Do you find that fact surprising? It is quite true. That striking fact raises the obvious question, "What made this incident so important, so significant in the memory of the disciples?" Let's keep that question in the back of our minds as we study Luke's account, which contains at least three elements: a feat accomplished, faith elicited, and a future embraced.

I. A Feat To Be Accomplished

It was, first, a feat to be accomplished. In some ways, The Feeding of the Five Thousand was the most impressive miracle (to the crowd at least) yet. For, you see, many of the others could have been explained away by those with the inclination to do so. This one could not. Everyone but the servants at Cana of Galilee might have thought some kind of switcheroo had occurred when the water was turned to wine. We have had faith healers who looked very impressive to their audiences exposed as frauds in our own day; maybe some of Jesus' healings could have been faked too. Jairus' daughter, after all, despite all appearances to the contrary, must have really just been asleep. Had not Jesus said so himself? The Woman with the Issue of Blood claimed to have been healed, but nobody noticed her at all until she did, and consequently nobody had exactly seen her bleeding beforehand. She was embarrassed and kept it hidden. Only the disciples, after all—not exactly the most objective and unbiased witnesses, as far as the Pharisees were concerned—saw the Miraculous Draught of Fishes or the Calming of the Storm or the Walking on the Water or the Transfiguration. But the

Feeding of the Five Thousand: This event could not be dismissed or explained away—and if it cannot be explained away, if we just have to deal with it as inescapably miraculous, then why bother trying to explain away the others? Then they all start mounting up as witnesses to the power of God in this Man!

Three factors made the Feeding of the Five Thousand into what today we would call a "media event." First is the fact that there were five thousand witnesses (not counting women and children), not an insignificant number even by today's standards. Second, they were in a desert (i.e., deserted, wilderness—not like the Sahara) place. I have been there. It is flat and grassy, and you can see a long way. The point is that there was literally no place where enough food to feed that big a crowd could have been stashed or hidden. While only a few at the Wedding in Cana saw the actual transformation of the water into wine, here everyone could see with his own eyes the five loaves being multiplied into five thousand. More bread and fish just kept coming—but from where? From Jesus' hands. There was no other place from which it could come. And third, the miracle met an immediate need, not just of one person among many onlookers, but of every single person in the crowd. They liked it so much that John says they were chasing Jesus all around the Sea of Galilee hoping for seconds. So they were all focused on what was happening. You cannot shut up five thousand people, and you cannot dismiss their testimony. Jesus was already popular; He was already being looked on as a person who might be the One who was coming. But this miracle ups the ante in several significant ways.

What then is the theological point, the spiritual significance of the feat Jesus accomplished here? It is in what is revealed about Jesus, and there are at least two revelations. In the first place, **He is revealed as the Lord of Creation**, the One who multiplies food in Nature. In his classic work *Miracles*, C. S. Lewis shows how many of the miracles Jesus performed take what God normally does slowly in Nature and speeds it up dramatically as a kind of flourished signature, signifying, "the One who *always* multiplies fish and grain is here." God turns water into wine all the time, but He normally uses a grapevine and takes several months to do it. He multiplies fish and bread all the time, but normally uses wheat plants and mommy and daddy fish to do it.[64] Even the pagans recognized that there was a divine power behind Nature's ability to reproduce so richly as to be able to feed mankind. In the pagan mind, Zeus presided over the thunder that signaled life–giving rain, Ceres presided over the grain as it was growing in the field, Poseidon presided over the fish of the sea, Bacchus over the grape in the vine, Persephone over the life–giving revival of Nature in the Spring. What those Greek pagans glimpsed through a glass darkly in a debased and fragmented form, Jesus revealed in all its unified and holy splendor: The God of Nature, Yahweh, the glad Giver of Life, is here! I can best sum it up with a sonnet:

---

[64] C. S. Lewis, *Miracles*, op. cit., 140–152.

The ancients worshipped what they did not know:
>Corruptible men and beasts and creeping things
>Enthroned in splendor, deathless. From below,
>They scaled the sky with such imaginings,

But for that trip they needed stronger wings.
>The glimpses filled their hearts with holy dread;
>They could not see the way the King of Kings
>Joins all the scattered hints into one Head:

Atropos, who snips thread after thread;
>Poseidon, master of the raging sea;
>Hera of the hearth and marriage bed;
>Life–giving power of Persephone;

Aphrodite's beauty; Ares' might;
>Zeus's thunder; and Apollo's light.[65]

So Jesus is revealed as the Lord of Creation, the original and unified One that the Greek and Roman pagans had fragmented into their multiple polytheistic deities.

Jesus is revealed in the second place not only as the Power that gives life and multiplies it in nature, but also more specifically **as the Old–Testament** *Jehovah Jireh*, "the Lord who Provides." But what does He provide here? What is the promise that He keeps? What is the need that He meets? It might not be what you think. If you read the story carefully, you will see something very interesting. He has commanded the disciples to feed the people, only to elicit their admission that they cannot. Then he tells them to seat the people on the grass anyway. Awkward! What is my point? The need being met here is not so much the people's need for full bellies, though of course that gets richly provided for. But the more important need that is met is the disciples' need to be able to minister! It is not the people's ability to eat so much as the disciples' ability to serve, not so much the people's need to be fed as the disciples' ability to feed them, that is being supplied by Jesus in this miracle.

Why does this matter? Because thus our Lord still provides for His servants today. For not one of us could so much as give a cup of cold water in His name in a way that would truly glorify Him apart from His grace. Do we wish to serve the Lord? After all He has done for us, what other desire could we have? Do we confess our utter inability to serve Him worthily? After all we have seen about how Wonderful He is, what other confession could we make? Then receive today His promise afresh and His provision anew! Do you have just five loaves and two fish? No talent or ability (that's probably an exaggeration—you've surely got a few loaves and a couple of fish worth)? No holiness in yourself (that's definitely not an exaggeration!) that could allow you to stand as Christ's ambassador, His representative before men? No? Well, then, you are

---

[65] Donald T. Williams, *Stars through the Clouds*, op. cit., 109.

in the same position as Jesus' disciples were on this day. And so, rejoice! He has not changed. It is your job only to make your inadequate loaves and fishes available. It is His job to make them enough. Let me repeat that: It is your job only to make your inadequate loaves and fishes available. It is His job to make them enough. And that leads us to our next point.

II. A Faith To Be Elicited

Not only is there a feat to be accomplished; this story also presents us with a faith to be elicited. The people got a good meal of fish and hush puppies, but the disciples received something far more significant. They got another of the series of lessons in faith that Luke seems to be presenting throughout his Gospel. We have already seen at the Stilling of the Storm that faith is an understanding of who Jesus is that produces confidence in His solution of our problems. We saw with the healing of the Woman with the Issue of Blood that it is a personal response to Jesus as Lord and Savior, not a superstitious trust in externals. What will Luke add to that understanding of faith today?

The disciples begin with a perception of a problem, a need to be met: What are we going to do with all these people out here in the middle of nowhere? And that was good. So they came to Jesus with a solution to the problem already in mind: We'd better send the people away to the villages to try to find some food and lodging. And that was not bad either. But as often happens, Jesus had a different solution in mind: *You* feed them! What? At this point, the disciples must have recognized that they were being asked to do the impossible. They freely confess their inability. And what is Jesus' response to that? Okay, tell the people to sit down in groups to facilitate our passing out the food!

It is this moment that I think is the most interesting and instructive moment in the whole story. For it shows that the disciples had learned something from those previous lessons. It is one of their best moments, one of their most impressive acts (they will have plenty of further opportunities to embarrass themselves before the Gospels are over!). And it was very simple. They obeyed. What is more, they did it immediately. Before Jesus had multiplied a single loaf or fish, they obeyed. Boy, were they sticking their necks out! They were going to look pretty foolish if something didn't happen! And Jesus has not even told them what He was planning to do. He just takes the pittance they have and tells them to arrange the people for food service. If only the disciples could have responded like this more consistently! If only we would.

The disciples obeyed, and in that obedience they learned another important lesson about faith, one whose elements are still present in every mighty work of God. We can express it in the form of an equation, or, since this is a story about food, a recipe if you will. **Need seen, plus desire felt, plus inadequacy confessed, plus Christ obeyed, equals the opportunity for God to work in ways that may be miraculous.** Let me repeat that. Need seen, plus desire felt, plus inadequacy confessed, plus Christ obeyed, equals the opportunity for God to work in ways that may be miraculous. We start with an awareness of a need and the desire to meet it. But we must add to that an awareness (and admission) of our own inability to meet that need, of the inadequacy of our resources. *Then* we add the critical element: a commitment to **obey** Jesus in spite of that inadequacy, a determination to obey Him in the face of that inability.

Now we have set the stage for God to meet the need—and He will do it by using those very resources that were so inadequate when they were still in our hands. It is your job only to make your inadequate loaves and fishes available. It is His job to make them enough. **And faith is the determination to obey in spite of our inadequacy; it is to consider our own inability irrelevant in the light of His ability; and it is to act on that basis.** Faith is the determination to obey in spite of our inadequacy; it is to consider our own inability irrelevant in the light of His ability; and it is to act on that basis. The more we do so, the more we will find our own paltry loaves and fishes multiplied.

III. A Future To Be Faced

Finally, there is in this story not only a feat to be accomplished and a faith to be elicited; there is also a future to be faced. In each of the four Gospels, this event is a turning point in the earthly life and ministry of Jesus. It marks the apex of His popularity with the multitudes, and understandably so. Who doesn't like a free lunch? But that popularity from this point on declines most precipitously. Why? Because Jesus now begins in each Gospel to concentrate His teaching increasingly, with ever increasing tension and intensity, mounting to a grand climax at the end, on preparing Himself and His disciples for the Cross. The people were ready to make Him king, but He had not come to be the kind of king they wanted (a Burger King?), and in their disappointment and disillusionment when He turned instead to the path of the Cross they turned from Him as fiercely as they previously had followed Him. From this moment He sets his face like flint to go to Jerusalem and take the way of the Cross. Only their lack of understanding kept even the Twelve following Him on *that* road.

It is not easy to obey, to sit people down at the table when you do not yet see any fish or bread to set before them. To their credit, the disciples passed that test. Would we? But **the real test of faith** is something greater even than that: It **is our commitment to follow Christ on this road, the road that leads to the Cross**. Will we walk with Him on the Calvary road when it means giving up the very popularity that seemed our greatest opportunity to serve him? I think the Evangelical movement was set up for this temptation in 1980, the "Year of the Evangelical" in popular media, and it has not done very well in handling the loss of popularity that inevitably comes when the world rejects our message. What forms might this temptation take for us? Will we walk with Christ on the Calvary Road even if it means giving up our very lives? It's kind of easy to say yes when that is only a theoretical possibility. But what about some of the forms that rejection might more realistically take in our actual lives? What about our jobs—or even just our ability to advance in them? Our reputations? Increasingly we will face such

237

things as the world continues in the direction it has taken over the last decade. Some of our fellow Christians have already experienced them. We had better be ready.

My friends, we are as inadequate to this as we would have been to feed five thousand people with five loaves and two small fish. But don't forget one thing: Those people got fed! And we can remember how they did when the even tougher obediences of faith are asked of us. And that memory can help us be faithful even then.

Conclusion

The Cross, Christ's sacrificial death for our sins, is at the center of the Gospel message. It is also at the center of the Christian life. We have foretastes of the Marriage Supper of the Lamb like the one we read about today. We have foretastes of it in the Communion meal that we will share in just a minute. But until our Lord returns, we will have those foretastes as refreshments and encouragements on the Calvary Road. So let us deny ourselves, take up our crosses, and follow Him (Luke 9:23). For that is to know life and know it more abundantly, both now and forevermore (John 10:10). Amen.

CROSS-BEARING: CONFESSION—AND FOLLOW-THROUGH

Luke 9:18 And it came about that while he was praying alone, the disciples were with him, and he questioned them, saying, "Who do the multitudes say that I am?" 19 And they answered and said, "John the Baptist, and others say Elijah; but others that one of the prophets of old has arisen again." 20 And he said to them, "But who do you say that I am?" And Peter answered and said, "The Christ of God." 21 And he warned them and instructed them not to tell this to anyone, 22 saying, "The Son of Man must suffer many things and be rejected by the elders and chief priests and scribes and be killed, and be raised up on the third day." 23 And he was saying to them all, "If anyone wishes to come after me, let him deny himself, take up his cross daily, and follow me. 24 For whoever wishes to save his life shall lose it, but whoever loses his life for my sake, he is the one who will save it. 25 For what is a man profited if he gains the whole world and loses or forfeits himself? 26 For whoever is ashamed of me and my words, of him shall the Son of Man be ashamed when he comes in his glory, and the glory of the Father and of the holy angels. 27 But I say to you truthfully, there are some of those standing here who shall not taste death until they see the kingdom of God."

Introduction

In our last study we saw the reason why all four Gospels include the Feeding of the Five Thousand: It is a turning point in the earthly ministry of our Lord Jesus Christ. From this moment when His popularity was at its height, He began increasingly to focus with ever mounting insistence and clarity on the centrality of the Cross to His mission and His identity, a message that was increasingly met with stunned bewilderment and rejection. The familiar passage before us today is the first example of that new focus. Matthew's version of the story is fuller and more familiar. Luke leaves out Jesus' praise of Peter's confession, his renaming of Simon as Peter ("a stone") and the controversial promise to build his church upon the rock—a different word in Greek that clearly does not refer to Peter the pebble but to the boulder–like truth of his confession, which in its fuller form was "Thou art the Christ, the Son of the living God." Why does Luke leave out these important details? Because his more compact narration has the effect of bringing together in close proximity the two ideas of confession and cross–bearing, thus bringing out or highlighting the point that our confession of Christ has consequences. In this manner, Luke forces us to consider the question: What are the consequences of confession? What are the demands of discipleship? What is the follow–through that flows from faith? What is the cost of commitment? What is the price of receiving pardon? What is the responsibility that comes with redemption?

The answer to that question is the main thesis of our message today: It is that **salvation is free, but it is not cheap.** In other words, Christ has already purchased it with His own blood. Nothing could be less cheap than that! We have nothing we could give to obtain what He already gives us freely. But though salvation is free, it is not cheap; and part of the meaning of the not–cheapness is that accepting this free gift is going to cost you something. Does that sound like a paradox? A careful reading of Jesus' words here is the key to understanding it. For they all drive us—as His mission drove Him—to the cross.

But let's get one question out of the way before we look at them. If a gift is really free, can it cost you something to receive it? Of course. When I was a poor pastor just out of grad school, one of our parishioners took pity on us and gave us an old bomb their family wasn't using as a second car so that my wife wouldn't be stuck at home when I was out doing hospital calls or something. The car was a completely free gift, with no strings attached. I never paid _____ _____ one cent for it. We named it "Ol' Yeller" because of its age and its faded color; it was an old Plymouth station wagon with a slant six in it. And it was, as I have said, totally free. Nevertheless, I actually had to count rather carefully the cost of whether or not I could afford to accept this completely free gift. In the very first week I had to pay and pay again for a license tag, motor oil, gasoline, and insurance. None of these payments went to the giver; none of them compromised the completely free offer of the gift. I could have paid for all those things separately, and none of those payments would have given me a car apart from Mrs. _____'s generosity. Those payments were not made—could not have been made—to receive the gift. They were simply inherent in the very nature of the gift itself. It could be that salvation is that kind of free gift—and it could be that not understanding this principle has been the cause of much confusion, leading some (Roman Catholics, for example) to deny the completely gracious character of the gift, as if we had to do at least a little work for it, and leading others (Antinomians) to deny that there is any price for us to pay in any sense. Okay, let's see if my experience with Ol' Yeller is consistent with what Jesus has to say to us here.

I. The Necessity Of Cross Bearing

Jesus' words are clear and plain: *"If anyone wishes to come after me, let him deny himself, take up his cross daily, and follow me."* They apply to anyone and therefore to everyone. They describe, not an optional, graduate level type of Christian life, but the Christian life, period. For no person who is not following Jesus can be said to be living the Christian life at all. Two facts about this cross bearing bring its necessity into focus.

1. Its Connection with Confession. First is the intimate connection between cross bearing and confession of Christ. Jesus brings this hard saying up as part of His response to Peter's confession of His Messiahship. The obvious question is, why say all of this hard, unpopular stuff about denying oneself and taking up the cross *now*? And the obvious answer is, to be sure that the disciples understand what confessing Jesus as their Messiah means. For Jesus, it means being rejected and killed and rising the third day. For Jesus, in other words, it means the Cross. And for the disciples, it means that they have a cross of their own to deal with. *"If anyone wishes to come after me, let him deny* *himself, take up his cross daily, and follow me."* Before you confess me as Messiah, in other words, you had better—in language the Lord uses elsewhere—count the cost.

Confessing Christ as Lord is part of the very definition of what a Christian is, part of the very definition of how to be saved, in one of the most familiar summaries of the Gospel in all of Scripture. *"That if you confess with your mouth Jesus as Lord and believe in your heart that God raised him from the dead, you shall be saved. For with the heart man believes, resulting in righteousness, and with the mouth he confesses, resulting in salvation"* (Rom. 10:9–10). This is really just a more elaborate version of the simpler *"Believe on the Lord Jesus Christ, and you shall be saved"* (Acts 16:31). This is so because "believe" never means just "entertain as an opinion" in the New Testament when salvation is in view. It means "place your trust in and therefore be committed to Christ as a person." A belief so timid and tentative as to remain unconfessed is hardly any ground for a warranted hope of salvation! Only God can judge the heart, and I will therefore not dogmatically deny that such people might be saved "yet so as by fire" or "by the skin of their teeth" (1 Cor. 3:15). But they do not represent the normative picture of saving faith we are presented in the New Testament.

All right, then: If we confess with our mouth Jesus as Lord and believe in our hearts that God raised Him from the dead, we shall be saved. Confession is simply that heart belief put into action. Confession is true heart faith made audible. It is not just saying the right words; it is the right words coming out of the mouth because first they are in the heart. Therefore, no one can legitimately claim to have saving faith who does not confess Jesus as Lord before men. And here's the connection. No one can truly confess Christ as Lord without denying himself, taking up his cross, and following Him. Without this, what could the word "Lord" in our confession possibly mean?

2. Its Character as Command. Not only is cross bearing part of the very meaning of confessing Christ as Lord; it is also His commandment for all His disciples. In verse 23 He addresses anyone who would come after him. Anyone. This teaching is not just for super–spiritual "saints"; it is for all His disciples. And what does he say to this "anyone"? Let him take up his cross. "Let him" is a third–person imperative in Greek. It is a command. It is not optional; it is not avoidable; it is an absolute requirement for anyone who would follow Jesus. It is commanded because it is part of the very nature of what confessing Christ as Lord is.

The logic of Christ's words is inescapable once we stop to think about them. Imagine a person who says, "I accept Jesus Christ as my personal Messiah, that is, as the divine Son of God who came to be my personal Savior and Lord—but I'm going to retain the right to be my own boss." Once the hidden caveat, the "fine print" in the second part of the sentence, is brought out into the open, we can only either confess it as sin and forsake it or give up our claim to have accepted Christ at all. It is sheer absurdity. Both things cannot be meant simultaneously. You might as well say, "I'm a circle with four corners." "I'm a square with three sides." You can say such things with your mouth, but you cannot mean them. They are not mean—able. They are meaningless nonsense. No one can truly confess Christ as Lord without denying himself, taking up his cross, and following Him. Doing this perfectly is not a requirement for salvation. No one in fact does it perfectly. But, however imperfectly, it must be what we are doing. Otherwise, what has become of our confession?

This is not adding some kind of works—righteousness requirement onto faith. It is what faith looks like. It is what faith is. It is as much as to say that confessing Christ as Lord is confessing Christ as *Lord*—not as something else. The relationship to Christ that saves us, that in fact constitutes salvation, is given to us as a free gift. There is nothing we could do to earn it. But this is what the relationship is! Why, you might well ask, would anyone want such a relationship? For only one reason: because He is Jesus. Because, in other words, we love Him, because He first love us and gave Himself for us. If you are playing at Christianity for any other reason than that, you might as well stop wasting your time right now. There is no other reason. If we are not interested in this, there is nothing in the Christian faith that could possibly interest us. But if you love Him . . . then you must be interested in the next point.

II. The Nature Of Cross Bearing

If cross bearing is an essential part of following Christ, we had better be sure we understand what it is. Our Lord uses two phrases to describe it that are both subject to much misunderstanding: deny yourself and take up your cross.

1. Deny Yourself. People think this is a hard saying, but most of them have no idea how hard it actually is. They are worried that Christ might ask them to deny themselves some particular thing which they might find hard to give up—like promiscuous sex, or money, or their comfortable lifestyle. I'm afraid it is much worse than that. What He asks is not that I deny myself some *thing*. What He asks is that I deny my *self*. It is the whole principle of "me first" that constitutes my sinful identity as a son of Adam that has to go. It is not my unique personality, created by God for his glory, that must be denied. Ironically, the denial of self is the only way in which *that* "self" can truly be affirmed. What I must deny is the *sovereignty* of self, the primacy of self. Whether or not the self thus denied gets to hang on to this or that tid—bit that it was formerly in the habit of calling its own is hardly the issue. Once self has been denied, that will no longer be an issue. We are being asked here to recognize Jesus as the absolute Lord of glory before whom our place is on our faces in the dust. We are being asked to consciously and with meaning make the Lordship we have already accepted in principle when we accepted Him absolute. We are being asked to say to Him—as he said to the Father—"Not my will but thy will be done."

Now, this goes against the grain of our age. Our age is telling us the very opposite. We are told that self—affirmation, self—expression, self—fulfillment is the path to joy. And we have accepted this lie on levels we are not even aware of. But it is a lie, and at our best we already know it. Which moments in your own life have given you the greatest joy? Manipulating another person for your own selfish desires or falling in love? Being a "hot dog" for your own glory or sacrificing yourself for the sake of the team's victory? If you answered the first option in either pair, you only prove that you have never known the second. I am here to tell you that our Lord knew what He was talking about. This principle is true even in the natural world because it is the very watershed of the spiritual life. If you want to be His disciple, deny yourself, take up your cross, and follow Him! You cannot confess Christ as Lord—you cannot invite Christ to take the throne of your life—if you are still sitting there.

2. Take Up Your Cross. The second phrase is commonly understood no better than the first. When most people speak of having a cross to bear, they are mindlessly using the Lord's words as a metaphor for some hardship in their life—and sometimes a fairly trivial one. My roommate's snoring; my body's propensity to snag and hang onto every calorie that passes near it; my unreasonable boss; you name it: This is (we say with a sigh) just the cross I have to bear. We wouldn't say such stupid things if we had lived in the first century, when the cross was the common method of execution. So let's translate the Lord's words into Twenty–First–Century language. "If any man would come after me, let him deny himself, sit down in the electric chair, and follow me." "If any man would come after me, let him deny himself, stick his head in the noose, and follow me." "If any man would come after me, let him deny himself, hold out his arm for the lethal injection, and follow me." "If any man would come after me, let him deny himself, walk into the gas chamber, and follow me." "If any man would come after me, let him deny himself, step in front of the firing squad, and follow me." Are we getting the idea? In the First Century, confessing Christ literally meant risking the martyr's death. It would be supremely foolish to do so without taking that into account! But there is a spiritual principle here that transcends the circumstances of the early Church.

Taking up the cross, in other words, is exactly parallel to the first phrase, to denying our self. As Christ laid down His life for us, so we are to lay down our lives for Him. And we are to do it daily. We consider ourselves, as Paul puts it in Romans, already dead to sin so that we can be alive to God (Rom. 6:1–11). Or, as he told the Galatians, Christ lives in us; it is no longer we who live, but the life we live, we live by faith in the Son of God, who loved us and gave himself for us (Gal. 2:20). If I have laid down my very life, what else do I have left to hold back? If the necessity of actual martyrdom arises, the decision has already been made in advance. Does this sound negative? It only seems so to people who do not know the Lord! Those who love him would give up their lives and more and count it all as dung for the surpassing value of knowing Christ (Phil. 3:7–8). It is not as if He is holding out on us until we make these nasty sacrifices. It is rather that because of who He is—because He is God, because He is Lord—we cannot truly have Him and keep control of our own lives. It is not an arbitrary requirement with which He could have dispensed. It is the very nature of the relationship He is freely offering us by grace alone: a relationship with God! Why do we insist on trying to settle for something less? *"If any man would come after me, let him deny himself, take up his cross daily, and follow me."*

Conclusion

Salvation is free, but it is not cheap. It cost our Lord Jesus Christ everything. But He made the payment in full simply because He loved us. Now, there is nothing you could give for such a great salvation. You must accept it as the free gift of His grace, His unmerited favor, if you are to have it at all. But accepting that gift will cost you something. It might in effect cost you some of your friends (you won't reject them, but they might reject you); it might cost you some of your possessions; it might cost you some of your habits. But those are superficial things. What it will ultimately cost you is your independence. What it will ultimately cost you is your *self*, your life. Nevertheless, I do not hesitate to ask you to count the cost, any more than our Lord Himself did. Why? You are only being asked to empty your hand so He can fill it. Deny yourself, take up your cross, and follow Him. And you will discover that it has cost you precisely everything that has been holding you back from the joy for which you were created. *"If you confess with your mouth Jesus as Lord, and believe in your heart that God raised him from the dead, you shall be saved."* What does that mean? *"If any man would come after me, let him deny himself, take up his cross, and follow me."* Let us follow Him indeed!

THE TRANSFIGURATION

Luke 9:27 *"But I say to you truthfully that there are some of those standing here who shall not taste death until they see the kingdom of God." 28 And some eight days after these sayings, it came about that he took along Peter and John and James and went up to a mountain to pray. 29 And while he was praying, the appearance of his face became different and his clothing became white and gleaming. 30 And behold, two men were talking with him; and they were Moses and Elijah, 31 who, appearing in glory, were speaking of his departure which he was about to accomplish in Jerusalem. 32 Now Peter and his companions had been overcome with sleep, but when they were fully awake they saw his glory and the two men standing with him. 33 And it came about that as these were departing from him, Peter said to Jesus, "Master, it is good for us to be here. Let us make three tabernacles, one for you, one for Moses, and one for Elijah"—not realizing what he was saying. 34 And while he was saying this, a cloud formed and began to overshadow them; and they were afraid as they entered the cloud. 35 And a voice came out of the cloud , saying, "This is my Son, my Chosen One; listen to him!" 36 And when the voice had spoken, Jesus was found alone. And they kept silent and reported to no one in those days any of the things which they had seen.*

37 And it came about that on the next day, when they had come down from the mountain, a great multitude met him. 38 And behold, a man from the multitude shouted out, saying, "Teacher, I beg you to look at my son, for he is my only boy, 39 and behold, a spirit seizes him, and he suddenly screams, and it throws him into a convulsion with foaming at the mouth, and as it mauls him it scarcely leaves him. 40 And I begged your disciples to cast it out, and they could not." 41 And Jesus answered and said, "Oh unbelieving and perverted generation, how long shall I be with you and put up with you? Bring your son here." 42 And while he was still approaching him, the demon dashed him to the ground and threw him into a convulsion. But Jesus rebuked the unclean spirit and healed the boy and gave him back to his father. 43 And they were all amazed at the greatness of God. But while everyone was marveling at all that he was doing, he said to his disciples, 44 "Let these words sink into your ears; for the Son of Man is going to be delivered into the hands of men." 45 But they did not understand this statement, and it was concealed from them so that they might not perceive it; and they were afraid to ask him about this statement.

Introduction

We come today to one of the strangest and most eerie stories in all of Scripture. Only our familiarity with it blinds us to its mystery and dulls the sense of awe we should have as we read it. In my attempt to explain its significance this morning, my outline is as simple as one, two, three: what it meant to the One (Jesus), to the two (Moses and Elijah), and to the three (Peter, James, and John).

I. Its Significance For The One (Jesus Christ)

This event in the life of Jesus takes on added meaning and importance if we look at it, not just as an isolated episode, but as it appears in the context of Jesus' life. When we think of it that way, we realize how many different threads of Luke's narrative it pulls together. We begin by recalling Jesus' baptism, for when Jesus came up out of the water, He heard the same Voice giving Him the same message (Luke 9:35, cf. 3:22). *"This is my beloved Son."* This cannot be a coincidence. So what was happening at the baptism, and how does it connect with what we find here on the Mountain?

If you can recall our treatment of that earlier passage, Jesus was submitting to a baptism of repentance for the remission of sin—a baptism He did not personally need. Yet He insisted on receiving that baptism anyway, because it was a symbolic way of identifying Himself with His people, whose sins He had come to atone for. It was an act of commitment to His ministry conceived as that of the ultimate Sin–Bearer. To this commitment the Father responds with approval and encouragement: *"This is my beloved Son! I am pleased with Him."*

That this was in fact the meaning of that experience to Jesus is confirmed by the fact that it is immediately followed by the Temptation in the Wilderness, in which Satan specifically tries to get Jesus to question His unique divine Sonship and renounce the way of the Cross. That temptation then continues through the crowd, who want Jesus to be a military messiah, and even through His own disciples, who share the same hope with the crowd and cannot understand all this dark talk about being delivered into the hands of the Gentiles, suffering, and being raised the third day. Now the multitudes have begun to forsake Jesus because He refuses to be their ongoing meal ticket, Peter has confessed Him to be the Messiah without understanding anything about what that confession means, and Jesus' efforts to convince the disciples about the necessity and meaning of what lies ahead have met with nothing but blank stares and denial. We are poised on the very brink of the chain of events that leads inexorably toward the final resolution, for coming right up in Luke 9:51 is that chilling statement that Jesus *"resolutely set His face to go to Jerusalem"*—that is, to the Cross. That is His response to what happens here!

When we look at the Transfiguration in this light, it is easy to sense the psychological and spiritual weight of the Cross beginning to grow in Jesus' mind, much as the weight of the One Ring grew in Frodo's as his steps took him closer to Mount Doom. Jesus tries to share His own burden with the disciples, but unlike Sam Gamgee, they just can't deal with it; it goes right over their heads. It is at this critical juncture in Jesus' life that the same Voice that had expressed its approval when He had formally committed himself to this mission of sin–bearing at the River Jordan returns with the same message here on the Mount of Transfiguration. He had gone up to the mountain to pray. We can now see this prayer as a significant step on that journey that would eventually lead to Gethsemane.

The Calvary Road has never been taken without a struggle—not even by our Lord Himself! Was He already beginning to say, *"If it be thy will, let this cup pass from me? Nevertheless, not my will but thine be done"*? At the very least His human nature needed strength and assurance—and understanding. He wasn't getting it from the disciples. And so the Father gives Him both encouragement and reassurance. He unveils His Son's glory for a moment to remind Him of what lies on the other side of the Cross. He sends Moses and Elijah, two men who did understand what He was going through and what He had come for, back from the dead to speak with Him of his imminent "departure." The word in Greek is actually εξοδος (*exodus*). Hmmm. I wonder what that is supposed to remind us of? And then the Father Himself descends upon the mountain in the traditional manner so familiar from the Old Testament. The same Cloud that hovered over Mount Sinai, the same Cloud that had overshadowed Tabernacle and Temple at their dedications, the same Cloud that had overshadowed the virgin Mary at her conception (no wonder the disciples were afraid to enter it!) now descends on the Mount of Transfiguration, and the Voice itself speaks from the Shekinah. *"This is my Son, my chosen one!"* And then it has a pointed word for the disciples, who had not been doing so very well: *"Listen to Him!"*

If the Lord Himself needed strength, encouragement, understanding, and assurance as He took the Calvary Road, how much more do we! As He prayed for it, how much more should we. And if Moses and Elijah were sent to meet these needs, how much more should we be sensitive to them in our fellow believers. If your path presents you with no such needs, I think you must question whether you are indeed on the path of discipleship. For as we have seen, it is the path of those who have denied themselves and taken up their Cross to follow Him. "Shall I be carried to the skies / On flowery beds of ease / When others fought to win the prize / And sailed through bloody seas?"[66] A spiritually stouter generation was wont to ask itself questions like that. We should do so again. Such needs are met for believers, as they were for their Lord, in a manner that is sometimes nothing short of glorious. But first they must be felt, as they can only be by those who have taken up their cross to follow Jesus.

II. Its Significance For The Two (Moses And Elijah)

As Jesus prepares to set foot on the last journey to Jerusalem and the Cross which would usher in the New Covenant, two representatives of the Old Covenant show up to see Him off. How did the disciples recognize them, you ask? Perhaps they appeared as they were traditionally remembered in Jewish tradition; perhaps Jesus spoke with them by name. In any rate, they appear as walking synecdoches. The synecdoche is a figure of speech in which a part stands for the whole, When the Texas rancher says he is running three hundred "head" of cattle, he means three hundred whole cows. So Moses and Elijah appear as living synecdoches, representing not only the Old Covenant

---

[66] Isaac Watts, "Am I a Soldier of the Cross," *Trinity Hymnal*, op. cit., no. 573.

247

in general but specifically the Law and the Prophets, that is the Old Testament in its totality.

What did these representatives of the Old Covenant have to say to the Embodiment of the New? The New American Standard says they spoke of the "departure" that Jesus was to make at Jerusalem. Literally, the word is *Exodus*, as we saw above, and that word is not there by accident. The Exodus from Egypt was God's greatest deliverance of his people up to that time. Moses himself had been there! So they come as living synecdoches and they speak of a life–giving synecdoche, for the deliverance from bondage in Egypt stands, as the part for the whole, for all of God's redemptive acts. And the point was that what was about to happen in Jerusalem was going to be the ultimate fulfillment of what had happened at the Red Sea.

So Moses and Elijah were there for Jesus' sake, as we saw above, but also for their own. For they had a stake in what had been prophesied so long ago. Their own salvation ultimately depended upon it. Peter, perhaps remembering this event with greater understanding, would later explain how *"As to this salvation, the prophets who prophesied of the grace that would come to you made careful search and enquiry, seeking to know what person or time the Spirit of Christ within them was indicating as he predicted the sufferings of Christ and the glories to follow"* (1 Peter 1:10–11). Therefore, they came to say, "We appreciate what you're doing" (the disciples didn't—yet); "We understand what you are doing" (the disciples didn't). In fact, Moses, who gave us the sacrificial system that Christ was about to fulfill; who had, like Jesus, experienced rejection by the very people he had come to deliver; Moses was in a position to know better than any other man or angel what our Lord was going through. Of course he wanted to be there to encourage Him. For in doing so, he could lift up his own head, finally knowing that his own redemption was drawing nigh.

III. Its Significance For The Three (Disciples)

The disciples, inner circle of the apostolic band though they were, were at the time pretty clueless about the meaning of what they were seeing and hearing. And Peter was typically clueless with his mouth open. Nevertheless, had they been paying better attention, there were a couple of things they might have profitably noticed (and would later notice as they remembered these things after the resurrection). One is that they were experiencing the fulfillment of Jesus' prophecy in Luke 9:27. *"But I say to you truthfully that there are some of those standing here who shall not taste death until they see the kingdom of God."* This verse has often been trotted out as an example of error in Scripture if not in Christ himself, for obviously the kingdom has not come even yet and none of the disciples are exactly still waiting for it among the living. But even a little attention to the context would make mincemeat of this arrogant assumption. Notice how verse 27 flows into verse 28. These three disciples were granted to see Jesus as He would not be seen again until John's prophetic vision of His Second Coming in the Book of Revelation. They were granted, before their deaths, to see the kingdom in the glory of the King as it will not be seen again until it comes indeed. And it is possible—just possible—that there are some alive in this generation who will not taste death until they see that same vision. Even so, come, Lord Jesus!

There was another important lesson for the disciples in the contrast between what they experienced on the Mountain and what was happening down in the Valley. In fact, this experience of theirs has become a paradigm, a pattern, and even a prototype for a kind of experience that God still grants his people to encourage and inspire them along the way. It is because of this passage (as well as Moses' trips up Mount Sinai) that we still speak to this day of "a mountain–top experience." Peter did what was very natural for someone having that kind of experience. He wanted to preserve it, to live in it, to hang on to it, to prolong it. That was the point of the "tabernacles" he wanted to build. But meanwhile the other nine disciples were in trouble down in the valley where they were failing to heal the boy with the seizures. Up to the mountaintop Jesus and the three had gone, but back down it they had to come to deal with the realities of ministry and of life. And guess what? God still gives His people such experiences, and they still have to come down from them, and for just the same reasons.

People make two mistakes regarding such a mountain top experience. One is Peter's: to try to hold on to it, prolong it, or (even worse) control it so we can repeat it at will. Some of our charismatic brethren have fallen into that rut, I'm afraid, and it produces only a caricature of real spiritual experience. The other and opposite error, often fallen into in reaction to the first one, is to despise such an experience, debunk it, or at least patronize it. Here one thinks of those denominations who have tempted us to call them "God's frozen people." I am convinced that one reason Peter, James, and John were up on that mountain is so they could learn better than either, for the Lord knew how badly the Church was going to need that lesson. The Lord's lesson here is obviously that both the Mountain and the Valley are essential to genuine and authentic Christian experience. We can expect to visit both, and it is naïve to think we can permanently live on the Mountain until we get to Heaven. But how do they relate to each other? Why go up the Mountain if you can't stay there? What the disciples had the opportunity to learn by experience has never been better explained than by Paul Stookey in one of the songs he wrote after his conversion:

> And I wonder if you've ever been to the mountain
> To look at the valley below?
> Did you see all the roads tangled down in the valley?
> Did you know which way to go?
> Oh the mountain stream runs pure and clear
> And I wish to my soul I could always be here,
> But there's a reason for living way down in the valley

That only the mountain knows.[67]

Conclusion

"There's a reason for living way down in the valley / That only the mountain knows." That line is too profound to be ruined with an explanation. So I will not ruin it. Let us be glad for our foretastes of eternity up on the Mountain because in their light we may better serve the Lord here and now down in the Valley. That way, and no other way, we may finally become so heavenly minded that we may be of some earthly good. May God make it so for our good and His glory. Amen.

---

[67] Paul Stookey, "John Henry Bosworth," *Paul And* (NY: Warner Brothers Records, 1971).

HE WHO IS GREATEST

Luke 9:46 And an argument arose among them as to which of them might be the greatest. 47 But Jesus, knowing what they were thinking in their heart, took a child and stood him by his side, 48 and said to them, "Whoever receives this child in my name receives me, and whoever receives me receives Him who sent me; for he who is least among you, this is the one who is great." 49 And John answered and said, "Master, we saw someone casting out demons in your name, and we tried to hinder him because he does not follow along with us." 50 But Jesus said to him, "Do not hinder him, for he who is not against you is for you."

Introduction

In our last few messages, beginning with the Feeding of the Five Thousand, we have seen Jesus reject the offer of a worldly throne and commit Himself to walk the way of the Cross. We have seen Him declare that if we want to be His disciples, we have to walk with Him on that path, denying ourselves, taking up our own crosses daily, and following Him. We have seen the masses desert Him over that message. We have seen even the twelve disciples' inability to make sense of this message as they respond to it with stunned incredulity. And we have seen the Father, on the Mount of Transfiguration, approve those very teachings of our Lord and exhort the disciples to *"Listen to Him!"* But listen though they might, the way of the Cross still does not make any sense to them. We can see this clearly in the conversation hinted at in our text today. Who is the greatest? I think we can imagine all too well how it might have sounded.

The Three must have insisted, "Well, it pretty much has to be one of us, doesn't it? After all, we got to see the resurrection of Jairus's daughter; we got to go up on the Mountain of Transfiguration while *y'all* were screwing up down in the Valley." To which the rest probably responded, not without a certain credibility, "Oh, he just takes *you* three along to keep you out of trouble!" Then John chimes in: "Hey, I'm the one who leans on the Master's breast." James: "Yeah, and he's going to get tired of you hanging on him like that all the time, too." Peter: "Hey, I'm the Rock, after all, the foundation of the Church!" Andrew: "Oh, yeah? If it wasn't for me, you wouldn't even be a disciple!" Matthew: "Well, I used to be a tax collector, so I clearly get the most improved award." Judas Iscariot: "Well, that's all well and good, but it's obvious that I'm the one He trusts the most—after all, He did make me the treasurer." Alrighty, then.

"And an argument arose among them as to which of them might be the greatest" (verse 46). What clearer symptom could we want of the fact of their complete failure to understand the way of the Cross? They were not denying self; they were affirming self. They were not taking up the cross; they were competing for a crown. They were not following Christ; they were pursuing their own self-interest, their own glory. They had not yet been liberated from the world's concept of greatness, what we have called the

"Gentile Paradigm" of leadership as superiority which allows you to "lord it over" your subordinates. They needed desperately to learn the principle that the Lord tries once again to teach them here: the world's concept of greatness is backwards, and the Christian concept is radical: *for he who is least among you, this is the one who is great"* (v. 48b). Well, there are two specific lessons they needed to learn then and that we need to learn now: And the first of them is about the very definition of greatness:

I. The World Finds Greatness In Status; The Lord Finds It In Service

The world finds greatness in status, and therefore orients itself around the pursuit of status. A dictionary definition of status is "position or rank in relation to others; position in a hierarchy of prestige." The key idea is rank "in relation to others." Status is a zero–sum game in which, as you go higher, everyone else ends up lower. It is not enough that I be recognized; I must be recognized as better than you. It is not enough that I be honored; I must be honored more than you. It is not enough that I be valued; I must be valued more than you, or it is worth nothing. This is the default position occupied by human beings in a fallen world. Sinners automatically think like this, though the more civilized among them have learned to hide it—even sometimes from themselves. You 4and I think like this, though hopefully Christ has already begun to teach us not just to hide it but to repent of it and forsake it. The disciples had at least not become hypocrites about it yet! They genuinely wanted to know who was the greatest.

Well, if that kind of superiority is what status is, how do you acquire it? What are the sources of status? In our society there seem to be mainly three: power, wealth, and celebrity.

Power is the most important of them all, perhaps because it is a key to getting the other two. Professional athletes make more money than the president of the U. S., and some movie stars get more publicity than he does. But he is the most powerful man in the free world. So you definitely want to be president. Unless you can be Batman. Always be Batman.

Only one person can be president of a nation or a company at a time, but everyone can pile up **wealth**—or, what may be more important, the appearance of wealth. That is why fads are so potent. You have to have the *right* possessions, or you lose status. My house has the most square feet. I trump your square feet with a Jacuzzi, or by parking a Lexus in my driveway. For about $35,000 you can get a good, reliable car that is even decently accessorized. For twice that, or even more, you can get a "luxury car." Is the luxury car really twice as good? How would we measure that? Is it really twice as comfortable? Twice as fast? Twice as reliable? No, it is only marginally better. In fact, it may be built on the very same frame and have the same engine and drive train as the standard model. So why don't we pay just marginally more for it? Because what we are buying is not a better car at all, but the status that having it confers.

The hollowest source of status of all is **celebrity**. Celebrity has been defined as being famous for being famous. Now, most of us aren't really famous, but we can pretend to be by playing the name–dropping game. Back in the mid–Eighties, Michael Jackson had a concert in Atlanta. It was announced that for fifty dollars you could "apply" for a ticket. If you were chosen, you would get to fork over another hundred or more, depending on where you wanted to sit. It was a sadistically brilliant publicity stunt. A sufficient number of idiots were falling all over themselves to get one of those coveted tickets. Why? Because his music was really that good? No, it was because the publicity created a kind of illusory sharing of his celebrity: you were "special" if you actually got to go. You were oner of the Chosen! (I would have paid real money to be spared; fortunately, *that* was still free).

Do you think believers are immune from such absurd temptations? Think again. A person I know once met a woman whose big thing was to get all the really big Evangelical celebrities—TV preachers, pastors of famous megachurches—to autograph her Bible. And he was dumbfounded to discover some of the names of people who had been silly enough to do it. I will not reveal them here, but they were people you have heard of. And oh, was she proud of those signatures! Then she offered him the opportunity to add his autograph too, right under . . . oh, that's right, I wasn't going to tell you. He said, "Lady, there is only one Name in that Book that matters, and it isn't mine." My friend had witnessed to or counseled prostitutes, adulterers, and gossips; I don't think he ever felt soiled by any of those encounters the way he did by this one. He was too polite to do so, but he wanted to rend his garment and cry, "Blasphemy!" that someone should demean the Word of God so. Yet his objections produced only an uncomprehending stare. (Did that qualify the lady to be one of the original disciples? Oh, never mind.) Why wasn't he granting her the status she had obviously earned by traveling around to these huge mega–churches and stroking the egos of their pastors? Maybe because it would have been a betrayal of everything the Lord is trying to teach us here.

What is the result of the quest for status? Spiritual impotence. It is great super–churches only half or less of whose "members" actually bother to show up on Sunday morning. It is "Christian" television modeled on secular media techniques developed to fuel and exploit the celebrity syndrome. It is a great hue and cry and impressive statistics but no spiritual reality; no real spiritual power. Why? Because it is the exact opposite of the way of the Cross. Those on this path have their backs to the Cross. And therefore they have their backs to Christ! Which of us has not been touched by this? To the extent that we have our backs to Him, he calls us to turn around and face him, to move towards him, again. And He does it in His unique, inimitable way: He does it by means of a little child.

"But Jesus, knowing what they were thinking in their heart, took a child and stood him by his side, and said to them, 'Whoever receives this child in my name receives me, and whoever

receives me receives Him who sent me; for he who is least among you, this is the one who is great'" (verses 47–8). This child is the Lord's alternative to the search for status. To "receive" this child—to accept him, to take him in, to care for him—is to receive Christ. Why? Because the child is weak, because he is insignificant, because he is a nobody—*precisely* for those reasons. He is utterly lacking in any ability to confer status on you. Nobody will be impressed that he has autographed your Bible! He is not going to give you one iota of power, wealth, or celebrity; in fact, he may cost you quite a bit of some of those things. So why serve him? Only one reason: love. Only one reason: because in so doing you are serving Jesus.

Who has status in the Kingdom of Heaven? Billy Graham? Spurgeon? They have their honor as faithful servants, no doubt. But who has *status?* The nursery worker! The nameless, unsung nursery worker has a status in the Kingdom that is not eclipsed by the famous preacher who has evangelized millions. How? Why? Because status as the world defines it is irrelevant in the Kingdom of God. All who are truly Christ's have everything in Christ. Comparing ourselves with others is therefore totally superfluous. It is worse than superfluous—it is counterproductive. The only thing that matters is pleasing the Lord, and to do that we must deny ourselves, take up our crosses, and follow Him. Specifically, we must follow His example and serve the brethren, especially the least of them. Why? The world finds greatness is status, but the Lord finds it in service. That is the first lesson we learn from this passage, and the second is like unto it:

II. The World Forms A Monopoly; The Lord Furthers The Ministry

The world forms a monopoly; the Lord furthers the ministry. That is the second point to be made here. How is it made? In verse 49, John tries to salvage the situation, which has become rather embarrassing for the disciples jockeying for position, by changing the subject to an encounter he has had with what he considers a potential rival, expecting the Lord to be pleased that he has put him down and discouraged him. Oops! But Jesus said to him, *"Do not hinder him, for he who is not against you is for you"* (v. 50). Why was Jesus not in fact pleased by John's care for the apostolic band's market share? Because John's motive for putting down the potential rival was one more manifestation of the very sinful pride that had been fueling his quest for status. Jesus was zealous for the glory of the Father. As long as that is maintained, it did not matter to Him which human being got the credit for the ministry. What matters to Him is that the ministry happens and that the least of these are served and the Father is glorified.

Ministry matters to Jesus. But those among us who are trying to build their own little kingdom have a different agenda altogether. Watch out for that attitude and flee it like the plague—because a spiritual plague it is, more deadly than COVID–19 or Cholera or even the Black Death, Bubonic Plague. How does it manifest itself? Let me count the ways.

254

Here is one. You don't have to be in a mega–church for this approach to manifest itself. It can happen in pitifully puny congregations and denominations. Show me a church with a closed and self–perpetuating board (i.e., one that chooses its own replacements without a congregational vote), and nine times out of ten it will be populated by people like John in this encounter. Why is it set up that way? Because perpetuating their own status matters more to them than accountability to the people they are supposed to be serving. Who is serving whom in a church like that? That is a question you do not dare to ask. Beware of a church where you do not dare to ask it. Beware of people who are in the church because they think it is the small pond in which they can be the big fish! Flee such a church like the plague, but more importantly, flee the attitude that generates it like the spiritual plague it really is.

There are lots of other ways you see this happening. You see it in certain denominations where it seems more important to them whether you are a member of their group than it does whether you are a Christian or not. It is one more manifestation of the search for status. And it can smack you in the face in good churches that are really trying to do the right thing. I remember a lady in the congregation I served in Marietta, GA, back in the early 1980s. She was upset because some people from a nearby trailer park were getting saved and coming to the church. You would think an Evangelical would be happy that her church was fulfilling the Great Commission, but no. She actually said to me, "I don't think these are the kind of people we want in our church." My chin hit the floor. I was so shocked I just stared back at her stupidly, not believing I had heard what I had just heard. My reaction went right over her head. She did not see a problem at all, and neither did her friends standing around her. When I suggested that maybe fulfilling the Great Commission was more important than maintaining her social status, she just sniffed and turned her back. She was still in that church after I was forced out.

It was one more manifestation, and a particularly ugly one, of the search for status—literally making status into an idol. When these kinds of attitudes prevail, servanthood is not the model and ministry is not the priority—unless we get the status of inflated numbers as a result. And so, in our missions programs, in our building funds, in our annual reports, we should be constantly examining our motives. Are we doing this to build His kingdom or to build our own empire? Are we doing this to gain status or to serve the least of these? The answer to that question will determine the kind of blessing we receive. For the world forms a monopoly, but the Lord furthers the ministry.

Conclusion

The concept of greatness through servanthood we see in this little child that the Lord set before His disciples—the little child He has set before us—is not just an arbitrary ethical rule the Lord made up. It is central to the very Gospel itself. How? The Gospel is the good news of salvation by God's grace alone accepted by faith alone. And grace is specifically and explicitly *unmerited* favor. The notion of fallen human beings earning salvation is anathema to Christ. This salvation can only be received as a gift by the undeserving. No one who believes he deserves salvation has it. For it is *"by grace through faith, and that not of yourselves . . . lest any man should boast!"* (Eph. 2:8–10).

Don't you see? In principle you gave up the world's view of greatness when you accepted Christ. How inconsistent it is for us to return to it in our practical lives after we are saved! Servanthood is not something tacked on to the Gospel, but something that flows inevitably from it. Therefore, to be a slave to status and to those means of achieving it we have been studying, to seek fulfillment and self–worth from the world, in the world's way, rather than from Christ in Christ's way, is to live in a manner utterly incompatible with the belief in the Gospel we profess to have. Thank God we are not saved by our consistency! But we must come to see this inconsistency as intolerable, because it is a betrayal of our Savior and our Lord. And it causes us to forfeit many of the blessings salvation brings: freedom from the tyranny of the opinions of the crowd, freedom from the rat race, and most of all the fulfillment that comes from denying ourselves, taking up our crosses daily, and following Jesus.

ON TO JERUSALEM

Luke 9:51 And it came about, when he days were approaching for his ascension, that he resolutely set his face to go to Jerusalem. 52 And he sent messengers on ahead of him. And they went and entered a village of the Samaritans to make arrangements for him. 53 And they did not receive him, because he was journeying with his face toward Jerusalem. 54 And when his disciples James and John saw this, they said, "Lord, do you want us to command fire to come down from heaven and consume them?" 55 But he turned and rebuked them, and said, "You do not know what kind of spirit you are of. 56 For the Son of Man did not come to destroy men's lives, but to save them." And they went on to another village.

57 And as they were going along the road, someone said to him, "I will follow you wherever you go." 58 And Jesus said to him, "The foxes have holes and the birds of the air have nests, but the Son of Man has nowhere to lay his head." 59 And he said to another, "Follow me." But he said, "Permit me first to go and bury my father." 60 But he said to him, "Allow the dead to bury their own dead; but as for you, go and proclaim everywhere the kingdom of God." 61 And another also said, "I will follow you, Lord, but first permit me to say goodbye to those at home." 62 But Jesus said to him, "No one, after putting his hand to the plow and looking back, is fit for the kingdom of God."

Introduction

In our last few messages, we have been studying a transitional period in the Lord's ministry. It began with the Feeding of the Five Thousand and the apex of His popularity; it proceeded to His rejection of the kind of throne the crowds wanted to give Him, and their rejection of Him in turn; and it led to His talking more and more to His disciples about the Cross for Him and the Way of the Cross for them. All of this leads up to Luke 9:51. *"He resolutely set his face to go to Jerusalem."* Or as the King James perfectly has it, "He set his face like flint to go to Jerusalem." This passage then marks the end of the Galilean ministry and the beginning of the long journey to Jerusalem and the Cross. It was a long journey and frequently interrupted, but there is also an inexorability about it. It took half as long to happen and twice as long to tell as the Galilean ministry, and it constitutes the central section of Luke's account of the Gospel.

After the birth narrative which serves as an introduction, then, Luke is organized like a three–act play. The first act in this play, set in Galilee, had asked over and over again the question, "What manner of man is this—who heals diseases, terrifies demons, raises the dead, and bosses around the winds and the rain?" In the transition to Act Two, Peter answers that question: *"Thou art the Christ, the Son of the living God!"* And Jesus responds, "Yes—and that means the Cross." The second act, on the way to Jerusalem, drives home with increasing, inescapable, and sobering clarity the implications of that response. And the third act will be passion week in Jerusalem, the

Crucifixion, and the Resurrection themselves: the climax toward which everything is building. Now at the very beginning of the second act, the journey to Jerusalem and to Act Three, there are some important lessons for us. This passage illustrates two truths about the nature of commitment to Christ. And the first one is what His servants can expect as they travel the Way of the Cross. We can call it "The Afflictions of His Servants."

I. The Afflictions Of His Servants

The **first of those afflictions**, and a major one, is rejection. **Rejection** is a major theme of Luke's Gospel because it was a frequent experience of our Lord. It is interesting to note a pattern: Each major phase of Jesus' ministry begins with rejection. One of the toughest to take must have been at Nazareth, his hometown, at the beginning of the Galilean phase (4:28–29). His own relatives and childhood friends respond to His preaching by saying, "Who does this young whippersnapper think he is?" Now in our passage today as we begin Act Two, He gets a very different reception in Samaria (9:53) than when He visited the Woman at the Well. They liked Him when He said you didn't have to worship in Jerusalem but rather in spirit and in truth. But now that their local chauvinism is no longer apparently being fed by His message, they turn hostile again pretty quickly. The mere mention of Jerusalem is apparently enough to set them off. Ironically, had they listened more carefully, they would have realized that this emphasis was not exactly complimentary to their hated rival! This was a pattern— initial enthusiasm that turns into rejection—that Jesus had to get used to. No wonder John would later summarize his whole ministry by saying, *"He came unto his own, and his own received him not"* (John 1:11).

Jesus had human feelings like we do, sin only excepted. He could not have been unaffected by these experiences. Surely they are part of the "many things" He had said He was going to suffer in Luke 9:22. His friends, the disciples, His best friends, the Three, His own family: None of them could understand Him. It began at least as early as His conversation with the doctors in the Temple. Can you hear the surprise in His twelve–year–old voice at the fact that his parents did not know He had to be about His Father's business? They just look back at Him, clueless. Can you hear the disappointment and frustration when he says to Philip, *"Have I been so long time with you and yet you do not know Me?"* (John 14:9). Can you hear His agony as He looks at the city of Jerusalem and says, *"How often I longed to gather you as a hen does her chicks, and you would not"*? (Luke 13:34). So when He enumerates the sufferings He would undergo for our sins, surely rejection is among them, and not the least significant.

How does this apply to us as the Lord's disciples? First, we should realize that it is Okay to desire understanding and acceptance and to hurt when they are not received. Do you? I do. Our Lord did! He was tempted, tested, in every way like as we are, and this is one of them. He understands. He has been there. But then we must also realize that He steadfastly preferred the pain of that rejection to compromise of His principles or His mission. Are we willing to follow Him in that? We must if we love Him and love lost sinners. The biggest reason why opportunities to witness for Christ are missed is not our inability to articulate the Gospel clearly or handle objections to it effectively (though some of us surely need work there), nor is it our failure to care (though none of us cares enough). If we are to be honest, we must admit that the biggest reason is simple fear of rejection. We are not willing to risk that pain, for it is surely among the greatest that we ever face.

How can we overcome that fear? We look to Jesus. But first, let's look at someone else who can help us look to Jesus and understand what we are seeing. Let me remind you of that great basketball movie, "Hoosiers." Gene Hackman's character, the coach, does what he knows is right even though it is sure to cause him to be rejected by most of the people in the little town, even when it is sure to cause him (in the short run) to fail. He had decided it was better to fail at doing what was right than to succeed in any other way. He comes within a hair's breadth of losing his job and being seen as a complete failure. And when the team finally starts to get what he has been trying to teach them and it turns its season around and goes on to win the state championship, it becomes very clear that it was his very willingness to fail that was the key to his success. Had he not accepted the possibility of rejection and been at complete peace with himself about it, he could never have been truly accepted.

Gene Hackman is a great example of this point in that movie, but I would also point you to an even greater one: our Lord Himself. He was despised and rejected of men, and it hurt Him more than we will ever be able to understand. But He also heard His Father say, "*This is my beloved Son in whom I am well pleased*" (Luke 3:22). He has had a mighty host of followers who were gladly ready to give their lives for Him, they loved Him so much. Someday every knee will bow and every mouth will confess that Jesus Christ is Lord, to the glory of God the Father (Phil. 2:10–11). He could never have had that joy if He had not been willing to face that pain. Neither could Hackman's basketball coach. And neither can we.

How then should we deal with rejection as disciples of the Lord Jesus Christ? In three ways. First, **expect it.** Those who reject Him will reject us as well, for the same reasons. Second, **accept it.** The joy that is set before you, acceptance by God, hearing the Father say, "*Well done, thou good and faithful servant*" (Mat. 25:21), is not worthy to be compared with the sufferings we undergo now—including the rejection that hurts so much. And, thirdly and most importantly, **respond to it** as our Lord did, not with rejection in turn, but with love. James and John reacted to rejection in the natural human way: They were hurt, and they wanted to strike back. But Jesus rebuked them. "*You do not know what kind of spirit you are of. For the Son of Man did not come to destroy men's lives, but to save them*" (9:55–6). Can I love those who reject me? Can you? No. But Christ has already done it. And Christ in us can do it still. Let us ask Him to do so in us, for the opportunity is certainly going to be presented.

I don't know which is worse: being rejected or having people make a big deal about wanting to follow you when they don't have the foggiest idea what you are really all about. Jesus had to deal with that in this passage too, and one of those men elicits from Him an expression of a **second form of affliction: poverty.** The Son of Man had nowhere to lay His head, worse off even than the foxes of the wood or the birds of the air (9:57–58). Possessions are not wrong in themselves. Indeed, they are necessary if we are going to continue to live and function in this world. And the Gospel is not negative about them. But following the Lord means they are not and cannot be your first priority. We had a missionary visit our church in Marietta who described the hut his family had occupied in Africa for a while: mud brick walls, a dirt floor, no plumbing or electricity. Someone asked John Loshbough how his family dealt with these conditions, and he said, "We never really thought about it. We were too busy enjoying the challenges and blessings of the Lord's work." He did not intend it so, but it was a rather strong rebuke of our materialism! Following Jesus means being willing to accept rejection; it also means being willing to accept poverty and deprivation if that is what it takes to get His work done. I doubt the Lord is asking any of us to give up indoor plumbing and electricity at the moment, but we should ask: What *have* we given up so that people like John Loshbaugh could be out there on the front lines of the Lord's service? Surely the answer should be something! This is part of what it means to follow Him.

II. The Urgency Of His Service (vv. 59–62)

The first truth this passage teaches us about the nature of commitment to Christ on the way of the Cross is the Afflictions of His servants: certainly misunderstanding and rejection, possibly deprivation and poverty, will be our lot if we are faithful. The second lesson is the Urgency of His service. The afflictions are worth it for many reasons, and one of them is how important the work is to which we are called, how great the needs of a desperate world, and how wonderful the Savior is that we offer it.

How do we see that urgency in this passage? There were three other people besides the disciples who wanted to follow Jesus—but only when it was convenient, only when they got around to it! The Lord does not seem to have been terribly impressed by or even interested in such followers. With our popularity collapsing around our ears, we would probably have been desperate for anybody who wanted to sign up; but Jesus was not. He had no time for people who were not serious.

The first guy lost interest pretty quickly when Jesus told him what his accommodations were going to be—less posh than those of the birds and the foxes. People are needlessly troubled by the second example. *And he said to another, "Follow me." But he said, "Permit me first to go and bury my father"* (verse 59). How could Christ be so harsh, so heartless, as to forbid this man from even attending his own father's funeral? But the fellow's father was in all probability not dead. This man's statement was an idiom which could well have meant, "My father is getting up in years. As soon as he dies, I will join up with your disciples." Jesus' reply then means, "Let the [spiritually?] dead put me off with such excuses. You've got more urgent business with the living! Are you serious or not?" The third bloke was apparently not serious either. *"I will follow you, Lord, but first permit me to say goodbye to those at home"* (60). Once he went back to "say goodbye," there was every likelihood that his family was going to try to talk him out of it. Jesus was on his way to Jerusalem to be *crucified*! He did not have time to mess around with people who wanted to talk big about following Him (and presumably get in line for the spoils of victory when the Kingdom came and the military Messiah they assumed Jesus to be overthrew the Roman Empire), but who were not serious about making the sacrifices required.

What of our situation today? Is there any urgency in our period of history? Well, do we believe that men and women are lost without Christ? Of over eight billion people in the world today, half of them have never even heard the name of Jesus, much less had the opportunity to hear a clear presentation of the Gospel. Only about half of the people groups (there are at least 1,600 of them with a population of 10,00 or more) have been reached.[68] How shall they hear without a preacher? Of all evangelical North American missionaries, it is estimated that only 19% of them are working in unreached people groups.[69] Could you have accepted Christ or grown in Him without any access to a Bible? Of 7394 known languages on the planet, only a little more than half have any Scripture at all, and only about 10 % have the whole Bible.[70] I know you've heard these kinds of statistics before, and you have probably learned to roll your eyes at them.[71] That's part of the problem.

Jesus in His response to these three potential volunteers makes two points about the urgency of His work. First, it comes before everything else, even the highest human obligations. Nothing is more important than family, but there comes a point where even they have to take a back seat to Jesus and His mission (verses 59–60). No, you can't put it off until the unspecified and constantly receding date when your father dies; no, you can't let your family talk you out of it, or even give them a chance to try. Second, it demands whole–souled, steadfast devotion. *"No one, after putting his hand to the plow and looking back, is fit for the kingdom of God"* (verse 62). Interestingly, in this passage it is not the man who *turns* back who is unfit for the kingdom, but rather the man who merely

---

[68] If we define an unreached group as "any sociolinguistic group in which there is no witnessing church movement capable of reaching that group, perhaps half of the people groups in the world have been 'reached.'" Robertson McQuilken, "Reached and Unreached Mission Fields" *Evangelical Dictionary of World Missions*, ed. A. Scott Moreau (Grand Rapids, MI: Baker, 2,000), 809.

[69] "Mission Stats," https://www.thetravelingteam.org/stats.

[70] Wycliffe World Alliance, https://www.wycliffe.net/resources/statistics/.

[71] The statistics are constantly changing, and different groups report them slightly differently depending on the definitions they use of key terms like "unreached." These therefore should be taken only as suggestive — but they certainly do suggest that we have a problem.

looks back (like Lot's wife). What happens if you just look back when you are plowing? You plow a crooked row. What an interesting description of a lot of Christian lives today! Henry David Thoreau is not a very good guide to theology, but he once gave some excellent advice on writing that applies to life as well: "A sentence should read as if its author, had he held a plow instead of a pen, could have drawn a furrow deep and straight to the end."[72] That is what the words and the lives of Jesus' disciples should look like too!

Conclusion

What shall we say to these things? Understanding the urgency of discipleship should make us willing, yea, eager, to embrace the afflictions. George Scott, a one–legged schoolteacher, reportedly once offered himself to Hudson Taylor as a missionary to China. "With only one leg," Taylor asked, "why do you think of going as a missionary?" Scott's response was classic: "I don't see those with two legs going!" Oh, that we could see that spirit in the Lord's servants again! Here's the question: Is the Lord's work something you fit in after everything else in your life, or is it your highest priority? He set His face like flint to go to Jerusalem for us, and we now know a bit more about what that meant. Would you prayerfully consider where He would have you to go for Him? It might not be a physical place at all, but then again it might—whether across an ocean or across the street. The important thing is that we are following Him. Where Jesus goes, we follow. Whether in the crudest literal manner or in other ways impossible to enumerate or anticipate, that is what it means to be a disciple.

---

[72] Henry David Thoreau, "A Vigorous Prose Style," 1849.

THE MISSION OF THE SEVENTY

Luke 10:1 *Now after this, the Lord appointed seventy others and sent them two and two ahead of him to every city and place where he was going to come. 2 And he was saying to them, "The harvest is plentiful, but the laborers are few; therefore, beseech the Lord of the Harvest to send out laborers into his harvest. 3 Go your ways; behold, I send you out as lambs in the midst of wolves. 4 Carry no purse, no bag, no shoes; and greet no one on the way. 5 And whatever house you enter, first say, 'Peace to this house.' 6 And if a man of peace is there, your peace will rest upon him. But if not, it will return to you. 7 And stay in that house, eating and drinking whatever they give you. For the laborer is worthy of his wages. Do not keep moving from house to house. 8 And whatever city you enter, and they receive you, eat what is set before you 9 and heal those in it who are sick, and say to them, 'The kingdom of God has come near you.' 10 But whatever city you enter and they do not receive you, go out into its streets and say, 11 'Even the dust of your city which clings to our feet we wipe off in protest against you; yet be sure of this, that the kingdom of God has come near.' 12 I say to you, it will be more tolerable in that day for Sodom than it will be for that city. 13 Woe to you, Chorazin! Woe to you, Bethsaida! For if the miracles had been performed in Tyre and Sidon which occurred in you, they would have repented long ago, sitting in sackcloth and ashes. 14 But it will be more tolerable for Tyre and Sidon in the judgment than for you. 15 And you, Capernaum, will not be exalted to heaven, will you? You will be brought down to Hades! 16 The one who listens to you listens to me, and the one who rejects you rejects me; and he who rejects me rejects the One who sent me." 17 And the seventy returned with joy, saying, "Lord, even the demons are subject to us in your name." 18 And he said to them, "I was watching Satan fall from heaven like lightning. 19 Behold, I have given you authority to tread upon serpents and scorpions, and over all the powers of the enemy, and nothing shall injure you. 20 Nevertheless, do not rejoice in this, that the spirits are subject to you, but rejoice that your names are recorded in heaven."*

Introduction

The division of labor in the work of God for the salvation of sinful mankind is something to contemplate. The Father conceives and initiates the plan of Salvation. The Son accomplishes it; He purchases and provides that salvation. The Spirit applies it to the lives of believers. And the Church responds to that provision and application by taking the message to the world. The last time we were together we saw the urgency of the Church's task: It requires the acceptance of the Lordship of Christ and the Way of the Cross; it sets us on the path of potential rejection and deprivation. It takes precedence over every other priority and demands full commitment, complete, unswerving, and unwavering devotion. Today the Lord sends out the Seventy disciples, expanding the earlier mission of the Twelve. In His instructions to them, we learn part of the reason for that urgency and something more about our proper response to it.

Many of these instructions that we have just read are the same as those given to the Twelve in chapter nine. Like the Twelve, the Seventy have the dual and coordinated task of preaching the message of the Kingdom and healing; that is, announcing the Good News of God's movement in Christ to reassert His rule over creation and working to provide foretastes of that coming rule with its defeat of Satan and all his works. Like the Twelve, the Seventy have a Word to speak and a Work to do, and they must always be kept together; for the Work is the Word lived and the Word is the Work explained. Like the Twelve, they are to take nothing for their journey, especially not a begging bag, bending over backward to avoid giving the unfortunate impression that they are in this for the money. Like the Twelve, they are to have stability in one house and not be moving around like a modern church–hopper. Like the Twelve, they are to make a distinction between the faithful and the apostate, shaking the dust off their feet where their message is rejected as their contemporary fellow Jews did when returning to Israel from Gentile lands All of this that you remember so well from that message we will not repeat here today, but we will rather focus on what is added to this picture with the mission of the Seventy. And the first thing is a fuller understanding of the reason for the urgency of that mission.

I. The Reason For The Urgency

The reason given for the urgency of their task (which is ours) is twofold. *"The harvest is plentiful, but the laborers are few"* (10:2). The first part of it is that **the harvest is plentiful.** Plentiful? Indeed, it is universal. All have sinned and come short of the glory of God. There is none that is righteous, no, not one. All we like sheep have gone astray. The wrath of God is revealed from heaven against all men who suppress the truth in unrighteousness—that is, against all men (Rom. 3:23, 3:10, Is. 53:6, Rom. 1:18). In other words, all human beings are rebels against God's kingdom, and as such they deserve and are headed for eternal punishment. But God so loved the world that he gave His only begotten Son that whosoever believeth in Him should not perish but have everlasting life (John 3:16). God commended His love to us in this, in that while we were yet sinners, Christ died for us Rom. 5:8). Therefore, a complete pardon, forgiveness, and eternal life are offered as a free gift by pure grace, unmerited favor, to all who repent and accept Jesus Christ as Lord and Savior, to all those who confess with their mouths Jesus as Lord and believe in their hearts that God has raised Him from the dead (Rom. 10:9).

This message is desperately needed by every single person on the planet, and we are commissioned to take it to every single person on the planet. *"Go ye into all the world and preach the Gospel to every creature, baptizing them in the name of the Father, the Son, and the Holy Spirit, teaching them to observe all things whatsoever I have commanded you"* (Mat. 28:19) Yet of the several billion of such persons alive today, roughly half have never heard a clear presentation of the Gospel and, what is worse, many of them do not live in a place where they are at all likely to. Truly, the harvest is plentiful!

The daunting size of the task would be bad enough were it not for the second part of the reason for its urgency: **the laborers are few.** Not only that, they are not as strategically deployed as they might be. We said last time that of the conservative Protestant North American missionaries, only 19% of them are working in unreached people groups. That is about 15,000 people trying to reach 799.7 million people.[73] That makes one witness for every 53,333 people. How would you like to be responsible for reaching that many people? Most of us find it a daunting task to reach just one!

Obviously, we have two problems. First, not enough people are going to the hardest places, and second, not enough people are going, period. But if we were to double the missionary force sent out and supported by conservative Evangelical churches in the next year—that would not be nearly enough, but if we could do just that much—if that many people volunteered to go, would we be able to find the support to send them? That is a very serious question, and the answer is probably not at our current level of mobilization. Statistically, the number of months of deputation it takes a new missionary couple to reach the field fully supported has been going up for the last couple of decades. A year used to be standard, but now some of them are still stuck at home after two years of raising support or more. We had an annual Faith Promise Pledge for missions at the church I pastored in Marietta, which supported what I thought was a pretty impressive missions program for a church of that size. Yet only about half of the families in that church participated in it. Interestingly, there was absolutely no correlation between a family's wealth and their participation at all, much less their level of participation. To have more people going, we would have to have more people giving, a much higher percentage of wealthier members giving proportionately to their ability, and more people at every economic level giving sacrificially. In other words, we would have to start acting as if we thought the task actually was urgent! The harvest is plentiful, and the laborers are few.

To say that the harvest is plentiful is simply to say that the opportunity is great. The problem is not the size of the harvest but the size of the labor force. We think we are a mission–minded church, we think we are doing well, for one reason: We are comparing ourselves to other churches rather than comparing ourselves to the need! That is why J. Robertson McQuilken wrote his classic book *The Great Omission*.[74] He asks, with so many unreached people, why are so few going to reach them? And he concludes that in order to get the job done, we will have to completely change our way of thinking. The mission of the church would have to become its first priority, rather than something it gets around to after it has done everything else.

How would our thinking need to change? Currently we assume that we are not supposed to go unless we receive a specific "call." But McQuilken suggests that when

---

[73] "Mission Stats," https://www.thetravelingteam.org/stats.
[74] Robertson McQuilken, *The Great Omission: A Biblical Basis for World Evangelism* (Downers Grove, Il: InterVarsity Press, 2001).

we consider what is at stake, the enormity of the need, and the lack of laborers, the presumption, the default setting, ought to be that we are going to go unless we are specifically called to *stay*. And it should go without saying that those who are called to stay are automatically called to help send others. Yet a church in which half the people are giving to missions is considered to be a mission–minded church! Brethren, we need to get serious. The harvest is plentiful, and the laborers are few.

II. The Response To The Urgency

The response to this urgency is laid out in the second half of verse two: And he was saying to them, *"The harvest is plentiful, but the laborers are few; therefore, beseech the Lord of the Harvest to send out laborers into his harvest."* This response to the urgency of the situation is not what we were expecting; it is not to *go*. You might have thought it would be, based on what I have been saying just now about Dr. McQuilken's thesis about how we need to change our default setting (which we do), but it is not. Rather, the response the Lord asks of us is to *pray*.

The response is to pray that God will send more workers. Is this a copout? No! To say that would be to deny the importance and the efficacy of prayer; to deny the importance and efficacy of prayer is to deny the power of God; and to deny the power of God is to deny the Christian faith. To make "going" the first–line response would be short–sighted. Why? Only God can truly send missionaries. This is not to contradict Dr. McQuilken's recommended change to our thinking—that we should think of going unless we are called to stay—but rather to add another layer to it: We need to start thinking of going *and* staying as *equally* a specific call from God on our life!

The commitment required for successful missionary service cannot be manufactured. If you were to go only because my statistics made you feel guilty, you would be better off to stay (and so would the mission field). Therefore, unless the going is preceded by the praying, the going will not be sustained or fruitful anyway. Unless the staying is preceded by the praying, the staying will not be sustained or fruitful anyway. So we don't start with going *or* staying; we start with praying. As usual, the Lord's solution is not the first thing we would have thought of, but it makes perfect sense and is the only answer that really has a chance to work.

Well, then: we are to "beseech" the Lord of the harvest to send forth workers into his harvest. The word *beseech* denotes an earnest and fervent pleading. Therefore, the Church should make it a perpetual priority of its prayers to agonize before God for the needs of the harvest, and specifically to ask that He would call forth more laborers to move into the fields, both at home and abroad. Leaders should model this priority and this practice before the people in their own public and private prayers. Services should be structured to remind us to include it. "Father, the need is so great! The laborers are so few! Please, you've got to send some more!" That is where everything that matters must begin.

When the Church starts being obedient about praying and meaning that, then a wonderful thing will happen. God will turn to some of us and say, "Okay, I hear you. You can go!" Look how verse three follows from verse two: We go straight from *"Beseech the Lord of the Harvest to send out laborers into his harvest"* to *"Go your ways. I am sending you out as lambs."* The sending comes right after the praying! It looks very much as if something very like this is just what happened with the Seventy. It is definitely what happened with Paul and Barnabas's first missionary journey. It was when it was fasting and praying that the church of Antioch heard from the Holy Spirit and recognized their call, and after fasting and praying that they sent them out (Acts 13:1–3). That was the beginning of the first major expansion of the Gospel. Could the same thing work today?

You see, if you pray that prayer with understanding, sincerity, and consistency, then it will not be long until you will *want* to go. You will actually be relieved when God says, "Yes. You can go!" And if you wish you could go but are not given that freedom, you will certainly be zealous to support those who can go in your place. You will certainly also be zealous to go to those who are at hand, not across the world but across the street. It always hurts me to hear people talking about budgets as if foreign missions and home missions were in competition for the same limited funds. If we had the dynamic the Lord intended—and we would have it if we would just obey his instructions about our prayer life here—then we would see that a heart for foreign missions is also the key to effective home missions. *"The harvest is plentiful, but the laborers are few; therefore, beseech the Lord of the Harvest to send out laborers into his harvest."*

Conclusion

If the disparity between the needs and the resources is so great, where do we start? We start right where the Lord told us to. *"The harvest is plentiful, but the laborers are few; therefore,* beseech *the Lord of the Harvest to send out laborers into his harvest."* Let us begin right now.

THE PRIVILEGES OF DISCIPLESHIP

Luke 10:17 And the seventy returned with joy, saying, "Lord, even the demons are subject to us in your name!" 18 And he said to them, "I was watching Satan fall like lightning from heaven. 19 Behold, I have given you authority to tread upon serpents and scorpions and over all the power of the enemy, and nothing shall injure you. 20 Nevertheless, do not rejoice in this, that the spirits are subject to you, but rejoice that your names are recorded in heaven." 21 At that very time he rejoiced greatly in the Holy Spirit and said, "I praise thee, oh Father, Lord of heaven and earth, that thou didst hide these things from the wise and intelligent and didst reveal them to babes. Yes, Father, for thus it was well pleasing in thy sight. 22 All things have been handed over to me by my Father, and no one knows who the Son is except the Father, and who the Father is except the Son, and anyone to whom the Son wills to reveal him." 23 And turning to the disciples, he said privately, "Blessed are the eyes which see the things you see, 24 for I say to you that many prophets and kings wished to see the things which you see and did not see them, and to hear the things which you hear and did not hear them."

Introduction

In our last few times together, we have been studying passages which speak of the rigors of discipleship: the hardships and rejection that Christ's followers may have to endure, and the total commitment demanded of them because of the very nature of who their Lord is and because of the urgency of the task He has given us, for the harvest is plentiful and the laborers are few. Today we catch a glimpse of what makes it all worthwhile. For along with the difficulties of discipleship come the delights of discipleship. Along with the burdens of discipleship come the blessings of discipleship. Along with the pains of discipleship come the privileges of discipleship. And so the Lord in this passage speaks of three joys of Christian discipleship, in ascending order of importance. They are, first, Victory over Satan; second, Vindication from Sin; and third, the Vision of the Son.

I. Victory Over Satan (v. 17)

The first of these privileges and joys of discipleship is Victory over Satan. *And the seventy returned with joy, saying, "Lord, even the demons are subject to us in your name!"* They realized that Christ's power over the minions of Satan was one of the signs that the Kingdom had come in Him, and now they were being included in His victory. That is a joyous thing indeed. And while Jesus wanted them to be even happier about more important things than this, He affirmed their joy by pausing to celebrate it with them. And He said to them, *"I was watching Satan fall like lightning from heaven"* (verse 18).

Hmmm. When did Jesus see this? Is it a reference to Satan's original fall from Heaven, "hurled headlong flaming with combustion down / To bottomless perdition, there to dwell / In adamantine chains and penal fire / Who durst defy the Omnipotent to arms"?[75] Certainly, that fall is not irrelevant; from it indeed the imagery of the statement is taken. But I find the verb interesting. It is in the Greek imperfect tense, and it could very well be translated, "I've been watching Satan fall." Not the aorist, "I watched him fall long ago" (though of course the Son had been there to see that), but "I've been watching him fall" at a more recent time in the past—when else in context but during the mission of the Seventy itself? Our Lord is implying that the original fall of Satan, the original defeat of Satan, his casting out of Heaven, the original thwarting and frustration of Satan's rebellion against God, is recapitulated or repeated or reenacted in the activity of the Church. Therefore, the seventy disciples are right to take joy in their victories over the demons in their ministry.

Jesus goes on to say in verse 19 that *"Behold, I have given you authority to tread upon serpents and scorpions and over all the power of the enemy, and nothing shall injure you."* Probably this was not intended as an invitation to the disciples to literally go out and start stomping with impunity on snakes and spiders, though the various snake–handling cults of the American South have taken it literally that way indeed. I have two reasons for rejecting that literal interpretation. First, miracles were never intended to be the kind of "show" that one sees in such groups. Second, the Greek conjunction καὶ (*kai*, "and') can also be used as the adverb "even," which makes good sense in the middle of this verse. I would translate, "Behold, I have given you authority to tread upon serpents and scorpions, even over all the power of the enemy, and nothing shall injure you." The serpents and scorpions are then not meant literally (though God could certainly grant a literal fulfillment when it was needed, as he did with the Apostle Paul when he was stung by a viper hiding in the firewood, Acts 28:5), but as a symbol for the power of the Enemy. The point of the passage in context is not primarily a promise of protection from poisonous creatures as such, but a promise of spiritual victory over the forces of Satan.

What then does this passage teach us? When the Church marches forward in faith and obedience, in the name of Christ, it can expect to experience substantial victory over sin, darkness, evil, etc. The Lord's teaching here is very much parallel to His promise that the Gates of Hell would not prevail against us (Mat. 16:18). That is a greatly misunderstood passage. Usually when I hear people quote it, they mean something like, "Whew! We're safe! The Gates of Hell will not prevail against us!" Well, when was the last time you saw a pair of city gates leave the walls and start chasing the enemy away across the battlefield? Gates are not an offensive weapon. They are defensive! When we attack Satan's kingdom—in faith and faithful obedience—its gates will not prevail against *us*! We will knock them down and liberate the captives they hold inside.

Why then do we see the Church in retreat? Why don't we see more of this kind of victory? Well, maybe it is because the army of Christ has adopted a defensive posture

---

[75] John Milton, "Paradise Lost" I.45-9, *John Milton: Complete Poems and Major Prose*, ed. Merritt Y. Hughes (Indianapolis: Odyssey Press, 1957): 213.

on the field of battle, not an offensive one. Maybe it is because she is unwilling to face hardship and rejection. Maybe it is because she has put her hand to the plow and turned back. Maybe it is a combination of all of these things. But we have Christ's promise that when the Church moves in faith and unity under the banner of the Cross, the fortresses of Satan will fall. Now, that is something to rejoice about. That is something we need to see a lot more of. But Jesus says it is overshadowed by two blessings that are even greater.

We started with Victory over Satan. The next occasion of rejoicing one is . . .

II. Vindication From Sin (v. 20).

The second privilege of discipleship, and one which we Evangelicals rightly emphasize in our presentations of the Gospel, is Vindication from Sin. "*Nevertheless, do not rejoice in this, that the spirits are subject to you, but rejoice that your names are recorded in heaven*" (20). It is surely not wrong to rejoice in success, in life or ministry. But in comparison to our own salvation, success is nothing. Why? At least three reasons are implied. First, we ought to be rejoicing in Christ's victory, not our own. Do not rejoice that the spirits are subject to *you*. In other words, we should rejoice in the *Lord's* success, and in His graciously allowing us to have a part in it, but we should beware of rejoicing overmuch in the fact that it came through us, lest we fall into pride.

Second, only if I adequately realize the depths of my own sinfulness will I be adequately impressed by the miracle of my own salvation. The fact that I came to faith is a greater victory for the Holy Spirit, a greater accomplishment for God, a greater testimony to the riches of the glory of his grace, than anything I have achieved for Christ since coming to faith—even if I have performed miraculous healing or even raised the dead! When I was saved and passed from spiritual death to life, that was a resurrection of sorts, and a harder one to pull off than the mere reversal of physical death. To forget this is not only to have a false perspective on the work of Christ and a false evaluation of myself; it is also to fail to appreciate the wonder of the fact that my name is written in heaven—it is to miss that greater joy.

And third, we must remember the surpassing value of salvation itself, not worthy to be compared to anything else. "*I count all things to be loss in view of the surpassing value of knowing Christ Jesus my Lord, for whom I have suffered the loss of all things, and count them but rubbish in order that I may gain Christ*," said Paul (Phil. 3:8). And that leads us to the third ground for rejoicing: not just the Victory over Satan and the Vindication from Sin, but the greatest of all . . .

III. The Vision Of The Son (vv. 21–22)

The third privilege of discipleship, and the crowning one to which all the others point and for the sake of which they exist, is the Vision of the Son: We get to see Jesus! I said we Evangelicals put a lot of emphasis on Vindication from Sin as what the Gospel is all about. And we are right to do so. You cannot put too much emphasis on that. But we may not have put enough emphasis on the third blessing. Why do our sins need to be taken out of the way? So that we don't have to go to Hell, surely—but there is a greater reason than that. It is so we can see with the eyes of our hearts un–blinded the greatest vision there is, for the sake of which the whole universe exists: the glory of God in the face of Jesus Christ!

At that very time He rejoiced greatly in the Holy Spirit and said, *"I praise thee, oh Father, Lord of heaven and earth, that thou didst hide these things from the wise and intelligent and didst reveal them to babes. Yes, Father, for thus it was well pleasing in thy sight. All things have been handed over to me by my Father, and no one knows who the Son is except the Father, and who the Father is except the Son, and anyone to whom the Son wills to reveal him"* (21–22). What did God hide from the wise and intelligent and reveal unto babes? Ultimately all the blessings and joys of this passage are focused in the revelation of Christ Himself. And so great is this joy that this is the only time in the Gospels where it is specifically recorded that Jesus rejoiced. What is a greater source of joy than the frustration of Satan? What is a greater source of joy than the forgiveness of sins? That which made the other joys possible: the grace of God in Christ, through which we know both the Father and the Son.

There is a Peanuts comic strip where Charley Brown has gone to Lucy's booth for counseling. "The trouble with you, Charley Brown," says Lucy, "is that you don't know the meaning of life." Charley Brown thinks about this for a moment and then asks, "Do *you* know the meaning of life?" "We're not talking about me," Lucy replies. "We're talking about you."

Well, what is the meaning of life? The Stoic finds it in self–control and indifference; the Epicurean in pleasure; the Buddhist in the Nirvana of non–being; the Humanist in the progress of mankind. How do they know? Which is right? It is no accident that the Existentialist would eventually conclude that there is no universally valid meaning for everyone, that in fact life is absurd. Yet what the great intellects, philosophers, prophets, mystics, and kings all sought but could not surely find, a child can know in Christ through faith. What a privilege is this! The meaning of life is to know God, to glorify him, and to enjoy him forever. And in Christ you can not only understand what it is; you can know it, experience it, live in it, bathe in it, luxuriate in it, exult in it through faith.

And God revealed this to babes. Our Lord rejoices not only in the "things" of the Gospel, its substantive content, but also in the *method* of it. That Man in his intellectual pride missed it but God has freely given it to "whosoever will" is wonderful to contemplate. Because otherwise, you and I would not be rejoicing in it today! When you really begin to understand the Gospel you will adore the Father not just for the benefits of it, but even more for the wonder and glory of it. You will find satisfaction, fulfillment, and joy just in contemplating it. I hope you are finding it even now. *"I count all things to be loss in view of the surpassing value of knowing Christ Jesus my Lord, for whom*

I have suffered the loss of all things, and count them but rubbish in order that I may gain Christ" (Phil. 3:8).

Conclusion

This is a lot to rejoice in. No wonder Jesus closed this passage by saying, *"Blessed are the eyes which see the things you see, for I say to you that many prophets and kings wished to see the things which you see and did not see them, and to hear the things which you hear and did not hear them"* (verse 23–24). Well, we cannot see Jesus Himself in the flesh as the disciples did. But we have the next best thing in the reminder of His incarnation and His death that He has left us. Blessed are the eyes which see the things you see, the hands that touch the things that you are about to touch, the lips that taste what you are about to taste, if indeed you know Jesus Christ as your Lord and Savior and can therefore participate with us in Communion! So let those of us who know Him rejoice in the Victory, the Vindication, and the Vision as we draw near to the One who is the Source of them all.

THE GOOD SAMARITAN

Luke 10:25 And behold, a certain lawyer stood up and put him to the test, saying, "Teacher, what shall I do to inherit eternal life?" 26 And he said to him, "What is written in the Law? How does it read to you?" 27 And he answered and said, "You shall love the Lord your God with all your heart, and with all your soul, and with all your strength, and with all your mind; and your neighbor as yourself." 28 and he said to him, "You have answered correctly. Do this and you will live." 29 But, wishing to justify himself, he said to Jesus, "And who is my neighbor?" 30 Jesus replied and said, "a certain man was going down from Jerusalem to Jericho, and he fell among robbers, and they stripped him and beat him and went off, leaving him half dead. 31 And by chance a certain priest was going down on that road, and when he saw him, he passed by on the other side. 32 And likewise a Levite also, when he came to the place and saw him, passed by on the other side. 33 But a certain Samaritan who was on a journey came upon him, and when he saw him he felt compassion. 34 And he came to him and bandaged up his wounds, pouring oil and wine on them. And he put him on his own beast and brought him to an inn and took care of him. 35 And the next day he took out two denarii and gave them to the innkeeper and said, 'Take care of him, and whatever more you spend, when I return I will repay you.' 36 Which of these three do you think proved to be a neighbor to the man who fell into the robbers' hands?" 37 And he said, "The one who showed mercy to him." And Jesus said to him, "Go and do the same."

Introduction

Few of Jesus' parables are more familiar or more superficially understood than the story of The Good Samaritan. It is usually interpreted simply as an object lesson on the duty of benevolence—and so it is. But it is also much more. To study it profitably, we need to see it in the context of the conversation with the lawyer in which it is embedded, and to look at the two questions the lawyer asked—and the answers Jesus didn't give!

I. Question Number One (vv. 25–28)

1. The Question: The first question is, "What must I do to inherit eternal life?" It is in some ways a very good question, but it probably was not asked because the lawyer wanted to know the answer. He asked it to "test" Jesus. This implies that he already thought he knew the answer, and he wanted to see if Jesus did too. We usually look down on him for that, and indeed there were a number of Pharisees and Scribes who did ask Jesus questions from ignoble motives, trying to trip him up. But I am willing to give this fellow the benefit of the doubt. There were a lot of people starting messianic movements in those days. I probably would have wanted to ask a few questions before signing up with one of them myself! When the elders of the church I served in Marietta were thinking of asking me to serve as its pastor, they had some pretty serious questions for me, and rightly so. So this man may have been sincere—but sincerity is not enough.

What was he going to do with the answer? That is the bottom line. And what will we do with it?

The lawyer probably thought he had come up with a pretty good question: It would simultaneously elicit Jesus' theology and make the questioner sound spiritual. But the question ironically shows the limitations of the lawyer's thinking. In fact, at one level he hasn't been thinking at all. "What must I do to inherit eternal life?" You can't "do" anything to inherit something! An inheritance depends entirely on the relationship you have with the giver, and on his will as expressed in his Will. The question may also reveal something more about the lawyer's spiritual state than he realized. As a lawyer (or Scribe), he was an expert in the Law of Moses, and he was probably very conscientious about keeping it. But all this had brought him no peace. If the question wasn't purely theoretical, it probably meant he was looking for some one thing he could do that would be so meritorious that it would give him an unshakable assurance of acceptance by God. The aorist participle he uses could be translated, "What one thing, having done it, will I as a result inherit eternal life?" If he was truly seeking, his question illustrates the failure of contemporary Jewish theology at this point, and it illustrates Paul's principle that *By the works of the Law shall no flesh be justified in His sight, for by the Law comes the knowledge of sin"* (Rom. 3:20).

2. The Answer: Jesus hardly ever gave anybody a direct answer to anything. He would usually either answer a question with a question or say, "Let me tell you a story." He uses the first of those tactics with the first question, and the other one with the second. Here He answers the question with a question: "What do you think?" Or, actually, He uses the form of that question appropriate for a Jewish lawyer: "What does the Old Testament Say?"

Jesus is setting us a very good example for our own witnessing here. Don't be too quick to just give your spiel and leave. Jesus always wanted to make the people He was talking with think for themselves, in order to give them the opportunity to think with Him. We should pay close attention to His method here. Until a person is thinking with you, it does no good to give him the Four Spiritual Laws, or take him down the Roman Road, or do whatever it is you use to present the Gospel. Once you have got people to that point, there are many good methods. So how do we get people thinking with us? It really helps to master the art of asking good Socratic questions. And to know what the right ones are going to be, we have to listen as well as talk. As you read Jesus' encounters with people in the Gospels, have an eye to how He does this. He is the best role model you're ever going to find.

Well, Jesus answers the question with a question, and the lawyer's answer to that question is in verse 27: Keep the Law! Now Jesus has him on the way to finding an answer to his original question. And so Jesus agrees with him: Do this and you will live. But wait. Why does Jesus agree? Why doesn't He carefully explain that salvation does not come by the works of the Law but by faith? First, because the lawyer was not just plain wrong. After all, Jesus had quoted the very same Old Testament passages Himself in answer to the question about what the greatest commandment was. If a person loved God with his whole heart, mind, soul, and strength, and his neighbor as himself, and did it consistently throughout his whole life, he would indeed merit eternal life. The trouble is that none of us has. The trouble is that none of us does. The trouble is that none of us can. So the right question, the question the lawyer *should* have been asking, is what kind of salvation can there be for *sinners*? But you can't ask—or answer—that question until you have come to see yourself as a sinner. That is why Jesus agrees with the preliminary answer. He does it to show its inadequacy!

In other words, why doesn't Jesus carefully explain that salvation does not come by the works of the Law but by faith? Perhaps because it does no good to explain such things until a person has learned by experience that Law–keeping as the path to salvation must inevitably fail. The theology of Grace is the answer to our experience of failure at keeping the Law. Until we admit that failure, we have no ear for Grace. Jesus agrees because the Law precedes the Gospel. It has to. We must see the Law's inability to save before we are ready for another solution. Man's pride will not allow him to accept a Savior who does all as long as man has any hope left of doing something. That hope must first be destroyed. That is why Spurgeon once said that "It is of no use trying to sew with the silken thread of the gospel unless we pierce a way for it with the sharp needle of the law."[76] So Jesus hits the ball right back into the lawyer's side of the court. "Do this and you will live. You *are*, aren't you?" Well, not exactly. Not with all his heart, not all the time. The lawyer now feels acutely a need that may have been only latent at the beginning of the conversation: the need to be justified! Now we are getting somewhere. Unfortunately, he is still trying to justify himself.

II. Question Number Two (vv. 29–36)

1. The Question: The second question is truly unfortunate. "But, wishing to justify himself, he said to Jesus, *And who is my neighbor*?" It is the wrong question once again, absolutely wrong. The proper response should be, "But I can't love God and my neighbor perfectly. Now what?" That would have been the response of a person ready to hear the Gospel. Instead, the lawyer tries to wiggle off the hook. Just who are these "neighbors" I am supposed to love? Maybe I can eliminate some of them and come closer to passing the test! He is looking for a loophole. The Pharisees, by the way, had defined the neighbor in this context as only one's fellow Israelite—which may help explain why Jesus chose a Samaritan as His example. The lawyer is trying to divert the conversation from his own need of Grace to a technical point of Jewish ethics. You can bet that Jesus is not going to let him get away with it!

---

[76] Charles Spurgeon, "On Preaching the Lawand the Gospel," https://paearly.com/blog/2018/3/7/charles-spurgeon-on-preaching-the-law-and-gospel

2. The Answer: The answer to this question is the familiar story of The Good Samaritan. But of course, it is, again, not an answer—that is, not an answer to the question the lawyer had asked. He wanted to know the answer to the question, "Who is my neighbor?" Instead, Jesus answers the question, "To whom should I *be* a neighbor?" But the most important thing for us to understand today is the way this answer is a pointed attack on the two things standing between this lawyer and salvation, the two things standing between him and his ability to appreciate the Gospel: his pride and his trust in the Law.

First, it was a frontal attack on the lawyer's pride. The hero of the story is a Samaritan. Most of you probably know that the Samaritans were a race of half–breeds despised by pure Jews. But you probably cannot imagine the true shock value of Jesus' choice of hero. I have often heard it compared to making a black person the hero in the pre–integration South. That gets us part of the way, but this was much worse than that, for it was theoretically (and actually) possible even for a Southern white who was a segregationist to have respect and admiration and even affection for a particular black individual. This was more like making a Jew the hero in a story told to Nazis, or a Nazi the hero in a story told to Jews. Do you think I am exaggerating? The Mishnah says that "He who eats the bread of Samaritans is like to one who eats swine's flesh."[77] I can tell you as a personal eyewitness that whites who employed black cooks in the old South did not feel the least bit defiled by eating their fried chicken. And it gets even worse. The synagogue prayer service at this time included a prayer that Samaritans not be partakers of eternal life.[78] Segregationists in the old South neither thought all blacks were going to Hell nor wanted them to. As bad as that racism was (and it was bad, make no mistake), it was nothing like this. Forget blacks and whites. As bad as that racial discrimination was, there was not enough hatred there to make this story work. To get the impact, you have to imagine yourself telling this story to modern Israelis with a member of the PLO or Fatah or Hamas as the hero.

What is my point? In order to get an answer to his question, the lawyer is forced to identify with the Samaritan! The Samaritan is the good neighbor, the one the lawyer has to be like if he wants to go to heaven. Gulp. When Jesus puts him on the spot, he cannot even bring himself to say that the Samaritan was the neighbor. He is forced into circumlocution, not to mention beating around the bush: "Er, the one who showed mercy." What is Jesus really asking him? "Can you put yourself on the same spiritual footing as a Samaritan? Can you accept the proposition that you may actually be farther from the kingdom than he is? Can you accept, in other words, the proposition that all men have to come by grace?" Unfortunately, he could not.

---

[77] Shebiith 8.10, Danby, *The Mishnah*, op. cit., 49.

[78] R. C. H. Lenski, *The Interpretation of St. Luke's Gospel*. Commentary on the New Testament. (Woodridge, Il: Hendrickson, 1961), 606.

So the answer was a frontal assault on the lawyer's pride. In the second place, it was a frontal assault on the lawyer's trust in the Law. This is another point that is obscured for modern readers unless they know something about ancient Jewish culture. Why didn't the priest stop to help the wounded man? It wasn't just that he was being callous. From a distance, the victim looked dead. He might have been dead. And, of course, if the priest touched a corpse, he would become ceremonially unclean. Check out Numbers 19:11–13 to see what he would have had to go through—a weeklong process—to become eligible to minister again. Otherwise, he would defile the sanctuary of the Lord and be cut off from Israel.[79] *"The one who touches the corpse of any person shall be unclean for seven days. That one shall purify himself from uncleanness with water on the third day and on the seventh day, and then he will be clean; but if he does not purify himself . . . he will not be clean. Anyone who touches a corpse, the body of a man who has died, and does not purify himself, defiles the Tabernacle of the LORD; and that person shall be cut off from Israel."*

Do you see what the Lord is doing here? It is absolutely brilliant! The lawyer has rightly quoted the Law of Love as the summary of the Law. But the very rigid adherence to the letter of the Law for which his party was known, symbolized here by the priest and the Levite, is in direct contradiction to the spirit of the Law on which he had so rightly focused. A person who truly understood the Law as the Law of Love would have risked putting himself through that week of ritual cleansing rather than leaving the victim of the mugging lying in the road. To cling to Law–keeping as the path to eternal life, as if Law–keeping were a matter of mechanically following a set of Rules, is contrary to the Lawyer's own definition of salvation: *"You shall love the Lord your God with all your heart, and with all your soul, and with all your strength, and with all your mind; and your neighbor as yourself. . . . Do this and you will live."* Yet the mechanical rule–keeping is precisely what all the lawyer's instincts and his Pharisaic tradition have trained him to do.

Do you see what has happened? Salvation by the works of the Law has just self–destructed right in front of this lawyer's very own eyes! And then Jesus concludes by telling him to be like a Samaritan. A more efficient method of calling into question every assumption of this man's whole religious life could hardly have been devised. Unfortunately, Jesus never gets to the Gospel as such. But the whole conversation is a classic example of what we have come to call "pre–evangelism." Instead of answering the lawyer's questions, Jesus has just made them harder, and he has done it in a way that sets up Paul's later clarity in Romans 3:20: *"By the works of the Law shall no flesh be justified."*

Conclusion

---

[79] Janes R. Edwards thinks that this point is discounted by the fact that the priest was going *from* Jerusalem, hence not on his way to perform Temple service. *The Gospel According to Luke*, PNTC (Grand Rapids, MI: Eerdmans, 2015), 321. But he would have needed the week of purification in any case, so the point stands.

We miss the pre–evangelism of Jesus' non–answers because of our ignorance of the First–Century Palestinian context and also because we have become used to the technical vocabulary for these same ideas that was later developed by the Apostle Paul in Romans, Galatians, and Ephesians, and which of course Jesus does not use here. I do not think I am reading Paul back into the Gospels; rather, I hope I have shown that Jesus' questions are the ones ultimately answered by (and only by) Paul's theology of Grace. Jesus in his own way completely demolishes the theology of salvation by works, right down to the ground, and replaces it with that Foundation other than which no man can lay, so that Paul can build on that foundation his theology of grace. Missing all of that, we have reduced this story to a Sunday–School lesson on helping the needy. And it is that, of course, but it is so much more. The main point of it is to anticipate Romans 3:20. *"By the works of the Law shall no flesh be justified."* The Law says, as the lawyer realized, "Love perfectly and you will live." But it is too late for that! Therefore, the Gospel says, "I will give you my life that you may love."

It takes an awful lot of work sometimes to get people to the place where they are ready to hear the Gospel. We can learn a lot by watching our Lord do some of that work here. Let us first make sure that we are people who can hear the Gospel ourselves. Why are there so many half–Christians? Maybe because so many have accepted the Gospel without being ready to hear it. They are not completely convinced that apart from Christ they can do nothing. At some level, even as they mouth the Gospel of grace, they are still trying to "Love perfectly and you will live." But the Gospel says, "I will give you my life that you may love." You can't have it both ways; only one way works, only one way is the power of God for salvation for those who believe (Rom. 1:16), and that is the way of the Gospel of salvation by Grace alone through Faith alone in Christ alone for the glory of God alone. Let us understand it and believe it so that we may be able to live it and proclaim it! Amen.

MARY AND MARTHA

Luke 10:38 Now as they were traveling along, he entered a certain village, and a woman named Martha welcomed him into her home. 39 and she had a sister called Mary, who, moreover, was listening to the Lord's word, seated at his feet. 40 But Martha was distracted with all her preparations. And she came up to him and said, "Lord, do you not care that my sister has left me to do all the serving alone? Then tell her to help me." 41 But the Lord answered and said to her, "Martha, Martha, you are worried and bothered about so many things. 42 But only a few things are necessary, really only one. For Mary has chosen the good part, which shall not be taken away from her."

Introduction

We come today to one of those precious gems of insight into the personal life of our Lord which only Luke records. It seems a very intimate and private encounter. Probably the disciples, including Matthew, John, and Peter (the source of Mark's information) were either on a mission or were lodged elsewhere and did not know of this exchange, but Luke heard the story from Mary or Martha (or their brother Lazarus) in the course of his research in Jerusalem. This family were all close friends of Jesus. You can read more about their relationship in John chapter 11 and the first part of chapter 12. Here, Luke points out their support of Jesus' ministry with a verbal parallel in the Greek that is lost in translation. When Martha "welcomes" Jesus in verse 38, it is the same verb that is translated "receive" in 9:53, when the Samaritan village did not "receive" Jesus because he was journeying to Jerusalem. The implication is that Mary and Martha did "receive" Him. The context loads the verb with extra meaning: They "accepted" Him as the Messiah. They did not just happen to be His hosts, but they were giving moral—and probably financial—support to His mission. In this as in other things, they serve as examples to us. In their relationship with Jesus as revealed in this passage, we find three elements that are still with us, affecting our relationship with Jesus: Busyness, Bitterness, and Blessing.

I. Busyness (vv. 40–41)

The first of those factors is busyness. Martha was "distracted" with all her preparations; in the Lord's words, she was "worried" about a great many things. She usually gets a bad rap in this story, and indeed her sister does come off better. But we are probably harder on Martha than she deserves. Both her activity—serving—and her motives for doing it—love for the Lord—were good things in themselves. Out of love and desire to serve, she was ministering to real physical needs. Indeed, she wanted to provide a sumptuous entertainment (Was her last name "Stewart"?) worthy of her Lord and Savior whom she thus delighted to honor. And this was good and right. Woe be to all of us if the Marthas suddenly disappear from the world!

It all reminds me of when I was a child and we had the preacher over for Sunday dinner. I tell you, Martha could have taken some lessons from my Mom, who managed to do the same kind of work extremely well and without complaining or even seeming to be flustered. The preparations had started the night before. Then we would rush home from church, and she would somehow get it all finished to perfection just in time to be served after only a few minutes of the rest of us (in Mary's role) entertaining this extremely lucky minister in the living room. Now, these meals were just too good to be described in mere prose, so with your indulgence—and apologies to Hee Haw's Grandpa Jones—let me set the table for you.

> Fried chicken, good and hot,
> Green beans (with fatback in the pot),
> Fresh–pulled corn cooked on the cob,
> Mashed potatoes with a great big glob
> Of butter running as it melts,
> Buttermilk biscuits—better loosen your belts.
> Top it off with apple pie
> And ice cream piled on way up high:
> That's what the Lord meant when he said
> To ask him for our daily bread.[80]

Oh, I can smell it now! What was really impressive about all this was the coordination it took. I could probably cook any one of those dishes and do it adequately—if that's all I had to worry about. But somehow my Mom kept it all going at one time and had all of it ready—indeed. done to perfection—at the same time. And this was before the invention of microwave ovens! Well, I couldn't do that if my life depended on it. Now, I know this was not the menu at Martha's house, but you can bet anything she was fixing Jesus the first–century Palestinian equivalent. Oh, yes, this was a good thing!

But even good things can get out of hand. And when they do, they risk becoming not so good. That's what happened to Martha here. She seems to have lost perspective on what she was doing. We can get so focused on the means that they swallow up the end, and we lose sight of our original purpose. This can happen in lots of ways in lots of good things that we do in life. A father works hard to provide for his family out of love—but if he is never at home, where is the love? A mother works hard to maintain a clean house out of love for her family—but can they live comfortably in it?

So we see that when we lose perspective, the activity may no longer be the good it was meant to be, even for the intended beneficiary. But this loss of perspective has a negative impact on us too. When activity gets the upper hand over aims, when procedures overwhelm their purpose, we become susceptible to anxiety. Martha was

---

[80] From my discussion of daily bread in Donald T. Williams, *The Disciple's Prayer* (Eugene, OR: Wipf & Stock, 2005), 88–9.

"worried" about a great many things. **Anxiety** may be defined as the useless and futile expenditure of emotional energy on fretting about what might go wrong. Anxiety can be debilitating. Ian MacLaren pointedly asks, "What does your anxiety do? It does not empty tomorrow of its sorrow, but it does empty today of its strength; it cannot make you escape evil, but it does make you unfit to cope with it when it comes."[81] And we suffer this emotional drain for something that is non–constructive and pointless. Can you do something about the situation? If so, then do it. If not, leave it in the Lord's hands. In neither case should you *worry* about it.

Two constructive **lessons about anxiety** emerge from this passage. First, **it can result from imbalanced priorities.** Martha put too much importance on a good thing. So if you suffer from anxiety, examine your priorities. When the Georgia Bulldogs lost the national championship on the last play of the last game of the season to great passes by Dan Marino of Miami and Todd Blackledge of Penn State the two years after Herschel Walker had helped them win it in 1980, I found it hard to sleep that night. Now, I still love my Dawgs and follow them faithfully, but that experience was a message to me. That second sleepless night was not an isolated event. It was a pattern, and it told me I was putting too much importance on a mere game. My priorities were out of whack and needed to be adjusted. I do better on the rare occasions when we lose now, and if I could not have gotten to that place, I might have needed to give being a fan up. I have one less source of anxiety in my life as a result, precisely because my priorities are better adjusted to reality than they used to be. It's a good thing Martha was not a Georgia fan!

First, anxiety can result from imbalanced priorities. Second, **anxiety is a choice.** Yes, it is! Despite some of your quizzical stares, the passage is clear. The difference between Martha and Mary was a *choice*. Mary had *chosen* the good part. Now, I can hear some of you saying, "It's not that simple. If I could just push a button and choose not to worry, I would." Well, I don't know about mashing any buttons. But listen to Phil. 4:6–7. "*Be anxious for nothing, but in everything by prayer and supplication with thanksgiving let your requests be made known to God, and the peace of God, which surpasses all comprehension, shall guard your hearts and your minds in Christ Jesus.*" We could accurately translate, "*Instead* of being anxious, pray and be thankful, etc." You **substitute** the one for the other. That is a choice.

I have heard that when Theodore Geisel (the secret identity of Dr. Seuss) wanted to quit smoking, he found he could not just not smoke. It drove him crazy. So he decided to do something else instead. He got one of those calabash pipes with a big bowl, filled it full of dirt, and planted a little flower in it. Then, every time he was tempted to smoke, he would take out the pipe, put it in his mouth, and then take out a little medicine dropper and water the flower. He couldn't just not smoke, but he could do something else instead. You may not be able simply to choose not to worry as such, but you *can*

---

[81] 1859, Alexander MacLaren, "Anxious Care," *Sermons Preached in Union Chapel, Manchester by Alexander McLaren* (Manchester, England: Dunnill, Palmer, and Company, 1859), 288.

choose to pray instead. You may not be able simply to choose not to worry, but you *can* choose to give thanks instead. And the result of those choices is that the peace of God will guard your heart and your mind! So in effect, worry is a choice, or at least a failure to make a better choice. Let us serve like Martha, but at the same time make better choices like Mary—and Dr. Seuss.

II. Bitterness (v. 40b)

If the first factor that affected their relationship with the Lord (and ours) was busyness, the second is bitterness. "Lord, she's left me to do all the work! Make her help me!" Martha wasn't just bothered by the fact that she was working. It was just as big a problem—maybe a bigger one—that Mary wasn't! Well, wasn't her accusation fair? Maybe—maybe not. Somebody has to entertain the guest until dinner is ready. That was my job when I was little, because I was a snotty little Sheldon Cooper of a kid who would ask the pastor abstruse (for my age) theological questions about his sermon, and fortunately the pastor we had thought that was cute and enjoyed playing that game with me. That was one occasion where my snottiness was actually useful! But Martha hasn't thought of that because she is too busy illustrating another psychological dynamic that still plagues us today. Too much busyness gives birth to anxiety, and anxiety when it has matured turns into bitterness.

Too much busyness gives birth to anxiety, and anxiety when it has matured turns into bitterness. You want a good definition of bitterness? I once lived next to a man who had three vehicles in his yard: a car, a van, and a light truck. And on each one of these vehicles was the same identical bumper sticker: "Please draft my ex–wife!" One would have been a statement; two was a pattern; three was a serious attitude!

So what is the connection between anxiety and bitterness? The **root of bitterness** is **self–pity.** When the worry that we can't be good enough festers into despair, we cry out, "It's not fair!" And then we look for someone to blame—someone besides us. It is easier to blame someone else for our problems than to admit that they started from our own misplaced priorities. But bitterness is perhaps one of the ugliest of all our emotional problems, and certainly one that closes us off effectively from the grace of God. For God's grace must be accepted with the open hand of faith; it only bounces off a closed fist.

And what is the **solution to bitterness**? It is to realize that **bitterness is a choice**, too! And the alternative to it is the choice to forgive. Now, maybe you cannot now forgive that person against whom you are bitter without a real struggle. But I'll bet there was a time when you could have, and you chose instead to harden your heart. Now maybe you cannot directly choose to change your feelings, but you can choose positively to love, positively to forgive, positively to close the books on that wrong—real or imagined—never to bring it up again, and to stop picking at the scab. And if you do make this choice, by God's grace, you will eventually find that you have in fact indirectly also chosen to change how you feel. Forgiveness is the path to emotional liberation and peace, both when we accept it from God and when we extend it to others because we ourselves have been forgiven.

III. Blessing (v. 42)

The first factor that affects our relationship with Christ is busyness; the second is bitterness; and the third, which lets us finish on a more positive note., is blessedness. So far, this has been a story about handling negative and hurtful emotions. And I keep saying that **the solution is to choose something.** What? "The good part" that Mary chose, which would not be taken away from her. And what did she choose? She chose **to listen to Jesus** as His disciple, to sit at His feet. She chose to make Jesus Himself her first priority. When we do that, then it does not matter whether it is our turn to sit or to serve (we will do both), for we are doing it all for the Lord, and both are simply and equally acts of love for Him. Mary chose to look at Jesus, to see Him for who He is: Messiah, Lord of All, Lamb of God who taketh away the sins of the world (John 1:29). She chose to sit at His feet and hear Him say, *"Seek ye first the kingdom of God and his righteousness, and all these things shall be added to you"* (Mat. 5:33). If we sit at His feet, we will also hear Him tell us how to seek first the kingdom: *"Go ye into all the world and preach the Gospel to every creature, baptizing them in the name of the Father, the Son, and the Holy Spirit, teaching them to obey all things, whatsoever I have commanded you"* (Mat. 28:19–20). To sit at those feet is to realize that anything we fret about, everything we are bitter about, is just absurdly, shamefully, sinfully petty in comparison. It is to be freed from all of that to walk with Him, love Him, and serve Him. Blessed are those who do so. For that is the good part indeed, and it shall not be taken away from them.

Conclusion

You cannot defeat negative emotions by a negative strategy, i.e., by trying not to feel them: not to be too busy, not to worry, not to be bitter, etc. But there is a positive strategy that does work: We can **choose to dwell on Christ Jesus**, His grace, His goodness, His glory. Like Dr. Seuss, we can choose to water the flower. We can force those negative emotional forces out of our lives by choosing consciously to focus on something else instead. We can choose to *"Be anxious for nothing, but in everything by prayer and supplication with thanksgiving let your requests be made known to God, and the peace of God, which surpasses all comprehension, shall guard your hearts and your minds in Christ Jesus"* (Phil. 4:6–7). We can choose the better part. And if we do, it will not be taken away from us.

JESUS ON PRAYER

Luke 11:1 *And it came about that while he was praying in a certain place, after he had finished, one of his disciples said to him, "Lord, teach us to pray, just as John also taught his disciples." 2 And he said to them, "When you pray, say: Father, hallowed be thy name. Thy kingdom come. 3 Give us each day our daily bread. 4 And forgive us our sins, for we ourselves also forgive everyone who is indebted to us. And lead us not into temptation." 5 And he said to them, "Suppose one of you shall have a friend and shall go to him at midnight and say to him, 'Friend, lend me three loaves, 6 for a friend of mine has come to me on a journey and I have nothing to set before him.' 7 And from the inside he shall answer and say, 'Do not bother me. The door has already been shut and my children and I are in bed; I cannot get up and give you anything.' 8 I tell you, even though he will not get up and give him anything because he is his friend, yet because of his persistence he will get up and give him as much as he needs. 9 And I say to you, ask, and it shall be given to you; seek, and ye shall find; knock, and it shall be opened to you. 10 For everyone who asks receives, and he who seeks finds, and to him who knocks it shall be opened. 11 Now suppose one of you fathers is asked by his son for a fish. He will not give him a snake instead of a fish, will he? 12 Or if he is asked for an egg, he will not give him a scorpion, will he? 13 If you, then, being evil, know how to give good gifts to your children, how much more will your heavenly Father give the Holy Spirit to those who ask him?"*

Introduction

There is probably nothing in the Christian life that is more advocated and less attempted, more urged and less understood, more recommended and less resorted to, or more praised and less practiced than prayer. That this should be so is a serious danger sign in the spiritual life. But one more exhortation—"You ought not to be so carnal; you ought to pray more"—probably would not do much good. Part of the reason for that is that many sincere Christians simply have not found prayer to be the meaningful experience it is cracked up to be. We assume meaningful prayer should come naturally, like talking to a friend, and we get frustrated and discouraged when it does not. But think about the differences between prayer and human conversation. In a conversation with a friend, I get immediate feedback. Through words, tone of voice, facial expression, and body language I have objective evidence of how my friend feels about what I have said—or whether he is even listening. With the invisible God there is none of that. To believe that prayer is more than a monologue requires a constant *exercise* of *faith*. Prayer starts sounding an awful lot like *work*. And what do you say to the High King of the universe? It is little wonder that we can end up feeling tongue–tied.

In short, we need instruction in prayer. If you feel that frustration, if you feel that need, then rejoice, and be of good cheer! For the disciples felt the same way. And so they asked, *"Lord, teach us to pray."* And more importantly, Jesus approved of their request. It seems it may have been their most intelligent question in the whole three years they spent with Him! For if you have been following these studies in the Gospel of Luke, you should realize by now how radically unusual the Lord's response was. He did not answer their question with a question. He did not say, "Well, let me tell you a story." For once, he gave a plain, simple, and straightforward answer. He approved of that request. And if it is your request today, he approves of yours too.

The answer Jesus gave is a condensation of the model prayer that we find in its full form in Matthew's account of the Sermon on the Mount. I have expounded that passage elsewhere.[82] But I don't want to just repeat what I said there today. Today we want to see how Luke's condensation of that more familiar material focuses our thoughts. It leads us to the following thesis: **Effective prayer is rooted in an understanding of who God is.** Let me repeat that: Effective prayer is rooted in an understanding of who God is; that is, it is rooted in theology. Two of God's attributes are especially brought into focus in Jesus' response here: His sovereignty and His goodness.

I. God's Sovereignty

First, Jesus' model prayer begins with a focus, not on ourselves and our needs, but on God, both as Father and as King. In other words, it is focused specifically on His Person and on His sovereignty. *"When you pray, say: Father* [the Person], *hallowed be thy name. Thy kingdom come"* [the sovereignty]. *Hallowed be thy name*? That pulls the two ideas together. "Hallowed" is an old–fashioned word for consecrate, sanctify, or make holy. God's name, in other words, is to be treated as holy. He is to be treated with all respect, reverence, and godly fear. Good praying then starts where Solomon says wisdom starts: with the fear of the Lord (Prvb. 1:7). Effective prayer is prayer that treats God as God.

Then God's sovereignty comes into even clearer focus in that His kingdom is to be sought above all else. *"Thy kingdom come"* is a Greek idiom, an expression for "May you reign; may you exercise your sovereignty, in heaven and on earth, in the world and in my own life." The longer version in Matthew uses Old Testament Hebrew poetic parallelism to "rhyme" a similar idea: Thy kingdom come; *Thy will be done*. Good praying then is praying that is concerned first of all not with ourselves and our needs, but with God. It starts with a concern for God's name (Person) and continues with a concern for His agenda (sovereignty). Effective prayer is prayer that is focused on the will of God.

What does this mean practically for the way prayer is supposed to function in our spiritual life? Obviously, for one thing, one cannot really pray at all until one has accepted Christ as Savior and as Lord. What we call "The Sinner's Prayer" is often presented as the only exception to this principle, but that is not really an accurate way

---

[82] Donald T. Williams, *The Disciple's Prayer* (Camp Hill, PA: Christian Publications, 1999; reprinted, Eugene, OR: Wipf & Stock, 2005).

to understand it. Rather, *"God, be merciful to me, a sinner"* (Luke 18:13) is simply and logically the first thing one says after one has accepted Christ as Lord and Savior, or as one is accepting Him as such. How so? As a sinner is the only way we can come to Him, and as Lord is the only Him we can come to. It is because Christ is Lord that His death puts Him in a position to be able to do something about our sins. It is what gives Him the authority to pardon them. So His sovereignty is entailed in His saviorhood. The model prayer begins the way it does to remind us of this fact. When we follow Christ's instructions for prayer, then, we begin by orienting ourselves properly to the God who is the Father of our Lord and Savior Jesus Christ, and to the Christ who is both Lord and Savior. This means that orienting ourselves to Christ's Saviorhood means precisely orienting ourselves to His sovereignty so that our prayers are focused on the holiness of His name and performance of His will.

If effective prayer is focused on the will of God, then it becomes a powerful re–shaper of our priorities. (Remember how Martha's had gotten out of whack last week?) And as that happens, it becomes a powerful promoter of our peace. By following the Lord's outline, we train ourselves in prayer to concern ourselves with the honor due to God's name and the allegiance due to His rule and kingdom before we finally concern ourselves with our own felt needs—though such is His grace that we are indeed encouraged to bring in those needs in their proper place. In other words, every time we pray this way we are reminded to *"Seek first the kingdom of God and His righteousness"* so that *" all these things may be added to us"* (Mat. 6:33). That means that every time we pray in accordance with the Lord's instructions we are reminded not to be anxious about what we shall eat or drink or what we shall put on, for our heavenly Father knows that we need such things, and if He feeds the birds of the air and clothes the lilies of the field, will He not also take care of us, despite our little faith?

Do you need to be reminded of such things as I do? Then make it a practice to pray as the Lord has taught us—not by reciting the model prayer as a formula (though there is nothing wrong with reciting it), but by using it as an outline. We take each petition and make it personal and specific in accordance with our needs and our situation. The path to peace then is not to focus on your needs, but on the sovereign God who is able to meet them. Effective prayer is focused on the will of God as the expression of the sovereignty of God.

Effective prayer is not only focused on the will of God; it is submissive to the will of God. Submission flows inevitably from the focus; without it, we would be rebellious, which is hardly an attitude conducive to prayer! In this as in everything, Christ Himself is our great example. *"Nevertheless, not my will but thine be done"* (Mat. 26:39). Practically, this means that we are prepared to accept a possible "No" or "Wait" or "Yes, but not the way you are thinking" as God's sovereign answer to our prayers. If you really stop and think about it in the light of our own shortsightedness, we really want it to work that way! Woe to the person who gets everything he thinks he wants.

This focus on God's will also explains the apparent "blank checks" that Scripture sometimes seems to promise us: If we ask in faith, we will get whatever we ask for. (Verses 8–9 imply that kind of thing here.) This is a rather strange promise, when even Jesus himself had to say, *"not my will but thine be done."* But, of course, these are prayers of faith, and faith involves bowing to God's will, coming to want what He does. Prayer that is truly submissive to the will of God will always get what it really wants, though not necessarily what it thought it wanted. Finally, this perspective drives us to the Scriptures. If effective prayer is focused on the will of God, where is that will revealed? Effective prayer flows from a heart that reads the Bible not just for information but to know and do the will of God; to know the will of God so we can pray in accordance with it.

In summary, until the purposes of God are more important to us than our petitions, until the demands of discipleship are more important to us than our desires, until the Law of God is more important to us than our lusts, until the will of God is more important to us than our wishes, we have not really begun to pray. And part of the purpose of prayer is to be gradually and continually helping us to get to that place.

II. His Goodness

The first attribute of God brought out by Jesus' instruction in prayer is His sovereignty; the second is His goodness. If we believe that God is sovereign and therefore able to answer prayers that are in accordance with His will, and yet we do not pray, it must be because we fear what that will might be! We wouldn't like to admit it, but it is true. Therefore, in the parables that follow the prayer, Jesus emphasizes the goodness of God as an encouragement to prayer.

First, we see His readiness to hear us in the story of The Friend at Midnight (verses 5–8). *"Suppose one of you shall have a friend and shall go to him at midnight and say to him, 'Friend, lend me three loaves, for a friend of mine has come to me on a journey and I have nothing to set before him.' And from the inside he shall answer and say, 'Do not bother me. The door has already been shut and my children and I are in bed; I cannot get up and give you anything.' I tell you, even though he will not get up and give him anything because he is his friend, yet because of his persistence he will get up and give him as much as he needs."*

Now, it seems to me that this parable is often misapplied. Its point is not that we should be persistent and nag God, as if God were like the lazy friend. The point is the *contrast* between God and the friend. If even a sorry friend like the one in the story would give you what you need, how much more will our Father? God is good, full of mercy and compassion, and He *wants* to give you what you really need just like you do your own children. You don't have to bang on the door to rouse Him; you don't have to beg and plead and nag and whine and wheedle. His ear is already turned toward us. We just have to ask. How do we get to the place where we really just have to ask? Effective prayer is focused on God's name and His will, and it is founded on faith in His goodness.

First, we see the Father's readiness to hear us in the story of The Friend at Midnight. Second, we see His benevolent kindness toward us in the Father's good gifts (verses 11–13). *"Now suppose one of you fathers is asked by his son for a fish. He will not give him a snake instead of a fish, will he? Or if he is asked for an egg, he will not give him a scorpion, will he? If you, then, being evil, know how to give good gifts to your children, how much more will your heavenly Father give the Holy Spirit to those who ask him?"* What kind of Father do we think God is? Well, we would never say He is going to give us a snake or a scorpion, but we often act—and pray—as if we thought exactly that. To improve our prayer lives then, we can do no better than to take our regularly scheduled prayer time (you do have one, don't you?) as an opportunity to meditate on God's sovereignty and His goodness.

Why don't we earnestly pray "thy will be done" in our lives, even when we understand that this is the foundation for all effective prayer? It is because we are afraid of what it might cost us. We might have to go to the mission field, we might have to give up our money or our time, we might have to forgive an enemy or love the unlovely. Well, yes, we might. Oh, horrors! But the truth is that God only asks us to do any of those things because He knows they are the best thing for us to do. Yet we treat Him as if we thought He were a Father who would give us a snake instead of a fish or a scorpion instead of an egg. How ludicrous!

God is good. He is not an ogre. How do we know He is good? Because He sent Jesus! Because Jesus is His Son! Because Jesus is the express image of His nature! Because, as Paul put it, *"God commendeth His love it us in this, that Christ died for us"* (Rom. 5:8). Because, as Paul put it again, if God did not spare His only Son, but delivered Him up for us, how shall He not also with Him freely give us all things (Rom. 8:32)? That is why we can believe and know that He is our loving Father who longs to give us the very best gift of all: the Holy Spirit (verse 13). In other words, He longs to give us all the benefits and all the blessings of salvation in Christ Jesus! In prayer as in every part of the Christian life, the key to all is faith. Do we trust Him? Are we willing to trust Him? Apart from faith it is impossible to please Him. With it, we experience Him as our loving Father, who will give us a fish or an egg, not a snake or a scorpion. Effective prayer is focused on God's name and His will, and it is founded on faith in His goodness.

Conclusion

Effective prayer then is like an arch with two foundations: the sovereignty of God and the goodness of God. It really does not function without both. In meaningful prayer, these two columns grow together into a gothic arch pointing to heaven. Effective prayer is focused on God's name and His will, and it is founded on faith in His goodness.

So meditate on these truths, as they come to us in the principles Paul expounded and the stories Jesus told, until you are saturated with them. And from them in your heart will flow effective and fervent and meaningful worship, praise, adoration, confession, intercession—and yes, petition too—until God becomes to you in your experience all that the Bible says He is in reality: your heavenly Father.[83]

---

[83] **NOTE:** For further teaching on the theology and practice of prayer, see my book *The Disciple's Prayer*, op. cit.

THE CRAVING FOR SIGNS

Luke 11:14 And he was casting out a demon, and it was dumb; and it came about that when the demon had gone out, the dumb man spoke, and the multitudes marveled. 15 But some of them said, "He casts out demons by Beelzebul, the ruler of the demons." 16 And others, to test him, were demanding of him a sign from heaven. 17 But he knew their thoughts and said to them, "Any kingdom divided against itself is laid waste, and a house divided against itself falls. 18 And if Satan also is divided against himself, how shall his kingdom stand? For you say that I cast out demons by Beelzebul. 19 And if by Beelzebul I cast out demons, by whom do your sons cast them out? Consequently, they shall be your judges. 20 But if I cast out demons by the finger of God, then the kingdom of God is come upon you. 21 When a strong man fully armed guards his own homestead, his possessions are undisturbed. 22 But when someone stronger than he attacks him and overpowers him, he takes away from him all his armor on which he had relied and distributes his plunder. 23 He who is not with me is against me, and he who does not gather with me scatters. 24 When the unclean spirit goes out of a man, it passes through waterless places seeking rest, and not finding any, it says, 'I will return to my house from which I came.' 25 And when it comes, it finds it swept and put in order. 26 Then it goes and takes along seven other spirits more evil than itself, and they go and live there. And the last state of that man is worse than the first." 27 And it came about that while he said these things, one of the women in the crowd raised her voice and said to him, "Blessed is the womb that bore you and the breasts at which you nursed." 28 But he said, "On the contrary, blessed are those who hear the Word of God and observe it." 29 And as the crowds were increasing, he began to say, "This generation is a wicked generation; it seeks for a sign. And yet no sign shall be given to it except the sign of Jonah. 30 For just as Jonah became a sign to the Ninevites, so shall the Son of Man be to this generation. 31 The Queen of the South shall rise up with the men of this generation at the judgment and condemn them, because she came from the ends of the earth to hear the wisdom of Solomon; and behold, something greater than Solomon is here. 32 The men of Nineveh shall stand up with this generation at the judgment and condemn it, because they repented at the preaching of Jonah; and behold, something greater than Jonah is here. 33 No one after lighting a lamp puts it away in a cellar or under a peck–measure, but on the lampstand, in order that those who enter may see the light. 34 The lamp of your body is your eye. When you eye is clear, your whole body also is full of light; but when it is bad, your whole body is full of darkness. 35 Then watch out that the light in you may not be darkness. 36 If therefore, your whole body is full of light, with no dark part in it, it shall be wholly illumined, as when the lamp illumines you with its rays."

Introduction

Have you ever wondered why God doesn't make it easier for us to believe? We know we walk by faith and not by sight, but we still wonder, if He is really there, why doesn't He show Himself more plainly and remove all doubt? Doesn't He want people to believe? Why doesn't He give us a sign? This passage gives us some answers to those questions, and it also shows us how the Lord's progress towards the Cross was increasingly provoking them in His confrontations with the Jewish establishment. While it may not be evident to a cursory reading, the Lord's words here are not just an arbitrary collection of sayings but constitute a careful, step by step refutation of the challenges presented to Him which focuses attention on the sign God *did* give and shows us the response of rational faith that is appropriate to it. Therefore, we want to look carefully at the intricacy of the argument, the sufficiency of the sign, and the function of faith.

I. The Intricacy Of The Argument

This passage consists mainly of a series of sayings and parables that might at first seem unrelated. But we should notice the comparison between verses 16 and 29, both of which deal with the issue of signs. "*And others, to test him, were demanding of him a sign from heaven*" . . . "*This generation is a wicked generation; it seeks for a sign. And yet no sign shall be given to it except the sign of Jonah.* Then we will see that it truly is one dialogue with a beginning, a middle, and an end, and that the middle is pertinent to the topic; it is not a digression. (This is why I have read such an unusually long passage this morning.) We can see this most clearly if we break this dialogue down into the eight units that make it up.

1. The Challenge (vv. 14–16). "*He casts out demons by Beelzebul!*" "*Give us a sign!*" To fully understand what is happening here we must realize that the crowd consists of three different groups of people. First are Jesus' supporters. They are not mentioned, but they are here, represented by the disciples and by part of the crowd. Second are the opposition. These people—probably the Scribes and the Pharisees and their disciples—had already made their minds up that Jesus is a dangerous heretic, and therefore his miracles, impressive though they may be, must be using demonic power. (We see that miracles *by themselves* don't prove anything. If you believed Jesus was wrong and dangerous, they would only confirm your worst fears about him.) Third, there is a "neutral" group, or a group that would like to have thought of themselves that way. They want further evidence. These are the people who ask for another sign. But their neutrality is really an illusion. They've already seen enough evidence to "demand a verdict," as Josh McDowell would put it.[84] What difference is one more bit going to make? One more sign won't do anything to resolve the dispute between the two ways of interpreting the miracles—they are divine or they are demonic—that are already on the table. It just asks the question that they are already faced with over again. And that question has to be answered on the basis of Jesus' character and His faithfulness to the Word of God. The demand for a sign sounds reasonable, but it was really just a delaying tactic on the part of the crowd, an evasion of their responsibility to deal with the

---

[84] Josh McDowell, *Evidence that Demands a Verdict: Historical Evidences for the Christian Faith* (Arrowhead Springs, CA: Campus Crusade for Christ, 1972).

evidence with which they had already been presented. At any rate, these are the challenges to which the Lord will now respond.

2. The Response, Part 1: The Opponents (vv. 17–20). Jesus first responds to the first group that spoke, to His opponents. To answer the charge that His miracles are being worked by demonic power, He offers what we may call "The House–Divided Defense." A house divided against itself cannot stand. First, this highlights the absurdity of the charge. Why would Satan want to thwart and hinder and mess up his own work? Look at the people who have been delivered. Are they more in Satan's power, deeper in bondage to him as a result? Or are they now glorifying God? Note how the tables are subtly being turned. Those who are putting forth the theory that Satan is behind Jesus' miracles now have the burden of proof: They must show that these miracles are advancing Satan's interests, not God's; they must explain what possible motive Satan could have for doing such things.

Then Jesus really turns the tables on His opponents. Why is it only *His* miracles that are being attributed to Beelzebul? Why not those of other Jewish exorcists? The opponents must now explain why, if they object to Jesus delivering someone from Satan, they support others who are claiming, at least, to do the same thing. They must now show cause why Jesus' exorcisms should be treated differently. This is an explanation they will not wish to give, for the only difference they will be able to find is that Jesus is doing the same thing with greater efficacy, using simple commands rather than complicated rituals, and having better success. Go ahead, talk to this dumb man (Hey, you *can* now!) and then ask yourself, is Jesus doing the work of God or of Satan? It has to be one or the other, and Jesus' opponents now have a burden of proof they will not be able to bear.

3. The Parable of the Strong Man (vv. 21–22). The parable is an elaboration of the House–Divided Defense. In context, then, the strong man is clearly Satan; his goods are the demon possessed people; the stronger man is Christ, and the plunder is the people delivered from Satan's grip. Thus the picture of opposition between the kingdoms of God and of Satan is reinforced. But something else is happening too: Jesus' own claim to be the Messiah is being advanced. For Satan is the strongest of all created beings. Who could possibly be stronger? Obviously, no mere created being could fit this role. Only the divine Son of God incarnate in human flesh will do. And the implication is that this is exactly what Jesus is.

4. The Response, Part 2: The "Neutral" Party (v. 23). "*He who is not with me is against me, and he who does not gather with me scatters.*" Jesus now turns to address those who want further evidence. In a transition to His full response to them, he shows that He considers their claim to neutrality suspect at the very start. In the war between God and Satan that He has been talking about, there is no room for neutrality. Think back to World War II, when the very survival of the Free World was at stake and very much in doubt. Imagine someone saying to the draft board, "Well, I refuse to serve—but that doesn't mean I'm for Hitler." It would have seemed a very unimpressive response even then; in the conflict of which Jesus is speaking, it is utterly ridiculous. As C. S. Lewis once put it, "There is no neutral ground in the universe; every square inch, every split second, is claimed by God and counterclaimed by Satan."[85] According to Jesus Himself in John 3:18, those who have not believed are condemned already. In other words, "neutrality" is the practical and moral equivalence of rejection. I am not saying that there is no place for people to consider the evidence and ask questions before committing themselves to faith. After all, false religions (and false, distorted versions of the true religion) abound, and careful critical thinking is therefore a requirement for God's people. But for people like the ones in this dialogue, people who have the Scriptures and have already been confronted by the claims of Christ and given sufficient reason to believe, "neutrality" is a mere evasion of responsibility.

5. The Parable of the Swept House (vv. 24–26). This parable is an elaboration of the response to the "neutral" party. The demon goes out, and when he returns, he finds the house swept. In other words, there has been an attempt at moral reformation in the flesh—but this does not hinder the demon from getting back in one little bit. The purpose of this parable is to illustrate the point just made about the ultimate impossibility of neutrality. It shows that the impossibility of neutrality flows not only from the wartime situation, but also from the very nature of human beings. We are spiritual creatures. The throne room of our souls is going to be occupied by someone or something. Ultimately, it can only be the Spirit of God or the Spirit of Iniquity. You say, "But I'm leading a perfectly good moral life without all those religious trappings. I believe in God, but I don't have to be a fanatic about it. I'm just as good and decent as you 'born again' people." Well, you may be right. Your house may be swept and in pretty good order. But there is a crucial question you are neglecting: *Who holds the key to it?* There is no neutrality! Unless Christ occupies the throne of your heart, its last state will be worse than the first.

6. An Interruption (vv. 27–28). We've all met examples of the woman who chooses this moment to break into the discussion: emotional, voluble, irrepressible, she cannot resist trying to wrest the attention to herself—though no doubt she would not have seen it that way. *"Blessed is the womb that bore you and the breasts at which you nursed!"* And suddenly every head turns to look—at her! I cannot resist the impression that she is trying just a little bit too hard to sound "spiritual." Is she sincerely praising Jesus or is she wanting everyone to notice what a devoted follower she is? Perhaps I am being unfair to her. Whatever her motives, she creates a potential distraction from the point Jesus is trying to make, which has nothing to do with His mother. But Jesus skillfully turns the interruption into an opportunity to advance the discussion into which it intruded: *"On the contrary, blessed are those who hear the Word of God and observe*

---

[85] C.S. Lewis, "Christianity and Culture," 1940; rpt. *Christian Reflections*, ed. Walter Hooper (Grand Rapids, MI: Eerdmans, 1967), 33.

it." In other words, we are still talking about the kingdom of God versus the kingdom of Satan, here, and the bottom line is the issue of your allegiance!

7. Summation (vv. 29–32). A wicked generation seeks for a sign. You've already had better signs than the Queen of the South or the Ninevites, and what are you doing with them? Nothing! You're going to get just one more, so don't miss it. The "sign of Jonah" as explained further elsewhere involves the parallel between Jonah being three days in the belly of the fish, as Jesus will be three days in the belly of the earth. But, as we know again from the Parable of Dives and Lazarus: If people will not believe the Word of God, they will not believe even if one came back from the dead. Once again, the supposed neutrality of the audience is nailed as the wickedness of rationalization, even as they are graciously given one more opportunity, when they are in a position to remember the sign of Jonah, to repent.

8. Conclusion (vv. 33–36). Perhaps the hardest part to connect to the dialogue as it has unfolded, the part whose relevance is hardest to see, is the Parable of the Lamp. It also appears in other contexts such as the Sermon on the Mount. Why does the Lord reprise it here? I think he is saying, "Open your eyes!" You say you want further evidence? The problem is not with the evidence but with the fact that you are not *seeing* what you've already been given. As long as your eyes are closed, as long as you continue to be willfully blind, what's the point of giving you more evidence? Open your eyes and look at what you've already been given!

II. The Sufficiency Of The Sign

Well, then. The theory that the signs have been wrought by Satan has been refuted and the people who ask for further evidence have been sent back to the evidence they have already been given. So what are we to make of that evidence? First, I want to head off at the pass a possible misapplication of this rebuke, which was delivered to people who were refusing to deal with the evidence that had already been presented to them. For there is a false spirituality abroad that would use this passage as an excuse to attack any use of evidence at all. And that is clearly not the issue here. It is not wrong to demand evidence for faith; it is wrong not to! We are commanded to test the spirits (1 John 4:1) and not swallow every religious claim that comes down the pike. The problem here was not that people demanded evidence, but that they were refusing to deal responsibly with the evidence they had been given. The problem was not with the evidence but with their hearts.

God has given us good and sufficient reasons to know that he is God and Jesus is his Son. First there is the created universe with its form, its complexity, and its beauty. It could not just have happened. Then there is the nature of man, his aspirations for goodness, truth, and beauty, for meaning and relatedness, for love. If evolution were true, why would the universe evolve a being with unslakable desires for so many things a purely secular universe cannot provide? Then there is Christ Himself, who fulfilled the sign of Jonah by rising from the dead in solid and verifiable history. And finally there is the Gospel, a set of Answers that fits the intractable problem of who we are like a key fits the wards of an intricate lock. The signs are all around us. They are good; they are sufficient; they are compelling. To ask for more is wicked ingratitude. Open your eyes!

III. The Function Of Faith

Finally, this exchange between the Lord and his critics can help us see what true faith is. Faith is not believing without evidence, much less believing in spite of it. It is a personal trust in and commitment to Christ as the Son of God in accordance with the evidence. The disciples, the Pharisees, and the "neutral" crowd of curious onlookers all saw the same evidence. There was adequate evidence for those who chose to trust Christ. But there were people there who were not prepared to trust Him no matter what the evidence said. Faith is that trust. Having compelling evidence does not keep you from needing to trust; it just makes that trust justified. But the trust still has to be exercised. That is what it means to be human, to be a person. Our brains are not automatic logic machines drawing conclusions dispassionately and inevitably and then committing us to them irrevocably. They present us with reasons for choices, but the choices are still ours to make, and we often make them against our better judgment. Do you see? We can appreciate the solidity of the foundation laid for our faith, the sufficiency of the evidence provided for it. These are reasons to trust, reasons to have faith, but they are not faith. Do not despise the evidence. Be grateful for it. But then act on it, and trust Christ. That is faith.

Conclusion

What we see here is that the ultimate issue is not the evidence. It is helpful to see how strong it is, and I would be happy to share it with you in greater detail when we have time.[86] But the ultimate issue is not the evidence. There was plenty of evidence available, but people dealt with it in different ways. Why? Because some wanted the truth, and some wanted their preconceived notions confirmed. Some wanted to know what was right, and some wanted to justify themselves and their own lifestyles. The evidence is important, but the ultimate issue is not the evidence. It is whether in your heart you are willing to listen to the evidence and follow where it leads. The ultimate issue is allegiance. Won't you give yours to Christ today?

---

[86] Those interested in my keeping that promise can see *The Young Christian's Survival Guide: Common Questions Young Christians are Asked about God, the Bible, and the Christian Faith Answered*, vol. 1 (Cambridge, OH: Christian Publishing House, 2019) and *Answers from Aslan: The Enduring Apologetics of C. S. Lewis* (Tampa, FL: DeWard, 2023).

CURSES OF CONSEQUENCE

Luke 11:37 Now when he had spoken, a Pharisee asked him to have lunch with him. And he went in and reclined at the table. 38 And when the Pharisee saw it, he was surprised that he had not first ceremonially washed before the meal. 39 But the Lord said to him, "Now you Pharisees clean the outside of the cup and the platter; but inside of you, you are full of robbery and wickedness. 40 You foolish ones, did not he who made the outside make the inside also? 41 But give that which is within as charity, and then all things are clean for you. 42 But woe to you, Pharisees! For you pay tithe of mint and rue and every kind of garden herb, and yet disregard justice and the love of God—but these are the things you should have done without neglecting the others. 43 Woe to you, Pharisees! For you love the front seats in the synagogues and the respectful greetings in the market places. 44 Woe to you! For you are like concealed tombs, and the people who walk over them are unaware of it."

45 And one of the lawyers said to him in reply, "Teacher, when you say this, you insult us too." 46 But he said, "Woe to you lawyers as well! For you weigh men down with burdens hard to bear while you yourselves will not even touch the burdens with one of your fingers. 47 Woe to you! For you build the tombs of the prophets, and it was your fathers who killed them. Consequently, you are witnesses and approve the deeds of your fathers, because it was they who killed them and you build their tombs. 49 For this reason also the wisdom of God said, 'I will send to them prophets and apostles, and some of them they will kill, and some they will persecute, 50 in order that the blood of all the prophets shed since the foundation of the world may be charged against this generation, 51 from the blood of Abel to the blood of Zechariah, who perished between the altar and the house of God; yes, I tell you, it will be charged against this generation.' 52 Woe to you lawyers! For you have taken away the key of knowledge; you did not enter in yourselves, and those who were entering in you hindered."

53 And when he left there, the scribes and the Pharisees began to be very hostile and to question him closely on many subjects, 54 plotting against him to catch him in something he might say.

Introduction

Ever since the Feeding of the Five Thousand, a very definite pattern in the way the Lord related to the Jewish establishment has been building to a head. Ever since His rejection of Messiahship as popularly understood, ever since His refusal to be the kind of king the people wanted, ever since His forthright declaration that His way would be the way of the Cross, ever since His promise that His disciples would have to travel that road too, His encounters have become increasingly confrontational—especially his encounters with the Scribes and the Pharisees. This one elicits a series of "Woes unto you!" because it involves a confrontation with **three religious attitudes which are under the curse of God: Formalism, Legalism, and Clericalism**. They are under His curse because they are the mortal enemies of true religion. Let's look at them each in turn.

I. Formalism

Formalism is the idea that conformity to outward forms—ceremonies, rituals, practices, creeds—is either central to genuine piety or sufficient for acceptance with God. It is not that any of these things are bad in themselves; in fact, they are all positive goods, some of which at least are essential to Christian faith. If you think we are against ceremonies, rituals, practices, or creeds, you have badly missed the point. The First-Century church was a liturgical church, and affirming that certain propositions about Jesus—summarized by the Creeds—are simply and literally true is essential to Christian identity. But necessary, versus essential and sufficient, are two very different things. And even if they were not, a mere outward conformity that does not flow from inward reality in the heart is only a caricature of faith anyway. Formalism is a mentality that is focused on, and satisfied with, that outward conformity. And it is deadly to real and vibrant Christian faith.

Jesus' example of formalism here is the Pharisees' ceremonial ablutions (verses 38–44). Few Jews were as zealous about them as the Pharisees, but most Jews would have gone along with them, especially as a guest in a Pharisee's house. Jesus seems to have provoked this exchange deliberately by omitting his. Why? Because he had just been with the crowd, the *am ha 'eretz*. In the Pharisaic mind, that was what made him unclean. No "righteous" Jew would eat with people like that. This emphasis was in fact a distinguishing mark of Pharisaic religion; that's why it was an important issue for Jesus' host. I strongly suspect that Jesus objected to the attitude of self-righteousness and contempt for the common people implied in the washings He was expected to observe, and pointedly omitted them for that reason.

When His host calls Him on it, Jesus responds with a two-fold analysis of formalism that exposes its weaknesses as an approach to faith. The first part is the Parable of the Cup. The Pharisees are so careful to wash the outside of the cup or the platter but leave the inside full of corruption. This parable always evokes a very vivid memory of my childhood for me. One of my most hated chores was washing dishes. Well: do any of y'all remember those old Boy Scout cooking kits? They had a frying pan and a plate that folded together around a pot and a cup on the inside. Well, I had been on a Scout campout with one of those. I made bacon and scrambled eggs in the frying pan the last morning, along with oatmeal in the pot—burning some of both—and then, always being willing to put off washing the dishes, I just folded the whole mess up together on the inside of the cooking kit, wiped off the outside, and took it home. I am ashamed to report that I would have made a good Pharisee, for I proceeded to stick this outwardly shining set of cookware in my closet without a further thought—until, about two weeks later, my Mom noticed a rather strange odor exuding from that closet. I am sure that several life forms unknown to biological science must have evolved in there in the interim. I got to see to their extinction under the watchful maternal eye, the folded maternal arms, and the tapping maternal foot. I would have been better off to have cleaned out the inside of the vessel in the first place!

Well, you are all enjoying a good laugh at my youthful folly, and rightly so. But is it not sobering to think that not only ancient Pharisees but many modern Christians take exactly the same approach to living the Christian life? Hey, it *looks* clean! All the t's are crossed and all the i's are dotted! What could possibly be the problem? After all, is this not the definition of true religion, to have a public image unspotted from the world? Ahem. Jesus wants us to understand that correct outward forms can easily be a mask for inward corruption. In the case of the Pharisees, it was a combination of self–righteousness and a lack of compassion and charity for the masses. What might it be in ours?

The second part of Jesus' analysis involves his jibes about the prophets' tombs. Your fathers killed the prophets, and you build their tombs. In modern terms, we might say, "Your father pulled the trigger, and you dug the grave and shoved the body in." There is both hypocrisy and self–deception here. The irony is that while outwardly the scribes are expressing their devotion to the prophets and their teaching, they were in fact not only rejecting their message but were about to follow in their fathers' footsteps by killing the greatest Prophet of all! Outward forms can cloak a commitment to something entirely different from—even opposite to—what the forms were originally designed to express.

What does all this mean for us today? We must make no mistake. Going through the motions does not save, even if they are correct motions. Now, of course, American Evangelicals and Fundamentalists don't have any problems with this, do we? That only happens in liberal churches, right? Hmmm. Have you ever known people who judge the spirituality of a church by whether it has an altar call at the end of every service? I am not against altar calls. They have their proper use and place. But to make them a formality is only to subject our worship to reductionism. If everything is evangelism, what happens to worship, edification, discipleship? You know what happens to those necessary functions in many of our churches: They disappear. It not only reduces everything to evangelism; it even hinders the very process of evangelism itself! Listen to me: The corruption of the altar call by formalism is one of the greatest hindrances to effective evangelism in the American Bible Belt. How many times have I heard someone say, "Of course I'm saved; I went forward when I was ten." Some of us have done the same thing with baptism. "Of course I'm saved; I was baptized when I was eleven." Does this person understand the Gospel? Does he have any real living faith in Christ as his savior or commitment to Him as his Lord? No. But he is saved, right? Sure, and a cup that has been washed only on the outside is ready to be used to serve your guests. Formalism is the idea that conformity to outward forms—ceremonies, rituals, practices, creeds—is either central to genuine piety or sufficient for acceptance with God. It is a mentality that is focused on, and satisfied with, that outward conformity. And it is deadly to real and vibrant Christian faith.

II. Legalism

Legalism is a word that has been abused almost to the point of becoming useless. To most people, a legalist is anyone who is committed to a lifestyle that is more strict than one's own. Needless to say, that is not what the Lord is talking about here. Used accurately, legalism is the mentality that depends on keeping the Law as the path to salvation. But it is easy to see why the word picks up the connotation of petty strictness. For if our focus is on keeping the rules, if keeping the rules is the key to spirituality, then the emphasis is naturally going to be on keeping rules, and the stricter the better, the stricter the more spiritual. Just as we must not be thought to be opposed to the right use of ceremony, ritual, practice, or creed when we oppose formalism, so also we are not against obeying God's Law when we oppose legalism. In a way quite parallel to formalism, legalism is a mentality that tends to substitute the outward observance for the inward reality. The focus gets put on keeping the rules rather than on why we should be following them in the first place: love of God and our neighbor. And that love is the only thing that enables us to follow them in the spirit in which they were meant to be followed. Without love, law keeping will quickly become ugly even while one's behavior is technically correct.

The Lord's examples of legalism are the tithes (verse 42) and the burdens (verse 46) which the Pharisaic mentality imposed on its followers. They took tithing to the point where they would go through their spice rack and carefully measure out a tenth of each jar—while ignoring the weightier matters of the Law, justice and love. The "burdens" refer to the whole system of rules they had generated to "put a hedge around the law" and make sure they never even came close to breaking it. If the Sabbath overtakes you on a journey, can you unload your donkey? You can untie his pack and let it fall to the ground by itself, but not actually lift it off; that would be work![87] The point is not that we should not tithe, or that we should not make the Sabbath a special day. The point is that once you start thinking of Law keeping as the path of salvation, once that rather than the grace of God becomes your focus, you inevitably get the cart before the horse and end up keeping a version of the Law that becomes a caricature of God's will—all the while that love and justice are being neglected with the very best of intentions.

Do we have a problem with legalism? Yes, we do, whenever we try to bind the conscience beyond what Scripture says. There are Christians who have made drinking alcohol the eighth deadly sin and abstinence from it the eleventh commandment. Am I advocating social drinking? That is not my point. My point is that teetotalism, while it

---

[87] The rabbinic rules for the Sabbath are summarized in two treatises of *The Mishnah*, "Shabbath" and "Erubin." *The Mishnah*, op. cit., 100–136.

is an honorable practice and may be a wise one in our society, is never commanded by Scripture, and therefore we do not have the right to make it a test of spirituality. Storehouse tithing, attending public theater, playing cards—we are less prone to turn these kinds of things into shibboleths than we were a generation or two ago. But there are still those who do. And to think that the problem of legalism has disappeared merely because some of the traditional outward manifestations of it have disappeared is to fall into the trap of formalism! Maybe our besetting sin is the opposite error, antinomianism. If so, the best way to fall back into legalism again is to become complacent about it. It is deadly to real and vibrant Christian faith. Let us be people who season everything with grace, who see God's unmerited favor manifested in our lives, who say, "There but for the grace of God go I," who do not neglect justice and love. Let us not be negative, even about legalism, but be people who are positively in love with the grace of God! That is our best protection.

III. Clericalism

Clericalism is not the belief that the Church should have clergy, a regular, called, equipped, set apart, and ordained ministry. Of course it should. Clericalism is the wrong kind of dependence on that clergy and their God–ordained ministry. It is the idea that there are two levels of access to God, and that ministers have a different, higher level than regular lay people. I always have a complex reaction when people ask me to pray for themselves or for a loved one because they know I am ordained. Of course, I am honored by their request and am glad to do it—but often I suspect that they are asking me because they think that as a minister my prayers will "count" more than theirs do. They do not. God is no respecter of persons; He does not play favorites. I and other ministers are gifted and called to be teachers of the Church, examples to God's people, and under–shepherds of the flock of Christ, our chief Shepherd. But we equip the saints to do what all God's people should be doing. We are not a special caste essentially different from other believers.

Jesus' examples of this error are the Pharisees' love of the chief seats in the synagogue (verse 43) and the scribes' withholding of the key of knowledge (verse 52). They gave the impression that only they could interpret Scripture; it was too high and holy and difficult a book for simple laymen to read for themselves. Well, I hope I never give that impression. I am here to help you learn to read the Bible profitably and interpret and apply it for yourselves, not just to do it for you. The interpretation and application of Scripture should be a joint project of the whole Church, in which we correct each other's errors of fact or emphasis. I am here to help it happen. Though I read Greek and have the gift of teaching and have skills of logic and analysis honed by training and practice, that does not give me the right to pontificate! I have no authority save the authority of the Word. You should be searching the Scriptures yourselves to see if these things be so (Acts 17:11). My job is to use my training to enable you to do just that.

We look down our noses at those churches which call their ministers "priests" and make them special mediators without which the members cannot approach God. But do we commit the same errors? We all know preachers who are little Protestant Popes, and congregations who are glad to have it so. The last thing we want to do is have to think for ourselves! We turn our media–savvy preachers into superstars and hang on their every word. But like formalism and legalism, this mentality is deadly to true spirituality and saps the Church of the strength it needs to witness effectively for Christ. Let us honor and respect our pastors and elders and follow them as they follow Christ and open the Scriptures to us. We do damage to ourselves spiritually when we despise them, but equally when we put them on the wrong kind of pedestal. Let clericalism, like formalism and legalism, never be named among us again!

Conclusion

Formalism; legalism; clericalism. We must beware of these attitudes, these mentalities, these approaches, in ourselves and in our leaders. Why? Because they are deadly; they make us like concealed tombs (verse 44), full of death even though nobody can see it. It is easy to spot these curses in other Christians or other churches; it is easy for them to lie hidden and unnoticed in our own circles, because their very nature is to make everything look outwardly Okay to those whose minds are abused by them. And so we must be vigilant against them, for otherwise we will be like the inside of my old Scout cooking kit even as the outside is bright and shiny. We must be vigilant against them, for otherwise they will bring defilement and spiritual sickness and death on us as individuals or as congregations, costing us the blessing of God. Woe to the Pharisees and Scribes in our midst! Woe to their mentality! And woe to us if we are not diligent to avoid these spiritual pitfalls. To do so, let us keep our eyes on Jesus, the author and finisher of our faith (Heb. 12:2). Amen.

COURAGE FOR CONFESSION

Luke 12:1 Under these circumstances, after so many thousands of the multitudes had gathered together that they were stepping on one another, he began saying to his disciples first of all, "Beware of the leaven of the Pharisees, which is hypocrisy. 2 But there is nothing covered up that will not be revealed, and hidden that will not be known. 3 Accordingly, whatever you have said in the dark shall be heard in the light, and what you have whispered in the inner rooms shall be proclaimed upon the housetops. 4 And I say to you, my friends, do not be afraid of those who kill the body, and after that have no more that they can do. 5 But I will warn you whom to fear: Fear the One who after he has killed has the authority to cast into Hell; yes, I tell you, fear him! 6 Are not five sparrows sold for two cents? And yet not one of them is forgotten before God. 7 Indeed, the very hairs of your head are all numbered. Do not fear; you are of more value than many sparrows. 8 And I say to you, everyone who confesses me before men, the Son of Man shall confess him also before the angels of God. 9 But he who denies me before men shall be denied before the angels of God. 10 And everyone who will speak a word against the Son of Man, it shall be forgiven him; but he who blasphemes against the Holy Spirit, it shall not be forgiven him. 11 And when they bring you before the synagogues and the rulers and authorities, do not become anxious about how or what you should speak in your defense, or what you should say. 12 For the Holy Spirit will teach you in that very hour what you ought to say."

Introduction

Everyone admires a person who has the courage of his convictions. Even if we do not agree with him, we respect him for standing up for what he believes—especially if it costs him something to do so. Yet, on the issue that matters the most, and about which we ought to have the strongest feelings, we often choke, and all our convictions evaporate. You know what I am talking about: opportunities to take a stand for the Lord or to share the Gospel. Well, Jesus knew it was not going to be easy. That is why He had said before, *"Blessed are you when men hate you and ostracize you, and insult you, and scorn you name as evil for the sake of the Son of Man"* (Luke 6:22). The disciples probably did not pay that much attention then, for then they were popular. But now, while the crowds are still big, they are increasingly hostile. And as for the Pharisees, well, they were as mad as a flock of wet hens. Therefore, Jesus addresses his disciples again: "Beware . . . be ready . . . be encouraged . . . be prepared . . . be sober . . . be confident." Let's see if we can hear him saying these things in the seemingly confusing welter of parables we have just read, which I believe actually hang together when we put ourselves into the place of the disciples. For the Lord is discussing three issues relevant to the confidence He wants to give them: The Hazard of Hypocrisy, the Basis for Boldness, and the Consequences of Cowardice. The first is . . .

I. The Hazard Of Hypocrisy (vv. 1–5)

1. The Definition of Hypocrisy (verse 1b). *"Beware of the leaven of the Pharisees, which is hypocrisy."* Normally, we think of hypocrisy as pretending to be something we are not. It can also be pretending not to be something that you are. The disciples don't think they have a problem with this, but they are going to have: All but one of them will flee from the Cross, and Peter is going to go so far as to deny that he even knew the Lord—pretending not to be a follower of Jesus when he really was. Nobody has captured that scene better than Thomas Hardy:

"Man, you too, aren't you one of these rough followers of the criminal?
All hanging hereabout to father how he's going to bear
Examination in the hall." She flung disdainful glances on
The shabby figure standing at the fire with others there,
  Who warmed them by its flare.

"No, indeed, my skipping maiden: I know nothing of the trial here
Or criminal, if so he be. I chanced to come this way,
And the fire shone out into the dawn, and morning airs are cold now;
I. too, was drawn in part by charms I see before me play,
  That I see not every day."

"Ha Ha!" then laughed the constables who also stood to warm themselves,
The while another maiden scrutinized his features hard,
As the blaze threw into contrast every knot and line that wrinkled them,
Exclaiming, "Why, last night when he was brought in by the guard,
  You were with him in the yard!"

"Nay, nay, you teasing wench, I say! You know you speak mistakenly.
Cannot a tired pedestrian who has legged it long and far
Here on his way from northern parts, engaged in humble marketings,
Come in and rest awhile although judicial doings are
  Afoot by morning star?"

"Oh, come, come!" laughed the constables. "Why, man, you speak the dialect
He uses in his answers; you can hear him up the stairs.
So own it. We shan't hurt ye. There, he's speaking now! His syllables
Are those you sound yourself when you are talking unawares,
  As this pretty girl declares."

"And you shudder when his chain clinks!" she rejoined. "O yes, I noticed it.

And you winced, too, when those cuffs they gave him echoed to us
here.
They'll soon be coming down, and you may then have to defend
yourself
Unless you hold your tongue, or go away, or keep you clear
When he's led to judgment near!"

"No! I'll be damned in Hell if I know anything about the man!
No single thing about him more than anybody knows!
Must I not even warm my hands but I am charged with blasphemies?"
His face convulses as the morning cock that moment crows,
And he droops and turns and goes.[88]

I'm afraid the scene is all too familiar. For in less extreme and dramatic forms, we have all stood there in that courtyard. We may not have denied the Lord quite so blatantly, but we have all swallowed our testimony out of shame, we have all let blasphemy against our beloved Savior pass unchallenged, we have all let opportunities to take a stand for Christ pass us by, as if we found the Lord of Glory to be an embarrassment! We have all, perhaps more quietly and less dramatically, but just as culpably, pretended not to be Christians when we were. It might be too strong to say that we are all hypocrites, for sometimes we do speak the truth in love and with integrity regardless of the cost. Some of you do so consistently. But we have all acted hypocritically at some time in the past, and we all have the potential to do so again. And so we all need to take to heart the teaching that our Lord is giving us here.

2. The Futility of Hypocrisy (verses 2–3). Jesus follows his warning about hypocrisy with an analysis of it. And his first point about it is its futility. *"There is nothing covered up that will not be revealed, and hidden that will not be known. Accordingly, whatever you have said in the dark shall be heard in the light, and what you have whispered in the inner rooms shall be proclaimed upon the housetops."* Whatever we are trying to achieve by pretending to be something different from what we are, the attempt will eventually not only fail but come back to haunt us. It will do so first in this life. If we try to live with a foot in each of two worlds, sooner or later those worlds will collide, resulting in a greater embarrassment than the one you were trying to avoid in the first place. Then you will have to decide: Which of the two faces you have been wearing is the real you? Do not presume that you know which it is in advance of that moment! The only safe course is to have only one face, be only one person whose heart is not divided. For the double–minded man, as James reminds us, is unstable in all his ways (James 1:7–8). How could he be otherwise? You can never trust him, for the part of his divided mind that made a promise to you may not be the part that is in the forefront when the time comes to keep it. Doublemindedness always gets exposed in the long run. But not only is there

---

[88] Thomas Hardy, "In the Servants' Quarters," *Modern British and American Poetry*, op. cit., 413–14.

307

the great probability that this will happen even in this life; there is also the certainty that it will happen in the next. *"There is nothing covered up that will not be revealed, and hidden that will not be known. Accordingly, whatever you have said in the dark shall be heard in the light, and what you have whispered in the inner rooms shall be proclaimed upon the housetops"* (verse 3). These are sobering words indeed.

3. The Motive for Hypocrisy (verses 4–5). Why do weak human beings who actually do love the Lord sometimes pretend that they don't? The Lord's brilliant analysis continues by explaining the source of hypocrisy. The motive for hypocrisy is misplaced fear. *"And I say to you, my friends, do not be afraid of those who kill the body, and after that have no more that they can do. But I will warn you whom to fear: Fear the One who after he has killed has the authority to cast into Hell; yes, I tell you, fear him!"* The "One" in verse 5 that we are to fear is God. It has to be God, for Satan has no authority over Hell. He is destined to be an inmate of that prison, just like unrepentant human beings, not its warden. Therefore, the point is that a two–faced testimony always comes from misplaced fear—from fearing men more than God. How supremely foolish!

It is not that we are to live in fear of God or of what He might do to us if our testimony or our walk is not perfect. It is confidence in His love for us, trust in His grace, that gives us the courage to stand for Him without compromise, not that kind of fear. The Christian life as modeled by Jesus is hardly one of constantly looking over our shoulder. But the true love of God is kept from turning into presumption by *godly* fear, which is a respect and awe before God so strong that it causes us to tremble before His majesty and holiness. That trembling, to have knees trembling like that which are then straightened and strengthened by our faith in His love for us, is the true biblical picture of how we are to relate to our heavenly Father. When we have learned this kind of fear, then we will be able to say, "Because I fear God, I need fear no man." That is the place to which our Lord is trying to help us come in this passage.

II. The Basis For Boldness

The second main point is the basis for boldness. In order to help us come to the place where we fear God and not man, Jesus now gives us three reasons for boldness, three reasons why we need not fall into hypocrisy. We can stand for Christ with integrity when we remember:

1. The Providence of God the Father (verses 6–7). If you wish to put your fear of the opinions of men back into perspective so that it can no longer overwhelm your fear of God, the first thing to remember is the Providence of God the Father. He is sovereign; He is in control of events. *"Are not five sparrows sold for two cents? And yet not one of them is forgotten before God. Indeed, the very hairs of your head are all numbered. Do not fear; you are of more value than many sparrows."* If not a sparrow can fall off a branch without the Father's knowledge, concern, and permission; if not even a hair can fall out of my balding head without that same awareness, concern, and permission on His part;

then how much more valuable to Him are you yourself! How much more is it true that nothing can happen to you which is not part of His plan!

This truth has two implications that are relevant to the boldness and integrity the Lord is trying to give us here. First, God is in control of events. Nothing can take Him by surprise. He will not allow anything to happen that will keep a person who truly wishes to reach Him from doing so. Second, even though He allows difficult times to come into our lives, when they do come, we can know that He knows about them, He cares about us in them, and He will be with us through them. He is greater than anything or anyone we might fear. And therefore, we can safely commit the outcome to Him.

2. The Promise of God the Son (verse 8). Not only can we rest in the surety of the Father's utterly competent providential love in the present, but we have the even greater motivation for faithfulness of the Son's astounding promise for the future. *"And I say to you, everyone who confesses me before men, the Son of Man shall confess him also before the angels of God."* Can we possibly comprehend what this means? The very Son of God himself will put his arm around your shoulder and stand with you before all the angels of God and say, "This is my disciple _____. He confessed me before men when it was hard to do so. And so I want all of you to know what he did, and to know that I am very pleased with him." I am abashed into silence at the prospect. I can hardly continue. Can we grasp this promise? It is not the promise of an easy road—a hard one, rather—but it is the promise of an inestimable reward at the end of that road. Let us be journeying, moving forward always and never taking another step backward. We are going to see the King!

3. The Provision of God the Spirit (verses 11–12). We have then the providence of God the Father and the Promise of God the Son. We also have the Provision of God the Holy Spirit. We cannot need, or ask for, greater motivation than what we have just been provided. But in our weakness, there is yet one thing more that we need. And our loving Savior has provided it by sending us His own personal Agent and Representative, the Holy Spirit, to strengthen us in those weaknesses. *"And when they bring you before the synagogues and the rulers and authorities, do not become anxious about how or what you should speak in your defense, or what you should say. For the Holy Spirit will teach you in that very hour what you ought to say."*

Note here the assumption of verse 11: You may expect to have opportunities to take a stand for Christ which will occur under pressure, in adverse circumstances, when you have had no opportunity to prepare. But note also the assurance of verse 12: you are not on your own in such times. This verse has been mightily abused as an excuse for laziness by preachers who think it is more spiritual not to prepare their sermons, but just let the Spirit put words in their mouths when they enter the pulpit. I would not want to lay to the Spirit's charge the vacuous nonsense that often comes out of such mouths! The KJV translation here was unfortunate: *"Take no thought for what you will say."* A more accurate translation would be "Do not be anxious, do not worry, about what you will say." It hardly commands thoughtlessness! This promise only applies to occasions when there has been no opportunity for preparation because of persecution, not because of our own laziness. But when God puts you in a situation for which you have not been able to prepare, he will not leave you high and dry. In such a situation, you can look to his help with confidence that it will be provided. When you stick your neck out for God in the right spirit, He will back you up.

III. The Consequences Of Cowardice

We have seen the hazard of hypocrisy and the basis for boldness. Finally, we look at the consequences of cowardice. Our Lord has given us every reason to be wary of hypocrisy and every provision we need to avoid it. But for those who do not avail themselves of that provision, there is a stern and sober warning. *"But he who denies me before men shall be denied before the angels of God. And everyone who will speak a word against the Son of Man, it shall be forgiven him; but he who blasphemes against the Holy Spirit, it shall not be forgiven him"* (verses 9–10).

What does this mean? It does not mean you have to have a perfect track record in witnessing for Christ in order to be saved. Peter denied the Lord, but he also repented. And for those who repent, there is forgiveness. But it does mean that the two–faced professing "Christian" is in danger of eternal damnation. Why? Because when you have two faces, you unavoidably raise the question of which is the real face and which the mask. Time will tell. When the chips are down, or when your life can be viewed as a whole, your real loyalty will show. You will either be among those who are confessed before the angels in verse 8 or those denied before them in verse 9. But it is horribly dangerous to assume which it will be! For many people fool themselves on the question. Many will think they belong to the Lord, many of them will even have done great things in his name, only to hear him say, *"Depart from me; I never knew you."* Therefore, the only safe thing is to have only one face. To eliminate hypocrisy, go back to the Lord's basis for boldness and dwell with those truths. Be fortified by those realities: the Providence of God the Father, the Promise of God the Son, and the Provision of God the Holy Spirit.

What is the "blasphemy against the Holy Spirit" mentioned here? If we look at the context where the Lord first used that phrase, in Mark 3:28–30, it is plain that it is a willful and stubborn attribution of Christ's work to Satan by one who ought to know better. It is a persistent, willful denial that Jesus is God, in resistance to the Holy Spirit, by one who knows better, that persists to the end of his life. It cauterizes the conscience. Therefore, if you are worried that you have committed it, that very concern is proof that you have not. It appears here because it is the ultimate form of the hypocrisy that Jesus is warning us about. If you are concerned that you may have committed this unpardonable sin, you have not. But you need to understand that it is the possible end result of playing games with God. The best way to be sure you never approach it is to be a one–faced, single–minded Christian. None of us has perfectly achieved that goal yet. Fortunately, we are not saved by our perfection, but by our faith in Christ's.

How do you know if you have that faith, saving faith? It shows itself by a life that confesses Christ before men in both word and deed. To the extent that we are one–faced and single–minded—perhaps I should rather say, to the extent that we are *becoming* one–faced and single–minded—we may have warranted confidence that we belong to Him. That confidence is an irrepressible fountain of joy that cannot be contained, for it looks forward to our being confessed before the angels by the Son of God! And from that fountain of joy comes a testimony that is truly not only consistent and sincere, but effective in bringing glory to His name.

Conclusion

Therefore, let us confess Christ clearly and consistently now, if we never have before. For much depends on it. When John Hooper, the 16th century English martyr, faced burning at the stake, he is recorded to have said, "Life is sweet and death is bitter. But eternal life is more sweet, and eternal death more bitter."[89] He was right. If we keep our minds focused on the Providence of God the Father, the Promise of God the Son, and the Provision of God the Spirit, we may not only taste the full sweetness of eternal life, but we may even avoid the momentary bitterness of this life that Peter felt when "the morning cock that moment crows / And he droops and turns and goes." Let it be so for our good and His glory.

---

[89] *Foxe's Book of Martyrs* on the martyrdom of John Hooper, https://www.exclassics.com/foxe/foxe268.htm

WHERE YOUR TREASURE IS

Luke 12:13 And someone in the crowd said to Him, "Teacher, tell my brother to divide the family inheritance with me." 14 But He said to him, "Man, who appointed me a judge or arbiter over you?" 15 And He said to them, "Beware and be on your guard against every form of greed; for not even when one has an abundance does his life consist of his possessions." 16 And He told them a parable, saying, "The land of a certain rich man was very productive. 17 And he began reasoning with himself, saying, 'What shall I do, since I have no place to store my crops?' 18 And he said, 'This is what I will do: I will tear down my barns and build larger ones, and there I will store all my grain and my goods. 19 And I will say to my soul, "Soul, you have many goods laid up for many years to come. Take you ease, eat, drink, and be merry."' 20 But God said to him, 'You fool! This very night your soul is required of you; and now who will won what you have prepared?' 21 So is the man who lays up treasure for himself and is not rich toward God."

22 And He said to His disciples, "For this reason I say to you, do not be anxious for your life, as to what you shall eat, nor for your body as to what you shall put on. 23 For life is more than food and the body more than clothing. 24 Consider the ravens: For they neither sow nor reap, and they have no store room nor barn, and yet God feeds them. How much more valuable are you than the birds? 25 And which of you by being anxious can add a single cubit to his life span? 26 If then you cannot do even a very little thing, why are you anxious about other matters? 27 Consider the lilies how they grow. They neither toil nor spin, but I tell you , even Solomon in all his glory did not clothe himself like one of these. 28 But if God so arrays the grass in the field, which is alive today and tomorrow is thrown into the furnace, how much more will He clothe you, O men of little faith! 29 And do not seek what you shall eat, and what you shall drink, and do not keep worrying. 30 For all these things the nations of the world do eagerly seek; but your Father knows that you need these things. 31But seek for His kingdom, and these things shall be added to you. 32 Do not be afraid, little flock, for your Father has chosen gladly to give you the kingdom. 33 Sell your possessions and give to charity. Make your selves purses that do not wear out, an unfailing treasure in Heaven where no thief comes near, nor moth destroys. 34 For where your treasure is, there will your heart be also.

Introduction

The American people seem to be the most interested in accumulating and using wealth of any people. We support magazines like *The Wall Street Journal* and *Changing Times*. We have supported Christian gurus on this topic like Gary North and Larry Burkett. So we ought to be the people most interested in what Jesus has to say about this topic—if we can stand it! So let us look, first, at the Petition of the greedy individual who suddenly emerged from the crowd, and then at the Principles about wealth, and the Practice of those principles, that flow from Jesus' answer to the fellow and from the parables Jesus gave to the disciples to follow up that discussion.

I. The Petition (verses. 13–14)

And someone in the crowd said to Him, "Teacher, tell my brother to divide the family inheritance with me." But He said to him, "Man, who appointed me a judge or arbiter over you?"

I want to spend most of our time on the principles Jesus gave us and their practice, but we do need to say a little bit first about the situation, the petition that provoked that discussion. This fellow that shows up in verse 13 really gets on your nerves. He pops up out of the very serious discussion already going on from the previous verses we looked at last time, of how important it is to be faithful in persecution and how the Holy Spirit will have your back if you get arrested and don't know what to say. *"Everyone who confesses me before men . . . the Son of Man shall confess him before the angels of God. But he who denies me before men shall be denied before the angels. . . . And when they bring you before the synagogues and the rulers and authorities, do not become anxious about how or what you should speak in your defense . . . for the Holy Spirit will teach you in that very hour what you ought to say"* (12:8–12). This is some pretty serious stuff about the coming of the Kingdom of Heaven and what it could potentially cost you. Then this guy pokes his way into that discussion, sticking out like the proverbial sore thumb. His tone reminds you of two toddlers fighting over a toy: "Mom, tell him to give me the . . . !" I think that must explain the uncharacteristic exasperation in Jesus' voice: "Man, . . ." It's very different from our Lord's response to anyone other than the Pharisees. *"Man, who appointed me a judge or arbiter over you?"* (12:14).

At least Jesus is answering a question with a question, which is indeed His normal procedure. But this question is interesting. It calls into doubt, not Jesus' authority—for the Father has given all judgment into Jesus' hands, so in one sense the answer is that God had made Jesus the arbiter over everything—but rather it calls into doubt the inquirer's motives. "I did not come into this world to settle your family squabbles arising out of your greed" would be a fair paraphrase. The word translated arbiter literally means "divider." Jesus had bigger fish to fry than dividing up this family's land according to this individual's whims. There is a lot we don't know about him and his situation. Was the other brother the older brother? The responsible one? Was this fellow trying to get what was coming to him early, like the younger brother in the Parable of the Prodigal Son? Is there a contrast with Abraham, who when dividing the land with Lot unselfishly allowed Lot the first choice in picking out his share? We suspect that in some way this man was putting pelf ahead of people, fees ahead of family, receiving ahead of relationships. Jesus had no intention of participating in that game.

II. The Principles

Well then, let's move on to the principles Jesus gives us in His way of rebuking this fellow. There are three principles, three fundamental truths about wealth and property, that are taught or implied by Jesus' response. The first is that **Property is From God and Depends on God.** This truth is firmly established in the Old Testament. Israel is warned as they are about to enter the Land that it is a good land that will support them well, but when they are enjoying its bounty, they should not forget how they got there. *"Otherwise, you may say in your heart, 'My power and the strength of my hand made me this wealth.' But you shall remember the Lord your God, for it is He who is giving you power to make wealth, that He may confirm His covenant which He swore to your fathers"* (Deut. 8:17–18). This point is emphasized in the Luke passage—indeed, the Old–Testament passage leading up to it is echoed—by Jesus' comment that the land of the rich man had been productive (Luke 3:12:16). It was the land, not his skill at farming it, which produced this bumper crop. It was due to God that he had it, and it was due to God's timing in his death that he did not get to keep it. Property is from God and depends on God. Your property is from God and depends on God. And that means all of it—every bit of it—every last penny.

It follows from this that the riches, the prosperity of this man, was not the problem. It had been the gift of God. The problem was not the rich man's wealth but his attitude toward it—thinking of it as his own, taking credit for it, using it to provide for his own laziness and leisure rather than as an opportunity to serve others. We learn from this that we should not take our job—and the health that allows us to work it—for granted. If you find your security there, rather than in God Himself, you are guilty of idolatry. And don't say, "Well, I have disability insurance." Don't dare God to prove to you that you are dependent on Him for your welfare! And if you think of your job as more a chance to prosper than an opportunity to serve, you are also guilty of idolatry. You are serving Mammon, not God. And no man can serve two masters.

The second principle is that, not only does property come from God and depend on Him, **Property Belongs to God and is Held Only on Loan from Him.** And it's not just your property. This is true even of your life itself. In verse 20, when the rich man's life is "required" of him, the world translated "required" is a technical term for the repayment of a loan. If your very life does not belong to you but is on loan from Another, and you are required to give an account of your stewardship of it, then surely that applies to your stuff as well. And, guess what? Dead people can't own anything. You never see a U–Haul trailer being pulled behind a hearse. All of us are under sentence of death because the wages of sin is death (Rom. 6:23). But we have been given our lives back because of Christ's death on the Cross. We have been "bought with a price" (1 Cor. 6:20). Therefore, everything we are and have belongs to Christ, and we hold it as stewards. What is a steward? It is a servant who manages the property of another for the benefit of the owner.

Okay, what does it mean if God owns all of my property (and time and talent) and has only loaned it to me? I have a friend named _____ _____ who usually has a book she's been wanting me to read, and she even keeps talking about loaning it to me. If she does, I get to read it, but I don't get to keep it. It's her book, so she can ask for it back at any time, and I will need to give it up. Also, just because it isn't my book, I need to take really good care of it. It would be horribly discourteous and ungrateful for me to give it back with the back cover torn and a few pages missing and water damage on some of the other pages. No matter how bad a book it may turn out to be, it is not mine, so I cannot give it away or toss it out.

You begin to get the picture. The rich man in the parable thought all his crops were his and he could do whatever he wanted with them. He forgot that his time, talent, and treasure were on loan and belonged to Another. So I need to stop thinking of my time, talent, and treasure as mine. They belong to God, and I am entrusted with them. Okay, what does this mean for my money? I need to be asking, not just what I would like to buy with it, but whether God wants what I'm proposing to buy with it. Does God want the oil changed in His car? Where does He want me to drive His car? Does God want a new roof on His house? Does God want His dishes washed? Does He want His grass cut? Watered? How often? To start thinking like that is to revolutionize your life. You might fear it would be oppressive. In fact, some of you might try to make it oppressive. If you are asking whether God wants His grass cut, how perfect does your yard have to be to satisfy Him? The key to avoiding that trap is to remember who God is, to remember His character. It is Jesus who is telling us this! It is the deep, deep love of Jesus that lies behind it. And He cares more about people than stuff. Yeah, He wants His grass cut, but He has better priorities than making you obsessive about it. You might fear it would be oppressive to think of Jesus as the owner of all your stuff, but I can tell you it is liberating if you remember who He is! You will make fewer stupid decisions when thinking that way, for one thing. And it doesn't mean you don't get to enjoy the stuff God has entrusted you with. You get to enjoy it, but you are no longer a slave to it, it can no longer pull you down into the rat race, because you realize that it was never yours to start with.

The third principle is kind of in your face: **The Person Who Does not Realize and Live by the Truth that He is not an Owner but a Steward is a Fool.** *"But God said to him, 'You fool! This very night your soul is required of you; and now who will own what you have prepared?' So is the man who lays up treasure for himself and is not rich toward God"* (Luke 12:20–21). Anybody who does not live in accordance with reality is a fool. Being this kind of fool may not cost you your life, as it did the man in the story. But it will cost you your peace of mind and it will cost you a lot of opportunities to achieve real happiness in the enjoyment of the wealth God has entrusted to you by using it for His glory. Don't be that fool!

III. The Practice

Having laid down some basic principles about a biblical philosophy of wealth and property in the story about the rich man, Jesus proceeds to make a couple of practical applications of those principles. There are basically two of them: Don't worry; do work—but work without worrying, which is a very different thing.

First, **Don't Worry!** *"And He said to His disciples, 'For this reason I say to you, do not be anxious for your life, as to what you shall eat, nor for your body as to what you shall put on'"* (verse 22). Look up at the ravens and down at the lilies and understand that the God who provides for them cares even more about you. The fool depends on himself—his skills, his continued health, the stock market, the economy. These are things we should use of course, but if you find your security there, you are a fool! The believer, on the other hand, owns nothing but is cared for by his heavenly Father. The Father will normally use the fruits of your labor to provide for you, but you are trusting, not in your labor, but in Him. This sets you free from the rat race, free to live—and to give. *"Sell your possessions and give to charity. Make yourselves purses that do not wear out, an unfailing treasure in Heaven where no thief comes near, nor moth destroys. For where your treasure is, there will your heart be also"* (verses 33–4). Unlike the man in the story, we are free to use God's resources as He would have us to because we care about His less fortunate children, and we can act on that care because we trust Him to take care of us.

So, the first principle is don't worry. The second is **Do Work.** *"But seek for His kingdom, and these things shall be added to you"* (verse 31). What does seeking the kingdom have to do with work? It clearly does in context because of the way it caps off this whole discussion. It transforms your idea of what (and Whom) you are working for. That is, while most of us have to work to make a living, our primary motive for working is not money anymore but God's glory and the advancement of His kingdom. This does not just apply to people who are doing "church work"; it is about the spread of the Gospel of course, but it is also about how we approach any calling we have in life. If we get that right, it will be something that is good in itself, and it will also aid in the spread of the Gospel as we enhance our credibility in the way we do that good work. Martin Luther is supposed to have said that a Christian cobbler works as a Christian not by putting little crosses on his shoes but by making good shoes and selling them to his neighbor at a fair price as an act of love.[90] The Christian makes shoes for the glory of God and for the love of his neighbor.

This is how we should think of our work. Can you take your job and put that phrase at the end of it? "I build houses for the glory of God and for the love of my neighbor, who needs a good place to live." "I fry hamburgers for the glory of God and the love of my neighbor, who needs to be fed." "I preach sermons for the glory of God and the love of my neighbor, who needs to be trained and edified in the faith." "I design airplanes . . . teach school . . . catch speeders . . . wait tables . . . balance books . . . play music . . . sell clothes . . . fix cars . . . for the glory of God and the love of my neighbor." If you cannot finish your sentence that way, you are in the wrong line of work! Almost every honest job can fit there, even if we don't think of it that way. A few of us might

---

[90] The quote may possibly be apocryphal, but it is thought-provoking nevertheless. http://www.lutheranlayman.com/2015/01/little-crosses-on-shoes-or-what-luther.html

need to quit our jobs, but most of us need rather to transform them by approaching them the way a Christian should.

When we do that, all these other things will be added to us. God will take care of us. To work primarily for money is to enter the rat race, to experience slavery, boredom, and foolishness. To work for the glory of God and the love or your neighbor is to experience freedom, fulfillment, and happiness. So guard your priorities. Don't automatically build bigger barns as if the whole goal of your life's work was your own comfort and security. Rather, invest your money, invest your treasure, talent, and time, where your heart should be, and it will follow them there. *"For where your treasure is, there will your heart be also"* (Mat. 6:21).

Conclusion

Jesus says to each of us in our greedy, materialistic society, "Don't be a fool!" Life does not consist in the multitude of things that a man possesseth (Luke 12:15). Don't be a fool! First be sure that you have put your faith in Him as your Lord and Savior to receive the forgiveness of sin and eternal life and become part of His Kingdom. *"For if you confess with your mouth Jesus as Lord and believe in your heart that God has raised Him from the dead, you shall be saved"* (Rom. 10:9). Then seek the kingdom of God and His righteousness, and all these things will be added to you. Amen.

THE FAITHFUL STEWARD or REASONS FOR READINESS

Luke 12:35 "*Be dressed in readiness and keep you lamps alight. 36 And be like men who are waiting for their master when he returns from the wedding feast, so that they may immediately open the door to him when he comes and knocks. 37 Blessed are those slaves whom the master shall find on the alert when he comes. Truly I say to you that he will gird himself to serve, and have them recline at table, and will come up and wait on them. 38 Whether he comes in the second watch, or even in the third, and finds them so, blessed are those slaves. 39 And be sure of this, that if the head of the house had known at what hour the thief was coming, he would not have allowed his house to be broken into. 40 You too, be ready, for the Son of Man is coming at an hour that you do not expect.*"

41 And Peter said, "Lord, are you addressing this parable to us, or to everyone else as well?" 42 And the Lord said, "Who then is that faithful and sensible steward whom his master will put in charge of his servants to give them their ration at the proper time? 43 Blessed is that slave whom that master finds so doing when he comes. 44 Truly I say to you, he will put him in charge of all his possessions. 45 But if that slave says in his heart, 'My master will be a long time in coming,' and begins to beat the slaves, both men and women, and to eat and drink and get drunk, 46 the master of that slave will come on a day when the slave does not expect him, and at an hour he does not know, and will cut him in pieces and assign him a place with the unbelievers. 47 And that slave who knew his master's will and did not get ready or act in accord with his will shall receive many lashes, 48 but the one who did not know it and committed deeds worthy of a flogging will receive but few. And from everyone who has been given much shall be required; and to whom they entrusted much, of him they will ask all the more."

Introduction

When last we looked at Luke's Gospel together, we saw the concept of stewardship in the parable of the farmer who built bigger barns because he did not realize that his wealth was a gift held in trust from God to be used for Him. For a Steward is a servant who manages the wealth of another for the benefit of the Master. Now Jesus gives us some insight on how to be a good Steward in the light of the fact that we pursue that calling while waiting for the Second Coming. "*Be ready, for the Son of Man is coming at an hour that you do not expect.*"

In a passage of great earnestness, Peter writes this in his second Epistle: "*Know this first of all, that in the last days mockers will come with their mocking, following after their own lusts and saying, 'Where is the promise of His coming? For ever since the fathers fell asleep, all continues just as it was from the beginning of creation. . . . But do not let this escape your notice, beloved, that with the Lord one day is as a thousand years, and a thousand years as one day. The Lord is not slow about His promises as some count slowness, but is patient toward you, not wishing for any to perish but all to come to repentance. But the day of the Lord will come like a thief, in which the heavens will pass away with a roar, and the elements will be destroyed with intense heat, and the earth and its works will be burned up. Since all these things are to be destroyed in this way, what sort of people ought you to be in holy conduct and godliness?"* (2 Pet. 3:3–4, 8–11).

Peter writes this way because of the instruction he got from the Lord here in Luke 12, the passage that is before us today. If in the First-Century people were becoming cynical about the Lord's return, surely we are even more susceptible to the argument they were making, with another two thousand years of business as usual continuing just as it has since the creation. Jesus and Peter both foresaw that we would find it hard to maintain a sense of urgency about the Lord's work that flows from expectancy about His coming. We are like I was my first year in seminary, when I had a job as caretaker for a mansion on Chicago's North Shore of Lake Michigan. I got a room in the house and salary for looking after the place. Well, my bosses, the Solovys, went on a trip to Europe for two weeks and left me in charge. I had the run of their mansion for the duration. And here's the thing: I knew the day and hour of their return, because I had to take their Lincoln Continental and pick them up at O'Hare when they got back.

I knew the day and hour of the master's return. So what did I do? I spent two weeks swimming in their pool and listening to their expensive stereo and playing another kind of pool in their billiards room when I wasn't studying. And then the last day I spent in a flurry of activity doing all the chores I was supposed to have been keeping up with every day. You can all see the point already. If I had not known the day and hour of the master's return, I would have had to approach those two weeks very differently. So, when it comes to the Lord's work, which way are we living? I just quit preaching and went to meddling, didn't I? Sorry. Jesus beat me to it. He gives us three reasons here why we need to be ready all the time: a command to stay ready, the conditions under which that command must be obeyed, and the consequences of obedience or disobedience.

The Command (vv. 35–36)

The first reason we need to be always faithful and always ready for the Master's return is that Jesus has commanded it. *"Be dressed in readiness and keep you lamps alight. And be like men who are waiting for their master when he returns from the wedding feast, so that they may immediately open the door to him when he comes and knocks"* (v. 35–6). That should be a sufficient reason in itself for those who love Him. *"If you love me,"* He said elsewhere, *"keep my commandments"* (John 14:15).

What is He commanding? Action! To be about His business. What the NASB translates as "Be dressed in readiness" is the old familiar idiom "gird up your loins" of the KJV. Modern men don't relate to that imagery very well because we don't typically wear long flowing robes anymore that need to be tucked up out of the way for strenuous physical activity. A literal modern equivalent might be something like "Put on your athletic supporter," or, maybe a little less graphically, "roll up your sleeves" is probably what we would say in a similar context.

I remember as a kid hearing a sermon on a parallel passage with a similar idea, Mark 13:37, which in the KJV is *"What I say unto thee I say unto all: Watch!"* I took it rather literally. That afternoon I went home and got out my telescope and sat in the back yard scanning the sky, watching for Jesus to come back. You can't see much besides blue sky in the middle of the day, which gets a wee bit boring after the first five minutes, so by the time my Mom called me in for supper I was starting to wonder if I had the right idea. I didn't.

The idea of watching is not scanning the horizon but rather staying on the alert, not going to sleep at your post, being always on the lookout for opportunities to share the Gospel or advance the Kingdom in other ways. Instead, do you ever find yourself muddling through the day just trying to make ends meet and survive while being spiritually half asleep? That's what the passage of time that Peter spoke of can do to you. So we need to be reminded periodically of the Lord's command: Gird up your loins; roll up your sleeves; stay spiritually involved; be on the lookout; watch!

The Conditions

So that is the command: stay on the alert. Here we also find a discussion of some of the conditions under which we serve, the situations in which we will find ourselves, hence the circumstances in which we obey it. The Lord is coming back, and we don't know when. We can't predict it, so we have to be ready all the time and can't take the approach I took at the Solovys' mansion. This unpredictability is emphasized three times in this short little passage. It might be in the middle of the night. *"Whether he comes in the second watch, or even in the third, and finds them so, blessed are those slaves"* (verse 38). The Romans divided the night into four "watches," so the second and third would be the ones when the temptation to drowsiness would be at its peak for anyone on duty. One thing is certain: Jesus' coming definitely will not be when you figure it will. *"You too, be ready, for the Son of Man is coming at an hour that you do not expect"* (v. 40). And this unpredictability is stressed yet again in verse 46. The master of that slave will come on a day when the slave does not expect him, and at an hour he does not know, and will cut him in pieces and assign him a place with the unbelievers.

What are the implications of these conditions of unpredictability? Surely one is that date–setting is totally ruled out. As if Matthew 24:36 were not enough! *"But of that day and hour no one knows, not even the angels of heaven, nor the Son, but the Father alone."* In case you missed it there, this passage should pretty much nail it down. You absolutely cannot figure it out. So stop trying! And don't listen to anyone who still does try. It's not your job to figure out when the Lord is coming. It's your job to be faithful, to occupy until He does.

Second, we need to be faithful in the light of our inability to figure out the timing of the Second Coming. That means we have to live in such a way that we cover the bases either way. What if it is really soon? What if it won't be for another thousand years? Our life should be such that we are prepared for both scenarios because they are both possible.

Okay, what if it is really soon? We are to live as if it could be at any moment. I don't think our preachers have done a great job of preparing us for that possibility. I don't know how many times I've been warned against whatever the sin *du jour* was of the sermon in question, "What if Jesus came back and found you doing that?" I suppose that would be pretty embarrassing, but the proper exhortation if you want me to flee that sin would be to remind me that He can see me doing it already, right now! Omniscience was an attribute of God last time I checked. Jesus' point is rather a positive one: Be found at your post! Never desert it! And realize that, whenever the Return might be, the amount of time we have to serve the Lord who bought us is finite. Even if the Second Coming is long delayed, your personal moment to see the Lord face to face could literally be at any moment.

So what do you need to be doing? What are you putting off? To break a bad habit? To apologize to your brother? To start reading your Bible on a less haphazard basis? To tell someone that you love him? To witness to your neighbor? To pay back a debt? Get on with it! Do it now. Do not put it off. Based on both the doctrine of the Second Coming and the reality of the brevity of life, for all you know this might be the last day you have to get it done. This doesn't mean you live constantly stressed out and under the gun. But even if you live to be a hundred and the Lord tarries, life is short. Believe me, it did not take me seventy years to become seventy years old! At least, that's not how it feels. The last half of that period especially happened in a day. Your moments are finite. Make them count!

On the other hand, what if it's going to be a long time? We need to live so we've got that base covered too. We take care of the environment. We plan for the future in case we are here to live in it, and in case our children and grandchildren are going to live in it. We plant trees even if we won't be around to enjoy their shade when they are big enough to cast it. We make every day count, both for the present and the future. We don't know when the burglar is coming, so we lock our door every night. We don't know when the pop quiz is coming (my students knew it would be in an hour when they thought not!), so we study every night. We don't know when the inspection is coming, so we are always at our post. We do this because we are commanded to and because the conditions under which we serve require it of us.

The Consequences

Okay, we are ready because we were commanded to be and because of the conditions in which we live. The third reason for readiness may be the best of all. There are consequences: great reward for faithfulness, and judgment for unfaithfulness. Verse 37 may be one of the most astounding verses in the Bible. Jesus will do what hardly any earthly master, however kind and benevolent, would ever think of doing. He will sit his faithful servants down at the table and wait on them Himself. *"Blessed are those slaves whom the master shall find on the alert when he comes. Truly I say to you that he will gird himself to serve, and have them recline at table, and will come up and wait on them"* (verse 37). It was unheard of for a master to do what Jesus says He will do for His servants who are found faithful. It foreshadows the radical act when He would wash the disciples' feet before the Last Supper. His love will be shown to us in ways so extravagant we will not know how to handle it! And it would be enough were He just to say, *"Well done, thou good and faithful servant. Enter into the joy of your Master"* (Mat. 25:21).

The consequences of unpreparedness are judgment. It is possible to find yourself in verses 45–47. *"But if that slave says in his heart, 'My master will be a long time in coming,' and begins to beat the slaves, both men and women, and to eat and drink and get drunk, the master of that slave will come on a day when the slave does not expect him, and at an hour he does not know, and will cut him in pieces and assign him a place with the unbelievers."* This is one who was thought to be a servant of the Master, but who ends up with the unbelievers. The best way to be unprepared is to be an unbeliever. The second–best way is to be a merely professing believer. You're not going to Hell because you occasionally get distracted by the cares of this life. We've all nodded off on our watch at one time or another. But this passage gives us a useful way to examine ourselves, whether we be in the faith. Is your faith genuine faith? Well, how does this passage inspire you to respond to the idea of the Second Coming? Does the reminder that Christ is coming back, and you don't know when, inspire you to serve the Lord even more faithfully, or does it inspire you to say, "My master will be a long time in coming," and to therefore live for yourself? That is the bottom line. People who do not relate properly to the Second Coming probably are not related properly to the First Coming either. How we relate to the Lord is the common denominator in both.

One little footnote before we close. Verses 47–48 are the basis for the idea that, just as there are degrees of reward in Heaven, so there are degrees of punishment in Hell. *"And that slave who knew his master's will and did not get ready or act in accord with his will shall receive many lashes, but the one who did not know it and committed deeds worthy of a flogging will receive but few."* God will do what is right. There might be some small comfort there for basically good people who died in their unbelief, though nothing can compensate for not being in Heaven with the Lord. But I'm afraid I've got bad news for you. The fact that you have just heard this sermon makes you ineligible for inclusion in the group that did not know the Master's will. I will be really bummed out if all I have accomplished today is to heighten the severity of your flogging! So avoid stripes altogether by taking Jesus as your Savior and Lord and by joining that group that will receive His table service at the Marriage Supper of the Lamb!

Conclusion

I can think of no better way to conclude this message than by returning to Peter's words, what may indeed be his commentary on this passage as he remembered it, those words we started with. *"Know this first of all, that in the last days mockers will come with their mocking, following after their own lusts and saying, 'Where is the promise of His coming? For ever since the fathers fell asleep, all continues just as it was from the beginning of creation. . . . But do not let this escape your notice, beloved, that with the Lord one day is as a thousand years, and a thousand years as one day. The Lord is not slow about His promises as some count slowness, but is patient toward you, not wishing for any to perish but all to come to repentance. But the day of the Lord will come like a thief, in which the heavens will pass away with a roar, and the elements will be destroyed with intense heat, and the earth and its works will be burned up. Since all these things are to be destroyed in this way, what sort of people ought you to be in holy conduct and godliness?"* (2 Pet. 3:2–3, 8–11). What sort of people ought we to be indeed? The sort who are found on the alert when the Master comes. Amen.

NOT PEACE BUT STRIFE

Luke 12:49 *"I have come to cast fire upon the earth, and how I wish it were already kindled!* **50** *But I have a baptism to undergo, and how distressed I am until it is accomplished.* **51** *Do you suppose that I came to grant peace on the earth? I tell you no, but rather division.* **52** *For from now on five members in one household will be divided, three against two and two against three.* **53** *They will be divided, Father against son and son against father, mother against daughter and daughter against mother, mother in law against daughter in law and daughter and law against mother in law."* **54** *And he was also saying to the multitudes, "When you see a cloud rising in the west, immediately you say, 'A shower is coming.' and so it turns out.* **55** *And when you see a south wind blowing you say, 'It will be a hot day,' and it turns out that way.* **56** *You hypocrites! You know how to analyze the appearance of the earth and the sky, but why do you not analyze this present time?* **57** *And why do you not even on your own initiative judge what is right?* **58** *For while you are going with your opponent to appear before the magistrate, on your way there make an effort to settle with him, in order that he may not drag you before the judge, and the judge turn you over to the constable, and the constable throw you into prison.* **59** *I say to you, you shall not get out of there until you have paid the very last cent."*

Introduction

Every Fall we are subjected on the 6:00 News to predictions of the harshness or mildness of the coming winter based on the bunions of the weather prophet, the chirping of crickets, or the thickness of the fuzz on wooly worms. Unfortunately (or fortunately, as the case may be), by the time winter actually arrives, we have had just enough time to forget what the predictions were, which prevents us from checking their accuracy. But Jesus tells us that there are some signs of the times that we had better pay attention to, because they are accurate and what they predict is upon us. We saw last time that we who serve the Lord should be always at our post and always on the alert because He is coming back and we do not know when; we do not know the day and the hour of that return. As Jesus continues His discourse about the End Times, we learn today that His return has implications for those who do not yet serve Him as well. A storm is coming, so they had better pay attention to the Signs of the Times and head for shelter before it is too late!

Jesus here makes three points to those who are not yet His disciples, parallel to the ones He made to those who already are, or at least profess to be, that we saw last time. If you are not yet a disciple of Jesus, you obviously need to pay attention! This message is for you. It has your name written on the outside of the envelope. Okay, what if you *are* His disciple already? Why do *you* need to pay attention today? Because it is part of His message for the non–Believer with which you have been entrusted! Every single person here today is either the recipient or the mail carrier. So what is that message? First, the weather forecast has been made: Judgment is coming! Second, the signs of that coming judgment are clear; you have no excuse if you ignore them. Third, there is only one logical response you can make to those signs: Repent, for the Kingdom of Heaven is at hand!

I. The Forecast Has Been Made: Judgment Is Coming!

To understand what Jesus is saying here, we must remind ourselves of what He has just been saying, as we saw last time. He is clearly talking about the day of judgment, when the master of the slaves (Himself) returns unexpected and rewards them for their faithfulness or lack of it. He concludes that section with a warning to the slaves who have not kept themselves ready: Those who knew the master's will and did not do it will receive many stripes; those who sinned from ignorance will only get a few. In this context, the statement about casting fire on the earth is doubtless a continuation of the same discussion. These are not revival fires or the tongues of fire associated with the coming of the Holy Spirit but the fires of judgment, flowing from a strong strand of Old Testament imagery. *"Therefore the Lord heard and was full of wrath, and a fire was kindled against Jacob and anger mounted also against Israel because they did not believe in God and did not trust in his salvation"* (Ps. 78:21–22). *"Seek the Lord that you may live, lest he break forth like a fire, oh house of Joseph, and it consume with none to quench it"* (Amos 5:6). *"Who can stand before his indignation? Who can endure the burning of his anger? His wrath is poured out like fire, and the rocks are broken up by him"* (Nahum 1:6). *"For all the earth will be devoured by the fire of my zeal"* (Zeph. 3:8). *"But who can endure the day of his coming? And who can stand when he appears? for he is like a refiner's fire"* (Mal. 3:2).

It is a strand of imagery picked up also by the New Testament. Peter was no doubt thinking of the Lord's words here when he said that *"the present heavens and earth are by his Word being reserved for fire, kept for the day of judgment and destruction of ungodly men"* (2 Pet. 3:7). And the Lord's audience would have remembered the fiery (ahem) rhetoric of John the Baptist, who had predicted that the greater One who was coming would baptize with the Holy Spirit and with fire. John made it clear that these were two alternative baptisms, for he immediately explains that the Lord's winnowing fork is in his hand, to separate the wheat for the barn but reserve the chaff for unquenchable fire (Luke 3:16–17). The wheat are those whom the Holy Spirit has called to faith and regenerated, and the barn is Heaven. The chaff then are the wicked, and the fire is eternal punishment. So it seems plain that when Jesus speaks of casting fire on the earth he is anticipating the Day of Judgment.

But wait a minute. Jesus seems to be looking forward to casting this fire! He wishes it was already kindled. How can this be, when the Lord takes no pleasure in the death of the sinner (Ezek. 33:11)? Well, truly He would prefer that they repent. But we are confronted here with the less comfortable fact that God is just as much just and righteous as he is merciful and gracious. Less comfortable, I say, but equally important, and indeed bracing in its own way if we can grasp it aright. God's justice is a good thing. It is not our favorite of his attributes—Grace, for certain very personal reasons having to do with our own need, will always be that. But it is a positive good nonetheless, and a necessary one. It is good that sin will one day be dealt with in such a fashion that it can no longer function. It is good that sin will one day be dealt with in such a fashion that it can no longer harm people. It is good that sin will one day be dealt with in such a fashion that it can no longer damage and defile the universe. It is good that sin will one day be dealt with in such a way that it can no longer hold the universe hostage. That is something which not only the Lord, but we too, should be properly looking forward to!

It is due to human recalcitrance, human stubbornness, human rebellion, and human unbelief, that this happy day will also involve a certain, shall we say, unpleasantness for the unrepentant. That is a sobering reality. It is the most grievous thing we know, and we should never make light of it. But if we let it keep us from looking forward to the establishment of God's righteous reign, it would be tantamount to giving Sin and Satan—and sinners—the right to highjack the universe and hold it eternally for ransom. Well, that is just what they want to do! But fortunately, the Ransom has been paid, and therefore anyone who really wants to can be in the Barn instead of the Trash Fire. The point is, as we saw last time, that the fire is coming. The very arrival of Christ on the planet the first time brings it nearer. And the Son of Man will come at an hour that we think not.

I cannot resist thinking that there is a second, and perhaps even more profound reason why the Lord is anxious to get this fire started. What He is really looking forward to is the Marriage Supper of the Lamb. He tells us in the most personal of His discourses, the great high priestly prayer of John 17, that He longs to have the people that the Father gave Him before the foundation of the earth with Him where He is, so that they may behold His glory and be one with Him and with each other. Well, that is the final consummation of all things. And the judgment is something that has to come first. I think the Lord wants this fire kindled because He wants to get it over with, so He can get it out of the way, so He can get to his Bride! When those of you who are married were waiting for your wedding day, was that waiting easy to do? Was it a matter of indifference to you how quickly it came? If there were things that had to be accomplished first, was getting them out of the way a happy thing? Think about what it means to use the biblical metaphor that the church is the Bride of Christ! The judgment is the last bit of work to be done, and then comes the Sabbath rest when the people the Father gave Christ will be with Him where He is and we will glorify Him by enjoying Him forever. No wonder He says, "how I wish it were already kindled!"

Fortunately for those who are not yet repentant, it is not kindled—yet. But it will be, and there are certain signs that it is getting closer. That is the point of this passage. Repent, for the kingdom of heaven is at hand! You can tell when a storm is coming, but you can't see this? You hypocrites! The forecast has been made. The clouds are already gathering on the horizon! So bring in the pets and the potted plants, board up the windows, get ready! The storm is coming.

In this context, the parable of the magistrate (verse 58–59) is not in this passage primarily about reconciliation with your brother. *For while you are going with your opponent to appear before the magistrate, on your way there make an effort to settle with him, in order that he may not drag you before the judge, and the judge turn you over to the constable, and the constable throw you into prison. I say to you, you shall not get out of there until you have paid the very last cent."* Your "opponent" is the Law, which accuses you of capital crimes; the magistrate is God, the constable is Satan, and the prison is Hell. So the point is, wake up! The forecast has been given, the clouds are gathering, and you are already on your way to appear before the judge. The urgency in the uncertain time of the Lord's return is a motivation for the believer to be faithful at his post, as we saw last time. It is also a motivation for the sinner to repent now, before it is too late. That is the focus of the Lord's words that are before us today.

II. The Clarity Of The Signs

Alright, the first point is that the forecast has been made: Judgment is coming. The second is the clarity of the signs of that impending judgment. With the improving technologies of Doppler radar, hurricane chasers, and satellite imagery, meteorologists are more reliable than they used to be, but weather forecasting is still an inexact science. If the next winter coming to us is a normal one for Northeast Georgia, I can tell you a couple of things with little fear of contradiction. First, we will probably get about two snowfalls that actually "stick" on the ground; second, neither of them will happen on a night in which they were predicted. When I was living in Chicago, the weather prophets failed to predict a devastating late spring snowstorm that hit right after studded snow tires had to be off the cars and thus paralyzed even that snow–hardened city. They were so embarrassed by this failure that for at least the next two years (after that I escaped back to Georgia and lost track, thank God!) they consistently overestimated every snowfall by about fifty percent, and predicted several that they probably suspected were not going to happen, lest they leave people unprepared again. It was laughably obvious that subjective factors like covering their own posteriors were trumping the science of meteorology in their predictions. We can all tell similar stories. But we still listen to the Weather Channel because their guess is in fact the best one available. And even without them we can tell some things. Hmm, south wind? Hot day. *"When you see a cloud rising in the west, immediately you say, 'A shower is coming.' and so it turns out. And when you see a south wind blowing you say, 'It will be a hot day,' and it turns out that way. You hypocrites! You know how to analyze the appearance of the earth and the sky, but why do you not analyze this present time? (verses 54–55)..*

By contrast, Jesus has given us signs of the approach of this storm that are absolutely infallible. Wait, didn't I just say last time that we could not predict the day or the hour? I'm glad you remember! They are infallibly designed *not* to tell us that, but to give us instead a trustworthy sense that the event is imminent and coming ever closer. The biggest sign of all is, as we have already indicated, the First Coming itself. Another list of phenomena whose increasing presence is a reminder that the end is drawing near is found in Matthew 24:3–14. They include false Christs (verse 5). My experiences in Uganda training national pastors in the 21st century have reminded me that cults are multiplying faster than we can keep up with them. Wars and rumors of wars are mentioned in verse 6–8. I won't bore you by reciting the current catalog of conflicts, which changes every year. Persecution of believers will escalate in verse 9. In many parts of the world today it is more dangerous to be a Christian than it has been since the Roman persecutions ended with Constantine. As for the coldness of believers in verse 13, just compare our churches to the ones in those persecuted countries.

Now, none of this so far is very specific to our time; it is a general description of the world at most times and in most places. It is hard to tell if these things are really on the increase or if we are just more aware of them because of better media coverage, or if it is that they affect more people because with increasing population density there are more people to be affected. But the last sign is different: *"And this Gospel of the Kingdom shall be preached in the whole world for a witness to all the nations, and then the end shall come"* (Mat. 24:14). We live in the first generation of which it can be truthfully said that this prophecy is being fulfilled, or at least is nearing its fulfillment. There is now, for the first time in history, no nation without at least some Christian witness, though there are still numerous "people groups" who are effectively unreached. What a dramatic and significant new development!

Does this mean the Lord will come back in our generation? How should I know? The point is that it means that He *could*. And when you see such a momentous thing happening in your very own day, the implication of these Scriptures is, "What more do you need?" It is too late to come in out of the rain after you are already drenched! The storm clouds are gathering, and the rumble of thunder can be heard in the distance. To pretend that we have not been warned is arrant hypocrisy. Repent, for the kingdom of heaven is at hand!

III. The Response: Take Action!

Okay, judgment is coming and the signs of it are sufficiently clear. What are non–Christians supposed to do about this? The same thing professing Christians were supposed to do in the last passage: Take action! If you are a Christian, be found at your post. If you are not a Believer, repent and believe so you can be assigned a post.

What the Lord is really doing here is explicating the urgency implicit in His favorite way of presenting the Gospel: "Repent, for the kingdom of heaven is at hand!" It is urgent for all the reasons we have been seeing for two sermons now. *"While you are going with your opponent to appear before the magistrate, on your way there make an effort to settle with him, in order that he may not drag you before the judge, and the judge turn you over to the constable, and the constable throw you into prison"* (verse 58).

In other words, now is the accepted time; today is the day of salvation. If you have never committed your life to Christ, if you have never admitted to Him that you are a sinner and cast yourself on His mercy and asked Him to forgive you and save you, if you have never confessed with your mouth Jesus as Lord and believed in your heart that God raised Him from the dead, what in the world are you waiting for? Don't let anything hold you back! It is that serious.

Conclusion

The forecast has been made. The signs are clear. The fires of judgment are coming. Will they refine you or destroy you? The difference is the blood of Christ shed for sin. Have you accepted Him? The forecast has been given, the signs are clear, the sky is dark, the clouds are gathering, and the thunder is rumbling. No one will be able to stand in that storm; there is shelter only under the blood of Christ. Have you come in? Will you come in? The forecast has been given, the signs are clear, the sky is dark, the clouds are gathering, and the thunder is rumbling. Therefore, choose ye this day whom ye will serve! For me and my house, we will serve the Lord.

REPENTANCE AND ITS FRUIT

Luke 13:1 Now on the same occasion there were some present who reported to him about the Galileans whose blood Pilate had mingled with their sacrifices. 2 And he answered them, "Do you suppose that these Galileans were greater sinners than all other Galileans because they suffered this fate? 3 I tell you, no, but unless you repent, you will all likewise perish. 4 Or do you suppose that those eighteen on whom the tower in Siloam fell and killed them were worse culprits than all the men who live in Jerusalem? 5 I tell you, no, but unless you repent, you will all likewise perish." 6 And he began telling them this parable: "A certain man had a fig tree which had been planted in his vineyard. And he came looking for fruit on it and did not find any. 7 And he said to the vineyard keeper, 'Behold, for three years I have come looking for fruit on this tree without finding any. Cut it down! Why does it even use up the ground?' 8 And he answered and said, 'Let it alone, sir, for this year too, until I dig around it and put in fertilizer. 9 And if it bears fruit next year, fine; but if not, cut it down.'"

Introduction

What an interesting passage we have here, and one full of questions. Do we know anything about these current events the Lord references? Who were these Galileans, what does this falling tower in Siloam have to do with anything, and what does either incident have to do with repentance? We might be tempted to think it doesn't matter much; just take it all as a generic warning that we need to repent of our sins and be satisfied. That would be a big mistake. So let me see if I can put you in a position to understand how this little exchange would have sounded to the people who first heard it.

Imagine that you are conducting services on the West Bank in modern Israel. Your congregation is a group of Palestinian Christians, and your biggest pastoral challenge is the atmosphere of hatred and distrust that exists between them and their Jewish neighbors. This atmosphere of hatred is fueled by an endless supply of atrocity stories on both sides—some true, some exaggerated and embellished, some made up, but all believed—selectively. That is, each side believes all and only those stories in which it is the victim and the other side is the perpetrator of the vilest atrocities. You've just preached on the signs of the times, when suddenly there is an interruption. "I'll give you a sign," somebody shouts. "The Jewish army came right into a Palestinian church and machine-gunned the congregation during Communion. They mingled their blood with the Communion wine right as they were receiving it! Now, what do you say to *that*?" [Dr. Williams spits this out with intense anger and a distorted face. Into the stunned silence which follows, he says:] Now you understand the dynamics of this conversation Luke reports. Until we understand those dynamics, we are not in a position to understand either what Jesus says in response, or the kind of person He would have to be to say it. When we do, we will begin to see something profound about the courage of the Christ and the requirement of repentance, and then conclude with a parable against presumption.

I. The Courage Of The Christ

The key to understanding this passage is to understand the dynamics of the "atrocity story," and in order to understand that, you have to put yourself in the place of the people who tell stories like that. The situation in first–century Palestine was strangely similar to the one that exists there today. Then it was the Romans who were the occupying army and the Jews who, oppressed in their own view, responded with what today we would call terrorism, terrorism which eventually led to the destruction of their society in AD 70. Please understand that I am making no political statement about who is right or wrong in today's struggle; I certainly do not have the wisdom to find a solution to it. I just want you to understand the situation that existed in this passage and to see how it parallels our own day. So the first thing we must reckon with is the fact that this story about the Galileans is in fact an atrocity story that came out of just the same kind of conflict and tensions as the ones we are familiar with.

Now, there is a very particular etiquette that applies to the atrocity story when it is not just a segment on the evening news but is told by the people directly concerned with it, and ignoring that etiquette can have serious, er, social consequences. The proper response to an atrocity story is to identify with the teller and the victims and condemn the perpetrators in the strongest possible terms. The person who tells the story is angry, and his feelings run deep. He is probably a relative of one of the victims. You are supposed to join in with a condemnation of the evil Romans and a celebration of their victims as freedom fighters and heroes. The last thing you want to do in that particular moment is to say, "Yeah, well, I suppose we'd better put our own house in order." *"Unless you repent, you will all likewise perish!"* Jesus just called the Jewish heroes sinners! To call his response "inflammatory" would be mild. Kenneth Bailey, who teaches at the Near Eastern School of Theology in Beirut and knows middle-eastern culture as well as any Westerner can, says that when his Lebanese students read this story, they cannot understand how Jesus avoided being killed on the spot![91] This is a very tense situation.

Then Jesus proceeds to make it even worse by bringing up the story of the tower (verse 4). This tower was probably part of Pilate's aqueduct, a seemingly beneficial public works project he had initiated. So what's wrong with bringing water into Jerusalem, for goodness' sake? Well, the project had been paid for by what the Jews considered a misappropriation of Temple funds.[92] They considered this an outrage. It was blasphemy. Abomination! Abomination! You can picture pious Pharisees rending their garments and spitting on the ground as they passed it by. And therefore, the men

---

[91] For an analysis of the genre of the atrocity story and its implications, see Bailey, *Through Peasant Eyes*, published together in a in one volume with *Poet and Peasant* (Grand Rapids, MI: Eerdmans, 1983), 74–80, esp. 78.

[92] Ibid., 77.

who worked on the project were considered collaborators and traitors, and their death when the tower collapsed was considered to be the judgment of God. You're expecting Jesus to condemn those evil Romans and those intolerably guilty scalawags who collaborate with them and had their well–deserved judgment coming—and He says *we* had better repent, or we will be just like them? Jesus is not exactly helping His cause here. He is not exactly ingratiating himself with his audience. This is not the way to win friends and influence people—or even to promote your own continued existence! It is in fact a good way to get yourself beaten to a bloody pulp if not killed.

What is Jesus doing here? He is putting the victims of the first atrocity on the same level as the Roman soldiers who perpetrated the Galilean massacre and treating the current crowd as no better than a bunch of hated collaborators. This would be equivalent to telling a group of holocaust survivors that Eli Wiesenthal the Nazi hunter has the same need of repentance as Adolf Hitler. Well, technically, he does, but that would not be a very popular message for that crowd in that context! It would be like telling a patriotic Israeli that Lt. Jani, the hero who died saving the victims in the raid on Entebbe, was on the same spiritual level, had the same need of repentance, as Idi Amin, who had captured them. Again, they are both fallen human beings. So it is true, but is this the time and place for that message? Or try telling a Palestinian radical to his face that his brother, the suicide bomber, is not a hero and martyr in Paradise at all but is on the same footing before God as the Israeli soldiers who bulldozed his house. Do you begin to understand the reaction of Bailey's students? Do you begin to understand the reaction of Jesus' audience? Truly you would be taking your life in your hands! That is not an exaggeration.

So why is Jesus doing this? It may be the most radical statement of universal depravity and the need for repentance—yes, that means you, and me, too—in all of Scripture. And it speaks volumes on how important Jesus thought that doctrine was. People need to understand this no matter how much it offends them, because until you get the profound seriousness of the problem of sin, you are not ready to contemplate the radical nature of the solution—nothing less than the Cross. And Jesus' audience thinks it is so righteous because it is on the "right" side; they feel so spiritually superior to their hated enemies. He is not going to let that assumption pass, not on your life—or His. Oh. Did I mention this applies to you and me?

This encounter speaks volumes about how crucially important Jesus thought the doctrine of sin was. It also speaks volumes about our Lord's character. How *did* He avoid being killed on the spot? This wipes away all those wimpy portraits of the "gentle Jesus meek and mild" that infest our Sunday–School literature. Jesus was the kind of man who would say such things. He was the kind of man who could say such things. He was the kind of man who did say such things—and then stare down the crowd and walk away after having done so! This man makes Captain America look like the ninety–pound weakling he was before his transformation. This man makes Chuck Norris look like a wimp. This man makes John Wayne look like a sniveling sissy. Now, that was a man! That is the Lord that we worship! That is the Lord we serve! That is the Lord we follow! No wonder so many of his disciples in history have been willing to lay their lives on the line for Him.

II. The Requirement Of Repentance (vv. 3, 5)

I have already mentioned that this passage understood in terms of these dynamics may be the most radical statement of the universality of sin in all of Scripture. It is Romans chapter two in dramatic terms. And we have stressed that Jesus thought the point was worth risking His life for. And therefore, we had better not miss the point. Before a righteous and just and holy God, the heroes of our stories need repentance no less than the villains. Let me try to make it as plain as Jesus did: George Washington needed repentance no less than Benedict Arnold or George III. Abraham Lincoln needed repentance no less than John Wilkes Booth. You and I need repentance no less than Adolf Hitler—Joseph Stalin—Mao Tse Tong—Pol Pot—Osama Bin Laden—Sadam Hussein—Vladimir Putin. Put that in your pipe and smoke it!

Now, I am not saying that there is no difference between the heroes and the villains or that it does not matter which role you take when your part in the story comes. It does. But they are all sinners in total and utter need of God's grace, His unmerited favor. They all stand in the same place at the foot of the Cross. And that is the place where we had better take our stand too. Unless we all repent, we shall all likewise perish. Being a hero rather than a villain is a good thing, an important thing, often a desperately needed thing—but it gives you no exemption from this principle. None whatsoever.

"Repentance" is the Greek word **μετανοια** (*metanoia*). It literally means to change your mind. It is a change of mind leading to a change of behavior. But it does not mean just turning over a new leaf. Not just any change of mind is biblical repentance. This is not just deciding to do better. You would probably fail if you did, and even if you succeeded it would not merit salvation. Biblical repentance means a change of mind about your own innocence and God's righteousness. It means accepting Jesus' perspective on human depravity *in this passage* as applying to you. It means a change of mind about your own need and God's provision. It means a change of mind about your own ability and God's grace. Most of all it is a change of mind about who Jesus is. Is He a myth devised by the early church? Is He just a great human teacher and moral example? Neither a myth nor a teacher nor an example is what we need. When we change our mind about Jesus and accept Him as the divine Son of God in human flesh, as the Lamb of God who taketh away the sins of the world (John 1:29), as *our* Savior from sin through His death and resurrection, as Lord of all and Lord of our lives, then we are ready to receive God's pardon for our sins and experience His power to change our lives. *That* change of mind is the only basis on which we can experience the change of heart that turns us from sin to God. That and nothing less is the change of mind, the repentance, that we need. It is not, obviously, something you can just up and decide to do. It is a change you must ask God to work in your heart. And unless we all repent, we shall all likewise perish.

III. A Parable Against Presumption (vv. 6–9)

Okay, the message of this incident is pretty radical. But what has the parable of the unfruitful fig tree got to do with it? Why have I risked an anticlimax by including it in this sermon, which has been pretty exciting up to this point? I mean, compared to these atrocity stories and Jesus' bold and daring use of them, who really cares if some stupid tree gets cut down or not? Well, remember that in the Old Testament, and in the usage of Jesus, a fig tree is often used as a symbol for Israel, for the people of God. And John the Baptist had told his converts to bear fruit worthy of repentance. So the topic of repentance, as it applies to the Jews in Jesus' audience, is still on the table, and so far nothing has happened to alleviate the tension and the intensity we have been seeing in this whole encounter. If we do not all repent, and that means you and me, we shall all likewise perish.

It's pretty important then that we understand what repentance is. I've just been working pretty hard to try to define it. So Jesus next *illustrates* repentance with the parable of the unproductive fig tree. *"A certain man had a fig tree which had been planted in his vineyard. And he came looking for fruit on it and did not find any."* Remember that John the Baptist had told his converts to bear fruit worthy of repentance. (Jesus and His audience would have remembered that.) That fruit refers to a change of life that manifests the reality of the change of mind that occurs when we repent and believe, when we accept Christ as Lord, receiving God's pardon and unleashing His power to bring us from darkness into light. The parable then advances the discussion by balancing two important points. The first is the necessity of real repentance as shown by its fruit. Those who do not manifest that fruit will be cut off, for thereby they prove that their repentance was not real. But the second is the patience of God with those who are not bearing the fruit they ought to be. The tree should be cut down for its lack of fruit, but it is being given another chance. To miss the first point leads to presumption; to miss the second leads to despair. The parable tries to make sure we don't miss either point and fall into either error.

To understand what is happening with this tree, we must go to Lev. 19:23–25, which gives the law for planting fruit trees. *"And when you enter the land and plant all kinds of trees for food, then you shall count their fruit as forbidden. Three years it shall be forbidden to you; it shall not be eaten. But in the fourth year all of its fruit shall be holy, an offering of praise to the Lord. And in the fifth year you are to eat of its fruit, that its yield may increase for you. I am the Lord your God."*

In other words, the first year in which the owner came looking for any fruit would be the fourth year of the tree's life. Any fruit found that year would have been taken to the Temple and offered as a firstfruits offering of praise to the

Lord. Starting in year five you can actually eat the fruit. So the owner has come for three years without finding any fruit (years four, five, and six), and now comes again. This fig tree is now at least seven years old, and it still has not made its offering of praise to God! So the owner has already been more than patient. Yet still the vineyard worker begs for one more chance—and the owner agrees. Let him cultivate and manure the tree for one more year, he begs. And then if it produces fruit, fine; if not, they will cut it down. (I love the KJV translation of the rationale: "*Why cumbereth it the ground?*").

The message is plain. Bring forth the fruit of repentance! God is more patient with us than we deserve, but there is a day of reckoning coming. Even now His gardener is digging and fertilizing—this sermon is, we might say, part of the fertilizer (Ahem! Let's not think about that metaphor too much.) Will we respond with true repentance, a real reckoning with who Jesus is that leads to a changed life, or are we just playing games? We need to repent—yes, you and I, even if we are heroes in the reckoning of men. Let us reckon with that need and be inspired by the courage of the Christ to respond to the requirement of repentance with fruit rather than presumption, while it is still called today.

Conclusion

Wow, what a passage! How are we to respond to it? Let us bow before not just the deity but also the sheer manhood of Jesus, who pulled no punches and refused to back down to the social pressure of the atrocity story and could get away with it. Let us open our hearts to the Gospel. Let us make like that fig tree should have acted and bear fruit. How? Let us sink our roots deep in Scripture, let us unfold our leaves to the light of the Lord, and bring forth the fruit of repentance to the glory of God and our own eternal joy. The Father is patient beyond our comprehension or our desert, but a day of reckoning is coming. Let us respond to that patience, to the love and the lordliness of His Son, before it is too late. For unless we all repent, we shall all likewise perish.

PARABLES OF THE KINGDOM

Luke 13:10 And he was teaching in one of the synagogues on the Sabbath. 11 And behold, there was a woman who for eighteen years had had a sickness caused by a spirit; and she was bent double and could not straighten up at all. 12 And when Jesus saw her, he called her over and said to her, "Woman, you are freed from your sicknesss." 13 And he laid his hands upon her, and immediately she was made erect again and began glorifying God. 14 And the synagogue official, indignant because Jesus had healed on the Sabbath, began saying to the multitude in response, "There are six days in which work should be done; therefore, come during them and get healed, not on the Sabbath." 15 But the Lord answered him and said, "You hypocrites, does not each of you on the Sabbath untie his ox or his donkey from the stall and lead him away to water him? 16 And this woman, daughter of Abraham as she is, whom Satan has bound for eighteen long years, should she not have been released from this bond on the Sabbath day?" 17 And as he said this, all of his opponents were being humiliated, and the entire multitude was rejoicing over all the glorious things being done by him. 18 Therefore he was saying, "What is the kingdom of God like, and to what shall I compare it? 19 It is like a mustard seed which a man took and threw into his garden, and it grew and became a tree, and all the birds of the air nested in its branches." 20 And he said again, "To what shall I compare the kingdom of God? 21 It is like leaven which a woman took and hid in three pecks of meal until it was all leavened."

Introduction

Having finished his account of Jesus' discourse on the Second Coming that we've been studying the last few weeks, Luke now moves on to another encounter and another conversation that continue to reveal Jesus as the Lord of glory. The key to understanding this passage is the word "Therefore" in verse 18. *"Therefore, He was saying, "What is the kingdom of God like, and to what shall I compare it?"* It tells us that Jesus told the parables of the Mustard Seed and the Leaven because He had just healed the woman and successfully defended having done it on the Sabbath. It demands that we ask the question, "What have these parables got to do with the healing of a stooped woman on the Sabbath?" The connection between the two bits of the story is the concept of the Kingdom of God.

How is that the connection? It is a very good question indeed. The answer is not at all obvious if we limit ourselves to our knowledge of English idioms. And what, you may ask, is an idiom? An idiom is a phrase or construction in a language whose meaning cannot be deduced from its constituent parts. For example, if I said, "You're pulling my leg," a person who was trying to learn English would have a hard time figuring out what I meant. He would be puzzled by the fact that he is not in any apparent way yanking on any of my ambulatory appendages. Looking up any or all of the words involved in a dictionary will not help him. Looking up the syntax in a grammar book will not help him. You just have to know the idiom to realize that it means "You're kidding." In Spanish it's "*Estas tomando mi pelo*," literally, "You're pulling my hair," which has nothing to do with the fibrous growth that is missing from the top of my head, either. Well, every language has these phrases, useful but hard on people dependent on a dictionary and a grammar book. And Greek is no exception.

The phrase "kingdom of God" in Greek ("*What is the kingdom of God like?*" verse 18) is an idiom that means primarily the reign or rule of God, and only secondarily the realm over which He is ruling (which would be the primary meaning of the word "kingdom" in English). English, in other words, has the primary and secondary meanings reversed from the Greek idiom. The word *kingdom* in English makes us think, first of all, of the realm or country that is being ruled—say, Great Britain, as in The United *Kingdom* of Great Britain and Northern Ireland. In Greek, you think first not of the country being ruled but of the *act of ruling*—King Charles doing whatever he would be doing to run the country if kings still actually ruled anymore. Imagine his meeting with the prime minister or addressing the House of Commons or issuing decrees in more than a merely ceremonial capacity. That's what we would mean by the phrase "Charles's kingdom" if we were speaking koine Greek—not Great Britain but his activity in ruling it.

We miss a lot of the nuances of the New–Testament teaching about the kingdom of God if we do not realize this. For example, in The Lord's Prayer, "Thy kingdom come" does not mean "May the nation or state over which you are going to rule come into existence"; it is closer to "May the time when you begin to exert your authority to take dominion and rule come; start reigning on earth now as you already do in Heaven." "The Kingdom of God is at hand" does not mean that the nation or kingdom is about to be set up so much as that God is about to take over, to enter decisively into history to rule it more proactively and directly rather than permissively and by a seemingly more distant Providence. The Kingdom itself is not therefore primarily any political or social entity such as the Church. It is rather the reigning and over–ruling activity of God that brings the Church into existence. That is why Jesus stresses that the kingdom is not of this world. It comes to any individual at the moment, and then to the extent, that Jesus begins to act as Lord in that person's life.

Alright, then. In verses 10–17 Jesus has prevailed, He has ruled, He has exercised dominion, in two ways. First, He has exerted His dominion over Satan as the perpetrator of disease by healing the woman. And second, He has exerted His dominion over the religious establishment by humiliating them in debate. So what He is saying is in effect, "You have just seen the triumph of the Kingdom of God over its enemies. You have just seen what happens when God asserts His authority to rule. And I am just getting started. This is not ephemeral; it is not a flash in the pan. This Kingdom is destined to triumph over everything. Let me tell you what it is like: It is going to happen just as surely as a seed grows into a tree, just as surely as leaven makes dough to rise." And now we understand how the "therefore" connects the Parable of the Mustard Seed and the Parable of the Leaven to the healing of the woman. Each parable has something important to tell us about the Kingdom of God. They are all focused on its triumph in both its external and internal aspects.

I. The External Triumph Of The Kingdom: The Growth Of The Church (vv. 18–19)

"What is the kingdom of God like, and to what shall I compare it? It is like a mustard seed which a man took and threw into his garden, and it grew and became a tree, and all the birds of the air nested in its branches." In this parable we can say that the mustard seed is the Gospel; the tree that grows from it is the Church; the man who plants the seed is God; the garden in which it is planted is Israel; and the birds of the air who come to nest in it are the Gentiles. The point is not that the Church is going to take over the world, but that the calling out from the Gentiles of a people for His name (Acts 15:14) is the triumph of God's rule, of the coming of the true King back into the kingdom of history.

The Parable of the Mustard Seed emphasizes the small beginning of the kingdom. The mustard seed is not in fact the smallest seed in nature, but it was the smallest seed that was planted in Palestinian agriculture, miniscule enough so that the large, potentially almost tree–like bush that resulted was particularly impressive as an example of growth. The Christian faith was not an impressive phenomenon in the beginning. It was just one more Jewish sect, just one more messianic cult. Such movements were a dime a dozen, and none of them lasted very long. The Sunday morning after the Crucifixion it consisted of eleven cowardly men and a few hysterical women. Those people had very little formal education. Probably only the men were even literate. Several were fishermen, one a very minor government official—a tax collector. Most of them were basically peasants. Until the miracle of the resurrection smacked them in the face so hard they couldn't miss it, not one of them really believed. All but one of the men were deserters, and their leading spokesman actually denied even knowing Jesus—three times! All of them were in hiding. Even after forty days of intensive post–resurrection training, they did not understand anything very well.

If you wanted to turn the world upside down, would you start with people like that? God did! The Apostle Paul wasn't just making it up when he wrote, *"Consider your calling, brethren, that there were not many wise according to the flesh, not many mighty, not many noble. But God has chosen the foolish things of the world to shame the wise, and God has chosen the weak things of the world to shame the things which are strong, and the base things of the world and the despised, God has chosen, the things that are not, that he might nullify the things that are, that no man might boast before God"* (1 Cor. 1:26–29).

And from such small beginnings, think of the way the kingdom has grown. At Pentecost, 3,000 people were converted in one fell swoop. The very persecution of the early Church is evidence that neither the Jewish, nor later the Roman, hierarchy, was capable of ignoring it. By the mid–sixties of the First Century—less than two generations later, with much of the first generation still living—there was a church in every major city in the Roman Empire, and the one in Ephesus was powerful enough to be a threat to the idol-making industry there. By the end of the First Century, the Kingdom had spread to people of every class, rank, station, and province of the Empire. By the end of the Twenty-First, it may well have spread to people of every tongue, tribe, and nation on earth.

What does this tell us? The kingdom of God is the rule of God. It is not about us, the citizens, but about Him, the One who rules, about His activity, about His glory. Small, even hopeless beginnings are no problem for Him. In fact, they only add to His glory when the finished result is seen. I expect just about any decent conductor could probably make the Atlanta Symphony or the New York Philharmonic sound good. It would take a special maestro indeed to get the same results out of a junior-high orchestra with little talent and no experience and unbalanced instrumentation. But that is what God is doing in His Kingdom. And it's a good thing, too. Otherwise, how many of us would even get to play? Now, look around you. There is also a very particular application to a small church like ours. Size is not relevant when Christ is at work; size is not relevant when Christ is building His Church. If God wills to use us, none of the things human beings normally think of are necessary. What is necessary? Why, that is the subject of the next parable.

II. The Internal Triumph Of The Kingdom: Personal Transformation (vv. 20–21)

And he said again, "To what shall I compare the kingdom of God? It is like leaven which a woman took and hid in three pecks of meal until it was all leavened." Here the woman is God, the leaven is the grace of God or perhaps the Holy Spirit, and the meal is you and me; the three pecks are perhaps the Church. The point here is not growth so much as transformation. The whole DNA of the mustard tree is in the seed. It just grows and unfolds. But leaven turns dough into a whole new thing: a loaf of bread instead of a cracker.

What new reality, what new kind of thing, do we see being produced in the New Testament? Peter, who denied the Lord, became one of His boldest ambassadors, saying with John that he would obey God rather than men (Acts 4:19) and continuing stubbornly to preach Christ after a close brush with death (Acts 5:42). The ignorant and unlearned men that had been the disciples now astonished the scribes with the power and clarity of their orations (Acts 4:13). And Saul of Tarsus, the most violent hater of Christ and persecutor of all who belonged to him, became his most ardent follower and most insightful spokesman. What happened to these people? Jesus happened! Christ had begun taking control of their lives, reigning in their hearts through His personal Agent and Representative, the Holy Spirit, acting as Lord. The Kingdom of God had come to them! God had started to rule them through His Son the King of Kings. And it changed them; it transformed them forever.

340

We should pay attention to the details of the description that Jesus chose to make of this transformation. Comparing the process to the leavening of dough tells us in the first place that **the transformation is inevitable.** If the leaven is good and the conditions are right, the dough is going to be different. What was formerly destined to be a cracker will now be home–made bread. The dough is not really given a choice, The leaven acts, and the dough cannot choose but rise. *"Therefore, if any man is in Christ, he is a new creature. The old things have passed away; behold, all things have become new"* (2 Cor. 5:17).

In the first place, the transformation is inevitable. In the second place, **the transformation is inexorable.** The leaven is hid in the meal until it is all leavened; the key word here is "until." Not one of you bakers will stop kneading the leaven into the dough when the job is only half done. The process of transformation can be slowed by cold, etc., but it cannot be stopped as long as the leaven is active. And that is what the whole concept of the Kingdom is about: the sovereign *activity* of God. It is His work, not ours.

In the first place, the transformation is inevitable. In the second place, the transformation is inexorable. In the third place, **the transformation is invisible.** The *results* are not invisible: they are the fruit of the Spirit, love, joy, peace, patience, kindness, goodness, faithfulness, gentleness, and self–control (Gal, 5:22–3); they are the light that we let shine before men so they can see our good works and glorify our Father who is in Heaven (Mat. 5:16). But the *process* of the transformation whereby these fruits are produced is invisible and mysterious. You cannot see it happening, but when you come back to the dough it is a loaf and not a cracker.

In the first place, the transformation is inevitable. In the second place, the transformation is inexorable. In the third place, the transformation is invisible. In the fourth place, **the transformation is extensive.** The leaven is hid until "all" of the meal is leavened. Jesus must become Lord of the whole person, not just his emotions, his inner life, or his "spiritual" life. As we have seen, He is Lord not just of our "tithe" but of all of our time, our talent, and our treasure. On the last day His Lordship will be extended to the whole Church, which will no longer on that day have tares among the wheat (Mat. 13:24–30). And on the last day it will be extended to the whole world, when every knee shall bow and every tongue confess that Jesus Christ is Lord to the glory of God the Father (Phil. 2:10–11).

In the first place, the transformation is inevitable. In the second place, the transformation is inexorable. In the third place, the transformation is invisible. In the fourth place, the transformation is extensive. And finally, **the transformation described here is intensive.** The process of "hiding" the leaven in the meal means *kneading.* You work it in, using whatever force is necessary, for as long as it takes, until the whole loaf is affected. If dough could speak, this would probably not be its favorite part of its preparation. If dough could speak, its speech at this point would probably involve a certain amount of complaining. If dough could speak, it would probably think it was ready for baking a long time before the baker was satisfied! This then is what it takes to make the Church grow like a mustard seed: not beginning with lots of smart and rich people but *continuing* with people into whom the leaven of God's grace is being kneaded day by day. I pray that this is the kind of church we are going to be.

Conclusion

To pray "thy Kingdom come" in The Lord's Prayer is to pray that in precisely this way God will take control of your life, to pray that Christ may act as Lord in your heart. It is to pray that the leaven of God's grace will be kneaded into you and the other members of University Church in such a way that the Church will grow, like a mustard seed, into a tree in which spiritual outcasts can find their spiritual home. Will you pray The Lord's Prayer like that? Let us do so together even now.

> Our Father who art in Heaven,
> Hallowed by thy name.
> Thy Kingdom come, thy will be done, on earth as it is in Heaven.
> Give us this day our daily bread,
> And forgive us our debts as we forgive our debtors.
> And lead us not into temptation. but deliver us from evil
> For thine is the kingdom, the power, and the glory
> Forever and ever. Amen.

THE NARROW GATE

Luke 13:22 And he was passing through from one city and village to another, teaching and proceeding on his way to Jerusalem. 23 And someone said to him, "Lord, are there just a few who are being saved?" And he said to them, 24 "Strive to enter by the narrow door. For many, I tell you, will seek to enter and will not be able. 25 Once the head of the house gets up and shuts the door and you begin to stand outside and knock on the door, saying, 'Lord, open to us!' then he will answer and say to you, 'I do not know where you are from.' 26 Then you will begin to say, 'We ate and drank in your presence and you taught in our streets.' 27 And he will say, 'I tell you I do not know where you are from. Depart from me, all you evildoers.' 28 Then there will be weeping and gnashing of teeth there when you see Abraham and Isaac and Jacob and all the prophets in the kingdom of God, but you yourselves being cast out. 29 And they will come from east and west, and from north and south, and will recline at the table in the kingdom of God. 30 And behold, some are last who will be first, and some are first who will be last." 31 Just at that time some Pharisees came up, saying to him, "Go away and depart from here, for Herod wants to kill you." 32 And he said to them, "Go and tell that fox, 'Behold, I cast out demons and perform cures today and tomorrow, and the third day I reach my goal. 33 Nevertheless, I must journey on today and tomorrow and the next day, for it cannot be that a prophet should perish outside of Jerusalem.' 34 Oh Jerusalem, Jerusalem, the city that kills the prophets and stone those sent to her! How often I wanted to gather your children together just as a hen gathers her brood under her wings, and you would not have it! 35 Behold, your house is left to you desolate, and I say to you, you shall not see me until the time comes when you say, 'Blessed is he who comes in the name of the Lord.'"

Introduction

Nothing is more fun than thinking about speculative questions in theology. I suppose the most famous one is "How many angels can dance on the head of a pin?" Would it surprise you to know that the answer to this question is actually known—and that I know it? Seriously, there are two answers with a certain amount of validity, each from a certain point of view. The first is that an infinite number, or else a number equivalent to the total number of angels God created, can do so. Why? Because angels are spiritual beings. Being finite, they have location, that is, they are not omnipresent; being not made of matter, they do not have extension in space, that is, they do not take up any room in our dimension (unless they are manifesting themselves to us in a temporarily assumed physical form, as they sometimes did in Scripture). So, like mathematical points, however many are dancing on the head (or even the point) of the pin, another one can always join them without pushing anyone off. The second answer? None, because angels, being good conservative servants of God, do not dance.

Seriously (this time, really), such questions have a legitimate use: the question about angels is a good way of finding out if a theology student actually understands the attributes of a spiritual being. But they are notorious and the butt of jokes because they can also easily be abused—for example, if a person used them as a smokescreen to avoid dealing with a pertinent personal issue. That is exactly what the questioner in verse 23 was doing. *"Lord, are there just a few who are being saved?"* You will notice that the Lord gives no answer to his question as it was verbalized at all. No number of saved people, whether small or large, is deducible from or even implied by anything He said. Many will be saved, many won't—but the pertinent question, the only question that matters, the question the man should have been asking, the question *you* should be asking, is which group will *you* be in? The important question is not how many people are going through the door, but rather where the door is, how to identify it and not confuse it with false doors, and how to make sure that you are going through it yourself. Once that is settled, then you try to take as many others through it with you as you can.

In other words, Jesus ignores the "presentation problem" and redirects the question to what really matters: The focus switches from others (the few), first to the door and then to the questioner himself. Are they few that be saved? None of your business. Above your paygrade. Wrong question. Let's analyze for a few minutes the question Jesus really wanted to answer: What is the door to salvation and how can we make sure we are going through it?

I. The Identity Of The Door

First, we need to nail down the Identity of the Door. The narrow door that Jesus actually wanted to talk about is of course our Lord himself, as He makes explicit in passages like John 10:7–9 and 14:6. He is the door of the sheepfold; he is the way, the truth, and the life. Through him we go in and out and find pasture; no one comes to the Father but by Him. Okay, if Jesus is the Door, what is on the other side? A door is an entryway. It is designed to give us access to that which is beyond it. What does Jesus give us access to, in other words?

First, **He gives us access to God:** *"No one comes to the Father but by me"* (John 14:6). The Door is the entryway to God's kingdom. Christ gives us this access to God first simply **by being who He is,** the eternal Son of God in human flesh. *"No one hath seen God at any time; but the only begotten God, who is in the bosom of the Father, he hath declared him"* (John. 1:14). Jesus is the invisible God made visible, the incomprehensible God made understandable, the unapproachably holy God made accessible. That is why *"there is only one God and only one Mediator between God and men, the man Christ Jesus"* (1 Tim. 2:5). But just as crucially, Jesus gives us access to God **by his Work on our behalf.** He died a substitutionary and sacrificial death on the Cross to pay for our sins, which otherwise would have separated us from a holy God forever. *"He who knew no sin was made sin for us, that by Him we might be made the righteousness of God"* (2 Cor. 5:21); He has *"canceled the certificate of debt consisting of decrees against us and taken it out of the way, by nailing it to the Cross"* (Col. 2:14); through Him, *"we who were far off have now been made nigh"* by the blood of Christ (Eph. 2:13). So infinite and high is this God that only by His own stooping to our nature in the incarnation of his Son could we ever reach Him. So holy is He that only through the blood of his Son shed for us could we be able to stand in His presence. Truly, Jesus is the way, the truth, and the life, and no one comes to the Father but by Him!

As the Door, Jesus first gives us access to God. Second, by giving us access to God, **Christ gives us access to all else that is Good, True, and Beautiful** as well. Even non–Christians grasp at these things for a while. But apart from the One who made and sustains these transcendental values, apart from the One who gives them their meaning by the way they reflect His own glory, there is no possibility of fully enjoying them even now, and no possibility of truly possessing and keeping them now or forever. In Christ, we have every spiritual blessing in the heavenly places (Eph. 1:3); in Christ we will inherit the new earth as well. In Christ we are joint heirs of all the good things God has made.

Among those great gifts is **Truth itself.** Bacon said that "the inquiry of truth, which is the wooing of it, the knowledge of truth, which is the presence of it, and the belief of truth, which is the enjoying of it, is the sovereign good of human nature"; Bacon said that "it is heaven upon earth to have a man's mind move in charity, rest in providence, and turn upon the poles of truth."[93] And Christ is the λογος (*Logos*), the Word of God, the light which comes into the world and enlightens every man (John 1:9). Isolated truths we may intuit or guess at even by that light reflected to us apart from faith; but there is no permanent and abiding relationship with the Truth as a whole, with Truth in its depths, with Truth as a saving reality, apart from Christ. He is the way, the truth, and the life (John 14:6). So central and foundational is Truth, that to know Jesus as the Truth is also to have access to Goodness and Beauty. For they are intimately related: Truth is the reflection of God's mind, Goodness of His character, and Beauty of His glory as they are imprinted on or reflected in the world He has made.

And so the third thing to which Christ gives us access is Life. In Him was life, and that life was the light of men; He came to give us life, and to give it more abundantly (John 10:10). For He is the Son of that One who is often and with reason called the living God. For He is that God whose Spirit, brooding over the surface of the waters, gave life to the world when it was without form and void (Gen. 1:2). He sends forth His Spirit and the deer calve; He withdraws it and they return to dust (Psalm 29:9, 104:29). And this divine life was so powerfully present in Christ that even the grave could not hold Him. So we who were dead in our trespasses and sins are made alive in Christ (Eph. 2:5). All that is meaningful, energetic, wholesome, dynamic, growing, and good about existing finds its source in Him. Thus the wages of sin is death, but the gift of God is eternal life in Jesus Christ our Lord (Rom. 6:23). Without Him we scratch out a pitiful

---

[93] Francis Bacon, "Of Truth," *Essays or Counsels Civil and Moral*, 1625. Hyder E. Rollins and Herschel Baker, eds., *The Renaissance in England: Non-Dramatic Prose and Verse of the Sixteenth Century* (Lexington, MA: D. C. Heath, 1954), 902.

biological existence for a few decades; but there is no permanent and abiding relationship with Life apart from Him. He is the way, the truth, and the life. He is the door of the sheep. That is the Door we are talking about!

II. The Narrowness Of The Door

The identity of the Door is Jesus. But there is a second truth about this Door that is taught here. Here as elsewhere, Jesus emphasizes a curious quality of this wonderful door: It is narrow. Strive to enter in by the narrow door. For strait is the gate and narrow the way that leads to life, and (relatively) few there be that find it (as He said on another occasion when He was not needing to avoid a wrongly asked question), while wide is the gate and broad the way that leads to death, and many there be that enter therein (Mat. 7:13–14). What is the point of this rather off–putting adjective, *narrow*? It highlights the specificity and the exclusivity of Christ's claims. There is only one Door that leads to God, to Truth, and to Life. There are a lot of other doors out there, opening on a lot of other paths, but you don't want to take them.

I remember once reading a short story entitled "The Black Door." A general offered a captured deserter a choice between the standard punishment for desertion, a firing squad, or whatever was behind the black door. He chose the firing squad over the unknown horror and chose like Hamlet rather to suffer the evil that he knew than fly to another that he knew not of. Afterwards, an aide asked the general what was on the other side of the door. "Freedom" was the answer. The consistent message of Scripture is that our choices matter; our choices in time affect eternity. This being the case, we need to know that Jesus is the Way, the Truth, and the Life. And we equally need to know that no one cometh to the Father but by Him.

No doctrine of the Christian faith is more unpopular in the modern world than this one. Our insistence on the exclusivity of Christ as the only way to God gets us branded as narrow, intolerant, and bigoted. So harsh and unforgiving is the response to this teaching that many even who still call themselves Evangelicals have begun to weaken and waffle on it, to fall into a horribly secular shuck and jive whenever it comes up, or even to abandon it altogether. At best we shy away from it. But it is a matter of spiritual life and death, as well as faithfulness to the clear and unequivocal teaching of our Lord. And therefore, it is both unfaithful and (ironically) *uncharitable* for us to compromise on it. If you want to drive to Atlanta from Athens and I tell you, "US 78 to the Southwest and 441 North or South are all good choices," have I been charitable to you, have I been a good neighbor? No. Two of those routes will take you to many places, but Atlanta is not one of them. We must do the truly loving thing and tell people forthrightly that the Door is narrow, and Jesus is the only Way.

At the end of the Nineteenth Century, the great London preacher Charles Haddon Spurgeon had already prophetically smelled the way the wind of doctrine was blowing and provided a response to it as wise as it was forthright: "Men must be told that they are dead and only the Holy Spirit can quicken them. This is thought to be discouraging teaching, and so it is. But men *need* to be discouraged from seeking salvation in a wrong manner."[94] Yes. People need to be actively discouraged from thinking that cigarette smoke is good for their hearts and lungs. They need to be actively discouraged from thinking that no one else ought to drink and drive, but *they* can get away with it just this once. They need to be actively discouraged from storing their guns and their ammunition together in unlocked cabinets when they have children in the house. And if they need to be discouraged from these things, then they surely need to be actively discouraged from seeking salvation in any other, for there is no other name given under heaven, whereby we must be saved.

III. The Need For Action

Finally, what do the identity and the narrowness of this Door mean for us practically? Jesus says we should *strive* to enter in by the narrow gate. The word translated "strive" is the Greek verb αγονιζομαι, (*agonizomai*), literally "to agonize or struggle." It is a word used in athletics, a verb for athletes doing an excruciatingly demanding and intense form of exercise such as wind sprints; one hears in it the desperately shouted gasp of a weightlifter trying to clean and press an almost impossible weight.

The point is not works for salvation. As long as the Door is open, all you have to do is walk through it. The problem is that the Door is not going to be open forever for anyone, and it is not always open even for you. Now is the accepted time; today the day of salvation! The point is the importance of getting yourself through the Door, any way you can, while you still can. You can't afford to just saunter up to it at some unspecified time in the very vague future when you might feel like it. Some people may get through that way, by the skin of their teeth, as it were, but you cannot afford to count on it. Run through the Door now, as hard as you can, while you still can! The house you are in is on fire! Get yourself and anyone else who will come with you out through the Door while you still can!

The point, in other words, is the supreme importance of getting through the Door combined with the unspeakable urgency of doing so. And it is also the realization that you may have to struggle against many obstacles to get through: Your own pride, your own stubbornness, the influence of society, possibly your own family and friends, and certainly the Enemy of our Souls will be trying desperately to hold you back. But whatever is trying to hold you back must be overcome at any cost, and overcome now, because the Door is not going to be open forever. *Once the head of the house gets up and shuts the door and you begin to stand outside and knock on the door, saying, 'Lord, open to us!' then he will answer and say to you, 'I do not know where you are from.'* (verse 25). So strive to enter by the narrow gate!

---

[94] Charles Spurgeon, *Lectures to My Students*, 2nd Series (1877; Lynchburg: The Old Time Gospel Hours, n.d.), 182.

Conclusion

This life is not purely an end in itself. Do not mistake me. In one sense it is. To obey God now, to love God now, to love God's people practically and sacrificially here and now, to glorify God right now: all this is worth doing for its own sake and needs no future life to justify it. But in another sense, this life is also truly not lived just for its own sake but as a preparation for the next one. At death or at the end of history, we must all live forever with what we have chosen in this life. And therefore, we need to ask ourselves some serious questions. And there are some questions, important in themselves, which are sometimes asked simply to avoid asking the only question that finally matters. What about those who have never heard the Gospel? Why does God allow suffering? How can a God of love send people to an eternal Hell? Are they few that be saved? Ahem.

I say some of these questions do have their own importance. Well, there is another set of questions that is more important still. Is Jesus the Door? Is He the only Door? We are in no position to wrestle with the one set of questions until we have dealt with the other. If the one set is used only as a smokescreen to avoid dealing with the other, they become no better than "Are they few that be saved?" And God's answer has not changed:

> *Strive to enter by the narrow door. For many, I tell you, will seek to enter and will not be able. Once the head of the house gets up and shuts the door and you begin to stand outside and knock on the door, saying, 'Lord, open to us!' then he will answer and say to you, 'I do not know where you are from.' Then you will begin to say, 'We ate and drank in your presence, and you taught in our streets.' And he will say, 'I tell you I do not know where you are from. Depart from me, all you evildoers.' Then there will be weeping and gnashing of teeth there when you see Abraham and Isaac and Jacob and all the prophets in the kingdom of God, but you yourselves being cast out. And they will come from east and west, and from north and south, and will recline at the table in the kingdom of God. And behold, some are last who will be first, and some are first who will be last."*

Strive to enter in. Agonize to enter in. Do it today. Before . . . the Door . . . is shut.

AFTER DINNER SPEECHES

Luke 14:1 *And it came about when he went into the house of one of the leaders of the Pharisees on the Sabbath to eat bread, that they were watching him closely. **2** And there, in front of him, was a certain man suffering from dropsy. **3** And Jesus answered and spoke to the lawyers and Pharisees, saying, "Is it lawful to heal on the Sabbath, or not?" **4** But they kept silent. And he took hold of him and healed him and sent him away. **5** And he said to them, "Which one of you shall have a son or an ox fall into a well, and will not immediately pull him out on a Sabbath day?" **6** And they could make no reply to this.*

*   **7** And he began speaking a parable to the invited guests when he noticed how they had been picking out the places of honor at the table, saying to them, **8** "When you are invited by someone to a wedding feast, do not take the place of honor, lest someone more distinguished than you may have been invited by him, **9** and he who invited you both shall come and say to you, 'Give place to this man,' and then in disgrace you proceed to occupy the last place. **10** But when you are invited, go and recline at the last place, so that when the one who has invited you comes, he may say to you, 'Friend, move up higher.' Then you will have honor in the sight of all who are at the table with you. **11** For everyone who exalts himself shall be humbled, and he who humbles himself shall be exalted." **12** And he also went on to say to the one who had invited him, "When you give a luncheon or a dinner, do not invite your friends or your brothers or your relatives or rich neighbors, lest they also invite you in return, and repayment come to you. **13** But when you give a reception, invite the poor, the crippled, the lame, the blind, **14** and you will be blessed, since they do not have the means to repay you; for you will be repaid at the resurrection of the righteous."*

*   **15** And when one of those reclining at the table with him heard this, he said to him, "Blessed is everyone who will eat bread in the kingdom of God!" **16** But he said to him, "A certain man was giving a big dinner, and he invited many. **17** And at the dinner hour he sent his slave to say to those who had been invited, 'Come, for everything is ready now.' **18** But they all alike began to make excuses. The first one said to him, 'I have bought a piece of land and I need to go out and look at it; please consider me excused.' **19** And another one said, 'I have bought five yoke of oxen, and I am going to try them out; please consider me excused.' **20** And another one said, 'I have married a wife, and for that reason I cannot come.' **21** And the slave came back and reported this to his master. Then the head of the household became angry and said to his slave, 'Go out at once into the streets and the lanes of the city and bring in here the poor and the crippled and the blind and the lame.' **22** And the slave said, 'Master, what you have commanded has been done, and still there is room.' **23** And the master said to the slave, 'Go out into the highways and along the hedges and compel them to come in, that my house may be filled. **24** For I tell you, none of those men who were invited shall taste of my dinner.'"*

Introduction

After dinner speakers have a reputation for being boring that is often well deserved. Jesus, on the other hand, was anything but boring. In fact, His few remarks here probably broke up the party! We can break them up into four discourses and one interruption and look at them in more detail in turn.

I. A Saying About The Sabbath (vv. 1–6)

We have seen Jesus teaching about the Sabbath before, and so it does not need much comment now. But we should notice that Jesus had probably been set up. The fact that the Pharisees were "watching him closely" in verse 1 implies that there is a good chance this sick man was a plant, a not–so–subtle attempt to get Jesus in trouble and discredit Him if He broke the somewhat arbitrary Pharisaical regulations that governed what constituted "work" on the Sabbath. But Jesus brilliantly turns the tables on His enemies and puts them on the defensive, simply by His way of phrasing his Socratic question and framing the dispute. "Is it lawful to heal on the Sabbath, or not?" Who wants to publicly come out against healing? And then He quickly follows up His advantage with another question: "Which one of you shall have a son or an ox fall into a well, and will not immediately pull him out on a Sabbath day?" Well, what could they say to that? The silence that followed was no doubt tense with Pharisaical embarrassment. They could not accept Jesus' conclusions, but neither could they oppose them without exposing the unloving and legalistic—and hence, ungodly—tenor of their own spirituality. Jesus, as He always did, had put them between the proverbial rock and the parabolic hard place.

II. Advice About Avoiding Embarrassment (vv. 7–11)

Having made His point, Jesus charitably relieves the company's embarrassment by changing the subject—though I'm not sure how much relief was actually provided! Noticing the guests jockeying for positions of honor at the head of the table, He offers them a sample of His typical shrewd, common–sense peasant wisdom. If you are interested in social recognition, you'll actually get more in the long run by taking a lower place and being asked to move up than by over–reaching and being sent to the back of the line in disgrace. The curious thing is that Jesus does not challenge the assumption that social advancement is a good thing and a worthy goal by attacking their pride directly. His comment here is open to a very cynical interpretation: You want to pursue pride? I'll give you a way to do it more efficiently!

I suspect this is one of those times that we Bible readers at the distance of two millennia suffer from not being able to see the twinkle in the dominical eye. The very absurdity of that literal interpretation gives the pompous guests an opportunity to laugh at themselves and realize they are taking themselves way too seriously. Anyone who was willing to receive instruction could have been corrected in a relatively painless manner; those who were not would find that their laughter had a hollow ring to it and left an empty taste in their mouths. As with most of Jesus' parables, the hearer will get out of it what he is capable of getting. Putting yourself forward can backfire; maybe we shouldn't be putting ourselves forward at all; maybe our whole focus on merit rather than a concentration on grace not only leads to social awkwardness but is what is keeping us outside the kingdom. It's all there. What you take away depends on you.

III. A Homily On Hospitality (vv. 12–14)

Now Jesus turns from the guests to the host with a similar application of the principle of grace to his social situation. When you throw a party, don't invite your friends or other rich people who can invite you back; invite the poor and the powerless instead, and your reward will be received in the Kingdom. This would be a very different affair than the Pharisee had actually arranged, a miserable failure of an attempt to make himself look good to his friends in the religious establishment by getting that idiotic peasant prophet from Nazareth to break the Sabbath, no doubt so he could lecture Him about Jewish ethics!

We have to understand Jesus' statement here in turns of the dynamics of that particular social situation. He is not forbidding us from inviting our friends and family over; otherwise, Mary and Martha and the New Testament Christians who practiced hospitality with their Christian brothers would be condemned. But He is saying that there is something drastically wrong with this man's attitude and motives. The principle that ties these two statements together is that of grace, unmerited favor. If salvation is by grace, if the Kingdom of God runs on the principle of grace, then whether you are a guest or a host you ought to live your whole life in that light of that grace. If you are a guest, don't be jealous of your own honor but take delight in the honor offered to your neighbor. If you are a host, treat your neighbors as God treats His people; that is, make a habit of showing your hospitality to those who have no claim on it and no way to repay it. That—not keeping a bunch of rigorous rules you made up to build a hedge around the Law but which show that you have no real understanding of the Spirit behind the Law—is the way to be godly, to be like your Heavenly Father.

Well—ahem. Are we supposed to apply this today? That's a stupid question. Is it in the text? Well, then, it applies to us. Okay, *how* are we supposed to apply it today? Now, that's a more intelligent question. For indeed the circumstances are a little different. Jesus' command was addressed to a rich man in a culture where to be rich meant you had a large staff of servants who would constantly be there to guard your house. Also, the poor would have literally been his neighbors—think of Dives and Lazarus—rather than being sequestered in their own neighborhoods or ghettoes. In that culture you would not have been putting your family or your property in danger by giving opportunistic but irresponsible people an opportunity to case a joint they would otherwise have been unaware of, as I did when one of my naive attempts to put this commandment into practice led to our checkbook and a credit card being stolen. We may not all be in a position to literally invite the poor home for a meal, as this man could very well have done with nothing much more to fear than the other rich neighbors looking at him funny.

But that does not mean that we cannot find ways to live out the spirit of Jesus' words here. Lew Rabbitt, the father of one of my childhood friends, did regular prison visitation, leading a Bible study in the local jail. He built a guest house on the hill above his own home and gained the trust of the local authorities to the point that they would often release a prisoner into his custody. Such a man, along with others who had recently been released and had nowhere to go, would be brought to that half–way house and helped to restart their lives. Lew would take them around and pester his friends until they gave jobs to these ex–cons, as well as holding daily Bible studies with them until they were able to move out and be on their own. We euphemistically referred to them as "the men on the hill." I have known people who go beyond nursing home visitation to the point of "adopting" a resident whose family is either dead or absent and uncaring, going to great trouble to bring them home for Christmas and other occasions so that some sense of family and belonging is restored to them in their last years. And perhaps there are some who are in a position to take the risks implied by a literal obedience. My point is, if you do not think you are called to do *that*, I won't say you are wrong, but you are not absolved from obedience. Be creative and find ways to apply the spirit of the commandment in a manner that will be meaningful in our culture and our society. You say, "It just isn't done!" So what? If you want to be like your Father in Heaven, you will do it.

IV. The Snide Sneer Of A Snippy Snob (v. 15)

Now, why would I give such a harsh heading to the person trying to inject such a fine spiritual sentiment into the proceedings? *"Blessed is everyone who will eat bread in the kingdom of God!"* Perhaps it is because I have met enough such people to become deeply suspicious of those who go out of their way to look spiritual by mouthing vaguely pious phrases with which no one could possibly disagree. Their noses are often stuck a bit too far up in the air. The obvious motive for this interjection is for people to notice how very spiritual the speaker is. I suspect he was thinking, "This folk rabbi claims to be the Messiah, and all he's got to offer is a bunch of lame–brained advice for entertaining? Let's talk about the *spiritual* banquet!" If so, he had profoundly missed the point. But Jesus would take his interruption as an opportunity to try and make it once again.

V. The Supper Of Salvation (vv. 16–24)

Okay., Jesus says in effect, you want to talk about the kingdom of God and the feast that awaits us there? Showing God's grace to the needy around you not spiritual enough for you? Okay, let's talk about that supper. Who do you think will really be eating it? Hmmm. It turns out to be, not the Pharisees, but some of the very ones Jesus wanted the host to be inviting to his house instead here and now!

To understand this exchange, we have to know something about both the biblical and the cultural background to it. The biblical background is the prophecy of Isaiah 25: 6–9. *"And the Lord of hosts will prepare a lavish banquet for all peoples on this mountain, a banquet of aged wine, choice pieces with marrow, and refined aged wine. And on this mountain He will swallow up the covering which is over all peoples, even the veil which is stretched over all nations. He will swallow up death for all time, and the Lord God will wipe tears away from all faces, and He will remove the reproach of his people from the earth—for the Lord has spoken. And it will be said on that day, 'Behold, this is our God for whom we have waited that He might save us. This is the Lord for whom we have waited; let us rejoice and be glad in his salvation!'"*

It is astounding how badly the Pharisees had missed the point of this prophecy. They expected to be the guests there. But the invitation had originally been made to all nations, and they had restricted it, first to Jews alone, and then only to legalistically unblemished Jews like themselves. Nevertheless, when the invitation was given in the coming of Christ, they hid behind their legalistic excuses, accusing him of breaking the Sabbath, for example, rather than responding to it.

Culturally, we need to understand the nature of invitations in the ancient Near East. An invitation is a two–step process. First is what *we* would call the invitation, which comes some time in advance. If you accept, you have obligated yourself to show up for the event, for the provisions would be bought (or slaughtered) on that basis. The second phase is the one represented by the slave in the parable. When the time came, he would be sent to fetch the guests and escort them to the now fully prepared feast. To refuse at this point without a truly grave and inescapable reason would be a terrible insult to the host. Yet that is exactly what the guests in the parable do. "I've bought a field and I have to go see it." Nobody would buy land sight–unseen today, and you definitely would not have done it then, for fertile land was at a premium. You would never buy a piece of property until you could recite every feature of it and list its productivity figures for generations. Nobody bought oxen without a test drive, any more than you would buy a used car that way today. In fact, the ox dealers would have a field right next to the auction where the buyers could test the animals out to see if they could plow before bidding on them. These excuses are on the level of "I've just painted my toenails, and I have to let them dry."

By this time the interpretation of the parable should be coming into focus. The man giving the banquet is God. The Banquet is salvation, the blessings of the Messianic kingdom. The first invitation was the Old Testament, and the prospective guests who had received that invitation are Israel, most pointedly its religious leaders. The slave bearing the second invitation is the preaching of the Gospel. He is greeted by the Jewish establishment with some really lame excuses. "I've just bought a house and I need to check out the neighborhood and see if the roof leaks." "I've just bought five used cars and I need to go see what year they are and whether they start." Those from the streets and lanes (names for roads in town) are the "unworthy" Jews, and those from the highways and hedges (roads outside of town) are the Gentiles. The people actually enjoying the banquet—strangely just like the one Jesus had suggested to the host, if he wanted truly to be like the Father—are those who had no prospects or expectations, in terms of their own righteousness, of being there.

What then is the significance of this parable for us? First it surely raises the question, "What is our excuse?" "The Church is full of hypocrites." "I will follow Christ someday, but not right now." Give me a break! Such statements are an insult to God's intelligence. They are even an insult to yours. Second, it underscores the fact that God's desire to save us exceeds man's willingness to be saved. No matter how rebuffed the master has been, he keeps sending the slave out until the house is full. Third, we must realize that the invitation has to be acted on. Were you raised in a Christian family? Are you a member of the church? Have you heard the Gospel all your life? That just puts you in the position of those who had received the first invitation. What will you do when the slave comes and says, "Now is the accepted hour, today is the day of salvation?" That is what will determine your eternal destiny. Say yes! Do not hesitate, do not squirm and make excuses. Come!

Finally, we who have already responded must realize the importance of persistence in evangelism. We must "go out into the highways and hedges and compel them to come in." This is not a reference to strong–arm tactics but rather an exhortation to urgency and to earnestness. Sometimes you did not get the standard two–stage invitation. The second round of guests only got the invitation to come right now. Palestinian manners required you to refuse such an invitation, lest it be only offered out of politeness. Normally the host would then say, "Okay, hopefully some other time, then." and that would be that. But if he really meant it, he would persist and convince you that, despite the full round of formalities having not occurred, he really meant it; he really wanted you to come. Then, and only then, it would be Okay to accept. That is what the word "compel" really means here. We see this being acted out, by the way, when Jesus met the two disciples on the Road to Emmaus. When they first asked Him to stay the night, He very correctly "made as if to go further," but then when they repeated their invitation, He very correctly accepted it (Luke 24:13–35), following the manners of the time to a T. So if we are the slave in the parable—and we are—we must not just say, "God has provided salvation in Christ, and you can take it or leave it." We must go out into the highways and hedges and compel, urge, beg them to come in.

Conclusion

The banquet is ready. The food is getting cold. When the hall is filled, the door will be shut. And my Master really wants you to be there! Yes, he really does. Won't you come with me? I am afraid we do not communicate such urgency because we do not feel it ourselves. Therefore, let us read these parables with full understanding and meditate on them until we begin to. Amen.

COUNTING THE COST

Luke 14:25 Now great multitudes were going along with him, and he turned and said to them, 26 "If anyone comes to me and does not hate his own father and mother and wife and children and brothers and sisters, yes, and even his own life, he cannot be my disciple. 27 Whoever does not carry his own cross and come after me cannot be my disciple. 28 For which one of you, when he wants to build a tower, does not sit down first and calculate the cost, to see if he has enough to complete it? 29 Otherwise, when he has laid a foundation and is not able to finish, all who observe it begin to ridicule him, 30 saying, 'This man began to build and was not able to finish.' 31 Or what king, when he sets out to meet another king in battle, will not first sit down and take counsel whether he is strong enough with ten thousand men to encounter one coming against him with twenty thousand? 32 Or else, while the other is still far away, he sends a delegation and asks terms of peace. 33 So therefore, no one of you can be my disciple who does not give up all his own possessions. 34 Therefore, salt is good' but if even salt has become tasteless, with what will it be seasoned? 35 It is useless either for the soil or for the manure pile; it is thrown out. He who has ears to hear, let him hear."

Introduction

When I was in seminary our budget was pretty tight and splurging a rare event, but there was one day that I thought I had enough saved up to take my wife out to a nice restaurant. "What can I order?" "Hey, for once, anything you want!" "Should we get desert?" "Hey, you only live once." Things were going quite well until I got the bill. "Uh, Marsha, do you have any money on you?" By pooling our resources, we managed to come up with enough to cover the tab plus at least a token tip. But we walked out of that place with exactly four cents to our name. Four little pieces of copper stood between me and public embarrassment! As for private embarrassment after we got back home . . . well, we won't go into that. Perhaps some of you have had a similar experience; maybe some of them did not end so fortunately. In any transaction, it is important to count the cost.

It can be important to count the cost even when you are being offered something for free. One time somebody gave us a dog. We did not pay one red cent for that dog. It was a completely free gift. But before the week was out, we had paid plenty in vet bills and dog food. You may remember from sermon XXXVI, on Cross–Bearing (Luke 9:18–27) that on another occasion a member of our congregation, perhaps feeling guilty for the low wages that the church was paying, gave us a car. It was completely free; I never paid one red cent for that car. But in order to accept this free gift, I had to pay through the nose for a tag and insurance—not to mention gas and oil (and, not too much later, repairs). I literally had to count the cost. I had to pause for some quick calculations to see if I could afford to accept that totally free gift! It was not immediately clear that I could do so. As we saw then, even a completely free gift with no strings attached whatever can end up costing you something.

Well, that idea becomes relevant once again as we consider the Lord's words about counting the cost of discipleship. Salvation is like that. Scripture accurately describes salvation as a free gift. *"The wages of sin is death, but the gift of God is eternal life in Jesus Christ our Lord"* (Rom. 6:23). *"For all have sinned and fall short of the glory of God, being justified as a gift by his grace through the redemption which is in Christ Jesus"* (Rom. 3:23–24). These words are absolutely true, and they are not in conflict with the Lord's words here. Salvation is a free gift. It can only come as a free gift. There is nothing you could do to earn it; it is not earnable. But accepting that gift will cost you something. And that is what our Lord is talking about in the passage before us today, in which we see the Calculation of the Cost, the Basis of the Bargain, and the Consequences of the Calculation.

I. The Calculation Of The Cost

What will accepting the free gift of salvation cost you? In a word, everything. The Lord here lays out three specific areas that add up to everything.

In the first place, accepting Christ as Lord and Savior will cost you your family, indeed, by implication, **all of your relationships**. Now, of course our Lord Himself maintained his relationship with His own mother right up to the end of His life, and almost His last act was to provide for her after His death by entrusting her to the care of the Beloved Disciple. So in one sense, the Lord does not take those relationships away at all, but rather transforms them. Nevertheless, it is a transformation which includes one of the hardest and most misunderstood sayings in all of Scripture: *"If anyone comes to me and does not hate his own father and mother and wife and children and brothers and sisters . . . he cannot be my disciple"* (Luke 14:26). What can this mean? How can the Lord want us to hate anyone, when we are supposed to love even our enemies? The attempt to explain this I have heard most frequently is that our love for our family must be like hatred only in comparison to our love for Jesus. But that sounds like a rationalization because it is; it doesn't really get the point. To understand Jesus' statement here, you have to understand what was to his original audience a common and familiar Old-Testament idiom.

Quite frequently in the Old Testament people—even God himself—are spoken of as "hating" others for whom they held no personal animosity or even necessarily any negative feelings at all. Often *hatred* does not mean literal "hatred" in any sense but is used as a metaphor for *rejection*. *"Jacob have I loved, but Esau have I hated"* means that God had rejected Esau as the heir of the Promise and chosen Jacob; it does not necessarily mean that God bore Esau any ill will. I think the clearest example of this usage is found in Genesis 29:30–31. In Genesis 29:30 we read that Jacob *"loved Rachel more than Leah."* This means that he did love Leah; after all, she bore him quite a few children, so their relationship was not without affection. But then in verse 31 we read that *"Now the Lord* saw that Leah was unloved," so he opened her womb, presumably to compensate her for Jacob's preference for her younger sister. The word that our squeamish translators have rendered as "unloved" is literally "hated." This when the very previous verse has just stated that Jacob loved her (albeit less than Rachel)! Love and hate are sometimes used as a *metaphor* for acceptance and rejection, or even for preference.

Luke 14:26 therefore has nothing to do with hating your parents, spouse, children, or siblings in the way that most non–Hebrews unfamiliar with the idioms of the Old Testament would understand hatred. We are of course supposed to love them more than ever in loving Christ, not the reverse. But it means that, when push comes to shove, we are prepared to reject them and choose Jesus, that in principle we have in fact already done so should they ever come between us and our relationship with Christ. They are to have no claims on us except those which are compatible with His claims, which are absolute and non–negotiable. A well–meant but shallow formula says, "Christ first; others second; self last." I say this formula is shallow, and the use of the metaphor of hatred in this passage for the choice being made points out how shallow it is. The real formula is "Christ first—period." There is to be no competition for the throne of your heart permitted at all. You must hate your father and mother. In other words, any claims from any other person in your life, no matter how close, which would ever conflict with the claims of Christ, must have already been rejected in advance. If you waver on that point, you have not yet really reckoned with what it means to be His disciple.

The second thing accepting this free gift will cost you is your self, or **your life**. Verse 26 includes *or even your own life* among the things to be "hated" or rejected, and verse 27 adds, *"Whoever does not carry his own cross and come after me cannot be my disciple."* To carry a cross is to be a person marked out for death, on your way to execution. The crowd looked to Jesus as their Messiah, and if He had turned out to be the kind of messiah they wanted, He would have led them in a rebellion against Rome. The Roman Empire executed traitors by crucifixion. They did it all the time. So Jesus is saying, "If you are not prepared to die for this cause, don't sign up! Count the cost." When the early Christians refused to participate in emperor worship, their refusal was misinterpreted as political disloyalty or treason, and many of them had to pay for it with their lives, often by crucifixion.

"Take up your cross" was not just religious language in the First Century! Any person who was not prepared to face the very real possibility of a martyr's death had no business becoming a disciple of Jesus. And in many countries to this day this demand is still a literal one. For us in the West right now it is not a literal demand, but it is no less real for that. We simply have the opportunity to explore its spiritual dimensions in death to self and sin. But whether spent in martyrdom or in daily service, your very life is what the free gift of salvation will cost you. You are not a true Christian if you are not ready to die for the cause of Christ. Am I saying you have to be that brave before you can be saved? No. The spirit is willing, but the flesh is weak (Mat. 26:41). What I am saying is that to truly give your life to Christ, the spirit must be willing.

The third thing Jesus lists in the cost to be counted is **our possessions** (verse 33). *"So therefore, no one of you can be my disciple who does not give up all his own possessions."* When I first studied this passage, I wondered at the order. After hating your father and mother and giving up your very life, possessions seemed somewhat anticlimactic. But then I remembered the comedy routine that Jack Benny made a career of. A robber sticks a gun in his face and demands, "Your money or your life!" Benny just stares at him. "Hey, didn't you hear me?" the robber asks. "I said your money or your life." Benny then waits for just the perfect split second of comedic timing and replies, "I'm thinking about it."

So there is a way in which this cost of accepting the free gift is climactic after all. It is easy to make the demand to give up relationships or our own life merely hypothetical. Our parents aren't opposing our call to the mission field, no one is holding a gun to our head and asking us to deny Christ, so we can easily pretend that we have yielded to the Lordship of Christ in those areas because it is not being put to the test. The question, "Who is Lord of your wallet?" has to be answered every day. Do I own its contents, or does Christ? Not all Christians are called to a life of poverty, but all are called to the concept of Stewardship. That is, we are called to think of (and treat) our property not as something we own but as something we manage for the true owner, Christ Himself. *"So therefore, no one of you can be my disciple who does not give up all his own possessions."*

II. The Basis Of The Bargain

That is giving up a lot! What could possibly be the basis of this bargain? It is important to see that these rejections, these yieldings, are not arbitrary requirements tacked on to the gift of salvation so that it is not a free gift after all. They are part of the gift. To accept it without accepting them is not to accept it at all. The basis of this truth lies in who Jesus is: Lord of all, the King of glory, the One in whom all things consist (Col. 1:17), the One to whom is given all judgment, rule, and power, the One who is Wonderful Counselor, Everlasting Father, Mighty God, and Prince of Peace (Isaiah 9:6), the One who is Head of his Body, the Church (Eph. 4:15), the One who is King of kings. To accept anyone less than this is not to accept Christ. And the basis of this truth lies also in what salvation is: union with Jesus Christ. Even our clichés reflect this truth. We speak of having a "personal relationship with Christ." Scripture speaks even more profoundly, describing salvation as like the grafting of branches into a tree (Rom. 11:17–24) or like being a body in relation to its head (Eph. 4:15–16) or like marriage (Eph. 5:22–32). Even justification by faith is not an impersonal transaction, as if we could say, "Yeah, sure, I'll take free forgiveness" and then go on our merry way as if nothing had happened. For the imputation of our sins to Christ and of His righteousness to us is based on the union: We are in Christ as before we were in Adam, and *that* is why there is now no condemnation (Rom. 8:1).

In other words, the objective, forensic declaration of righteousness, the objective imputation of righteousness, *counts*, and it counts precisely *because* of the *relationship* we enter into with Christ when we take Him by faith as Savior and as Lord. The mystical union is not something extra tacked on to a merely legal justification. (Justification is more than legal, but it is not less; Romans 5–8 flows out of Romans 3–4.) Our union with Christ is essential to salvation, the very essence of it. It is because we belong to Christ, because faith relates us to Him in this very particular way, that God counts us as righteous for His sake.

Now, this relationship is not one that can exist between equals. This is not Jim Croce saying, "If you're going my way, I'll go with you."[95] It is us saying to Christ, "*Whither thou goest I will go, and whither thou lodgest I will lodge. Your people shall be my people and your God my God*" (Ruth 1:16). Christ is the Teacher; I am the disciple. He is the Master; I am the servant. He is the Lord; I am the vassal. He is my God; I am His creature. You can no more get married and keep your independence than you can accept Christ as Lord and Savior and still say of your other relationships, your life, or your property, "This is mine." Not to see this is not to see that Jesus is God; not to accept it is not to accept that Jesus is God; not to relate to Jesus in this way is not to be related to him as your *God*. It is not to be a true Christian. And therefore, these rejections, these yieldings, are not arbitrary requirements tacked on to the gift of salvation so that it is not a free gift after all. They are part of the gift. To accept it without accepting them is not to accept it. Salvation is free, but it is not cheap. You cannot buy it; you cannot earn it. You can only receive it as a free gift by faith. But accepting it will cost you everything you have and are. Therefore, count the cost!

III. The Consequences Of The Calculations

Well, there are consequences to these calculations. If you have become a Christian, a follower of Jesus, without counting the cost, count it now. You will thus discover whether or not you are truly in the faith. None of us is able in ourselves to give any of these things up. None of us perfectly does so. Only by God's grace and Christ's constant help through His personal agent and representative, the Holy Spirit, can we enact these surrenders at all. But, thank God, we are not saved by our performance but by God's grace, which grants us this relationship with Christ through faith. Nevertheless, counting the cost will tell you if you have that relationship. A Christ who is not Lord can save no one; a Christ who is not God is not Lord; a Christ who *is* God and Lord to you is One to whom you *want* to make these sacrifices. The spirit is willing, but the flesh is weak. Here as in every other aspect of the Christian life, we must often pray, "*Lord, I believe; help thou mine unbelief*" (Mark 9:24). The question is, are you willing

---

[95] Jim Croce, "I got a Name," *Jim Croce, Photographs and Memories: His Greatest Hits* (NY: ABC Records, 1974).

to pray in such terms? Do you want to be His? That is the infallible sign that you have already begun to be.

I am struck by the fact that the Lord did not hesitate to ask us to count the cost. In fact, He went out of his way to do it when the multitudes were following him a bit too thoughtlessly. He was much more secure in the Gospel as the power of God for salvation than we are! He did not downplay the cost of commitment. And therefore, in our witnessing, we should not do so either. We are far too apologetic, and as a result we present a gospel that is less than the Gospel. Let us have the confidence that our Savior had that there are people out there who are looking for a Cause worth giving their lives for, and let's offer it to them. Let us learn to have the confidence He had that, when we have fully counted the cost, it will still be plain to those who are called that following Christ is royally worth it. Do we not believe it ourselves? Let me ask you to consider it right now.

If you are not a believer, I want to challenge you to count the cost at this very moment. I will not hide from you that you must give up everything. You must give up your self–righteousness, any idea of deserving salvation. You must give up all conflicting loyalties, your relationships, your life, your possessions. And what do you get in return? Only Christ. Only Christ! But it is only *Christ*. And in Him, the forgiveness of all your sins, a clean conscience, peace with yourself and with God, eternal life, and a cause big enough to give point to living the rest of this life and indeed all of eternity. You get a personal relationship with God thought faith in His Son Jesus Christ. That is all. And so I ask you to count the cost, and to count it seriously and carefully.

Conclusion

There you have it. Now the cards are all on the table. There is no fine print. You are offered as a free gift salvation and all that it means. It will only cost you everything. Jesus was not afraid to make this offer forthrightly and plainly and without flinching, and neither am I. When I accepted the Lord as my Savior, I was too young to fully understand the cost. I have been learning about it ever since. Sometimes the lessons have been hard. I am still learning them. But I have never regretted this transaction for one single moment. I don't think you will either. He who has ears to hear, let him hear what the Spirit says about the One whom to know is life eternal.

JOY IN HEAVEN

Luke 15:1 Now all the tax gatherers and sinners were coming near him to listen to him, 2 And both the Pharisees and the Scribes began to grumble, saying, "This man receives sinners and eats with them." 3 And he told them this parable, saying, 4 "What man among you, if he has a hundred sheep and has lost one of them, does not leave the ninety–nine in the open pasture and go after the one which is lost until he finds it? 5 And when he has found it, he lays it on his shoulders, rejoicing. 6 And when he comes home, he calls together his friends and neighbors, saying to them, 'Rejoice with me, for I have found my sheep which was lost!' 7 I tell you that in the same way there will be more joy in heaven over one sinner who repents than over ninety–nine righteous persons who need no repentance. 8 Or what woman, if she has ten silver coins and loses one coin, does not light a lamp and sweep the house and search carefully until she finds it? 9 And when she has found it, she calls together her friends and neighbors, saying, 'Rejoice with me, for I have found the coin which I had lost!' 10 In the same way, I tell you there is joy in the presence of the angels of God over one sinner who repents."

11 And he said, "A certain man had two sons. 12 And the younger of them said to his father, 'Father, give me the share of the estate that falls to me.' And he divided his wealth between them. 13 And not many days later, the younger son gathered everything together and went on a journey into a distant country, and there he squandered his estate with loose living. 14 Now when he had spent everything, a severe famine occurred in that country, and he began to be in need. 15 And he went and attached himself to one of the citizens of that country, and he sent him into his fields to feed swine. 16 And he was longing to fill his stomach with the pods that the swine were eating, and no one was giving anything to him. 17 But when he came to his senses, he said, 'How many of my father's hired men have more than enough bread, but I am dying here with hunger! 18 I will get up and go to my father, and I will say to him, Father, I have sinned against heaven and in your sight. 19 I am no longer worthy to be called your son; make me as one of your hired men.' 20 And he got up and came to his father. But while he was still a long way off, his father saw him and felt compassion for him and ran and embraced him and kissed him. 21 And the son said to him, 'Father, I have sinned against heaven and in your sight; I am no longer worthy to be called your son.' 22 But that father said to his slaves, 'Quickly bring out the best robe and put it on him, and put a ring on his finger and sandals on his feet, 23 and bring the fatted calf, kill it, and let us eat and be merry. 24 For this son of mine was dead and has come to life again; he was lost and he has been found.' And they began to be merry. 25 Now his older son was in the field, and when he came and approached the house, he heard music and dancing. 26 And he summoned one of the servants and began inquiring what these things might be. 27 And he said to him, 'Your brother has come, and your father has killed the fatted calf because he has received him back safe and sound.' 28 But he became angry and was not willing to go in. And his father came out and began entreating him. 29 But he answered and said to his father, 'Look! For so many years I have been serving you, and I have never neglected a command of yours, and yet you have never given me a kid that I might be merry with my friends. 30 But when this son of yours came, who has devoured your wealth with harlots, you killed the fatted calf for him.' 31 And he said to him, 'My child, you have always been with me, and all that is mine is yours. 32 But we had to be merry and rejoice, for this brother of yours was dead and has begun to live, and was lost and has been found.'"

Introduction

I've chewed off a huge hunk of Scripture today, a much larger portion than I would normally try to cover in one message. But really the Text gave me no choice. All three of these parables are joined as a single, unified response to the same singular objection, the complaint that Jesus could not be righteous—and hence could not be the true Messiah—because He was eating with sinners. So they demand to be treated together because if we don't, we will miss Jesus' most important point.

The main body of this chapter is one of the Lord's most familiar stories, perhaps His greatest masterpiece of parabolic art. Unfortunately, it is also one that we are accustomed to read out of context. So well did our Lord tell this story that many of the ideas we derive from it are true anyway—but they are subordinate to the one we miss. One way we can tell how we have missed the main point is to see how we have messed up the title. You see, we call it the Parable of the Prodigal Son, but in context it is clearly meant to be the Parable of the Older Brother. For it is the climax of a series of three parables, all of which are Christ's response to the Pharisees' complaints about Jesus' habit of hanging out with sinners. It is addressed to the Scribes and the Pharisees, who appear in the parable *as* the Older Brother. And while it does indeed tell us much about the Prodigal's folly and need of repentance, and about the Father's mercy and forgiveness, its main point is directed against the self–righteous attitudes of the Older Brother—the Pharisees. All three parables are here primarily to condemn Pharisaic self–righteousness and invite such older brothers to rejoice with Christ in the salvation of *sinners*. Today we will look at three points these parables combine to make, the first two on the way to making the main one: The Mercy of God, The Merry–Making of the Angels, and the Meanness of Self–Righteousness.

I. The Mercy Of God

The mercy and forgiveness of God the Father is not the main focus of these parables, but it is certainly illustrated by them. The first, the **Parable of the Lost Sheep**, shows us **His tender compassion.** It is not in Scripture, but it may well have been in the mind of the original audience: Jewish tradition tells a story of Moses when he was caring for Jethro's flock. He had lost a lamb in just such a fashion, went on a long search for it, and when he found it he carried it back to the fold draped over his shoulders, just like the shepherd in the parable, as illustrated in many religious paintings. When he did this, God appeared to him and said, "You have had compassion on man's sheep; I will put you in charge of *my* sheep, Israel."[96] So Jesus uses a traditional picture of compassion to make His point. God's compassion for sinners is something we desperately need, so it is quite natural that we focus on it. But we must not forget that the main reason for portraying it here is to contrast it with the lack of any such compassion on the part of the Pharisees. We may well be encouraged to seek God's forgiveness by these stories, and indeed rightly so. But the main point of them is how we are going to treat those who are still mired in their sins, especially if those sins have a certain social stigma attached to them. Let us not forget how God treated us when we were lost!

The second story, the **Parable of the Lost Coin**, emphasizes **God's tireless initiative** in pursuing the lost. The emphasis here is on the carefulness of the search. Many religious people will tell you that God is prepared to accept you if you clean up your act and make yourself presentable and come to Him. But Scripture says that He commends His love for us in this, in that while we were *yet sinners* Christ died for us (Rom. 5:8). And it is also while we are yet sinners that His Holy Spirit woos us and calls us. Jesus was eating with these sinners not because they had repented—they were still tax gatherers at the moment—but in hopes that they would repent. We are not saved because we have cleaned up our act; we clean up our act because Christ has saved us. This is not a trivial distinction. By the first method, the method of works, there can be no flesh justified. By the second method, the method of grace, salvation is possible even for you and me. And if once we have been saved by grace, then we can never again afford to despise those who are still lost, or whose act is still (like ours, were we completely honest) still in the process of being cleaned up in response to God's gracious forgiveness.

The third parable, **The Prodigal Son**, is the climax of the series, showing us not only the Father's tender compassion and his tireless initiative, but also **His totally incomprehensible grace.** A lost sheep is just silly and foolish; a lost coin has no responsibility at all for its condition. But the Prodigal Son has been inexcusably wicked and gotten only what he deserves. His father had every right to disown him. Yet he not only accepts him back—to do so as a hired man would have been unmerited favor—but he runs to meet him half–way, interrupts the son's very proper speech about being unworthy, and loads him with robe, ring, and sandals. Instead of taking him out to the woodshed he gives him honor which even his responsible older brother had never earned. Well, if that is our Father's attitude, and we pride ourselves on being His true sons, then how should we relate to our own long–lost brothers? Hmmm.

II. The Merrymaking Of The Angels

The mercy of God is tied to the merrymaking of the angels. There is another important point made in passing on the way to the main point. **There is joy in heaven over every sinner who repents.** Every one of these three parables ends with a party,

---

[96] Plummer, *The Gospel according to S. Luke*, op. cit., 369n.

and the three parties are climactic in their own way. In the **Parable of the Lost Sheep**, there is more joy in heaven over one sinner who repents than over ninety–nine so–called "righteous" who need no repentance. Well, it wouldn't take very much joy to be more joy than that! Who are these supposedly righteous people who allegedly need no repentance? I think we must hear the biting sarcasm in our Lord's words here. We don't need the Apostle Paul's careful theological analysis in Romans—where there is none righteous, no, not one, but all have sinned and fallen short of the glory of God (3:10, 23)—to realize how ironic the statement is. For the "righteous" are obviously the Pharisees (the very word *Pharisee* means "righteous one"). And while they are ironically given their own chosen title, it can hardly be applied to them with a straight face. For the whole point of the trio of parables is that they do very much have something to repent of—the bad attitude of the Older Brother! Unless your righteousness exceeds that of the Scribes and Pharisees, you will nowise enter into the kingdom of heaven! For that, you had better forget about your own righteousness and be clothed with the righteousness of Christ.

Well, then, Heaven is happier about a sinner who repents than about unrepentantly self–righteous Pharisees. Lest in the irony of that statement we miss how really happy that is, we have the other two parables. In the **Parable of the Lost Coin**, the comparison with the so–called righteous drops away and there is just joy in heaven over repentant sinners, period, a joy that is absolute and in need of no comparison. And then in the **Parable of the Prodigal Son** (er, excuse me, Older Brother), we have a detailed description of the celebration. Fatted calf was not normal fare. This veal was reserved only for very special occasions. And this occasion was so special that the Older Brother could hear the music and dancing before he even got back to the house. Not bad for a consort of acoustic harps and lyres with no amplification! Well, if the angels throw a big party when a sinner repents, should we be sticking our snooty noses in the air and making ominous comments about the "wrong kind of people" who are being attracted to the church? I have actually heard that comment made with a straight face (though not here, thankfully), and I bet some of you have too. Hmmm.

III. The Meanness Of Self Righteousness

The mercy of God and the merrymaking of the angels are here. But the context, as we have been showing, points them out as here for the sake of then main point Jesus was making at this moment: the point that was called forth by the Pharisees' complaint. It is made by implication in the first two parables, and then rubbed in when we get to the Parable of the Elder Brother. The Pharisees must have been livid at the unflattering portrait being painted of them. It gives us a veritable anatomy of self–righteousness.

In the first place, we see that **self–righteousness involves a false view of one's own merit.** It is not just that the Pharisees lacked compassion for sinners, but otherwise their claim to be righteous had credibility or validity. No, their claim to righteousness is false through and through, from beginning to end. The Elder Brother claims in verse 29 that he has never neglected the Father's commands. Well, that is how the Pharisees saw themselves, but the parable undermines their claim radically. For in the very act of making his claim to perfect obedience, the Older Brother is resisting the Father's will, in fact, refusing his entreaty to come in and join the party, to help welcome his brother home! He claims to have obeyed all his commands, but he is refusing a very serious entreaty, which I would think is coming much more from the Father's heart than a command to go harvest the crops. So the Older Brother's claim to perfect obedience is patently fraudulent, absurdly and even comically so. And that is just the beginning.

In the second place, we see that **self-righteousness is not only delusional and deceptive; it is also joyless.** The joylessness of the Older Brother is profound; it goes far beyond missing the party that's going on in the house. For he is missing the celebration of his brother's homecoming because he has an essentially joyless relationship with his father. He has turned their relationship into a business relationship, turned it into a job. Fatted calf? I've served you all these years and you never gave me even a kid! So the kid is compensation for service, now? The father's reply is poignant. You've missed the point! All I have is yours. All you had to do was ask. Ironically, the Older Brother is actually *asking* to be treated as a hired hand, to be compensated for superior service rendered rather than loved freely as a son. The Father's love has always been there for him, but he is too self-centered to recognize it, much less receive it. Meanwhile, the Prodigal, who knows he is unworthy to be treated as a son and would think it a great favor to be treated as an employee, is given all the honor the Father can bestow. The metaphor of a feast is often used as an image of salvation, from the Wedding Feast of chapter 14 to the Lord's Supper to the Marriage Supper of the Lamb This parable is no exception. The self-righteousness of the Older Brother has not only kept him outside of the feast; the joylessness inherent in that self-centered orientation would have kept him from enjoying it even if he had come in. He thus calls his own salvation into very serious question.

Here's a sobering thought. **What if instead of the Father it had been the Older Brother who first met the Prodigal** on his way back to the house? Do you think the Prodigal would have been encouraged to pursue reconciliation with the Father? Or would he not rather have been driven to despair? I'm afraid I just summarized an awful lot of church history. I hope that pattern is not repeating itself among us! What am I saying? Do not think that because you are not an Older Brother this parable has nothing to say to you. For even after we have come in and joined the party, the tendency to adopt the Older Brother's attitude to those who are still outside is most insidious. And once we have been working in the field for some time while some of our younger brothers still delay to come back home, the tendency to adopt the Older Brother's attitude to those who are still outside is even more insidious. Let us beware of his attitude and nip it in the bud whenever it rears its ugly head.

Conclusion

I suspect there are three kinds of people who might be here today. First, there may be some **Prodigal Sons** who are still in the Far Country. Maybe you aren't yet eating pig slop—but why wait until you get that low? Come back home today! The Heavenly Father will not reject you if you truly repent.

It is not unlikely that we have some **Older Brothers** in our midst. You are outwardly righteous, upright, religious—but it is ultimately *self*-righteousness. You would never spend your inheritance on harlots or eat pig slop, but you are not by that any closer to the heart of the Father who ran to welcome his returning son. You think you are worthy to be called his son; but that very thought is proof that you are not. You must humble yourself just like the Prodigal whose sins are less respectable but not by that more sinful if you want to be saved.

And the third type? Most of us, I hope, are **Prodigals who know it and have already returned.** We can praise God for his indescribable love with a whole heart that knows whereof it speaks. But we must beware of coming to take our acceptance by the Father for granted so that we subtly begin to turn into Older Brothers. The "holier than thou" are some of the most damaging people to the cause of Christ on this earth. Let us never forget who we are: people not worthy to be called sons (or even servants) who are being treated to fatted calf; beggars, in other words, telling other beggars where we found bread.

THE UNJUST STEWARD

Luke 16:1 Now he was saying to the disciples, "There was a certain rich man who had a steward, and this steward was reported to him as squandering his possessions. 2 And he called him and said, 'What is this I hear about you? Give an account of your stewardship, for you can no longer be steward.' 3 And the steward said to himself, 'What shall I do, since my master is taking the stewardship away from me? I am not strong enough to dig; I am ashamed to beg. 4 I know what I shall do, so that when I am removed from the stewardship, they will receive me into their homes.' 5 And he summoned each one of his master's debtors, and he began saying to the first, 'How much do you owe my master?' 6 And he said, 'A hundred measures of oil.' And he said to him, 'Take your bill and sit down quickly and write fifty.' 7 Then he said to another, 'And how much do you owe?' And he said, 'A hundred measures of wheat.' He said to him, 'Take your bill and write down eighty.' 8 And his master praised the unrighteous steward because he had acted shrewdly; for the sons of this age are more shrewd in relation to their own kind than the sons of light.

9 And I say to you, make friends for yourselves by means of the mammon of unrighteousness, that when it fails, they may receive you into the eternal dwellings. 10 He who is faithful in a little thing is faithful also in much; and he who is unrighteous in a very little thing is unrighteous also in much. 11 If therefore you have not been faithful in the use of unrighteous mammon, who will entrust the true riches to you? 12 And if you have not been faithful in the use of that which is another's, who will give you that which is your own? 13 No servant can serve two masters. For either he will hate the one and love the other, or else he will hold to the one and despise the other. You cannot serve God and Mammon." 14 Now the Pharisees, who were lovers of money, were listening to all these things, and they were scoffing at him.

Introduction

Today we come to one of the most misunderstood passages in all of Scripture. If we are not careful, we will think Jesus is praising dishonesty. The steward in question had all the financial records; he was what today we would call an accountant. Therefore, when he falsified the records to curry favor with the master's debtors, there was no way the master could prove otherwise. What he was doing in effect was embezzlement. He has already been fired, probably for other examples of dishonesty. So while he is cleaning out his office he cheats his employer one more time so that his employer's debtors will owe him big time once he is on the street looking for a new gig.

This is all pretty bad. So how can the master praise him? The key to the Lord's point here is verse 8b: *"For the sons of this age are more shrewd in relation to their own kind than the sons of light."* In other words, the story illustrates how the unbeliever takes more pains to prepare for his future in this world than a lot of believers do for theirs in the next! The believers should take note and step up their game—*their* game, a very different one from the one the steward is playing! The point is the relative value of money and spiritual things. Then as now, most people—even if they say they believe otherwise—live as if the things of this world were of supreme and lasting value. And they are wrong! By pointing out their mistake, Jesus teaches us something about the deceptiveness of wealth, but also about its proper use—the Deceptiveness of Wealth and the Deployment of Wealth.

I. The Deceptiveness Of Wealth

First, the deceptiveness of wealth. More than once in this passage Jesus calls money the "mammon of unrighteousness," or "unrighteous mammon." Why? It cannot be because money is evil in itself. If it were, Jesus could hardly have appointed one of the disciples as treasurer for the group! The Old Testament is quite clear that material wealth is one form that blessing from God can take. Deut. 28:1–11 is very clear: The reward for obedience will include God's blessing on *the produce of your ground, the offspring of your beasts and the increase of your herd and the young of your flock.* This is a pretty impressive description of wealth and prosperity for an agricultural people that climaxes in verse 11 with the explicit promise that God will make them *abound in prosperity.* Deut. 8:16–18 is even more explicit: the very power to make wealth comes from God. This is not a prosperity Gospel that promises material blessing such that we can "name it and claim it" (or, more accurately, perhaps, "blab it and grab it"). But it does affirm that wealth and prosperity are a good thing that can be one of the ways in which God blesses His people.

But that's not all. The command *"Thou shalt not steal"* could not be one of the Ten Commandments unless the Bible recognized a right to private property. Indeed, God establishes that right by giving this commandment (Ex. 20:15). And lest we think this is only an Old Testament idea, in Luke 12:16 (if you can remember that far back!) the wealth of the Rich Fool is also said to have been a gift from God. His problem was not that he had it but the selfish way he planned to use it. The Christian position about our relationship to money, then, is not one of Renunciation but of Stewardship. (We've talked about that concept before.) We are to be the *masters of* what God has given us and use it for good rather than being *mastered by it* for evil. Did you hear me? We are to be the masters of what God has given us and use it for good rather than being mastered by it for evil. We are given it to enjoy and to use for Him.

Nevertheless, there is none of God's good gifts that so readily lends itself to evil if we are not careful. Paul warns us about this in 1 Tim. 6:6–10. Some depraved people think godliness is a means of gain. It actually is, when it brings contentment, and we should be content if we have food and clothing. *"But those who want to get rich fall into temptation . . . for the love of money is a root of all sorts of evil."* This verse is often misquoted as "Money is the root of all evil." But it does not say that. Money is not evil in itself, but the *love* of it is, and so close are the two intertwined for most of us that the Lord anticipates Paul's warning here by noting how easily wealth can lead us into unrighteousness, so easily that we would do well never to forget the connection between the two. Calling the thing by the name the Lord gave it—unrighteous mammon—can help us remember this.

There are several **reasons why money, though not inherently evil in itself, is nevertheless inherently deceptive and dangerous**. First, **it comes claiming to have value in itself** when it is really only a tool, a means of achieving or attaining other good things that are what is actually valuable. Every coin and bill has what we call a "face value." It proclaims itself as "worth" so many dollars or pounds or francs or marks (or, today, euros) or pesos. Even in the days when currency was made of or backed by actual precious metals, it was what you could *do* with the gold or silver to bring goodness and blessing to your family and others that mattered, not the metal itself. And, of course, today the "value" of money is even farther removed from its physical form. As Traherne reminds us, people "rejoice in a piece of gold more than in the sun and get a few little glimmering stones and call them jewels and admire them because they are resplendent like the stars and transparent like the air and pellucid like the sea. But the stars themselves, which are ten thousand times more useful, great, and glorious, they disregard."[97]

The first reason why money is deceptive is that it comes falsely claiming to have value in itself. The second is that **money will try to convince us that it is ours**, when in fact we are nothing but its stewards. A steward is a servant who manages the resources of another for the benefit of the owner. Now, there are great rewards in being a good and faithful steward. Verse 12 hints at them. If we are faithful in the use of God's wealth entrusted to us for the support of our families and the advancement of His kingdom, He will give us that which is our own. And what is that? It is our heavenly reward which can never be taken away from us; it is ultimately Himself. Wealth is good only in so far as it is an opportunity to do good, an opportunity to be faithful stewards of God's property entrusted into our care. When we view it thus, it is liberating. When we try to own it, it becomes a ball and chain.

So money comes falsely claiming to have value in itself and falsely claiming to be ours. Finally, if we do not watch our money like a hawk and constantly be reminding it that it is our servant, **it will quickly come before us masquerading as a master.** The Lord speaks of this in verse 13. No man can serve two masters. And then He explains: the two masters are God and Mammon. How subtly does even the smallest amount of wealth switch roles when we are not looking! But it is easiest to see when the amounts grow larger. The story is told of a man giving a testimony in church. "I was destitute. I only had one dollar to my name. But I put it into the offering plate. I gave God everything I had, and he honored that gift, so that today I am a millionaire." And then a voice from the back pew was heard saying, "Brother, I dare you to do it again!" How

[97] Thomas Traherne, "Five Centuries of Meditations," *Seventeenth Century Prose and Poetry*, op. cit., 697.

is it that we know this is not going to happen? Why do we feel the impossibility in our very bones? Could it be because our own wealth has subtly begun the transformation from servant to master? We even say we work for money—as if money were our boss. Let us look to it. We can only have one Master, and Mammon isn't it!

II. The Deployment Of Wealth

So much for the Deceptiveness of Wealth. Jesus equally here wants to teach us about the Deployment of Wealth. Money is a good blessing from God as long as it remains a means to an end and not the end in itself; it is a good blessing from God as long as it is held in trust from him and not grasped as our own; it is a good blessing from God as long as it remains a servant and not a master. And it is most insidious at sneaking from the good side of those equations over to the bad side when we are not looking. Yet we cannot renounce it completely and still live in this world, much less serve God in it. So we have to learn to master our money, to remember that it is only a means and spiritual things are the end. How can we do that?

It helps to remember that the Christian does not work for money. He works for God: for the glory of God, the good of his family and his fellow man, and the spread of the Gospel, trusting God to supply his needs. God will normally do this through his work and the income it brings him. But as soon as the income becomes the main thing, we are slipping back into the acceptance of all those deceptive lies that money is prone to tell us. If we can keep focused on the proper mentality, though, we are no longer slaves to our jobs or to money but are set free to use what God gives us in those ways that alone are ultimately fulfilling. We are set free to use what God gives us for His glory.

That is the point of the cryptic advice in verse 9. "*And I say to you, make friends for yourselves by means of the mammon of unrighteousness, that when it fails, they may receive you into the eternal dwellings.*" It starts off sounding parallel to what the unrighteous steward did, but suddenly ends talking not about a cushy retirement on earth but rather the eternal dwellings in Heaven. In other words, if we are good stewards of God's wealth, it will have an impact on our eternal reward in heaven. (It doesn't mean we earn salvation by giving our money away; salvation is a gift, not something that can be earned. So what the Lord is talking about is our reward for faithfulness as His stewards when we get to heaven.) In other words, even though wealth is dangerous and deceptive, God can free us to use it for our enjoyment and His glory in ways that prepare for our mansions in heaven rather than the kind of temporal dwelling the unrighteous steward of the parable was thinking of.

What we have here is an argument *a fortiori* (an argument to the stronger). If wicked men show such dishonest cleverness to provide for their temporal futures, how much more should the Christian use his honest brains to think of ways of providing for his eternal future! We should make it a point to be creative and intelligent in investing what God gives us in the things we believe in. Two brothers got to heaven to discover that one of them had been assigned a mansion that made the Biltmore House look like a hovel, and the other was given a one–room shack that was barely standing up. He was floored by the difference. "What is this?" he asked in bewilderment. The angel in charge replied, "I know it's a bit meager, but we did the best we could with the materials you sent up."

This is not about feeling guilty every time you spend a cent on yourself. God has given us some of His money to manage for Him, and He has told us how He wants us to use it—which includes using some of it to enjoy life! We are to take care of our families. In the Old Testament this included what was called the "rejoicing tithe," money you were supposed to set aside so you could go to Jerusalem during the required festivals and have a party: You *"bind the money in your hand and exchange it for whatever your heart desires"* so you can rejoice before the Lord (Deut. 14:26). This is not about guilt but about freedom. For when we trust God to take care of us, when we see our money as His, held in trust, then we are free to use it in ways that advance His kingdom—and this is a great joy.

How do we begin to make sure that our enjoyment of money is not just an excuse to be selfish but serves Kingdom values? That becomes the important practical question, doesn't it? Can I make a simple suggestion? Think in terms of a "graduated tithe." This is not a commandment from Scripture; it's just a suggestion from me, which I therefore ask you not to obey but simply to consider as a possibly wise way of putting the principles we have been seeing into practice.

So what is a "graduated tithe"? Figure out how much money you require to live reasonably, including a reasonable amount for recreation and things you enjoy. (This includes a regular tithe to support the Lord's work budgeted into that figure—not because we are still "under the Law" but because ten percent is a convenient place to start, remembering how absurd it would be for us, with all the privileges of the New–Testament Gospel that we enjoy, to be *less* generous than the Old–Testament saints were.) Then when God gives you more than that, instead of automatically spending it on yourself, multiplying your conspicuous consumption and inflating your lifestyle, advance your tithe *on the surplus*, as it grows, from ten to twenty, thirty, forty percent or more. This will give you the opportunity to do more to support missionaries, Christian schools, etc. than most other people with the same income are free to do. Why aren't they free? They usually just let their surplus disappear into a black hole or spend it to support a lifestyle that isn't worth what they are putting into it and does not reflect what we Christians say we actually value. Don't be like that!

My friends, we can defeat the deceptiveness of wealth and use it as God intended, we can be the masters of it rather than the servants, but it will take a well thought–out and consistently executed lifelong plan if we are to do it. This is just one suggestion about a way to do that. If you can think of a strategy that you like better or that fits your personality or the circumstances of your family better, go for it! But do something; don't just be passive. If we take the path of least resistance, we will wake up one day to find we have been listening to the lies just like everyone else. Then regret over lost opportunities will be greater than the memories of indulgence. Instead, let us make friends for ourselves by means of the mammon of unrighteousness, that when it fails, they may receive us into the eternal dwellings.

Conclusion

Do you value material things and spiritual things aright? To answer that question, examine what you are investing in. Are you the master or the slave of your money? To answer that question, examine how hard it is to turn loose of it in the ways that God wants us to. If you find that you struggle to do so and you are a Christian, then you have two masters. This is an intolerable position! Love and hold to God with all your heart—and you will discover that you will be set free to enjoy the money He has given you even more.

DIVES AND LAZARUS

Luke 16:14 Now the Pharisees, who were lovers of money, were listening to all these things, and they were scoffing at him. 15 And he said to them, "You are those who justify yourselves in the sight of men, but God knows your hearts; for that which is highly esteemed among men is detestable in the sight of God. 16 The Law and the Prophets were proclaimed until John; since then the Gospel of the Kingdom of God is preached, and everyone is forcing his way into it. 17 But it is easier for heaven and earth to pass away than for one stroke of a letter of the Law to fail. 18 Everyone who divorces his wife and marries another commits adultery; and he who marries one who is divorced from a husband commits adultery. 19 Now there was a certain rich man, and he habitually dressed in purple and fine linen, gaily living in splendor every day. 20 And a certain poor man named Lazarus was laid at his gate, covered with sores 21 and longing to be fed with the crumbs which were falling from the rich man's table. Besides, even the dogs were coming and licking his sores. 22 Now it came about that the poor man died, and he was carried away by the angels to Abraham's Bosom; and the rich man also died and was buried. 23 And in Hades he lifted up his eyes, being in torment, and saw Abraham far away and Lazarus in his bosom. 24 And he cried out and said, 'Father Abraham, have mercy on me and send Lazarus, that he may dip the tip of his finger in water and cool my tongue; for I am in agony in this flame.' 25 But Abraham said, 'Child, remember that during your life you received good things, and likewise Lazarus had bad things; but now he is being comforted here, and you are in agony. 26 And besides all this, between us and you there is a great gulf fixed, in order that those who wish to come over from here to you may not be able, and that none may cross over from there to us.' 27 And he said, 'Then I beg you to send him to my father's house— 28 for I have five brothers—that he may warn them, lest they also come to this place of torment.' 29 But Abraham said, 'They have Moses and the Prophets; let them hear them,' 30 But he said, 'No, Father Abraham, but if someone goes to them from the dead, they will repent!' 31 But he said to him, 'If they do not listen to Moses and the Prophets, neither will they be persuaded if someone rises from the dead.'"

Introduction

This is one of those passages of Scripture which seems simple enough on the surface, but the more we think about it the more we find there is to it. We have to start by realizing that it is the continuation of a conversation that was already going on. It is obviously a continuation of the discussion of wealth in the Parable of the Unjust Steward. You remember him: the guy who cheated his master because he was focused only on unrighteous mammon and not true riches. That's what the Pharisees in verse 14 were mocking the Lord about. But it is also a continuation of the discussion of the Gospel of the Kingdom which began with the Parable of the Great Banquet, where all the invited guests begged off and were replaced by the lame, the blind, and the poor. The Gospel is mentioned in verse 16. While pursuing those topics it incidentally gives us some fascinating insights into the next life and its relation to this one in the new Parable of Dives and Lazarus. And if that were not enough, it ends with a grand tribute to the sufficiency of Scripture. Let's examine each of these aspects of the passage in turn.

I. As A Continuation Of The Discussion Of Wealth

First, this passage is a continuation of the discussion of wealth in the Parable of the Unjust Steward. The rich man in this parable (traditionally knows as "Dives," though the text does not actually give him a name) is clearly an example of a person who has the kind of worldly values satirized in the Parable of the Unjust Steward: We are not owners, but stewards; we should be investing the wealth that God entrusts us with in the things of the Kingdom; if the sons of this age put so much dishonest effort into preparing a place in this life, how much more should we be using our honest brains to prepare for our place in the next! I'm sure you all remember those lessons perfectly and are practicing them diligently!

The Pharisees, on the other hand, were making fun of Jesus' teaching on wealth because they were lovers of money, and this next major parable is obviously designed to take the wind out of their sails. Like them, Dives is an example of a person who has not "made friends" in the eternal dwellings with unrighteous mammon, but rather hoarded it. Having been selfish—indeed, callous and cruel—in his use of unrighteous mammon, he is impoverished when it comes to the true riches of the spirit. Having been selfish in the use of Another's property (God's), he is destitute of anything he can call his own. Having served Mammon for earthly reward, he is rejected by God in terms of heavenly reward. When he arrives in the afterlife, his folly is revealed, and its results are inescapable. Thus the scoffing Pharisees are given an opportunity to recognize the path that they have chosen and repent. They are also given a warning of what will happen if they do not.

Dives is an object lesson to the Pharisees of what they truly are—and of what they will become if they do not repent. He is a sad negative object lesson to us of the truth of Jim Elliot's dictum that it seems practically every serious Christian of my generation had memorized: "That man is no fool who gives up what he cannot keep in order to gain what he cannot lose." He is a way for Jesus to re–emphasize what he had said back in verse 13: No man can serve two masters. You will either love the one and hate the other or cling to the one and despise the other. You cannot serve God and Mammon. Apparently, the Lord thinks we need to be reminded of all of that. So let us take that reminder to heart.

II. As A Continuation Of The Discussion Of The Gospel

Second, our passage is also a continuation of the discussion of the Gospel going all the way back to the Parable of the Great Banquet. It has been a little while now since we studied the Parable of the Banquet in Luke 14:15–24 (Sermon LIV), so perhaps a little review is in order. This is the banquet to which the Jews were invited by the Old Testament. But when the time came for it to be served, they all had lame excuses—they had bought a house sight unseen and had to check it out, they had bought a used car (actually, a yoke of oxen) and had to test drive it, etc. So the servant was sent out into the highways and the hedges—i.e., to the Gentiles—to bring in the lame and blind and destitute. The Master's hall was filled with the "unworthy," with people who had no claim on any right to be there except that they had responded to the invitation. It is a wonderful picture of salvation by grace, by God's unmerited favor. The banquet is for sinners, for those the Pharisees would have considered unworthy to be there. The people they approved of are conspicuous by their absence. And the Master delights to honor whosoever will come, but you have to act by accepting the invitation.

These themes are followed up in the Parable of the Prodigal Son, where the elder brother (undoubtedly a Pharisee) ends up missing the party while the unworthy Prodigal is welcomed in by grace. And now this parable hits the same themes again. The person the Pharisees would have considered unworthy, manifestly devoid of God's favor as shown by his very poverty, ends up in Abraham's bosom, while Dives (again, undoubtedly a Pharisee) is excluded. The man without claims or expectations is welcomed with open arms by the Father of the Faithful (Abraham). Meanwhile, the fine upstanding Pharisee (who undoubtedly tithed his mint, anise, and cummin while Lazarus, the homeless man right at his doorstep, was desperate for his garbage after the servants had swept it out) finds himself in outer darkness. Salvation, in case you had not already gotten this, is once more by *grace*; it is for sinners who repent, not for the self–righteous who think they need no repentance.

Not only does this reiteration of the Gospel show up in the parable of Dives and Lazarus, it also makes sense of the prologue leading up to it, which might seem unrelated if we have not been following these trains of thought that go back at least a couple of chapters. The Pharisees scoffed because they knew the Old Testament theme that wealth can be a form of blessing from God. Their mistake was that they had *equated* wealth with blessing, and hence looked down on the *Am ha 'Aretz*, the "people of the land." These were poor people who did not have either the leisure to study the Law and all its interpretations nor the free time to concern themselves with the minutiae of those interpreted observances so beloved by the Pharisees. So in verse 16, Jesus reminds them of the good news of the Kingdom: that *sinners* could be saved! The translation of this verse is difficult. A better rendering might be, "all kinds of people are taking it by storm," in other words, rushing into it with abandon. The emphasis is on *everyone*—not just the self–righteous spiritual elite approved by the Pharisees.

Now, Jesus does not want them to misunderstand. He does not mean that the Law has been abolished. In verse 17, it would be easier to destroy the whole universe than overturn one dot of an i or crossing of a t of the Law. (The Hebrew "jots" and "tittles" were marks parallel to those strokes in English handwriting.) The Law itself—as opposed to the many Pharisaical interpretations of it and interpolations of their own human doctrine into it—is still valid, still defining the will of God in such a way as to drive us to repentance and to Christ. That must be why divorce is brought up seemingly out of the blue in verse 18: it is an example of the truth laid down in verse 17, that the Law cannot be overturned, so it is not really out of the blue at all. Divorce is still wrong, and those Pharisees who allowed it for trivial reasons (as opposed to adultery and desertion, mentioned as exceptions elsewhere) were hypocrites. The point is that grace does not overturn the Law. But salvation is still by grace and not by the works of the Law. For once again, in this third picture of the Kingdom of God (the first two are the Great Banquet and the Prodigal's Party), the upstanding and respected person (Dives) is excluded, and the one who has no claim other than grace (Lazarus) is admitted. The Gospel of the Kingdom that John had come to announce and that Jesus had come to preach is a Gospel of grace, *unmerited* favor. That is the point.

III. As A Glimpse Of The Next Life

In the process of making that point about grace, Jesus in the third place gives us a glimpse of the next life. Some modern interpreters have pooh–poohed this passage as giving us any insight into the next life, arguing that Jesus was merely describing it in terms familiar to his contemporaries without necessarily endorsing them except as providing a setting for his story about Dives and Lazarus. In arguing this way, they press a half–truth until it becomes a complete lie. Jesus often went out of his way to disagree with the assumptions of his contemporaries. One could say that this regrettable tendency was the thing that eventually got Him crucified. He contradicted them so often, so insistently, and so stubbornly that He got Himself lynched as a dangerous heretic! He was not exactly shy about contradicting cherished Jewish beliefs. Therefore, when He does not contradict them, the presumption is that He accepts them. And therefore, we can legitimately look to this parable for some hints about what the next life will be like. On the other hand, we must remember that it is a parable, and in a parable the details exist for the sake of the main point. It is seldom safe to turn a parable into an allegory. So it is good for us to remember that they are only hints: The main point of this parable is not to satisfy our curiosity about the next life, but to bring self–righteous Pharisees to repentance. Therefore, we should not press the details too hard. Nevertheless, there are some important features of the next life that are relevant to the main point, and which we should therefore take to heart.

The most important of those features is that there will be a parting of the ways in the next life based on decisions made in this life. I repeat: There will be a parting of the ways in the next life based on decisions made in this life. Decisions we make here and now set our feet on one of two paths, which lead to blessing or punishment, acceptance or rejection, bliss or misery, Heaven or Hell. These two destinations are real, and the experience of them will be real. No doubt the flames are symbols. We are told that we cannot imagine what Heaven is really like—it hath not entered into the heart of man what God hath prepared for those who love him (1 Cor. 2:9)—so I suspect the same principle holds for Hell as well. Therefore, I am willing to believe the flames are symbolic. But they are symbolic *of something*. You do not want to find out what that something is! The people in the next life are conscious. They are conscious of their identity, of their surroundings and their condition, of their pasts, of what they are enjoying or suffering, of what they have been granted or of what they are missing (just one drop of cool water!). And most importantly, their destinies are final. The great gulf of verse 26 is a stark reminder that there is no second chance. The decisions we make in this life really count. It is not a game. Today is the day of salvation! And therefore, we must repent while it is today.

IV. As A Commentary On The Sufficiency (And Majesty) Of Scripture

Finally, in the course of making all these other points, the passage is a commentary on and a celebration of the sufficiency of Scripture. There is a parting of the ways that begins in this life and is made final in eternity. And which way you take depends on whether or not you believe the Word of God. How you respond to Moses and the Prophets (and now the Apostles) right now is what will make the difference. And Moses, the Prophets, and the Apostles are completely adequate to play this pivotal role. If a person will not believe them, he would not believe even if he saw a Resurrection. And in fact, the Resurrection when it happened confirmed the truth only to those who had already believed Moses and the Prophets—though they had not understood them very well until then! This Book must be pretty important.

Familiarity breeds contempt! It has blunted the edge of our awe and dulled us to the wonder of this Book. It is really a library of sixty–six books by some forty different authors written over a millennium and a half. Yet it manifests an amazing unity that could only come from the one Mind which inspired it. It alone has an accurate diagnosis of our problem (sin) and an adequate prescription for its cure (the Blood of Christ); it alone has the answers to our deepest questions. It is, as it were, the missing page of Nature's book. The miracles—and I do not use the word lightly—of its composition, its preservation, and its effects are staggering. It has been used by the Holy Spirit to bring some of us, natural men who could not understand the things of the Spirit of God because we would not receive them (1 Cor. 2:14), from darkness to light! After all, it is the Word of God.

If you can shut your mind and close your heart to the Bible, then truly nothing can get through to you—not even a Resurrection from the dead! Moses and the Prophets are indeed incomplete without the Resurrection of Christ; but then the Resurrection of Christ would be meaningless without Moses and the Prophets. They stand or fall together. And for two thousand years now they have stood together! This Book is powerful and sharper than any two–edged sword (Heb. 4:12). So let us use it, in our own lives and in our witness. For if Jesus was right, we can surely do so with confidence.

Conclusion

Do you want to be set free from the bondage to two masters? Do you want to receive forgiveness? Do you want to invite others to the Banquet of the Kingdom? Do you want to experience the true riches? Do you want to experience real growth? *"If they do not listen to Moses and the Prophets, neither will they be persuaded if someone rises from the dead."* If the Bible as the living Word of Christ cannot teach you to do these things, nothing can. Read it daily, meditate on it hourly, and be here again next week to look into its pages once more!

UNWORTHY SERVANTS

Luke 17:1 And he said unto his disciples, "It is inevitable that stumbling blocks should come, but woe to him through whom they come! 2 It would be better for him if a millstone were hung around his neck and he were thrown into the sea than that he should cause one of these little ones to stumble. 3 Be on your guard! If your brother sins, rebuke him, and if he repents, forgive him. 4 And if he sins against you seven times a day and returns to you seven times, saying, 'I repent,' forgive him." 5 And the apostles said to the Lord, "Increase our faith!" 6 And the Lord said, "If you had faith like a mustard seed, you would say to this mulberry tree, 'Be uprooted and be planted in the sea,' and it would obey you. 7 But which of you, having a slave plowing or tending sheep, will say to him when he has come in from the field, 'Come, immediately sit down and eat'? 8 But will he not say to him, 'Prepare something for me to eat, and properly clothe yourself and serve me until I have eaten and drunk, and afterward you will eat and drink'? 9 He does not thank the slave because he did the things which were commanded, does he? 10 So you too, when you do all the things which are commanded you, say, 'We are unworthy slaves; we have only done that which we ought to have done.'"

Introduction

Most scholars have assumed that this passage is just a collection of miscellaneous sayings that Luke wanted to get in, so he lumped them together here. I think there is a train of thought discernible in these verses nonetheless, and that it is the key to understanding each part. The topic is offenses. We have first offenses against others (verses 1–2, with the warning not to be a stumbling block). Then we have offenses against oneself (verses 3–4, with the command to forgive them). The disciples feel that they do not have sufficient faith to produce such costly forgiveness, so they ask for their faith to be increased in verse 5. The Lord responds to this request with the Parable of the Mulberry Tree in verse 6. The point of it is not working "miracles." The casting of the tree into the ocean is symbolic of any difficult task, and the task in focus here is forgiveness. So the point is, "Don't worry about how much faith you have; quantifying your faith is merely a distraction. Just use what little you do have, and obey (i.e., forgive)!" Then the Parable of the Slave warns them that, when they have forgiven one another, they must not think of themselves as super–spiritual or especially deserving of God's favor. They have only done what they were supposed to do.

Throughout this discussion, seven practical principles for the Christian life emerge. Let's look at them in order.

I. The Principle Of Reality (v. 1a)

The first principle is the reality principle: "*It is inevitable that stumbling blocks should come*" (verse 1). This is a crucially important realization. We live in a world that is currently full of things for us to feel discouraged about. "Nones" are the fastest growing religious demographic. Young people are leaving the church in droves. The world is increasingly hostile to Christianity, and corrupt Christians keep giving them excuses to be. But Christians should be the last people to be discouraged, certainly the last people to be disillusioned by such things—not just because God is sovereign but because Christian theology is rooted in reality; it is the only philosophy that deals seriously with how messed up this wonderful world really is.

The Christian story begins with the creation of the world and moves immediately to the Fall of the human race and the Curse it brought on all of creation. The world we live in is abnormal. "The time is out of joint," says Hamlet. "O cursed spite / That ever I was born to set it right."[98] But the time is *always* out of joint, and it will continue to be until Christ returns. Stumbling blocks are an inevitable and unavoidable part of time's current way of flowing. And therefore, there is no point in cursing or even complaining about it. Christians do not need to curse because they are under no pressure to pretend that everything is Okay. They might suffer from depression, but they should not be a people subject to disillusionment. They should be people who know better than that.

I suppose some of the people most in danger of disillusionment are the followers of what is falsely called "Christian Science." For they believe that evil is not real. It is an illusion, an "error of the mortal mind." The story is told of a man who used to meet his Christian Scientist friend every morning when they went out to check their mail. What's the matter?" his friend asked him one morning." "It's my wife. She's been sick for a long time, and we can't figure out what's wrong with her." "Oh, she's not really sick," the Christian Scientist responded. "Sickness isn't real. It's just that she thinks she's sick. It's an error of the mortal mind." The next day the fellow looked even more depressed. "What is it?" his friend asked. "It's my wife again. She's been diagnosed with cancer." "But cancer doesn't really exist," the Christian Scientist tried to comfort him. "She only *thinks* she has cancer. It's an error of the mortal mind." The third day was still worse. "Now they say that the cancer is inoperable." "Operable, schmoperable," the Christian Scientist responded. "She just needs to get victory over these negative thoughts. Cancer doesn't really exist. She only thinks she has it. It's an error of the mortal mind, I'm telling you." Finally, the fourth day came. "Boy, you look terrible. What is it now?" "Well, it's my wife again. Now she thinks she's dead."

The informed Christian is a person set free from the terrible burden of having to pretend that because God's in his Heaven, all's right with the world—at least, yet! We know that we live in a fallen world, and we know that God has not exempted us from sharing in the sorrow and frustrations that flow from that fact. Peter tells us in 1 Peter 2:21 that "*You have been called for this purpose, since Christ also suffered for you, leaving you an example for you to follow in his steps.*" Like our Master, we are to suffer in and for a

---

[98] "Hamlet," act I, scene v, lines189-90; *The Complete Works*, op. cit., 896.

dying world. Our suffering is not redemptive in the same sense as His, but we point to His redemptive sufferings by following His example of identifying with the sufferings of a fallen world. And that is why we can face cancer, theft, tragedy, even betrayal, not without sorrow, but without disillusionment and therefore without bitterness. We live in this fallen world by the hope of redemption, not by the folly of an earthly utopia. And that is surely one of the greatest gifts our Lord has given us.

II. The Principle Of Responsibility (vv. 1b–2)

The first principle in this passage is the reality principle; the second is the principle of responsibility (verse 1): *"It is inevitable that stumbling blocks should come, but woe to him through whom they come!"* The responsibility principle flows from the reality principle: In the real world, actions have consequences. When I taught college full–time, I saw a constant stream of freshmen who had never been held responsible or accountable before in their lives. They cruised through public high schools making Bs while coming out functionally illiterate. Then there is a huge culture shock when they get to college or university and find out that we professors think they are still responsible for knowing (and practicing) all the things they never learned in the first place—just because they were supposed to have! Welcome to the real world.

It is inevitable that stumbling blocks are going to come, but you don't have to be the source of them. If you choose to be, then it would have been better to have had a millstone tied around your neck and be thrown into the sea (verse 2). God holds us responsible for our participation in the ongoing rebellion against Him that surrounds us. That is a sobering reality indeed, but it carries hope with it, for it means that our beliefs, our choices, and our actions matter. They have meaning. If we were not held responsible, they would have none. So get used to the burden and the blessing of significance! Which it is, burden or blessing, will depend on what you follow: Christ or your own lusts.

III. The Principle Of Rebuke (v. 3)

Reality; responsibility; the principle of rebuke is next: *"If your brother sins, rebuke him, and if he repents, forgive him"* (verse 3). This flows from the principle of responsibility. Your fellow believer is your brother or sister in Christ. Therefore, Christians are responsible to and for one another in the church. We cannot just let sin pass unremarked and undealt with, for doing so hurts not only the sinner and the victim but also their relationship and the whole body of Christ. This is not about being a busybody. The principle of rebuke comes into play when your brother *sins*, not just when you happen find him annoying. And you go to him to restore his relationship with Christ and with yourself; you do not go to anyone else about it (unless he is stubborn in unrepentance, but that comes later). You go to him in love, not self–righteous condemnation, and you do it privately (Mat. 18:15). Why? Because love between brothers and sisters in Christ is so important that nothing can be allowed to compromise or interrupt it. Why? Because, as the Lord explains in John 17:21–23, it is by whether we love one another or not that the world will judge whether Christ has come in the flesh. The Gospel will be only as believable to a lost world as we are, and we will be only as believable as our love is. Therefore, we cannot let real sin pass. If your brother sins, rebuke him—but do it in the way the Lord requires.

IV. The Principle Of Repentance (vv. 3b–4)

Reality; responsibility; rebuke; next is the principle of repentance. If your brother sins, rebuke him. And if he repents, forgive him. The principle of repentance gives us the proper response to rebuke by people who are living by the principles of reality and responsibility. The Greek word μετανοια (*metanoia*), repentance, means a change of mind leading to a change in behavior. In the context of sin against another person, that behavior includes restitution. Repentance is a commitment, with God's help, to forsake the sin and to make it right with those the sin has hurt. Repentance is a prerequisite to forgiveness: "If he repents," we are to forgive him. I should have a forgiving attitude toward the unrepentant. I should in other words earnestly desire the opportunity to forgive him and be prepared to do so, not holding any grudge against him so that nothing puts him off from acknowledging his sin and asking for forgiveness. I have, in other words, already forgiven him in my heart. But the transaction of forgiveness can only be complete when there is repentance on the part of the offender.

God himself does not forgive the unrepentant! To do so would be to transgress his own principles of reality and responsibility. That is part of the reason why forgiveness is so costly that it demanded the Cross. God offers the forgiveness purchased there as a free gift to anyone who believes. But true faith includes repentance. Repentance does not atone for sin—only the blood of Christ can do that. But repentance simply accepts forgiveness and the atonement it is based on with a sincere heart. To say that one accepts forgiveness while fully intending to continue the very sin for which one has asked it is simply to speak nonsense. That is not faith but hypocrisy, and God knows the difference! We often do not, which is why we must give the benefit of the doubt to those who repent seven times in one day, yea, seventy times seven. Nevertheless, the principle remains valid that repentance is the prerequisite for forgiveness. Forgiveness cannot be perfect and complete where it does not find repentance.

V. The Principle Of Restoration (vv. 3–4)

Reality; Responsibility; Rebuke; Repentance; Next come Restoration. The principle of repentance applies mainly to the offender, the one asking for forgiveness. The principle of restoration applies mainly to the offended, the one granting forgiveness. Restoration is the ultimate goal of rebuke. Let us be very plain about this. Forgiveness of the repentant is always mandatory for followers of Christ. Always. This is true for several reasons. It is true because of how important love between Christian brothers and sisters is: The very credibility of the Gospel depends on it. And it is true because Christ has forgiven us. Repentance is a commitment not to repeat the offense. The offender may fail in that commitment, but he must at least intend it. Forgiveness is a commitment never to bring the offense up again. When repentance and forgiveness are a mutual commitment between two people, then and only then is the relationship fully restored. This restoration is always the ultimate goal. How often we settle for avoiding confrontation instead while the witness of the whole Body suffers! Let us repent of our own disobedience in this area so that God can forgive us and we can then go on truly to forgive and restore others.

VI. The Principle Of Reliance (vv. 5–6)

Reality; Responsibility; Rebuke; Repentance; Restoration: The sixth of our principles is the principle of Reliance, that is, reliance on Christ by grace through faith. *"And the apostles said to the Lord, 'Increase our faith!' And the Lord said, 'If you had faith like a mustard seed, you would say to this mulberry tree, 'Be uprooted and be planted in the sea,' and it would obey you.'"* When the disciples realize what the Lord is asking of them, they say in effect, "Lord, we need help!" A life of consistent repentance toward those we have wronged and forgiveness toward those who have wronged us is not something that comes natural to us. In fact, it cuts right across the grain of the biggest impediment to spiritual progress, our sinful pride. The disciples rightly know that they are not capable of these things. So they cry out for help, and the Lord responds with the Parable of the Mulberry Tree.

The mulberry tree apparently had deep roots, and it was very hard to get a fully grown one out of the ground. And so casting a mulberry tree into the sea had become a proverb for doing the impossible. Therefore, the Lord is saying, in effect, "You are right. You can't live this way—except through faith. Faith is a radical reliance on God to do what would otherwise be impossible in and through you. But the problem is not the size or amount of your faith. It is not the power of the faith in the individual, but the power of the God in whom he puts his faith, that matters. If you have any faith at all, just exercise it, just trust in the Father completely, and this impossible thing will be done. Don't worry about the size of your faith; just use the mustard seed you've got, and God will work this miracle in you." And the miracle, the impossible thing, being discussed, is obviously forgiveness, not tree–tossing or any other publicly impressive act we might be dreaming up. Oh, if only we would read the Scriptures in context, they would make so much more sense—and call us to account more effectively, too!

VII. The Principle Of Reward (vv. 7–10)

Reality; Responsibility; Rebuke; Repentance; Restoration; Reliance. Seventh and last for today is the principle of Reward—though it might not sound like that at first. When you have learned to trust in God's grace and He has enabled you truly to repent and forgive your brother, do not think that you are anything special. A slave doesn't expect any reward just for doing what he's told, what he's supposed to do. This parable is not here to tell us that God is stingy and is going to treat us like the slave in the example. It is here to remind us that the Christian life is not about merit but about grace. When you have done everything, you have not earned any reward. The mightiest saints of history—Paul himself, Augustine, Luther, Calvin, Wesley—did not deserve any reward.

It is simply not possible for us who have been redeemed by the infinitely precious blood of Christ to give more than what we owe so that God owes us anything back. We must not think we deserve to be treated any differently from the slave in the parable. But that is so that we will be able fully to appreciate the indescribable grace we are going to receive anyway. For we have already seen back in Luke 12:36–7 that Christ is going to treat his faithful servants precisely as no human master ever did: "*Blessed are those slaves whom the master shall find on the alert when he comes. Truly I say to you that he will gird himself to serve and have them recline at table and will come up and wait on them.*" The Prodigal Son gets sandals on his feet and the best robe on his back and a ring on his finger and a fatted calf on his plate. And this our Lord will do for those who have only done what they ought to have done and hence are not worthy of any special treatment! The reward we could not have earned by merit will be richly bestowed by grace. Oh, the matchless wonder of the riches of the glory of His grace! Praise Him!

Conclusion

These seven principles are essential to a faithful Christian life: the principles of reality, responsibility, rebuke, repentance, restoration, reliance and reward. And they lead us to a place that is blessed indeed. It is the place where we combine the humility of verse 10, the humility of unworthy servants who have only done their duty, with awed praise for undeserved grace. Don't you see how this necessitates the principle of restoration? Who are we, who do we think we are, when we have received such grace, not to forgive? And are you not impelled to worship and praise the God of such grace, who delights to honor unworthy servants like ourselves? I certainly am. Let us be reminded of all that we owe to Christ as we once again remember the Lord's sacrifice for us in the way that He taught us.

THE TEN LEPERS

Luke 17:11 And it came about while he was on the way to Jerusalem that he was passing between Samaria and Galilee. 12 And as he entered a certain village, ten leprous men who stood at a distance met him. 13 And they raised their voices, saying, "Jesus, Master, have mercy on us!" 14 And when he saw them, he said to them, "Go and show yourselves to the priests." And it came about that as they were going, they were cleansed. 15 Now one of them, when he saw that he had been healed, turned back, glorifying God with a loud voice, 16 and he fell on his face at his feet, giving thanks to him. Now he was a Samaritan. 17 And Jesus answered and said, "Were there not ten cleansed? But the nine—where are they? 18 Was no one found who turned back to give glory to God but this foreigner?" 19 And he said to him, "Rise and go your way; your faith has made you well."

Introduction

The story of the ten lepers who were healed and the one who returned to give thanks is as familiar as any of the stories we remember from Sunday School, and the obvious lesson about gratitude that it conveys is just as familiar. But as usual, this incident turns out to be more than just a simple Sunday–School story. It illustrates at least three principles that are essential to a healthy Christian life: Help is found in the Perception of Infirmity; Healing is found in the Path of Obedience; and Happiness is found in the Practice of Appreciation.

I. Help Is Found In The Perception Of Infirmity (vv. 12–13)

First, help is found in the perception of infirmity. I'm going to spend most of my time on this point because even though it is simplicity itself, it is one we work awfully hard to miss. It is sitting right smack in the middle of one of our worst blind spots. It might seem too obvious to be stated, were it not for the level of denial about our spiritual neediness that surrounds us in the modern world and has even infected our own minds to some extent. Yes, it has; yours, and mine too. We prefer to think we are doing just fine. There's nothing wrong with us that a run of better luck wouldn't cure. We've learned to say that we are saved by grace, by God's unmerited favor, But we act like we really think that Christian life can work just fine based on our own strength, our own wisdom, and our own unaided efforts—once we get around to exerting them.

These lepers, by contrast to us, did not have this problem. They certainly knew that they were sick. They could not deny it; they were reminded of it every day. Why were they standing afar off? Because they were not allowed to approach healthy people. If a healthy individual passed by, the lepers had to cover their mouths and cry out, "Unclean! Unclean!" It would be rather difficult in such circumstances to pretend that I am Okay, and you are Okay, and all of us are Okay. We would know that we are not Okay. There would be no room for doubt. And so these men cried out in desperation,

"Jesus, Master, have mercy on us!" And He did. The first step to healing was the recognition that they were unclean. The first step to healing for us would be the same recognition. But, man, is that hard for us to admit!

Help is found in the perception of infirmity. Somehow this all too obvious truth seems to be one of the hardest lessons for us to learn. Everyone who does counseling will tell you the same tale: People will not come for help until after they have allowed their problems to become so ingrained and so compounded and so festered that their situation is desperate, often past curing. How many times have you asked someone if they know the Lord only to receive the response, "Well, I'm trying." They are trying to live a good life, they are trying to keep the Golden Rule, they are going to turn over a new leaf and start coming to church as soon as life is a little less hectic—as if any of this was the least bit relevant as an answer to the question! We just won't give up the notion that we can do something about our spiritual lostness; we won't give up the notion that salvation is by works. But it is absolutely essential that we give these comfortable notions up if there is to be any help for us at all.

We are familiar with the fact that the Pauline epistles emphasize the truth that salvation is by grace, God's unmerited favor, alone, accepted by faith, our believing and trusting response, alone, apart from works, lest any man should boast. What I want you to see today is how this little incident brings into focus the fact that the same emphasis is strung all throughout the Gospels, and especially the Gospel of Luke. How has Luke emphasized it already? It is not the well that need a physician, but the sick. Christ did not come to call the righteous, but sinners. There is more joy in heaven over one sinner who repents than over ninety–nine so–called "righteous" who need no repentance. Who came to the Wedding Feast? Not the upstanding citizens first invited, but the poor, the crippled, the blind, the lame. Who got fatted calf? The Prodigal who had realized and admitted his unworthiness, not the elder brother who thought he had it coming. Who was in Abraham's Bosom? Not the rich man who thought he had it all together. Hmmm. Do I detect a pattern here? Help is found in the perception of infirmity.

Do you see? Until you reckon with the fact that you are a miserable, inexcusable sinner who is helpless to do anything about it, the greatest Good News ever proclaimed has nothing to say to you. The first prerequisite to finding salvation, and therefore the infallible common denominator of all true Christians, is that they are needy. They are needy and they know it. They are needy and they are not afraid to admit it. They all without exception say, "Nothing in my hands I bring; / Simply to thy Cross I cling."[99] If they do not say that, then they have no understanding of the Gospel at all. But when they do understand and accept that truth, then they are ready to understand the opening line of Jesus' greatest sermon: *Blessed are the poor in spirit, for theirs in the Kingdom of Heaven"* (Mat. 5:3).

---

[99] Augustus Montague Toplady, "Rock of Ages Cleft for Me," *Trinity Hymnal*, op. it., 499

Are you weary and heavy laden? Are you frustrated? Are you suffering? Are you sad and lonely? Are you burdened with problems you can't handle, much less solve? Are you oppressed by guilt which no good works can assuage? Good news! Good news! The Gospel is for you! Jesus came for you! The Bible was written for you! Take heart! Help is found in the perception of infirmity.

Are you satisfied with yourself? Do you have it all together? Are you successful? Are you enjoying the good life? Can you handle anything life throws at you? Then I pity you—for God Himself can do nothing for you except to strip away the comfortable veneer of your smugness so you can see yourself as you really are: a spiritual leper. Help is found in the perception of infirmity. Help is found in the perception of infirmity! Only there! Yes, it really is. Cry out to Jesus like the lepers before you are brought that low!

II. Healing Is Found In The Path Of Obedience (v. 14)

Help is found in the perception of infirmity. But there is a second principle illustrated by these lepers: Healing is found in the path of obedience. Verse 14 may be the most intriguing verse in this whole passage. "*And when he saw them, he said to them, 'Go and show yourselves to the priests.' And it came about that* as they were going, *they were cleansed.'* As they were going! Do you get that? They had to start back on their journey to be examined by the priest *before* they were cleansed. To understand what is happening here, we need to know something about the Old Testament background. The explanation is found in Leviticus 14:1–8.

> *Then the Lord spoke to Moses, saying, 'This shall be the law of the leper in the day of his cleansing. Now he shall be brought to the priest, and the priest shall go out to the outside of the camp. Thus shall the priest look, and if the infection of leprosy is healed in the leper, then the priest shall give orders to take two live clean birds and cedar wood and a scarlet string and hyssop for the one who is to be cleansed. The priest shall also give orders to slay one bird in an earthenware vessel over running water. As for the live bird, he shall take it, together with the cedar wood and the scarlet string and the hyssop and shall dip them and the live bird in the blood of the bird that was slain over the running water. He shall then sprinkle seven times the one who is to be cleansed from the leprosy, and shall pronounce him clean, and he shall let the live bird go free over the open field. The one to be cleansed shall then wash his clothes and shave off all his hair, and bathe in water and be clean. Now afterward, he may enter the camp.*

So seriously was leprosy taken that there was a definite ceremonial as well as hygienic process for restoring the leper who was healed. Before he could re–enter society and stop crying "Unclean!" he had to be certified as healed by the priest, who would then restore him to ceremonial as well as hygienic purity. If these ten men were healed, they would have to go through the same procedure before they could return to their families. But the curious thing about this incident is the order of the events. Jesus does not heal them and then remind them that they need to go see the priest. No, he tells them to go to the priest, and then heals them only after they were already on the way. He requires of them a pretty impressive act of faith expressed in obedience. Imagine setting out on that journey with your skin still white and necrotic! They must have wondered what Jesus was thinking. And then imagine the joy of discovering that healing is found in the path of obedience.

Salvation is by grace through faith alone apart from works. You will not be saved by coming up with an impressive act of obedience. But obedience is the natural expression of faith. Faith is not an optimistic outlook, though living by faith might give you one. It is not correct doctrinal opinions, though it is important to believe in the truth God has actually revealed to us rather than some garbled version mixed with lies. Faith is the radical trust in Christ as the Son of God that commits you to Him. It believes that what God says is so and believes it so sufficiently that it is willing to act on it. *"But thanks be to God that, though you were slaves to sin, you became obedient from the heart to that form of teaching to which you were committed,"* says Paul in Romans 6:17. Faith is the empty hand that receives Christ and his blessings. And therefore, *"faith is the victory that overcomes the world"* (I John 5:4). The lepers believed Jesus and showed it by acting on his instructions, and therefore the supernatural power of God to heal them was unleashed. Healing is found in the path of obedience.

It follows that believing and then obeying God is the most practical step you can take to solving your problems. For the Word of God is inspired, and this makes it adequate for training us in righteousness until we are fully equipped for every good work (2 Timothy 3:15–17). You cannot become a Christian by your efforts to obey the Word of God, but once you have become a Christian by faith, that faith will make you want to obey it and put you in touch with the Power that can enable you to obey it. And to the extent that you are not a hearer of the Word only but also a doer (James 1:2), your life will be blessed.

What? Is the God who made us male and female and performed the first wedding not able to teach you how to have a good marriage? Does the God who is our heavenly Father not know how to raise children? Is the God who owns the cattle on a thousand hills not able to help you manage your money? Is the God who designed the whole universe not able to help you set your priorities? Is the God who transformed Peter from a big-mouthed coward to a saint and martyr, the God who transformed Paul from a persecutor of the church to the greatest missionary and theologian who ever lived—is He not able to help you break a habit? The answers to these problems and many more are all found in the Bible, and as we go through it over time, they are being expounded here every week. If through laziness and inattention we are ignorant of these instructions, if through rebellion or unbelief we are disobedient to them, then we condemn ourselves to being defeated by the effects of sin even after we have been forgiven for the guilt of sin. We have forgotten that healing is found in the path of obedience.

II. Happiness Is Found In The Practice Of Appreciation (vv. 15–19)

Help is found in the perception of infirmity. Healing is found in the path of obedience. And yes, the obvious Sunday–School lesson is here in the story too: Happiness is found in the practice of appreciation. On one level this is just common sense. It is very difficult to be truly grateful and seriously depressed at the same time. But there is a spiritual dynamic at work as well as a psychological one when the One to whom we are grateful is Christ. Being thankful to anyone is psychologically healthy, and expressing that thanksgiving doubles the benefit. But when we are overflowing with gratefulness *to God*, then a spiritual dynamic is added which multiplies those benefits exponentially.

Only one of the ten lepers turned back to thank Jesus for what He had done, and not only is he commended for having done so, but he is also the only one who is recorded as loudly (significant word!) glorifying God. I don't know that we need to be *too* hard on the others. No doubt they were very excited and were awfully anxious to have that interview with the priest, which is after all what Jesus had told them to do. In that excitement as they rushed toward the temple, they were not necessarily ungrateful. But if they felt gratitude, they did not stop to express it. What is unique about the one leper is the fact that he did; he went out of his way to personalize his thanksgiving. And for this he was rewarded with a more intimate relationship with the Lord. You could call it a reward, or you could say that this enhanced relationship was inherent in the very act of returning to give thanks itself. Either way, it is impossible to believe that the one leper did not emerge from the experience as the one most blessed of all. He had not only learned that help is found in the perception of infirmity and that healing is found in the path of obedience; he also learned that happiness is found in the practice of appreciation. I said the *practice* of appreciation. Don't just feel grateful (though that is a start, and a good and healthy one). Express it! Express it to God privately in your own devotions but also publicly, in our exhortation and testimony time for example. It will do wonders for your emotional outlook and your spiritual life.

Conclusion

Well, there it is. Do you want to experience the fullness of the Christian life? Do you want to know joy inexpressible and full of glory? Do you want to experience victory over sin and its effects in your life? Do you want to know the peace the passes understanding? Then remember to practice daily these three principles illustrated by the story of the ten lepers. Help is found in the perception of infirmity. Don't scrimp on that one; it is the door to all the rest. Healing is found in the path of obedience. Obedience is the natural expression of real saving faith. And happiness is found in the practice of appreciation. Let us therefore give glory to God even as the one leper did: As we turn to Communion, let us receive it as, the sign and the seal of the New Covenant and thus the reminder of all that we owe to Christ and the tremendous price He paid for it! Let it be our way right now of starting to practice appreciation, of following the example of the One Leper and coming back to kneel at the feet of the One who has healed us. Amen.

IN THE DAYS OF NOAH

Luke 17:20 Now, having been questioned by the Pharisees as to when the kingdom of God was coming, he answered them and said, "The kingdom of God is not coming with signs to be observed, 21 nor will they say, 'Look, here it is!' or 'There it is!' For behold, the kingdom of God is in your midst." 22 And he said to the disciples, "The days shall come when you will long to see one of the days of the Son of Man, and you will not see it. 23 And they will say to you, 'Look there! Look here!' Do not go away and do not run after them. 24 For just as the lightning, when it flashes out of one part of the sky, shines to the other part of the sky, so will the Son of Man be in his day. 25 But first he must suffer many things and be rejected by this generation. 26 And just as it happened in the days of Noah, so shall it be in the days of the Son of Man. 27 They were eating and drinking, they were marrying and being given in marriage until the day that Noah entered into the ark and the flood came and destroyed them all. 28 It was the same as happened in the days of Lot. They were eating, they were drinking, they were buying, they were selling, they were planting, they were building; 29 but on the day that Lot went out from Sodom it rained fire and brimstone from heaven and destroyed them all. 30 It will be just the same on the day that the Son of Man is revealed. 31 On that day, let not the one who is on the housetop and whose goods are in the house go down to take them away, and likewise let not the one who is in the field turn back. 32 Remember Lot's wife! 33 Whoever seeks to keep his life shall lose it, and whoever loses his life shall preserve it. 34 I tell you, on that night there will be two men in one bed; one will be taken and the other left. 35 There will be two women grinding at the same place; one will be taken and the other left. 36 Two men will be in the field; one will be taken and the other left." 37 And answering, they said to him, "Where, Lord?" And he said to them, "Where the body is, there also will the vultures be gathered."

Introduction

The Pharisees in this passage ask Jesus a question: When is the Kingdom coming? It is a question we are still interested in today. And the only answer we are ever going to get to it is still the one Jesus gave long ago. When is the Kingdom coming? Any time. At a moment when you think not. Therefore, be ready for it always. Okay, what can we learn about the Kingdom from Jesus' way of answering the question on this occasion?

I. The Kingdom Looked For (vv. 20–21)

The first thing we see in this passage is the Kingdom looked for. Scripture leaves us in a kind of creative tension with regard to the coming of the Kingdom of God. We are supposed to watch and wait for it, to look for it, to live in expectancy of it, but we are not supposed to speculate about the day or the hour (to which all that expectancy naturally tempts us), but rather be about the King's business as we wait. We should live as if Jesus might come back today, and that means . . . planting a tree that won't give fruit or shade for many years to come. And somehow these two seemingly contradictory things must be held as wholly compatible. Theologians call this tension the paradox of the "already, but not yet." So this passage raises an urgent question: How do we do that?

I remember when I was a little boy, we had a sermon on watching and waiting for Jesus to come back. I'm afraid I took it rather literally. I went home and got out my telescope and spent the whole afternoon gazing up into the heavens, trying to be the first to catch Him in the act of returning! When you are pointing a telescope up into an endless blue sky, you don't see very much that is interesting or edifying. At that point, I don't think I had the tension quite right. And neither did the Pharisees—or the disciples, *yet*, for that matter. When is the kingdom coming? Well, it's not coming with signs to be observed. You can't say, "Look! It's over there!" In fact, it is already in your midst.

What did Jesus mean by this? Was He contradicting what He had said back in 12:54–56? You see the clouds coming out of the west and you expect rain; you feel the south wind blowing and you expect a hot day. Well, if you can read the signs of nature, shouldn't you also be able to read the signs of the times? First we are supposed to read the signs, and then there aren't any to read! But the contradiction is only apparent. The word "signs" does not actually appear in the original Greek text of our verse 20. It literally says that the kingdom is not coming "with observations." In other words, the Pharisees were looking for the wrong kind of sign. They wanted to see some indication that a renewed Jewish empire to replace the hated Roman occupation was coming. Well, no matter how hard they might look, they weren't going to see anything because they were looking for the wrong kind of thing. Neither their political speculations nor our dispensational charts are going to help us. Because the whole time the real Sign was standing right in front of them, and they missed it. *"For behold, the kingdom of God is [already] in your midst"* (verse 21b).

What does that mean, "in your midst"? The phrase has been translated two different ways to reflect the two possible meanings it can have. Is the Kingdom "within" you, or is it "in your midst"? "Within you" appeals to those for whom religion is a private, inner affair of the heart, a matter of one's own interior landscape. This reading has the virtue of contrasting with the Pharisees' crass, outward, political concept of the kingdom. But this is almost certainly not what Jesus meant, precisely because he was talking to the Pharisees. They were the people who had rejected him as Messiah. They were probably the least poor in spirit of all the groups in the land. Their hearts had no room for grace, because they were full of self–righteousness. To say that the Kingdom of God was "within" *them* is to render the Kingdom all but meaningless.

What Jesus meant then was that the Kingdom was *in their midst*. In other words, the Kingdom was already present in the person of the King, Jesus himself, who was literally standing in the middle of the group—standing right in front of them. Now, the

Kingdom can be an inner reality in one sense. It is within us to the extent that Jesus reigns as King in our hearts and indwells us through His personal agent and representative, the Holy Spirit. But it is not the essence of the Kingdom to be inward or subjective; it is the essence of the Kingdom to be Christocentric. Christ is to reign over our private inner lives *and* over our outward public selves, over our subjective feelings *and* all that is outward and objective. If you want the Kingdom to come, let King Jesus reign. The Kingdom is that realm over which the King's authority holds sway. It may start in the hearts of believers, but its very nature is that it must reach out from there to conquer the whole world. Francis Schaeffer captured the idea well in his phrase, "The Lordship of Christ over the total culture."[100] The Kingdom was already in their midst in the person of the King, but in that larger sense it had not—and still has not—"come." That is why we end up talking about a *"Second* Coming." Well, why is that second coming needed, if Christ has already conquered Satan's kingdom on the Cross?

Why is that second coming needed if Christ has already conquered? Here's an analogy to help you answer that question. When was the United States born? When did the rule of King George III come to an end in the colonies? Was it when we signed the Declaration of Independence? Or was it when General Cornwallis was defeated? Or was it when we ratified the Constitution? When does a new person become the next president? Is it when he wins the election? Or is it when the electoral college meets to make it official? Or is it on Inauguration Day? There is a certain truth in all those answers, and it is no different with the coming of this Kingdom. The Old Testament prophets published the Declaration of Independence, as it were; General Cornwallis was defeated on the Cross; but the day we await when the Son returns will be the ratification of the Constitution. Or we can say that the prophets were the television networks projecting a winner; the Cross was the actual defeat of the opponent; the Resurrection was the meeting of the electoral college; and the Second Coming will be Inauguration Day.

So that is what we are looking at; that is the place we occupy in history. In other words, Satan is still in the White House. (Beware: This is an analogy, not a political allegory! I'm saying absolutely nothing about that building's current occupant one way or another.) Satan is still in the White House, but he is a lame–duck president whose days are numbered. The transition has already begun, but opposition to the reign of the new administration still continues. But the rule of King Jesus is now inevitable. The main difference is that the date of this Inauguration has not been published. That is where we are.

II. The Kingdom Longed For (vv. 22–23)

---

[100] Or over "the whole spectrum of life," Francis Schaeffer, *A Christian Manifesto* (Westchester, IL: Crossway, 1981), 63.

So much for the Kingdom looked for. Next we have the Kingdom longed for. Jesus now turns to the disciples and tells them that the day is coming when they will long for the Son of Man but not (yet) see Him. That is the period we are in.

We cry out, "How long, oh Lord?" Why? Because we love Jesus above all things and want to see Him face to face. That should be the main reason for our longing. But there is another reason that is also real and legitimate and cannot be dismissed: because, as a lame duck, Satan knows his time is limited and wants to do all the damage he possibly can before his term finally expires. Indeed, as that unknown date nears, his activity increases in intensity, so that there will be wars and rumors of wars, pestilence and famines in diverse places, persecution, affliction, tribulation—all the troubles that so many prophetic passages warn of. They will just naturally escalate as the time draws near.

Okay, how are we supposed to respond to this situation? Jesus says that our response should be patience and discernment. *"And they will say to you, 'Look there! Look here!' Do not go away and do not run after them."* In other words, we are not to get antsy and run off after tangents and on false trails in our desire for relief. Why not? Because when the Kingdom does come, we will know it. That indeed is the point of the next section.

III. The Kingdom Likened To (vv. 24–30)

The Kingdom looked for; the Kingdom longed for; now we have the Kingdom likened to. Jesus now continues his explanation by giving two analogies, two comparisons to help us understand the coming of the kingdom. The first is that the coming of the Son of Man will be like lightning that shines from one end of the sky to the other (verse 24). Two things about this comparison are pertinent. First, such lightning is unmistakable. This is not a flicker in the distance. It is one of those dramatic bolts that lights up the whole sky and transforms night to day for a split second. It brings you up short and rivets you to the spot. You know exactly what has happened. You are not saying to yourself, "I wonder if there's a thunderstorm about?"

Do you understand? If you are asking yourself whether anything—say, something like the war in Ukraine—might be the prelude to the Second Coming, the answer is no, it is probably not. If they tell you He is in the wilderness, do not even go to see. When the real thing happens, you won't be asking; you will know. In that moment every prophecy, every loose end of interpretation, will fall into place in your head for the first time, and it will all make sense, and you will say, "Of course! Why didn't I see it before?" But you will not see it before. You will not figure out the day or the hour—probably not even the generation—no matter how hard you try, no matter how elaborate and painstakingly you have constructed your chart. Nevertheless, do not worry. When it comes, it will be like lightning that shines from the East unto the West, unmistakable. You will know.

Second, lightning is not only unmistakable, it is sudden. It is immediate, not gradual. Do you know the Peanuts cartoon where Snoopy is on top of the doghouse working on his novel? He has written, "Suddenly, a shot rang out." And Lucy says, "That is a cliché. I think you should change it." So Snoopy scratches his head for a moment and then writes, "Gradually, a shot rang out." Well, it is just as ridiculous to say, "Gradually, a bolt of lightning lit up the sky." The coming of the Kingdom will not be the culmination of a long, slow process of improvement as the Post–Millennialists expect. That does not mean we should not work for improvements and pray for the peace of the city where we are placed. But we should not expect those efforts to bring in the Kingdom. Its coming will be supernatural, not the culmination of natural processes. All the Scriptural imagery which describes that Day agrees with this image. It will hit us like a bolt of lightning.

The second analogy is that the coming of the kingdom will be like the days of Noah (and Lot). When I was growing up, my preachers liked to portray the description of those days as a reference to the wickedness of those generations. Well, both of those generations were indeed exceptionally wicked—but that is not the point being made here. None of the things they are described as doing—marrying and giving in marriage, eating and drinking, buying and selling, planting and building—are inherently sinful. The point is that life was going on very normally; they were practicing and experiencing business as usual. And then suddenly and without warning those very normal lives were interrupted; suddenly they were over. Life is just going along, you are unconcerned with spiritual things, and then, boom! The flood comes or the brimstone falls and it's all over. Wham! The books are closed, and the spiritual commitments you have made, the spiritual commitments you might not even realize you have made, are sealed for eternity. No one will tell you, "This is your last opportunity to repent. You have one week to put your house in order." You wouldn't believe them if they did, but they won't. They're not going to. They do not know the day or the hour. I do not know the day or the hour. I do not know that this is your last chance to bow before Jesus as Lord. But it could be! For the day of the Lord will come like lightning, it will come like a fire or a flood, it will come without warning, it will come (as another familiar description puts it) like a thief in the night. But it will come. Will you be ready?

IV. The Kingdom Lost Out On (vv. 31–37)

The Kingdom looked for—you can't know the day or the hour, The Kingdom longed for—we should long for it indeed. The Kingdom likened to—it will hit you like a lightning bolt or a flood. And some people will not be ready. Therefore, we have our final point, a sobering one: the Kingdom lost out on.

The central figure of the last part of this passage is Lot's wife. She is the perfect example of one who was not ready. How so? She left Sodom along with Lot—but she looked back. Her feet were walking away from Sodom, but her heart was not, and her eyes betrayed that fact. She therefore shows that those whose primary attachment is to this world and the things of this world are in trouble. They are in sho'–'nuff, bad–off trouble! Remember Lot's wife!

Maybe this is why Jesus said, "*If anyone wishes to come after me, let him deny himself and take up his cross daily and follow me*" (Luke 9:23). Maybe it's why he said, "*If anyone comes to me and does not hate his own father and mother and wife and children and brothers and sisters, yes, and his own life, he cannot be my disciple*" (14:26). Maybe it's why he said, "*For where your treasure is, there will your heart be also*" (12:34). Why did he say these things, culminating in the exhortation to remember Lot's wife? If your chief desire is for this world, you will be allowed to have it. Mrs. Lot was a professing believer in Yahweh, but when the test came, she showed that her heart was in Sodom.

When the Kingdom comes, there is going to be a parting of the ways—so we had better be in the right way now! This parting of the ways is illustrated by the pairs of men and women who are caught when the kingdom breaks into their daily lives. One was taken and the other was left. Those who are "taken" are the ones who are rescued, taken out of the flood or the conflagration like Noah or like Lot. Those who are "left," like Lot's wife and Noah's neighbors, are left to judgment and destruction. It is a graphic illustration of the fact that the commitments we make now will be sealed for eternity then. The very purpose of time is that it is the arena in which those choices for eternity are to be made. The passage ends with a strong warning to those who have not made themselves ready for the Kingdom by submitting to the King and recognizing His right to reign now. We end with the vultures gathering over their bodies, in an image that simultaneously reminds us that the coming of the Kingdom will be unmistakable— everybody knows what buzzards are after when we see them circling—and gives us a sobering and chilling picture of the fate of those who are "left." The Pharisees ask their question hoping for an encouraging affirmation of their political cause. But they are left with the foreboding feeling that they have just been pictured as buzzard bait. The kingdom was among them, it was in their midst, but they had already rejected it. Well, the King is not *physically* present in our midst this morning. But blessed are they who have not seen, and yet have believed (John 20:29)!

Conclusion

The storm clouds are gathering. We have gotten used to them. But someday, when we least expect it, in the midst of business as usual, lightning will strike. It will strike you unless you find shelter. And the only shelter that will avail on that day is the Cross of Christ. Won't you give your life to Him today? Give up your rebellion, your claim to be sovereign over your own life, acknowledge Him as your true and rightful King, and receive his pardon. And then you will become a citizen of the Kingdom, and then you can join us in waiting expectantly for it to come. Amen.

PARABLES FOR FEAR AND PRESUMPTION

Luke 18:1 *Now he was telling them a parable to show that at all times they ought to pray and not lose heart,* *2* *saying, "There was in a certain city a judge who did not fear God and did not respect man.* *3* *And there was a widow in that city, and she kept coming to him, saying, 'Give me legal protection from my opponent.'* *4* *And for a while he was unwilling. But afterward he said to himself, 'Even though I do not fear God nor respect man,* *5* *yet because this widow bothers me, I will give her legal protection, lest by her continual coming she wear me out.'* *6* *And the Lord said, "Hear what the unrighteous judge said!* *7* *Now shall not God bring about justice for his elect who cry to him day and night, and will he delay long over them?* *8* *I tell you that he will bring about justice for them speedily. However, when the Son of Man comes, will he find faith on the earth?"*

9 *And he also told this parable to certain ones who trusted in themselves that they were righteous and viewed others with contempt.* *10* *"Two men went up into the temple to pray, one a Pharisee and the other a tax gatherer.* *11* *The Pharisee stood and was praying thus to himself, 'God, I thank thee that I am not like other men: swindlers, unjust, adulterers, or even like this tax gatherer.* *12* *I fast twice a week; I pay tithes of all I get.'* *13* *But the tax gatherer, standing some distance away, was even unwilling to lift up his eyes to heaven, but was beating his breast, saying, 'God, be merciful to me, the sinner!'* *14* *I tell you, this man went down to his house justified rather than the other. For everyone who exalts himself shall be humbled, but he who humbles himself shall be exalted."*

Introduction

We come today to two parables, "The Unjust Judge" and "The Pharisee and the Publican," which were delivered on different occasions and on different topics. I choose to treat them together because they are connected by the common themes of prayer, fear, and presumption, and because I think they shed interesting light on each other. Both are very familiar, and the basic point of each is well known. But a more detailed look at their background and setting makes them come to life.

I. The Unjust Judge

Background

First, let's look at the background to "The Unjust Judge." The first parable is very interesting in the light of an account by H. B. Tristram of a courtroom in Iraq (before the Gulf wars), in Kenneth E. Bailey's fascinating book *Through Peasant Eyes*.[101] The proceedings were conducted in an open courtyard with an unruly crowd milling about. At one end, on a raised dais, sat the judge on cushions, surrounded by secretaries and other functionaries. The plaintiffs in the crowd had all pushed their way through to that

---

[101] Op. cit., 134.

end of the courtyard and were crying for attention—but the judge and his cronies acted as if they did not even hear them. Meanwhile, the prudent slipped certain envelopes to the secretaries, who then conferred together. They finally went and whispered to the judge, who then called out the first case to be heard—in order of the highest bribe. But there was a poor woman there who screamed so loud she even disturbed the chaos. She was repeatedly told to shut up, but she only screamed the louder, "Not until he hears me!" "Not until he *hears* me!"

It was so bad that it was impossible for normal business to be conducted; nothing could happen except the woman screaming bloody murder and the secretaries trying to shush her. Finally, out of sheer exasperation, the judge himself interrupted the secretaries. "What in Allah's name does that wretched woman want?" It turned out that she was a widow whose only son had been drafted, which according to Iraqi law meant she should have been exempt from taxes. But the tax collector kept harassing her anyway. "Let her be exempt!" the judge cried impatiently, and so the corrupt business of the court was able to resume and things returned to normal. One of the bystanders explained to Tristram, "It was an open and shut case. If she had had the money for a bribe, she would have been heard days ago." Hmmm.

It is truly remarkable how little the Near East has changed in some ways since biblical times. In verse 2 of the biblical story, we read that the unjust judge neither feared God nor respected man. Literally, it says that he had no shame before men. In other words, he was shameless, moved neither by justice nor pity—only by bribes. So the parallel between Tristram's account and the biblical parable is so exact it's uncanny. Only the names have been changed—to protect the guilty.

Interpretation

So then, what does this understanding of the background tell us about the interpretation of this parable? I have often heard Jesus' story cited in favor of importunity in prayer. (Importunity? Who uses that word? Well, "stubborn insistence," which is what importunity means, sounds less pious, doesn't it?) But that interpretation misses its point entirely. The whole story turns on the *contrast* between God and this judge, a figure who would have been all too familiar to Jesus' audience. The contrast: therefore, the point is not that we should yell, scream, and pitch a fit like the woman did in order to get our way with God. The point is that because God is so different from the judge, we do not need to. Because our heavenly Father is a righteous and good judge, we should be encouraged to pray reverently and respectfully. If even the unjust judge who cared only for bribes could be got to hear the woman, how much more will God, who is good and just and loves us, hear His people when they are in need? (Students of logic will appreciate the Lord's deft use of the *argumentum a fortiori*, the argument from the lesser to the greater.)

In other words, we should pray readily and wait in faith for God to answer. He will indeed bring justice for his people speedily. And if the answer seems to be delayed (like the children of Israel languishing in Egyptian slavery for 400 years), we should not be discouraged. It is not because we have not given God a big enough bribe or pitched a loud enough fit. He is not like the judge in the parable. "In the corrupted currents of this world," says Shakespeare's Claudius,

> Offense's gilded hand may shove by justice,
> And oft 'tis seen the wicked prize itself
> Buys out the law. But 'tis not so above.
> There is no shuffling; there the action lies
> In its true nature, and we ourselves compelled,
> Even to the teeth and forehead of our faults
> To give in evidence.[102]

What would we give God as a bribe anyway? Church attendance? Fasting? Tithes? Good works? What could we give Him that we do not already owe Him? If we wanted to play that game, we would swiftly find ourselves not in the plaintiff's place but in the dock as defendants! Bribes will neither help us be heard, nor will they get us off. We can only trust to God's wisdom and his mercy, as well as His justice. His wisdom and His goodness mean that relief from the injustices of this life is coming as speedily as it can.

That word "speedily" is a challenge to our faith, is it not? Relief from injustice does not always seem to some "speedily" to us. I am sure it did not seem speedy to the generations of Israelites who perished in Egyptian slavery while waiting for the 400 years to elapse! So let me offer four reasons why we should still believe what Jesus said in spite of appearances to the contrary, four reasons why "speedy" might indeed mean years of painful waiting.

First, life is a complicated web of relationships, and there are other people besides us who have to be considered. Why did Israel's slavery have to last as long as it did? For one reason, they could not invade the Holy Land and kick out and slaughter its inhabitants until "the iniquity of the Amorites was full" (Gen. 15:16). The current inhabitants needed to come to fully deserve the fate that was about to befall them. We have no idea what the effects of the deliverance we ask for might be on other people; but God has to consider such things. Israel's deliverance came, when all things were considered, as speedily as it could.

Second, waiting in itself is spiritually good for us. It is an exercise we need to develop our faith. God certainly asks us to do a lot of it! In the third place, there is one additional thing we must never forget. We are not just plaintiffs in a world of injustice; we are also soldiers in a great spiritual war. There is hardship to be born for the Kingdom. The setting for this parable is the material on the Last Judgment that we saw

---

[102] "Hamlet," act III, scene iii, lines 57-64; *Complete Works*, op. cit., 913.

at the end of chapter 17 last week. It is only there, at that Judgment, that all tears will be wiped away.

In the meantime, because of who our heavenly Father is, we should pray, and we should wait patiently. He hears us now; sometimes He grants us temporal relief now; and when all is made right, it will then be seen that He has brought justice speedily indeed. In the meantime, why does He seem to delay? The fourth reason is because opportunity for repentance is still being given to those who need it. And we mustn't complain about that because it was given to us! For at least these four reasons, then, relief from injustice does not always happen immediately. Life is complicated and we cannot know all the side–effects of what we ask for; waiting is good for us; we are soldiers, not private citizens; and opportunity for repentance is still being given. These reasons do not answer all of our questions, but they can help us or to see, to at least be able to believe, to have faith, that because God is just and because He cares, it really is coming as speedily as it can.

II. The Pharisee And The Publican

Background

Alright, let's look at the background to "The Pharisee and the Publican." Jesus chooses these two figures as His examples because Pharisees had the reputation of being the most righteous people in Israel, and Publicans had the reputation for being the least. Publicans truly were despicable sinners—collaborators who worked for the hated Roman overlords as tax collectors, getting rich off of exploiting their fellow countrymen. If you want to upset the applecart of people's expectations, this is the way to do it!

The setting for this parable is not private prayer but public worship. These two men were at the Temple for either the daily morning or evening atoning sacrifice as it was practiced in the Temple at that time. When the blood of the sacrificial lamb, sprinkled on the altar, had covered the sins of Israel, the way to God was symbolically opened. At that moment incense would be offered, a signal to the people that it was a propitious time for their prayers to rise up to God along with the incense and the "soothing aroma" of the sacrifice. That is the moment at which you would make your prayer.

If you remember, we saw Zacharias participating in this rite at the very beginning of Luke's Gospel. It was at that moment, when he was inside offering the incense, that the angel Gabriel revealed to him that he would be the father of the Forerunner, John the Baptist. "*And the whole multitude of the people were in prayer outside at the hour of the incense offering*" (Luke 1:10). Even if you were not at the Temple, that is the time at which you would pray if you had any petition, across the whole land of Israel. Fascinating. This dynamic is crucial for fully understanding the teaching of this familiar story.

Interpretation

So then, what does this understanding of the background tell us about the interpretation of this parable? We here find two men who, for different reasons, stand out from the crowd of worshippers who have come to the service. When the NASB in verse 11 says that the Pharisee prayed "to himself," it would probably be better translated "by himself." Both of these men were standing alone, apart from the rest of the congregation, though for different reasons. One of them thought he was too good to be part of the congregation; the other thought he was not good enough. Let me repeat that: One of them thought he was too good to be part of the congregation; the other thought he was not good enough.

By the way, we should not let ourselves be distracted by either of those feelings from full participation in the life of the Body. As we are all sons of Adam and daughters of Eve, all sinners saved, if at all, by grace, unmerited favor, I can assure you that any feeling that you are too good to be part of this or any other Christian community is a sheer delusion. And since we are saved by the grace, the unmerited favor, portrayed in this parable, I can assure you that any feeling that you are not good enough is perfectly accurate. It is also a colossal exercise in irrelevance, a missing of the point as great as any that can be imagined. What is the point? I'm glad you asked that question!

The type of service these two men were attending highlights both the pride and the humility that they manifest. At the very moment of sacrifice, the Pharisee shows no awareness that he has any need for an atoning sacrifice. He is really not even praying at all, but boasting. Pious Pharisees at this time would pray, "God, I thank you that you did not make me a Gentile, unlearned, or a woman." So Jesus was giving an example of a familiar type that his audience knew well.

When the Publican asks for God's mercy, on the other hand, what he actually says is 'ιλασθητι μοι, "hilastheti moi": literally, "Make atonement for me." "Make atonement for *me*." It is a very pointed reference to the lamb being sacrificed at that very moment. The Publican knows what he needs; yet so burdened is he by his sins that he has no confidence his prayer could possibly be answered. He shows this by beating his breast, and even more eloquently, by not looking up to heaven. The standard Jewish posture for prayer was not kneeling with bowed head but standing with head looking up and arms lifted as if to receive from heaven the blessing that was being requested. What he is saying, rather desperately, is, "If only I could be included in this atonement when the priest gives the benediction! But I am afraid I am so unworthy that it can never happen."

What a great summary of the Gospel of salvation by Grace through Faith alone this story is! It is telling that Jesus uses the word "justified" in his comment at the end. (Yes, Jesus uses that word; no, contrary to many liberal theologians, it was not an alien concept made up and added to the simple teaching of Jesus by the Apostle Paul.) Acceptance with God is not something that can be earned; it can only be received as a gift, a gift given to those who are willing to admit their abject need. And the gift is based on an atoning Sacrifice which does no good at all to those who do not think they need one.

Okay, so who is justified? Who is declared righteous? Not the one who outwardly looks righteous, certainly not the one who thinks he is righteous, but the one who, with absolutely no claim in himself, casts himself unreservedly on God's mercy, on his Grace. The publican is simply an extremely clear and unmistakable example of what is true of all of us. If he is to be accepted by God as just, it has to be due to the righteousness of Christ imputed to him, for he has no righteousness of his own to bring. And all the "good" works of the Pharisee serve only to hide from him his true condition, as desperately needy for that imputed righteousness as the tax collector beside him — if not more.

Conclusion

What do we take away from this story? You may be saved and not know it: The Publican knew he needed atonement, he wanted it, he asked for it, and the Lord says he had it — but he did not dare to think he had it. The very feeling of unworthiness that made him eligible for it ironically prevented him from being so daring. Ah! If only he had known the love of Jesus for lost sinners as it would be expressed sacrificially on the Cross, he could have dared. He could have dared with confidence, with confidence that was justified because it was placed not in himself but in the Lord. As it was, he shows that it is possible to be saved and not know it.

You may also be lost and not know it: The Pharisee viewed himself as a good man and did not think he needed forgiveness, certainly not atonement. He therefore did not want it or ask for it — and Jesus says he did not have it. If only he could have seen the contrast between his own ugly self–righteousness and the beautiful holiness of Jesus' character, he would have been overwhelmed by his need. And if only he had known the love of Jesus for lost sinners as it would be expressed sacrificially on the Cross, he might too have dared to accept it. As it was, he shows that it is possible to be lost and not know it.

You can be lost and not know it. You can be saved and not know it. But you can also be saved and know it. How? By coming to God like the Publican, on no other basis. How then can you know it? You have one advantage he did not have: You have heard the parable in which he was only a character. You have seen the love of Jesus for lost sinners expressed not only in this parable but also sacrificially on the Cross. Believe, then, that God is your heavenly Father and is nothing like the unjust judge. Do not insult Him with a bribe, with claims of fasting and tithing and church attendance and good works. but cast yourself on His mercy like the Publican — and then believe also in His response: "I tell you, this man went down to his house justified." Let it be so today

.

AS A LITTLE CHILD

Luke 18:15 And they were bringing even their babies to him so that he might touch them, but when the disciples saw it they began rebuking them. 16 But Jesus called for them, saying, "Permit the children to come to me and do not hinder them, for the kingdom of God belongs to such as these. 17 Truly I say to you, whoever does not receive the kingdom of God like a child shall not enter it at all."

Introduction

One of the most touching and appealing vignettes in all the recorded life of Christ is this short passage we come to today: His blessing of the children. Its emotional impact is immediate, poignant, and simple; but it is also fraught with profound theological significance. Therefore, I want to look closely with you at four aspects of the scene which you may not have thought about before: the Identity of the Characters, the Intentions of the Carriers, the Attitude of the Christ, and the Implications for the Kingdom.

I. The Identification Of The Characters

The first thing we want to consider is the identification of the characters, the people who appear in this fascinating little three–verse scene. For we need to understand exactly who these people are in order to understand fully the significance of what they were doing. Matthew and Mark in their descriptions of this event both use the general word παιδια (*paidia*), which could be translated "children." But Luke uses the more specific term βρεφη (*brephe*), which refers specifically to nursing infants. Thus, we must revise our view of the scene, created by Sunday School art that makes the group of children include toddlers and others even older, focusing naturally on the age of the Sunday–School children for whom the quarterly in question was written—usually beginners, primaries, or juniors. There was at this time a custom among the Jews whereby parents would bring their children to the local rabbi for his blessing on their first birthday.[103] It is doubtful that this whole group of children were all having their first birthday that day, but what was happening here is probably very much in the spirit of that custom. Luke's careful use of the word *brephos*, nursing infant, is consistent with this idea. So let us imagine that these children are babies about a year old.

There is another probably false assumption we make about this scene, and that involves the parents. I seem to remember it being depicted with a focus on the mothers of these children as the ones bringing them, probably from the assumption that the fathers would have been at work. But Luke uses a masculine pronoun for the parents.

---

[103] Plummer, op. cit., 421.

That means that it was quite specifically the *fathers* who had brought them! And this again is consistent with Jewish culture.

In the Old Testament (as well as the New), the father is the head of the family. In the Old Testament one of the things this meant is that he took the lead in the religious training of his children; it was his primary responsibility. He was to be the source of godly example and spiritual leadership in his home. In this both parents participated, both parents cooperated, but the father took the lead. Solomon shows us this practice in Proverbs: *"Hear, my son, your father's instruction and do not forsake your mother's teaching"* (Prvb. 1:8). Both parents are mentioned, but the father comes first. He continues by comparing the discipline of the Lord to that of an earthly father toward the son in whom he delights (3:11–12). And though mothers are included as part of the team, it is primarily the fathers who are held accountable for religious instruction and whose instruction sons are exhorted not to ignore (4:1–5). In Exodus, it is the father who answers the children's questions about the Passover, *"What does this night mean to you?"* (Ex. 12:24–27). In modern Judaism the eldest son asks, "Why is this night different from every other night?" and the father answers by telling the Passover story.

In the New Testament we see that same basic pattern. In Eph. 6:1–4, children are to honor both parents, but it is specifically the father in verse 4 who is not to exasperate the children but *"bring them up in the nurture and admonition of the Lord."* Again, the mother is not being excluded from this duty, but the father is being asked to take the lead in it; the father is being tasked to see that it gets done. God wants Christian fathers to be intimately involved in raising their children, indeed, to be the one who takes the initiative in seeing that they are brought up in the nurture and admonition of the Lord.

If this is true, then current trends must give us pause. By one count, 17.8 million children in this country, that is, nearly 1 in 4, live without a biological, step, or adoptive father in the home; 19.5 million are without their biological father. When fathers are present, they often spend a horribly small amount of quality time with their kids.[104] It has been well said, "The biggest problem in this country is that we think raising children is something that can be done in your spare time." Now increasingly with the demands of the two–income household, mothers are falling into the same pattern. That is a huge problem, but it is not the one this passage addresses. What it says, it says to the Dads: **You** are the one responsible to bring your children to Jesus! Rearrange your priorities in any way you have to in order to see that it gets done.

II. The Intentions Of The Carriers

So that was the identity of the characters. The next thing we need to think about is the intentions of the carriers. What were these parents—these fathers—doing as they

---

104   National   Fatherhood   Initiative,   https://www.fatherhood.org/father-absence-statistic#:~:text=According%20to%20the%20U.S.%20Census%20Bureau%2C%2017.8%20million,City%20twice%20or%20Los%20Angeles%20four%20times%20over, accessed 4/1/24.

brought their babies to Jesus? If they were following the Jewish custom of bringing their one–year–olds to the rabbi for his blessing, they were performing a very significant act of faith which involved the expression of a deliberate choice. They were bringing their children to Jesus instead of to their normal local rabbi! This was a radical choice with potentially costly consequences. For Jesus has already been rejected by the religious establishment. John in his Gospel shows us what that meant. After the resurrection of Lazarus, the chief priests and the Pharisees had given orders that *"if anyone knew where [Jesus] was, he should report it"* so they could arrest Him (John 11:57). They had threatened that anyone who accepted Jesus as the Messiah should be excommunicated from the synagogue (John 12:42). As a result, many even of the leaders who believed were following Jesus secretly. Secretly? Not these families! Not these fathers!

This then was not just a nice, pious act by these fathers; it was a serious declaration of loyalty to Jesus as the one they looked to as their Messiah, no matter what the local rabbis said. They were taking their spiritual responsibility for their children very seriously. They had asked the question, "Where is God's blessing for my children to be found?" And they had answered that, as far as they were concerned, it was to be found with Jesus and not with the rabbinical establishment. So to Jesus they went, even at the risk of exclusion from the synagogue. How great and how real this risk was is shown by the level of fear Peter had as expressed in his denial of even knowing the Lord later on. How ironic that Peter was among the disciples rebuking these men for showing greater faith and commitment than even he had yet developed—except in his big talk! No wonder Jesus was so upset with the disciples for thinking these children were not worth His important time.

Fathers, do you see the example these men set for you? You too are responsible to have your family loyal to Christ and his Gospel. Today, that means being sure that they are part of a church that believes and teaches the Bible and preaches the biblical Gospel without compromise. Like these fathers, you must not do the convenient thing. The church to which your family should belong is not the one with the most exciting programs or the most comfortable building or the most charismatic leader. It is the one where the Gospel is rightly preached and the sacraments are rightly administered. And some pretty significant sacrifices are in order if that is what it takes to belong there.

III. The Attitude Of The Christ

So we have seen the identity of the characters, not mothers and toddlers but fathers and infants. We have seen the intentions of the carriers, to take their children to the true Messiah even if the religious establishment did not approve. And that leads us to what may be the most interesting thing of all: the attitude of the Christ. The irony continues with the disciples actually presuming to rebuke these fathers for wasting Jesus' valuable time. The disciples are guilty here of the same gross insensitivity which would prevent them from understanding what Jesus was really about until after the resurrection. Their apparent assumption was that the Lord was too busy with much more important things, like his controversies with the Pharisees, to waste his time on a bunch of whining babies who had no public–relations value that they could see in the slightest.

In those assumptions of course they had missed the very thing that all those controversies were about: the salvation of people like those who were coming. They missed the significance of the faith of these fathers and how valuable that would be to Jesus—far more valuable than refuting all the Pharisees (who weren't really teachable anyway) in the world. And they had missed the value of the kids themselves. In addition, they had forgotten the lesson of Luke 9:46–48, when Jesus had interrupted their argument about who was the greatest by standing a (slightly older) child in their midst and telling them to be like that. Jesus was not happy with them. In fact, He felt strongly about it. Mark says He was indignant—the only time that word is used about Him. Forbidding the little children was a serious offense! Parents—especially Dads—does Jesus have any reason to be indignant with us?

So much for Jesus' attitude toward the disciples. His attitude toward the children however was one of compassion and love. In the way He valued them He was in sharp contrast with His times. Only in the Culture of Death which has given rise to the abortion industry in our own time have we surpassed ancient pagans in callousness toward the lives of children. A letter from this period has survived from one Hilarion, away on a business trip, to his wife who was living in Egypt, and who had written to tell him she was pregnant. "If it is a male," he writes back, "receive it; if female, throw it out."[105] If female, throw it out! Decadent Romans who had more children than they thought their budget would support would "expose" them—simply leave them in the wilderness for wild animals to find. The Jews knew better, and Jesus raises the value of children even higher than that. Remember that these are only one–year old babies. They will not even remember this encounter. Yet Jesus still considers the time spent with them worthwhile. Jesus changed the world for the better, even for people who do not believe in Him, and our traditional Western compassion for children is an example of this fact—though we are departing from it again after almost two millennia of its influence.

IV. The Implications For The Kingdom

So we have seen the identity of the characters, not mothers and toddlers but fathers and infants. We have seen the intentions of the carriers, to secure for their children the blessing of the true Messiah even if the religious establishment did not approve. We have seen the attitude of the Christ, who approved the fathers, reproved the disciples, and loved the children in ways that would have seemed radical in His own times. The last matter we must consider is the implications of all this for the Kingdom.

---

[105] *Sententiae Antiquae,* https://sententiaeantiquae.com/2018/07/15/if-it-is-a-girl-a-letter-about-child-exposure/

What are we supposed to learn from all of this? What are we supposed to do about it? Does it have anything to do with *our* relationship to the Kingdom, yours and mine?

"Whoever does not receive the kingdom of God like a child," says Jesus, driving home the lesson of the encounter for his disciples, *"shall not enter it at all"* (verse17). But how do we enter the kingdom like children? The age of these children is the key to understanding how they serve as a model for entry into the kingdom. Usually we emphasize their faith—and indeed other passages do speak of that. Children are not suspicious; they are very trusting. There is some truth in that observation. But while the faith of a child is appealing, and while we should have that kind of trust in our heavenly Father once we have been convinced that the claims of Christ are valid, the faith of a child is also dangerous. The less romantic might call it not faith but gullibility. It is one of the things that makes the career of child molesters pursuable. So Scripture balances the appeal to childlike faith with appeals to have an adult faith, to grow up beyond the milk of the word to solid meat. But that is not what this passage is talking about anyway.

The fact is that these one–year–olds were not capable of saving faith in Christ, whether childlike or not. Some of them probably squalled and kicked when he took them, as they sometimes do at an infant baptism or dedication today. They were not of an age to make a rational decision to trust and follow Jesus as their Messiah or not. They did not even know what a Messiah was. Hence the word "faith" does not appear in this particular account. So what was it about these children's way of receiving Jesus' blessing that He could have been pointing to? There is only one thing it could be. It was their utter and complete helplessness.

It was their utter and complete helplessness! Remember that this passage comes in context right after the story of the Pharisee and the Publican, which also emphasizes the sinner's total dependence on God's grace, His unmerited favor. The Pharisee thought he had done a lot to earn God's favor; the Publican knew he had done nothing. It was the one who acknowledged his helplessness and threw himself on God's mercy, the one who brought nothing to the Temple but his need, who went away justified. In like manner, a baby cannot do anything to get Jesus' blessing but to be passively brought and to receive. And so, how do we enter the kingdom of God? We must come to Christ not like the Pharisee but like the Publican. We must come not like the Pharisee but like these little babies. What does that mean?

It means, in other words, that we can no more be saved by our own merit than a baby can earn his milk by his labor. We can no more be saved by our own effort than a baby can produce his own milk. We can no more be saved by our own works than a baby can buy his own milk in the store. Jesus loses no opportunity to reiterate in his own inimitable way the doctrines that would later come to be called justification by faith alone and salvation by grace alone, through faith alone, in Christ alone, apart from works.

I am not addressing the topic of infant baptism. Bring your children to Jesus always, at every age, in ways appropriate to that age; and if you believe in infant baptism by all means make it one of those ways—just don't assume it will save them unless they later come to personal faith as a result of those later ways appropriate to those later ages. Just bring them to Jesus. Bring them to Jesus as you are coming yourself, coming as they do, coming as little children for His blessing which comes by grace through faith—because that is who He is.

Conclusion

Jesus' teaching on salvation was radical. It was the opposite of what people always assume. We always put the focus on ourselves, not on Him. We will do good deeds, we say, we will keep the Golden Rule, we will come to church, we will tithe, we will be baptized, etc., etc., etc. But all this misses the point completely. It ironically demeans the free gift of God which is too great and too high ever to be earned. And it does nothing to deal with our sin, whose guilt can only be removed by the Cross.

Therefore, come to Christ as a little child, a nursing infant whose only contribution to the situation is probably to throw up on His shoulder. And then after He wipes it off, just snuggle up there and let Him love you. Come to Him as one wholly helpless, utterly dependent on God's grace, bringing nothing by which you can claim admittance except your very neediness itself. Come with the works of a little baby so you can grow up into costly confession and tried testimony and deep devotion in weekly worship, and other good works too, all done not to be saved but because you have been saved by grace through faith alone. At whatever physical age you come, come like this. For to those who come thus, admittance and welcome into the kingdom are freely given. But those who come in any other way will never enter into it at all.

THE RICH YOUNG RULER

Luke 18:18 *And a certain ruler questioned him, saying, "Good Teacher, what shall I do to inherit eternal life?"* **19** *And Jesus said to him, "Why do you call me good? No one is good except God alone.* **20** *You know the commandments: 'Do not commit adultery, do not murder, do not steal, do not bear false witness, honor your father and mother.'"* **21** *And he said, "All these things I have kept from my youth."* **22** *And when Jesus heard this, he said to him, "One thing you still lack: sell all that you possess and distribute it to the poor, and you shall have treasure in heaven; and come follow me."* **23** *But when he heard these things he became very sad, for he was extremely rich.* **24** *And Jesus looked at him and said, "How hard it is for those who are wealthy to enter the kingdom of God!* **25** *For it is easier for a camel to go through the eye of a needle than for a rich man to enter the kingdom of God."* **26** *And they who heard it said, "Then who can be saved?"* **27** *But he said, "The things impossible with men are possible with God."* **28** *and Peter said, "Behold, we have left our homes and followed you."* **29** *And he said to them, "Truly I say to you, there is no one who has left house of wife or brothers or parents or children for the sake of the kingdom of God,* **30** *who shall not receive many times as much at this time, and in the age to come, eternal life.*

Introduction

We come today to one of the saddest passages in all of Holy Scripture. For here we have a young man who asked the right question, who came to the right place to get the answer, and whom Jesus loved—but one who apparently went into eternal darkness because he loved something else more than Jesus. What can we learn to help us—and others—avoid the same tragedy? To learn it we will have to examine the Personality of the Ruler, the Problem he Posed, the Pedagogy of Jesus in answering him, the Predicament of the Wealthy, who in the natural course of things cannot be saved, and then finally the Payment of the Disciples, who, having made the commitment the Rich Young Ruler could not make, receive many times more at this time and in the age to come, eternal life.

I. The Personality Of The Ruler (Cf. Mk.10:17, Mt. 19:20)

This tragic man has come to be known as the "Rich Young Ruler" because of the full portrait we get of him by comparing Luke's account of his encounter with Christ to those of Matthew and Mark. We know that he was rich and a person of some importance. Matthew tells us that he was young, and therefore no doubt ambitious, a man on the fast track to success, undoubtedly greatly aided by his father's bank roll. He had many characteristics that are still often typical of youth to this day. He shows the impetuosity of youth in Mark 10:17, where we read that the young man *ran* up to Jesus and knelt before him. He had the enthusiasm of youth. "Good Teacher" was not the customary greeting for a rabbi; for most people, "Teacher" would suffice. Perhaps this young man was over–reaching a bit, over–anxious to make a good impression. He had the promise of youth. He was obviously a man of great aptitude and intelligence and drive. Normally even his privileged birth would not have sufficed to make him a ruler, a position usually reserved for elders in that society. He had the idealism of youth. He was asking the big questions and was prepared to make an impressive sacrifice in order to earn favor with God. Unfortunately, he also had the naivety of youth. He was not prepared for the radical kind of commitment Jesus asked of him. He did not really understand what a serious commitment it was, and went away disheartened, for he had never realized that to Jesus the Kingdom was not a game but a life–consuming cause that demanded all we have and are.

Would this young man realize his promise or waste his life? We are shocked and sobered when he turns away. Mark says that Jesus loved him. It is clear that Jesus wanted to recruit him. So why then did He run him off with such a heavy demand? In the answer to that question lies the lessons about discipleship which the passage asks us to learn.

II. The Problem He Posed (v. 18)

So here is the problem he posed. The question the Rich Young Ruler asked is one we have heard before. "What must I do to inherit eternal life?" The lawyer of Luke 10:25 asked exactly the same thing. In both cases, Jesus answered by referring his questioner to the Law. The lawyer, possessed perhaps with a bit more self–knowledge and realism, squirmed, and wanted to evade the response by asking for a definition of his neighbor which led to the Parable of the Good Samaritan. The Rich Young Ruler in his youthful brashness is undeterred. Keep the Law? Okay, he wants to know, been there, done that, what's next? Those who know Jesus well must be shuddering at this point. They know the Ruler is asking for a comeuppance. He is going to have to have to be brought down to earth, and brought down hard, not because Jesus is harsh but because with a person like this it is the only way He can bring him to a point of decision that will actually mean anything.

The question itself is interesting. Our English translations cannot quite do it justice. The verb is in the Greek aorist tense, which implies an action completed at a point in the past. We could accurately render it, "What great thing, when once I have done it, will guarantee me eternal life?" It is a question laden with assumptions which have to be knocked out of the way before the real question can even be answered. Surely the Ruler was not ignorant of Jewish theology. He would have believed that the path to salvation was keeping the Law. But he had a problem: Perfect law–keeping—by his own standards—had not given him peace or assurance about his acceptance with God. We must give him credit at least for realizing honestly that it had not. Perhaps that was the thing that made the Lord want to reach out to him. But he was asking the right question in the wrong way, for his way of phrasing it implies that he has come expecting a certain kind of answer. Like every proud though hopeless human sinner, he wants something he can do—some great act of love or devotion or sacrifice or penance—that will enable law-keeping to do what it can never do, take away sin and make us right with God. At least, unlike the Pharisee who was praying next to the Publican, he knew he had not done enough. But he was still convinced that if he just did one more thing, if it was something impressive enough, he would make it.

The young man's question was a standard question that the rabbis got all the time. And they had a standard way of answering it: Keep the Law, study the Torah so you can keep it with greater detail and precision, and even though you have not kept it perfectly, this will produce merit to cover your sins and make you acceptable if you do it often enough and hard enough and sincerely enough and well enough. Perhaps he had already asked the Rabbis and gotten that answer. But there is a fundamental problem inherent in that answer. How do you ever know when you have done enough? The Rich Young Ruler did not know *that*. It isn't knowable—but without that component he can never have peace or assurance. In any case, his very record of excellent progress on that path which left him no nearer peace with God than when he began sets Jesus up perfectly to give a different answer. If we understand that answer in the context of the encounter as we have described it here, we will see that it is a radically different answer indeed.

I expect there is someone here today who wrestles with peace and assurance. If you do, ask yourself if it is possible that you are bringing a similar set of assumptions to the question as the Rich Young Ruler did—even if you have never made them explicit enough to be conscious of them. They are endemic to the human race. If so, pay special attention to the answer Jesus is about to give. It might at first seem to make your problem worse, but if you really get it, the radical answer it gives and the profound freedom it enables will take your breath away.

III. The Pedagogy Of Jesus

Even if you do not worship Jesus as God, you must admire His skill as a master teacher here. For He deftly uses the Socratic Method to expose his student's inadequate assumptions and give him an opportunity to reach a better understanding. He asks first, *"Why do you call me good?"* Only God is good. Jesus is not denying that He is good, or that, like God—indeed, as God—He deserves that title. But He sees that the impetuous young man is not really thinking about what he is saying. Does he realize the implications of his greeting? Do we, as the readers?

Then Jesus reminds the Ruler that he knows the commandments. Why would Jesus say this? Surely, he is not accepting the premise that the young man can be saved by keeping the Law! And of course, the One who told us that to be saved in that way our righteousness would have to exceed that of the Scribes and the Pharisees (who were the Olympic athletes of righteousness) was not saying any such thing. But He was starting where the young man was. He was giving him an opportunity to confess his inadequacy, to confess his sins. The Law cannot save, but we must confront the Law and its demands, we must compare ourselves to its standard, before we are ever in a position to hear the Gospel with understanding. You cannot be saved until you know that you are a sinner, and the Law is the perfect instrument for bringing us that knowledge. Unfortunately, verse 21 shows that the Ruler had not made the comparison very profitably. How can he claim to have kept the Law perfectly all his life? Only by limiting his concept of law keeping to that which is outward, only by ignoring Christ's teaching in the Sermon on the Mount that lust and hate are sin even if we have not committed the outward acts of adultery and murder to which they lead, only then can any of us make such a ridiculous claim. And even then it will have little credibility. Yet the Ruler apparently makes it in all sincerity. Wow!

Jesus' answer is radically different: It is salvation by grace. No, it is not salvation by voluntary poverty, though it may look that way at first. People read it that way because, like the Ruler, they are looking for something they can *do* to be saved (though I haven't noticed many of them following the procedure laid down here, even if they do read it that way!). And it is because they have not noticed or have forgotten that this story flows right out of the blessing of the children with its proclamation that we have to enter the kingdom as a little child, that is, as one helpless to do anything but receive. That in itself should prevent us from turning the command to sell all the Ruler had into the Deed–in–Addition–to–the–Law that he was looking for. Instead, what Jesus was actually doing was offering the Rich Young Ruler an invitation to join his inner circle of disciples, to turn the Twelve into Thirteen. Selling his possessions was simply the preliminary to making that kind of radical commitment. The selling was in that sense a prerequisite to the following. Do you see? This is Jesus' answer to the question, "What saves when the Law can't?" And the answer is a relationship with Christ as His disciple! There is *nothing* you can *do* except receive it. But the Ruler has to ask himself first whether he is willing to be saved on that basis. And—we can hardly stand it!—he turns away in sadness because he was a man of many possessions. Don't be that guy!

IV. The Predicament Of The Wealthy (vv. 24–7)

Jesus shakes his head sadly, more sadly than the Rich Young Ruler is shaking his as he departs. And then he gives his famous parable of the Camel and the Needle's Eye. I love C. S. Lewis's little poetic paraphrase of it:

> All things (e.g., a camel's journey through
> A needle's eye are possible, 'tis true.
> But picture how the camel feels, spread out
> In one long bloody trail, from tail to snout![106]

The point of the parable is exactly what it says: that it is impossible for the rich to be saved. I expect you may have heard explanations about a gate in the Jerusalem city

---

[106] C. S. Lewis, "All Things," *The Collected Poems of C. S. Lewis: A Critical Edition*, ed. Don W. King (Kent, OH: Kent State Univ. Pr., 2015), 426.

walls called the Needle's Eye that camels had to kneel to get through and a spiritualized application about humility. Unfortunately, though that story circulates through sermons and even commentaries, there is no solid evidence that such a gate ever existed. There is a very similar proverb in the Talmud involving an elephant, used consistently as a proverb for the impossible.[107] The disciple's question, "Then who *can* be saved?" confirms what Jesus was saying: the salvation of the wealthy is flatly impossible. It isn't going to happen in the normal course of nature. Fortunately, with God, there are miracles.

Why is this so? Well, wealth has a tendency to insulate us from any sense of need, making the recognition and admission of absolute neediness which is the prerequisite to receiving a salvation that is by grace, unmerited favor, alone, next to impossible to conceive. Wealth is an insidious god, and you cannot serve God and Mammon. It is insidious. It sneaks up on us. We do not intend to put our wealth before God and trust in it instead of Him, but it takes a special effort (and lots of grace) not to do it. You will remember our discussion of the deceptiveness of wealth in sermon LVII, on the Unjust Steward in Luke 16:1–14

You've heard the story of the man who gave a testimony about how he had given his last dollar in the offering like the Widow's mite, and God had honored that sacrifice and made him a millionaire. Then someone jumped up in the back of the church and yelled, "Brother, I dare you to do it again!" How is it that we are all so sure he did not? Finally, the wealthy are often high achievers. It makes it psychologically very hard for them to accept charity—and of course that is the only way salvation can be accepted, as God's free and undeserved gift, not as our achievement.

All salvation is humanly impossible. Whenever it happens, it takes a miracle. None of us can possibly be saved, but with some it is more impossible than others! And so let the wealthy beware. And let us all pause for a while in the sobering moment following that realization before hearing the Good News: With man it is impossible, but with God, everything is possible. My salvation and yours was and is a miracle. It is one more reason not to think it can ever depend on your works. A miracle is something God has to do.

V. The Payment For Disciples (v. 30)

"And he said to them, '*Truly I say to you, there is no one who has left house of wife or brothers or parents or children for the sake of the kingdom of God, who shall not receive many times as much at this time, and in the age to come, eternal life.*'" To receive salvation, we must first give up everything, starting with any pretension that we will ever be able to save ourselves. But what we receive in return is—well, salvation. It is eternal life. Even if we got nothing in this life, eternal life would be worth any sacrifice. But the wonderful

---

[107] Plummer op. cit., 425.

thing is that even in this life we are better off as disciples of Jesus than as people who possess all the world has to offer.

Most of us are not asked to give up our wealth, but rather to hold it in trust and use if for Christ and his kingdom. But even if we were, the trade would be more than worth it. Am I promising you houses and lands and a loving family in this life? Not necessarily. What I am saying is that even if you go through everything that happened to the Apostle Paul in 2 Cor. 11:23–33, imprisonments, beatings, shipwrecks, hunger, thirst, exposure, rejection, you will be—as he was—happier than you would have been as a successful secular person, happier than he would have been as a rich and respected Pharisee without Christ.

Do you still not believe it? Listen to Paul's own words in Phil. 3:8, which will make the best conclusion this message could possibly have:

Conclusion

"More than that, I count all things to be loss in view of the surpassing value of knowing Christ Jesus my Lord, for whom I have suffered the loss of all things and count them but rubbish in order that I might gain Christ."

SPIRITUAL BLINDNESS

Luke 18:31 And he took the twelve aside and said to them, "Behold, we are going up to Jerusalem, and all the things which are written though the prophets about the Son of Man will be accomplished. 32 For he will be delivered to the Gentiles, and will be mocked and mistreated and spit upon, 33 and after they have scourged him, they will kill him; and the third day he will rise again." 34 And they understood none of these things, and his saying was hidden from them, and they did not comprehend the things that were said. 35 And it came about that as he was approaching Jericho, a certain blind man was sitting by the road begging. 36 Now hearing a multitude going by, he began to inquire what this might be. 37 And they told him that Jesus of Nazareth was passing by. 38 And he called out, saying, "Jesus, Son of David, have mercy on me!" 39 And those who led the way were sternly telling him to be quiet; but he kept crying out all the more, "Son of David, have mercy on me!" 40 And Jesus stopped and commanded that he be brought to him; and when he had come, he questioned him, 41 "What do you want me to do for you?" And he said, "Lord, I want to regain my sight." 42 And Jesus said to him, "Receive your sight; your faith has made you well." 43 And immediately he regained his sight, and began to follow him, glorifying God. And when all the people saw it, they gave praise to God.

Introduction

Well, this is an interesting pairing of episodes. Luke doesn't beat us over the head with it, but sometimes a Gospel writer can say a lot just by his choice of events to record and how he arranges them. Here, the healing of a blind man is pretty obviously . . . the healing of a blind man. But its placement calls attention to the fact that in verses 31–34 we are dealing with a different—and darker—kind of blindness.

If you are like me, you probably have to resist the temptation to feel superior to the disciples in the first part of our passage today. Jesus' words about His upcoming suffering are not terribly obscure, even given that the disciples did not have the advantage of hindsight that we have in understanding them. "How could they have missed it?" we ask. We would not have missed it! Right. That is why I want to talk to you today about spiritual blindness and hardness of heart. I'm not going to talk about the meaning of Jesus' words, for I think that in our post–Resurrection and post–Pentecost hindsight they are clear enough. Their significance cannot be stressed too much, but I have spoken about that on multiple occasions. So today I am going to focus on the spiritual blindness and hardness of heart that lay behind the disciples' lack of comprehension of them. For it was a much more serious problem than the physical blindness of poor Bartimaeus in the episode which follows. (We know his name from Mark's account.) So we will look at spiritual blindness—its nature, its seriousness, its difficulty, and, by God's grace, maybe even its cure.

I. Spiritual Blindness: What It Is

What is spiritual blindness? Perhaps the easiest way to explain what spiritual blindness and hardness of heart are, is to start by giving some examples. Here are some statements I hear all the time doing church work, trying to share the Gospel. I bet you have heard some of them too.

"Well, I'm just not very religious." Ah, I reply, but I am not talking about religion—I'm talking about truth. This often produces either a blank stare, or else even hostility; it's hard to get past either one. "Oh, I am a Baptist (or Methodist or Presbyterian—insert denomination of your choice)." Ah, I reply, that's very nice, but what about your relationship with the Lord? More blank stares or else hostility. "I'm spiritual but not religious." Now it's my turn to give the blank stare, though hopefully not the hostility. It's better to have the presence of mind to say, "That is very interesting. What do you mean by those terms?" Bottom line: It is awfully hard to connect with people on spiritual things—harder, we often feel, than the mere difficulty of the concepts involved could ever possibly explain. Surely something else is at work: spiritual blindness and hardness of heart.

But wait: You encounter the same phenomenon when dealing with believers on certain subjects, too. What about the spirit which tolerates a lack of theological integrity in the church? "Oh, I feel led to stay in and be a witness where I am." What kind of witness? Talking to a sinner from inside a church that preaches liberal theology, that does not believe the Bible, that does not take seriously the problem of original sin and nothing less than the blood of Christ as its only cure, is like trying to reform a drunk by taking him to a bar and buying him a gin and tonic! Why is this so hard for some people to see? Or what about the multitude who watch Charles Stanley or some other media preacher on TV on Sunday morning but have no relationship to an actual local congregation? Do their Bibles somehow not contain Hebrews 10:25, which commands us not to forsake the assembling of ourselves together? Somehow, they can read right past that verse (I have watched some of them do it right in front of my eyes!) without ever being struck by the strange outlandish notion that it might apply to them. It goes right over their heads, or maybe around their heads, or perhaps more accurately through their heads without leaving behind any evidence of its passage. They see the words, but somehow, they do not register. If you point them out so that they are prevented from ignoring them, however kindly, you are right back to the blank stare or hostility.

Oh, but we are just getting started. How many times have you heard someone say, in effect, "I am going to get serious about the Christian life—Bible reading and prayer—faithful church attendance—tithing—witnessing (insert practice of your choice)—*tomorrow*. I really will. But, you see, things are just a little hectic right now." *Right now*? I know people who have been saying this for years! Yet they seem blissfully ignorant of how hollow it sounds or of how little likelihood there is that "things" will be any less "hectic" tomorrow than they are today, so that they could achieve their laudable spiritual goals without the trouble of prioritizing and making sacrifices. What about the man who consistently works eighty plus hours a week and tells you that what matters is not quantity but quality time with his family! Right. As if he is not too exhausted for there to be any "quality" if and when he does get home. Or how about people who routinely turn on the television to be entertained by adultery and blasphemy? I am not saying we should never hear or read or watch stories involving those topics. Then we would have to stop reading the Bible! But instead of being driven to our knees by such content, we laugh at it! And our faces are mighty pious when we come to church on Sunday morning. *"And they understood none of these things, and his saying was hidden from them, and they did not comprehend the things that were said."*

Ouch! If I haven't stepped on *your* toes, it is probably only because I did not go on multiplying my examples long enough. So be grateful that it is high time to move on from examples to a definition. Spiritual blindness is the inability to receive spiritual things which Paul described in 1 Cor 2:14. *"The natural man does not receive the things of the Spirit of God, neither can he know them, for they are spiritually discerned."* This inability is total in the unbeliever until the Holy Spirit converts his heart. It remains partially present in the more or less carnal believer, hindering and thwarting the ongoing work of God in his life. It is progressively relieved by the process of sanctification, of growth in grace, but it will never be completely absent from our lives until we see Christ face to face. It has nothing to do with intellectual limitations or stupidity. It affects brilliant minds just as much as slow ones. It is a spiritual dullness, a spiritual denseness, an ability to hear the truth without dealing with it or being dealt with by it, which ultimately stems from our fallen and rebellious natures, encouraged by the Enemy of our souls. It is something that each one of us wrestles with at one point or another. And it was certainly operative in the disciples before the Resurrection, as we see in the passage that is before us today. It may not be at the same point for us as it was for them, but at some point we are each as capable of this blindness as they were.

II. The Seriousness Of Spiritual Blindness

Second question: How serious is spiritual blindness? It is interesting that Luke pairs this story with the healing of blind Bartimaeus. The comparison with physical blindness helps us understand the seriousness of the disability we are dealing with here. It raises the question of which of the two is the greater problem. How can we get a handle on the answer?

Students in the university system of Georgia used to have to pass a test to enter their junior year, a test I used to get to grade. Do they still take the Regents Test, the Rising Junior Exam? One of the essay questions they used to have to choose from was, "Which of your five physical senses—sight, hearing, touch, smell, taste—would you least like to lose?" Well, there were a few gluttons who wrote on taste, and a handful of musicians who picked hearing, but ninety percent of the respondents and more always chose sight. I understand. Hearing is a close second, but I think I would pick sight too.

417

I remember when I got my first pair of glasses after a couple of years of progressively finding the chalkboard in school harder to read. I was in the seventh grade. I could not stop taking them off and putting them back on, fascinated by the contrast and appalled by how much I had been missing. How had Miss Mims acquired all those wrinkles all of a sudden? I had also not adequately appreciated how her eyes lit up when a student got something right. That made even the wrinkles beautiful.

Okay, if physical sight is valuable to us, how much more should spiritual vision be? It would be a great tragedy to miss the light of this world, but how much greater to miss the Light of which our sun is only a symbol! It would be a great tragedy to miss so much earthly beauty, but how much greater to miss the beauty of holiness, the beauty of the glory of God in the face of Jesus Christ, the beauty of heavenly and eternal life! Nothing could be more serious. Spiritual blindness is a terrible thing: It can cost you God's blessing in this life and Heaven in the next.

III. The Difficulty Of Curing Spiritual Blindness

Our third point, flowing from its seriousness, is the difficulty of curing spiritual blindness. It is curious, as I have noted, that Luke leads us right into the story of the healing of blind Bartimaeus. I do not know whether he did it on purpose or not (I strongly suspect he did), but the juxtaposition of these two stories certainly helps bring out the difficulty of curing spiritual blindness. How? Look at the contrast between the results. One type of blindness got cured—the one you might think was more difficult—and the other did not. At least, not yet.

Physical blindness is much easier to cure than spiritual blindness—even for the Lord Jesus Christ Himself! All it took was one simple request from Bartimaeus, and his physical sight was restored. But the disciples were constantly asking, "Teach us to pray—explain this parable—show us the Father." Give them credit for trying. Yet still they did not see. It took one word from Jesus to cure Bartimaeus's physical blindness. All the eloquence of the eternal Word, every discourse, every parable and hard–hitting illustration of the Son of Man, every plain and blunt statement such as we read today from the greatest Teacher who ever lived, were not sufficient for the disciples' spiritual blindness. One moment was enough to remove the scales from Bartimaeus's physical eyes. Three years day and night had not yet sufficed for the disciples. If I can say it without heresy, if I can utter it without blasphemy, the one thing that seems difficult even for an omnipotent God is to remove the cataracts of spiritual blindness from the hearts of men. Don't get me wrong—Omnipotence is sufficient for this task. But every bit of that omnipotence and nothing less is what it takes!

IV. The Cure For Spiritual Blindness

Fourth, what is the cure for spiritual blindness and hardness of heart? I wish I knew! (Actually, I do. It would be more accurate to say I wish I knew an easier answer.) Part of the answer is the prescription for preconceived notions that we saw back in chapter seven when John the Baptist's assumptions got the better of him and caused him to question if Jesus really was the Messiah. (See Sermon XXVI, "Just the Facts.") Go back to the facts; go back to your relationship with Jesus. But sometimes there is a spiritual dynamic at work that makes it hard to do that. Go back to the facts? Not all the Bible reading in the world, in and of itself, will suffice to do it. Not all the good expository preaching in the world, in and of itself, will do it. Go back to your relationship with Jesus? Well, yes, but how?

Ultimately, without neglecting those necessary means, we must wait on the mysterious illuminating and convicting work of the Holy Spirit. That is what took the disciples from Luke 18:34 to Luke 24:45 — from *"And they understood none of these things, and his saying was hidden from them, and they did not comprehend the things that were said,"* to *"Then [Jesus] opened their minds to understand the Scriptures."*

Then He opened their minds to understand the Scriptures! Oh, is that not where we too want to be? So let us push on one step farther. What was it that unleashed the power of the Holy Spirit in the disciples' lives so they could complete that journey? It was the Cross! It was the death, burial, and resurrection of Christ which brought home to them in an inescapably personal way the spiritual truths they could not yet see. And so, if we truly want the Spirit to do His work of enlightening our eyes to the truths of Scripture and how they apply to us, perhaps we should seek Him for that ministry at the place where the disciples found it: at the foot of the Cross.

Truly, the Cross is the place where we have the most hope of receiving this cure. How did that work in the disciples' case? The death of Christ for these disciples was the death of all their hopes, all their dreams, their whole life's work. And as such, it was also the death of all their safe assumptions and all their preconceived notions. The death of Christ was also, perhaps most significantly, the death of all their pride. It was the death and crucifixion of any pretense that they were anything but a bunch of clueless cowards, useless deserters, and fickle traitors. The death of Christ was then inescapably to them that *death to self* which makes possible the resurrection of faith, understanding, and responsiveness to the Word of God. Only after that death were the disciples ready — only then *could* they be ready — to accept a suffering Messiah and salvation by grace, God's unmerited favor, alone. If we want to receive the same gift of sight, then we too must stand at the foot of the Cross and receive by faith that death. That is the place — the only place — where the Spirit's ministry of illumination, which is the only answer to the problem of spiritual blindness, can be found.

Conclusion

For all of us, as for the original disciples, the only cure for spiritual blindness is to be driven to our knees at the foot of the Cross. And so I plead with you this morning: go there first, on your own, before God has to drive you! Would you pray this prayer with me? If God gives you the ability to pray it and truly mean it, and to keep praying it and meaning it as a regular part of your devotions, I think it could take us an important step at least in that direction.

"Father, I do not know where my blind spots are—if I did, they wouldn't be blind spots—but I am willing to admit that I must have some. I ask you to drive the sharp, two-edged sword of your Word through where it needs to penetrate. I am willing and ready to suffer whatever death to self is necessary to make this penetration possible. And I am ready and willing to make whatever changes may be necessary in response— for your Son said, *'He who is willing to do His will is he who will know the doctrine, whether it be of God'* (John 7:17). Make us willing for the sake of your Son, and for His glory."

Amen.

THE CONVERSION OF ZACCHAEUS

Luke 19:1 And he entered and was passing through Jericho. 2 And behold, there was a man named Zacchaeus; and he was the chief tax collector, and he was very rich. 3 And he was trying to see who Jesus was, and he was unable because of the crowd, for he was small in stature. 4 And he ran on ahead and climbed up into a sycamore tree in order to see him, for he was about to pass through that way. 5 And when Jesus came to the place, he looked up and said to him, "Zacchaeus, hurry and come down, for today I must stay at your house." 6 And he hurried and came down and received him gladly. 7 And when they saw it, they all began to grumble, saying, "He has gone to be the guest of a man who is a sinner!" 8 And Zacchaeus stopped and said to the Lord, "Behold, Lord, half of my possessions I give to the poor, and if I have defrauded anyone of anything, I will give back four times as much." 9 And Jesus said to him, "Today salvation has come to this house, because he too is a son of Abraham. 10 For the Son of Man has come to seek and to save that which was lost."

Introduction

This familiar story is essentially a passage about what it means to be saved. There is no concept which is more central to the Christian faith or less understood by the general populace and by many professing Christians. Jesus said, *"Today salvation has come to this house, because he too is a son of Abraham. For the Son of Man has come to seek and to save that which was lost."* But what is this salvation that had come to Zacchaeus? How is salvation related to conversion? To being "born again?" And what is conversion? Is it essentially a decision? A commitment? An experience? A relationship? A transaction? Or in some sense all of these things. And more? To understand Luke's answer to these questions, we had better begin by defining some terms.

First, **religious awakening:** that which happens to the congregation when the sermon is over. Okay, for those of you to whom that definition does not apply, let's get serious. First, **salvation.** To be saved is to be rescued, delivered, brought from danger to safety. It is what a lifeguard does to a person in danger of drowning. To understand what spiritual salvation is, we have to ask, rescued or delivered from what? And the biblical answer is, from sin, that is, from its reality, its penalty and its effects, the sum of which is damnation and spiritual death. And what is sin? It is at its simplest disobedience or even any lack of conformity, inward or outward, to the law of God. It is what causes all men to fall short of the glory of God (Rom. 3:23). It is whatever is not of faith (Rom. 14:23). It is knowing to do good and doing it not James 4:17). It is all unrighteousness (1 John 5:17); it is rebellion, and its wages is death (Rom. 6:23). So Scripture would describe it. Salvation then is being delivered or rescued from all of that: from sin itself, from its degradation, and from its consequences in this life and the next.

Conversion is basically a word for change. Jesus said, *"Truly I say to you, unless you are* converted *and become like children you shall not enter the kingdom of heaven"* (Mat. 18:3). You have to be changed, converted, turned into something you are not. Interestingly, modern automotive technology has given us a perfect illustration of the New Testament usage of this word. Have you ever heard of a "conversion van?" It is a van whose normal insides have been stripped out and replaced with luxurious seating and appointments. Instead of the standard benches, you now have captain's chairs, tables, a mini–fridge, maybe a couch hiding a fold–a–bed. In just that way, a sinner who has been converted is the same on the outside but has new "equipment" on the inside. Old things have passed away and behold, all has become new.

Born again is a metaphor Jesus used to describe **conversion** when he was talking to Nicodemus: "You must be born again" (John 3:3). It emphasizes that the change which takes place is nothing less than supernatural: It involves receiving new spiritual life from above and adoption into God's family, a new relationship with the Father. So how do all these terms relate? Do you have to be **converted**, i.e., **born again**, to be **saved**? Jesus said so flatly to Nicodemus. But little Zacchaeus has his own way of illustrating these truths. His familiar Sunday–School story emphasizes four essential points about salvation and conversion.

I. Salvation (And Hence Conversion) Is Needed By All

First, salvation (and hence conversion) is needed by all. Nicodemus was a son of Abraham, and a pretty righteous one, and yet he still needed to be saved. Zacchaeus was a son of Abraham, and not quite so righteous a one, and he too still needed to be saved (verse 9). The Jews tended to assume that because they were the people of God they were automatically saved, just by being in the right human family. But the New Testament launches a frontal assault on that assumption almost from its very first word. Don't even think it, said John the Baptist: God is able to raise up children to Abraham from these stones! (Mat. 3:9). In modern terms, people often assume that they are saved because they are members of a church, or because they were baptized, or because they grew up in a Christian family. But nothing could be further from the truth.

As the cliché has it, God has no grandchildren. All men have sinned and fallen short of the glory of God, and they are saved by faith in Christ's work on the Cross— not by their parents' faith or their church's faith! You have to personally admit that *you* are a sinner and ask for God's forgiveness, confessing with *your* mouth that Jesus is Lord and believing in *your* heart that God raised him from the dead (Rom. 10:9). There is nothing in Scripture about your parents or your pastor being able to do it for you! All need salvation because all are sinners. Your family, your church, your culture, your personal uprightness in human terms, and your sincerity have nothing to do with it. If you are a sinner (and you are), you need a savior. And if you want your own way and have therefore been disobedient to God in anything (and you have), you are a sinner.

That is why even a "good" person needs to be saved. He needs to be converted from self to God in his basic orientation. Zacchaeus certainly did. And so do you.

II. Conversion (And Hence Salvation) Is Available To All

All right, salvation (and hence conversion) is needed by all. The second point is that conversion (and hence salvation) is available to all. Zacchaeus was a tax collector. Now, tax collectors are not exactly the most popular of all public servants today, but it is probably impossible for you to conceive how despised they were in the first century. As we saw back in sermons XVII and LI with the conversion of Levi and the parable of the Publican and the Sinner, Judea was crushed under the heel of the occupying Roman army, and the tax collectors were Jews who were getting rich by collaborating with the enemy. Not only that, but they were notorious for taking advantage of their fellow Jews. A tax collector was expected by his Roman masters do deliver a certain sum, and anything he collected beyond that he got to keep for his services. So the incentive to cheat his fellow Jews was built into his job. Zacchaeus was no doubt the most hated and despised man in Jericho, and for good reason. He had earned — *earned* — all the contempt that we have for a thief, an extortioner, and a traitor, combined. If I can use so low a word in the pulpit here in the South, he was a *scalawag*! That is the only thing worse than a carpetbagger. And he was not just any tax collector; he was the chief of them, the head honcho, the worst of the bunch.

Zacchaeus, in other words, was a truly despicable person who, in order to pursue his job at all, had made a profession out of hardening his heart. He was not only the lowest of sinners, but he had made a continual practice of killing in himself every ounce of compassion and fellow–feeling for his countrymen. Statistically, he was the last person you would ever expect to be able to repent and be converted and be saved. And that is the point. If Jesus could save Zacchaeus, he can save anybody! He can save you. Salvation (and hence conversion) is needed by all. Conversion (and hence salvation) is available to all. Do you remember the story of the Rich Young Ruler from just a few weeks ago? Do you realize what just happened? The camel just went through the needle's eye! Who then can be saved? With God, all things are possible.

III. Salvation Is, In Essence, A Personal Relationship With Jesus Christ

All right, salvation (and hence conversion) is needed by all. The second point is that conversion (and hence salvation) is available to all. The third point Zacchaeus show us is that salvation is, in its essence, a personal relationship with Jesus Christ. I know that sentence has become a bit of an Evangelical cliché. But if we can de–cliche it, we will see that it contains a profound truth.

Zacchaeus is the perfect paradigm, the perfect picture, of a concept of salvation that has been the theme of the whole Gospel from the beginning. Jesus does almost nothing but offer the invitation, "Come and follow me!" But this person needed to bury his father first, and that one had bought a pair of oxen and needed to check them out. The rich young ruler went away sorrowful because he had many possessions. The disciples were those who had accepted the invitation. So when Jesus invited Himself to Zacchaeus' house, the key to Zacchaeus' salvation is that he hurried down from the tree and received him gladly. That makes all the difference between being saved and being lost. Think of the parable of the marriage feast: It is the very significant relationship of table fellowship that is the Bible's constant picture of what salvation is—climaxing in The Lord's Supper that we will share later today as it anticipates the Marriage Supper of the Lamb.

You see, man assumes, "If I do my best, God will accept me." But man's best is only filthy rags, not a wedding garment. We have it all backwards. We think, because conversion is a necessary component of salvation, we'd better get busy and change ourselves. But you cannot make the change that is required. You can only make yourself a more respectable sinner. That is the best you can do, and it is not enough. The reality is, because God has accepted us—if we accept that—we are enabled to do more than our best. You don't change yourself so God will accept you; it is the fact that God has accepted you in Christ that changes you! The change flows from the relationship. In other words, based on your personal relationship with Jesus Christ—that you take Him as your personal Lord, God, Savior, Messiah, and follow Him—based on your having that relationship with Christ, God counts your sins as Christ's, His sacrifice as the payment for your sins, and His righteousness as yours. That is what we mean by "justification by faith."

It is important to see that justification by faith is not a mere legal fiction. It is *rooted* in the *relationship* you have with Christ when you accept the invitation to follow Him, a relationship that flows from the very incarnation itself, and which is of such a nature that it makes it right for God to treat you that way instead of treating you as you deserve. It is right because Jesus has become your official Representative as the Second Adam; As Adam was the head of the human race, so Christ is the Head of restored humanity and thus relates to you in such a way as to make the substitution just and right. (That is a topic for another day.) And because it is a relationship with the very Lord of Glory himself, it does things to you. Because of that relationship you will never see the flames of Hell. Because of that relationship you will never be the same again. Or, to put it another way, God doesn't grant you forgiveness and justification because you have sufficiently converted yourself; conversion, the change, flows from the nature of justification. It is all contained in the *relationship*. When Jesus invites Himself to dinner, say yes! And this leads us to the fourth point:

IV. There Is Therefore No Salvation Without Conversion (Change)

All right, salvation (and hence conversion) is needed by all. The second point was that conversion (and hence salvation) is available to all. The third point Zacchaeus show us is that salvation is, in its essence, a personal relationship with Jesus Christ. And the fourth is that therefore, there is no salvation without conversion.

How do we see that here? From the very moment that his new relationship with Jesus began, Zacchaeus began to be a new person. It did not take him long to show it. *"Behold, Lord, half of my possessions I give to the poor, and if I have defrauded anyone of anything, I will give back four times as much"* (verse 8). On hearing this, Jesus announces that salvation has come to Zacchaeus's house—not as a reward for his repentance, but because this dramatic change in Zacchaeus was the evidence that his new friendship with Jesus was real. Conversion is not a new leaf we turn over to assure God's acceptance; it is the new attitude which comes with a new relationship with God's Son and which leads to a new heart and therefore new behavior.

We are not saved by perfect obedience, because we cannot render it. We are not saved by imperfect obedience, because God cannot accept it. So we can only be saved by grace, God's unmerited favor, His offer of friendship based on the sacrifice of Calvary. And so Jesus does not say, "Shape up and we will see." He says, "Come and follow me—yes, you, just as you are, right now. Just as you are, without one plea but that my blood was shed for thee. Leave your nets—your tax table, like Matthew—your sycamore tree—and come. Nothing will ever be the same again, but all you have to say right now is, 'Yes.'"

I once heard Leighton Ford say, "God loves you just as you are, but he loves you too much to leave you that way." That's right. But all Jesus is asking of you right now is a real "Yes." He will take care of the rest. But don't you see: If you do respond with a *real* "yes," it will by its very nature involve making right what is wrong. Wanting to do so is part of the "yes," and the ability to do so flows from the relationship thus established, for you are now no longer attempting to do it alone. You can't say, "Yes, Jesus, I will follow you—as long as you are going where I was going to go anyway." That is not a "yes!" It's a "no" disguised as a yes. And, oh yes, He knows the difference. So there is no salvation without conversion, without a change in your life. Why? Because you cannot enter into a relationship with Jesus and not be changed by it. The change is not the ground, but it is the evidence that salvation has come to this house. We cannot judge because only God sees the heart, but if there has been no change it is *prima facie* evidence that there has been no justification and hence no salvation. You cannot know Jesus and stay the same.

Conclusion

Salvation (and hence conversion) is needed by all. Conversion (and hence salvation) is available to all. Salvation is, in its essence, a personal relationship with Jesus Christ. And therefore, there is no salvation without conversion. You cannot be in a relationship with Jesus and stay the same person that you were before.

The rich young ruler kept all his wealth, and much sorrow with it. Zacchaeus gave away half of his and did it with great joy. What was the difference? One of them said a real "yes" to a real relationship with Jesus as Lord and therefore Savior, and the other did not. Jesus still says, "Come and follow me." What is your answer today?

GOD'S BUSINESS

Luke 19:11–27 And while they were listening to these things, he went on to tell a parable, because he was near Jerusalem and they supposed that the kingdom of God was going to appear immediately. 12 He said, therefore, "A certain nobleman went to a distant country to receive a kingdom for himself and then return. 13 And he called ten of his slaves and gave them ten minas and said to them, 'Do business with this until I come back.' 14 But his citizens hated him and sent a delegation after him, saying, 'We do not want this man to reign over us.' 15 And it came about that when he returned, after receiving the kingdom, he ordered that these slaves to whom he had given the money be called to him in order that he might know what business they had done. 16 And the first appeared, saying, 'Master, your mina has made ten minas more.' 17 And he said to him, 'Well done, good slave; because you have been faithful in a very little thing, be in authority over ten cities.' 18 And the second came, saying, 'Your mina, master, has made five minas.' 19 And he said to him also, 'And you are to be over five cities.' 20 And another came, saying, 'Master, behold your mina, which I kept put away in a handkerchief. 21 For I was afraid of you, because you are an exacting man; you take up what you did not lay down and reap what you did not sow.' 22 He said to him, 'By your own words I will judge you, you worthless slave. Did you know that I am an exacting man, taking up what I did not lay down and reaping what I did not sow? 23 Then why did you not put the money in the bank, and having come, I could have collected it with interest?' 24 And he said to the bystanders, 'Take the mina away from him and give it to the one who has the ten minas.' 25 And they said to him, 'Master, he has ten minas already.' 26 'I tell you, to everyone who has shall more be given, but from the one who does not have, even that which he has shall be taken away. 27 But these enemies of mine who did not want me to reign over them, bring them here and slay them in my presence.'"

Introduction

In this age of Yuppies and upward mobility, no topic captures the imagination of a certain type of person more than "investment strategy." Should you be in money market funds, mutual funds, certificates of deposit, or IRAs? These are not unimportant decisions, because your economic freedom in your last years, with all the opportunities for serving the Lord such freedom would bring, is at stake. But a far more important decision than how you invest your money is how you will invest your life. For unless you are already investing your life in making disciples for Jesus now, any economic freedom you might gain through investing your money wisely will just be wasted in the future. Jesus' parable here is about both. It is about investing money on the surface, but ultimately it is about how we should be investing our lives.

Jesus told this parable to combat the preconceived notions that the Jews had about the coming of the kingdom of God—preconceived notions we have run into before in this series. They were expecting Jesus to overthrow the Roman Empire and replace it with a glorious and righteous Jewish one, and as he got closer to Jerusalem, they were expecting him to do it then and there. That is the point of the word "immediately" in verse 11: They were expecting the Kingdom to come "immediately." But Jesus gives them an entirely different scenario. He is going away to receive a Kingdom that seems to have little to do with the people he is talking to, most of whom appear in the story as rebels against the master rather than as His triumphant supporters in the war with Rome. He will apparently bring this Kingdom with Him when He returns at an indefinite time in the future. In the meanwhile, their place in that kingdom depends on how faithful they are to Christ while He is gone. They may be great, ruling ten or five cities, or small, losing even the responsibility they started out with, or outside the Kingdom altogether and slain in the King's presence. In hindsight, we can see that the nobleman in the story was Jesus, the trip his Ascension into Heaven, his servants the Christians, and his enemies the unbelievers, especially the unbelieving Jews who would refuse his reign as soon as they realized it didn't fit their preconceived notions.

So there are two lessons here. First, the kingdom is not coming "immediately," i.e., right then in the lives of the people Jesus was addressing, and unless they repent, it won't be coming for them at all. Second, their status in the kingdom when it does come will depend on their faithfulness to Jesus now and during the long wait they are actually facing; their faithfulness will depend on their relationship to Him; their relationship with Him will depend on their attitude toward Him; and their attitude will depend on their concept of Him. Did I say "theirs"? I might as well say "yours." We can see how this all plays out in our own lives by asking two questions. First, do you believe in Jesus Christ enough to take Him as your Lord? And second, do you love Jesus enough to live for him?

I. Do You Believe In Jesus Christ Enough To Take Him As Your Lord?

Do you believe in Jesus enough to take him as your Lord? Most of the people in the crowd did not. They are the ones in the parable who did not wish Him to reign over them (verses 14, 27). Since these people are slain in the last verse, it is clear that the Lordship of Christ is the thing that separates the lost from the saved.

To understand why this is so, we have to examine the relationship between the Lordship of Christ and the Kingdom. And that relationship is not hard to see once you put the question that way. In the Kingdom of God, Jesus is the King. Those then are the citizens of the kingdom who have embraced His kingship. For in Scripture there are only two masters, Christ and the Devil. There are only two kingdoms, the Kingdom of God and the kingdom of Satan. There are only two paths, the path of light and the path of darkness. There are only two gates, the narrow gate that leads to life and the broad one that leads to destruction. There are only two final dwellings, only two homelands, Heaven and Hell. There are only two conditions, saved and lost. Hard as it may be for Post–Modern people to understand, there really are no other choices. And your relationship to Christ determines how you are related to each of these decidedly and inescapably binary pairs. (Do you begin to realize why certain enemies of Christ today are so insistent on being "non–binary"? It is not an accident.) To ask which kingdom you belong to is the same question as to ask which king you serve. If you serve Elizabeth I, you are an Englishman. (I use Sixteenth–Century examples because that is the Century I naturally inhabit.) If you serve Philip of Spain, you are a Spaniard. It is as simple as that.

Satan loves to encourage this watered–down Christianity that surrounds us in which you can have Jesus as your Savior without having him as your Lord. Why? Because it encourages professing believers to avoid the only question that matters and hence allows them to avoid ever becoming real Christians. He has even used an essential Christian doctrine, the doctrine of salvation by grace alone apart from works, in such a way that it seems to support this nonsense, as if insisting on the Lordship of Christ is somehow to reintroduce works into the plan of salvation. To name this view accurately, I am forced to employ three highly precise and technical theological terms: Balderdash! Horsefeathers! Fishfuzz!

Yes, nonsense it is: heretical nonsense. I choose my words carefully. And I think I can show you just how nonsensical this pseudo–Gospel is. Let us just imagine two hypothetical "believers." One of them says, in effect, "Okay, sure, I want to take advantage of Jesus' blood to pay for my sin so I can avoid going to Hell, but as for running my life, He can go jump in the lake!" He might be too pious to say it in those words, at least not in public, but that is what his attitude amounts to. The other says, "Yes! Now I see! Jesus died for *me*, to pay for *my* sins. I deserve Hell but He offers me Heaven as a free gift purely by grace—at the price of his blood! [He might be compelled to break into song, the whole thing is so wonderful.] *What wondrous love is this?*[108] *Amazing grace, how sweet the sound!*[109] *Oh, marvelous grace of our loving Lord!*[110] *And can it be that I should gain an interest in my Savior's blood? Died he for me who caused his pain, for me who him to death pursued? Amazing love! How can it be that Christ my God should die for me?*[111] Okay: How can I then deny Him anything who has given everything for me while I was yet a sinner? I will probably fail Him a hundred times, but what else can I do? I *must* follow Him! I *must* serve Him! I *must* obey Him!"

Now you tell me: Which one of these two understands the Cross? Which one of them understands and embraces salvation by grace alone? Yes, it is still grace alone because he is not saying, "If I obey enough, If I obey well enough, if I obey sacrificially enough, maybe Jesus will save me." No. That will not do at all. He is saying, "Jesus has saved me freely by pure grace; *therefore*, I want to follow Him!" The whole Gospel, the power of God for salvation to them that believe, is contained in that one little conjunctive

---

[108] Anon., "What Wondrous Love is This?" *Trinity Hymnal*, op. cit., 261.
[109] John Newton, "Amazing Grace," *Trinity Hymnal*, op. cit., 460.
[110] Julia H. Johnson, "Marvelous Grace of our Loving Lord," *Trinity Hymnal*, op. cit., 465.
[111] Charles Wesley, "And Can it Be that I should Gain?" *Trinity Hymnal*, op. cit., 455.

adverb *therefore*, powerfully so if you understand how it functions in the context of that sentence. "Jesus has saved me freely by pure grace; *therefore*, I want to follow Him!"

Again, then: Which one of these two understands the Cross? Which one understands and has accepted salvation by grace alone? Which one of them understands and has accepted the Gospel? There is only one of them who does, and I don't even need to tell you which one it is. The first statement is not only nonsense, it is blasphemous nonsense, damnable nonsense. You are a citizen of the kingdom—a forgiven and pardoned citizen—if and only if you acknowledge the authority of the King. For He is the One who must give you that pardon by grace alone. And so I repeat: In the final analysis, the question on which the forgiveness of sin, eternal life, salvation, belonging to the kingdom of Heaven depends really turns out to be "Do you believe in Jesus Christ enough to take him as your Lord?" Or, in other words, "Will you have this man to reign over you?"

But there is a second question the passage also raises. The first one deals with whether or not we will be in the kingdom. The second deals with how far in we will be. And it is

II. Do You Love Jesus Enough To Live For Him?

The first question, do you believe in Jesus enough to take him as your Lord, differentiates the slaves of the master from his enemies. This second question differentiates the first two servants from the third servant. Do you love Jesus enough to live for him? It is this question, actually, and not their relative success in making money, that is the difference between the first and the third servants. Do you see that? Let me try to show you.

The key to the failure of the third servant is his attitude toward the Master. What does he say when his turn comes to give an account? "*Master, behold your mina, which I kept put away in a handkerchief. For I was afraid of you, because you are an exacting man*" (verses 20–21). Contrast that with the excitement in the voice of the first servant: "*Master, LOOK! Your mina has made ten minas!*" The first servant is happy because he knows the Master he loves will be pleased with him. The third is afraid because his Master is an exacting man—or, as the King James familiarly put it, "a hard taskmaster."

But where did the third servant get this idea? To whom was the Master a hard taskmaster? Not to the first servant, or the second! They received an extravagant reward for their faithfulness, all out of proportion to what they had done. For each mina you make your boss, he puts you over an entire city? I found a source from 1962 that listed a mina as worth sixteen 1962 dollars. Well, I remember that when it was introduced in 1963 a Ford Mustang cost $2368.00. The price was on signs everywhere you turned. It would cost at least fifteen times that today. So let's say a mina is worth about $240.00 in today's money (2024). It's close enough to give you the idea. You make your master 240 bucks and you get for your reward . . . an entire city! Do *you* want in on that contract? Do you want to work for that boss? Or are you going to be basically saying that he makes

Scrooge before he was visited by the ghosts look generous? Where does this third servant get off?

It is very significant that the master says he will judge the third servant by his own words. You call me a hard taskmaster? Okay, I'll show you what one is really like. Take away his mina and give it to servant number one! Perfect love casteth out fear, and the love of this servant for the One he had taken as Lord was not sufficient to do so. His hard words about the master became a self–fulfilling prophecy. So here is the question that will determine the quality of your Christian life: Do you serve Jesus out of love or fear? Recall our two hypothetical believers. The first one was not a believer at all. He was just mouthing words without the slightest understanding of what they mean. The second one was full of love for his Lord, love that casts out all fear. He *died* for us! Do you understand? How is anyone who did that going to turn around and be mean to us? We can trust Him. We can cast everything on Him. Unfortunately, it is possible to forget that first love, or have it squelched by legalistic teachers who have spent too much time with the third servant. And so we can be in the kingdom but hide our mina in a handkerchief. Don't be that guy!

We hide our mina out of fear. But the opposite of fear is love! Let us think about the first two servants as they appear in contrast to the third. They show us the nature of loving service.

First, loving service takes risks and is willing to be vulnerable. Why not? What does it have to fear? The very nature of doing business is risk taking. How could the first two do that? Well, what do you think would have happened if they had come back and said (honestly said), "Sir, we did our best with your money, but the stock market crashed, or a tornado hit our store and the insurance company wouldn't cover it, or we were robbed on our way to the bank." You can tell they assume the Master would understand because they were willing to take the risk of investing his money. They were willing to take risks because they had confidence that their master would not be unjust or harsh, and that was the key to their success.

Second, loving service gives glory to God and does not need to horde it for the self. Hear what the first servant said in verse 16: Not, "My brilliant investment strategy has paid off," or "Look what I have done," but *"YOUR mina has made ten minas."* By contrast, the third servant is completely focused on himself—*he* was afraid, *he* put the mina in the handkerchief. We are naturally selfish people. The only way I know of not to be focused on myself is to be filled with love for someone else. That is what took the first servant from "I have gained" to "*Your* mina has multiplied." The third servant's focus on himself is totally unproductive. The first servant gives all the glory for his success to the Master. Love is the difference!

Third, loving service is rewarding. Can you hear the excitement in verse 16? *"Master, LOOK! Your mina has made ten minas!"* The first servant was happy and fulfilled before he ever gave his report, because he knew he had pleased the master he loved, had served him well. Because of love, the service itself was rewarding, irrespective of any reward that might be forthcoming. And then he received the master's response! Are there any more joyful words in any language than *"Well done, thou good and faithful servant"*? (Mat. 25:21). Note also: the reward of faithfulness is further responsibility. He was put over ten cities. Forget this nonsense about Heaven being a bunch of boring nerds sitting on clouds playing harps! We will be fulfilled because we will have meaningful work to do in which we can serve our Lord and receive His pleasure forever. What? The reward of faithfulness is more work? Isn't that a punishment? In human companies, it often is. But in heaven it is reward indeed: meaningful work to do to serve our King whom we love! What could be better than that? (I know it is also called the Sabbath Rest, but that does not mean we won't have meaningful things to do. Ruling cities does not sound like being a cloud–potato!)

Conclusion

These then are the two most important questions you will ever ask or answer: Do you believe in Jesus enough to take him as your Lord? Do you love Him enough to live for Him? A "yes" to the first question should lead straight to a "yes" to the second. Sometimes it tragically does not. But if we see Him for who He is, we will desire nothing but to say to them both, "Yes! Now I see! Jesus died for *me*, to pay for *my* sins. I deserve Hell but He offers me Heaven as a free gift purely by grace—at the price of his blood! *What wondrous love is this? Amazing grace, how sweet the sound! Oh, marvelous grace of our loving Lord! And can it be that I should gain an interest in my Savior's blood? Died he for me who caused his pain, for me who him to death pursued? Amazing love! How can it be that Christ my God should die for me?* Okay: How can I then deny Him anything who has given everything for me while I was yet a sinner? I will probably fail Him a hundred times, but what else can I do? I *must* follow Him!"

And follow Him I shall. Will you join me?

THE TRIUMPHAL ENTRY

Luke 19:28 And after he had said these things, he was going on ahead, ascending into Jerusalem. 29 And it came about that when he approached Bethphage and Bethany, near the mount that is called Olivet, he sent two of his disciples, 30 saying, "Go into the village opposite you, in which as you enter you will find a colt tied, on which no one has ever sat. Untie it and bring it here. 31 And if anyone asks you, 'Why are you untying it?', thus shall you speak, 'The Lord has need of it.'" 32 And those who were sent went away and found it just as he had told them. 33 And as they were untying the colt, its owners said to them, "Why are you untying the colt?" 34 And they said, "The Lord has need of it." 35 And they brought it to Jesus, and they threw their garments on the colt and put Jesus on it. 36 And as he was going, they were spreading their garments in the road. 37 And as he was approaching, near the descent of the Mount of Olives, the whole multitude of the disciples began to praise God joyfully with a loud voice for all the miracles which they had seen, 38 saying, "Blessed is the King who comes in the name of the Lord; Peace in heaven and glory in the highest!" 39 And some of the Pharisees in the multitude said to him, "Teacher, rebuke your disciples." 40 And he answered and said, "I tell you, if these become silent, the stones will cry out!"

41 And when he approached, he saw the city and wept over it, 42 saying, "If you had known in this day, even you, the things which make for peace! But now they have been hidden from your eyes. 43 For the days shall come upon you when your enemies will throw up a bank before you and surround you and hem you in on every side, 44 and will level you to the ground and your children within you, and they will not leave one stone upon another, because you did not recognize the day of your visitation." 45 And he entered the temple and began to cast out those who were selling, 46 saying to them, "It is written, 'And my house shall be a house of prayer,' but you have made it a robber's den." 47 And he was teaching daily in the temple, but the chief priests and the scribes and the leading men among the people were trying to destroy him. 48 And they could not find anything that they might do, for all the people were hanging upon his words.

Today we need a second passage:

Zechariah 9:9. "Rejoice greatly, oh daughter of Zion! Shout in triumph, oh daughter of Jerusalem! For behold, your king cometh unto thee. He is just and endowed with salvation, humble and mounted on a donkey, even on a colt, the foal of an ass."

Introduction

Since we have reached Palm Sunday today, and since it is such a significant day in the life of our Lord in preparation for what was coming on Good Friday and Easter, it is good that we come in Luke's Gospel to that auspicious and appalling event when the King rode in triumph into Jerusalem seated on a donkey to receive the fickle adulation of the crowds. We want to receive Him as King today with equal enthusiasm but less fickleness, hopefully as a result of greater understanding. So today we need to join that crowd on the slopes of the Mount of Olives with the ancient city of Jerusalem laid out in front of us on the opposite hill, the Temple Mount, across the Brook Kidron.

We come then to a great crisis in the life of the Lord Jesus. It is Sunday. By Friday He will be dead; by the next Sunday, risen again. So He declares himself openly as Messiah by riding into Jerusalem in deliberate fulfillment of Zechariah 9:9. *"Rejoice greatly, oh daughter of Zion! Shout in triumph, oh daughter of Jerusalem! For behold, your king cometh unto thee. He is just and endowed with salvation, humble and mounted on a donkey, even on a colt, the foal of an ass."* Do you get how shocking that must have been, given His previous reticence about accepting that title—King, Messiah—because of His contemporaries' misunderstanding of it? (*Messiah* means "anointed one," and the anointing is specifically the anointing with oil that marked David out as the future king.) Well, why do it now? It was a deliberate and calculated act designed to provoke a final show–down with the Jewish religious establishment. For us, it not only reveals Jesus as King, but it also tells us much about what kind of king He is. He was a King facing a great crisis; He was a King who felt a great compassion; and He was a King who was filled with a great cause. So here is the question for us today: Will we, unlike the crowds in the story, be able to receive Him as such?

I. He Was A King Who Faced A Great Crisis

Jesus was first a king who faced a great crisis. To understand why, we have to ask, who was this man, and why was He on his way into Jerusalem at this time? We know a lot from the rest of Scripture. He was the Lamb of God who taketh away the sin of the world (John 1:29). For without the shedding of blood there is no remission of sin (Heb. 9:22). Yet the blood of bulls and goats cannot take away sin (Heb. 10:4). But God was determined to redeem a people for his name. And so the Father had long ago started the preparation for His plan to achieve this seemingly impossible task. We know that preparation as the Old Testament with its Exodus, its Passover, its Temple worship, and its sacrificial system. It is all coming to fulfillment now, and that fulfillment is about to unfold right before our eyes.

The people sensed that all of their history, indeed, all of human history had led up to this moment, but they did not fully get how it had done so. Focused on a military Messiah who would deliver them from Rome, they had forgotten the greater element of God's promises to David. For every drop of blood from every goat or bull slain on every Jewish altar for two thousand years had been just so many ticks of the clock that kept beating, beating, beating until they led to this moment, when the Lamb of God would indeed take away the sins of the world, able and authorized to do so because He was the Second Adam and the King of all creation. They knew something important was happening, but they did not fully grasp that the souls of men were at stake; the salvation of all creation was on the line. And so, contrary to their expectations, their King was the Lamb of God who would be sacrificed.

So why was Jesus entering the City as a conquering King? Why accept that title and its acclamation now? Because it was as King as well as Lamb that Jesus would suffer. Because it would not do for this great act, the very climax of history, to be done in a corner! It would not do for the Son of Man to be beheaded in some out of the way dungeon like John the Baptist. It would not do for Him to be stoned by some Jewish mob in a back alley. This thing must be done publicly, openly, etched deep onto the pages of History by the very lackeys of imperial Rome.

And therefore, to that end, in deliberate fulfillment of Zechariah 9:9, the King entered His city. All Israel was in a messianic fervor, yearning for the overthrow of Rome, the liberation of Jerusalem, and the restoration of the glory of the Solomonic kingdom—for that was their understanding of Old–Testament prophecy. The inhabitants of Jerusalem knew Zechariah 9:9 like we know John 3:16. *"Rejoice greatly, oh daughter of Zion! Shout in triumph, oh daughter of Jerusalem! For behold, your king cometh unto thee. He is just and endowed with salvation, humble and mounted on a donkey, even on a colt, the foal of an ass."* They knew exactly what that donkey meant. It was intentional. It was pre–arranged. It was provocative.

In her radio play *The Man Born to be King*, Dorothy L. Sayers not unreasonably interprets the conversation between the disciples and the donkey's owners as cloak–and–dagger sign and countersign.[112] And if there was any doubt about the messianic meaning of what was happening, it was confirmed. When the Pharisees desperately pleaded with Jesus to rebuke his disciples, He cast the challenge back in their teeth, refusing to stop the demonstration He had occasioned. He was casting down the gauntlet. The King has come! The ball is now in your court, Jerusalem. The King has come! Will you accept Him or reject Him? That is, will you accept Him as the King He is, or reject Him because He refuses to be the kind of King you wanted? Will you bow to Him or spit at Him? Will you worship Him or mock Him? Will you serve Him or betray Him? Will you follow Him or kill Him? Either way, the die is cast. You must make your choice . . . And you must make it *now!*

If it was a crisis moment for Jesus, then it was for the people too. It was, as verse 44 says, the day of their "visitation." *Visitation* is an Old–Testament theological word having to do with those great moments like the Exodus when God "visited" his people for judgment and salvation. In Exodus it had meant the ten plagues, the Passover, the crossing of the Red Sea on dry ground, the destruction of the pursuing Egyptian army and the giving of the Law. Now that kind of time has come for them again, and they did not even know it.

But it was not just for first–century Jerusalem. For every people—for every man and woman—there are those times of visitation, of opportunity, when God is accessible and grace for repentance is offered. Such moments are a crossroads, a time of decision

---

[112] Sayers, op. cit., 203.

in which is fulfilled the Scripture which says that now is the day of salvation. Well, when the church of Jesus Christ gathers in His name to proclaim such a text from the Word of God as this, we must believe that by the appointment of God such a time of visitation has come for us today. Therefore, if you have never given your life to Christ, if as a believer there is something you need to confess and put right with Him, do not resist in the day of visitation lest not one stone of your life be left upon another, as was literally fulfilled for Jerusalem when the Roman legions crushed it for its rebellion in AD 70. Bow before the King today!

II. He Was A King Who Felt A Great Compassion

Jesus was a King who faced a great crisis. He was also a King who felt a great compassion. The time of Jerusalem's visitation had come, and she did not even know it. And so in verse 41 Jesus weeps over the city. There are two Greek words translated "to weep." The first. δακρυω (dakruo) means to shed tears silently, to weep; these are the tears Jesus famously shed at the tomb of Lazarus, sympathizing with the tears of his friends but knowing He was about to turn them into rejoicing by raising Lazarus from the dead. The second, κλαυω (klauo), on the other hand, means to shed those tears aloud, not to weep but to sob. It is that second verb that is used here.

These were not stoic tears. They were gut–wrenching. Jesus was sobbing in agony over the fate of most of the City, which would reject Him and His salvation. If you had been standing there you probably would have been embarrassed by it. Oh, the irony! Surrounded by all the joy and celebration of people who thought they were going to receive deliverance from Rome, Jesus wept, knowing that they were going to reject Him and crucify Him and that most of them would be lost forever, missing the deliverance, not from Rome but from Satan and sin, that He had actually come to bring them. He could hardly stand it. His tears were not tears of self–pity, though given the rejection He was about to experience and the form it would take, that would have been justified. "If only *you* had known!" He cries. It was the lostness of Jerusalem that moved Him so deeply.

Have you ever felt unappreciated? Have you ever been misunderstood? Have you ever been rejected? You are in good company! Hold on by faith to Jesus Christ, for He has been there. It is Okay that such rejection hurts. He understands that. But His tears were not for Himself but for the ones rejecting Him. What will give you strength when you go through such experiences? What will enable you to carry on with grace and courage when your witness for Jesus is rejected or even ridiculed? That could happen in normal times, but it is even more likely, and more likely to be a strong and bitter rejection, in these times into which we are moving in this increasingly post–Christian world,

What can sustain you and enable you to persevere in faithfulness in such times? Only one thing: the compassion of our Lord Jesus Christ Himself! We can and should shout hosannas (He did not rebuke them; indeed, He pointedly refused to do so). There is a time to shout condemnations of evil (He did that too, on more than one occasion). But what will keep us from disillusionment and bitterness when those messages are rejected or even laughed at and held in contempt? What will keep our messages from deserving that contempt? The bottom line is this: Are our hearts broken for a sinful world? Are our hearts broken for a sinful world? When we love like Jesus and weep like Jesus, then we will have the strength to withstand rejection. But even more: when we love like Jesus and weep like Jesus, then some of those lost people will see His compassion, and some of them will accept His love.

III. He Was A King Filled With A Great Cause

Jesus was a King who faced a great crisis. He was a King who felt a great compassion. He was also a King who was filled with a great cause. No sooner did Jesus arrive in Jerusalem to all these shouts of hosanna than He went to the Temple and continued His challenge to the religious establishment by throwing out the moneychangers. Why would He do that? Because of His zeal for the honor of His Father, because of His zeal for the glory of God, and therefore His zeal for His House. The Temple was supposed to be a house of prayer, but they had made it a den of thieves. How exactly had they done that?

There were two rackets being practiced in the Temple at this time. To understand them is to understand what Jesus meant by calling it a den of thieves. Why did there need to be moneychangers in the first place? Because you could not use regular money in the temple (which might have Caesar's picture on it—a graven image!) [Dr. Williams shows 1st–Century coin.] So you had to exchange your regular currency for what was called "the shekel of the temple." You've seen the Forex booth in the airport? They had one right there in the Temple. Well, that was not wrong in itself. The problem was that an exorbitant exchange rate was being charged for that shekel, so that the Temple was getting rich at the people's expense—clean contrary to the Old–Testament prohibitions of usury. Well, why would you need these special shekels? Because of the second racket. Any animal you brought to sacrifice must of course be a male of the flock without blemish. Of course, a priest would be glad to inspect it for you, and his eagle eye could invariably spot an unfortunate blemish you had overlooked. But, not to worry: The Temple considerately kept a supply of certified "unblemished" animals on hand for you to purchase—at ten times the going price! No wonder Jesus was angry.[113]

This act of cleansing the temple was also in fulfillment of prophecy. Just as the donkey Jesus rode into Jerusalem was in fulfillment of Zechariah 9:9, so the cleansing of the temple was in fulfillment of Malachi 3:1–3. *"'Behold, I am going to send my messenger, and he will clear the way before me. And the Lord whom you seek will suddenly come to his temple, and the messenger of the covenant in whom you delight, behold, he is coming,' saith the*

---

[113] See Edersheim, *Life and Times*, op. cit., 364–74 for a detailed description of these practices.

Lord of hosts. *'But who can endure the day of his coming? For he is like a refiner's fire and like fuller's soap. . . . For he will purify the sons of Levi and refine them like gold and silver so that they may present unto the Lord offerings in righteousness.'"* This was not lost on the religious leaders or on the people either. And the leaders' anger at being called out in front of the people no doubt added to the determination they already had to get rid of this troublesome lay rabbi, a determination that would be fulfilled in the course of the very next week.

Jesus was a King filled with a great cause, the redemption of his people and the glory of His Father. He could not enter the Temple without cleaning it out. Do not think He can come to live in your heart without cleaning it out either! For since the rending of the veil at Calvary, the temple of God is now the hearts of His people, which are indwelt by the Holy Spirit. So what is in yours? Pride? Envy? Bitterness? Anger? Laziness? Apathy? Greed? Gluttony? Impure lusts? Willfulness? Unbiblical priorities? Do not think Jesus can come in there without turning over some tables! It's not that you have to clean it up first. He could never come if that were the case. You cannot clean it up without His help. Salvation is by grace, not by works. But be prepared for some changes when He comes!

If we are followers of this King, we must be a people who are zealous for the purity of God's house. This is so whether we think of our personal lives as individuals or of the church. We and our churches must be pure in doctrine, pure in morals, pure in purpose. What is your purpose? What is your church's? If it is anything less than the glory of God, then we are not walking worthily of our calling, seeing that we have a King who was filled with a great cause.

Conclusion

The Triumphal entry is all about the kingship of Jesus. He was a King who faced a great crisis and who brings one into our lives. He was a King who felt a great compassion and calls us to feel it and live by it too. He was a King who was filled with a great cause, the glory of God. And for His servants, it is enough that they be like their Master.

THE WICKED HUSBANDMEN

Luke 20:1 And it came about on one of the days while he was teaching in the Temple and preaching the gospel, that the chief priests and the scribes with the elder confronted him, 2 and they spoke, saying to him, "Tell us by what authority you are doing these things, or who is the one who gave you this authority?" 3 And he answered and said to them, "I shall also ask you a question, and you tell me: 4 Was the baptism of John from heaven or from men?" 5 And they reasoned among themselves, saying, "If we say, 'from heaven,' he will say, 'Why did you not believe him?' 6 But if we say, 'from men,' all the people will stone us to death , for they are convinced that John was a prophet." 7 And they answered that they did not know where it came from. 8 And Jesus said to them, "Neither will I tell you by what authority I do these things."

9 And he began to tell the people this parable: "A man planted a vineyard and rented it out to vine growers and went on a journey for a long time. 10 And at the harvest time he sent a slave to the vine–growers in order that they might give him some of the produce of the vineyard; but the vine–growers beat him and sent him away empty–handed. 11 And he proceeded to send them another slave, and they beat him and treated him shamefully and sent him away empty–handed. 12 And he proceeded to send them a third, and this one they also wounded and cast out. 13 And the owner of the vineyard said, 'What shall I do? I will send my beloved son. Perhaps they will respect him.' 14 But when the vine–growers saw him, they reasoned with one another, saying, 'This is the heir. Let us kill him that the inheritance may be ours.' 15 And they threw him out of the vineyard and killed him. What therefore will the owner of the vineyard do to them? 16 He will come and destroy these vine–growers and will five the vineyard to others." And when they heard it, they said, "May it never be!" 17 But he looked at them and said, "What then is this that is written, 'The stone which the builders rejected, this became the chief corner stone?' 18 Everyone who falls on that stone will be broken to pieces, but on whomever it falls, it will scatter him like dust." 19 And the scribes and the chief priests tried to lay hands on him that very hour, and they feared the people; for they understood that he spoke this parable against them.

Introduction

The next episode in Luke's Gospel is the challenge to Jesus' authority and His response, the Parable of the Wicked Husbandmen. It is important to note that our passage today follows immediately after the Triumphal Entry and picks up on its theme, the kingship of Jesus. So let's remember that He has just ridden into the city on a donkey in fulfillment of Zechariah 9:9: "*Rejoice greatly, oh daughter of Zion! Shout in triumph, oh daughter of Jerusalem! For behold, your king cometh unto thee. He is just and endowed with salvation, humble and mounted on a donkey, even on a colt, the foal of an ass.*" He was claiming the kingship, even if it was not the kind of kingdom, as we saw last week, that the Jews were expecting. And so we saw Jesus revealed as a King facing a great crisis (the

Crucifixion), as a King who felt a great compassion (for the lost sheep of Jerusalem), and a King filled with a great cause (the glory of his Father and the salvation of men).

Well, that cause, zeal for His Father's glory, led Him to cleanse the temple, and that act naturally led to the challenge to His authority we read of today. *"By what authority are you doing these things?"* So this week we will focus on the Authority of the King. It is a topic of great relevance in our day, when we hear people saying, "No one has a right to tell me how to worship; no one has a right to tell me what to believe; no one has a right to tell me how to live." Never has Western society been more like the Book of Judges, in which *"Every man did what was right in his own eyes"* (Judges 21:25). So we must ask: Is there anyone who has the authority to tell us how to worship, what to believe, how to live? And we will find the answer in the passage before us today.

I. The Challenge To Jesus' Authority (vv. 1–8)

The situation we read about today flowed right out of the events which had just happened. Jesus had ridden into Jerusalem in fulfillment of prophecies that proclaimed Him as the King, the Son of David. Not only had He made such claims, He had acted on them, and started stepping, yea, stomping, on certain rather sensitive toes. He had just shut down a rather nice and profitable business the priests had been operating on the side in the Temple, in which they were taking advantage of the people. So it is not at all surprising that we find them saying, *"Tell us by what authority you are doing these things, or who is the one who gave you this authority?"* (verse 2). Or, as we might put it, "Who do you think you are? Who told you that you could do that? Who died and left *you* king?" For only the Messiah himself would have had the authority to go over the High Priest's head to reform the temple worship, and they certainly did not want any messiah who was going to mess up their little racket.

Jesus' response to their question was typical: It was to ask one of his own: What do you think about John's baptism? From God or men? Jesus often found a question to be the best answer to a question. His response was not an evasion, but a surprisingly direct answer. For the Baptist had proclaimed Him Messiah; John had already answered the question they were asking Jesus. John had called him the Lamb of God who taketh away the sins of the world (John 1:29). Jesus, who came after John, was before him, and John was not worthy to untie his sandals. So their question about Jesus' authority had already been answered. What did they think of the prophet who had answered it? The response they give about John then entails their response to Jesus as well.

The exchange is wonderfully ironic. These men have come to challenge Jesus' authority, but all they succeed in doing is discrediting their own authority as religious teachers of Israel. They know they are trapped. If they say John was from God, they have to admit that Jesus is the Messiah. But if they deny it, they will be in trouble with the people, who all hold John as a prophet. So what do they do? They punt. They chicken out and say they do not know. *Do not know?* Are they not the official teachers of the Jewish religion? How can they not know whether the most popular preacher of their day save Jesus himself is legitimate or a fraud? Are they not responsible for having an informed opinion on such a topic? It's their job! It is no wonder they show up in the parable as the vinedressers who get replaced.

There are some lessons for the contemporary church in this little exchange. Surely there is a basic competence in theology and a basic intellectual integrity required of its ministers, its teachers. Their job is to lead the people, to disciple them, to train and equip them to do the ministry of the church and to speak the gospel with intelligence and integrity into their world. Surely then our pastors are responsible to keep themselves informed about the world as well as grounded in the Word. How else are they to shepherd the flock of God? They should have some idea whether the popular religious teachers of their own day are from God or from men. They should have some expertise in how to tell shepherds from hirelings and sheep from wolves, and they should say so with reference to the truth rather than to what will make them popular. When I was pastoring in Marietta, Georgia, we had a good Christian bookstore—one which actually sold books, if you can believe that. The manager got to know me, so when I was in there, he would often refer people who had questions about what the best book was on a particular topic to me. One such customer was asking me whether the Moonies were a legitimate Christian group or a cult. "Why haven't you asked your pastor about this?" I asked. I got a look like, "Where did you fall to earth from, Pluto? That is the craziest idea I ever heard." This person found it a crazy idea that his "preacher" should be expected to know any such thing. I find it a crazy idea that he should presume to stand in the pulpit when he does not. And yet "shepherds" like this are the rule, not the exception in our day. It is no wonder the sheep are being led astray into the false pastures of Health and Wealth and moral relativism and neopaganism, or worse cults still.

Christians, we need to return to the foundations, one of which is the primacy of truth. Jean Luc Picard said to a wavering Wesley Crusher that "The first duty of every Starfleet officer is to the truth, whether it's scientific truth or historical truth or personal truth! It is the guiding principle on which Starfleet is based. And if you can't find it within yourself to stand up and tell the truth about what happened, you don't deserve to wear that uniform!"[114] Does this not apply even more to Christians in general and ministers of the Gospel in particular? Yet these priests had no concern for the truth, and therefore they had no answer to the Lord's question. And what do you look for when you read the Bible or hear it expounded? A "blessing?" The confirmation of your preconceived notions? Or are you really open to what God is telling you? Jesus said, "*If you abide in my word, then you are truly disciples of mine, and you shall know the truth, and the truth shall set you free*" (John 8:31–32). Let us be free indeed!

II. The Basis Of Jesus' Authority

---

[114] Episode "The First Duty," *Star Trek: The Next Generation*.

441

The challenge to Jesus' authority had failed, and so that authority is affirmed and confirmed. But what do we mean when we say this? What kind of authority did Jesus have? There are at least three kinds of authority, and Jesus had them all.

The first is what we might call **"informational authority."** I learned my Greek from Dr. Dale Heath at Taylor University and my Hebrew from Dr. Gleason Archer at Trinity Evangelical Divinity School. These men were known as "authorities" on biblical languages. What does that mean? Dr. Heath did not order or command the genitive singular of λογος (logos) to be λογου (logou). But he knew it so well that when he told you that such was the case, he spoke with authority. What he said on that topic had weight; it could be trusted. You need not be afraid to build on it. Now, Jesus had much more than this kind of authority, but He did not have less. When He spoke of the nature and character of the Father, of the Law and of Grace, He knew whereof He spoke. He spoke with authority, not as the scribes. The scribes dickered and argued and quoted one another and found no end in wandering mazes lost; but Jesus said, "Thus saith the Lord." Or even more dramatically, "Ye have heard it said [by the rabbis] . . . But *I* say unto you . . ." This is what the people meant when they said that Jesus was not like the scribes. In verse 17, Jesus is the stone which the builders rejected but which has become the corner stone. His words are foundational. You can trust them; you can rest on them; you can build on them. He speaks with authority, not as the scribes.

Second is what we might call **"delegated authority."** That is the kind of authority that _____ _____ has as our church treasurer. Because she has been duly appointed and authorized, she has the authority to write checks in the name of the church, and the bank will honor her signature and transfer the money. It will not honor yours, because that authority has not been delegated to you. Did Jesus have this kind of authority? Yes. In verse 13 he is the Son sent by the Father; therefore, all authority is given unto him in heaven and earth.

Finally, there is what I will call **"inherent authority."** This is authority by right of creation. The act of creation is what makes someone an author, and an author has *author*–ity. Even on a human level we recognize that if you make something, that act of creation gives you certain rights to determine how the thing you made will be used. If I write a book, only I have the authority to sign a contract for it to be published. If you pirate the book and publish it without my permission, it is wrong. Why? Because you did not make it! Creation creates rights. But our rights are only derivative, because we had to get our materials from God; we even got the minds we used to come up with the ideas from God. God has that right absolutely because He created the universe out of nothing. He does not owe anybody anything. This is the highest form of authority. And because Jesus was with the Father when the world was made, it belongs to Him. In the parable, this is expressed by the fact that the owner "planted" the vineyard. That is what gives him a right to its fruit.

So Jesus as the King of the Kingdom has informational authority: He speaks the truth and can be trusted to do so. He has delegated authority: The Father has committed all judgment into His hand. And He has inherent authority: He not only planted the vineyard; He created the world and designed the grapevine. All authority is given unto Him, in Heaven and on earth and under the earth. Thanks be to God!

III. The Extent Of Jesus' Authority

Because he is the Son of the Father who planted the vineyard, Jesus has all authority over everything, over every aspect of life. But two areas of authority are emphasized here. The first is that He has **the authority to order the worship of God**. He has the right to tell us how to worship. It is of course the case that this challenge to His authority flowed from His daring to reform temple worship without even bothering to consult the high priest or give him the time of day. That is what brings that issue to the forefront. It is precisely Jesus' authority to do just that which is at issue here. When He says that God is a Spirit and those who worship Him must do so in spirit and in truth, we must listen, and we must realize that any other worship is not acceptable worship at all. When He says not to make His Father's house a den of thieves, then we had best not do so. When He has His apostle say not to forsake the assembling of ourselves together, we had best not think it is Okay to just watch a religious service on TV. These are not just nice things to do; they are the orders of the One who has the right to order them. The One who has the right to expect it and the authority to demand such things requires them of us.

The second area of Jesus' authority is emphasized by the parable he told in response to the whole situation. He has **the authority to receive the fruit of the vineyard**. In the parable, the vineyard of course is the people of God. Let us say that the fruit is the fruit of the Spirit from Galatians 5:22–23. In hindsight I think that is a legitimate application. So let us picture the Lord coming to us and looking for love, joy, peace, longsuffering, kindness, goodness, and self–control, against which there is no law. These are not just nice goals for our personality. They are the fruit of the vineyard, what the vines are supposed to be producing, and Jesus has a right to expect to find that fruit when He visits it. It is His vineyard after all! But what kind of grapes are growing there? If He comes and finds hate for love, complaining for joy, anxiety for peace, impatience for longsuffering, selfishness for kindness, scheming for goodness, or an unfaithful, harsh, undisciplined spirit for self–control, then how are we different from the wicked vinedressers of the parable? They cast out and killed the son of the owner, and we crucify the Son of Man afresh!

Conclusion

Have you thought about the fact that the Lord Jesus Christ has authority as King? This means the right to expect things from us. It specifically means the right to determine what is the true worship of God and what is not. It means the right to receive the fruit of the vineyard. That is part of what it means to call Him "Lord." He is not a hard taskmaster, but He has the authority and the right to receive our worship and to determine what that is, and the authority and the right to expect fruit from His vineyard. That means we have a responsibility to render it to Him. Did I say responsibility? Yes. But let us rather call it the privilege. For what else can it be when He has given everything for us? Let us then worship Him in spirit and in truth and yield ourselves to His Spirit, that He may find fruit in due season when He comes. Amen.

RENDERING TO GOD AND CAESAR

Luke 20:19 And the scribes and the chief priests tried to lay hands on him that very hour, and they feared the people, for they understood that he spoke this parable against them. 20 And they watched him and sent spies who pretended to be righteous in order that they might catch him in some statement so as to deliver him up to the rule and authority of the governor. 21 And they questioned him, saying, "Teacher, we know that you speak and teach correctly, and you are not partial to any but teach the way of God in truth. 22 Is it lawful for us to pay taxes to Caesar or not?" 23 But he detected their trickery and said to them, 24 "Show me a denarius. Whose likeness and inscription does it have?" And they said, "Caesar's." 25 And he said to them, "Then render to Caesar the things that are Caesar's, and to God the things that are God's." 26 And they were unable to catch him in a saying in the presence of the people, and marveling at his answer, they became silent.

Introduction

Probably the least popular branch of the federal government is the Internal Revenue Service or I. R. S., known to readers of "Snuffy Smith" as "The Infernal Revenue Service." It was no different for first–century Palestine, except that the intensity of hatred and resentment was infinitely greater (as we saw when we studied Zacchaeus a few weeks ago), since the taxes were collected corruptly and were going to an occupying power. Therefore, this question represented the perfect opportunity for the Pharisees to get Jesus in trouble—and they desperately wanted to get Him in trouble because he had just claimed the kingship in his Triumphal Entry into Jerusalem and then disrupted their very profitable business ventures in the Temple as we saw recently. In reading this exchange we see two things: a conspiracy for the First Century, and a commandment for the Twenty–First.

I. A Conspiracy For The First Century

The indispensable background for understanding this encounter is the passage we studied two weeks ago, referred back to in verse 19, "*that very hour*." This whole encounter flows from the Triumphal Entry, which led to the Cleansing of the Temple, which led to the Challenge to Jesus' Authority, which led to the Parable of the Evil Vineyard Workers, in whom Jesus' opponents clearly recognized a not–so–flattering portrait of themselves. They wanted to lay violent hands upon Jesus then and there but could not because of their fear of the people. So instead, they sent spies to try to trip Him up in front of the people so that He would lose their support and become more vulnerable. As usual, their plots backfire and blow up in their faces.

Why the spies? Because Jesus was on to the leaders. He would have recognized them immediately, and His guard would have been up. So these sneaky fellows come pretending to be "righteous," i.e., sincere seekers and potential disciples. They begin by trying to butter Him up in verse 21. *"Teacher, we know that you speak and teach correctly, and you are not partial to any but teach the way of God in truth."* Beware of people who introduce themselves that way! The hidden implication is, "It's safe for you to say something really controversial, because we aren't going to turn you in." As if Jesus had ever shown any signs of being worried about such a thing! And as if they had not pretty clearly signaled to a person as perceptive as Jesus the fact that they were up to no good.

Why this particular question about taxes, though? These spies were hoping to impale Jesus on the horns of a dilemma. *"Is it lawful to pay taxes to Caesar or not?"* If Jesus says no, He will be in trouble with the governor, and the spies can denounce Him to Pilate as a rebel against Roman rule. If He says yes, He will immediately lose the support of the crowd, who hate the occupation with a passion. Brilliant strategy! The Lord is damned if He does and damned if He doesn't. Either way, they are thinking, they will be rid of this burr in their saddles, this troublesome prophet with the radical ideas. And they cannot imagine that there is any way out of this devilishly clever (see what I did there?) dilemma they have created. But once again—surprise, surprise!—Jesus is too smart for them.

Jesus rarely answered questions with a simple, straightforward "yes" or "no," though how He was going to avoid it here was hard for His opponents to conceive. But imagine their chagrin when they heard the response: *"Show me a denarius."* Oops! *"Whose likeness and inscription does it have?"* And they said, "er . . . er . . . Caesar's." And He said to them, "Alrighty then [That's the Amplified Version], *render to Caesar the things that are Caesar's, and to God the things that are God's."*

This is not just a clever response; it is actually brilliant truly brilliant, a typical example of Jesus' uncanny ability to turn the tables on His enemies. It was a principle of law accepted by the Jews at this time that the sovereignty of a state extends as far as its coins are good. This is accepted by most people. I have a few British Pounds, continental Euros, Indian Rupees, and Ugandan Shillings left over from my mission trips. What do you think would happen if I tried to spend them at Walmart? Not going to work? Why not? Because we don't live in Britain., Europe, India, or Uganda. A second legal principle that goes along with the first one is that the right of coinage implies a right of taxation. Whoever backs the money and makes it legal tender has the right to collect the taxes. So the spies must have known they were trapped as soon as Jesus asked them for that denarius. But what can they do? One of them reluctantly pulls the coin from his purse and hands it over. Ahem. Just whose face and inscription is on this coin? Between the lines of Luke's text there is suddenly much hemming and hawing and shuffling of Sadducaic sandals and Pharisaic feet. Why, it's Caesar's! Oops.

Well, then. *"Render unto Caesar the things which are Caesar's, and unto God the things which are God's."* Oh, my. The fact that the coin was handed over by one of the questioners means that the Jewish establishment has already accepted the legitimacy of Roman rule, the authority of Caesar. Jesus has just cut the whole ground right out from under their feet. The result is that the anger of the crowd at "Render unto Caesar" is deflected from Jesus to their own leaders, who were up to their ears in complicity and collaboration. Wow! Getting into a controversy with Jesus—especially one in which you are insincere and trying to trick Him—is a really bad idea.

But there is more to it than that. The head of Caesar on the coin is technically a "graven image." So what is this Jewish fellow doing with such a coin? Out of deference to fierce Jewish religious feelings on such matters, the Romans allowed special coins to be minted for Palestine with the head left off so that pious Jews could do business without violating their scruples.[115] (This may help explain, by the way, the references in Revelation 13:16f to the opponents of the Anti–Christ being unable to buy and sell without his "mark"—he will apparently be less sensitive to such feelings than Caesar was!) Well, you could get the special coins if you wanted them, but lots of people didn't bother. So the questioner has not only been forced to out himself as a Roman collaborator; he has also revealed himself as one who loves money more than God. He is breaking the commandment against graven images! In other words, if you would spend a coin like *that* on *anything*, why suddenly balk at paying it in taxes? To the people in the crowd, that would be straining at a political gnat after having swallowed a blasphemous camel!

So Jesus' opponents, in an effort to get him into trouble with the crowd, have succeeded only in turning its murderous anger on themselves. No wonder they decided to "become silent." As H. L. Mencken once said, "Before a man opens his mouth, it is always safe to assume he is a fool. After he speaks, it is seldom necessary to assume it."[116] Once again, Jesus has allowed these spies of the Pharisees and the priests to dig their own hole and then fall into it. When the wisdom of man pits itself against the Wisdom of God, can we expect any other outcome?

II. A Commandment For The 21st Century

The first century confrontation is fascinating, but there is a lesson for us in our own century in it as well. And the first and most obvious part of that message is: pay your taxes! Render unto Caesar. If you are going to enjoy the benefits of government, you need to help pay for them. If you like being protected from crooks and foreign armies and having roads to drive on, you need to help pay for these things. If you like having a currency (the coins, the denarii) that is recognized as legal tender so that you do not have to use the barter system, then you have to give some of it back to make the whole system work.

Now, lots of questions remain unanswered and left for us to wrestle with. How much is it legitimate for the government to ask for? What if it is spending some of that

---

[115] See Plummer, op. cit., 465–6.

[116] Qtd. in John Algeo and Carmen Acevedo Butcher, *Problems in the Origins and Development of the English Language*, 5th ed (Boston, MA: Thomson Wadsworth, 2005), 24.

money on things we disapprove of, yea, on things that God forbids? What if it is being irresponsible with it and throwing it down any number of ratholes? Surely such questions need to be addressed through legitimate political channels. And Scripture does not give us easy answers to them, not answers so clear that we can automatically treat our political opponents who are fellow believers as enemies and heretics. But it does uphold the basic principle that we do have a fundamental obligation to help support the government—even a very imperfect one like that of the Roman Empire.

Jesus here foreshadows what Paul will teach us in Romans 13:1-7. Government is ordained by God. Even an imperfect government—the only kind we have these days—exists by His permission and wields authority He has given it. The benefits of living under even an imperfect government are great when compared to the difficulties of living in the chaos that inevitably results from anarchy. For the earliest Christians it was a *very* imperfect government, the Roman Empire as it descended into corruption under Nero. But look what it gave them: the *Pax Romana*, the Roman roads, a world unified under one language (Greek), all of which were absolutely essential to the impressive success the Gospel had in those early years; and all of which were provided by a government that required the worship of Caesar! The early Christians disobeyed Rome where they had to, but they honored it where they could, and in doing so they were consistent not only with Paul's teaching but also with Jesus' hints in our passage today. They understood that in a fallen world even an imperfect government—even a *bad* government—is better than anarchy, better than no government at all. If you don't believe it, it is because you have never lived under anarchy. Let us pray that you never get that opportunity to learn this lesson!

"But what about Hitler or Idi Amin or Pol Pot or Sadam Hussein or Vladimir Putin?" somebody may ask. Could there be a tyrant so evil that Romans 13 would not apply to him? Paul's instruction is based on the premise that even Rome had a general tendency to punish evil and reward good. What if there were a government that reversed that formula completely? Surely Nazi Germany tempts one to think there could be. The Anti–Christ will be such a ruler, if no one else has been. But whether there may be exceptions or not, let us be sure we do not miss the general rule: Our leaders should be honored, obeyed except when they command us to disobey God, and supported by our taxes. Otherwise, we *"oppose the ordinance of God."*

Well, the obvious lesson is "Pay your taxes." Render unto Caesar. But there is another which is maybe less obvious but even more important. We are also supposed to render unto God. Render what? To Caesar we render taxes and qualified obedience—obedience, that is, *up to a point*, the point where he commands us to disobey God. What do we render to God? Well, to answer that question let's go back to the thing which set up the first part of Jesus' answer: the portrait of Caesar on the denarius. What gives Caesar a right to your taxes? The image of Caesar on your coins. Because his image is on the coin, he has a right to the coin. Okay, then, what bears the image of God? You do.

Man himself and Woman herself are together the image of God. You may need to give Caesar your coin; what you render to God is your *self*. God has the absolute right to your whole self, body, soul, and spirit. He has an absolute right to all your worship, all your obedience, all your loyalty, all your resources (of which you are the steward, not the owner), all your devotion, all your love. To give any of it to anything else is idolatry, it is treason, it is rebellion, it is disobedience, it is sin.

The basic principle of what we owe to God and to Caesar then is clear. But applying it, especially in reference to the state, requires some thought, because one of the things God requires is obedience *to* the state, but only up to a point. Where exactly is that point? Let me try to give some practical guidance in dealing with that problem as it applies to our own democracy.

Implicit in the contrast between what we owe to God and to Caesar is the principle of limited government. You owe Caesar your taxes, but you do not owe him your soul. Or to put it another way, there is only one Messiah, and the state is not it. Your ultimate allegiance is to God, and thus any state that asks for *that* kind of allegiance commits treason against the very God who grants it its existence and authority. God has ordained the powers that be, and He permits some pretty corrupt ones to exist at times. But He has preferences about the kind of government we should have. He disapproves of totalitarian government in principle, because it usurps some of His prerogatives. If He disapproves of totalitarianism, then He must approve of limited government in principle. If He approves of limited government, then He favors those forms which support and enable it, such as separation of powers and checks and balances.

I'm not just saying this because I happen to be a classical political conservative. It is not just implicitly but explicitly biblical. You can see it in the Old Testament. Why was it forbidden for the same man to hold both the kingship and the priesthood? Because then one man would have too much power. It is the first articulation of the principle of the separation of powers in history, and Saul got into the serious trouble that eventually spelled the end of his reign by violating it when he offered sacrifices himself rather than waiting for Samuel in 1 Samuel 15;9f.

So what is the upshot? We should thank God for the privilege of enjoying the freedoms we have as Americans, the foundations for which were laid by Him in the Old Testament. Some at least of our founding Fathers were aware of this and knew what they were doing when they incorporated such principles as the separation of powers into our Constitution. We should be thankful specifically for that. And therefore, we should oppose tyranny here and everywhere, and we should never take our freedoms for granted—even as we live in submission to the legitimate authority of government, even corrupt governments.

These principles are important, and it is important that we understand them because they are not simple—the complexities and corruptions of the actual governments we have to live under make them sometimes difficult to apply. So let's take another shot at trying to articulate them and their application. God permits totalitarian governments to exist, and when Christians live under them, they are to obey them as far as they can. But they should never legitimize their totalitarian claims by obeying them where they overstep their authority and ask us to disobey the laws of God. The Christian has not only the right but the obligation to disobey any law which commands disobedience to God. (This is not just laws we don't like, by the way. They specifically have to command disobedience to God to be in this category.) But when we have to disobey the government, we must not do so in such a way as to imply any disrespect for the government's legitimate authority. There is a fine line here, but we may be required to walk it more and more as our own society sinks deeper into secularism. We must always remember both sides of the equation: Render unto Caesar the things which are Caesar's, and unto God the things which are God's. Caesar gets your coin; God—and only God—gets your soul.

Conclusion

These then are the ground rules: render unto Caesar the things which are Caesar's, and unto God the things which are God's. What do we render to Caesar? Acknowledgement of his limited authority; honor; our limited obedience; taxes; prayers for his wisdom that we might live our lives in peace. What do we owe to God? Everything that we have, are, or ever hope to be; our whole selves, body, soul, and spirit; our worship, our adoration, our ultimate allegiance. To each, his own. Render unto Caesar the things which are Caesar's, and unto God the things which are God's. Amen.

NOT OF THE DEAD BUT THE LIVING

Luke 20:27 Now there came to him some of the Sadducees (who say that there is no Resurrection), 28 and they questioned him, saying, "Teacher, Moses wrote for us that if a man's brother dies, having a wife, and he is childless, his brother should take the wife and raise up offspring to his brother. 29 Now there were seven brothers, and the first took a wife and died childless, 30 and the second, 31 and the third took her, and in the same way all seven died, leaving no children. 32 Finally the woman died also. 33 In the Resurrection, therefore, which man's wife shall she be? For all seven had her as wife." 34 And Jesus said to them, "The sons of this age marry and are given in marriage, 35 but those who are considered worthy to attain to that age and the Resurrection from the dead neither marry nor are given in marriage. 36 For neither can they die any more, for they are like angels and are sons of God, being sons of the Resurrection. 37 But that the dead are raised, even Moses showed in the passage about the burning bush, where he calls the Lord 'the God of Abraham, Isaac, and Jacob.' 38 Now, he is not the God of the dead, but of the living, for all live to him." 39 And some of the scribes answered and said, "Teacher, you have spoken well." 40 For they did not have courage to question him any longer about anything.

Introduction

Have you ever been witnessing to someone, and the unbeliever asks a question like "Where did Cain get his wife?" "What about those who have never heard the Gospel?" "Who made God?" "Can God make a stone so big he can't lift it?" "Why do innocent people suffer?" The purpose of such questions is usually not to seek truth but to evade it, not to find truth but to ridicule it, as you discover pretty quickly if you actually try to answer them. Well, the Lord found Himself in just that kind of conversation in the passage that is before us today. From the way He handled it we can learn three things: something about God, something about the Resurrection, and something about how to handle questions.

I. Something About God

The most important thing we learn is something about God himself: He is not the God of the dead, but of the living. That this is so flows from His own inmost nature. He is uniquely "the living God," contrasted throughout the Old Testament with the false gods "made with hands." But this God is different: powerful, active, dynamic—alive! *"The voice of the Lord is powerful; the voice of the Lord is majestic. The voice of the Lord breaks the cedars; yes, the Lord breaks in pieces the cedars of Lebanon. He makes Lebanon skip like a calf, and Sirion like a young ox. The voice of the Lord hews out flames of fire. The voice of the Lord shakes the wilderness; the Lord shakes the wilderness of Kadesh. The voice of the Lord makes the deer to calve and strips the forests bare, and in His temple everything says, 'Glory!'"* (Psalm 29:4–9).

This God is no mere abstract idea, no mere idol whether made with mind or hands. He is the living God; He actually *does* things! *"Has any people heard the voice of God speaking from the midst of the fire as you have heard it and survived? Or has a god tried to go take for himself a nation from within another nation by trials, signs, and wonders and by war and by a mighty hand and by an outstretched arm and by great terrors, as the Lord did for you in Egypt before your eyes? To you it was shown that you might know that the Lord, he is God, and there is no other besides him"* (Deut. 4:33–35). He is not only alive, but He is the Source of all life, from the day He first breathed it into us at the Creation. Because He is alive, His Word also lives, and is living, active, powerful, sharper than any two–edged sword (Heb. 4:12). Supremely this life is seen in His Son, for *"in him was life, and that life was the light of men"* (John 1:4). He is the living God, so alive that He is the Source and Origin of all other life, the Lord and giver of life.

If that is who God is, then of course He must be the God, not of the dead, but of the living. For to be in relationship with Him is to receive life from Him! So if this is who God is, then it says something also about we who are His people. Throughout the Scriptures, salvation is described in terms of life, and damnation in terms of spiritual death. This theme comes into special focus in John's Gospel. *"Truly, truly I say to you, an hour is coming in which the dead shall hear the voice of the Son of God, and those who hear shall live. For just as the Father has life in himself, even so he gave to the Son also to have life in himself"* (John 5:26–7). *"To whom shall we go?"* asked the disciples, *"You have the words of eternal life"* (John 6:68). Jesus said, *"I am the Resurrection and the life"* (John 11:25). He said, *"I am the way, the truth, and the life"* (John 14:6). He said, *"I am come to bring life, and that more abundantly"* (John 10:10). And in his great high priestly prayer he gives the classic definition of salvation: *"This is life eternal, that they might know thee, the only true God, and Jesus Christ whom thou hast sent"* (John 17:3). Because salvation is a relationship with God through Jesus Christ, and because God is the living God, therefore we will live forever. You cannot know Him, you cannot be in a relationship with Him, you cannot be connected to Him, and not live. He is the living God; life rubs off on us when we are near Him.

If all this is true, then what does it say about the Christian life here and now? Our God is not the God of the dead but of the living! Therefore, we of all people should be full of life. Think of the adjectives that derive etymologically from various words that mean "life": vivacious, vivid, lively. This may not hit us as hard as it used to because we are protected from fully experiencing the contrast between life and death the way our ancestors did. Funeral homes have sanitized death and anesthetized us to some of the contrast between death and life. I will never forget visiting an African village where a man had just died. I will never forget seeing him laid out on the dirt floor of his hut for his wake. I will never forget watching his sons dig his grave with their own hands right outside his front door. With no embalming and a warm climate, he had to be in it the next morning. This death had come right into the middle of life, and it had to be dealt with very directly by the people it touched the closest.

We are protected from fully experiencing the contrast between life and death the way our ancestors did. This is not all bad, but it has a downside if it keeps us from fully appreciating the contrast. We can still see it if we know how to look. Life is beautiful; death is ugly. Life is good; death is evil. Life is wholesome; death is decadent. Life is joyous; death is sorrowful. Life is healthy; death is diseased. Life is whole; death is decayed and rotten. Life is active; death is impotent and immobile. Hear in this context once again the words of Jesus: *"I am come to bring life, and that more abundantly"* (John 10:10). Therefore, for a Christian (or a church) to be cold, dull, and passive, for a Christian (or a church) to take the path of least resistance, for a Christian (or a church) to be apathetic, boring—in other words, dead—is for that Christian (or that church) to deny the Lord who bought them! He is not the God of the dead, but of the living. Therefore, let us *live* for Him!

II. Something About The Resurrection

We learn something pretty important and life–giving then about God. Because God is not the God of the dead, but of the living, we can also learn something about the Resurrection from this passage. First, we learn the certainty of it. Because our Father is both the living God and the God of the living, nothing can stop it. Death is the strongest natural force we know of. Life (in the natural order of things) can be reversed, but death cannot. Every life comes to an end, but death (in this world) lasts forever. The utmost that science can do is to put it off for a little while. Once death has come (fully come), nothing can undo it or reverse its work. Oh, I know we can reverse it medically in a few cases, but only in the first few minutes, not when it is complete. But though death is strong, it is not stronger than the living God! He is not the God of the dead, but of the living, and our ultimate resurrection is the fruit of that truth.

We learn not only the certainty of the Resurrection, but something of the nature of it as well. Jesus' argument from the nature of God strictly and by itself proves only the *immortality* of Abraham and of those who share the faith of Abraham: If Abraham is one of God's people, and God is the God of the living, then Abraham must live; indeed, he must live forever. The form in which he will live is not specified by the argument as such. But Jesus does not stop with immortality; He goes on to argue for *the Resurrection of the body*. Why? How does He get there? He gets there because He has added or assumed something as background which does indeed yield that conclusion when combined with the stated premise. (In logic, this is technically known as an *enthymeme*, a syllogism with one premise left unstated or understood.) That unstated premise is the unity of human nature.

The unity of human nature: We are not just a body, as in modern secularism; we are not just a spirit which happens to live in a body (or be trapped in it), as in many forms of paganism. We were made to be the unique point in the universe where matter and spirit come together, a unity of body and spirit that integrates those two parts of God's creation as one. Sir Thomas Browne called us "that great and true *amphibium*, whose nature is disposed to live, not only like other creatures in diverse elements, but in divided and distinguished worlds."[117] Therefore, if Man was created to be a unity of body and spirit, he cannot be fully alive without his body. And therefore, the Resurrection is necessary for us to enjoy eternal life as fully human beings. Therefore, as God is the God of the living, and as He made us to be a unity of body and spirit, a bodily Resurrection is required.

The Resurrection has implications then for the way we conceive ourselves and the way we conceive the Christian life. The body is not our problem. Actually, as I age, my body presents me with certain problems, but the body is not ultimately my problem. My (metaphorical) heart is; my will is. Full humanity includes the body, and forms of spirituality that denigrate or despise it are sub–Christian. The spirit does not feel itself imprisoned in the body because spirit is good and the body is evil. It feels the body as a burden only because in a fallen world the body is perishable. That is why it groans for redemption—but not redemption *from* the body, but rather the redemption *of* the body, redemption *for* the body. Gerard Manley Hopkins put it well:

> Like a dare-gale skylark scanted in a dull cage,
> > Man's mounting spirit in his mean house, bone house dwells—
> > That bird beyond the remembering his free fells;
> This in drudgery day–laboring out life's age.
> > Though aloft on turf or perch or poor low stage
> > Both sing sometimes the sweetest, sweetest spells,
> > Yet both droop deadly sometimes in their cells
> > Or wring their barriers in bursts of fear or rage.
> No that the sweet fowl, song–fowl needs no rest—
> > Why hear him, hear him babble as he drops down to his nest,
> > But his own nest, wild nest, no prison.
> Man's spirit will be flesh bound when found at best,
> > But unencumbered: meadow down is not distressed
> > For a rainbow footing it, nor he for his bones risen![118]

We learn something about the Resurrection: its certainty and its nature. I don't know about you, but I need this reminder badly. I find it easier to make Jesus' historical Resurrection real to my imagination than I do my future one. Living in a secular world has corrupted my mind in that way. You know what helps me more than arguing with

---

[117] Sir Thomas Browne, *Religio Medici*, in Witherspoon and Warnke, op. cit., 339.
[118] Gerard Manley Hopkins, "The Caged Skylark," 1889; *The Poems of Gerard Manley Hopkins*, 4th ed., ed. W. H. Gardner and. N. H. MacKenzie (London: Oxford Univ. Pr., 1967), 70

myself about the Resurrection? Reminding myself that we serve the living God does! Maybe it will be so for you too.

III. Something About Handling Questions

There are, finally, some important and very practical lessons here about how to handle this type of insincere question the Sadducees brought. Such questions are usually asked as a diversion, an attempt to avoid the real issue. The first lesson is, **do not get sidetracked by accepting the assumptions implied by the question.** The Pharisees, who believed in the Resurrection, had heard this chestnut from the Sadducees before, and they had a standard answer for it: the woman would belong to the first brother.[119] But look what they have done. They have tacitly accepted the assumption that the next life will be just like this one, a mere continuation of it into a limitless future. Because they have accepted that assumption, their answer is not really an answer at all. For the Sadducees want to make the point that the doctrine of the Resurrection is absurd—look at the absurdities that follow from accepting it! And the standard answer left them still able to maintain that attitude. What about the other six brothers? Jesus cuts deeper by getting past the assumption and showing how little any of his opponents really understood about that time which will be so fresh and new that it has not even entered into the heart of man what God has prepared for us (1 Cor. 2:9), that time to which the sufferings of this life are not even worthy to be compared (Rom. 8:18).

The second thing we learn from Jesus' example is, **do not ignore or evade the evasive question,** but answer it; only **answer it in such a way that you focus the conversation back on the real issues of the Gospel,** especially who God is. This is exactly what Jesus did here. Does it really matter whose wife the lady would be? No, as it turns out, the Sadducees are asking the wrong question. But Jesus uses the topic to raise the question they should be asking. Who is God? Do we have a low or a high view of God? If we think of God rightly, the Resurrection will take care of itself. Do we have a high and exalted view of God? Ultimately, the Gospel hinges on this. We will never be properly convicted of sin, and so we will never see the necessity of the Cross, until we see the holiness, justice, and righteousness as well as the love of God. We are not ready to talk about anything else until we see that He is not the God of the dead, but of the living. So don't be thrown off by the question, and don't ignore it, but use it to get back to the central issue, as Jesus did.

So, where did Cain get his wife? We do not know specifically, but we do know that ultimately he got her from the same place that Adam did, from the God who supplies all our needs. What about those who have not heard? Well, of course we are very concerned about them, and we know that God wants them to hear—that's why I'm telling you! Who made God? God is not the kind of person who could *be* made. He is the necessary Being required to get the whole making thing started. Can God make a

---

119 Plummer, op, cit., 468.

stone so big he cannot lift it? God is a God not only of power but also of wisdom and of truth. He can do anything that is consistent with His own character. Contradicting Himself is not one of those things—so, no, He cannot make a stone so big He cannot lift it. But He can do something even more astounding than that: He can forgive our sins, cleanse us from all unrighteousness, give us eternal life, and—most astounding of all—make life worth living for an eternity. Why do the innocent suffer? Who is innocent? I'm not—are you? I'm afraid we're all sinners. The real question is why do the guilty enjoy life? Because God is gracious! And you have no idea how gracious—but let me tell you. There is only one documented time in history when an innocent man suffered, and that was Christ dying on the Cross—for my sins and yours.

Do you see? Do not ignore or evade the evasive question but answer it *in such a way* that you focus the conversation back on the real issues of the Gospel, especially *who God is*. The point is not for you to memorize these responses—though there's no harm in that if you think it would help. But the real point is to learn to think about all of life as related to God and his Gospel so that we can naturally practice following Jesus' example in this encounter and point people to the One who is not the God of the dead, but of the living.

Conclusion

God is not the God of the dead, but of the living, because He is the living God. And therefore we who are the people of God should not be the dead, but the living. Part of that life in us should be the ability to respond to questions and objections as people who know the living God, people for whom all of life revolves around Him. For the purpose of our answers is the same as the purpose of the Resurrection itself: that men and women might be brought into the presence of the living God.

DAVID'S SON AND DAVID'S LORD

Luke 20:39 And some of the Scribes answered and said, "Teacher, you have spoken well." 40 For they did not have courage to question him an longer about anything. 41 And he said to them, "How is it that they say Christ is David's son? 42 For David himself says in the book of Psalms, 'The Lord said to my lord, "Sit at my right hand 43 until I make thine enemies a footstool for thy feet."' 44 David therefore calls him 'Lord,' so how is he his son?" 45 And while all the people were listening, he said to his disciples, 46 "Beware of the scribes, who like to walk around in long robes and love respectful greetings in the marketplaces and chief seats in the synagogues and places of honor at banquets, 47 who devour widows' houses and for appearance' sake offer long prayers. These will receive the greater condemnation."

Introduction

Last time, we looked at the way the Lord answered a difficult (and impertinent) question: Which of the seven successive brothers who died childless and received the previous bother's widow as his wife according to the custom of Jewish Levirate Marriage would be married to her in the next life? We saw that Jesus refused to accept the hidden assumption behind the question, which is that the next life will be just like this one so that she would have to be married to one of them, and that He used their evasive question to get back to what really mattered: Who is God? He is not the God of the dead, but of the living. In this passage, we see the Lord complete His turning of the tables on his critics by *asking them* an equally difficult, but highly pertinent, question: How can the Messiah be both David's son and David's Lord? Jesus does not answer the question. He only asks it because, if we really understand the question itself, simply asking it is enough. You see, if we can just get people to ask the right questions, we have won half the battle already. I'd like to look at three aspects of this question for a few minutes this morning: the Purpose of the Question, the Point of the Question, and the Practicality of the Question.

I. The Purpose Of The Question

First, the Purpose of the Question. To understand this question, we must first ask the right questions about the question, and the first of those is, "To whom was the question addressed?" The "them" of verse 41 is the "scribes" of verse 39. You remember these guys. They had been trying to trap Jesus in several embarrassing questions, but he had turned the tables on them so many times that they had run out of questions and decided it was time for a strategic withdrawal. But though they had run out of questions, Jesus was not through with them yet. Now He turns and asks *them* a question. Note first of all His grace in this. Though they do not deserve it, the scribes get one last chance to listen, to repent, to make their sarcastic praise of verse 39, "Teacher, you have spoken well," actually sincere and genuine — to find forgiveness and eternal life.

But note also their response. [*Moment of silence.*] Would you like to hear it again? [*Moment of silence.*] There isn't any. They are not concerned at all with the answer, with the truth. They are only concerned with how the discussion makes them look, and they have decided that any further conversation with Jesus can only be embarrassing to them. And so they get what they wanted most to avoid but what they were really asking for all along: the blast of verses 46–47. Beware of the scribes! They are total hypocrites, only concerned with how they look (hence the long robes and the greetings) and not at all with truth or love (hence they devour widows' houses—they were the first century equivalent of our televangelists living high on the hog—a kosher hog in this case no doubt—off of the social security checks of the followers they have deluded.) Beware the scribes indeed!

But though embarrassment was the end result the scribes had chosen, it was not the Lord's purpose in the exchange. The aim of this wonderful Socratic question was to make them think, to get them to re–examine their inadequate assumptions, to take a fresh look at their interpretation of the Old Testament. It became an embarrassment precisely and only because they refused that opportunity. But *we* do not have to refuse it! The point of the question is not to deny that the Messiah is the son of David (which everybody knew, and which Luke actually goes out of his way to establish), but to point out the one–sidedness of their understanding of this truth. There was more to it than was dreamt of in their philosophy!

In other words, if the Messiah were only the son of David, how could he also be the Son of the Father, the inheritor of the Vineyard, with authority to cleanse the Temple, etc.? For since the days of Saul there had been a strict separation of powers which kept the secular ruler from also performing the functions of the priesthood. What possible king could there be to whom this rule would not apply? The Messiah that God was actually sending was bigger than the one they were expecting, in other words; bigger than they could even imagine. But now in dealing with Jesus' question they would have the opportunity either to become open to that possibility or to reject it. And they made the choice we would expect of them, very tragically so.

II. The Point Of The Question

So the purpose of the question was to give Jesus' audience a chance to learn something important about who He was. What was the point of the question? Jesus' question showed, negatively, the inadequacy of the scribes' preconceived notions about the Messiah. But positively, it leads us down the path to the very depths of Christology and reveals Jesus as both God and Man, one Person with two natures. That the Messiah was to be Man was widely known. Of this there was no doubt. He would be the son of *David*—a certifiably human king. And so Jesus was, born of a woman descended from David, tempted in every point like as we are, yet without sin. With this they had no problem—though some in our day do! I remember getting almost burned at the stake once for asking the teens in a high–school Bible class to consider the possibility that

Jesus might have had zits when he was a teenager. Oh, no, we had better not let the humanity of our Lord become *that* real to us! Well, except for sin, he was in every way the son of David.

But he was also David's Lord. Now, who was David? He was the king, the high king (like Peter of Narnia), the greatest king, the king to whom every subsequent king would be compared: They all either did or did not follow the Lord their God like their father David. If they followed, it was either with or without a full heart, like their father David. Now, where among men can we find a person with greater authority than David? Where among men can we find a person to whom David would need to bow, whom David could rightly call, "my Lord"? We cannot. There is only one authority in Israel higher than David, and that is Yahweh Himself! "The Lord said to my Lord"—Yahweh said to Adonai—"sit at my right hand" (Psalm 110:1). David's son would be his Lord, enthroned with Yahweh. That is, David would have a son who would share the glory and sovereignty of Yahweh himself. This is never said of any mere Hebrew king, or of any (other) mortal man.

Though the implications are not spelled out here because the scribes refused to participate in the conversation, the question drives us to a destination which is nothing less than the fully worked out theology of the incarnation of our Lord: Son of David, David's Lord, two natures in one Person, fully God and fully Man, the God–Man, God incarnate. He is David's son and David's Lord. David's son is not hard to believe. David's Lord takes some believing. But both at the same time? Yet that is the only adequate description possible for the Jesus we have seen presented in Luke's Gospel. Yes, He is David's son—but haven't you noticed?—the Old Testament also calls Him David's Lord. And how does He inhabit, how does He fill out that designation? Diseases and demons, loaves and fishes, winds and waves, even death and destiny bow to His authority. Let us worship Him as such.

III. The Practicality Of The Question

The purpose of the question then was an opportunity to learn who Jesus is. The point of the question is to impel us down the road that leads to Nicaea and Chalcedon and the Creeds that declare Jesus to be fully God and fully Man. What then of the practicality of the question? There is a tendency in the church today to demand that sermons be "practical," and this demand is urged in such a way as to imply that one cannot be both "practical" and "doctrinal," certainly not "practical" and "theological," at the same time. I agree about the practicality, but I would just point out that the Bible writers seem to have a different notion of what is practical than we do. For them, nothing is more practical than doctrine! So, no, this morning we are not going to have some neat set of seven steps to a better marriage or more health and wealth. We are going to get far more practical than that. We are going to let you know whether it is right for you to worship, serve, live for, and die for this man Jesus of Nazareth or not—and if so, how. The way we will do this is looking at three roles Jesus plays in the lives of believers for which it is absolutely essential that He be both David's son and David's lord.

First, that Jesus be understood as both David's son and David's Lord is absolutely essential to His **fulfilling His role as our example.** How can he be an example to us if he is not a man, a real man, a human being like us, tempted in all ways like as we are? Could an angel do it?

> The Tree–ness of the tree they know—the meaning of
> Arboreal life, how from earth's salty lap
> The solar beam uplifts it, all the holiness
> Enacted by leaves' fall and rising sap;
> But never an angel knows the knife–edged severance
> Of sun from shadow where the trees begin,
> The blessed cool at every pore caressing us—
> An angel has no skin.
>
> They see the Form of Air; but mortals breathing it
> Drink the whole summer down into the breast.
> The lavish pinks, the field new–mown, the ravishing
> Sea–smells, the wood–fire smoke that whispers, "Rest."
> The tremor on the rippled pool of memory
> That from each smell in widening circle goes,
> The pleasure and the pang—can angels measure it?
> An angel has no nose.[120]

No, to be relevant to us, our Example must be One who has lived *our* life. How will He do that if he is not a man? But how also can He do it if He is not sinless? For if He is a sinner like us, He is no safe and perfect example for us to follow. And how then can He be sinless unless He is more than just another son of Adam? Christ must be both David's son *and David's Lord* if He is to serve as our perfect example. Those theologies which present Christ as a merely human example, then, fail on their own terms. Unless He is much more than that, He cannot be even that. But neither can He be less. Jesus absolutely has to be David's son and David's Lord.

Second, that Jesus be understood as both David's son and David's Lord is absolutely essential to His **fulfilling His role as the Mediator between us and God.** Greek philosophy and Christian theology both deal with the question of how there can be any connection between finite humanity and the infinite, but they do it in radically different ways. Greek philosophy posited an infinite series of intermediary beings between the infinite purity of God and the finite impurity of Man. But this just reinforces the infinite and unbridgeable distance between us and leaves God unreachable. If you

---

[120] C. S. Lewis, "On Being Human," 1946; *Collected Poems,* op. cit., 338–9.

have to go through an infinite series of mediators, you never reach the end of the series. But with one hand, as it were, Jesus reaches up and touches the Father with his divine nature; and with the other He reaches down and touches us with His humanity. In His very person the estrangement between God and Man is bridged. So Paul rightly stresses to Timothy that there is one God and one Mediator between God and men, the Man Christ Jesus (1 Tim. 2:5). In Christ *our humanity* has been seated at the right hand of the Throne on high. There is no other way that finite human beings can be the sons and daughters and friends of God. Jesus absolutely has to be David's son and David's Lord.

Third, that Jesus be understood as both David's son and David's Lord is absolutely essential to His **fulfilling His role as our Redeemer.** How, if He is not a man, can He atone for the sins of mankind? And how if His life is not of infinite value—how, if He is not God—could His death atone for all the sins of all who believe on Him? Only a man is eligible to die for human sin; only a sinless man is qualified to die for human sin; and only God is able to die for the sins of all believers and come back from death to live forever as their Redeemer and Savior and Lord. The theological language of the Apostles' and Nicene Creeds (one substance with the Father), and the technical language of the Chalcedonian Creed (two natures, **ουσια,** *ousia* in one person, **'υποτασισ,** *hypostasis*), are inevitable once these two simple phrases are accepted: David's Son and David's Lord. Why? Without them there is no salvation. Only the biblical Christology can support the biblical Soteriology; only the biblical Savior could provide the biblical salvation; only the Person of Christ could do the work of Christ. It is absolutely essential: David's son and David's Lord.

If Jesus was not fully God and fully Man; if He was not David's son *and* David's Lord; then we are lost, without a Guide, separated from God, without salvation, and yet in our sins. But if He is David's son and David's Lord, then we can worship Him, serve Him, die for Him, live for Him, and live forever with Him. That is the difference it makes.

Conclusion

Our Lord Jesus Christ was David's son and David's Lord. Since that is not the usual language we use for the staggering paradox of who He is, I hope we can use it to brush away some of the cobwebs and see Him once again for the mind–boggling thing He is. Yet, to look at the way most of us worship Him and live for Him, you would get the impression that He was rather boring. Listen! I would almost rather you disbelieved the truth about Christ than to be bored with it. For to be bored with it means you are not yet, or no longer, taking it seriously.

The Christian faith makes three affirmations. You can call them bone–chilling, you can call them blood–curdling, you can call them shocking. But to call them boring is to say that you are not paying attention to them. 1. A mother held a baby to which she had just given birth, and it was her Creator. He was David's son and David's lord. 2. The God of Love came to us in human form (He was David's son and David's lord), and we were so threatened by it that we hung Him on the gallows rather than let Him upset the status quo. 3. The Man we killed walked out of his grave and is still alive and is coming again. He was David's son and David's lord.

You may not understand it; you may not comprehend it; you may not be able to explain it. But if you *believe* it, then you have got to be deeply moved and inexorably transformed by it. Let our worship of Him and our service to Him from now on reflect an awareness of these things! Amen.

THE WIDOW'S MITE

Luke 20:45 And while all the people were listening, he said to his disciples, 46 "Beware of the scribes, who like to walk around in long robes and love respectful greetings in the market places and chief seats in the synagogues and places of honor at banquets, 47 and who devour widows' houses and for appearance' sake offer long prayers. These will receive the greater condemnation."

What do these scribes at the end of chapter 20—who, after all, were already covered in last week's sermon—have to do with the poor widow in the first verses of chapter 21? Why have I chosen awkwardly to straddle this chapter break in such a curious fashion? I'm glad you asked that question! Keep it in the back of your mind and hang on to see if I can answer it before I'm done.

21:1 And he looked up and saw the rich putting their gifts into the treasury. 2 And he saw a certain poor widow putting in two small copper coins. 3 And he said, "Truly I say to you, this poor widow put in more than all of them. 4 For they all out of their surplus put into the offering, but she out of her poverty put in all that she had."

Introduction

How much did you put into the offering box today (or this month, if you get paid monthly)? Ten percent? Of your gross? Of your net? Were you happy about it? How much did you keep? What did you give up to put in what you did? Do you know what the amount is *really* worth? Well, I do not want to know the answers to these questions. But there is Someone who does know them—and I'm not talking about our Treasurer, _____ _____, either. What can this passage teach us about our giving and how we may please the Lord in it? That is the question which the Text places before us today in Jesus' response to the giving He observed at the Temple. Let's see if we can notice some things about the passage that can help us answer it

I. Jesus Notices Our Giving (vv. 21:1–2)

The first thing to notice here is that God notices what we give and why we give it. Now, of course, we all know this; we all know that God knows everything. But the doctrine of omniscience is too abstract to easily provide much practical help. "Everything" is such a huge thing that any particular thing can easily get lost (to our minds) in the shuffle of that vastness of infinite knowledge, so that we operate quite contentedly without realizing that any number of particular things—including some decidedly inconvenient ones—are included. But while we can thus easily forget that what we are doing at the moment is included in the divine omniscience, God doesn't have our limitations. He is able to attend to every single detail as if it were the only thing He needed to notice and give it a whole eternity of attention. This too we know when we stop to think about it.

Unlike God, though, we cannot think about everything all the time. Our minds are inescapably dependent on the concrete and the specific to give meaning to the abstract and the universal—and vice versa. Therefore, it is most useful for us to stop and watch this little scene, to notice Jesus noticing the rich people and the widow. As we do so, let's keep both perspectives in mind because we really need both. Without the doctrine of omniscience, the story is just some strange thing that happened two thousand years ago. Without the story, the doctrine might seem meaningless and irrelevant. Put them together, and your life may be changed forever!

So, in the light of all we know about God, let us watch His Son watching the people filing past the offering box outside the temple. He takes notice of what they are doing. He sees the rich putting in an impressive amount that really amounts to a pitiful pittance of their abundant surplus. And He sees the widow putting in everything she had. He sees the general patterns and the individual acts. He sees the objective amounts and the subjective cost. He sees the thrusting out of the hands and the pulling back of the hearts—with one exception that everyone else fails to notice. He hears all of our talk about tithing, but He also knows that only 5 to 10% of church members give a full tithe, and the average American church member actually gives only a little more than four percent.[121] He sees not only the surface, but also the substance; not only the amount, but also the attitude; not only the dollars but also the desires; not only the practice but also the priorities; not only the coins in the hopper, but also the condition of the hearts. And that leads us to a simple but disturbing question: Do we give in the light of this vision of His? Does the Lord in us find the cheerful giver which Scripture says He loves (2 Cor. 9:7)? He found one in a poor widow once. And it made Him sit up and take notice.

II. The Value Of The Widow's Gift

The second thing to consider here is the value of what was being given. What was the value of the widow's gift? We can answer that question from four different perspectives, each of which has something to teach us.

1. To Society. The value of this offering to society was practically nothing. The coin the widow used was a λεπτον (*lepton*), the smallest and least valuable coin that was minted at that time. In her honor we call it the "widow's mite" to this day. Here is a *lepton* [holds it up]. I would like to tell you that this is one of the actual *lepta* that the widow put into the offering box, but since I am trying to tell the truth this morning, I'd better not say that. But it is just like hers, an actual coin from the New–Testament period. This one apparently fell out of someone's purse into the Pool of Siloam, where I bought it from a worker at an archaeological dig who was finding beaucoups of them. You can see that it is about half the size of one of our pennies [holds it up], half the size of the denarius next to it in this sleeve, and that might give you an idea of its value.

---

[121] "Church Giving Statistics for 2024," https://careynieuwhof.com/church-giving-statistics/

We can imagine it as much like our penny—though of course the analogy is not perfect, since prices vary so much from age to age and society to society. To put its purchasing power into perspective, we can say that eight *lepta* were equal to one *assarion*, and sixteen *assaria* amounted to one *denarius*, which was a standard day's wage of a common laborer.[122] If we take a modern minimum wage of $7.50 an hour and multiply it times eight hours, we get a *denarius* of $60.00. Dividing that by sixteen and again by eight gives us a lepton of forty-seven cents. (This analysis has illustrative value only.) Two of those, then as now, made a paltry pittance indeed.

2. To the Temple. What was this offering's value to the Temple? The widow's two cents was, if it were possible, worth even less to the temple than it was to society. Its value was so small that the temple considered such coins not even worth the time it took their staff to count them. They had even passed a law that you could not put in one *lepton*. Therefore, two *lepta* was quite literally the smallest contribution that was allowable, the smallest contribution it was legal to make.[123] We can be sure that the treasurer rolled his eyes at them when he pulled them out of the offering box. He might have even muttered some uncomplimentary opinions about the giver's character and even her ancestry under his breath.

3. To the Widow. What were the two *lepta* worth to the widow? The English translation says that the widow put in "all that she had." In Greek it is παντα του βιου (*panta tou biou*), literally, "all her life," or maybe in effect "all her living." The meaning is probably not that it was her whole life's savings, but rather that it was all she had to "live" on that day, all she had been able to scrape together to keep life in herself on that particular day. Therefore, she might have had a very simple decision to make. This day, this particular day, should she eat, or should she give? She could not do both. And she chose to give. Obviously, this was not a choice she could make every day; if she did, she would die. But there were days when this was the decision she would make, and this was one of them. Such was her love for the Lord that she viewed her two cents in those terms.

Oh, how zealous we feel if we give up steak for hamburger or peanut butter for the Lord! I do not mean to despise or put down those who have done that. I have done it myself, when I was an impoverished seminary student, an impoverished graduate student, and an almost as impoverished pastor of a small church. I honor you who have done it, and I believe our Lord does too. But think of this widow! We are not in her league. The story is told of a millionaire giving a testimony in church. "I had only one dollar, and I put it in the plate. I gave all I had. And God has honored that decision, which is why I am a millionaire today." And then a cynical voice was heard from the

---

[122] William Hendriksen, *Exposition of the Gospel According to Luke* (Grand Rapids, MI: Baker, 1978), 920.
[123] Plummer, op. cit., 475.

back of the church. "Brother, I dare you to do it again!" How do we know that isn't going to happen?

What is my point? Not that you should hand over all your possessions to University Church (God forbid!), but just to get us to think about the fact that we always give what we value less to gain something that we value more. Look at this pen. [Pulls pen out of pocket.] It is a perfectly good ink pen. In another church, I had a parishioner named Mark. "Mark," I asked, "how about if I trade this pen [one of its predecessors, actually] to you for Binky?" Binky was Mark's first car—a bomb and probably unsafe at any speed, but he loved it. No? I could not get him to make that deal! He must have thought Binky was worth more than the pen—at least it was to him if nobody else!

That's the way it works. You will never give something you love for something you do not care about. You will never keep what you do not care about if you can buy with it something you really want. Therefore, every single one of your economic transactions reveals your priorities. If you want to know what you really value, just take a look at your budget. If you don't have a budget, you can reverse–engineer it to figure it out by looking at your check book. See what you are giving for what. And see what place the Lord's work has in that list of priorities. I am not suggesting it should be what it was for the widow. You have bills. You may have a family to take care of. But if you love the Lord like she did, it will show up in your checkbook *somewhere*. If it doesn't, your claims to love the Lord are nothing but empty words.

4. To the Lord. To society, the widow's mite was worth practically nothing. To the Temple, it was worth less than nothing. To the widow, it was all she had. This leads us to the most important question of all: What were those two *lepta* worth to the Lord? To Jesus, the widow's two cents was worth more than all the pelf of the wealthy—more than all their generous offerings put together.

How did Jesus figure that? Let's "get the picture," as Larry Munson used to say when calling a Georgia football game. The priests have just announced that we need a new Xerox machine for the Temple. How much? Two thousand shekels. So Benjamin Bank Balance pulls out his check book, signs the check with a flourish, tears it out, and says, "Here, this should take care of it." The Temple needs to purchase five new radio stations for its outreach ministry to the Diaspora. How much? Six hundred thousand shekels. No problem. Daniel Deposit Slip whips out his checkbook. "Here, this should take care of it." The Temple needs a new educational wing. How much? Two million shekels. No problem. Malachi Moneybags whips out his checkbook. "Here, this should take care of it." (I would say they whipped out their credit cards, but this is ancient Israel after all.) And then a little half–starved anonymous widow chucks in two cents—*and she gave the most*? You'd better believe it! For Jesus noticed that the others gave out of their surplus and did not suffer for it. But she gave out of her very lack. Her gift was an expression of love for God which said that He was more to her than her living. And that is what was worth the most to the Lord Jesus Christ.

III. The Contrast With The Scribes

This third thing I want us not to miss is the contrast with the scribes. Did you wonder why we started this passage with the scribes from the end of chapter 20, the scribes from last week? It is because they are a part of this story, though this fact is obscured by an unfortunate chapter division. The link is the fact that the word *widow* occurs in both passages. The scribes added this to their long list of impious posturings, that they "devoured widows' houses." In other words, they were hitting them up for contributions, like the infamous televangelists of not so long ago who became notorious for air–conditioning their doghouse with money given from old ladies' social security checks. Or I think of another one I actually heard on the radio saying, "If you don't have the hundred dollars to keep this ministry on the air, borrow it! And the Lord will repay you ten or twenty or a hundred–fold." Had this preacher—both the evil asker and his gullible givers—never read 1 Corinthians 8:12? Paul is talking about the collection he was taking up for the poor saints in Jerusalem. *"For if the readiness is present, it is acceptable according to what a man has, not according to what he does not have."* Oh, my.

Oh, my! We bow our heads in shame at the greed and selfishness of these brazen theological shysters preying on the naïve and foolish people of God while giving the enemies of the Gospel every excuse to blaspheme. But they are not a new phenomenon. They were practicing their inexcusable trade in the First Century, and they were called the scribes. And the widow's story follows theirs partly to allow Luke to draw a contrast between their motives and hers. Their religion was all for show, prestige, and profit. She was simply motivated by love for God. And that—more than any figures or percentages or dollar amounts—is what got Jesus' attention. We must believe it still does.

Conclusion

Now, I do not know what you give, or what should give, and I do not want to know. I do know your situation is more complicated than the widow's in the story, but I also know that it would be wrong for us to allow that fact to get us off the hook of what the Lord is trying to teach us through her example. I could give you a formula, but it would not solve the problem of wrestling with these decisions, decisions with which I struggle too. The first check I write after my pension and social security checks come in each month is to University Church for ten percent of my net, and then I give something more outside of UC to missions and other worthy Christian projects. I wish I could give more than I do. I'm not even close to being in the widow's league, but then I'm not in competition with her. The Lord did not give her to us as a legalistic standard but as a person whose heart He wanted us to see. So that's what I give. (I use myself as an example not because I am particularly righteous, but because it is the example I know.) I do it not out of legalistic obedience to the Old–Testament Law but because I cannot imagine, with all the privileges I have as a New–Testament believer, being less generous than the Old–Testament saints were and because I want the Lord's work to prosper. Ten percent is as good a place to start as any. But as I said, I am not giving you this as a formula for you anymore than the widow's mites are, but just as an example. Only you can decide what your example should look like.

My main point today then is not *what* we should be giving but *why*—because the why is, for our Lord Jesus Christ, that which determines the value of the what. And the why, if we clearly understand it and get it right, will also be what helps us to calculate our own what. You see, we must realize that each family and each individual is going to face a financial audit at the Day of Judgment. And as you prepare your books for that audit, I want you to understand how the Lord counts money. For He said, *"Truly I say to you, this poor widow put in more than all of them."* Why? Because she loved God. Within the bounds of responsibility, good stewardship, and Christian liberty, go thou and do likewise.

END-TIMES DISCOURSE, PART I

Luke 21:5 And while some were talking about the temple, that it was adorned with beautiful stones and votive gifts, he said, **6** *"As for these things which you are looking at, the days will come in which there will not be left one stone upon another which will not be torn down."* **7** *And they questioned him, saying, "Teacher, when therefore will these things be? And what will be the sign when these things are about to take place?"* **8** *And he said, "See to it that you are not misled. For many will come in my name, saying, 'I am he,' and, 'The time is at hand.' Do not go after them.* **9** *and when you hear of wars and disturbances, do not be terrified. For these things must take place first, but the end does not follow immediately."*

10 *Then he continued by saying to them, "Nation will rise against nation and kingdom against kingdom,* **11** *and there will be great earthquakes, and in various places plagues and famines, and there will be terrors and signs from heaven.* **12** *But before all these things, they will lay their hands on you and will persecute you, delivering you to the synagogues and prison, bringing you before kings and governors for my name's sake.* **13** *It will lead to an opportunity for your testimony.* **14** *So make up your minds not to prepare beforehand to defend yourselves,* **15** *for I will give you utterance and wisdom which none of your opponents will be able to resist or refute.* **16** *But you will be delivered up even by your parents and brothers and relatives and friends, and they will put some of you to death.* **17** *And you will be hated by all on account of my name.* **18** *yet not a hair of your head will perish.* **19** *By your endurance you will gain your lives.* **20** *But when you see Jerusalem surrounded by armies, then recognize that her desolation is at hand.* **21** *Then let those who are in Judea flee to the mountains, and let those who are in the midst of the city depart, and let not those who are in the country enter the city,* **22** *because these are the days of vengeance, in order that all things which are written may be fulfilled.* **23** *Woe to those who are with child and to those who nurse babes in those days, for there will be great distress upon the land and wrath to this people,* **24** *and they will fall by the edge of the sword and will be led captive into all the nations, and Jerusalem will be trampled underfoot by the Gentiles until the times of the Gentiles be fulfilled.* **25** *And there will be signs in the sun and moon and stars, and upon the earth dismay among the nations, in perplexity at the roaring of the sea and the waves,* **26** *men fainting from fear and the expectation of the things which are coming upon the world. For the powers of the heavens will be shaken.* **27** *And then they will see the Son of Man coming in a cloud with power and great glory.* **28** *But when these things begin to take place, straighten up and lift up your heads, because your redemption is drawing near."*

29 *And he told them a parable: "Behold the fig tree and all the trees.* **30** *As soon as they put forth leaves, you see it and know that summer is now near.* **31** *Even so, you, too, when you see these things happening, recognize that the kingdom of God is near.* **32** *Truly I say to you, this generation will not pass away until all things take place.* **33** *Heaven and earth will pass away, but my words will not pass away.* **34** *Be on your guard that your hearts may not be* *weighed down with dissipation and drunkenness and the worries of life, and that day come upon you suddenly like a trap. 35 For it will come upon all those who dwell upon the face of the earth. 36 But keep on the alert at all times, praying in order that you may have strength to escape all these things that are about to take place and stand before the Son of Man." 37 Now during the day he was teaching in the temple, but in the evening he would go out and spend the night on the Mount that is called Olivet. 38 And all the people would get up early in the morning to come to him in the temple to listen to him.*

Introduction

We are looking today at one of the most difficult passages to interpret in all of Scripture. There are a number of perplexing questions which make it so, questions which the people of God have asked through the years. What parts of this discourse refer to the destruction of Jerusalem by the Romans in AD 70, and what parts to the Great Tribulation? What is the meaning of verse 32? Jesus says that this generation will not pass away until all is fulfilled—but surely not everything in this passage has been fulfilled yet? But that generation is long gone. And those questions are just the tip of the iceberg. Why is this passage so difficult? Couldn't Jesus have made it plainer?

Part of the problem is the general difficulty of interpreting unfulfilled prophecy. Once the prophecy has been fulfilled, there is no difficulty at all. But until the fulfillment has arrived, you are trying to solve a math problem without having all the data. Another source of our difficulties might be a discrepancy between the questions we are asking and the ones Jesus was actually trying to answer. For these reasons, we are going to need to take two weeks on this passage—not just because of its length. (I apologize for giving you such a seemingly undigestible lump of Scripture, but it is one unit, and arbitrarily dividing it would be an act of interpretation in itself.) Today we will look at the general problems surrounding the interpretation of prophecy, and then next week, with that background, perhaps we will be in a position to look specifically at this prophecy in itself. So I would urge you to suspend judgment and hear me out, for I am afraid that much of the confident assertions that many of you have heard about these matters were made by preachers who had not taken the time to think through what we are going to think through today.

I. The General Difficulty Of Unfulfilled Prophecy

There is an inherent problem in understanding any statement about the future before that future has actually come. Suppose in, say, July of 1985, some sybil had said, "President Reagan will get a knife in the gut next week." Let us assume this seer can actually perceive the future, but that the utterance is simply made and left unexplained. What can it mean? Will the president be assassinated by a knife attack? Or will his opponents in congress simply make some cutting remarks? No one could know for sure until the week had passed—at which point it would turn out that Reagan had surgery. Or suppose our sage from that era pronounced that George Burns would not see his one hundredth birthday party. We might well assume that this meant he would die at ninety–nine. But that reasonable assumption would turn out to be false. In fact, he was still alive but unable to attend the bash they threw for him at Caesar's Palace. Go ahead. You try to make a meaningful factual statement about the future which is not capable of more than one interpretation. It is not as easy as you might think.

Lest we think that this difficulty only applies to hypothetical examples made up for the purpose, let us think about the greatest predictive prophecy of the entire Old Testament, the Suffering Servant passage of Isaiah 53. The Servant was crushed and put to grief, he bore our sins, by his stripes we are healed. Let us imagine it is 700 BC. You have not read one word of the New Testament. Would you be able to discern the specific death of the Cross of Calvary in this prophecy? Be honest. You would not. You would have a general idea of what God was promising to do, but it would only be *after the fact* that you would be able to see that Calvary and Calvary alone is the fulfillment, which covers every base, dovetails every detail, and fulfills the meaning behind it all most profoundly.

Well, yes, you might say, but Scripture gives us the advantage of context. The prophecies do not appear alone, but in a matrix of meaning created by other prophecies and other teachings of Scripture, which should help us narrow down to the correct interpretation. Well, context is supremely important and wonderfully helpful, but in the case of predictive prophecy even context is not sufficient. At least, it wasn't sufficient to allow anyone—*anyone*—to correctly predict how messianic prophecy would be fulfilled before the first coming of Christ. You see, when you try to look at Isaiah 53 *in context* of other Old Testament statements, the problem only grows worse. There are at least four semi–messianic figures discussed in the Old Testament. There is the Messiah himself, the son of David who would restore the Davidic throne and reign on it forever. There was the Prophet like Moses (Deut. 18:15, 34:10). There was the Suffering Servant of Isaiah 53. And there was the Danielic Son of Man. Now, pay close attention to what I am about to say, for it may be the most significant fact in this whole section of this message. There is not one single verse in the entire Old Testament which identifies these four promised Figures as the same individual. Not one. Not even a hint. There is of course also no verse which says they couldn't be, either. The question is left open.

Well, the Jews made some assumptions about these four Figures, and if you had lived then you probably would have made the same ones. They tended to assume they were separate persons. The one identification they absolutely refused to make was that of the Messiah with the Suffering Servant.[124] The Messiah would of course be the Davidic king who would restore Israel to its Solomonic glory by overthrowing the Roman Empire. One can easily imagine a scenario in which the Prophet like Moses would be a distinct person who would basically serve as his Press Secretary. And the Suffering Servant would be a military hero who would sacrifice himself in the war

---

[124] See Oscar Cullmann, *The Christology of the New Testament*, trans. Shirley Guthrie and Charles A, M, Hall (Philadelphia, PA: Westminster Press, 1963), 55–6.

against Rome, thereby allowing the Messiah to win that war and bring in the kingdom of God. Do not laugh. Something like this is what almost every pious Jew took for granted as the obvious meaning of the Old Testament prophecies when Jesus appeared on the scene. This preconceived notion was so deeply embedded in the minds of His own disciples that even after their forty–day graduate seminar in Old Testament prophecy after the Resurrection, at the very moment of Jesus' Ascension into Heaven, they were asking, "*Is now the time you are going to restore the kingdom to Israel?*" (Acts 1:6). Jesus was rejected by the Jewish establishment as a dangerous heretic. His heresy? The strange and novel notion that the Messiah and the Suffering Servant were one and the same Person.

Now, here's the point. These two conflicting interpretations of Old Testament prophecy could not have been decided based on the Old Testament alone. Was the Messiah the Suffering Servant or not? It is not just that they *were* not so decided—they *could not* have been. It simply does not give us the necessary data for deciding between them. Both are theoretically possible scenarios based on the words of the prophecies. Now, the correct interpretation was decided, in no uncertain terms, by the Resurrection of Christ. Had Christ's life and work contradicted the prophecies, had the Old Testament said plainly that the figures were separate individuals, then no strange event, however impressive, could have overturned the Word of God, for not one jot or tittle of it can pass away until all is fulfilled (Mat. 5:18). Christ is revealed as the perfect fulfillment by the Resurrection—but you could not have known the details of this in advance. The perfect fulfillment of the prophecy is only seen after the fact.

I repeat: Nobody figured the First Coming out before the fact. What makes us think we are going to do any better with the Second Coming? When Christ appears, we will see that all the prophecies dovetail perfectly, and we will see *how* they dovetail perfectly. I would be very surprised if anyone sees this perfectly until it has happened.

II. The Nature Of Prophecy

What we have been seeing surely shows us our misunderstanding of the very nature of biblical prophecy. It is not, as our popular teachers have often called it, "history in advance." Surely our brief look at Isaiah 53 makes this plain. One sees why this definition is popular. Prophecy does indeed often refer in advance to events that will become history in due time. But one cannot read them *as* history to see what they will actually look like *in* history until those events have *become* history. The English word *prophecy* comes from the Greek προφημι (*prophemi*), which means "to speak forth." The essence of the prophetic message is not so much foretelling as it is forth–telling. The prophet gives the message of God, which is primarily a message of repentance. He gives this message of repentance in the theological context of God's covenant and His promises, based on an understanding of God's purposes in history. That is how predictions become a part of the message. God promises that certain effects will follow from repentance and others from rebellion, and so they do. He promises that He will send his Son as the ultimate answer to our need for repentance, and so He does. But the predictions—better, promises—are not given to enable us to write history in advance. They are given as signs by which we may recognize the hand of God *when it moves* in the fulfillment of His promises. *"And they questioned him, saying, 'Teacher, when therefore will these things be? And what will be the sign when these things are about to take place?'"* (Luke 21:7). They might better have asked, "What will be the signs by which we will know when it has *taken* place."

In other words, the purpose of prophecy (so far as prediction is concerned) is not to allow us to *predict* what God will do in the future, but rather it is to enable us to *recognize* it when He does it. When God visits His people, He doesn't want them to miss it. That is why prophecy has a predictive element. Its ultimate purpose is not to help us to predict the future but to drive us to repentance and faith so that we will respond properly to God's mighty acts in the future when they do come. Prophecies are clear enough so that we are without excuse if hindsight and our knowledge of Scripture do not allow us to recognize the fulfillment of God's promises when it happens. They are not clear enough to let us correlate our daily newspapers with our concordances. And that is a simple and unavoidable fact.

The practical conclusion of this discussion is rather appalling. It is that ninety percent of Evangelical and Fundamentalist study of prophecy has been a pure waste of time! It is worse than a waste of time. It is all about sensationalism and the satisfaction of idle curiosity and has very little to do with the reasons for which prophecy was given in the first place: to drive us to repentance. It is a futile attempt to figure out in advance facts which prophecy by its very nature does not allow us to know until we recognize them after the fact. Did the resettlement of Israel by the Jews put us into the Last Days? (I mean the *last* Last Days—in one sense the Last Days began with the Cross.) Maybe— maybe not. The current nation of Israel could be swept into the sea by the Arabs tomorrow, and God could have them back in the land again a thousand years from now. Is Gog and Magog Russia? Is the European Union that evolved from the European Common Market the revived Roman Empire? Are we living in the last generation? I do not know. And neither do you. And neither does the next popular preacher who confidently tells you that he does. He *cannot* know these things, and the very claim that he does proves that he does not even understand what biblical prophecy is. He is trying to teach you to read between the lines when he does not even understand the lines themselves.

I am sorry if I disillusion some of you, but I must tell you the truth. This same Jesus is coming as you have seen Him go (Acts 1:11), in power and glory to judge the quick and the dead. This we may, indeed must, cling to dogmatically. But beyond that, hold to the predictive details lightly. They will sort themselves out when the Lord appears, and it will all make sense then. In the meantime, what do we do? We wait faithfully! What else? Whether you are Pre–, A, or Post–Mill, whether you are Pre–, Post–, or Mid–Trib, you must do that.

III. The Purpose Of Prophecy

We have seen the difficulty of interpreting unfulfilled prophecy, which flows in part from a misunderstanding of the nature or prophecy, which is a message of repentance in the context of the promises of God which do have a bearing on the future. It does not let us predict the future so much as recognize God's hand in it when it comes. So what is the purpose of prophecy? **The purpose of prophecy is not primarily to predict the future, but to teach you to live in the present in the light of eternity.** Let me repeat that. The primary purpose of prophecy is to teach you to live in the present in the light of eternity—which does indeed include certain promises that God makes about the future. But the focus is not on figuring out the future but on living a life of repentance and faithful witness in the present.

Now we are ready to start turning our attention back to the passage that is before us, the End–Times Discourse of Luke 21. Notice how it begins and ends with this concern. The whole conversation begins as a discussion of the impermanence of temporal things (verses 5–6). "Oh, you think the Temple is impressive, do you? I tell you that not one stone is going to be left on another." Herod's temple was an impressive edifice indeed. It had already been forty–six years in the making at the time of Christ (John. 2:20), and it would not be finished until AD 63, tragically only seven years before its destruction. Josephus tells us that it was made of white marble and looked like a mountain of snow. The doors were plated with gold. If you looked at them in direct sunlight, they would blind you. Its columns were forty–foot–high monoliths made each from a single block of marble.[125] One can understand why the Jews were proud of it. But Jesus says it's all coming down. The real Temple is the one He plans to build in the hearts of His followers, where the Holy Spirit will dwell.

The disciples want to know when that destruction is going to happen, and so the middle of the discourse deals with that question, laced with warnings about not being deceived and about being prepared for persecution. In all of this, Jesus' main point seems to be not when it's going to happen but about what we should do to be ready for it. And at the close he focuses on that point very specifically, with a strategy for prophetic living, that is, living in the light of eternity and of God's promises.

> **34** "Be on your guard that your hearts may not be weighed down with dissipation and drunkenness and the worries of life, and that day come upon you suddenly like a trap. **35** For it will come upon all those who dwell upon the face of the earth. **36** But keep on

---

[125] Flavius Josephus, *The Wars of the Jews* V.5-6; cf. *The Antiquities of the Jews* XV.xi.1-4; *The Works of Josephus*, trans. William Whiston (Lynn, MA: Hendrickson, 1980): 555-6, 334-6. Cf. also the summary in Hendricksen, op. cit., 922–7.

the alert at all times, praying in order that you may have strength to escape all these things that are about to take place and stand before the Son of Man."

First, don't get bogged down (verse 34, lit. "weighed down"). When the trivial hassles of life get to you, when they threaten to distract you from the business of the Kingdom, remember that this life is all temporal. A day will come when not one brick of your house will be left on another, but the people around you will live forever either in Heaven or in Hell. So don't get bogged down by the cares of this life. Second, **stay alert.** Be on guard. Keep on the alert at all times. God has given us a promise of Christ's return and a task to accomplish before it happens. Don't miss your opportunities to give your testimony for Him—and don't sleep through Christmas! Finally, **pray for strength,** strength to live faithfully and be able to "stand" before the Son of Man. We are to be alert, to watch, not so we can read the prophetic score card and check off all the prophetic checkpoints in the newspaper, but so that we can minister and love and serve and witness and stand.

That is Jesus' purpose in giving us this prophetic message. I am not going to ignore the predictive questions. I will deal with some of them next week. But let us not miss the point. The point is not for you to figure out the "when." It is for you to not get bogged down, to stay alert, and to pray for strength so that you may be faithful—whenever the End comes.

Conclusion

I do not know who Gog is. I do not know who the Antichrist is, or whether he is already alive. I do not know if the Millennium will be Pre, A, or Post (though I have what I think is an informed opinion). But I do know this: Next week when we study the details of Jesus' predictions, if we want to get out of it what He put in it for us, then we must bring to it this question. We must not ask how it helps us refine our prophetic timeline and perfect our dispensational chart. We must ask, *how do these things help me live in the present in the light of the future, yea, of eternity?* If we ask that question, we might be able to answer it. If we answer it, we can ask God to help us live in the light of the answer. This we will attempt next week if God permits. And if we can do that, and if we are faithful, alert witnesses in the meantime, we will do well.

END–TIMES DISCOURSE, PART II

Luke 21:5 And while some were talking about the temple, that it was adorned with beautiful stones and votive gifts, he said, 6 "As for these things which you are looking at, the days will come in which there will not be left one stone upon another which will not be torn down." 7 And they questioned him, saying, "Teacher, when therefore will these things be? And what will be the sign when these things are about to take place?" 8 And he said, "See to it that you are not misled. For many will come in my name, saying, 'I am he,' and, 'The time is at hand.' Do not go after them. 9 and when you hear of wars and disturbances, do not be terrified. For these things must take place first, but the end does not follow immediately."

10 Then he continued by saying to them, "Nation will rise against nation and kingdom against kingdom, 11 and there will be great earthquakes, and in various places plagues and famines, and there will be terrors and signs from heaven. 12 But before all these things, they will lay their hands on you and will persecute you, delivering you to the synagogues and prison, bringing you before kings and governors for my name's sake. 13 It will lead to an opportunity for your testimony. 14 So make up your minds not to prepare beforehand to defend yourselves, 15 for I will give you utterance and wisdom which none of your opponents will be able to resist or refute. 16 But you will be delivered up even by your parents and brothers and relatives and friends, and they will put some of you to death. 17 And you will be hated by all on account of my name. 18 yet not a hair of your head will perish. 19 By your endurance you will gain your lives. 20 But when you see Jerusalem surrounded by armies, then recognize that her desolation is at hand. 21 Then let those who are in Judea flee to the mountains, and let those who are in the midst of the city depart, and let not those who are in the country enter the city, 22 because these are the days of vengeance, in order that all things which are written may be fulfilled. 23 Woe to those who are with child and to those who nurse babes in those days, for there will be great distress upon the land and wrath to this people, 24 and they will fall by the edge of the sword and will be led captive into all the nations, and Jerusalem will be trampled underfoot by the Gentiles until the times of the Gentiles be fulfilled. 25 And there will be signs in the sun and moon and stars, and upon the earth dismay among the nations, in perplexity at the roaring of the sea and the waves, 26 men fainting from fear and the expectation of the things which are coming upon the world. For the powers of the heavens will be shaken. 27 And then they will see the Son of Man coming in a cloud with power and great glory. 28 But when these things begin to take place, straighten up and lift up your heads, because your redemption is drawing near."

29 And he told them a parable: "Behold the fig tree and all the trees. 30 As soon as they put forth leaves, you see it and know that summer is now near. 31 Even so, you, too, when you see these things happening, recognize that the kingdom of God is near. 32 Truly I say to you, this generation will not pass away until all things take place. 33 Heaven and earth will pass away, but my words will not pass away. 34 Be on your guard that your hearts may not be weighed down with dissipation and drunkenness and the worries of life, and that day come upon *you suddenly like a trap.* **35** *For it will come upon all those who dwell upon the face of the earth.* **36** *But keep on the alert at all times, praying in order that you may have strength to escape all* *these things that are about to take place and stand before the Son of Man."* **37** *Now during the* *day he was teaching in the temple, but in the evening he would go out and spend the night on* *the Mount that is called Olivet.* **38** *And all the people would get up early in the morning to come* *to him in the temple to listen to him.*

Introduction

One of the all–time best ways to make a fool of yourself is by trying to interpret unfulfilled prophecy, especially if your interpretation involves the setting of dates. William Miller infamously calculated the return of Christ for Oct. 22, 1844. A lot of people foolishly gathered on a hillside to await the event. They were disappointed.[126] In 1969, Hal Lindsey in *The Late Great Planet Earth* said that the European Common Market would become the United States of Europe by 1980.[127] Even if we take the European Union as the fulfillment of this prophecy, 1980 was a bit early; the Maastricht Treaty creating it went into effect in 1993. When I was a little boy, I remember hearing Billy Graham say in a televised crusade that he thought Christ would come back before his children graduated from high school. They have been married and serving the Lord for some time now, and *their* children graduated high school many years ago. One of the best sellers of the late 1980's was *88 Reasons Why the Lord will Come Back in 1988* — followed by the inevitable sequel, *89 Reasons Why the Lord will Come Back in 1989*. I was eventually driven by all this nonsense to commit the following limerick:

> Though it's something the Bible berates,
> Still it keeps coming out of our pates:
> We can't seem to resist
> Much less cease or desist
> The incessant resetting of Dates![128]

Well, I would like to get through this message without giving you one more example to add to our Eschatological Hall of Shame. Therefore, let's begin by remembering what we learned last week. First, we should never forget the general difficulty of interpreting prophecy that is still unfulfilled, which can be summed up in the maxim that hindsight is always better than foresight. Nobody got the First Coming right until after it had happened, so why should we think we will do any better with the Second Coming? Second, prophecy is not "history written in advance." That is, its function is not to allow us to predict the future but rather to give us signs by which we

---

[126] See Walter R. Martin, *The Kingdom of the Cults: An Analysis of the Major Cult Systems in the Present Christiam Era* (Minneapolis, MN: Bethany Fellowship, 1968), 362.

[127] Hal Lindsey, *The Late, Great Planet Earth* (Grand Rapids: Zondervan, 1970), 96.

[128] Williams, *Stars through the Clouds*, op. cit., 275.

may recognize the promised work of God *when it happens*. We saw that Isaiah 53 was fulfilled perfectly by the Cross and Resurrection, but you could only see that after the fulfillment took place. Third, our purpose in studying biblical prophecy must therefore be in line with the purpose for which it was given: to lead us to repentance. It is not there to enable us to predict the future so much as to enable us to live faithfully in the present in the light of eternity, in the light of God's purposes and His promises.

Now, having said all of that, let's finally look at the actual predictions our Lord made in this passage. Any solutions I offer beyond "This same Jesus will return as ye have seen Him go" (Acts 1:11) and "He will return in glory to judge the quick and the dead" (The Nicene Creed) should be taken as appropriately tentative, held to if we find them helpful, but not turned into dogmas. Why then examine the details at all? For one thing, to be accurate about what was said and not said so we can avoid the kind of preconceived notions that hindered Jesus' own generation from recognizing the fulfillment of those prophecies that dealt with the First Coming.

I. AD 70 Versus AD 2000 + ?

The most difficult problem in this passage is trying to figure out how it can relate both to the Lord's time and to our own. Verse 32 says that "this generation" would not pass away until all takes place. The most obvious meaning of "this generation" would be the generation to whom the Lord was speaking. But while much of what the Lord spoke of may have taken place in the sack of Jerusalem in 70 AD, surely He did not return in the clouds with power and great glory (verse 27) at that time. That Return is supposed to be an unmistakable event like lightning that shines from the east into the west, and all eyes are supposed to see it (Mat. 24:27, 30). The attempts of "preterists" (who believe the Lord has already returned) to get around those details are nothing short of lame. Yet if "this generation" does not mean "this generation," how are we supposed to be able to understand anything? You have to have some sympathy with the desire of preterists to understand everything as having been fulfilled in the past, even if you cannot accept their view. So this is a difficult problem indeed. Let us try to solve it in steps. The first step is to understand what did happen in AD 70 and see how the Christians of that time at any rate understood it.

The first thing to notice is that the disciples' question in verse 7 is focused on the Lord's prediction of destruction for the Temple. His declaration that not one stone would be left on another is what prompts their question: When shall *these* things be? Therefore, the answer has to be understood as relevant to the question, relevant to the destruction of the Temple, which did in fact take place in 70 AD. Matthew's version of the question in Mat. 24:3 shows that the Second Coming is also in view, for he adds a second part to the question, " . . . *and what will be the sign of your coming and of the end of the age?*" The "and" in Matthew's account shows that the questions of the destruction of the Temple and of the Second Coming are separate questions but also related questions. It also shows that full preterism—everything was fulfilled in AD 70—can't be right. We need to try to see how the destruction of the Temple and the Second Coming are related. Meanwhile, in Luke, the primary emphasis is on the destruction of the temple.

Therefore, I am inclined to think that everything up to Luke 21:24a must be seen as having been *in some sense* fulfilled in AD 70. ("In some sense"? Hang on. We'll get back to that.) Jerusalem was trampled underfoot then, but the "times of the Gentiles" have not yet been completed. Look at some of the specific details that would have been understood as having been fulfilled in AD 70 by the Christians living at that time. The "wars" of verse 9 certainly included the Jewish revolt against Roman rule which led to the sack of Jerusalem and the destruction of Herod's temple in reprisal. The earthquakes of verse 11 were thought to correspond to the eruption of Mount Vesuvius and the destruction of Pompeii in AD 63. The famine of that verse was experienced by the citizens of Jerusalem during the Roman siege. And as for signs in the heavens, Josephus records a comet which hung ominously "like a sword" over Jerusalem.[129] First–century Christians saw the persecution of Nero in the 60s as having been described quite accurately by verse 12.

The thing which confirms the fact that the believers of the time were thinking this way is their response to the warnings of verses 20–21. *"But when you see Jerusalem surrounded by armies, then recognize that her desolation is at hand. Then let those who are in Judea flee to the mountains and let those who are in the midst of the city depart and let not those who are in the country enter the city."* They interpreted that material quite literally, and it saved their lives. According to many accounts, including early church historian Eusebius, the Christian community in Jerusalem were the only people to leave before the city was surrounded. They evacuated to Pella, a village outside the Roman lines, and thus became the only major group of inhabitants to survive.[130] For once, a literal interpretation of prophecy turned out rather well. And if you are thinking that the devastation of that war doesn't fit the horrific details of the passage, recall that Josephus records that one million Jews died from famine or the sword, and that 97,000 of them were scattered as Prisoners of War throughout the Empire: They *"fell by the sword and were led captive into all the nations"* (21:24a).[131]

But wait! Why did I say, "fulfilled *in some sense*" in AD 70? If everything through verse 24a was fulfilled in 70 AD, does that mean that there won't be wars and rumors of wars at the end of time? No, it doesn't. Those wars are prophesied by other passages — 1 Thes. 5:1–4, 2 Thes. 2:1–4, 2 Tim. 3:1 — and they seem to continue even here in verses 25, etc. In other words, though a primary fulfillment of these words had to do with the destruction of the Temple, that destruction was also a foreshadowing of the

---

[129] Josephus, *The Wars of the Jews*, VI.v.3, *Works*, op. cit., 582.
[130] Though some question the historicity of this event. See Hendricksen, op. cit., 937.
[131] Josephus, op. cit., VI.ix.3, p. 587.

Great Tribulation which is still to come. Similar conditions will occur. This passage can be about the historic destruction of the Temple and *still* be relevant to the end times. Plummer says it well: The passage refers to the destruction of Jerusalem *"regarded as the type of the end of the world."*[132]

After all, it would not be the first "double fulfillment" in messianic prophecy. When it comes to biblical prophecy, double fulfillment is definitely a "thing." Isaiah's virgin who shall conceive was a woman who was alive when he spoke, and whose child after she had conceived would not be old enough to distinguish good and evil before God destroyed the two kings Ahaz feared (Is. 7:14–16). She is also the virgin Mary (Mat. 1:23). "Out of Egypt I have called my son" (Hos. 11:1) refers to the Exodus. It also refers to Mary and Joseph's flight to Egypt to protect the baby Jesus from Herod (Mat. 2:15). It does not mean the Apostles were cheating when they applied to Jesus those prophecies that originally had a different meaning. They recognized that God works in patterns that repeat themselves. It is reasonable to expect that we will see the same pattern with prophecies about the Second Coming.

II. The Sequence Of Events

We can now make a more educated guess at the sequence of events. More educated, but still only a guess—I have not forgotten what I said last week! First comes the sack of Jerusalem and the destruction of the Temple, described through Luke 21:24a, which took place in AD 70. Then the Times of the Gentiles begin (24b). We may still be in that time, or it may have ended in 1948 (with the founding of modern Israel) or 1967 (with the recapture of Jerusalem). Many have thought these dates significant, but they cannot be more than guesses before the fact. The Arabs could push Israel into the sea tomorrow, and God could have the Jews back in the land again in a thousand years. We do not know. Next comes the Great Tribulation itself, described apparently in verses 25–26. After that is the Second Coming of Christ, in verse 27.

What is the significance of the sequence? The destruction of the Temple was God's judgment on Israel for its rejection of the Messiah. It is also the most profound statement He could have made that pre–Messianic, or non–Messianic, Judaism is obsolete. Christ has come! The religion of the Old Testament alone is over. Those who would follow the true God must now follow Him on into the New Testament, or not follow Him any longer at all. The detailed fulfillment of those parts of the prophecy related to AD 70 show the certainty of the fulfillment of the whole sequence. By trusting in and obeying these words, first–century Christians in Jerusalem saved their skins, as they were intended to do. Therefore, by trusting in and obeying the rest, by being on guard against dissipation, by alertness, and by prayer (verses 34–36), we may be faithful in our own day or even be enabled to stand in the Last Day. Don't miss that: the same practices that will let you stand in any day will let you stand in the Last Day. There is

---

[132] Plummer, op, cit., 485; emphasis in the original.

an organic unity to the whole sequence of events. The fulfillment of the first part sets in motion the fulfillment of the rest. And therefore, whether we are somewhere in the middle or close to the end, we may lift up our own heads, for our redemption draweth nigh.

III. The Meaning Of Verse 32

Are we now in a position to understand what Jesus meant when he said that *"this generation will not pass away until all things take place"*? I hope so. There have been many attempts. Hal Lindsey and his school maintained that it means the generation born in 1967. (This would mean that the Second Coming would be expected by 2007, which would mean Lindsey's pre–tribulation rapture should have happened in 2000. Oops!) Even if history had not already eliminated that option, it really made no sense even in the 1960s. Jesus' words were *this* generation, not *that* generation. It really would help if people would pay attention to the text! Many others hold that Jesus was talking about the Jewish race: Jewry itself is the generation that will not pass away. God will preserve the Jews in existence until the Second Coming. This would alleviate the burden of seeing everything fulfilled within forty years or so of the 30s AD. But if Luke had meant us to think that Jesus meant the Jewish race, he could have used the Greek word for race, **εθνη** (*ethne*), rather than the word for generation, **γενεα** (*genea*), to translate the Lord's Aramaic. So that solution doesn't work either. Besides, it does nothing to answer the disciples' question of *when* the *destruction* would take place.

I think the solution lies in combining the organic unity of the sequence of events with the clearer perspective provided by comparing this passage with Matthew's fuller version in Matthew 24. In Matthew, the disciples ask a double question: when will *all these things* (i.e., the destruction of the Temple) be, and what will be the sign of *your coming*? When Jesus said that "all these things" would take place before the current generation passed away, he was referring specifically to the first part of the question as phrased by the disciples. And indeed, the Temple was destroyed about forty years, or one generation, later. The phrase "all these things" *could* be taken to refer to everything being discussed, which includes the Second Coming. It is by forgetting the way the original question was phrased that we have taken it that way, creating the problem. But there is no problem if we pay sufficient attention to the context, which should tell us that the generation is a plain and simple generation, the one then living, and that "all these things" is an answer to the question that generation was asking, about the destruction of the Temple. In other words, it is not "*all* these things" but "all *these* things," i.e., the sack of Jerusalem and the destruction of the Temple, which would happen in the lifetime of the people asking the question. The Second Coming has turned out not to be in that generation after all. Will it be in ours? Possibly. But nobody knows.

Conclusion

What then is the bottom line? We cannot swear that we live in the last generation, but we do live in "the last days." They started when Jesus accomplished His first mission with the Cross and Resurrection. And we live in the "times of the Gentiles." They started when the Temple was destroyed. They may very well have progressed through verse 24 of Luke 21. In other words, while Jesus' prophecy will not in fact let us calculate the time frame (based on figuring out who the "generation" is), it does tell us that an organic, unified series of events leading to the Second Coming has already begun to be played out. It has already been set in motion with the fulfillment of the first part concerning the destruction of the Temple; it is in that sense "at hand." Therefore, we should live in readiness, whether the final cascade of events toward the end should begin in our own generation or not. That is the point. The readiness, as Hamlet said, is all.[133] What does that mean in practical terms?

A former parishioner's father was told by his physicians that he only had a few months to live. As a result, he had to decide what the most important thing was in his life. Was it to build a new house, to buy a new car, to get one more promotion? Not in that time frame! It was to bring about a reconciliation between two of his children who had become estranged. To see that happen before he died was all that mattered to him. And so he rose from his death bed to drive one of them to that reunion with the other. Why? Because he had been served notice. The end was near! Therefore, he had to discern what was really important.

Well, brothers and sisters, we were all served that notice in 70 AD when the Temple was destroyed and the series of events described by our Lord as leading to the end of the world was set in motion. So we had also better decide what is important in life. What is? *"Be on your guard that your hearts may not be weighed down with dissipation and drunkenness and the worries of life, and that day come upon you suddenly like a trap. For it will come upon all those who dwell upon the face of the earth. But keep on the alert at all times, praying in order that you may have strength to escape all these things that are about to take place and stand before the Son of Man."* Don't get bogged down in temporal affairs. Keep on the alert. Pray for strength that you may maintain your witness for Christ with integrity and faithfulness no matter what they may do to you. That is how to be ready while waiting for the Second Coming, whether it be in our lifetime or not. That is how to stand today, and it will be how to stand on any day, even the Last Day. So said our Lord Jesus Christ. Let us listen to Him; let us follow Him.

---

[133] *Hamlet*, act V, scene ii, line 233; *Complete Works*, op. cit., 931.

THE LAST SUPPER

Luke 22:1 Now the Feast of Unleavened Bread, which is called the Passover, was approaching. 2 And the chief priests and the scribes were seeking how they might put him to death, for they were afraid of the people. 3 And Satan entered into Judas, who was called Iscariot, belonging to the number of the Twelve. 4 And he went away and discussed with the chief priests and officers how he might betray him to them. 5 And they were glad, and agreed to give him money. 6 And he consented and began seeking a good opportunity to betray him to them apart from the multitude.

7 Then came the first day of Unleavened Bread on which the Passover Lamb had to be sacrificed. 8 And he sent Peter and John, saying, "Go and prepare the Passover for us, that we may eat it." 9 And they said to him, "Where do you want us to prepare it?" 10 And he said to them, "Behold, when you have entered the city, a man will meet you carrying a pitcher of water. Follow him into the house he enters. 11 And you shall say to the owner of the house, 'The Teacher says to you, "Where is the guest room in which I may eat the Passover with my disciples?"' 12 And he will show you a large, furnished upper room; prepare it there." 13 And they departed and found everything just as he had told them, and they prepared the Passover.

14 And when the hour had come, he reclined at the table, and the apostles with him. 15 And he said to them, "I have earnestly desired to eat this Passover with you before I suffer, 16 for I say to you, I shall never again eat it until it is fulfilled in the Kingdom of God." 17 And when he had taken a cup and given thanks, he said, "Take this and share it among yourselves, 18 for I say to you, I will not drink of the fruit of the vine from now on until the Kingdom of God comes." 19 And when he had taken some bread and given thanks, he broke it and gave it to them, saying, "This is my body which is given for you; do this in remembrance of me." 20 And in the same way he took the cup after they had eaten, saying, "This cup which is poured out for you is the new covenant in my blood. 21 But the hand of the one betraying me is with me on the table. 22 For indeed the Son of Man is going as it has been determined; but woe to that man by whom he is betrayed!" 23 And they began to discuss among themselves which one of them it might be who was going to do this thing.

Introduction

As we consider the passage of Scripture before us today, we ought as it were to remove the shoes from off our feet like Moses at the Burning Bush, for we are standing on holy ground. At last, the Lord comes to the crisis up to which His whole life has led, the crisis up to which Luke's whole narrative has led. We have been in Passion Week since the Triumphal Entry way back in chapter 19. But now we come to the very night in which He was betrayed. As we enter with the Lord and the Twelve into that Upper Room, we may learn something both about the Savior Himself and the Supper He instituted: something, that is, about the Passover Lamb and about the Lamb's Passover.

I. The Passover Lamb

The whole context—and that is why I read such a long passage again this morning—focuses our attention on our Lord Jesus as the Passover Lamb. In verses 2–6, His betrayal by Judas, and thus His own sacrificial death, is foreshadowed. In verse 7, what we have come to call the Last Supper takes place on the very day on which the ritual Passover lamb was sacrificed. Clearly the Last Supper is a Passover Seder, but Luke carefully mentions only the unleavened bread and two of the cups. Why is there no mention of the main course, the lamb? Because none of Luke's words will be allowed to distract attention from Jesus, the true Passover Lamb, for whose real sacrifice all this symbolic meal serves as preparation—indeed has served so since the very first Passover lamb was sacrificed by Moses himself. Then we return to the topic of betrayal in verse 21–23, making the whole passage a kind of betrayal sandwich. It is no accident that this account of the Last Supper begins and ends with reference to the betrayal which will hand this innocent Victim over to the religious authorities. Everything is here to point to one inescapable fact: the words of John the Baptist are about to be fulfilled. *"Behold, the Lamb of God, which taketh away the sins of the world!"* (John 1:29).

If the point of this passage is to present the Lord Jesus Christ as the true fulfillment of Passover, as the Lamb of God who taketh away the sins of the world, then we must pause to think about that ancient Jewish feast which commemorated Israel's deliverance from slavery in Egypt. The night before the tenth plague, each Israeli family slew the Passover lamb and painted its blood on the lintel of their doorpost, so that when the Angel of Death saw the blood he would pass over that house and spare it. There are at least six features of that historic sacrifice that are relevant to understanding what was happening with Jesus here.

In the first place, **the sacrifice of the Passover lamb was <u>substitutionary</u>.** It was God's provision to protect His people from His wrath and judgment in the final plague poured out on the Egyptians, the coming of the Death Angel to smite the firstborn. One can put it no plainer than to say that the lamb died *instead of* the firstborn son; the lamb died *in his place*; the lamb died that he might live. The lamb died as a substitute for the son. And so it was with the death of our Lord. *"For the Son of Man did not come to be served, but to serve, and to give his life a ransom for many"* (Mark 10:45). *"For while we were still helpless, at the right time, Christ died for the ungodly. For one will hardly die for a righteous man, though perhaps for the good man some would dare even to die. But God demonstrates his love toward us in this, in that while we were yet sinners, Christ died for us"* (Romans 5:6–8). The Greek "for us" can accurately be translated "in our place." *"For the love of Christ constrains us, having concluded this, that one died for all"* (2 Cor. 5:14). *"I have been crucified with Christ; and it is no longer I who live, but Christ lives in me. And the life I now live in the flesh I live by faith in the Son of God, who loved me and gave himself up for me"* (Gal. 2:20). Christ became identified with us to the point that he could take our sins, be identified with them, and be punished for them in our place. *"He made him who knew no sin to be sin* *on our behalf, that we might become the righteousness of God in him"* (2 Cor. 5:21). Like the Passover lamb of old, Christ died in our place. The sacrifice of the Passover Lamb was substitutionary.

In the second place, **the sacrifice of the Passover lamb was propitiatory.** That is, it covered the sin of His people from God's sight, and thus averted His judgment. They showed this by sprinkling the blood as a sign on their doorposts, so that when the Death Angel came, he could say, *"When I see the blood, I will pass over you."* They were covered, protected from judgment, by the blood. This is why the feast which celebrated that deliverance was called "Passover." The sacrifice of the Passover lamb was propitiatory. And so it was with the death of our Lord. *"For all have sinned and fall short of the glory of God, being justified as a gift by his grace through the redemption which is in Christ Jesus, whom God displayed publicly as a propitiation in his blood through faith"* (Rom. 3:23–25a). *"And when you were dead in your transgression and the uncircumcision of your flesh, he made you alive together with him, having forgiven us all our transgressions, having cancelled out the certificate of debt consisting of decrees against us, and which was hostile to us. And he has taken it out of the way, having nailed it to the cross"* (Col. 2:13–14). Because he died as our substitute, Christ's death covers our sin, cancels it, takes it out of the way, and protects us from the judgment which would otherwise inevitably befall it. Like the Passover lamb of old, Christ died to protect us from judgment. The sacrifice of the Passover Lamb was propitiatory.

Third, *the sacrifice of the Passover lamb was obligatory.* It was obligatory, that is necessary, essential, indispensable. Without it, without the blood sprinkled on the doorposts and the lintel, there would be weeping and wailing and gnashing of teeth, there would be the death of the firstborn the next morning. Good intentions would count for nothing. Only a faith in God's promises that was serious enough to produce obedience and lead to the sacrifice and the sprinkling would distinguish you from the Egyptians. There were no exceptions. The sacrifice of the Passover lamb was obligatory. And so it is with the death of our Lord. *"There is no other name given under heaven, whereby you must be saved"* (Acts 4:12). Good intentions are worth nothing; sincerity will not avail. Only the blood of Christ applied to your heart by faith will save you in the day of judgment. The sacrifice of the Passover Lamb was obligatory.

Fourth, **the sacrifice of the Passover lamb was freely available.** Anyone could choose to participate. All who trusted in God's promise and who sacrificed the lamb and sprinkled his blood would be saved—even Egyptians. Though God had chosen Israel as His special possession and His peculiar people, then as now He was no respecter of persons, and His salvation was made available to anyone who responded to Him in faith. And so it is with the death of our Lord. *"For God so loved the world that he gave his only begotten Son that whosoever believeth in him should not perish but have everlasting life"* (John 3:16). Is there a more bracing, a more exciting, a more inviting and encouraging and heart–stopping word in the English language than that one little word in this context, *whosoever*? The sacrifice of the Passover Lamb was freely available.

Fifth, **the sacrifice of the Passover lamb was <u>totally</u> efficacious.** There is no record of any family who sacrificed the lamb and sprinkled the blood who was not spared. The faithful were distinguished from the rebellious with infallible efficiency, and those protected by the blood were spared with inexorable effectiveness. The promise of God was a thing you could trust, a thing you could lean your whole weight on, a thing you could stake your life and indeed your eternity on. And so it is with the death of our Lord. *"There is therefore now no condemnation for those who are in Christ Jesus"* (Rom. 8:1). No condemnation! None! Not one word of condemnation for any of them! *"But as many as received him, to them he gave the right to become children of God, even to those who believe in his name"* (John 1:12). *"If you confess with your mouth Jesus as Lord and believe in your heart that God raised him from the dead, you shall be saved. For with the heart man believes, resulting in righteousness, and with the mouth he confesses, resulting in salvation. For the Scripture says, 'Whoever believes in him will not be disappointed'"* (Rom. 10:9–11). This is what the sacrifice of Christ has done. It is the most powerful act in the history of the universe, as was shown when its first fruit was our Lord's own resurrection from the dead. It has never failed, it will not fail, it cannot fail to save those who trust in it with all their hearts. The sacrifice of the Passover Lamb was totally efficacious.

Finally, **the sacrifice of the Passover lamb was celebrated as a <u>continual memorial</u> in Israel.** After a millennium and a half, Jesus and his disciples celebrated that memorial in the Upper Room in this very passage. And two millennia more have passed since then—to what effect? To this very day observant Jews around the world still hold that feast on the day of Passover. To this day the father still asks the oldest son, "Why is this day different from every other day?" To this day the cups of wine, the unleavened bread, the bitter herbs, and the Passover lamb are served at a table with one empty seat. So powerful was the sacrifice of that Old Testament shadow of Christ that the hope of that people has not died yet, and is still expressed in the confession, "Next year in Jerusalem!" The sacrifice of the Passover Lamb was celebrated as continual memorial by God's people. And so it is with the death of our Lord. *"This do, as oft as ye do it, in remembrance of me,"* He said. And so we shall obey His commandment once again this very morning. The sacrifice of the Passover Lamb was substitutionary, it was propitiatory, it was obligatory, it was freely available, it was totally efficacious, and it was celebrated as a continual memorial in Israel. It was the perfect picture, the perfect prophecy, the perfect object lesson to prepare for the Lord Jesus Christ, whose death fulfilled all these truths in the most profound way imaginable. Truly, He was the Passover Lamb who taketh away the sins of the world (John 1:29).

II. The Lamb's Passover

But do you see what else is here? If Jesus was the Passover Lamb, then the Lord's Supper, the Eucharist, Holy Communion, is the Lamb's Passover. It was from the context of the Passover Seder that Jesus plucked those elements which became the Lord's Supper. It was *that* unleavened bread, *that* wine, already associated with the Old Testament redemption, that He chose to represent His own body and blood, which He was about to sacrifice for us. Do you hear all this in His words which we still repeat whenever we celebrate Communion? *"This is my body which is given for you; this do in remembrance of me." "This cup is the new covenant in my blood which is poured out for you." "This do, as oft as ye do it, in remembrance of me."*

There are many things in life which are so important that you do not want to forget them. That is why we still re–enact the Thanksgiving celebration of the Pilgrims. It is why we still celebrate the Fourth of July, the day we declared our independence as a nation, based on the self–evident truth that all men are created equal and are endowed by their Creator with certain inalienable rights. It is why we celebrate birthdays and anniversaries. And rightly so. But those things, deserving of a memorial as they are, pale into insignificance next to this, along with Christmas and Good Friday and Easter. *"This do, as oft as ye do it, in remembrance of me."*

It is because Jesus was the Passover Lamb that Communion is the Lamb's Passover. Why is this day different from every other day? Christian liturgies do not typically include that question in the celebration of Communion, but maybe they should. Why, also, is it different even from the Jewish Passover? Because Jesus was the Passover Lamb, the reality to which the Old Testament sacrifice pointed. Do you hear that question in your mind when you receive the bread and the wine? "Why is this day different from every other day?" Do you supply the answer? "Because on the First Day of the Week we remember that Jesus rose on Sunday, having died for our sins as the Lamb of God who taketh away the sins of the world" (John 1:29). You should.

And do you remember another New Testament phrase we often quote? *"Whenever we eat the bread or drink the cup, we do show forth the Lord's death until he come."* "Until He come!" Do not miss the fact that the institution of The Lord's Supper immediately follows His long discussion of the Second Coming that we studied the last two weeks. To receive Communion is a historical memorial and an eschatological affirmation, simultaneously looking back the Cross and ahead to the Marriage Supper of the Lamb. That is why *"until he come"* is an essential part of it, following inexorably from "show forth the Lord's death."

When we hear that phrase, we should also hear that other affirmation from the Jewish feast which is our antecedent. "Until He come!" "Next year in Jerusalem!" Do you not hear it ringing from the bread and from the wine? It is implied right here in our passage. *"I will not drink of the fruit of the vine from now on until the Kingdom of God comes."* Do you hear it? "Next year in Jerusalem!" Next year in Jerusalem! My friends, because Jesus was the true Passover Lamb, because this is the Lamb's Passover, because all of this really happened as Luke records it, this bread and this wine is God's promise to every person who believes in Christ and confesses His name. It is God's promise that we are forgiven; it is God's promise that we are accepted; it is God's promise that we are going home!

Conclusion

What our Lord said to the Twelve in verse 15 he says to you right now. *"I have earnestly desired to eat this Passover with you."* He earnestly desires you to receive Him by faith as your own personal Savior and Lord so that you may truly partake of these symbols of His body given and His blood shed for us, in remembrance of what He did for you. The sacrifice of the Passover Lamb was substitutionary, it was propitiatory, it was obligatory, it was freely available, it was totally efficacious, and it was celebrated as a continual memorial in Israel. The sacrifice of God's true Passover Lamb can therefore be all those things for you as well. And therefore, *"If you confess with your mouth Jesus as Lord and believe in your heart that God raised him from the dead, you shall be saved. For with the heart man believes, resulting in righteousness, and with the mouth he confesses, resulting in salvation. For the Scripture says, 'Whoever believes in him will not be disappointed'"* (Romans 10:9–11). Do so now, that you may join us! For this we shall do in remembrance of Him. Christ our Passover is sacrificed for us. Therefore, let us keep the feast (1 Cor. 5:7–8).

FINAL INSTRUCTIONS

Luke 22:24 And there arose also a dispute among them as to which one of them was regarded to be the greatest. 25 And he said to them, "The kings of the Gentiles lord it over them, and those who have authority over them are called 'benefactors.' 26 But not so with you, but let him who is greatest among you become as the youngest, and the leader as the servant. 27 For who is greater, the one who reclines at the table or the one who serves? Is it not the one who reclines at the table? But I am among you as the one who serves. 28 And you are those who have stood by me in my trials. 29 And just as my Father has granted me a kingdom, I grant you 30 that you may eat and drink at my table in my kingdom, and you will sit on thrones judging the twelve tribes of Israel."

31 "Simon, Simon, behold Satan has demanded permission to sift you like wheat. 32 But I have prayed for you, that your faith may not fail. And you, when once you have turned, strengthen your brothers." 33 And he said to him, "Lord, with you I am ready to go both to prison and to death!" 34 And he said, "I say to you, Peter, the cock will not crow today until you have denied three times that you know me."

35 And he said to them, "When I sent you out without purse and bag and sandals, you did not lack anything, did you?" And they said, "No, nothing." 36 And he said to them, "But now let him who has a purse take it along, likewise also a bag, and let him who has no sword sell his robe and buy one. 37 For I tell you that this which is written must be fulfilled in me, 'And he was numbered among the transgressors.' For that which is written about me has its fulfillment." 38 And they said, "Lord, look, here are two swords." And he said to them, "It is enough."

Introduction

All people naturally feel that a great deal of solemnity and significance attaches itself to the last words of great men. Sometimes they have risen to great moments of eloquence and profundity. "I only regret that I have but one life to give for my country." —Nathan Hale, about to be hanged. "Be of good cheer, master Ridley, and play the man, and by God's grace we shall light this day such a candle in England as shall never be put out!" —Hugh Latimer, as he faced martyrdom through burning at the stake. "Eighty–six years I have served Him [the Lord Jesus Christ] and he never did me wrong. How can I blaspheme my King who saved me?" –Polycarp, refusing to curse Christ in order to save his life. "Let us cross over the River and rest in the shade of the trees." —Stonewall Jackson. "Fight on!" —Francis Schaeffer.

Our Lord Jesus Christ was granted by the Father to give his final instructions to His followers twice: once before His death (here in this passage) and again before His ascension into Heaven (the Great Commission). These are not literally His last words—those would be the Seven Last Words from the Cross—but they are His final instructions to His followers before his impending death, before leaving them. Since they are instructions for His disciples, they are then also His last instructions for us. Let us hear them as such. They include a great commandment; a great caution; and a great counsel.

I. A Great Commandment (vv. 24–30)

This is not what we have come to call the Great Commandment—that we love God with all our heart, mind, soul, and strength, and our neighbor as ourselves (Luke 10:27). Nor is it the New Commandment that flows from it—that we love one another as Jesus has loved us (John 13:34). But it is a great commandment that fits right with those and is a necessary part of a life in which they are being obeyed: Let the one who aspires to be great among you be the servant of all.

The context of this teaching is of course the argument over which one of the disciples was the greatest (verse 24). This dispute was probably a reaction to the prophecy that one of them would betray the Lord, which we read last time. As the disciples tumbled over one another to distance themselves from any suspicion that they were that one, their protestations of loyalty and devotion would easily have escalated in extravagance until they overflowed into another argument over which one of them was indeed the greatest. John chapter 13, where we see the incident of the Foot Washing, fits here in the life of our Lord. It was part of Christ's response to this same squabble on the same occasion. We learn from John that He not only *taught* that they should be servants of one another, but *modeled* it, performing Himself the office of a menial servant and washing the disciples' feet. How humbled the disciples must have been by that! The climax of John's account is Jesus' words, "*A new commandment I give to you, that you love one another, even as I have also loved you. . . . By this shall all men know that you are my disciples, if you have love for one another*" (John 13:34–5). The words we have read today are part of that same conversation. It fills out our understanding of that love by showing us one form it should take: "*I am among you as one who serves*" (verse 27).

It is not the first time this issue has come up. On another occasion Jesus had responded to the same argument by standing a little child in the midst of the group and telling the disciples that they would have to become like little children if they wanted to enter the kingdom. They still at this point have not learned the lesson. Like them, I suspect we also need a reminder. Once again, the Lord has emphasized that the path to greatness in the Kingdom is the path of sacrifice and servanthood. It was important enough to be part of Jesus' final instructions as he was about to leave the world. And John tells us why: "*By this men will know that you are my disciples.*" What do people know about us?

The promise of reward in verses 28–30 for those who learn the lesson, "*that you may eat and drink at my table in my kingdom, and you will sit on thrones judging the twelve tribes of Israel,*" should be a powerful encouragement and incentive. God has indeed destined us for greatness. The disciples would sit on twelve thrones judging the tribes of Israel! But the path to true greatness is not grasping for greatness, but rather the path of laying down your life for the brethren. Don't lord it over one another like the Gentiles! Let the one who is greatest be the servant of all. For I am among you as one who serves. And it is enough for the servant that he be like his Master.

II. A Great Caution (vv. 31–34)

So there is a Great Commandment for us as we await the Lord's return: to love one another and to show it by being the one who serves. There is also a Great Caution. Peter still hasn't figured out this whole servant thing. He is still asserting his greatness, professing his readiness to follow Christ to prison or to death. And so the Lord delivers a warning that was especially for Peter but has an application to all of us. We will return to Peter when we reach the part of the story in which his denial occurs. For today, let's concentrate on what we can learn about our own weaknesses and our own situation.

We have a great Enemy who is constantly looking for opportunities to trip us up, and we should not take him lightly. But neither should we live in fear of him, but rather with confidence in the One who is greater. There is a twofold message here. First, Peter, Satan is going to *"sift you like wheat."* What does that mean? He is going to mess with you to the point that you will think you are going to come apart. You may feel like wheat feels when it is being ground into flour! But the second part is that Jesus has prayed for Peter. Satan will only be allowed to go so far, and Peter's faith will not be destroyed.

There is a twofold lesson here, and we need both parts of it. We have a great Enemy; we should be sober. But he can only go as far as he is permitted; we should be confident. Peter had a misplaced confidence in his own faithfulness, and hence lacked a proper sobriety which left him vulnerable to temptation. It led to his denying the Lord. Others have the opposite problem: They fall into despair. We are to do neither, but rather walk in sober confidence because we are trusting not in our own faithfulness but in Christ's.

When you next come into temptation, remember two things. First, Satan is on a leash! He hates you and wants to trip you up and destroy your testimony. He wants to do you harm. But he can only go as far as he is permitted. What he intends as harm, God will use as training in righteousness to strengthen you spiritually. If you want to get stronger physically, you can't just wave your arms around. You have to have some weights in your hands. You have to work against resistance. What Satan intends as harm, God can use as spiritual resistance training to make you stronger. Which it will be depends on your response. But it is Christ, not Satan, who is in control. Never forget that.

The second thing to remember is even more astounding. Jesus is praying for you! Christ our great Mediator, Christ our Intercessor, is praying for you that your faith will not fail. It is not just an abstract truth that Christ, not Satan, is in control during times of temptation. What this detail of Jesus praying for you does is to make it a highly specific and personal truth. Christ is praying for *you*! In other words, He is taking a personal interest in your situation. He knows all about it, and He is in your corner. He is pulling for you, and He is putting that into very practical action by praying to the Father for you. He will keep Satan on his leash so that you will not be tempted above what you are able; but it is more than that. He is personally interested in you, personally invested in your success—to the point of shedding his blood.

When you enter into temptation, then, don't just remember that God is sovereign. Remember that Christ is praying for you at that very moment. *That* is why it is always possible for you to stand; it doesn't just depend on you. You can ask for strength to make the right decision in that moment, and you are asking Someone who has already beat you to that prayer, who got there ahead of you, because He really wants to answer it. It is in the light of that astounding fact that we experience the reality that faith is the victory that overcomes the world.

III. A Great Counsel (vv. 35–8)

So we have a Great Commandment, to love and serve one another, and we have a Great Caution, the Satan wants to sift us but Christ is praying for us. Finally, we have a Great Counsel. *"But now let him who has a purse take it along, likewise also a bag, and let him who has no sword sell his robe and buy one. 37 For I tell you that this which is written must be fulfilled in me, 'And he was numbered among the transgressors.' For that which is written about me has its fulfillment." 38 And they said, "Lord, look, here are two swords." And he said to them, "It is enough."*

This last section is one of the most misunderstood in all of Scripture. People talk about it as if they thought the swords were the point—if you'll pardon the expression. Does the Jesus who told us to turn the other cheek really want us to sell our cloaks to buy swords? Why were two enough, when the instruction seemed to apply to all twelve of the disciples? Having encouraged the disciples to acquire swords, why does Jesus turn around and condemn Peter for using his in the Garden of Gethsemane? How does this passage relate to the prooftexts for and against pacifism? These are all exercises in missing the, er, point.

The key to understanding this whole conversation is verse 37. The reason for the change in directions for Christian missions is the fulfillment of the prophecy that Jesus was to be numbered among the transgressors. Why does that mean that we should suddenly start taking bags and spare sandals and even swords when before when we went out two by two we took none of those things and suffered no lack? The point is that before when the disciples were sent out, Jesus was popular, and they basked in His popularity. People mostly received them with enthusiastic hospitality and catered to their every need. But now the situation has changed. Now they are going to be looked at as criminals. In other words, what Jesus is saying in his usual graphic way is, "Get used to hard times." The sword for which they were to trade their robes was a symbol, technically a metonymy, for how hard those times were about to get. The disciples—like some of their equally dense descendants—took the swords literally, and the two who had them (we know one was Peter) proceeded proudly to pull them out in demonstration of how prepared they were (i.e., greater than the others—ahem). Can you hear the sadness and resignation in Jesus' voice when he says, "It is enough"? It was not an estimate that one sword for every six followers is the right ratio! I think it was something like, "Never mind. You guys still aren't ready to understand yet. Never mind. Pentecost is coming. It will be Okay. Then. I'm just dropping the subject for now. Sigh."

The point of the sword then is that it is an illustration of the kind of commitment that was going to be required for the hard times that were coming. Jesus' counsel to us is not to buy a sword—or a Smith and Wesson. Whether or not you are going to own firearms you will have to decide on other grounds. What *is* the point? It is to be prepared to give up anything and everything if only we can go on fighting, if only we can continue the spiritual struggle for the souls of men and women. It is to be prepared for opposition that might even lead to martyrdom. It is to be a good soldier of Jesus Christ, not entangling yourself with the affairs of this life, as Paul would later apply it to Timothy.

Summary

Do you hear what Jesus is saying? God has destined you for greatness, true greatness, not the false counterfeit pursued by men who lord it over one another. Therefore, practice servant leadership now and love one another; therefore, beware of your own weakness and trust in God when Satan attacks you; therefore, have the firmest commitment to life as spiritual warfare, so that the true Kingdom may indeed come.

Conclusion

Last instructions are significant ones, and Jesus' two sets should be taken together. The very last set, the Great Commission, gives us our purpose and our mission, to make disciples of all nations. These last words in the Upper Room give us the attitudes we will need to successfully carry that mission out. Show me a church which has a servant spirit flowing from genuine love from Jesus in its hearts—show me a church which is humble and which puts itself in the hand of God so it can learn and grow through its trials and temptations—show me a church which is prepared for hardship and is committed, whose most valuable possession is its sword—and I will show you a church where people are getting saved and believers are being strengthened. May God help us increasingly to be such a church.

GETHSEMANE

Luke 22:39 And he came out and proceeded as was his custom to the Mount of Olives, and the disciples also followed him. 40 And when he arrived at the place, he said to them, "Pray that you may not enter into temptation." 41 And he withdrew from them about a stone's throw, and he knelt down and began to pray, 42 saying, "Father, if thou art willing, remove this cup from me; yet not my will, but thine, be done." 43 Now an angel from heaven appeared to him, strengthening him. 44 And being in agony, he was praying very fervently—and his sweat became like drops of blood falling down upon the ground. 45 and when he rose from prayer, he came to the disciples and found them sleeping from sorrow, 46 and said to them, "Why are you sleeping? Rise and pray that you may not enter into temptation."

Introduction

We come today to a very solemn and strategic portion of Scripture. For though the Lord Jesus Christ was a man of sorrows and acquainted with grief throughout His earthly ministry, though He had accepted the role of Sin Bearer at His Baptism, and though it is His long obedience to the Father which has brought Him to this moment, still it is here that the sufferings, the Passion of Jesus Christ, begin in earnest. G. Campbell Morgan said, "As I ponder it, through that darkened window there is a mystic light shining, showing me the terrors of the Cross more clearly than I see them even when I come to Calvary."[134] And so it is. By that light we may see something of the Mission of Christ, something of the Submission of Christ, and something of the Commission of Christ to us.

I. The Mission Of Jesus Christ

First, the mission of Christ. In order to understand this passage, we must ask a question whose answer might at first seem obvious, but which turns out to be anything but. Why is the Lord so upset over his impending death that He sweats, as it were, drops of blood? Well, you say, He knows that He is going to be betrayed and rejected and killed—killed in one of the most gruesome ways ever devised by the sick mind of man. Indeed, He does. But many of His followers have since faced their own equally gruesome deaths with courage and even joy—with an equanimity that Jesus himself seems to lack here. How can this be?

The Apostle Paul said, *"And now, behold, bound in spirit, I am on my way to Jerusalem, not knowing what will happen there, except that in every city the Holy Spirit solemnly testifies to me that bonds and afflictions await me. But I do not consider my life of any account as dear to myself, in order that I may finish my course"* (Acts 20:22–25). A little later when his friends tried to dissuade him from going, he said, *"What are you doing, weeping and*

---

[134] Qtd. in Norval Geldenhuys, *Commentary on the Gospel of Luke* (Grand Rapids, MI: Eerdmans, 1951), 377.

breaking my heart? For I am ready not only to be bound, but even to die at Jerusalem for the name of the Lord Jesus" (Acts 21:13). And he wrote to the Philippians, "*For me to live is Christ, and to die is gain*" (Phil. 1:21). He was not talking about a peaceful death like a ripe fruit falling from the branch, but about being beheaded. Yet there is nothing in any of these passages about the passing of any cups from the Apostle Paul!

And it is not just the Apostle. Ignatius of Antioch, on his way to martyrdom in Rome at the turn of the Second Century, wrote, "May nothing seen or unseen begrudge me making my way to Jesus Christ. Come fire, cross, battling with wild beasts, wrenching of bones, mangling of limbs, crushing of my whole body, cruel tortures of the Devil—only let me get to Jesus Christ!"[135] A few years later, Polycarp, the disciple of John, on being offered the chance to live if he would only curse Christ, replied, "Eighty–six years have I served him, and he never did me any wrong. How can I blaspheme my king who saved me?"[136] These were not just empty words, for those men proceeded to die as bravely as they had written or spoken. Years later, as Hugh Latimer was being led out to be burned at the stake for his testimony for the Gospel of Christ, he turned to his fellow prisoner and victim Nicholas Ridley and said, "Be of good cheer, master Ridley, and play the man, and we shall this day by God's grace light such a candle in England as shall never be put out!"[137] It would almost be worth a burning at the stake to be remembered for words like that. (I said "almost"—don't get any ideas.)

Now, let me ask you: Is it possible that the One who was the very source of the life, strength, and courage that allowed so many of His followers to face death with courage and even joy—is it possible that He should face it himself with less confidence and peace and serenity than they? Is it possible that the stream should rise higher than its Source? Is it possible that Jesus' disciples should outshine their own Master in bravery? That the Lion of Judah should be less bold in the face of death than we mice? No, no, a thousand times no, it is not possible! So what are we to make of all this sweat like blood and this desperate–sounding request that the Cup might pass away?

There is only one thing that we can make of it. The only answer is that the Cup did not represent the pains and the agony of physical death, even that cruelest of prolonged tortures, death on a cross. I submit to you that what made even the Lord of Glory so upset was the fact that in less than one day He faced the prospect of being identified with, of bearing, the sin of the human race—your sin and mine. That was a burden so great and oppressive—especially to this holy One—that even Omnipotence could well shrink from bearing it. And shrink He did.

---

[135] Ignatius of Antioch, "To the Romans," *Early Christian Fathers*, ed. Cyril C. Richardson, The Library of Christian Classics, vol. 1 (Philadelphia, PA: Westminster Press, 1953), 105.

[136] "The Martyrdom of Polycarp," *Early Christian Fathers*, op. cit., 152.

[137] Quoted in many versions which ultimately go back to Foxe's *Acts and Monuments* or *Foxe's Book of Martyrs*. https://en.wikiquote.org/wiki/Hugh_Latimer

What is coming to a head here is a whole stream of Scriptural teaching that overflowed into drops of sweat like blood on the brow of our Lord. Isaiah had said it well, looking forward to the Cross: *"All we like sheep have gone astray. Each of us has turned to his own way. But the Lord has caused the iniquity of us all to fall on him"* (Is. 53:6). And looking back on it, Paul described Christ as having been *"displayed publicly as a propitiation in his blood"* (Rom. 3:25). The word "propitiation" simply means precisely what Isaiah had said: the iniquity of us all, and with it the full display of the Father's wrath and displeasure against sin, fell on the shoulders of Christ. He goes on to explain the basis of our reconciliation with God: *"He made him who knew no sin to be sin on our behalf, that we might become the righteousness of God in him"* (2 Cor. 5:21). And he concludes that *"Christ redeemed us from the curse of the Law, having become a curse for us—for it is written, 'cursed is everyone who hangs on a tree'"* (Gal. 3:13). Christ was about to die a propitiatory death as our Substitute. He who knew no sin was about to be so closely identified with our sins in the Father's eye that Paul could say He would *be* sin. That was His mission, the very reason for which He had come. And only in Gethsemane do we begin fully to see what it meant to him.

The Cup that Jesus wanted to pass from Him then was the emotional and spiritual agony of being associated with our sin. Think of the worst sin ever committed. What do you think it was? Hitler and the holocaust? The even greater genocides committed by Stalin or Mao or Pol Pot? The degradation of pornography? The callousness with which our society values no-fault promiscuity over the sanctity of human life in abortion? The betrayal of Christ by Judas? The betrayal of the entire human race by Adam and Eve? The greatest sin ever? Not an answerable question. But never mind. Do not think of that. Think of the worst guilt and shame *you* have ever felt personally! Think of the one shameful act you are really glad I am not going to ask you to share to the group. Then multiply that by infinity and try to imagine its impact on a heart totally pure, untainted, uncalloused, unjaded, undulled by sin. You begin to get just an inkling of what our Lord subjected Himself to for us!

Worst of all, He would have to face the displeasure of His heavenly Father, the One whose will was His meat and drink (John 4:31–34), the One with whom He had been in perfect unbroken loving communion for all of eternity. But now it would be very different. The hatred of sin which drove the moneychangers from the temple—the hatred of sin which rained fire and brimstone on Sodom and Gomorrha—the hatred of sin which slew the firstborn of Egypt—unleashing all the righteous judgment against sin held back for all the millennia of human history, concentrated now in all its infinite force: That is what would nail Jesus Christ to the Cross! No wonder, in spite of His great love for us, in spite even of His great devotion to the Father's will, He prayed, "Father, if it be thy will—Father, if there is any other way—Father, let this Cup pass from me!"

Brothers and sisters, Sin is a terrible thing! When you are less than honest in your financial dealings—when you repeat that bit of idle gossip—when you allow those angry and bitter words to escape from your lips—when you allow your mind to dwell on impure thoughts, much less act them out—when you put anything ahead of God in your life—you are guilty of sin. And it took nothing less than the agony of Jesus Christ on the Cross, foreshadowed by His agony in Gethsemane, to atone for it. Do you want to know what sin is? Ultimately, look at Jesus Christ on the Cross. Do you want to know what sin is? First, look at Jesus Christ in the Garden. George Herbert expressed it well:

> Who would know Sin, let him repair
> Unto Mount Olivet. There shall he see
> A man so wrung with pains that all his hair,
> His skin, his garments bloody be.
> Sin is that press and vice that forceth pain
> To hunt its cruel food through every vein.

And then you may begin to understand why the Cross is such Good News. For He did bear it there—all of it—so that we would not have to bear it anymore, if only we will give our hearts to Him! And so Herbert continues:

> Who would know Love, let him assay
> And taste that juice that on the cross a pike
> Did set again abroach. Then let him say
> If ever he did taste the like.
> Love is that liquor, sweet and most divine,
> That my God feels as blood, and I as wine.[138]

II. The Submission Of Jesus Christ

Are you beginning to understand what this moment meant to our Lord? Well, there is yet more to be revealed. We have seen the Mission of Jesus Christ, to bear our sin. We also see something almost inexpressible about the Submission of Jesus Christ, to the will of the Father. The burden of sin was so great, so painful, so oppressive, that even Omnipotence shrunk from bearing it. But the love of our Lord Jesus was so great that He committed himself to bearing it anyway. It is not until we begin to understand what the Cross meant to our Lord that we can begin to understand the depths of His love expressed when he said, "*Yet not my will, but thine, be done*" (verse 42).

There are actually two different Greek words translated "will" in verse 42. "If it be thy will, ει βουλει (*ei boulei*), let this cup pass from me; nevertheless, not my will but thine, πλην μη το θελημα μου αλλα σου (*plen me to thelema mou alla to sou*) be done." Βουλομαι (*boulomai*) means to make plans and carry them out; θελημα (*thelema*) is preference or desire. So we could translate our Lord's words more fully thus: "If it is in accordance with your plan [to atone for the sins of the race], let this cup pass;

---

[138] George Herbert, "The Agonie," *The Works of George Herbert*, ed. F. E. Hutchinson (Oxford: Clarendon Press, 1941), 37.

nevertheless, it is not what I prefer, but what you do; that is what I embrace as needing to happen." If there is any other way to atone for the sins of our people, please, let's find it! But if not, I am fully committed to doing this thing, no matter how costly. Or, as Paul would put it later, *"God commendeth his love to us in this, in that while we were yet sinners, Christ died for us"* (Rom. 5:8).

We must understand what the crucifixion meant to our Lord so that we can understand the way His submission to the Father's will manifests His love both for us and for the Father. What could cause the Son of God to take on his pure unsullied shoulders this burden from which even Omnipotence shrank? Only the love of God. *"God commendeth his love to us in this, in that while we were yet sinners, Christ died for us."* Yes, knowing full well the cost, He embraced it for us. What wondrous love is this? To bear the fearful curse for my soul![139] We cannot see very far into these depths, but the least glimpse must be enough to change our lives forever.

Some of you are holding back on your Christian commitment because you are afraid of what you might have to give up. I can only say this. Take a long, hard look at the Lord Jesus Christ kneeling here in the Garden of Gethsemane. And if you still don't want to follow Him, then don't. But for me, I have to look also from Him to the disciples, sleeping as Jesus was making His peace with the Father's will—and doing it for them! And what I see then is our Lord longing for someone to step out from the crowd, to say, "This man cannot stand alone!" That would not be the disciples, not yet; later it would. They did not yet understand—but now some of us do. Can we not watch with him one hour? Not that we could be of any help in bearing that burden—none whatsoever.

But we could cast ourselves at His feet!

I don't know about you, but I cannot look at this scene which is before us today and find myself in any other place than on my face at His feet. Only there can I too be submitted to the will of the Father as I should be.

III. A Commission From Jesus Christ

There is the Mission of our Lord Jesus Christ, to bear our sins; there is the Submission of our Lord Jesus Christ, to the will of the Father; there is also a Commission from our Lord Jesus Christ: We are to watch with Him and pray. Specifically, we are to pray that we do not enter into temptation. The prayer is not that we will not experience trials. To "enter into" temptation is an idiom that means to yield to it—to say, in whatever trials may come to us, something different from what Jesus said in His: *"Nevertheless, not my will but thine be done."* To understand what the disciples *should* have been praying, we must attend to what Jesus *was* praying. The lesson for us is that, in whatever our trials may be, we should face them as Jesus faced His. And the only way we can do that is by facing them *with* Him. When that kind of temptation comes, then

---

[139] Anon., "What Wondrous Love is This?" *Trinity Hymnal,* op. cit., 261.

prayer itself, communion with God, is the only way through. And when we find ourselves needing to pray that way, we can now have the added encouragement of knowing that our Lord has been there—indeed, in an infinitely worse place—before us. When we need the strength to say, "*Nevertheless, not my will but thine be done,*" the One sitting at the right hand of the Throne as our Mediator is this very One we are watching in the Garden this morning. If you do not turn to Him in your time of trouble for the strength to pray as He prayed, then it is as almost if you are letting those drops of blood–like sweat fall to the ground in vain.

Conclusion

What then do we learn from this strategic and sobering scene? We learn to hate sin as God does, because of what it did to our Lord. We learn to love Jesus as we should, because of what He let it do to Him instead of to us. We learn to love God the way Jesus did, who was obedient unto death, even death on a Cross. And so we learn to pray, daily, hourly, constantly, that we may not enter into temptation. Why?

> Who would know Sin, let him repair
> Unto Mount Olivet. There shall he see
> A man so wrung with pains that all his hair,
> His skin, his garments bloody be.
> Sin is that press and vice that forceth pain
> To hunt its cruel food through every vein.
>
> Who would know Love, let him assay
> And taste that juice that on the cross a pike
> Did set again abroach. Then let him say
> If ever he did taste the like.
> Love is that liquor, sweet and most divine,
> That my God feels as blood, and I as wine.

Amen.

THE ARREST OF JESUS

Luke 22:47 While he was still speaking, a multitude came, and the one called Judas, one of the twelve, was preceding them. And he approached Jesus to kiss him. 48 And Jesus said to him, "Judas, are you betraying the Son of Man with a kiss?" 49 And when those who were around him saw what was going to happen, they said, "Lord, shall we strike with the sword?" 50 And a certain one of them struck the slave of the high priest and cut off his right ear. 51 But Jesus answered and said, "Stop! No more of this." And he touched his ear and healed him. 52 And Jesus said to the chief priests and officers of the temple and elders who had come against him, "Have you come out with swords and clubs as against a robber? 53 While I was with you daily in the temple, you did not lay hands on me. But this hour and the power of darkness is yours."

Introduction

Of twenty–four chapters in his Gospel, Luke devotes twenty–two to the last three years of Jesus' life. Of those twenty–two, five and a half are devoted to the last week of it and the forty days that followed that. Of 1, 151 verses, 268 are devoted to the one week between the Triumphal Entry and the Resurrection. In other words, twenty three percent of the book is devoted to less than one percent of the time Jesus spent in public ministry, to .0005% of his life. This ratio is similar to that in the other Gospels, and it points out the supreme importance of these events that we are covering in these last few messages. We will therefore look at each episode in some detail, starting with the one we have before us today, the arrest of Jesus. In this account of that gross miscarriage of justice, I would like to highlight three points that are not necessarily related conceptually. I confess that, for once, my points are related only by alliteration and their near simultaneity of occurrence as parts of this episode. But they are all important parts of it which need to be considered. They are The Perfidious Kiss, the Petrine Cut, and the Power of the Curse.

I. The Perfidious Kiss (v. 48)

We start in verse 48 with the Perfidious Kiss. *And Jesus said to him, "Judas, are you betraying the Son of Man with a kiss?"* I want to preface my remarks about this verse by reminding you of an important bit of theology: the reality of the incarnation of our Lord. Jesus was God. He was the same person as the eternal Logos, the Second Person of the Trinity. At every moment of eternity and at every moment (save one) of his earthly life, He enjoyed perfect communion with the Father. By that personal connection to the Godhead, He still possessed all the attributes of God, including omniscience. But for the sake of our redemption, He had also taken on human nature, and that human nature was also absolutely real. So the divine Person emptied Himself of His glory and His prerogatives and identified Himself with us so closely that He normally limited himself to operating through that finite human nature. As a result of His self–discipline in that ongoing self–sacrifice, He really experienced our life as we live it. He never cheated, as it were, by using His divine power to make His earthly life easier. Do you remember the Temptation, when He refused to turn stones into bread even though He was practically starving after forty days and forty nights of fasting? The bottom line of that discipline is one of the most incomprehensibly astounding facts about Him. It is incomprehensibly astounding, and it is absolutely essential to our redemption: As a result of His incarnation, the totally self–sufficient One could get hungry; the omnipotent One could get tired; and the living God could die.

One further implication is particularly pertinent here: The constant experience of omniscience is part of the glory that our Lord laid aside in order to come to us and identify himself with us as our Head, our Lord, our Substitute, and our Savior. As God, He still had omniscience—the Father could give him any information he needed to pursue his ministry. But he normally limited himself to operating through the few paltry million neurons of the finite human brain that came with the very human man Jesus of Nazareth. You see this clearly in Matthew 24:36. Speaking of his Second Coming, Jesus said, *"Of that day and hour no one knows, not even the angels in heaven, nor the Son, but only the Father."* How could the divine and therefore omniscient Son not know this? Because there was only room for a finite amount of knowledge in the finite human brain He was using. The day and hour of the Second Coming was on a "need–to–know" basis, and He didn't need to know. (Neither, apparently, do His modern disciples, despite the rather arrogant and disobedient attempts by many of them to figure it out.) My point in this long theological digression is to bring into focus one of the strange paradoxes of the divine–human Messiah. Jesus (in one sense) knew everything, but he was capable of being surprised.

And that is part of what makes this the unkindest kiss on record. The word order in the original Greek of verse 48 puts a strong emphasis on the word "kiss." **Ιουδα, φιληματι** τον υιον του ανθρωπου **παραδιδως**? *"Iouda, **philemati** ton huion tou anthropou paradidos?"* "Judas. . . with a KISS you betray the Son of Man?" Jesus knew that Judas was going to be the betrayer, but He was not expecting the method to be so cruel as this. He loved Judas; Judas was one of his closest friends. He knew that Judas had been driven to this action, perhaps by disillusionment over Jesus' failure to be the military messiah everyone was expecting. But Jesus was affected by the level of brazen hypocrisy of that kiss; He was shocked and hurt by the meaning behind that kiss. This kiss cut deep. It was worse than He expected.

The words still echo through history. *"Et tu, Brute?* Then fall, Caesar!"[140] "Judas . . . with a KISS?" No one has captured it better than Michael Card:

Why did it have to be a friend who chose to betray the Lord?

---

[140] Shakespeare, "Julius Caesar," act III, scene 1, line 77; *Works,* op. cit., 829.

And why did he do it with a kiss? That's not what a kiss is for.
Only a friend betrays a friend; a stranger has naught to gain.
And only a friend comes close enough to ever cause so much pain.[141]

"Et tu, Brute?" "Judas . . . with a KISS?" It was 1986. I had just resigned from my pastorate in Marietta, Georgia, because the Board had refused to back me in a matter of church discipline that was biblically required of us. As a reward for my integrity, I was out of work for a year, put on the shelf. It felt like I had been abandoned. "Lord, I really could have used some backup!" The worst part was the way I had been betrayed by a man on that Board that I had thought was my friend. He had been telling me, "Yes, we need to do this. I've got your back!" I will never forget that crucial moment at the Board meeting when instead of backing me up, he just lowered his head and refused to make eye contact. It's been almost forty years now, and I think I've gotten over it, until something reminds me and that knife–wound in my back suddenly cuts as sharply and aches as badly as it did when it was fresh.

It was the most depressing period of my life. I questioned my calling and my very identity. It was hard not to feel betrayed by God, not just by _____. But I doggedly kept reading my Bible and praying, though I was not feeling any comfort from it. Then, at my lowest, I happened to come to this passage as I was having my devotions as is my custom in the Greek New Testament. And I saw for the first time the emphasis on that word. "Judas—with a KISS?" And I broke down and wept like a baby. "Oh, my goodness!" I sobbed. "Now I get it. You went through *that* for me!" Betrayal hurts. I simply pause on it for a moment once again today as one small insight into the sufferings of Jesus Christ for our redemption.

II. The Petrine Cut (vv. 49–51)

So the first thing we notice is the Perfidious Kiss. Everything else in the sermon is probably going to seem anticlimactic after that. Forgive me. It needs to be covered. The first thing we notice is the Perfidious Kiss. The next is the Petrine Cut. *And when those who were around him saw what was going to happen, they said, "Lord, shall we strike with the sword?" And a certain one of them struck the slave of the high priest and cut off his right ear. But Jesus answered and said, "Stop! No more of this." And he touched his ear and healed him* (verses 49–51). We know from John's account (18:10) that the impetuous disciple who drew his sword was our old friend Simon Peter Surprise, surprise! What impresses me here is the astounding level of his gross misunderstanding of the situation. We have already seen a couple of weeks ago that he missed the point of Jesus' advice to sell your cloak and buy a sword. No doubt he was one of the two who pulled theirs out then to show they were ahead of the curve. The sadness in Jesus' sigh, "It is enough," went right over his head.

---

141 Michael Card, "Why?" https://www.songlyrics.com/michael-card/why-lyrics/

But that was not the only thing that had gone over his head! After all this time Peter was still looking for a military Messiah to overthrow the Roman oppressor. After all this time he still did not realize that Jesus had come to die a sacrificial death for sin. He did not understand that, because Jesus was the innocent Lamb of God, it was important that it be plain that His trial was irregular and unjust. Therefore, Peter almost blew it by giving the temple officials a legitimate excuse for arresting Jesus. He was not a very good swordsman. No doubt, his blow was intended not just to cut off the servant's ear, but to cleave his skull. Give me Aragorn and Gimli at my side, not Peter, if I ever have to go up against any orcs! But despite the incompetence of His disciple in using both the physical and the spiritual sword, Jesus stayed in control of the situation. He rebuked Peter and healed the ear (so much for a legitimate excuse to arrest Him), and things proceeded according to the Father's plan after all.

Peter's stroke here shows us something we have noted before in these studies: the power for evil of preconceived notions. Just think of what Peter had heard that should have told him different; listen just to a part, from Luke's account, of what he had managed to miss, reinterpret, or ignore. *"The Son of Man must suffer many things and be rejected by the elders and chief priest and scribes, and be killed, and be raised up on the third day"* (Luke 9:22). On the Mount of Transfiguration, he had heard Moses and Elijah talking with Jesus about *"his departure [Greek, exodus] which he was about to accomplish in Jerusalem"* (9:31). *"Let these words sink into your ears, for the Son of Man is going to be delivered into the hands of men"* (9:44). *"Whoever does not carry his own cross cannot come after me and be my disciple"* (14:27). The Son of Man will come in power and glory, *"But first he must suffer many things and be rejected by this generation"* (17:25). *"And he took the twelve aside and said to them, 'Behold, we are going up to Jerusalem, and all things which are written through the prophets about the Son of Man will be accomplished. For he will be delivered to the Gentiles and will be mocked and mistreated and spat upon, and after they have scourged him, they will kill him; and the third day he will rise again'"* (18:31–33). *"But when the vine growers saw him, they reasoned among themselves, saying, 'This is the heir; let us kill him that the inheritance may be ours'"* (20:14). *"And in the same way he took the cup, saying, 'This cup which is poured out for you is the New Covenant in my blood'"* (22:10). *"For I tell you that this which is written about me must be fulfilled, 'He was numbered among the transgressors'"* (22:37).

This teaching was brutal in its bluntness; it was incisive in its clarity; it was unparalleled in its authority; it was more than sufficient in its quantity, indeed abundant to the point of tedium in its repetitions. Yet Peter not only missed it, but he was so far out of harmony with the Lord's real purpose that his zeal served only to threaten to wreck God's plan for our redemption. How clueless can you be? Well, when we were natural men and women, we were just as bad. *"For the natural man receives not the things of the Spirit of God, neither can he know them, for they are spiritually discerned"* (1 Cor. 2:14).

What are the lessons we should take away from this near fiasco? Sincerity is not enough; zeal is not enough; good intentions are not enough. A sound and accurate understanding of biblical doctrine is absolutely essential equipment for Christian service and faithful discipleship. Judas with evil intentions betrayed Jesus with an insincere act of love. Peter with the noblest of intentions almost betrayed him with an ignorant act of war. And if we are not grounded in sound doctrine, we are capable of doing exactly the same thing.

Let us then beware lest our own assumptions cheat us of the truth of Scripture! My experience as a preacher tells me that the people of God have an almost infinite capacity to listen to the Word of God read and expounded without ever hearing a single solitary thing they do not already believe. It never even occurred to Peter that his assumptions might be wrong! Has it occurred to you? Let us begin with an awareness of the problem. That, combined with a sincere love of God's truth, unmerciful honesty with ourselves as we read and hear, and conscious dependence on the Holy Spirit, is half the battle.

III. The Power Of The Curse (v. 53)

So there was a Perfidious Kiss; there was a Petrine Cut; and finally there is the Power of the Curse. *And Jesus said to the chief priests and officers of the temple and elders who had come against him, "Have you come out with swords and clubs as against a robber? While I was with you daily in the temple, you did not lay hands on me. But this hour and the power of darkness is yours"* (verses 52–3). These are among the most mysterious and chilling words ever spoken: *"This hour is yours, and the power of darkness."* Evil is about to do its worst, and that worst—the torture and murder of God—is a horrible thing to contemplate. The power of darkness refers to human nature in its typical depravity and degradation, egged on by a power literally diabolical. It is not a pretty picture. This was something that human nature did. Our human nature. Therefore, we must presume that we, apart from grace—you and I, had we been there—would rather brutalize an innocent man who had spent the last three years doing nothing but good to the undeserving than let Him challenge our preconceived notions and upset our comfortable *status quo*. And this hour was given to us for that purpose so that, while we were yet sinners, Christ could die for us.

Yet even in these most chilling of words are hidden the seeds of hope. *"This* hour is yours," Jesus says to the mob. *This* hour; not every hour. As James R. Edwards puts it, "The 'hour' has arrived when these climactic forces conspire against Jesus. They are free to kill God's Son and Servant—and they will—but they are not free to determine the consequences"[142] Norval Geldenhuys says, "In that hour the evil powers of darkness, Satan and his henchman (men and spirits alike) are being permitted by God

---

[142] James R. Edwards, *The Gospel According to Luke*, The Pillar New Testament Commentary (Grand Rapids, MI: Eerdmans, 2015), 651.

to bring the Son of the Highest down into the grip of humiliation, suffering, and death—not because He is not mighty enough to prevent all this, but because He voluntarily delivers Himself to be sacrificed for the salvation of guilty mankind"[143]

Again: *This* hour, Jesus said. Not every hour; not the hour of sunrise on the third day after the Crucifixion. Not *any* hour after that! The Evil Power in the universe was strong enough to kill the Son of God. But it was not strong enough to prevent His resurrection! J. C. Ryle sums it up well: "Our Lord's enemies could not take and slay Him until the appointed 'hour' of His weakness arrived. Nor yet could they prevent His rising again . . . . When He was led forth to Calvary, it was 'their hour.' When He rose victorious from the grave, it was His"[144]

And *because* He rose victorious, now *every* hour is His forevermore. And that includes this hour. It includes the darkest hour you have ever known; it includes the darkest hour you have coming. If we belong to Him, it is the same in our lives. If you are a Christian, the power of darkness may be given an hour in your life. But God reserves eternity for Himself! Because Christ rose victorious, in Him we will rise too—even over death. And if over death, then certainly in Christ you can rise over whatever you are struggling with in this hour of your life. That hour belonged to the mob and to the power of darkness. This one, and every other one that will ever come, belongs to Jesus.

Conclusion

Remembering the Perfidious Kiss and the Petrine Cut, then, let us beware of betraying the Lord who endured so much for us. Judas did so intentionally by his nefarious treachery. Peter almost did so unintentionally by his impetuous stupidity. And remembering the Power of the Curse and how it was overcome, let us realize that by God's grace we need do neither, if we cling to this One who was so faithful to us. As we receive Communion today, let us renew our vows of faithfulness to Him in the light of these great truths.

---

[143] Geldenhuys, *Commentary on the Gospel of Luke*, op. cit., 581.
[144] J. C. Ryle, *Expository Thoughts on the Gospels* (Grand Rapids, MI: Baker, 1977), 2:432.

BEFORE THE ROOSTER CROWS

Luke 22:54 And having arrested him, they led him away and brought him to the house of the high priest; but Peter was following at a distance. 55 And after they had kindled a fire in the middle of the courtyard and sat down together, Peter was sitting among them. 56 And a certain servant girl, seeing him as he sat in the firelight, and looking intently at him, said, "This man was with him too." 57 But he denied it, saying, "Woman, I do not know him." 58 And a little bit later, another saw him and said, "You are one of them too!" But Pete said, "Man, I am not!" 59 And after an hour had passed, another man began to insist, saying, "Certainly this man also was with him, for he is a Galilean too." 60 But Peter said, "Man, I do not know what you are talking about." And immediately, while he was still speaking, a cock crowed. 61 And the Lord turned and looked at Peter. And Peter remembered the word of the Lord, how he told him, "Before a cock crows today, you will deny me three times." 62. And he went out and wept bitterly.

Introduction

We come today to consider a depressing topic denominated by an ugly word: *backsliding*. Webster defines backsliding as "a loss of zeal in religion or morals." Therefore, only a Believer can really backslide, for only he has any true zeal to lose.

Yet backsliding is a word I hesitate even to use, for it seems to me a word much abused. I hear people say of someone, "He is a backslidden Christian" when there is no evidence of any love of God, no hatred of sin, no regular attendance at public worship, no commitment to a Bible–believing church, no regular Bible reading or prayer as part of the person's life, etc. All this is true of the person, and he does not seem to be the least bothered by it or concerned about it. But this is not the description of a person who is backslidden so much as of a person who is lost! I fear that many whom we think of as backslidden Christians are really just lost sinners; many people we think of as backslidden Christians are really apostates. It is not ultimately possible for us to judge, for only God sees the heart. But Scripture is plain that the kind of person I have been describing, the kind of person we might be tempted to describe as "contentedly backslidden," is in a spiritually perilous position indeed. We should not give people the false hope of applying to them the doctrine of eternal security as to "backslidden Christians" when they give no evidence of real conversion in their lives in the first place!

Yet this is a topic that we must discuss, for it is a thing that happens. We lose our first love, we begin to drift, to grow cold, to become spiritually aimless. A real Christian can lose, for a time, not his connection with Christ or his relationship with Him, but his joy in Him and his testimony for Him. If he is a real Christian, he will not be able to do so contentedly or with impunity. If he is a real Christian who was truly converted, not just one who professed faith for a while, he will not be able to do so permanently. And all this we see in the example of Peter in the sad passage that is before us today. It can teach us something about the Beginnings of Backsliding, the Bitterness of Backsliding, and the Way Back from Backsliding, the way beyond it.

I. The Beginnings Of Backsliding

Backsliding does not happen overnight or out of the blue. It has its beginnings in a slowly growing neglect of our walk with the Lord. And therefore, there are early warning signs, as it were. Brothers and sisters, I want you to look for these early warning signs in yourselves this morning, and to take them even more seriously than you would the early warning signs of cancer! You know full well that if you find a lump in your breast that was not there before, if you notice a change in the size, shape, or color of a mole, you need to get yourself to the physician without delay. And if you see these early warning signs of backsliding, you need to get to your knees with the same alacrity. For they are the signs of a spiritual cancer potentially as dangerous to your soul as physical cancer is to your body. What are these signs?

1. The first and most important is a **Proud Self–Confidence**, a confidence in the flesh. Peter's failing here did not come on him out of the blue this night. It has its origins in things that were already going on in his life. For we recently heard him saying, with absolutely no clue what he was talking about, *"Lord, I am ready to go with you both to prison and to death!"* (Luke 22:33). Look back to that passage, and you will see that this is the statement that caused the Lord to predict Peter's betrayal, his denial three times before the crowing of the cock.

Scripture is replete with warnings on this score. What did Paul say? *"I find then the principle that evil is present with me, to one who wishes to do good. For I joyfully concur with the Law of God in the inner man, but I see a different law in the members of my body, waging war against the law of my mind and making me a prisoner of the law of sin."* This conflict comes to a climax in the agonizing cry, *"Wretched man that I am! Who will set me free from the body of this death?"* And the answer is *"Thanks be to God through Jesus Christ our Lord!"* (Rom. 7:21–25a). If we ever forget that law in our members and think we can live the Christian life by our own strength or in our own wisdom apart from moment by moment upholding by the grace of God: from that moment the process of backsliding has begun. On our own small scale we will come to experience the bitter irony in the contrast between Peter's "I am ready!" and his "I don't know what you are talking about." The moment we forget that we are only branches, the moment we try to live the Christian life without abiding in the Vine, the moment we forget that *"Apart from me ye can do nothing"* (John 15:5); from that moment we are on the path which will lead us, if we follow it, to that fire in the courtyard.

A Christian should indeed be supremely confident. But it must be confidence in our Lord Jesus Christ, and not in ourselves. Pride goeth before a fall. When you think you stand, take heed lest ye fall. When you think you are safe from sin and temptation, you are the most vulnerable. Self confidence in spiritual things is the sign of a hard or a shallow heart with little understanding either of the power of sin or of Christ in your life. It is the first step on the road to spiritual impotence and unreality. It is the first step on the path of backsliding.

2. The next early warning sign is a **Neglect of Bible Reading and Prayer**. Do you remember that in our message from last time we rehearsed the multitude of verses, statements by the Lord that Peter had heard, which clearly taught the necessity of a suffering Messiah? Yet when the crisis came, we found Peter drawing his sword to cut off the servant's ear (22:50). Peter had had the teaching of the Lord's prayer and the example of Jesus' prayer life, and yet in the Garden we found him falling asleep despite the Lord's exhortation to pray that he enter not into temptation (22:40, 45–6). Somebody has not been paying attention! Somebody's attention to the Word of God has been only perfunctory at best. If Peter had indeed been praying *"Lead us not into temptation"* and meaning it, would he have behaved differently in the courtyard? Alas, Alas! We will never know.

The Bible and Prayer are two of the most important lifelines of the Christian life. By extension we can add to them Christian fellowship, regular attendance at public worship and the sacraments, and Christian service: the means of growth. To grow lax in these things, to grow neglectful of them, is to be like an athlete who eats only junk food, who never runs laps or visits the weight room, who is late to practice or absent from it—and then wonders why his performance drops off! To neglect these things is a sign either of pride ("I don't need them") or of a lack of love for Jesus ("I don't want them"). In either case, it is a danger sign of the greatest magnitude.

3. When sinful pride and confidence in the flesh leads us to neglect of Bible study and prayer, unless these problems are corrected, they will eventually produce the third symptom—no longer an early warning sign, but a sign of great and critical danger. And that is a **Deliberate Distancing of Oneself from the Lord** and from spiritual things. We see it in Peter in verse 54: He was *"following the Lord afar off,"* as the King James says, or *"at a distance,"* as the NASB renders it. Pride and neglect can be passive; we can slide into them almost without noticing. But now there is an active choice. We are still following—we aren't apostates—but not too close! We find other places to be on Sunday morning. Increasingly minor and trivial excuses become acceptable reasons for missing worship. At this point spiritual things may become actually distasteful to us. We therefore avoid them, because they remind us of how far we have fallen, how unworthily we are walking. Instead of witnessing for the Lord, we begin to avoid the topic. A worldly lifestyle may start to creep in. All of this bothers us, at least a little—if it didn't, it would be a sign that we are not truly Christians at all—but we are not yet ready to do anything about it. But listen: Things will get worse still if they do not get better. Our danger is great.

4. The final stage of this process comes when with Peter we reach verse 55. *"And after they had kindled a fire in the middle of the courtyard and sat down together, Peter was*

sitting among them." There is now **a Positive Effort to Melt into the Crowd** and be just like the world. We have not yet denied Christ openly, but we are following him afar off. And if this process continues unchecked, we will find ourselves in verse 57: *"Woman, I do not know him."* It is inevitable. Peter did not mean to say this. He never thought he would hear such words come out of his mouth. And he still did not mean them. But he said them. Do you think you are better able to navigate such waters than our Lord's Apostle? Beware! If even the faintest beginnings of these warning signs are detectable in your life, your danger is great.

II. The Bitterness Of Backsliding

So those are the Beginnings of Backsliding: proud self–confidence, neglect of Bible reading and prayer, following afar off, melting into the world. Now we are in a position to understand the true Bitterness of Backsliding. And fortunately, there is no need to linger over it and analyze it like we did the Beginnings. But we do need to note it. Now we are ready to hear verse 62: *"And he went out and wept bitterly."* The one who is truly a backslidden Believer is a person like Peter. The one who has tasted the good things of the Lord and maybe even professed faith in Christ and joined the church but never been truly converted has a different problem. For him, this process (the current buzz word is "deconstructing") simply leads him out of a faith that never really took hold in his life. But the backslidden Believer is a person who, like Peter, really does love the Lord deep down, but who, like Peter, has presumed on his relationship with Christ rather than really living by faith in him. And so he will come to a point where the knowledge of his denial, the knowledge of his betrayal, the knowledge even of his neglect, will be a far more bitter experience to him than he ever could have imagined when he was letting himself slip. Some never reach that crisis of bitter anguish. But they experience a loss of meaning, of purpose, of fulfillment, of joy—for what? For the path of least resistance? For the approval of men? Dust and ashes! Dust and ashes! Dust and ashes.

III. Beyond Backsliding

What then is the cure for this spiritual cancer? How do we get Beyond Backsliding? Like with any physical disease, the best cure is never to let it get started. The best treatment is prevention! And so I plead with you to examine yourself today. Do you see any of the early warning signs? Admit them! Confess them! Forsake them! Do not give this horrible syndrome a chance to get started in your life.

But it may be that there is someone here today who is already far gone along this path. You have already begun to feel the bitterness of backsliding, and maybe like MacBeth you think that you are so far in that to go back were as tedious as to go on.[145] Is there hope for you? Yes! You are not yet so far gone as Peter was. So let us pay careful attention to what got Peter started on the road to recovery. What snapped him out of

---

[145] Shakespeare, "MacBeth," act III, scene iv, lines 136-8; *Works,* op. cit., 1205.

his pattern of denial and got him started on the road to the sorrow that led to repentance and restoration? The answer is found in verse 61: *"And the Lord turned and looked at Peter. And Peter remembered the word of the Lord."*

The Lord turned and looked at Peter! What do you think Peter saw in that look? Was it a reproachful "How could you!"? Was it a triumphant "I told you so!"? We know the Lord Jesus better than that. And we also know human psychology well enough to realize that such glances might have produced shame, self–hatred, or despair, but would have been very unlikely to produce godly sorrow leading ultimately to repentance. I think we know very well what Peter saw in that look: a sad but compassionate "I love you!" I love you? Think of it! At the moment His whole life had led to, at the turning point of all of history, before captors out to kill Him, facing mockery and brutality, Jesus had time to think of Peter. I love you! No wonder Peter's denials came to an abrupt halt. There was no doubt a lot of shame, self–hatred, and despair present in Peter's tears at first, especially until after the resurrection. But there was also the godly sorrow leading to repentance, at least embryonically, and we know this because of the outcome. For we know what is coming when Jesus appeared to the disciples on the shores of the Sea of Galilee at the end of John's Gospel. *"Peter, do you love me? Feed my sheep"* (John 21:15–17).

Backslidden Christian, can you see that gaze? It is directed at you even now! Jesus still loves you. In spite of all your sin, in spite of all your neglect of His provision for you, in spite even of your betrayal and denial, He still loves you. If that does not stop you in your tracks and turn you around and make you start to follow him again, nothing will. But it can! What it did for Peter it can do for you as well. You may need spiritual counsel, you may need to make some adjustments in your approach to living the Christian life, you may be burned out on "doing church" or trying to follow Christ in your own strength. There may be lots of adjustments you need to make, things you need to learn or unlearn. But the path back to spiritual health doesn't *start* with any of that. It starts with coming back to the basics. "Jesus loves me, this I know / For the Bible tells me so." Will you come back today?

Conclusion

Backsliding is a horrible spiritual cancer, but there is preventive medicine: Never forget how much Jesus loves you. Recognize the early warning signs that you have forgotten Jesus' love, and act on them before they become serious. Never entertain the thought that you can live the Christian life apart from Christ. Never neglect your Bible, your Prayers, your Church. Never get into the habit of following afar off. By this and by God's grace we can avoid the bitter experience of Peter. But even if you are already there, the way back starts in the same place. If you have forgotten how Jesus loves you, remember it. And you can remember it best by looking to that place to which all these verses are driving us: the Cross. By that Cross and God's grace you may also experience the restoration of Peter. May the Lord grant it to the glory of his Son. Amen.

THE SANHEDRIN TRIAL

Luke 22:63 And the men who were holding Jesus in custody were mocking him and beating him, 64 and they blindfolded him and were asking him, saying, "Prophesy! Who is the one who hit you?" 65 And they were saying many other things against him, blaspheming. 66 And when it was day, the Council of Elders of the people assembled, both chief priests and scribes, and they led him away to their council chamber, saying, 67 "If you are the Christ, tell us." But he said to them, "If I tell you, you will not believe, 68 and if I ask you a question you will not answer. 69 But from now on the Son of Man will be seated at the right hand of the power of God." 70 And they all said, "Are you the Son of God, then?" And he said to them, "Yes, I am." 71 And they said, "What further need do we have of witnesses? For we have heard it ourselves from his own mouth."

Introduction

The passage we have before us today is a great study in contrasts. Now, contrast is one of the most effective methods of definition. Try to imagine being able to understand darkness apart from light, evil apart from goodness, hunger apart from satisfaction, sickness apart from health, or sorrow apart from joy. Therefore, contrast is a technique frequently used by both visual and literary artists to bring out those features of their subject that they especially want us to notice. Can you remember in Hans Holbein the Younger's portrait of Henry VIII the way the rich, elaborately textured ornamentation of the royal robes contrasts with the bare, flat background? In Leonardo Da Vinci's portrait of the Mona Lisa he achieves a similar effect of highlighting in the opposite manner, as the simple folds of her garment contrast with the rich and complex tapestry of the landscape behind her. So also in his account of the Sanhedrin Trial, Luke uses the same technique of contrast to highlight at least three important ideas in his portrait of the Lord Jesus Christ.

Appearance And Reality

The first important contrast is between Appearance and Reality. Experience teaches us that they often do not coincide. The clouds that look like solid mountains from a distance dissolve into mist when you enter them. A stick half submerged in water looks bent for all the world—but it is really still straight. And the world sure looks flat from here; but it did not look that way at all to Neal Armstrong and Buzz Aldrin looking back from the Moon.

So it is in the trial of Christ by the Sanhedrin. The appearance—what you would have seen with the outward eyes if you had been in the gallery—was not very inspiring. The prisoner not only looks weak and helpless, but rather undignified, inglorious, and even pitiful. He even looks guilty. After all, why else would he refuse to answer the questions put to him? We all know what people assume when someone takes the Fifth

Amendment. And all that "You will see the Son of Man" stuff sounds like whistling in the dark. I doubt any of us would have been able to see through that appearance to the reality.

And what was the reality? From now on the Son of Man—a rather splendid character from the Book of Daniel of which no one would have been reminded looking at this scene—will be sitting at the right hand of Power (a euphemism for the right hand of God). This disheveled, pitiful looking object of mockery was the Word that was with God and was God (John 1:1), the Light of the World which enlightens every man. Look! There he stands. He looks nothing like any of that. Can you not trust your own eyes? Apparently not.

Was this prisoner weak? Well, His weakness was real, but it was not the whole story; there was more to it than that—though right now, that is all that appearance will show you. Was He weak? Tell that to the demons who screamed in terror at His approach, the lame who are still walking and the blind who are seeing even now, the widow of Nain whose son rose up out of his funeral shroud, or the moneychangers who were helpless to prevent the overturning of their tables in the face of His wrath. Tell it to the disciples, who just a few pages ago were asking, "What manner of man is this, that even the winds and the waves obey him?" (Oh, by the way, where are those disciples? Hiding. Why? Because they were still men of little faith. So this contrast is going to teach us something about the meaning of biblical faith, too.) Was the prisoner inglorious? He had not seemed so on the Mount of Transfiguration. Was He guilty? Guilty of being a false Messiah? Not according to the Voice of God, which at both His Baptism and on the Mount of Transfiguration had proclaimed Him "My beloved Son, in whom I am well pleased . . . my chosen one" (Luke 3:22. 9:35). Nor according to John the Baptist, who had called Him "The Lamb of God who taketh away the sins of the world" (John 1:29). But try to see any of that here. What are you going to believe?

Now, none of the things we have just rehearsed were, as Paul says in Acts 26:26, "done in a corner." So for the disciples, what they seemed to be seeing at this moment vanquished even their own memories. So what we seem to see here must be false; what we do see here then is a very useful definition of faith. How do you tell the difference between Appearance and Reality? By faith: faith in the Wod of God. The disciples were defeated by appearance because of their little faith; the Sanhedrin were deceived by appearance because of their lack of faith. How then does this help us understand what faith is?

Well, how do you know that the stick half submerged in the water is really still straight, despite its appearance? Two things tell you so. First, you remember that it was straight before you stuck it in the water. And, second, this memory is strengthened if you know something about the laws of optics, the different way the light rays are bent by passing through the thicker medium of water as compared to air. Based on the conjunction of these two factors, you have confidence in sticking (ahem) to your belief in the straightness of the stick in spite of its currently crooked appearance. Do you see? Experience interpreted by Doctrine is the foundation of Knowledge. Experience—you remember the stick is straight—plus Doctrine—you understand based on the laws of optics why it looks crooked—constitute your Knowledge of the stick's straightness. So what is faith? Faith is the ability to stick to your well–grounded knowledge of the stick's straightness when what you see at the moment seems to contradict it.

The situation here is no different. Experience—the disciples' (or the elders') memories of Jesus' mighty works—plus Doctrine—their understanding of Old Testament theology as often explained by Jesus—should have allowed them to see what was really happening here instead of what their eyes seemed to be presenting them. Thus, like us looking at the stick in the water, they should have walked by faith and not by sight. Why didn't they? Why do we ourselves have no trouble having faith in the straightness of the stick (and it really is faith, because to sight the stick looks bent) but often allow ourselves to be plagued by doubts when, say, God's promises seem to be delayed or we see the righteous suffer? Well, because there is a lot more at stake in what we see when we are looking at Jesus' trial. But it may help to realize that the stakes really do not change what faith is or how it works.

Faith is the ability to trust in what you know on good grounds to be true over what you seem to see for the moment. Let me repeat that: Faith is the act of trusting in what we know on good grounds to be true over what we seem to be seeing at the moment. Faith is not belief we have without evidence, still less belief contrary to evidence. People may well lack or fail to demand good grounds for what they believe, but that is their problem; it is not the essence of faith! Have you noticed that in Scripture faith is never opposed to or contrasted with knowledge? Never. How could it be, when the disciples had accepted Jesus as their Messiah based on their experience as interpreted by their understanding of biblical doctrine? Just as we have. Faith is not opposed to knowledge, but to sight (2 Cor. 5:7). Faith is the ability to trust in what you know on good grounds to be true over what you seem to see for the moment. Faith is not the opposite of knowledge or of evidence. Faith is being faithful to what we know. Faith is believing, against sight, that the stick in the water is still straight.

By the way, do you remember the series of definitions of faith Luke has given us? It seems to be one of his major themes. If we put them all together, we begin to have a fuller understanding of this crucial spiritual reality—for if Justification is by faith alone, and if faith is the victory that overcomes the world, then there is nothing more important for us to grasp than the true nature of biblical faith, for we can neither become a Christian nor live the Christian life without it. So let's review this theme. In "The Stilling of the Storm," we saw that Faith is an understanding of who Jesus is that produces confidence in His solution to the problem. In "The Healing of the Centurion's Servant," we saw that Faith involves an admission of our own unworthiness, an acceptance of Jesus' authority, and an ascription of excellence to him. Those were the elements of the faith that Jesus commended in the Centurion. At "The Feeding of the Five Thousand," we saw that Faith can be expressed as an equation: an awareness of our need plus an admission of our inability to meet that need plus a determination to obey Jesus in spite of that inability sets the stage for the need to be met by Jesus through our very inability, using our inadequate resources. And here we realize that Faith is the ability to trust in what you know on good grounds to be true over what you seem to see for the moment.

Do you begin to see what it means to exercise faith? Faith is not just "naming it and claiming it" (or "blabbing it and grabbing it"). It is not a belief we have in the absence of evidence or reason. Putting all these definitions together we can say that Faith is a very specific response to God's Word, based on God's character, focused on God's Son, and enabled by God's Spirit, whereby we contradict sight by affirming that the stick is still straight. And when you see that, you truly understand that it is by this faith alone that we are justified, and by this faith alone that we overcome the world.

Treatment And Desert

If faith is trust in God's Word based on His character, it is good that our other two contrasts allow us to focus on that character as revealed in His Son. The next one is the contrast between the Treatment Jesus Received and what he Deserved. I guess you could say that this contrast flows from the first one. Our Lord was treated in accordance with Appearance, and not in accordance with Reality, as the Sanhedrin walked by sight and not by faith. What did he deserve? Worship, adoration, obedience, love, devotion, service. What did he receive? Abuse, spite, brutality, cruelty, mockery. Once again, the contrast could hardly be more stark.

Our observation of this contrast has implications, both for our understanding of life and of salvation. As for life: Life isn't fair! I know you didn't need me to tell you that. But perhaps we do need Jesus' example to make us take it seriously. Life isn't fair. God is just, but the world is fallen, and so His justice is not always seen or experienced now. (Do you see why we took most of our time with the first contrast? Rightly understanding Appearance and Reality is basic to everything else!) Even our Lord and Savior was not exempt from the suffering often brought by this fact.

Now, this is in one sense a very sad reality. But in another, it is a powerfully liberating truth! It can set us free from the disappointment and disillusionment that can be such a sharp challenge to our faith. Life isn't fair! That is often a tough enough fact to face. It is made far worse if you somehow expect that life should be or will be fair.

We already know that life isn't fair. Promotions, tragedies, recognition, and distress are not necessarily or always distributed according to merit. Like Hamlet, we all face the slings and arrows of outrageous fortune, the heartache and the thousand natural shocks that flesh is heir to, the whips and scorns of time, the oppressor's wrong, the proud man's contumely, the pangs of despised love, the law's delay, the insolence of office, and the spurns that patient merit of the unworthy takes.[146] The whole creation groans and suffers the pangs of childbirth until now (Rm. 8:22), longing to be delivered from the futility imposed on it by man's rebellion. The world is out of kilter, and God's people are not exempt from their share of the effects. Yet often we catch ourselves thinking that for some reason we should be—and if we are not, we begin to doubt God's love for us. The disappointments of life are hard enough to take as they are; they are made doubly hard by the assumption that they somehow mean that God has let us down.

Well, God has not let you down! The Appearance that He has forgotten us is not Reality. How do we know this? We know it by looking hard at this scene. Life was infinitely more unfair to Jesus than it has been to you. And if He could bear it because of His love for us, His love for the Father, and the joy that was set before Him; well, then, maybe with His help we can bear the infinitely more trivial examples of temporary unfairness that life has dealt to us. Those examples are the Appearance. But these momentary sufferings are not even worthy to be compared either with those of our Lord or with the unimaginable joy that has been prepared for us (Rom. 8:18). And that is the Reality. The disappointments we face are real and sometimes grievous; they can be heavy burdens to bear. But do not make them worse by the wholly unjustified assumption that life in a fallen and sinful world is, was ever meant to be, or ever could be, fair.

There is an implication here for salvation too. Jesus got the opposite of what He deserved so that we also could get the opposite of what we deserve. He was made sin that we might become the righteousness of God (2 Cor. 5:21). He died that we might live. He was a man of sorrow and acquainted with grief (Is. 53:3) so that we might have joy unspeakable and full of glory in Him forever (1 Pet. 1:8). No, life isn't fair. It's better than fair. We don't get justice, even if we are foolish enough to think we want it. In the long run, we get grace. What could be better than that?

Humiliation And Glorification

Our final set of contrasts is that between the Humiliation and the Glorification of our Lord. These classical theological categories are brought together here in this passage like they are nowhere else. As the mockery, the cruelty, and the shame built toward the climax they would have on the Cross itself, in the very depths of His Humiliation, Jesus looked at the stick in the water and knew that it was straight. And so He said, *"But from now on the Son of Man will be seated at the right hand of the power of God."* No truer words of defiance were ever spoken.

Jesus' earthly life was the time of His Humiliation, when His glory was veiled. Small flashes of that glory got out from between the folds of His robe, as it were, and the lame walked, the blind saw, the dead were raised, demons fled in terror—and sins

---

[146] Shakespeare, "Hamlet," act III, scene ii, lines 58-74; *Works*, op, cit., 906.

were forgiven. But mostly it was the time of His Humiliation, and His glory was veiled. Imagine then the effect when He comes again in His power and glory! Well, it doesn't hurt to try. But we all know we have been told already that we really cannot imagine what that will be like (1 Cor. 2:9)!

From now on, Jesus said, the Son of Man will be sitting at the right hand of Power on high. He has already been raised from the dead. He has already been exalted to the right hand of the throne of God. Do you get what that means? It is now the glorified Christ with whom we have to do! It is the glorified Christ who sent His Holy Spirit to indwell us as His personal agent and representative until He returns. It is the glorified Christ who is now the head of His body, the Church. It is the glorified Christ who sits at the right hand of God to make intercession for us, to represent us as His people to the Father. It is the glorified Christ who is going to come for His own in power and glory, in like manner as the disciples saw him go. It is the glorified Christ whom we proclaim as the Light of Life, the Savior of the World, and the Lord of All. It is the glorified Christ whom we represent in the world and to the world. We proclaim His Humiliation leading to the Cross as the price of our redemption; but we also proclaim that God has raised Him from the dead and made Him Lord and Christ. It is all there in that earliest summary of the Gospel, the Apostolic Kerygma: *Kyrios Christos*, Jesus Christ is Lord! And it is because that is who Jesus is that our faith, our response to God's Word based on His character as revealed in His Son, is truly the victory that overcomes the world.

We ourselves live still in our own period of Humiliation. But lift up your head! For we are not the dupes of Appearance but the inheritors of Reality. We are not the slaves of sight, but conquerors who have caught the character of contrast. We walk by faith and not by sight. And the glorification of our Lord is present Reality that will be seen at his Appearing, but in the light of which we can live already. We walk by faith and not by sight.

Conclusion

We see Christ here anticipating His Glorification in the midst of His Humiliation, and we understand that it is the now glorified Christ who, in the days of His Humiliation, allowed Himself to be insulted, mocked, blindfolded, spit upon, brutalized, and nailed to a Cross—that He might pay for my sins and yours. What is one to say to this? We love Him because He first loved us. Let us remember that the stick in the water is still straight and walk by faith, even as the world is still fooled by apparent sight into believing in His guilt over His glory. Let us proclaim Him as the Lord of straight sticks with full confidence and boldness. And let us cast ourselves at His feet as we remember Him at His Table.

HEROD AND PILATE

Luke 23:1 Then the whole body of them arose and brought him before Pilate. 2 And they began to accuse him, saying, "We found this man misleading our nation and forbidding to pay taxes to Caesar, and saying that he himself is Christ, a king." 3 And Pilate asked him, saying, "Are you the king of the Jews?" And he answered him and said, "It is as you say." 4 And Pilate said to the chief priests and the multitudes, "I find no guilt in this man." 5 But they kept on insisting, saying, "He stirs up the people, teaching all over Judea, starting from Galilee even as far as this place." 6 But when Pilate heard it, he asked whether the man was a Galilean. 7 And when he learned that he belonged to Herod's jurisdiction, he sent him to Herod, who himself was in Jerusalem at that time. 8 Now Herod was very glad when he saw Jesus; for he had wanted to see him for a long time, because he had been hearing about him and was hoping to see some sign performed by him. 9 And he questioned him at some length; but he answered him nothing. 10 And the chief priests and the scribes were standing there, accusing him vehemently. 11 And Herod with his soldiers, after treating him with contempt and mocking him, dressed him in a gorgeous robe and sent him back to Pilate. 12 Now Herod and Pilate became friends with one another that very day; for before they had been at enmity with one another.

Introduction

There are many things we could notice in this passage that is before us today. We could pause to appreciate the irony in the fact that the one who was to give the order for Jesus' execution is forced many times to pronounce His innocence. We could examine the way Pilate's indecision at the outset, passing the buck to Herod although he has already been convinced of Jesus' innocence, sets up his final betrayal of justice and of Jesus. (We will spend some time on that next time, perhaps.) We could notice how the cruel mockery and savage brutality of Jesus' treatment adds to the tale of His sufferings on our behalf. We could marvel at the patient submission of Jesus to His Father in all of this, and at the commitment and love for both the Father and for us that it implies. But these are all points that will continue to come out as we work our way through the story of Jesus' trial leading to His crucifixion in the coming weeks. For today, I want to focus our attention on verses 8–9. "*Now Herod was very glad when he saw Jesus; for he had wanted to see him for a long time, because he had been hearing about him and was hoping to see some sign performed by him. And he questioned him at some length; but he answered him nothing.*"

You could summarize this whole message in one phrase: **The necessity of seeking God with the proper motives**. The necessity of seeking God with the proper motives: That is precisely what Herod does not do. So let's look at some of the improper motives as exemplified by Herod and then say a bit about the proper ones.

Improper Motives

What was motivating Herod? He had been wanting to see Jesus for a long time. You might think that an encouraging sign, but first we have to ask why he wanted to see Him. Unfortunately, it was not because Herod thought Jesus was the Messiah or because he even had any interest in the Messiah. Alas, it was only out of **idle curiosity**. He wanted to see Jesus perform a sign; he wanted to see a miracle. For Herod, Jesus was nothing more than a sanctified sideshow. And we have seen all through Luke's Gospel how Jesus felt about that kind of thing. "*A wicked and adulterous generation seeks for a sign*" (Mat. 16:4). It started with his own hometown when he preached at the synagogue in Nazareth, where his old friends were wanting to see the things they had been hearing about. But there is no recorded example of Jesus ever responding positively to such a request. Miracles were performed in response to need and in response to faith, in response to needy faith; they were never done to overcome dishonest doubt or to satisfy idle curiosity. So it is not terribly surprising that Jesus refused even to speak to Herod. There was nothing there in Jesus' eyes worth responding to. Even Pilate got an answer to some of his questions! Herod got nothing at all. And this is always what happens to a wicked generation that comes to God seeking a sign (Luke 11:29).

Well, we certainly don't have that problem—do we? We feel quite superior to our Pentecostal and Charismatic brethren who are constantly trying to manufacture signs. Most of us would probably be made quite uncomfortable if we were given a sign like that! But maybe we have our own versions of coming to Christ out of idle curiosity. Have you ever read your Bible to prove a point, rather than to meet God and submit to His Truth? Do you ever come to church hoping for a certain kind of experience— aesthetic, uplifting, inspiring—rather than to meet the God the experience is supposedly about? Have you ever engaged in a theological discussion to "hear some new thing" rather than to know God and His will better? One thinks of the answer Calvin is supposed to have given to the person who asked him what God did before he created the heavens and the earth. "God was not unoccupied before he made the heavens and the earth; he was busy making Hell for idle questioners!" Do we not have our own ways of turning God into a sideshow? Some churches do it blatantly, others subtly, but none of us is immune from the temptation.

I remember seeing a tent at the Fair one time which claimed to contain the world's largest bull. For a dollar you could go into the tent and see the bull. I was running low on cash right then, so I passed up this opportunity of a lifetime. Had it been free I might have gone in. Others perhaps would not have bothered except for the fact that the fee made it seem like something worth doing. Either way, we would be satisfying our curiosity, for lack of anything better to do. And where a bull is concerned, I suppose there is nothing wrong with that. Now, let me be blunt and clear here. How many of you would have gone in to see the bull? Several would. And why not? Nothing wrong with that. But how many of you would be prepared to sell everything you have for the privilege?

Hmmm. Do you see what I'm driving at? Lots of people come to church the way the crowds went to see that bull. Lots of people come to church the way I might visit a showroom to pass time while my car is in the shop. I would be killing time by engaging in an innocent fantasy about my next ride. Any salesman hoping I might actually buy a car would have been destined for disappointment. You can't come to Christ that way! He is the pearl of great price. The only way you can come at all is to sell all you have to buy that field (Mat. 13:45–6). That is the wonderful paradox of the Gospel. God's grace, the salvation that is in His Son, is a free gift. You could never earn it or deserve it if you wanted to; it can only be received as a gift. But this is a completely free gift that costs you everything! And to come to Christ in any other way just simply isn't serious. In fact, it really isn't to come at all. Curiosity without commitment is ultimately blasphemous. It treats God like a sideshow. And it gets no response from the Lord whatsoever—except those awful words, *"Depart from me; I never knew you"* (Mat. 7:23). So Herod's idle curiosity and the response it provoked form an important lesson for us today.

A short digression on this idea of a free gift that costs you everything: Is that even a coherent idea? Well, yes, it is, as I think I've mentioned before: Once upon a time when I was pastoring a small church in Marietta, GA, and living on a tight budget, one of our parishioners took pity on us and gave us a second car so my wife wouldn't be stuck at home while I was out doing pastoral visitation. (It seems my congregation insisted on being in hospitals strung out over the entire Atlanta metro area, and it would have broken some kind of immoveable natural law for two of them to be in the same hospital.) The car was an old bomb, but still functional, and we were grateful to have it. It was a totally free gift. I never paid _____ _____ one red cent for that car. But before the first week was out, I had paid through the nose for a tag and title, insurance, gas, and motor oil. I literally had to stop and count the cost of whether I could afford to accept a free gift! Apparently, Jesus knew what He was talking about when He told us to think of salvation that way.

End of digression. We now return you to your regularly programmed sermon.

There are other improper motives for coming to Christ, maybe less insulting to him on the surface, but not so when we really understand them. There are those who come out of idle curiosity. There are also those who come out of **selfish indulgence.** What does James say? *"You have not because you ask not. You ask and do not have because you ask amiss, to spend it on your lusts"* (James 4:2–3). This is the "What I can get out of it" syndrome. What's in it for me? Health and wealth? The opportunity to be a big fish in a small pond (the church)? How did that great philosopher Janis Joplin put it? (I'm probably paraphrasing a bit.)

> Oh Lord, won't you give me a Mercedes Benz.
> My friends all have Porsches; I must make amends.
> I'm trying to cut back on *most* of my sins,

So Lord, won't you give me a Mercedes Benz![147]

If idle curiosity treats God like a sideshow, this treats him like a vending machine. It might at first seem to have more to do with faith, but in the long run it is at least as blasphemous. God is the ultimate End to which all things must be oriented if they are to be fulfilled in their creaturely nature. It is nothing less than idolatry to treat Him as a mere means to some other end, however noble. For then that end is more important than God himself who gives it—the very definition of idolatry. And many of the ends we seek Him for aren't noble at all; they are just plain selfish. Prosperity Gospel, anyone?

Idle curiosity; selfish indulgence. Another improper motive people have for coming to Christ is **personal protection,** whether from temporal disaster or eternal Hell. This seems to have been part of what motivated Herod. For this is not the first time we have heard of his desire to see Jesus. Back in Luke 9:9 we read that he wanted to see Jesus because some people thought he was John the Baptist come back from the dead. Apparently one reason Herod had for wanting to see Jesus was to reassure himself, to confirm that this was not the case. He was superstitious and did not want to be haunted by John, whom he had beheaded! Do not think that modern Christians are immune from this motive either. We are all too familiar with those who think of Christ as a fire insurance policy. No flames of Hell for them! But then they go on about their earthly lives as if their "faith" in Christ made no difference at all. Just in case there is a Hell, we'd better take out the policy by "going forward" at the altar call Of course, after that, we can live just as if Christ were not part of our life at all—which may be evidence that in fact He is not, since we are saved by *faith* in Him, that is, by the trust that commits us to Him, not by merely professing faith or having some kind of religious experience. If idle curiosity turns God into a sideshow and selfish indulgence turns Him into a vending machine, this reduces Him to a fire extinguisher, or maybe a security blanket.

Now, I am not denying that salvation has some pretty impressive fringe benefits, escape from eternal damnation being not the least of them. We receive forgiveness, peace with God and with ourselves, meaning, purpose, fulfillment, love, belonging, and maybe material blessings too (though there is no guarantee of that). But these are all fringe benefits of salvation, byproducts of our relationship with Christ. And we only enjoy them when they are not the central thing. To make them the central thing is no longer to be worshiping God at all but treating Him as a means to those ends—as a sideshow, a vending machine, or a fire extinguisher. And that is the very opposite of worship.

---

[147] Janis Joplin, "Mercedes Benz." You can hear the original here: https://video.search.yahoo.com/search/video?fr=mcafee&p=Janis+Joplin%2C+Oh+Lord+won%27t+you+give+me&type=E211US739G91653#id=1&vid=e8e500fd6d090760f6108624cd081e09&action=view

The common denominator of all these improper motives is that they treat God as a thing; they do not treat God as God. Be not deceived; God is not mocked! He can tell the difference. He can infallibly distinguish the person who comes to Christ in faith from the one who is merely playing religious games for his own ends while remaining his own God. So let us indeed desire to see Christ above all things. But let us not be modern Herods as we do so. That way lies futility—and blasphemy. And therefore, that way lies death.

The Proper Approach

Okay, if idle curiosity, selfish indulgence, and personal protection are not proper motives for coming to Christ, what is? The answer is found in Hebrews 11:6. *"And without faith it is impossible to please Him, for he who comes to God must believe that He is, and that He is a rewarder of those who seek Him."* Wait a minute. Rewarder? Doesn't that sound perilously close to everything you have been warning us against? Yes, perilously close—but not the same, not when you come to it through the lens of first part of the verse.

What is that lens? Those who come to God must come in faith, believing that He is. Believing that He is what? Believing that He is God! We have a whole generation of Christians who have insufficiently reckoned with the fact that God is God. What can get this across that you have not already heard a thousand times? He is the Creator of all else that exists, and therefore absolutely sovereign over it, including you and me. He is omnipotent, all powerful. He is holy. You are totally dependent on his good pleasure for your next breath, even if you use it to curse Him. He owns and has an absolute right to your worship, your obedience, to all you have and are, for without Him you would not be. And shall we then *dare* to use Him for a sideshow, a vending machine, a Band–Aid, a security blanket? To come to Him that way is not to come to Him at all.

But then—and only then—we come to the next glorious phrase. He is a Rewarder of those who seek Him! When you come to Him in faith, He will not annihilate you. The fire of His holiness will not burn you to ash, because if you come to Him in faith you are covered by the blood of His Son, clothed in the white robes of Christ's righteousness, and that is what the Father will choose to see. When you come to Him in faith, you are seeking first the Kingdom of Heaven and His righteousness— and *then* He rewards you, then you find that "all these things" are added unto you (Mat. 6:33)! *Then* you will be forgiven, you will have your sins wiped away and never counted against you, you will be adopted and loved and given a purpose and eternal life in which to fulfill that purpose. *Then* He will meet all your needs, including the things the gentiles seek. *Then* you will be astounded by His mighty works, flooded by His blessings, healed of all your wounds, and wrapped in His loving arms forever. You will find all these things because you came not for them but for Him—and they are *in* Him. They are nowhere else to be found.

Conclusion

And this is the wonder. This is the God who so loved the world that He sent His only begotten Son that whosoever believeth in Him should not perish but have eternal life (John 3:16). This is who He is. He is God! Is it any wonder then that He said, *"Seek ye first the kingdom of heaven and his righteousness, and all these things shall be added to you"*? (Mat. 6:33). Herod had it all wrong. You cannot seek those things for their own sake. You must seek Him first. And knowing who He is, how else can we respond to Him? What else would we want to seek? Come to Him even now! And in that coming you will find the One whom to know aright is life eternal. Amen.

PILATE'S TRIAL

Luke 23:13 *And Pilate summoned the chief priests and the ruler and the people* **14** *and he said to them, "You brought this man to me as one who incites the people to rebellion, and behold, having examined him before you, I have found no guilt in this man regarding the charges you made against him.* **15** *No, nor has Herod, for he sent him back to us. And behold, nothing deserving death has been done by him.* **16** *I will therefore punish him and release him."* **17** *(Now he was obliged to release to them at the feast one prisoner.)* **18** *But they cried out all together, saying, "Away with this man, and release for us Barabbas!"* **19** *(He was one who had been thrown into prison for a certain insurrection made in the city, and for murder.)* **20** *And Pilate, wanting to release Jesus, addressed them again,* **21** *but they kept on calling out, saying, "Crucify, crucify him!"* **22** *And he said to them the third time, "Why? What evil has this man done? I have found in him no guilt demanding death. I will therefore punish him and release him."* **23** *But they were insistent, with loud voices asking that he be crucified. And their voices began to prevail.* **24** *And Pilate pronounced sentence that their demand should be granted.* **25** *And he released the man they were asking for who had been thrown into prison for insurrection and murder, but he delivered Jesus to their will.*

Introduction

Human parents are fallible. If you doubt the truth of this proposition, just ask any teenager. Therefore, though in the main our parents do a good job of raising us, probably each of you who lived in a house with brothers and sisters can remember being blamed and punished at some point for something you (for once) didn't actually do. It is one of the hardest things in life to take. But imagine that the judge knew you were innocent and condemned you—and punished you—anyway! That is what the Lord Jesus Christ endured voluntarily for us. In this passage which narrates that condemnation, I want you to notice three things: the innocence of the Christ (who took our place), the implications of the criminal (whose literal place Christ took), and the inevitability of the compromise (on the part of Pilate).

I. The Innocence Of The Christ

The first thing we notice is something the passage emphasizes and reiterates: the innocence of the Christ, It is nothing less than astounding how many times Pilate officially pronounced the innocence of the man he finally condemned. It started last time way back in 23:4. *"I find no guilt in this man."* But instead of letting him go, Pilate passed the buck and sent him to Herod. Herod then mocked Jesus but did not condemn him, and sent him back to Pilate, who reiterates his original verdict in 23:14. *"You brought this man to me as one who incites the people to rebellion, and behold, having examined him before you, I have found no guilt in this man regarding the charges you made against him."* In verse 15 Pilate acknowledges Herod's corroborating judgment: *"No, nor has Herod, for he sent him back to us. And behold, nothing deserving death has been done by him.*" In verse 20 the same statement is made again, to no avail. In verse 22 Pilate asks, "*What evil has he done? I have found no guilt in him demanding death.*" Pilate actually belabors the innocence of the Man he is about to condemn!

John 18:33–38 helps to explain Pilate's unexpected verdict. "*Are you the king of the Jews?*" he had asked Jesus point blank, only to receive the cryptic reply, "*My kingdom is not of this world.*" Hmmm. Pilate was satisfied that, contrary to the charges being made against Him, Jesus was not an insurrectionist, whatever He was. That is, He had no political ambitions that needed to concern a professional guardian of the interests of Rome. If the Jewish leaders found his religious views annoying, why that was all the more reason for Pilate to want to release him. Pilate found the religious views of the Jewish establishment annoying—very annoying—extremely annoying, as we shall see.

On a deeper level, it was important that Jesus' innocence be officially recognized because of the very nature of the sacrifice He was about to make for us. Jesus was about to die as the fulfillment of the Passover Lamb. And Exodus 12:5 required that the Passover Lamb be "*an unblemished male of the flock.*" If Christ was to die a substitutionary death for our sins, a death that would pay the penalty for all our sin forever ("*for the wages of sin is death,*" Romans 6:23), then it was absolutely necessary that He be sinless Himself. Otherwise, His death would only pay the penalty for His own transgressions. If you owe a hundred dollars, and I have a hundred dollars, I could pay the money for you—but not if I owed it too. Jesus' innocence did not depend on Pilate's verdict, but it was part of God's plan that the verdict be unmistakably proclaimed for all the world to hear. There was no cause of death in this man, and that is why his Death could be a sacrificial death and count for us.

II. The Implications Of The Criminal

If the first thing we notice is the innocence of the Christ, the second is certain implications of the criminal. It has long and often been noted that Barabbas is a perfect illustration of the substitutionary nature of the atonement. The cross on which Christ was crucified was literally Barabbas's cross. It had been erected for him; it had his name on it, as it were. And now he would be walking away from it a free man. Did he look back and see that other Man on his cross? Did he shudder at the thought that if it were not for that Man's agony, he would be there himself at that moment? Did he ever stop to think about it? We will never know. But I would suggest that we stop to think about it this morning. For Barabbas is the patron saint of every believer. We can all look up at that cross and see another Man hanging where we by all rights ought to be.

We all know that salvation is a free gift of God's grace, His unmerited favor, simply accepted by faith. "*For the wages of sin is death, but the free gift of God is eternal life in Jesus Christ our Lord*' (Romans 6:23). "*For by grace are ye saved through faith, and that not of yourselves, not of works, lest any man should boast*" (Ephesians 2:8–10). Thinking about Barabbas enables us to see more clearly both that this is so and why it has to be so.

Let us imagine that Barabbas walks up to Jesus and says, "How about you get up on that cross in my place and let me off? If you do that, I'll go to synagogue every week—at least when it's convenient—I'll tithe a full ten percent, and I'll try to be reasonably nice to people." Kind of ridiculous? Okay, suppose he promised to fast himself almost to death, to pray seven times a day, to wear a hair shirt, and to beat himself with whips every night, while spending every waking moment in self–denying service to mankind—if only Jesus would replace him on his cross. This is only marginally less insulting than the first deal! Do you see?

I hope you find this kind of proposal as disturbing and revolting as I do: not only absurd, but blasphemous. I almost hesitated to speak it. But I did it to make a point. Is that not what we are doing if we allow the Gospel to be tainted with the slightest tinge of the notion of salvation by works? Whether it be the superficial deal of American Protestants or the harrowing self–denial of medieval monasticism makes no essential difference. You cannot even think of making any deal like that with God, not if you actually think about what you are doing. You can only discover that Jesus has in fact, in an act of incomprehensible love and inscrutable grace, already mounted your cross and died there. All you can do is accept it as a gift. To treat it any other way is incomprehensible once we see it in these terms—not only incomprehensible but insulting and blasphemous. Salvation involves the forgiveness of your sins, not because God has winked at them, but because Jesus has paid for them in full. Because of the very nature of what salvation is, it can only be by grace alone through faith alone in Christ alone, apart from works completely, accepted as a free gift by the empty hands of faith. Every form of salvation by works is a blasphemous insult to our Savior. Once you have walked in Barabbas's sandals, you can never be unaware of that fact again.

But we must notice something else while we are still standing in Barrabas's sandals. The very same fact that makes works for salvation absurd makes works from salvation imperative. How does Ephesians 2:8–10 continue? *"By grace ye were saved through faith, and that not of yourselves, not of works lest any man should boast—for we are his workmanship, created for good works, which God hath prepared beforehand, that we should walk in them."* Why? The very same fact that makes works for salvation absurd makes works from salvation imperative. Barabbas might have looked up at that central cross on the hill, shrugged his shoulders, and walked away. Why? Because he was only a symbol, an illustration, of the believer. He did not have to have any faith to be the recipient of the gift of life and freedom. He just had to be in the right place at the right time. For him, nothing other than the incomprehensible vagaries of Roman politics was needed as an explanation.

But it is not like that for real believers! For us, the gift of eternal life won for us by Christ on our cross is given to those who believe in Him. *"For God so loved the world that he gave his only begotten Son that whosoever believeth in him might not perish but have everlasting life"* (John 3:16). Therefore, *"If you confess with your mouth Jesus as Lord and believe in your heart that God hath raised him from the dead, you shall be saved"* (Romans 10:9). To be the recipient of this gift is to know and understand that Jesus took your place on your cross voluntarily because He loves you. Can you be the recipient of such sacrificial love, the beneficiary of such a costly gift, and still be the same person? Can you do anything other than follow Christ even when it is inconvenient? Can you do anything other than follow Christ even to the ends of the earth? Can you do anything other than follow Christ even into the jaws of death if it comes to that? If you can do anything else, you cast doubt precisely by that something else on the supposition that you have ever actually believed at all. The response of one who acknowledges himself a sinner and truly believes that Jesus has replaced him on his cross out of love must be something far more profound than any of the bargaining we laid out a few minutes ago. Do you see? The very same fact that makes works for salvation absurd is what makes works from salvation imperative—imperative and inevitable.

III. The Inevitability Of The Compromise

Finally, we must examine the inevitability of the compromise. We've seen the innocence of the Christ, which contrasts starkly with the guilt of Barabbas. Pilate, alas, saw the innocence of Christ and the guilt of Barabbas, but did not see anything much beyond that. He had no experience of or understanding of the salvific dynamics we have just been discussing. Pilate was not the great evil villain imagination has made him. He was a normal human being a lot like we would have been without Christ. He found himself caught in an impossible political vice, and he yielded to the pressure and executed an innocent man. When we understand those pressures, we will understand why he did it. And we will also get a very practical lesson in compromise that will help us be faithful to our own role as the recipients of God's inestimable gift.

Pilate seems to have been a decent man and a good administrator who tried to do the right thing. If he had a weakness, it was that he had never been able to understand the religious sensibilities of this difficult people he had been sent to govern. Two incidents which illustrate that weakness had made his position somewhat precarious. When his troops had first marched into Jerusalem and displayed their standards, the Jews had a conniption that led to a riot. Why? Roman legionnaires had a ceremony where they sacrificed to their standards. It was idolatry. Abomination! Then there was the incident of the shields that had been hung from the windows of the fortress Antonia. Imagine some pious Jew looking up as he passes and stopping dead in his tracks. He reaches up to the little tear that he carries, closed with soft, thin thread, in the collar of his tunic so he can ceremonially "rend his garment," and cries in a loud, nasal voice, "Abomina–a–a–tion!" For the shields have pictures on them—the Roman eagle. Graven images! And there is another riot.

Rome wanted the peace kept in Judea, and it knew that the Jews would not compromise their fanatical religious beliefs. The Jews had therefore been granted a number of dispensations, privileges no other Roman provinces enjoyed, so they could

530

practice their beliefs unhindered. But Pilate kept running afoul of them anyway. About one year before this trial took place, he had received a letter from Caesar, which basically said, "I don't want to hear about any more complaints over the way you handle Jewish religious issues." So when the Jews said, as is recorded elsewhere, *"If you don't do what we want, you are no longer a friend of Caesar"* (John 19:12), they were not making an idle threat. There was actually a club in Rome called the *Amici Caesari*, the friends of Caesar. The members were officials of the Roman administration, including provincial governors. So the Jews were saying, in effect, "If you don't crucify Jesus, we are going to complain to Caesar one more time, and you will get kicked out of the club!" This is more than just the threat that Pilate would lose his job. Caesar's method of asking for the resignation of one of his officials might well be to command him to commit suicide— which he would have to do, because otherwise his property would all be confiscated and his family left in abject poverty. Do you begin to understand the kind of pressure Pilate was facing?[148]

Pilate was a normal human being. He was not a moral monster. He was a relatively decent, ordinary man under extreme pressure. It would have taken an extraordinary moral hero to have sacrificed his own life (or at least risked it) for the sake of abstract justice and this weird Jewish nutcase. And Pilate was not that. So he tried as hard as he could to do the right thing, but he finally gave in. Any of us might well have done the same thing in similar circumstances. We cannot excuse Pilate's act of injustice, but we can understand it. And in doing so, we can understand that "There but for the grace of God" any one of us might well have gone.

But extraordinary moral heroism is sometimes required of ordinary people! How, if we find ourselves in such a position, are we to stand—to be willing to give our lives for the One who gave His for us? That is the final question I want us to consider as we contemplate this scene. Do you see that, given the nature of the pressure he was under, the first moment of wavering really made Pilate's final downfall inevitable? Once Pilate tried to pass the buck by sending Jesus to Herod, his doom was sealed. He had already shown weakness; he had already tipped his hand that he was looking for a way out, that he was uncomfortable with the situation, that he was operating from a position of weakness. His only chance to get through this trial with his own integrity unscathed was to unwaveringly do the right thing from the very first moment, with no sign of compromise tolerated. But once he wavered, the birds of prey were circling for the kill. Once he wavered at all, his blood was in the water and the sharks were galvanized into their feeding frenzy. Once he wavered at all, the buzzards started circling around a very promising dinner.

---

[148] The material in this section is based on Paul Maier's biographical reconstruction of Pilate's life, a novelistic account but based on accurate historical information: Paul L. Maier, *Pontius Pilate: A Biographical Novel* (Garden City, NY: Doubleday, 1968). The description is on pages 167f, and the historical factual basis is laid out on pages 362–3.

What is the practical lesson for us? Don't set yourself up for compromise! When you are asked to do something you know is wrong, if you dither and scrape your feet and say, "Well, I don't know . . .", you are setting yourself up for a fall. You are sending the signal that you can be bought, and you are making it harder for yourself to say a final "no" at any later point. So let your first "no" be final by being forthright: "I'm sorry, but I am not going to do that, because it would be displeasing to my Lord." It's not open for discussion or negotiation—is it? If not, present it as if it were not from the get–go. Otherwise, you will eventually fall, even when you are under less severe pressure than Pilate faced here.

Conclusion

To have received the incredible gift Jesus gave us when He replaced us on our cross is to want to stand for Him without compromise. But where are we to find the strength to do it? For the spirit is willing but the flesh is weak. But the strength comes from the same One who gives us the desire. For He is with us through his personal Agent and Representative, the Holy Spirit. Christ and Christ alone can enable us to stand as strong and unwavering as He Himself did in the trial we have been studying today. So look to Him and live for Him; look to Him and live!

THE VIA DOLOROSA

Luke 23:26 And when they led him away, they laid hold of one Simon of Cyrene, coming in from the country, and placed on him the cross to carry behind him. 27 And there were following him a great number of the people and of women who were mourning and lamenting him. 28 But Jesus turned to them and said, "Daughters of Jerusalem, stop weeping for me, but weep for yourselves and your children. 29 For behold, the days are coming when they will say, 'Blessed are the barren and the wombs that never bore and the breasts that never nursed.' 30 Then they will begin to say to the mountains, 'Fall on us,' and to the hills, 'cover us!' 31 For if they do these things in the green tree, what will happen in the dry?"

Introduction

As we follow the sufferings of Jesus Christ, who, like Paul, "finished the course and kept the faith" (2 Tim. 4:7), we are come to the very last lap: the Road of Griefs, the "*Via Dolorosa.*" This is that sorrowful path that will lead directly to Golgotha, to the Cross. Every detail that is recorded about our Lord's steps on that path is laden with significance and helps to tell us why He was going that way. Let's look at two of them together today: the contributions of Simon of Cyrene and of the faithful daughters of Jerusalem.

I. Simon Of Cyrene (v. 26)

The first of those details is the role of Simon of Cyrene. The conscription of Simon out of the crowd to bear the cross speaks volumes about the exhaustion being suffered by our Lord on this last lap of His journey. He had had no sleep the night before. He had been mocked and beaten by Herod's soldiers and scourged by Pilate's preparatory to the crucifixion itself. The scourging was done with a whip of nine thongs that had bits of metal and rocks imbedded in them. It would literally rip chunks of flesh out of your body. Some people did not survive the scourging. The centurion had to be careful that Jesus did not die before the crucifixion itself. That very public display of what happens to people who rebel against the Empire was, in Rome's eyes, the whole point of the affair. He was not motivated by compassion. He would not have used his authority to draft Simon unless he had thought he was needed.

We can tell then that Jesus had been beaten so badly and lost so much blood that the centurion in charge was afraid he might not make it. Otherwise, he would have been forced to carry His own cross, His own instrument of execution, the symbol of His crime and His criminality, as a final form of humiliation. Jesus was so weak by this point that the centurion grabbed Simon out of the crowd, not out of mercy but out of fear that Jesus would not make it to Calvary otherwise. Jesus was not able to carry His own cross as normally prescribed by the Roman crucifixion ritual. Not only had the preliminary torture been more than what was normally born — two beatings instead of one, loss of a night's sleep because of the hurried–up nature of the whole affair—but the burden of the psychological and emotional suffering of being the innocent sin–bearer (which we saw in Gethsemane) was also weighing Him down. It is impossible for us ever to fully grasp the whole nature or extent of the sufferings of Christ for us.

What are the implications of these facts? For one thing, it is one more nail in the coffin (if you'll pardon the expression) of the "Swoon Theory," the favorite liberal idea that Jesus did not really die but only lost consciousness on the cross and was later revived in the cool of the tomb, causing people to mistakenly believe he had been supernaturally resurrected. It is one of those theories that explains everything except the actual facts. I hope you know some of the standard answers to this silly idea. When the soldier checked Jesus to see if he was dead by thrusting the spear into His side, "blood and water" came out. In other words, the solid parts of His blood and His plasma had already separated, a clinical sign of death. Then there is the incredible expectation that a man whose wrist and ankle bones had been shattered by the spikes driven through them could somehow move the stone door from the inside of the tomb, when it took four whole and strong men to do it from the outside—with handholds! And here let us remember that we are asking this of a man who by the time of Easter morning had not eaten in three days and who had already lost so much blood and become so weak through the beatings He had received before even being nailed to the cross that a professional executioner was concerned that He might not even make it to Calvary. I reject the Swoon Theory because, quite frankly, believing it requires more faith, and a more gullible faith, than believing that God raised His Son supernaturally from the dead in fulfillment of prophecy!

The Swoon theory is dead, and if people would just think critically about the facts of the case, it would never be resurrected again. But there is a more profound implication here than that. For we must not leave this moment without some appreciation for what it contributes to the humiliation of Christ as part of His sacrificial sufferings for us. This One who before His incarnation had known omnipotence, this One whose will upholds the stars, this One whose power holds all things together (Col. 1:17)—keeps the atoms from flying apart—this One now needs help even to die. I simply pause on it for a moment as one more small insight into the sufferings of our Lord Jesus Christ for us.

We can learn a lot from thinking about what this moment meant to Christ. But we do not exhaust its meaning until we think about it from the viewpoint of Simon of Cyrene, too. He had not known Christ before this happened, as far as we know. But apparently as a result of this encounter, he came to know Him! Mark 15:21 mentions that Simon was "the father of Alexander and Rufus"—as if every one of Mark's readers would have known who those people were. They were apparently fairly prominent members of the early church. This is confirmed by the fact that in Romans 16:13 Paul greets "Rufus and his mother," who was apparently still living in the late fifties, though apparently by that time Simon himself had died. It would seem that something about this encounter with Jesus convinced Simon that He really was the Messiah, for his family was still active, indeed, well known, in the early church more than two decades later.

Therefore, just as Barabbas is the perfect picture of the doctrine of penal substitution, of the vicarious substitutionary atonement as we saw last time, so Simon of Cyrene is the perfect picture of the Christian life. For how had Jesus defined the Christian life back in Luke 9:23? *"If any man would come after me, let him deny himself, take up his cross daily, and follow me."* Simon did this both literally, with Jesus' actual cross at this moment, and later in its spiritual meaning too. And what was the result? Jesus would not have made it to Calvary without either a miracle or Simon. God could have sent a miracle, but He chose to send Simon. Think of it! Without the help of a weak mortal, the work of the Omnipotent would have been incomplete.

Now, that is pretty astounding, but think of this: Even today, Christ will not normally make it into the hearts of people without someone to tell them about the Gospel. God is not dependent on us; He could send a miracle. But He rarely does. He could send a miracle, but He usually sends a man. What does Paul say? *"How then shall they call upon him in whom they have not believed? And how shall they believe in him of whom they have not heard? And how shall they hear without a preacher? And how shall they preach unless they are sent?"* (Romans 10:14–15). God could send a miracle, but He usually sends a man. And it is costly. That is why we need to take up our crosses and follow Jesus. That is what the Christian life is all about.

Why do we fear taking up our cross? It is taking up the cross that gives meaning to your life! It transformed Simon of Cyrene from a nobody to the head of one of the most prominent families in the Roman church, a family of pillars who were important enough to be mentioned not only in the Gospel of Mark but also in Paul's Epistle to the Romans. If Simon had not taken up the cross, we would never have known or cared if any of them had existed. And what of you and me? When I was young, I was for some reason very ambitious. I wanted to do something very big and important with my life. My earliest dream was to be an astronaut, and I was bitterly disappointed when it became plain that I was going to grow too big to fit the size limitations demanded by the Mercury, Gemini, and Apollo space capsules of those days. Then I decided I wanted to be the next C. S. Lewis. Yes, I know, pretty ridiculous. I pass for a scholar, a writer, and an apologist in our debased times, but I know full well I am not even worthy to have sharpened Lewis's pencil. But supposing I had achieved all that without Christ? What would it mean? Nothing. Or suppose that, being faithful to Him, I achieved absolutely nothing (by the world's standards). What would that mean? Everything! It is taking up the cross, and nothing else, that gives meaning to your life. Simon's last service then is to remind us of the old couplet,

Only one life: 'twill soon be past;
Only what's done for Christ will last.[149]

II. The Weeping Women (v. 27f).

There is another group of people Christ met along the *Via Dolorosa*: the weeping women. Not all of the multitude forsook Him. These women, no doubt including the ones who had followed Jesus from Galilee to minister to Him, were following Him not to mock but to mourn. They contrast with the disciples, all of whom except John ran away, and they remind us that God always preserves a remnant of the faithful, even in times of great apostasy.

So what does it mean to be part of the Faithful Remnant? It means, among other things, that you will be tempted to think you are alone when you are not. Elijah thought he was alone when there were seven thousand prophets who had not bowed the knee to Baal (1 Kings 19:18). Athanasius earned the nickname *contra mundum*, "Athanasius against the world," when he stood without compromise against the heresy of Arianism, the denial of the deity of Christ, even when it got him exiled from his bishopric. But he was brought back from exile and lived to see the victory of orthodoxy over Arianism. Martin Luther was accused of innovation, but he found kindred spirits not only in Wycliffe and Huss of a century earlier and in the early Fathers, but also in Melanchthon and others as his recovery of the Gospel gave rise to the Reformation.

Do you ever feel alone? Alone in general, but particularly alone as a follower of Jesus trying to be faithful in very discouraging times for the church? I know I do. A figure from Greek literature that I strongly identify with is the prophetess Cassandra, whose curse was that she would always tell the truth but never be believed. We live in a day when the truth of the Gospel is being co-opted by the spirit of the age even within what we thought were conservative churches, schools, and para-church organizations. The old-style theological liberals are dying on the vine, but so are the teachers of sound doctrine. What prospers is heretical aberrations like the Health and Wealth gospel. It is easy to feel alone and isolated. That's why I love the reply of one of Flannery O'Connor's characters who, when told, "People have quit doing that," responded, "They ain't quit doing it as long as I'm doing it."[150]

Do you feel alone? Don't give up! We are not alone. If we are the Faithful Remnant, then we know that God will preserve us. We cannot all live in an age of church history when real revival is in the air and the true Gospel and sound doctrine are in the ascendancy. God may send such a time again; He may not. What matters is that we as

---

[149] C. T. Studd, "Only One Life, 'Twill Soon Be Past," https://bibleapologetics.org/c-t-studd-a-poem-to-meditate-on/

[150] Flannery O'Connor, "Wise Blood," *Three by Flannery O'Connor: Wise Blood, A Good Man is Hard to Find, The Violent Bear it Away* (NY: Signet Classics, New American Library, 1962), 122. Hazel Motes is not a good role model, but he did have a good response!

the current corps of the Faithful Remnant be found faithful in the day in which we are called to live. They ain't quit doing it as long as we're doing it! Let us keep following Jesus even if it feels like all we can do is to weep.

Jesus' response to these women is easy to misunderstand. *"Daughters of Jerusalem, stop weeping for me, but weep for yourselves and your children. For behold, the days are coming when they will say, 'Blessed are the barren and the wombs that never bore and the breasts that never nursed.' Then they will begin to say to the mountains, 'Fall on us,' and to the hills, 'cover us!' For if they do these things in the green tree, what will happen in the dry?"* (28–31).

I don't think it was a rebuke to them so much as an expression of love and compassion for them. At this moment when Jesus needs help even to die, He is more concerned for these women than for Himself. For he foresaw the judgment that was coming on Jerusalem. Normally barren women were looked on as cursed. For them to be seen as blessed is a great reversal and an indication of how abnormal, how terrible, those times would be. A green tree is one that is not ready for burning. So what Jesus is implying is, "If this is what happens to an innocent Lamb now, what will happen to the wicked then?" He is looking ahead with a double perspective, both to the troubles that would come to Jerusalem in AD 70, and to the Great Tribulation and the Final Judgment. So, don't weep for me, Jesus is saying; weep for your nation and for the judgment that will be faced by all who by rejecting me are not covered with the blood I am about to shed. If God's judgment for your sin doesn't fall on me now, it will fall on you then. Now that is something to weep for!

It is easy to give when all of your own needs have been met. But what do you do when you are hurting, discouraged, beaten to a bloody pulp, and at the end of your rope? Do you give in to self–pity, or are you still more concerned for others than for your own problems? Our Lord was. And so He calls us here to look beyond the ends of our noses. These ladies were sad to lose the Lord that they loved, they were still loyally trying to show that love, but they really had no understanding of what was going on around them. They did not yet understand that the judgment of God on human sin was falling on Christ, and that it is coming for the whole world unless they put their faith in Him and in what He was doing there. We who do understand these things should love the Lord even more than they did and take up the cross the way Simon of Cyrene did.

When we take Communion, we weep for the suffering of our Lord and for our sins that caused it, and rightly so. But we also look beyond that to the Resurrection and the Great Commission and the coming Judgment. Therefore, maybe what the Lord is saying to us is, "Do not weep for me. Weep for your own generation—and then do something about it!" And so let us recognize the love of our Lord Jesus Christ demonstrated here for us. It was a costly love, a love with commitment that calls on us to take up the cross like Simon and weep for our generation like the women. Therefore, as we remember that love, let us respond to it by letting it live within us to the spread of the Gospel and the glory of God.

Conclusion

African theologian Philip Muinde puts that response this way: "Following the despised Galilean means a willingness to say, 'Lord, I will follow whithersoever thou goest,' not only to be excited about the Triumphal Entries but also to travel the Via Dolorosa. It is voluntarily to embrace a faith which exposes Self to fresh denial, disgrace, and death. It is also to acknowledge and identify with the Lordship of Jesus Christ at every moment, whatever the cost. It is to be crucified with Christ, and continually to unlearn Self and learn Him."[151] And so it is. Let us follow Him.

> Only one life: 'twill soon be past;
> Only what's done for Christ will last.

Amen.

---

[151] Philip Muinde, unpublished paper, Trinity Evangelical Divinity School, 1975.

THE THIEF ON THE CROSS

Luke 23:32 And two others also, who were criminals, were being led away to be put to death with him. 33 And when they came to the place called The Skull, there they crucified him and the criminals, one on the right hand and the other on the left. 34 But Jesus was saying, "Father, forgive them, for they do not know what they are doing." And they cast lots, dividing up his garments among themselves. 35 And the people stood by, looking on. And even the rulers were sneering at him, saying, "He saved others; let him save himself if this one is the Christ of God, his Chosen One." 36 And the soldiers also mocked him, coming up to him and offering him sour wine, 37 and saying, "If you are the King of the Jews, save yourself!" 38 Now there was also an inscription above him, "This is the King of the Jews." 39 And one of the criminals who were hanged there was hurling abuse at him, saying, "Are you not the Christ? Save yourself and us!" 40 But the other answered and rebuking him said, "Do you not even fear God, since you are under the same sentence of condemnation? 41 And we indeed justly, for we are receiving what we deserve for our deeds. But this man has done nothing wrong." 42 And he was saying, "Jesus, remember me when you come in your kingdom." 43 And he said to him, "Truly I say to you, today you shall be with me in Paradise."

Introduction

We have been studying in the last few weeks the most profound and inexhaustible theme in all the Bible: the love of Jesus Christ for His own. For we have seen something of the magnitude of the price He paid for our redemption. We have seen His agony in Gethsemane, His betrayal by His friends, His rejection by His people, His mocking by Herod, His condemnation by Pilate, and His stumbling beneath the Cross on the *Via Dolorosa*. And now, finally nailed and dying, we see Him still steadfast in His commitment to commend God's love to us in this, *"that while we were yet sinners, Christ died for us"* (Rom. 5:8). In the passage we reach today, all of this is revealed in two ways: by the Prayer of the Savior, and by the Penitence of the Sinner.

I. The Prayer Of The Savior (v. 34)

The prayer of the Savior is as simple as it is profound. *"Father, forgive them, for they know not what they do."* The most astonishing thing about this whole prayer may be the context in which it was uttered. Let's let one of the Roman soldiers, the centurion in charge, set the stage for us:

THE CENTURION SPEAKS
Sonnet XLIX

No question but it was a dirty job.
> The scourging by itself was bad enough;
> To drive the spikes, though, really takes a tough
> And calloused character. The women sob,

The victim screams, and even as the mob
  Cries out for more, men wince. The really rough
  Part comes when all four soldiers huff and puff
  To raise upright the heavy wooden stob,
For then the man's own weight begins to work:
  The tendons crack, the flesh begins to tear—
  And when he thinks it's more than he can bear,
  They drop him in the socket with a jerk.[152]
And after we did *that*, He said (it's true!),
  "Forgive them, for they know not what they do."[153]

One feels out of one's depth trying to say anything at all about such a mystery as this. But a few things we may attempt, as homage more than exposition. Something we need to consider is **the Objects of this Prayer.** Who is the "them" that Jesus wants the Father to forgive? The nearest antecedent to the pronoun in the Text would be the Roman soldiers. They certainly fit the criterion: they literally had not much of an idea what they were doing. They were just following orders. They certainly had not gotten up that morning and thought, "Hey, I know, I think I'll murder God's Son today." Yet they still needed forgiveness, for they had heard Pilate declare Jesus innocent, and so they knew that they were following unethical orders. They ought rather to have resigned or even faced death themselves rather than execute an innocent man. But isn't that the way it is with all of us? We rarely have a full knowledge of what we are doing, for good or for ill. We all resemble way too often and way too much Yoda's description of Luke Skywalker: "Never his mind on where he was, what he was doing." But we do know enough to know better. Yet Jesus wants people like us to be forgiven! He said this of these soldiers even as they were continuing the job of torturing and killing him. When you are tempted to think that you are too far gone to turn back, you need to remember that Jesus apparently intended for you to overhear this petition. For it applies to you as well.

The second group to be considered is the crowd on the hillside. These are the people who have been calling out for Jesus to be crucified and are now gawking at Him and mocking Him. Their guilt is greater than that of the soldiers; they have less excuse than the soldiers, because many of them had heard Jesus' teaching and seen His miracles. But still they did not have a full understanding of what they were doing. They did not really know what it meant for Jesus to be the Messiah in the first place, and they were caught up in an unthinking mob reaction. They are in their own way parallel with many of us, with our Christian backgrounds and our many opportunities to hear the

---

[152] Many authorities believe that the victim would actually have had his hands nailed to the crossbeam, which would then have been lifted up onto the upright stake that was permanently fixed in the ground. In any case, the suffering would have been extreme.
[153] Williams, *Stars Through the Clouds*, op. cit., 154.

Gospel. Truly they were, even more clearly than the Roman soldiers, without excuse — yet Jesus wants them to be forgiven too. From the very Cross on which they had demanded for Him to be nailed, He asked for it.

But there is a group here to whom I fear this prayer does not apply. The Jewish rulers, the high priests and the Sanhedrin, do not fit the criterion (not knowing what they do) at all, for their ignorance was willful and culpable. Luke has shown them in this light consistently. *"The Pharisees and the lawyers rejected God's purpose for themselves"* (7:30). *"The one who rejects you rejects me, and he who rejects me rejects the One who sent me"* (10:16). *"Woe to you, lawyers! For you have taken away the key of knowledge. You did not enter in yourselves, and those who were entering in, you hindered"* (11:52). Was the baptism of John from heaven or from men? And the Pharisees shuck and jive and equivocate, and Jesus tells them, *"Neither will I tell you by what authority I do these things"* (20:8). *"If you are the Christ, tell us."* But he said to them, *"If I tell you, you will not believe, and if I ask you a question, you will not answer"* (22:67–8). No sin is excusable. The forgiveness for which Jesus prays is not dependent on that; it is dependent on God's love and Christ's atonement. But there is no forgiveness possible while the attitude of willful ignorance and knowing rejection prevails. As long as we are like *that* — well, if you will pardon the expression, we don't have a prayer.

But for those who do not willfully remain ignorant and stubbornly turn away, **the Importance of this Prayer** can hardly be sufficiently emphasized. Not only does it reveal the unsearchable love of Christ, who at the very climax of His physical suffering prays for those who are causing it; not only does it reveal the spirit of forgiveness that we as his followers should also have; but what greater encouragement to our own repentance could there be? "I'm not good enough and never could be." No, you're not; no, you couldn't; but what of that? This forgiveness isn't about your worthiness; it's about Christ's. "You don't know what I've done!" No, I don't. But it would have to be worse than this not to be covered. Don't even try to convince me of that! There is only one sin that excludes anyone from this forgiveness, and that is a knowing rebellion against the truth that Jesus is the Messiah, an insistent hardening of your heart against Him, a willful rejection of the truth about Him that you really know is true. The only thing that can exclude you from the power of this prayer is a stubborn refusal to accept it. Whatever the burden you are carrying, you can be forgiven! Give your life to Christ today! Having prayed such a prayer for such sinners at such a time, He will not refuse you.

It remains then to consider **the Effects of this Prayer.** Was it answered? Not for every individual in any ultimate sense, of course. They would all still have to make an individual decision to accept or reject God's forgiveness. But a sure welcome by the Father into the Kingdom was guaranteed by it to whosoever would come. And consider the fact that the whole crowd of these people was not immediately exterminated for their presumption in killing and mocking the Son of God, as they ought to have been!

Why not? As a generation, they were granted forty more years of opportunity for repentance before judgment fell on them in 70 AD with the destruction of Jerusalem by the roman army. Was that not an answer to this prayer?

By the way, it is also the ultimate **refutation of "Christian" Anti–Semitism**. Are the Jews as a people to blame for the Crucifixion, as some Anti–Semites insist? So what if they are? We are required to have the same attitude toward them as our Lord did, and which He expressed here. Ahem. And some of them, no doubt as a result of this prayer, were among the three thousand added to the church in Acts 2:41, or the others from Jerusalem who continued to be added in Acts 6:7. And let us not forget that the very fact that you are here today is an answer to this prayer! But there is one more effect of it that was much more immediate, and that is the response of the Thief on the Cross himself— which leads us to our next point.

II. The Penitence Of The Sinner (vv. 39–43)

The most immediate effect of Jesus' prayer was the salvation of the convert we know as The Thief on the Cross. How do we know he was genuinely saved? First, because Jesus said so: *"This day you will be with me in Paradise."* But what interests me even more is the **Evidence of Conversion** shown by this man who had, of all men, the least opportunity to show any. There always is evidence of real conversion to Christ, you know. And if the Thief showed it, no other convert has any excuse not to! There is no genuine conversion without the accompanying evidence—though it is not always equally easy to see it. Even the classic passage that most clearly eliminates the idea of salvation *by* good works also eliminates the idea of salvation *without* them. *"For by grace are ye saved through faith, and that not of yourselves, it is the gift of God that no man should boast. For we are his workmanship, created unto good works, which God prepared beforehand, that we should walk in them"* (Eph. 2:8–10). Salvation is never *by* good works, but it is always *unto* good works. Therefore, any real conversion to Christ will always manifest itself in at least five ways. Even the Thief manages to exhibit them all in the few minutes of life he had left.

First, there is **a Change of Attitude toward Jesus Christ.** From Mark's account of this event (15:31–32), we know that at first both criminals were mocking Jesus. Something—I suspect Jesus' prayer might have had something to do with it—caused one of them to change his mind. He goes from mocking Christ to defending Him, from participating in sin to rebuking it, from disbelief to trust, from dismissal to petition, from unbelief to faith. No one who is indifferent to the person of Christ can claim to have been converted to Him or saved by Him, whatever rigmarole he might have gone through during an altar call at some earlier point in his life, no matter what formula he recited at the instigation of some over–zealous soul winner, no matter his baptism as an infant. The first sign of true conversion is a change of attitude toward Christ himself.

The **second sign of true conversion** is the sincere and heartfelt **Confession of Sin.** The Thief show this very clearly. *"And we indeed justly, for we are receiving what we* *deserve for our deeds*" (verse 41a). Salvation is about the forgiveness of sin. It is only for sinners—indeed, for people who have come to know what it is to be a sinner, who have at least some inkling of the exceeding sinfulness of sin. In Alcoholics Anonymous, every member introduces himself by saying, "Hello, I am so and so, and I am an alcoholic." They aren't *practicing* alcoholics anymore; they are hopefully recovering alcoholics, though they may still stumble. But the first step to recovery is to fully face their problem and own up to it. The true church of Jesus Christ we could call "Sin–aholics Anonymous." "Hello, my name is Don Williams, and I am a sinner." Can you say that? If we stumble at that point, we have not even made the first step in the journey. The first sign is a change of attitude toward the Person of Christ. The second sign of true conversion is the sincere and heartfelt confession of sin.

The **third sign of true conversion** is a **Public Confession of Jesus Christ as Savior and Lord.** Our Thief doesn't have much chance to do this, but he takes the chance he has. "*But this man has done nothing wrong.*" And he was saying, "*Jesus, remember me when you come in your kingdom*" (verses 41b–42). The confession is by implication: By asking Jesus to remember him on *coming into His Kingdom*, he publicly confesses that he has come to accept Jesus as the true Messiah (King) and put his faith in Him. "*For if you confess with your mouth Jesus as Lord and believe in your heart that God has raised him from the dead, you shall be saved*" (Rom. 10:9). The third sign of true conversion is a public confession of Jesus Christ as savior and lord.

First, a change of attitude toward the Person of Christ; second, a sincere confession of sin; third, a clear confession of Jesus as personal Lord. The **fourth way that true conversion shows itself** is through **the Exercise of Faith.** The only opportunity our Thief has for that is his very act of turning to Christ itself. But surely it is an exercise of faith in Christ, and one that stands in stark contrast to many other people standing around in this scene. The great exegete Alfred Plummer captures the contrast nicely: "Some saw Jesus raise the dead and did not believe; the Thief sees Jesus being put to death, and yet believes."[154] And so should we. The fourth sign of true conversion is the exercise of faith in Christ.

First, a change of attitude toward the Person of Christ; second, a sincere confession of sin; third, a clear confession of Jesus as personal Lord; fourth, the exercise of faith. **Finally,** true conversion always manifests itself in **a Change of Behavior.** It is in that change of behavior that we see the Thief's original change of attitude. Once he stole and tried to circumvent the law and justify himself; now he confesses that the law is just and he is a sinner. Once he reviled Jesus himself; now he not only stops doing it but cannot stand to have it done and rebukes the other thief. There is very little opportunity for this man to show his faith in his life, but in the few minutes he has, he

---

[154] Alfred Plummer, *The Gospel according to St. Luke,* op. cit., 535.

avails himself of the opportunity. True conversion always manifests itself in a change of behavior.

A change of attitude toward Jesus Christ; confession of sin; public confession of Christ as Savior and Lord; the exercise of faith in Christ; a change of behavior: These were the signs of true conversion in the Thief on the Cross. They are the signs of true conversion in all men. They are the signs of true conversion in us. Let us examine ourselves, whether we be in the faith.

The Thief is of course the classic example of the "**deathbed conversion**." Yet he surpasses many of us in the clarity and forcefulness of his testimony for Christ, both in word and in deeds. Deathbed conversions may be real. This one shows that even they can manifest the signs of true faith. But be warned: If you *plan* to have a deathbed conversion, you put yourself in the category of those who "know" and thus potentially exclude yourself from Jesus' prayer. That is a very dangerous thing to do!

What then are **the Implications of this Conversion**? We could mention that it **refutes the doctrine of Purgatory,** since this man had no opportunity to do penance for all his misdeeds; he would be with Jesus in Paradise *this day*. We could mention that it **refutes the doctrine of "soul sleep,"** for that very day—not thousands of years hence— the Thief was promised the enjoyment of Christ's presence in Paradise. But much more significantly, we should emphasize the way in which it **reinforces the doctrine of salvation by grace alone.** This man had no opportunity to work his way to heaven. How could just a few words spoken in duress make up for his entire misspent life? He of all men was saved by God's unmerited favor, by grace, by grace supremely, and by grace alone. And we should stress that he simultaneously emphasizes that fact that there is no salvation without repentance and a changed life—as the result, not the cause, of that salvation. If even the Thief on the Cross could manifest the signs of true conversion, surely we should expect to find them in ourselves if our faith is real! And we should not miss the fact that he completes the lessons of Jesus' prayer for forgiveness. The characteristic note of Scripture always combines encouragement with warning. For both thieves heard the encouragement of Jesus praying for the Father to forgive them—but only one responded in faith and repentance. J. C. Ryle summarized that lesson well: "One was saved that no sinner might despair; one was lost that no sinner might presume."[155] Let us then do neither!

Conclusion

What then do we learn from all of this? Everybody needs to be forgiven. Anybody can be forgiven. Not everybody will be forgiven. If you are not sure that you have been, then come and speak to me or one of the elders after the service and let us help you leave knowing that you are forgiven and will be saved. Why? Because Jesus

---

[155] J, C, Ryle, *Expository Thoughts*, op. cit., 471.

himself asked for it. And therefore, he that cometh unto Him, He will no wise cast out (John 6:37).

No question but it was a dirty job.
  The scourging by itself was bad enough;
  To drive the spikes, though, really takes a tough
  And calloused character. The women sob,
The victim screams, and even as the mob
  Cries out for more, men wince. The really rough
  Part comes when all four soldiers huff and puff
  To raise upright the heavy wooden stob,
For then the man's own weight begins to work:
  The tendons crack, the flesh begins to tear—
  And when he thinks it's more than he can bear,
  They drop him in the socket with a jerk.[156]
And after we did *that*, He said (it's true!),
  "Forgive them, for they know not what they do."[157]

---

[156] Many authorities believe that the victim would actually have had his hands nailed to the crossbeam, which would then have been lifted up onto the upright stake that was permanently fixed in the ground. In any case, the suffering would have been extreme.

[157] Williams, *Stars Through the Clouds*, op. cit., 154.

THE DEATH OF CHRIST

Luke 23:44 And it was now about the sixth hour, and darkness fell over the whole land until the ninth hour, 45 the sun being obscured. And the veil of the temple was torn in two. 46 And Jesus, crying out with a loud voice, said, "Father, into thy hands I commit my spirit." And having said this, he breathed his last. 47 Now when the centurion saw what had happened, he began praising God, saying, "Certainly this man was innocent." 48 And all the multitudes who came together for this spectacle, when they observed what had happened, began to return, beating their breasts. 49 And all his acquaintances and the women who accompanied him from Galilee were standing at a distance, seeing these things. 50 And behold, a man named Joseph, who was a member of the Council, a good and righteous man 51 (he had not consented to their plan and action), a man from Arimathea, a city of the Jews, who was waiting for the kingdom of God, 52 this man went to Pilate and asked for the body of Jesus. 53 And he took it down and wrapped it in a linen cloth and laid him in a tomb cut into the rock, where no one had ever lain. 54 And it was the preparation day, and the Sabbath was about to begin. 55 Now the women who had come with him out of Galilee followed after, and saw the tomb and how his body was laid. 56 And they returned and prepared spices and perfumes.

Introduction

Considered by bulk, the center of Scripture is Psalm 80:13. Considered by time (counting only datable events), it is somewhere in I Kings. Considered by significance, a good candidate has to be the passage we have before us today. It is no exaggeration to say that every word of Scripture either looks forward to or reflects back on the meaning of this event, the hinge or fulcrum on which all of history turns and the fulfillment of God's purposes for mankind depends: the voluntary sacrifice for sin of God the Son, the death of Christ. Here we see three witnesses who testify to the meaning of that death, along with three ways in which our response to those witnesses relates us to it.

I. The Significance Of His Death: Three Witnesses

The Sun (v. 44)

The first witness that testifies to the meaning of this death is the Sun, which simply refused to shine on the scene unfolding below it. It appears that this darkness was a local phenomenon. A regular eclipse of the sun would not produce "darkness" for a full three hours, and if the phenomenon had been worldwide, no doubt the astrologers of the time would have reported it. No meteorological phenomenon is mentioned as accompanying this darkness. So it was not just a coincidence of weather; it's not just that it was a cloudy day. No, for three hours from noon to 3:00 PM, during the time when the light of the sun should have been at its brightest, darkness fell over this hillside as a sign to those present.

A sign of what? Surely any Jew who noticed the phenomenon and tried to understand its significance would do so in the light of the use of light and darkness in the Old Testament; and we may add to it for our understanding the New Testament, as it records the fulfillment of the Old and then reflects upon it. For light comes from God and is always associated with Him. It first appeared when God said, *"Let there be light!" And there was light* (Gen. 1:3). *"The Lord is my light and my salvation,"* says David in Psalm 27:1. So light is associated not just with God but with God and with salvation. *"Arise! Shine! For your light has come, and the glory of the Lord has risen upon you"* (Isaiah 60:1). Light also figures in Messianic prophecy. And so when those prophecies were ready to be fulfilled, Zacharias had prophesied that *"The sunrise from on high shall visit us, to shine upon those who sit in darkness and the shadow of death, to guide our feet into the way of peace"* (Luke 1:78–9). And then the glory of the Lord shone round about the shepherds, and they were sore afraid; and in the temple Simeon had taken the baby Jesus from his mother's arms and called Him *"a light of revelation to the Gentiles"* (Luke 2:32, quoting Isaiah 49:6). And John would therefore conclude, *"God is light, and in him there is no darkness at all"* (1 John 1:5).

So what is the meaning of this darkness? Not that God was not present or at work on that hillside, nor that His purposes were not being fulfilled. But the Jewish nation had rejected their Messiah, and in so doing they had rejected God and they had rejected light. They were being given a symbolic taste of the darkness they had chosen. Have you ever visited a great cavern like Mammoth Cave in Kentucky? Once the guide had taken you deep into the cave, many miles underground and away from the light of the sun, did he turn off the artificial lights just for a moment so you could "see" the cave the way it appears naturally? And then perhaps, before turning the electric lights back on, he lit a single match. And how it shone in that darkness! Before it was lit, that was a darkness so deep you literally could not see your hand in front of your face; it made no difference at all whether your eyes were open or shut. Without Jesus Christ, you are in darkness that deep, spiritually. The purpose of life, the meaning of life, the intentions of your Maker and Judge toward you: All these things are that dark to you apart from Christ! And such darkness is not just *around* fallen men and women; it is *in* them. If the light in you is darkness, how deep is that darkness? (Mat. 6:23). But the light shines in the darkness, and the darkness cannot overcome it (John 1:5). But we are anticipating the Resurrection to say that, and that is not until next week!

The Veil Of The Temple (v. 45)

The second witness to the meaning of what is happening here is the Veil of the Temple. It was the great curtain that separated the Holy Place from the Holy of Holies, that last inner sanctum into which the High Priest came but once a year, bearing blood, on the Day of Atonement. Why was this great curtain hung? Because our sins have separated us from our God, and therefore to come into His presence is death. It is why the children of Israel were forbidden to touch the Mountain in Exodus 19 when the glory of God descended on it. That is why there was a veil before the Holy of Holies, where dwelt the presence of God. You can read about its construction for the Tabernacle in Exodus 26:31–33. And the Gemara tells us that forty years before the destruction of Herod's Temple—which would put us right about the time of the crucifixion—the doors of the Temple suddenly flew open of their own accord and the menorah went out![158] In that same disturbance, perhaps one of the earthquakes that accompanied the death of Christ, the Veil was ripped in two, and for the first time since it was hung the Holy of Holies stood open. What could this mean?

The significance of this event is explained by the book of Hebrews: The old High Priest had entered the Holy of Holies once a year on the Day of Atonement bearing blood to atone for his own sins and the sins of the people. But now, *"when Christ appeared as a great high priest of the good things to come, he entered through the greater and more perfect tabernacle not made with hands, that is to say, not of this creation; and not through the blood of goats and calves, but through his own blood, he entered the Holy Place once for all, having obtained eternal redemption. For if the blood of goats and bulls and the ashes of a heifer sprinkling those who have been defiled sanctify for the cleansing of the flesh, how much more will the blood of Christ, who through the eternal Spirit offered himself without blemish to God, cleanse your conscience from dead works to serve the living God?"* (Heb. 9:11–14). The Day of Atonement has been fulfilled! Because Christ has died as a vicarious, substitutionary sacrifice in atonement for our sins, the way to God has been opened to all men by faith. What only the high priest could do once a year, every believer can now do at any time: enter into the direct presence of God without fear, because our sins have been taken out of the way forever, having been nailed to the Cross. And therefore *"we have confidence to enter the holy place by the blood of Jesus"* (Heb. 10:19). And *"there is therefore now no condemnation to those who are in Christ Jesus"* (Rom. 8:1). Hallelujah!

The Words Of The Savior (v. 46)

What could possibly add to the testimony of the Veil without anticlimax? Only one thing: the third witness to the meaning of this death is the Savior Himself. *"Father, into thy hands I commit my spirit"* (Luke 23:46). He has already said, *"Father, forgive them, for they know not what they do"* (verse 34). He has already said, *"My God, my God, why hast thou forsaken me?"* (Mat. 27:46). He has already said, *"It is finished"* (John 19:30). And now he says, *"Father, into thy hands I commit my spirit."* Jesus was on that Cross so that we could be forgiven. He bore our sins in His body on the Tree, and experienced the very separation from God that is the essence of the death which is the wages of sin, an experience that was so excruciating that it tore from His lips that horrible cry of dereliction. And He had finished His work of sin bearing and propitiation and atonement. And now, His own relationship with the Father restored, He commits His life into the Father's hands and gives up the ghost. Despite the necessary cry of agony

---

[158] See Plummer, op. cit., 538. Josephus also refers to this event, *Antiquities* XV.v.2, *Works*, op. cit., 320.

in the middle as He bore the full penalty for our sin, there is no final conflict here between the Father and the Son. They are at one in their love of us poor sinners. That love has caused Christ to submit to the Cross voluntarily. And now He is received back into the favor of the Father. Do you see what this means? His sacrifice for us has been accepted! And therefore His Resurrection—and ours—becomes inevitable. From that moment, He will be our Mediator and our Advocate. From that moment, He who humbled himself even to death on the Cross will be exalted to the very right hand of the Father's throne on high.

Some modern thinkers reject the biblical view of the atonement as an example of "divine child abuse." How little they understand of human sin, of divine justice, and most of all of divine love! It was the Son's love as much as the Father's that led Him to that Cross for us. And the last word we hear from Him is no longer agony; it is back to the characteristic note of trust that has been the essence of His relationship to the Father from the beginning. Do you understand? *"Father, into thy hands I commit my spirit."* It is because He died for our sins—it is because He said this to the Father right as He was doing so—that we too can have hope. If Christ at such a moment as this could commit His spirit in complete trust into the Father's hands—then so can we. So can we—at this moment and at the moment of our own deaths. For this death has taken away the sting.

II. The Responses To This Death

The Centurion (v. 47)

There are three witnesses to the meaning of this death, and there are also three responses recorded by those who heard and saw their testimony. The first one is that of the Centurion. *"Now when the centurion saw what had happened, he began praising God, saying, 'Certainly this man was innocent'"* (verse 37). We must not exaggerate the understanding of which he was capable at this point, but something about the death of Christ impressed this battle–hardened soldier, this veteran of so many executions. Luke records that he was impressed that Jesus must have been an innocent man. Matthew adds that he was very afraid (for, after all, he had just executed a man who was innocent in his own judgment), and that he also proclaimed Jesus a son of God. He need not have had a very sophisticated understanding at that moment of what that meant. But he was impressed by Jesus as by one who told the truth. Unlike most of the people here, he actually stopped to think about what was happening. According to tradition, he went on to become a believer. If indeed he went on to faith and commitment, it was because he was paying attention here. Don't just give a conventional response to Christ defined by what other people are doing, whether it be uninformed respect or unthinking condemnation. Look at Him! Listen to Him! Pay attention! And deal honestly with what you see, as this Centurion obviously did. Then you may indeed be led to faith in Christ.

The Crowds (v. 48)

If the response of the Centurion is encouraging, that of the crowds is sobering. *"And all the multitudes who came together for this spectacle, when they observed what had happened, began to return, beating their breasts"* (verse 48). These are the same people who had been shouting, "Crucify him!" Well, they have gotten what they wanted. And it has left an empty taste in their mouths—indeed, worse than empty. They began to return, beating their breasts. This is sorrow of a kind, but there is no indication that it is a godly sorrow leading to repentance. They got what they wanted. Why aren't they happy?

There is a very basic principle that these people illustrate. Jesus is the Way, the Truth, and the Life (John 14:6). He came to bring us life, and to bring it more abundantly (John 10:10). In Him was life, and that life was the light of men (John 1:4). This is life eternal, that we may know the Father as the only true God, and Jesus Christ whom He has sent (John 17:3). To reject Christ is to reject life. There is a pleasure in sin for a season, but the end thereof is death. There is a pleasure in sin for a season, but it leaves an aftertaste. The taste it leaves in your mouth is emptiness, ashes, bitterness. It may seem sweet now, but the day is coming when you will choke on it. And you will walk away beating your breast and wondering what happened.

The Disciples (v. 49ff).

The final response is that of the disciples. I find the response of some of Jesus' disciples—not the Twelve, except maybe for John, but Joseph of Arimathea and the women—very intriguing indeed. Remember that none of them yet really understands the purpose of the Cross or the hope of the Resurrection. Therefore, they should conclude that Jesus' death is proof that he was a false Messiah and forsake Him. But they just couldn't do that! They could not bring themselves to forsake Him, for reasons they did not yet understand. But faith always finds a way to show itself, as we saw with the Thief on the Cross. Here it does so in loving service even when all is lost, service performed anyway even when everything seems hopeless and futile. They had no idea that the Resurrection was coming. But unlike Peter and the rest, they did not care if people realized they loved Jesus. They did not care if they were tarred by the brush of His guilt and His failure and His shame. They were going to see that He got a decent burial, they were going to anoint Him, and if the soldiers came for them as a result, so be it! They loved their Master, and that was all they needed to understand. They loved Him, and that was that.

We have the advantage of the Resurrection, the whole New Testament to explain it, and the Holy Spirit to apply it to our hearts. But do we have the loyalty and commitment and love for Jesus that they had without any of that? How faithful are we when things are discouraging—but never anywhere near so discouraging as this? How faithful are we when we are just not in the mood? Maybe that is actually the measure of the depth of the hold that Jesus really has on us. Maybe that is really the measure of our faith.

Conclusion

The Veil of the Temple has been torn! The way to peace with God, forgiveness, eternal life, meaning, purpose, and love is now open because Christ died. So how do we respond to this situation? We can be like the crowd and choke on dust and ashes. Or we can be like the centurion and actually pay attention and respond honestly to what we see. And we can be like the disciples and commit ourselves to Jesus and love Him and serve Him, and in that love and that service find life. What is your choice today?

THE APPEARANCE TO THE MARYS

Luke 24:1 But on the first day of the week at early dawn they came to the tomb bringing the spices which they had prepared. 2 And they found the stone rolled away from the tomb, 3 but when they entered they did not find the body of the Lord Jesus. 4 And it happened that while they were perplexed about this, behold, two men suddenly stood near them in dazzling apparel. 5 And as the women were terrified and bowed their faces to the ground, the men said to them, "Why do you seek the Living One among the dead? 6 He is not here, but he has risen. Remember how he spoke to you while he was still in Galilee, 7 saying that the Son of Man must be delivered into the hands of sinful men and be crucified, and the third day rise again?" 8 And they remembered his words, 9 and returned from the tomb and reported all these things to the eleven and to all the rest. 10 Now they were Mary Magdalene and Joana and Mary the mother of James; also the other women with them were telling these things to the apostles. 11 And these words appeared to them as nonsense, and they would not believe them. 12 But Peter arose and ran to the tomb. Stooping and looking in, he saw the linen wrappings only; and he went away to his home, marveling at that which had happened.

Introduction

For the last few messages on Luke, we have been studying in detail the darkest, most shameful, and most sorrowful hour of human history. But it was also the hour when the victory was won, the backs of Satan, Sin, and Death were broken, and redemption was purchased. This was already true when our passage begins, though it was not yet evident. But God was about to change that with the Resurrection of our Lord from the dead. This great event was first announced to the Women, who have therefore been called "the first preachers of the resurrection." Let us listen to what they have to say, as they first report their experience of the resurrection and then show its effects in their lives.

I. The Experience Of The Resurrection

The experience of the resurrection of Jesus for these women began not in joy but in grief, indeed in an anguish whose intensity can hardly be imagined by us at this safe distance from what they were going through. They had just experienced a whole series of the very hardest things for human beings to take. The first was **the Dashing of their Hopes.** Nothing is harder to live with, nothing harder to accept. It can be tough to get over even in trivial matters. I remember all too well the Sugar Bowls of 1982 and 1983. After my beloved Georgia Bulldawgs had won the national championship in the 1981 Sugar Bowl, we had a chance at it again the next two years, had it in our grasp, only to be deprived of the prize by last–minute, unbelievably heroic plays by Dan Marino and Todd Blackledge of the Miami Hurricanes and the Penn State Nittany Lions. I could not get to sleep either of those New Year's nights, with my mind compulsively replaying the games and generating an endless stream of one futile "if only" after another. Well, what if you had, not a mere national championship in college football, but the very Kingdom of Heaven longed for by Israel for generations just within your grasp? Only one week ago it must have felt like it was actually going to happen, like it was actually beginning during the Triumphal Entry. But now, inexplicably but inexorably, it had all suddenly fallen apart. Hope deferred makes the heart sick, but hope ripped out of one's very grasp at the moment when it seemed it was being fulfilled at long last can almost make the heart stop! Such was their experience.

But it wasn't just the dashing of their hopes. They also had to endure **the Trauma of Tragedy.** Nothing is harder to reconcile oneself to than the death of a loved one, especially if that death is totally unexpected. Viola Kilbourne was a missionary to Japan who was on furlough in Atlanta my junior year of high school and attended my church. Having two teenage daughters, she opened her home to our youth group and became for that year a second mother to us all. On her next furlough, she ended up living next door to the campus of Taylor University where I was now a senior in college, because her daughter Kathy was a freshman there, and so my ties to that family were picked up as if no time had intervened at all. One Sunday morning I showed up at their door to pick Kathy up for church because we were supposed to sing a duet that day. She came to the door in one of those deathly calms that masks a horrible inner turmoil. "I don't think I can come today. Mother was killed this morning." She had been out riding her bicycle for exercise and was hit by a drunk driver and thrown 200 feet through the air. It felt like I had just been hit, like someone had just punched me in the solar plexus. There was a literal physical shock, a numbness worse than any pain. It took me weeks to get over it. Imagine how bad it was for the family themselves! And yet it was even worse for these women. They had no idea it was coming, for it is plain that Jesus' attempts to forewarn them had not registered with them anymore than it had with the male disciples. One minute Jesus seems poised to ascend the throne of David, and then somehow before you know it you are watching Him be brutally murdered. How can this be happening? Truly the horror of it is hard to imagine.

So we have the dashing of our hopes and the trauma of tragedy. Then, on top of all of this, there came **the Frustration of the Sabbath.** Why is the Sabbath frustrating? Don't we welcome a day of peace and quiet in which to sort everything out? No! These are those old–fashioned women, like some of our mothers or grandmothers, for whom work is therapy. There is only one way they know how to deal with grief, and that is by preparing spices and anointing the body. But then as soon as they get the spices prepared, boom! The Sabbath comes. And they have to sit on their hands and chew their grief like bitter cud for a whole day in which they can do absolutely nothing about it. The frustration must have seemed intolerable. No wonder they were up at the crack of dawn on the first day of the week. How will they get the tomb open? Never mind! We'll worry about that later; something will turn up. But right now we've got to *do* something!

And so there they are at the tomb with their spices at the very first moment of anything you would remotely be able to call sunrise, only then to meet the final straw. After all that anticipation, after all that agony of waiting through the exquisite torture of forced inactivity—the tomb is open and the body is gone!!! *Now* what? Almost as great a wonder as the resurrection itself is the fact that they survived all this trauma to meet the angels and hear the Good News.

Well, I think we have not paid enough attention to what these women went through. But what is the significance of doing so now? For one thing, it helps us grasp **the Psychological Realism of the Narrative.** These were real human beings reacting to incredible stress just the way we might have, had we been in their place. If you need any help to believe in the historical reality of the resurrection story and the truthfulness of its narratives, these women are one more piece in that puzzle. When you look at them as real human beings in the context of this narrative, it all makes sense. Not only that, but in Jewish eyes women were not considered reliable witnesses. Their testimony would not have been allowed to count in a court of law! So what are they doing here? There is only one reason why the Gospel accounts would make them "the first preachers of the resurrection," and that is that this is exactly how it happened. It's not the kind of story anybody would have made up.

But there is more to it than that, as we think about **the Implications of their Anguish.** What these ladies have been through up to this moment is a picture of what human life is without the victory and hope that the resurrection brings. They had known their hopes dashed, and all our hopes are groundless if indeed Christ did not rise—yea, as Paul put it, we would be of all men most miserable (1 Cor. 15:19). If Christ was not raised, then it really does not matter what we do with our lives because once we are dead. we won't remember any of it, and it will be just as if we had never been. All they could think of was their grief at their loss, and as we stumble through life toward death, that loss is the definitive story of our lives, death the final word about us. How tragic! What they thought was meaningful action was frustrated by the intervening Sabbath, and everything we do is equally meaningless and pointless if this life is all that there is. But the resurrection puts an end to all of that! Sorrow is turned to joy, despair to hope, defeat to victory, frustration to fulfillment! Christ is risen.

II. The Effects Of The Resurrection

Such was the experience of the resurrection. I also want us to look at the effects of the resurrection on these earliest of the early Christians. These are the first such effects reported, and they remain definitive for valid and normal Christian experience two millennia later. Their presence in you is the sure sign of the reality of the resurrection in your life; their absence raises serious questions about whether you really believe the words that come out of your mouth. What are they?

REJOICING: First, they rejoiced. This is not explicitly stated. It does not need to be. Death has been defeated! The final Enemy has been neutralized! The one you love most in all the world has been restored to you! Why do you seek the Living One among the dead? Belief that God has raised Jesus Christ from the dead is the starting point of all true Christian faith. So how could joy not be the characteristic note of those who believe in Him? The fruit of the Spirit is love, *joy*, peace (Galatians 5:22). Why? Because it is the resurrection of Christ that unleashed the power of Pentecost. We count it all *joy* when we encounter various trials (James 1:2). Why? Because it is the resurrection that guarantees ultimate victory over those trials. We *rejoice* if we are counted worthy to suffer shame for His name (Acts 5:41). Why? Because it was in the resurrection that God gave Him a name that is above every name and declared Him to be both Lord and Christ. In 2 Corinthians 6:10 we are sorrowful yet rejoicing. In 1 Peter 1:8 we have joy inexpressible and full of glory. In Philippians 4:4 we are exhorted to rejoice always, and again I say rejoice! This is the characteristic note of the life that believes what these women have to tell us. What else could it be? How could it be anything else? Is your life full of this joy, or are you living as if Christ were still in the tomb?

REMEMBERING: First, they rejoiced. Second, **they remembered** (verse 8). They remembered that Jesus had told them what was going to happen. We know that He had done so repeatedly and insistently. But this message was so far outside the framework of His disciples' preconceived notions, so far outside the framework of their expectations, so unconnected to any of their plausibility structures, that they did not know what to do with it. They must have spiritualized it in some way and then forgotten it. But now it all came back to them. The resurrection was what made it all fall into place. Its effect was to focus their attention anew on the words of Jesus. For now they made sense. Now they were the words not of a would–be Messiah but of the risen Lord. Many people knew that Jesus spoke with authority, not as the scribes. But now His words resonated with authority and truth in a completely new way. This is one sure mark of whether you really *"believe in your heart that God hath raised him from the dead"* (Rom. 10:9): Do you remember His words?

RETURNING: First they rejoiced; second, they remembered; in the third place, **they returned** (verse 9a). Whenever we have a fresh experience with the Lord, the natural temptation is always to try to prolong it, or, worse, to reproduce it. Neither ever works. This is what caused Peter to want to build those tabernacles on the Mount of Transfiguration. But the Lord knew why that mountain–top experience had happened: because they were needed down in the valley. Paul Stookey says it so well, as you may remember from our discussion of The Transfiguration:

> And I wonder have you ever been to the mountain
> To look at the valley below?
> Did you see all the roads tangled down in the valley?
> Did you know which way to go?
> Oh, the mountain stream runs pure and clear
> And I wish to my soul I could always be here,

But there's a reason for living way down in the valley
That only the mountain knows.[159]

The temptation was to hang about on the mountain and savor the mountain–top experience, but Jesus and the three were needed down in the valley where the other disciples had failed to heal the boy with the demon. The temptation might be to hang around the tomb, to try to prolong that experience. But the resurrection is a call to action! The focus of ministry is there. The women returned from the tomb to tell the disciples. And that leads us right to the next point.

REPORTING: What were the effects of the resurrection in the lives of these women? They rejoiced; they remembered; they returned. And finally, **they reported** (verse 9b). They reported to the apostles what had happened. Who cares if the apostles don't believe us at first? Who cares if they think we are crazy? News like this has to be *told*! To really grasp the reality of the resurrection is to be a witnessing Christian. How could it be otherwise?

Imagine this scenario. Everything happens just as Luke tells it through verse 8 — and then nothing else follows. Finally, about three weeks later, Peter and John happen to run into Mary Magdalene. "Hey, Mar', how you doing? What happened to you after the death of the Lord? Did you ever get to anoint the body?" "Oh, yeah," Mary replies. "Didn't I tell you? Jesus rose from the dead that morning!"

It is harder to believe in that scenario than it is to believe in the resurrection itself! Let me be very plain. If you can keep news like that to yourself, you raise serious questions about whether you really believe it is true. So why are most of us acting more like the Mary Magdalene of my version of the story rather than the much more believable one in Luke's? There is something seriously amiss here. Don Francisco certainly hit the nail on the head: "I got to tell somebody!"[160] Don't you? Yes, we do!

Conclusion

Listen in conclusion to what is surely one of the clearest and most definitive statements in all the New Testament about how one becomes a Christian: *"If you confess with your mouth Jesus as Lord and believe in your heart that God raised him from the dead, you shall be saved. For with the heart man believes, resulting in righteousness, and with the mouth he confesses, resulting in salvation"* (Romans 10:9–10). Do you believe in your heart that God raised Jesus from the dead? If you did, you would certainly confess it with your mouth. In fact, you would do just like these women did: you would rejoice, you would remember, you would return, and you would report. Your reporting would be given

---

159 Paul Stookey, "John Henry Bosworth," *Paul And* (NY: Warner Brothers Records, 1971).
160 Don Francisco, "Got to Tell Somebody," https://www.youtube.com/watch?v=7VknKAoxDiI. See also "He's Alive," https://www.youtube.com/watch?v=NyPBVwOCYmM. Sadly, Francisco has developed some doctrinal deficiencies over time, but these songs remain classics that capture well the reality of what it must have been like.

credibility by your rejoicing and authority by your remembering, and they would all then give point to your returning.

Isn't that what the Christian life should look like? I'm not talking about that mythical state, the "deeper Christian life." This is what life should be like if it is Christian at all. So listen to the testimony once again of the first preachers of the resurrection, and may God grant you faith to believe it now if you never have before. Is Jesus risen? Then rejoice, remember, return, and report, to the glory of our risen and living Lord. Amen.

THE MAN WHO CAME TO DINNER

Luke 24:13 And behold, two of them were going that very day to a village named Emmaus, which was about seven miles from Jerusalem. 14 And they were conversing with each other about all these things which had taken place. 15 And it came about that while they were conversing and discussing, Jesus himself approached and began traveling with them, 16 but their eyes were prevented from recognizing him. 17 And he said to them, "What are these words that you are exchanging with one another as you are walking?" And they stood still, looking sad. 18 And one of them, named Cleopas, answered and said to him, "Are you the only one visiting Jerusalem and unaware of the things which have happened here in these days?" 19 And he said to them, "What things?" And they said to him, "The things about Jesus the Nazarene, who was a prophet mighty in deed and word in the sight of God and all the people, 20 and how the chief priests and our rulers delivered him up to the sentence of death and crucified him. 21 But we were hoping that it was he who was going to redeem Israel. Indeed, besides all this, it is the third day since these things happened. 22 But also some women among us amazed us. When they were at the tomb early in the morning 23 and did not find his body, they came saying that they had seen a vision of angels who said that he was alive. 24 And some of those who were with us went to the tomb and found it just exactly as the women also had said; but him they did not see. 25 And he said to them, "Oh foolish men and slow of heart to believe in all that the prophets have spoken! 26 Was it not necessary for the Christ to suffer these things and to enter into his glory?" 27 And beginning with Moses and with all the prophets, he explained to them the things concerning himself in all the Scriptures. 28 And they approached the village where they were going, and he acted as though he would go farther. 29 But they urged him, saying, "Stay with us, for it is getting toward evening, and the day is now nearly over." And he went in to stay with them. 30 And it came about that when he had reclined at the table with them, he took bread and blessed it and, breaking it, he began giving it to them. 31 And their eyes were opened and they recognized him; and he vanished from their sight. 32 And they said to one another, "Were not our hearts burning within us while he was speaking to us on the road, while he was explaining the Scriptures to us?" 33 And they arose that very hour and returned to Jerusalem and found gathered together the eleven and those who were with them, 34 saying, "The Lord has really risen and has appeared to Simon." 35 And they began to relate their experiences on the road and how he was recognized by them in the breaking of the bread.

Introduction

The account of the Disciples on the Road to Emmaus has always been one of my favorite Easter stories because of the fascinating questions it raises. Who was the second disciple? Why couldn't they recognize Jesus at first? I do not know the answer to the first question, but I think I can venture a good guess: Mrs. Cleopas. And as for the second question, I think I can also shed some light on it later on. But I love this passage even more for the important lessons it teaches us about the meaning of Easter.

I. The Reality Of The Resurrection

The first thing we learn here is something about the reality of the resurrection. This is only one of several accounts of resurrection appearances. Paul tells us that there was a total of some five hundred people who saw Jesus alive at some point between his Death and his Ascension (I Cor. 15:6). We know about the eleven (several times) and the women, the Maries, Salome, etc. But there were many other followers of Jesus to whom he appeared during this time. This story lets us put a name on at least one of them. This tells us that the resurrection was not some tiny, ingrown, tightly woven conspiracy, but a widely experienced phenomenon not limited to the inner band. And it is curious that all these stories have certain features in common.

For example, Jesus is always recognizably Jesus, but recognizing him is often not a simple matter. It is the same body that was killed, with the scars to prove it, but it has powers not normally seen before the resurrection, such as the ability to walk through walls and appear in a locked room, or, as in this case, to appear and disappear. These appearances, these encounters, had the hard, knobby, unyielding feel of reality. They involved eating fish or bread, things that almost seemed normal, but they were never quite what you expected. This appearance is no exception, and it confirms that we are dealing with a phenomenon that was stubbornly itself and very, very real. Nobody would have made up stories with rough edges like this: women as the first eyewitnesses, other eyewitnesses who couldn't even tell whom they were talking to! The only reason to write it this way is that this is how it happened.

I do not see how one can read these accounts, with all the rough edges of stubborn reality about them, and think that the resurrection was just a way of talking about the fact that the significance of Jesus' life and teachings survived his death. I do not see how one can read these accounts, with all the rough edges of stubborn reality about them, and think that the resurrection was just a way of talking about the fact that the impact of Jesus' life continued in His disciples. I do not see how one can read these accounts, with all the rough edges of stubborn reality about them, and think that the resurrection was even just a way of talking about the fact that His Spirit lived on in their hearts. The resurrection of Jesus from the dead was bodily, objective, physical, and real. The body was not just missing from its tomb; it could meet you on the road and walk with you and carry on a conversation. It could share in the breaking of bread. It said, "*A spirit hath not flesh and bones as ye see I have*" (Luke 24:39). Its hands and side could be touched. The resurrection was dynamic and powerful: the dead body from the tomb was alive, transformed, more alive even than it had been before—as ours will be when it returns. And it was real. I'm going to suggest that these very rough edges of the narrative confirm that conclusion; they do not compromise it. It was very, very real.

II. The Reportage Of The Resurrection

The second thing we learn is something about the reportage of the resurrection. The resurrection was real; it was also well documented. The resurrection of Jesus from the dead is the best attested event of ancient history. We have many eyewitnesses, whose accounts are consistent enough to be believable and varied enough to save them from any charge of collusion. We have the witness of the women, of the eleven, and of Cleopas. We have the empirical evidence of eyes and hands and senses; and they stand for the five hundred who saw the risen Lord. The Jewish establishment dealt with their testimony in a curiously consistent way. They never tried to refute them; they never appealed to contradicting evidence. They just tried to kill them. It was the only way they could shut them up. In every way these witnesses have the ring of truth.

But more compelling even than the eyewitness testimony of the observers, more compelling than the witness of the women, is the witness of the Word. Is that not why Cleopas and his friend were "prevented" from recognizing Jesus at first (verse 16)? I think it was so that in verses 25–27 Jesus could explain the Scriptures to them, so they could hear that testimony and base their faith on *that*, rather than on the less reliable witness of their own senses. Notice that word, "prevented" (verse 16). It is not just that they did not recognize Him at first; they were *prevented* from doing so. It is a word that implies a divine act with a purpose; and that purpose was that they should hear the Word and believe it. There is no doubt that the body they saw was the same body that they had known. The nail prints prove that. But there were natural factors in their failure to recognize it which meant that the "preventing" was easy to achieve. They were full of sorrow and confusion, and they were not expecting to see Jesus alive again. It was easy for the resemblance not to register as anything more than a cruel coincidence. If you saw me on the street the week after my funeral, would you think, "Oh, right, there's Don; he must have risen from the dead," or would you not rather think, "Boy, that dude looks an awful lot like Don"? But after Jesus had opened the Scriptures to them, in His characteristic act of breaking the bread, it all suddenly hit home; it all fell into place. And He vanished from their midst.

It seems there was a point Jesus wanted to make here. Empirical evidence alone is not enough as a basis for such a radical and life–changing belief. The passage focuses our attention on the importance of the human eyewitnesses but also on the even greater importance of the witness of the Word of God. It is when what the two disciples saw and heard fit what the Word had prophesied that real faith in Christ as the living Lord was born in them. The Scriptures confirm the empirical evidence: These are not just weird, isolated facts; they are fulfilled prophecy. And the empirical evidence confirms the Scriptures as well: These are not just theoretically possible interpretations; they are the authoritative explanation of what God has actually done in the real world of space and time and experience. The witness of the senses and the witness of the Word mutually confirm one another: they fit together like two pieces of a puzzle. It is no wonder that their hearts burned within them as their minds were being prepared for the inevitable conclusion. And then, in the breaking of the bread . . . Boom! Wow!

III. The Reason For The Resurrection

So, then, the Reality of the Resurrection is manifested by the Reportage of the Resurrection; and both are rooted in the Reason for the Resurrection. Jesus' explanation of the Scriptures' testimony to Himself points us to the reason why all of this was happening. Was it not necessary, He asked, that the Christ should suffer and then be raised? Why necessary? We do not get to hear the whole explanation as they heard it that night, but the rest of the New Testament is there to give it to us. And part of it is hinted at in verses 44–48, where, as we will see next week, Jesus gives a similar explanation to the larger band of disciples.

Why was the resurrection necessary? It was necessary, for one thing, to fulfill the Scriptures. God keeps His promises. And what had He promised to do in passages like Isaiah 53, which the early church, no doubt due to Jesus' own emphasis here, made central to their understanding of Him? He had promised to take away our sins. *"For He was pierced for our transgressions; He was crushed for our iniquities. . . . All of us like sheep have gone astray . . .But the Lord has caused the iniquity of us all to fall on Him"* The resurrection is the Father's declaration that He has accepted the sacrifice of the Son. Behold, it says, the promised Lamb of God, who has now on the Cross taken away the sins of the world! Behold the One who gave his life a ransom for many! The resurrection was finally necessary so that we would realize that God the Father has formally accepted the sacrifice for sin of God the Son, and that therefore we can believe that *"there is now no condemnation for those who are in Christ Jesus"* (Rom. 8:1).

IV. The Relevance Of The Resurrection

The Reality of the Resurrection, the Reportage of the Resurrection, and the Reason for the Resurrection lead us inexorably to the Relevance of the Resurrection. Look again at verse 26. Was it not necessary for the Christ to suffer *and then to enter into His glory*? The reason for the resurrection is that it is God's vindication of His Son and His acceptance of His sacrifice on our behalf. The relevance of the resurrection is that it is God's promise to *us* of eternal life. "Life! Life! Eternal life!" as Bunyan's Pilgrim shouted on his way out of the City of Destruction.[161]

But look at the specific features of this resurrection, of Christ's resurrection body. This is not just a promise of infinite duration to life as we live it now; it is a promise of a radically transformed quality of life and a radically realized purpose for life, one that could make a life of eternal duration worth living. Jesus, in other words, entered *into His glory*—and He now turns and offers to share that glory with us. The glory of God is ultimately what this is all about. It is a cause big enough to live for, and it gives to life lived in its presence a quality that makes eternal duration appropriate and desirable. We see the first glimmers of that glory in the resurrection. It is what makes the promise of eternal life not only possible but desirable. The thing that beats at the heart of the

---

[161] John Bunyan, "The Pilgrim's Progress from this World to That which is to Come," 1678; *The Works of John Bunyan*, 3 vols., ed. George Offor (Edinburgh: Banner of Truth, 1999), 3:90.

universe and keeps all the planets and electrons going in their orbits is an unbelievable splendor of powerful love—loving enough to give itself as a sacrifice for sin and powerful enough to overcome even the last enemy, Death. No wonder the hearts of the disciples burned within them on the road. Do not yours as well? If you have never done so before, believe on the Lord Jesus Christ now, confess with your mouth Jesus as Lord and believe in your heart that God raised Him from the dead, and you shall be saved.

Conclusion

There can be no better conclusion to these thoughts than the words of J. I. Packer from his classic book *Knowing God*:

> When the New Testament tells us that Jesus Christ is risen, one of the things it means is that the victim of Calvary is now loose and at large, so that anyone anywhere can enjoy the same kind of relationship with him as the disciples did in the days of his flesh. The only differences are that, first, his presence with the Christian [for now] is spiritual, not bodily, so invisible to the physical eyes; second, the Christian, building on the New Testament witness, has access from the start to these truths which the original disciples only grasped gradually. Third, Jesus' way of speaking to us now is not by uttering fresh words, but by applying to our consciences those words of his [and his apostles recorded in the New Testament]. But knowing Jesus Christ still remains as definite a relation of personal discipleship as it was for the twelve when he was on earth. The Jesus who walks through the Gospel story walks with Christians now, and knowing him involves going with him, now as then.[162]

The Reality of the Resurrection is conveyed to us by the Reportage of the Resurrection, which tells us the Reason for the Resurrection and the Relevance of the Resurrection. Jesus Christ is risen! (He is risen indeed.) And what does that mean? Jesus Christ is Lord. Jesus Christ is real. And Jesus Christ is the way, the truth, and the life. No one comes to the Father but by Him (John 14:6). Are you coming?

---

[162] J. I. Packer, *Knowing God* (Downers Grove, Il: Intervarsity Press, 1973), 33.

THE LUCAN GREAT COMMISSION

Introduction

We finish our long series on the Gospel according to Luke by watching him shift his focus from the ministry of Christ to the mission of the church, in anticipation of Luke volume 2, the Book of Acts. You know the mission of the church very well: It is the Great Commission of Matthew 28. It is to go into all the world and make disciples of every nation. So I would like to begin by reminding you briefly of things that should be obvious from reading that version of the Commission, things I am sure you have heard before. Then I will try to give you a fresh perspective on the Great Commission by examining the *other* passage in which it was given, the same Commission but in different words: Luke 24.

First, what should be obvious: The Great Commission is to make disciples. There is only one imperative verb, one commanding verb, in the Matthew passage, and it is not to *go*; it is to *make disciples*. It would be better translated, "As you are going into all the earth, make disciples of every nation." We have to "go" in order to reach every nation, but going is not our Commission. We have not fulfilled it by going but by making disciples when we get there. And it is not to make *converts*. It is to make *disciples*. We have to make converts in order to make disciples, but the Commission is not fulfilled until we have made those converts into disciples of Jesus. And what is a disciple? It is a learner. And what kind of learner in this context? Jesus defines that for us: It is someone who follows his Master, confesses Him before men in Baptism, and wants to learn and to follow, is in the process of learning to follow, all things whatsoever that Master has taught us. Making a convert is simply the first step in what we were sent to do: make disciples.

Now let us look at the other time when Jesus commissioned his disciples. It will confirm what we should have seen in Matthew: that the Great Commission is about the Gospel, and the Gospel is about Jesus. It is found in Luke's conclusion to his Gospel, Luke 24:44–48. It sums up the forty days of grad school, as it were, that Jesus conducted with His disciples after the Resurrection.

Luke 24:44 Now he said to them, "These are my words which I spoke to you while I was still with you, that all things which are written about me in the Law of Moses and the Prophets and the Psalms must be fulfilled." 45 Then he opened their minds to understand the Scriptures. 46 And he said to them, "Thus it is written that the Christ should suffer and rise from the dead the third day, 47 and that repentance for forgiveness of sins should be proclaimed in his name to all the nations, beginning from Jerusalem. 48 You are witnesses of these things."

So central is The Great Commission to the life of the Church that our Lord gave it more than once. The version in Matthew 28 is more familiar: But we also have much to learn from Luke's version. The two passages go together, and both are essential to understand our purpose in this world until our Lord returns. Both passages make Evangelism—taking the Gospel, the Good News of what God has done in Christ for our salvation, to all nations—central to that purpose.

In the case of Luke's version, we note that it was given at the end of the forty days Jesus spent with his disciples between the Resurrection and his Ascension, *"opening their minds to understand the Scriptures."* At the climax of that time, like all good teachers, He was summing up the central points He did not want His disciples to miss. That makes this summary of the Gospel, the very core of our Lord's own teaching, especially crucial for us. We can learn from it something about the Foundation of the Gospel, the Facts of the Gospel, the Fruit of the Gospel, and the Function of the Evangelist.

I. The Foundation Of The Gospel (vv. 44–46a)

The first thing we note is the foundation of the Gospel, which is the Word of God. "Now he said to them, *'These are my words which I spoke to you while I was still with you, that all things which are written about me in the Law of Moses and the Prophets and the Psalms must be fulfilled.' Then he opened their minds to understand the Scriptures. And he said to them, 'Thus it is written'* . . ." (Luke 24:44–46a).

"Thus it is written." Our message, in other words, is not our own; it is based on the Word of God. Thus the Gospel that we preach does not begin with "I think," or "I suppose," or even "I feel." It begins with "Thus is it written." That is the foundation of the Gospel. And that is why we must proclaim it.

This feature of the Gospel helps explain why Christianity is of necessity an evangelizing, a proselytizing religion. It explains why we cannot leave people alone, why we cannot just accept that they are different, respect their culture and their beliefs, follow Starfleet's Prime Directive of non–interference, and mind our own business. For, you see, every other religion is the product of man's search for meaning. As such, they can afford to dialogue with each other, share their results as equals, take an academic interest in one another's beliefs, and take or leave them as their fancy dictates. There is no sense of urgency, for everyone is still looking. But the Christian faith is not the product of Man's search for meaning; it is the proclamation of God's kingship, the planting of His flag on the territory of our souls. Christian faith is not the product of history but the producer of history. The Christian faith did not evolve from my culture; it was announced by my Creator. And therefore, my faith is not a progress report on my search for God; it is the successful conclusion of God's search for me.

We present the Gospel, in other words, as Truth. If it is not truth, it is not worth presenting. What we have to share is not an elevated emotion, it is not another set of pious platitudes, it is not just a noble sentiment. It is truth given to us by God through written revelation. It is a message from God to men with which we have been entrusted as the messengers. And it is a message that comes with the highest authority—not mine, not yours, but God's. That is why we must proclaim it.

You must understand that this truth revolutionizes our approach to witness and evangelism. That which was lost has been found! The Gospel is like the shot fired into the air by the member of the search party who finds the missing child so that everyone else can converge on that spot. That is the spirit with which we should proclaim it. Now is the day of salvation! God has not left us in darkness.

Good news! Good news! This is not our speculation; it is His speech. He has not left us in darkness. He has spoken. And so I am not sharing "my faith" (as if anyone cared what I thought about such exalted matters). I am sharing God's truth. This is not arrogant, because it is not my message. I am not telling you that I have figured out what all the sages could not. I am telling you the Good News that God has found us. We should speak with the spirit of excitement and expectancy (as well as humility) appropriate for people in such a position. And our presentation of the Gospel should bring the unsaved into contact with Scripture. It is Scripture, not my religious experiences, that is sharper than any two–edged sword. My "testimony" is only the opportunity for bringing the message of Scripture to bear on unbelievers. For then perhaps Jesus will open their eyes to understand it, as He did for the disciples after the resurrection and as He has done for us since. And then—and only then—will they hear and believe and be saved.

II. The Facts Of The Gospel (v. 46)

Next we come to the facts of the Gospel. *"Thus it is written that the Christ should suffer and rise from the dead the third day, and that repentance for forgiveness of sins should be proclaimed in his name to all the nations, beginning from Jerusalem."* Thus it is written: that is how the Gospel begins, that is its foundation. And its content, the structure built on that foundation, is that the Christ should suffer and be raised again so that repentance for forgiveness of sins can be proclaimed in His name. The message is from God; the salvation is from God. God has spoken; He is not silent. God has acted; He is not unmoved by our plight. The Christian Gospel is unique among the religious messages of the world in that its focus is not what we must to do but what God has done: not what we must do to find God, but what God has done to find us.

And what has He done? *"...that the Christ..."* The first thing He has done is to come to us Himself in his Son. *"For the Word became flesh and dwelt among us, and we beheld his glory, glory as of the only begotten of the Father"* (John 1:14). *"No man has seen God at any time. But the only begotten God who is in the bosom of the Father, he hath declared him"* (John 1:18). And this One was the Way, the Truth, and the Life, and no one comes to the Father but by him (John 14:6). And therefore, *"let all the house of Israel know for certain that God has made him both Lord and Christ, this Jesus whom we crucified"* (Acts 2:36). And all this He proved by raising Him from the dead. The Gospel is first of all the Good News that God has sent His Son. Good news! Good news! This is the Gospel! This is good news indeed.

But then what follows? " . . . *that the Christ* **should suffer . . .**" No wonder it took Jesus forty days to open the minds of his disciples to understand all that was written about Him in the Old Testament, for this is the very theme of that book. From the sacrificial system to the Day of Passover to the Day of Atonement to the Suffering Servant passage in Isaiah, the whole Old–Testament dispensation was a preparation for this suffering. For without the shedding of blood there is no remission for sin (Heb. 9:22). Why were Adam and Eve not immediately destroyed when they disobeyed God? Because the Christ would suffer. Why were animals slain to replace the fig leaves Adam and Eve had futilely woven to cover their shame? Because the Christ would suffer. Why the blood of all those bulls and goats on every Jewish altar for thousands of years? Because the Christ would suffer. Why the call of Abraham? So the Christ could come and therefore suffer. Why the sacrifice of Isaac? Because the Christ would suffer. Why the preservation of a remnant and their return to the Land? Because the Christ would suffer.

And why did he have to suffer? Because *"God commendeth his love toward us in this, that while we were yet sinners, Christ died for us"* (Rom. 5:8). He was the Lamb of God who took away the sins of the world (John 1:29). Sin is so evil that nothing less than this death, nothing less than His death, could have atoned for it. But He has paid all the price of it forever! And therefore *"if we confess our sins, God is faithful and just to forgive us our sins and cleanse us of all unrighteousness"* (1 John 19). *"For God so loved the world that he gave his only begotten Son, that whosoever believeth on him should not perish, but have eternal life"* (John 3:16). All because the Christ should suffer. Good news! Good news! This is the Gospel! This is good news indeed.

But that is not all. *". . . that the Christ should suffer* **and rise from the dead the third day."** The resurrection is God's way of saying that the sacrifice of His Son for sin has been accepted. It is God's warrant to us that Satan has been defeated and the debt of sin cancelled for believers forever. But even better than that (if anything could be), it means that our Lord who loved us even unto death is given back to us alive. He lives now to impart the life that is beyond death, to be our living King and Mediator, and to bring us to glory with Himself. Good news! Good news! This is the Gospel! This is good news indeed.

And what follows from that? The **proclamation of repentance.** *". . . that repentance for forgiveness of sins should be proclaimed in his name to all the nations, beginning from Jerusalem"* (verse 47). Do you see the beauty of the logic of the Gospel? Why does this come right after the resurrection? Because the resurrection of Christ is what gives repentance its point. Before Christ suffered, what good would it do to repent? You could promise not to sin anymore, but you would not be able to keep the promise, and even if you could, you would still be guilty of your former sin and thus still worthy of death.

But now that Christ has suffered, you can be forgiven. So now repentance is no longer futile; now it can lead to a restored relationship with God, to forgiveness, to salvation, to eternal life. And now that He has been raised from the dead, there is another way repentance becomes worth doing. Because now the power of the risen Lord is unleashed through His Holy Spirit, so that we have help in following through on our repentance. And we have the promise made more sure that, because He lives, so shall we.

So the suffering and resurrection of Christ leads to repentance. And repentance means changing your mind, laying down the arms of your rebellion against God, believing in Christ as your Savior, and turning from sin to follow Him. Does that mean you must stop sinning to be saved? Not exactly. It would be more accurate to say that you are saved to stop sinning. Salvation is God's work, not ours; your forgiveness is based on Christ's sacrifice, not on your success at reforming yourself. Salvation is through faith in Christ's work, not through the success of your own. To say that salvation is not by works is to say that it does not depend on your works but on Christ's work, not on your acceptability but on Christ's. But we must turn to Him in faith to receive the free gift of salvation, and turning to Him means turning away from sin. You will no doubt still stumble and even fall from time to time. But you must truly turn to Him. And that turning is repentance.

Do you understand? Because Christ suffered, because Christ rose, repentance can be proclaimed and sins forgiven. Your sins. And mine. Good news! Good news! This is the Gospel! This is good news indeed.

III. The Fruits Of The Gospel (v. 47)

The foundation of the Gospel (the Word of God); the facts of the Gospel (that the Christ should suffer); they lead to the fruit of the Gospel. Because the Christ has suffered and been raised, *"repentance for the forgiveness of sins"* is proclaimed in His name to all who believe. Forgiveness of sin means the thing that has separated us from God is taken out of the way and we are restored to our position as sons and daughters of the Father. And that gives us love, joy, peace, eternal life, and a purpose for living great enough to make eternal life desirable. And all of that starts with forgiveness.

It astounds me how shy we are of talking about this word, so central to every New Testament summary of the Gospel as it is. But in order to talk about forgiveness, we must talk about sin. And we are afraid that if we talk about sin we will be seen as judgmental. But if we don't, we must try to preach the Gospel without talking about the central need we all have as fallen human beings. Forgiveness! To have a conscience that is really clean—not just seared or asleep, but really free from guilt. To know that you are as acceptable to God as Jesus Christ is. To have no need to be ashamed. To receive this, not because you deserve it, but because God loves you and has paid for your sin forever in the death of Christ. Maybe the most important thing we can do today is to recover the joy of forgiveness. That means first recovering a sense of the sinfulness of sin. We cannot communicate this to others until first we have felt it ourselves. Then we will be filled with such joy that we will not need to motivate ourselves—indeed, we will not be able to restrain ourselves from proclaiming repentance for forgiveness in His name. Good news! Good news! This is the Gospel! This is good news indeed.

IV. The Function Of The Evangelist (vv. 48–49)

The foundation, the facts, and the fruit of the Gospel lead to the function of the evangelist. *"Repentance for forgiveness of sins should be* **proclaimed** *in his name to all the nations, beginning from Jerusalem. You are* **witnesses** *of these things."* If this is the great Gospel we have been given, what then are we to do with it? The actual function of taking the Gospel to the nations is carried by two words in this passage. First, repentance for forgiveness in Jesus' name is to be **proclaimed**. This verb captures the public side of evangelism. We have a message to deliver. We are not talking about ourselves; we are proclaiming what God has done. Remember what we said about the Foundation of the Gospel. If we lose this spirit, we lose something essential to the spread of the Good News.

But that is not the only side of it. We are also referred to as **witnesses** of these things. A witness is someone who is able to speak with first-hand authority. He is someone who has seen something with his own eyes. Let's say I hear a loud bang and look up to see that two cars have collided. I saw what happened, but because I was not paying attention I did not see how or why it happened. So if I am called as a witness to determine which driver was at fault, I will be useless, and my testimony will be disallowed. I did not see it. My speculation is of no interest to the court, and my testimony only hearsay. I am dismissed.

Now, the disciples were literal eyewitnesses to the resurrection, people whose testimony is therefore very important indeed. We cannot equal them in that, but our testimony is also relevant. For we can give personal testimony to the ongoing reality of the resurrection, experienced in the saving power of the blood of Christ. And that is what we are called to do. Proclamation is the public side of evangelism, and witness is the private, or better, the *personal* side. Evangelism is most effective when the two are combined, that is, when we are heralds to the Good News (like we said under the Foundation of the Gospel) who can add the clear and firm testimony of our own eyes, our own life experience, that the news we proclaim is true and real and powerful for salvation—because it has saved us. But of course, to give that testimony, we must first have experienced and be experiencing these things.

Therefore, the first step to effective witness is to take the Gospel seriously ourselves. When Ghandi was asked why, as a student of Christ, he had not become a Christian, he is supposed to have replied, "If Christ has done such a poor job of saving you, why should I ask him to save me?"[163] Ouch! What a tragic indictment this is, when

---

[163] The statement is attributed to Ghandi, but I have not been able to find confirmation that he actually said it. The challenge remains, whoever the source was!

the Gospel is the power of God to salvation for those who believe. The first step to effective witness is to be transformed by the Gospel ourselves.

And what a Gospel it is! *Thus it is written that the Christ should suffer and rise from the dead the third day, and that repentance for forgiveness of sins should be proclaimed in his name to all the nations. You are witnesses of these things.* Good news! Good news! This is the Gospel! This is good news indeed.

Conclusion

So let me ask you some key questions today as members of University Church. Has Christ opened your mind to understand the Scriptures? Do you see that thus it was written, that He should suffer and rise from the dead? Have you repented and believed in Him for the forgiveness of your sins? Have you confessed with your mouth Jesus as Lord and believed in your heart that God has raised Him from the dead? Are you ready to proclaim that Good News and be a witness to its saving power? I hope and trust that you are. May God grant that it may be so, more fully and practically so than ever before to the glory of His Son Jesus Christ!

EPILOG: FAREWELL AND ASCENSION

Luke 24:49 *"And behold, I am sending forth the promise of Father upon you, but you are to remain in the city until you are clothed with power from on high." **50** And He led them out as far as Bethany, and He lifted up His hands and blessed them. **51** While He was blessing them, He parted from them and was carried up into heaven. **52** And they, after worshipping Him, returned to Jerusalem with great joy **53** and were continually in the Temple praising God.*

Luke ends his Gospel with an anticipation of volume two, the Book of Acts, which begins with a fuller account of the Ascension so briefly recorded here. A full exposition of that event would then properly come from the first chapter of Acts. But before we leave Luke's first volume, we should pause to reflect on how the Ascension functions as a bridge to the other book, where we have a shift in focus from the ministry of Christ to the mission of the church—which might not be a wholly new focus after all.

Luke tells us in the introduction to Acts that his Gospel was about *"what Jesus began to do and to teach"* before He was *"taken up into heaven"* (Acts 1:1–2). This implies that Acts is about what Jesus continued to do and teach—now through His personal Agent and Representative, the Holy Spirit, and the Spirit's ministry through the Apostles.[164] Perhaps, then, we should have named the second volume "The Acts of the Holy Spirit" rather than "The Acts of the Apostles." (Luke did not give his book that title, of course; it was added later.) And ultimately the acts of the Holy Spirit are the acts of Jesus—what He continued to do and teach. To understand that is to understand what Jesus *continues* to do, through the calling, regenerating, and sanctifying work of the Spirit, and what He continues to teach, though the recorded words of His Apostles inspired by the Spirit and applied to His current disciples by the same Spirit.

Ironically, then, the Ascension of Christ into Heaven provides closure to the earthly life of Jesus by opening up for us the wider stage He entered by leaving that earthly life. For He is now seated at the right hand of the Father, where He rules as Head of His Body, the Church (Eph. 1:22–3). And thus He continues through His Church the mission He gave it before He departed: to proclaim the forgiveness of sins in His name as His witnesses, to make disciples of all nations. If the ending of Luke's Gospel seems abrupt, it is because it is as much a beginning as an ending. It demands the Acts and the rest of the New Testament, which is there to help us channel the "power from on high." That is how Jesus continues to do and to teach, to be the Lord of Lords and King of Kings and Savior of the world.

---

[164] For more on this view of the Spirit's role see Donald T. Williams, *The Person and Work of the Holy Spirit,* op. cit.

I hope that, as we conclude this account of things accomplished, you will see the Lord Jesus Christ looking out at you from its pages, saying to us what He said so many times when He was here on earth:

"Follow me!"

Selected Bibliography

This bibliography makes no pretense of being complete or comprehensive or any such thing. I just thought it might be useful to have a list of books that were particularly central in forming my vision of what preaching and exposition are all about in the life of the church, books I found particularly helpful in my attempts to understand and expound the life of Christ as portrayed by St. Luke, and books that managed to get themselves cited at some point in the exposition.

The Philosophy And Art Of Interpretation, Preaching, And Ministry

Baxter, Richard. *The Reformed Pastor*, ed. William Brown. 1656; Edinburgh: Banner of Truth, 1980.

Blamires, Harry. *The Christian Mind*. London: S.P.C.K., 1963.

Edwards, Jonathan. *A Treatise Concerning Religious Affections*. 1746; New Haven, CT: Yale Univ. Pr., 1959.

Gordon, David Stott. "John W. Montgomery: God's Universal Man." *Tough–Minded Christianity: Honoring the Legacy of John W. Montgomery*, ed. William Dembski and Thomas Schirrmacher. Nashville, TN: Broadman & Holman, 2008.

————. "Sir Philip Sidney: The Faith and Practice of an Elizabethan Christian." MA Thesis Trinity Evangelical Divinity School, 1995.

Herbert, George. *A Priest to the Temple, or The Country Parson*. in *The Works of George Herbert*, ed. F. E. Hutchinson. Oxford: Clarendon Press, 1941.

Jeffrey, David Lyle, ed. *A Burning and a Shining Light: English Spirituality in the Age of Wesley*. Grand Rapids, MI: Eerdmans, 1987.

Kaiser, Jr., Walter C. *Toward an Exegetical Theology: Biblical Exegesis for Preaching and Teaching*. Grand Rapids, MI: Baker, 1981.

Kantzer, Kenneth S. "Course Notes for Systematic Theology 511, Intro. to Theology." Typescript. Trinity Evangelical Divinity School, 1973.

Lloyd–Jones, D. Martyn. *Preaching and Preachers*. Grand Rapids, MI: Zondervan, 1982.

Longman, III, Tremper, *Literary Approaches to Biblical Interpretation*. Grand Rapids, MI: Zondervan, 1987.

Montgomery, John Warwick. *The Suicide of Christian Theology* Minneapolis, MN: Bethany Fellowship, 1970.

Orme, Alan Dan. *God's Appointments with Men: A Christian Primer on the Sacraments*. Athens, GA: University Church Press, 1982.

Ryken, Leland. *The Word of God in English: Criteria for Excellence in Bible Translation*. Wheaton, IL: Crossway, 2002.

————. *Words of Life: A Literary Introduction to the New Testament*. Grand Rapids, MI: Baker, 1987.

Schaeffer, Francis A. *The Church Before the Watching World: A Practical Ecclesiology*. Downers Grove, IL: InterVarsity Press, 1971.

————. *The God Who is There: Speaking Historic Christianity into the Twentieth Century*. Downers Grove, IL: InterVarsity Press, 1968.

——. *The Great Evangelical Disaster*. Westchester, IL: Crossway, 1984.

——. *No Final Conflict: The Bible without Error in All that it Affirms*. Downers Grove, IL: InterVarsity Press, 1975.

Stott, John R. W. *Between Two Worlds: The Art of Preaching in the Twentieth Century*. Grand Rapids, MI: Eerdmans, 1982.

Van Gorder, Paul R. *The Church Stands Corrected: Solutions for Today's Church Problems*. Wheaton, IL: Victor Books, 1976.

Wells, David F. *No Place for Truth: Or Whatever Happened to Evangelical Theology?* Grand Rapids, MI: Eerdmans, 1993.

Williams, Donald T. *Inklings of Reality: Essays toward a Christian Philosophy of Letters*, 2nd ed. Lynchburg, VA: Lantern Hollow Press, 2012.

——. *Ninety–Five Theses for a New Reformation: A Road Map for Post–Evangelical Christianity*. Toccoa, GA: *Semper Reformanda* Publications, 2021.

Luke And The Life Of Jesus

Aland, Kurt, ed. *Synopsis Quattuor Evangeliorum*. 7th ed. Stuttgart: Wurttemberische Bibelanstalt, 1967.

Archer, Gleason. *Encyclopedia of Bible Difficulties*. Grand Rapids, MI: Zondervan, 1982.

Bailey, Kenneth E. *The Cross and the Prodigal: Luke 15 Through the Eyes of Middle–Eastern Peasants*. Downers Grove, IL: InterVarsity Press, 2005.

——. *Poet and Peasant and Through Peasant Eyes: A Literary–Cultural Approach to the Parables in Luke*. Grand Rapids, MI: Eerdmans, 1983.

Bauckham, Richard. *Jesus and the Eyewitnesses: The Gospels as Eyewitness Testimony*. Grand Rapids, MI: Eerdmans, 2006.

Bruce, Alexander Balmain. *The Synoptic Gospels*. The Expositor's Greek Testament, ed. W. Robertson Nicoll, vol. 1. Grand Rapids, MI: Eerdmans, n.d.

Bruce, F. F. *Jesus and Christian Origins outside the New Testament*. Grand Rapids, MI: Eerdmans, 1974.

——. *New Testament History*. Garden City, NY: Anchor Books, 1972.

Calvin, John. *Commentary on a Harmony of the Gospels in Matthew, Mark, and Luke*. Calvin's Commentaries, vols. XVI–XVII. Trans. Rev. William Pringle. Grand Rapids, MI: Baker, 1981.

Creed, John Martin. *The Gospel According to St. Luke: The Greek Text with Introduction, Notes, and Indices*. London: MacMillan, 1930.

Cullmann, Oscar. *The Christology of the New Testament*, trans. Shirley Guthrie and Charles A, M, Hall. Philadelphia, PA: Westminster Press, 1963.

Danby, Herbert. *The Mishnah, Translated from the Hebrew with Introduction and Brief Explanatory Notes*. Oxford: Oxford Univ. Pr., 1933; rpt. Peabody, MA: Hendrickson, 2019.

Douglas, J. D., ed. *The New Bible Dictionary*. Grand Rapids, MI: Eerdmans, 1970.

Edersheim, Alfred. *The Life and Times of Jesus the Messiah*. Grand Rapids, MI: Eerdmans, 1971.

Edwards, James R. *The Gospel According to Luke*, The Pillar New Testament Commentary. Grand Rapids, MI: Eerdmans, 2015.

Geldenhuys, Norval. *Commentary on the Gospel of Luke: The English Text with Introduction, Exposition, and Notes*. The New International Commentary on the New Testament. Grand Rapids, MI: Eerdmans, 1951.

Green, Joel B. *The Gospel of Luke*. The New International Commentary on the New Testament. Grand Rapids, MI: Eerdmans, 1997.

Guthrie, Donald. *New Testament Introduction*, 3rd ed. Downers Grove, IL: InterVarsity Press, 1973.

Harrison, Everett F. *A Short Life of Christ*. Grand Rapids, MI: Eerdmans, 1968.

Hendriksen, William. *Exposition of the Gospel According to Luke*. New Testament Commentary. Grand Rapids, MI: Baker, 1978.

Josephus, Flavius. *The Works of Josephus*, trans. William Whiston, Lynn, MA: Hendrickson, 1980.

Lenski, R. C. H. *The Interpretation of St. Luke's Gospel*. Commentary on the New Testament. Woodridge, IL: Hendrickson, 1961.

Liefeld, Walter L. *Luke*. The Expositor's Bible Commentary, vol. 8, ed. Frank E. Gabelein. Grand Rapids, MI: Zondervan, 1984.

Maier, Paul L. *Pontius Pilate: A Biographical Novel*. Garden City, NY: Doubleday, 1968.

Marshall, I. Howard. *The Gospel of Luke*. The New International Greek Testament Commentary. Grand Rapids, MI: Eerdmans, 1978.

McGrew, Lydia. *Hidden in Plain View: Undesigned Coincidences in the Gospels and Acts*. Tampa, FL: DeWard, 2017.

———. *The Mirror and the Mask: Liberating the Gospels from Literary Devices*. Tampa, FL: DeWard, 2019.

Metzger, Bruce M. *The New Testament: Its Background, Growth, and Content*. Nashville, TN: Abingdon, 1965.

Morgan, G. Campbell, *The Crises of the Christ*. Old Tappan, NJ: Fleming H. Revell, 1936.

Neil, Stephen. *The Interpretation of the New Testament, 1861–1961*. London: Oxford Univ. Pr., 1966.

Plummer, Alfred. *The Gospel According to S. Luke*, 5th ed. The International Critical Commentary. Edinburgh: T & T Clark, 1922.

Porter, H. "Sabbath Day's Journey," *The International Standard Bible Encyclopedia*, ed. James Orr. Grand Rapids, MI: Eerdmans, 1946.

Ryle, J. C. *Expository Thoughts on the Gospels*, 4 vols. Grand Rapids, MI: Baker. 1977.

Sayers, Dorothy L. *The Man Born to be King: A Play–Cycle on the Life of our Lord Jesus Christ*. Grand Rapids, MI: Eerdmans, 1943.

Miscellaneous

Algeo, John and Carmen Acevedo Butcher, *Problems in the Origins and Development of the English Language*, 5th ed. Boston, MA: Thomson Wadsworth, 2005.

Bacon, Francis. "Essays or Counsels, Civil and Moral," 1625. Rollins, Hyder E. and Herschel Baker, eds., *The Renaissance in England: Non–Dramatic Prose and Verse of the Sixteenth Century*. Lexington, VA: D. C. Heath, 1954.

Bevington, David, ed. *Medieval Drama*. Atlanta, GA: Houghton Mifflin, 1975.

Browne, Sir Thomas. *Religio Medici*, 1682. In Seventeenth Century Prose and Poetry, 2nd ed. Alexander M. Witherspoon and Frank J. Warnke, eds. NY: Harcourt Brace Jovanovich, 1982.

Bunyan, John. *The Works of John Bunyan*, 3 vols., ed. George Offor. Edinburgh: Banner of Truth, 1999.

"Church Giving Statistics for 2024," https://careynieuwhof.com/church-giving-statistics/

Conan Doyle, Sir Arthur. *The Annotated Sherlock Holmes*, 2 vols. Ed. Sir William Baring–Gould. NY: Clarkson, N. Potter, 1997.

Croce, Jim. "I Got a Name," *Jim Croce, Photographs and Memories: His Greatest Hits* NY: ABC Records, 1974.

Donne, John. "Devotions Upon Emergent Occasions," 1624. *Seventeenth Century Prose and Poetry*, 2nd ed., ed. Alexander M. Witherspoon and Frank J. Warnke. NY: Harcourt, Brace, Jovanovich, 1982.

Edwards, Jonathan. "Sinners in the Hands of an Angry God," 1741. *The Works of Jonathan Edwards*, 2 vols. Edinburgh: Banner of Truth, 1974.

Herbert, George. *The Works of George Herbert*, ed. F. E. Hutchinson. Oxford: Clarendon Press, 1941.

Holmes, Michael W. *The Apostolic Fathers: Greek Texts and English Translations of their Writings*, 2nd ed. Trans. J. W. Lightfoot and J. R. Harner. Grand Rapids, MI: Baker, 1993.

Hopkins, Gerard Manley. *The Poems of Gerard Manley Hopkins*, 4th ed. W. H. Gardner and N. H. MacKenzie, eds.. London: Oxford Univ. Pr., 1967.

Lewis, C. S. "Christianity and Culture," 1940; rpt. *Christian Reflections*, ed. Walter Hooper. Grand Rapids, MI: Eerdmans, 1967.

———. *The Collected Poems of C. S. Lewis: A Critical Edition*. Ed. Don W. King. Kent, OH: Kent State Univ. Pr., 2015.

———. "Is Theology Poetry," 1945; rpt. *The Weight of Glory and other Addresses*, ed. Walter Hooper. San Francisco, CA: HarperSanFrancisco, 1980.

———. *The Last Battle*. 1956; NY: Harper Collins, 1984.

———. *Mere Christianity*. NY: MacMillan, 1943.

———. *Miracles: A Preliminary Study*. NY: MacMillan, 1947.

Machen, J. Gresham. *Christianity and Liberalism*. 1923; Grand Rapids, MI: Eerdmans, 1981.

———. *The Virgin Birth of Christ*. NY: Harper, 1930.

MacLaren, Alexander, *Sermons Preached in Union Chapel, Manchester by Alexander MacLaren*. Manchester, England: Dunnill, Palmer, & Company, 1859.

Marlowe, Christopher, "The Tragical History of Doctor Faustus." *The Norton Anthology of English Literature*, ed. Stephen Greenblatt et al. NY: Norton, 2013.

Martin, Walter R. *The Kingdom of the Cults: An Analysis of the Major Cult Systems in the Present Christiam Era*. Minneapolis, MN: Bethany Fellowship, 1968.

McDowell, Josh. *Evidence that Demands a Verdict: Historical Evidences for the Christian Faith*. Arrowhead Springs, CA: Campus Crusade for Christ, 1972.

McQuilken, Robertson, *The Great Omission: A Biblical Basis for World Evangelism*. Downers Grove, IL: InterVarsity Press, 2001.

———. "Reached and Unreached Mission Fields." *Evangelical Dictionary of World Missions*, ed. A. Scott Moreau. Grand Rapids, MI: Baker, 2000: 808–9.

Milton, John. *John Milton: Complete Poems and Major Prose*, ed. Merritt Y. Hughes. Indianapolis, IN: Odyssey Press, 1957.

"Mission Stats." https://www.thetravelingteam.org/stats.

Montgomery, John Warwick, *In Defense of Martin Luther*. Milwaukee, MN: Northwestern Publishing House, 1970.

Noyes, Russell, ed. *English Romantic Poetry and Prose*. NY: Oxford Univ. Pr., 1956.

O'Connor, Flannery. *Three by Flannery O'Connor: Wise Blood, A Good Man is Hard to Find, The Violent Bear it Away*. NY: Signet Classics, New American Library, 1962.

Packer, J. I. *Knowing God*. Downers Grove, IL: InterVarsity Press, 1973.

Piper, John. "The Supremacy of God in Missions through Worship," *Mission Frontiers*, July–August 1996, https://www.missionfrontiers.org/issue/article/the–supremacy–of–god–in–missions–through–worship.

Richardson, Cyril C., ed. *Eary Christian Fathers*. The Library of Christian Classics, vol. 1. Philadelphia, PA: Westminster, 1953.

Rollins, Hyder E. and Herschel Baker, eds., *The Renaissance in England: Non–Dramatic Prose and Verse of the Sixteenth Century*. Lexington, MA: D. C. Heath, 1954.

Schaeffer, Francis A. *A Christian Manifesto*. Westchester, IL: Crossway, 1981.

———. *The Church at the End of the Twentieth Century*. Downers Grove, IL: InterVarsity Press, 1970.

Shakespeare, William. *Shakespeare: The Complete Works*, ed. G. B. Harrison. NY: Harcourt, Brace, and World, 1958.

Sibbes, Richard, "The Soul's Conflict with Itself and Victory over Itself by Faith," 1635. *Works of Richard Sibbes*, 6 vols. Ed. Alexander B. Grossart. Edinburgh: Banner of Truth Trust, 1973.

Spurgeon, Charles, *Lectures to My Students*, 2nd Series. 1877; Lynchburg:, VA The Old Time Gospel Hour, n.d.

———. "On Preaching the Law and the Gospel," https://paearly.com/blog/2018/3/7/charles–spurgeon–on–preaching–the–law–and–gospel.

Stookey, Paul. "John Henry Bosworth." *Paul And*. NY: Warner Brothers Records, 1971.

Thoreau, Henry David. "A Vigorous Prose Style." 1849.

Tolkien, J. R. R. *The Hobbit*. 1937; NY: Ballantine, 1973.

———. *The Return of the King*. NY: Ballantine, 1955.

Traherne, Thomas. "Five Centuries of Meditations," 1674? *Seventeenth Century Prose and Poetry*, 2nd ed., ed. Alexander M. Witherspoon and Frank J. Warnke. NY: Harcourt, Brace, Jovanovich, 1982.

Trinity Hymnal. Rev. ed. Atlanta: Great Commission Publications, 1990.

Untermeyer, Louis. *Modern British and American Poetry*. NY: Harcourt, Brace, & World, 1955.

Williams, Donald T. *Answers from Aslan: The Enduring Apologetics of C. S. Lewis*. Tampa, FL: DeWard, 2023.

——. *The Disciple's Prayer*, Eugene, OR: Wipf & Stock, 2005.

——. *The Person and Work of the Holy Spirit*. Nashville: Broadman, 1994; rpt. Eugene, Or: Wipf & Stock, 2002.

——. *Stars through the Clouds: The Collected Poetry of Donald T. Williams*, 2nd ed. Lynchburg, VA: Lantern Hollow Press, 2019.

——. *The Young Christian's Survival Guide: Common Questions Young Christians are Asked about God, the Bible, and the Christian Faith Answered*, vol. 1. Cambridge, OH: Christian Publishing House, 2019.

Witherspoon, Alexander M. and Frank J. Warnke, eds. *Seventeenth Century Prose and Poetry*, 2nd ed. NY: Harcourt, Brace, Jovanovich, 1982.

Wycliffe World Alliance. https://www.wycliffe.net/resources/statistics/.

Index Of Greek Words And Phrases Discussed

Index Of Scripture Passages Cited

This study examines one book of the Scriptures in a manner impregnated with the rest of the Scriptures. This index is then one of its most important features if it enhances your ability to emulate the noble Bereans and *"examine the Scriptures daily, whether these thigs be so"* (Acts 17:11). Trying to trace every appearance of every verse of Luke's Gospel would quickly become too tedious and overwhelming to be useful. The basic units of Luke's narrative will therefore be tied to the sermon in which that unit is covered and not broken down further. We will try to trace more fully here the way the rest of Scripture appears in the study to shed light on the Lucan passages in a less predictable manner. As the child sang to Augustine, *"Tolle, lege*, take up and read,"

Index Of Names

General Index

www.ingramcontent.com/pod-product-compliance
Lightning Source LLC
Chambersburg PA
CBHW080834120626
46553CB00009B/2430